Procedures & Theory

FOR ADMINISTRATIVE PROFESSIONALS

6e

Patsy Fulton-Calkins, Ph.D.
Director of the Bill J. Priest Center
University of North Texas
Denton, TX

Karin M. Stulz, M.A.E.
Assistant Professor
Northern Michigan University
Marquette, MI

SOUTH-WESTERN
CENGAGE Learning™

Australia • Brazil • Japan • Korea • Mexico • Singapore • Spain • United Kingdom • United States

SOUTH-WESTERN
CENGAGE Learning™

Procedures & Theory for Administrative Professionals, 6E
Patsy Fulton-Calkins, Karin M. Stulz

Vice President of Editorial, Business: Jack W. Calhoun

Editor-in-Chief: Karen Schmohe

Acquisitions Editor: Jane Phelan

Senior Developmental Editor: Dave Lafferty

Consulting Editor: Dianne Rankin

Editorial Assistant: Connor Allen

Marketing Manager: Valerie Lauer

Marketing Coordinator: Kelley Gilreath

Senior Marketing Communications Manager: Terron Sanders

Senior Content Project Manager: Kim Kusnerak

Production Technology Analyst: Adam Grafa

Senior Technology Project Editor: Mike Jackson

Manufacturing Coordinator: Kevin Kluck

Production Service: Newgen

Copyeditor: Nancy Ahr

Art Director: Bethany Casey

Internal Designer: c miller design

Cover Designer: c miller design

Cover Images: © GettyImages, Inc.

Internal Images: © GettyImages, Inc.

Photography Manager: Deanna Ettinger

Photo Researchers: Sylvia McDonald/Terri Miller

For product information and technology assistance, contact us at
Cengage Learning Academic Resource Center, 1-800-423-0563

For permission to use material from this text or product,
submit all requests online at **www.cengage.com/permissions**
Further permissions questions can be emailed to
permissionrequest@cengage.com

Above & Beyond is a registered trademark of 1Soft Corporation, Blue River, OR. Access, Excel, Internet Explorer, Microsoft, Microsoft ActiveSync, Microsoft Windows, Outlook, PowerPoint, Windows Live, and Windows Vista are registered trademarks or trademarks of Microsoft Corporation. Ask.com is a trademark of Ask.com. BlackBerry is a registered trademark of Research In Motion Limited. Dragon Naturally Speaking is a registered trademark of ScanSoft, Inc. Google is a trademark of Google Inc. Lycos is a registered trademark of Lycos, Inc. Mac OS is a registered trademark of Apple, Inc. Norton Internet Security is a trademark of Symantec Corporation. United States Postal Service, Postal Service, Post Office, StampsOnline, Express Mail, Priority Mail, Delivery Confirmation, First-Class Mail, Parcel Post, Global Express Guaranteed, ZIP Code, Standard Mail, Registered Mail, Media Mail, Signature Confirmation, Certified Mail, Priority Mail International, First Class Mail International, and Express Mail International are trademarks of the United States Postal Service. Yahoo! is a registered trademark of Yahoo! Inc.

Student Edition ISBN 13: 978-0-538-97529-2
Student Edition ISBN 10: 0-538-97529-6
Student Edition with CD ISBN 13: 978-0-538-73052-5
Student Edition with CD ISBN 10: 0-538-73052-8

South-Western Cengage Learning
5191 Natorp Boulevard
Mason, OH 45040
USA

Cengage Learning products are represented in Canada by Nelson Education, Ltd.

For your course and learning solutions, visit **school.cengage.com**

Printed in the United States of America
3 4 5 6 7 11 10

THE FOUNDATION FOR A FUTURE

In today's dynamic workplace, administrative professionals must be able to adjust to a diversified workforce with emerging technologies and be prepared to function in an expanding global marketplace. From hard skills to soft skills, *Procedures & Theory for Administrative Professionals, 6E* equips you to handle whatever workplace challenges may come your way by providing instruction and activities directed toward technology, communication, and human relations.

Its emphasis on critical thinking, creative thinking, and lifelong learning gives you opportunities for unique solutions and ideas. Reflecting a changing marketplace, the sixth edition includes a host of new topics, ranging from business etiquette and e-commerce to globalization and security, and is packed with career tips, professional pointers, and critical-thinking activities.

Comprehensive and practical, *Procedures & Theory for Administrative Professionals, 6E* is an excellent resource for learners seeking entry-level assistant positions, preparing for promotion opportunities, or transitioning to a job of greater responsibility.

ANCILLARIES FOR THE STUDENT

In addition to the main text, there is a supporting workbook (ISBN: 0-538-73053-6) that includes hands-on projects and applications for each chapter.

Technology Toolbox is a robust distance-learning resource that includes chapter resources with quizzes, flash cards for vocabulary review, enrichment critical-thinking activities, Web links, and more.

TOOLS FOR THE INSTRUCTOR

An **Instructor's Resource CD-ROM** is available to instructors who adopt a textbook for class use (ISBN 0-538-73054-4). The CD contains ExamView testing software and test bank, *PowerPoint* presentations, data files, solutions files, tests in *Microsoft Word* format, and the manual pages.

A supplementary **eBook CD-ROM** is also sold separately (ISBN 0-538-73051-X). This digital material offers the same rich photos, graphics, and easy-to-read fonts as the printed text! Students view the PDF files on their computers.

South-Western/Cengage Learning maintains a **Web Site** to support this text. Both students and instructors may access the Web site at *academic.cengage.com/officetech/ fulton-calkins*. The site provides instructor resources and information about related products. Student resources on the site include data files and links to related sites.

POWERFUL FEATURES

Critical-Thinking Activity

On Monday, Kim Chang had a problem with Joleen March, the administrative assistant who works in the office next to her. They have been friends for several months and usually take their morning and afternoon breaks together. On Monday, Kim was extremely busy and could not take a break at either time because her employer had an emergency situation occur. Kim needed to get several documents ready for her employer's supervisor. As Kim was leaving her workstation at five in the afternoon, she saw Joleen. Kim smiled and said, "I have had a terrible day; nothing seemed to go well." Joleen replied in an angry voice, "Well, apparently you forgot about our coffee breaks and my birthday also." Kim started apologizing to her; however, Joleen walked away. Kim does care about their friendship; however, she believes that Joleen has definitely overreacted to the situation. After all, she had to get the work done for her employer.

How should Kim handle the situation? What steps can she take to cope with the stress and communicate clearly with Joleen?

Critical-Thinking Activities require students to use critical-thinking skills to solve problems presented through a real-world situation.

e-portfolio

internet

Web activities incorporate the use of technology into each chapter.

Integrated throughout the text, coverage of soft skills "rounds out" the office education process, helping students become proficient in this critical area.

RESOLVING CONFLICT

- Identify the issues causing the conflict. Is it power, resources, recognition, or acceptance? Many times the need for these items is at the heart of the conflict.

- Be willing to listen to the other person. Ask questions to determine what the other person wants or needs. By understanding the needs of the other person, you may be able to find ways to resolve the conflict.

- Identify points of agreement. Work from these points first. Then identify points of disagreement.

- Create a safe environment for discussion. Meet in a neutral location and use a tone that is accepting of the other person's views and feelings. Let the other person tell you how he or she is feeling. Share your feelings with the other person.

- Be objective. Many times individuals act too quickly when a conflict occurs. Step back, collect your thoughts, and try to see the situation as objectively as possible.

- Do not seek to win during a confrontation. Negotiate the issues and translate the negotiation into a lasting agreement.

- Listen actively. Watch the individual's eyes and notice body language to help you determine whether you are communicating effectively.

Insightful coverage of anger, stress, and time management includes tips for managing these aspects as part of everyday behavior.

End-of-chapter Workplace Applications provide activities for skill improvement tied directly to goals, critical thinking, team building, and written and oral presentation. New topics include business etiquette, identity theft, e-commerce, professional image, PDAs, and much more.

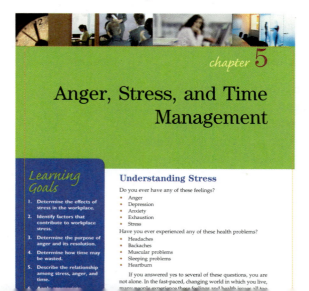

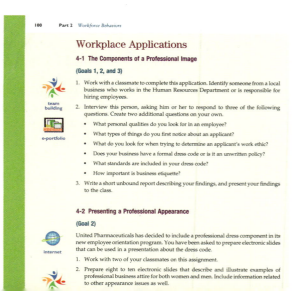

INSPIRING NEW ADDITIONS

Focus On . . . emphasizes the importance of various topics such as e-mail and visual aids.

Career Profile

Human Resources Associate

Attracting, training, and retaining qualified workers is important to the success of organizations. Workers in Human Resources Departments handle these vital tasks. Human resources employees can be found in almost all industries and in small, medium, and large companies. Human resources, training, and labor relations managers and specialists held about 820,000 jobs in the United States in 2004. About 21,000 specialists were self-employed, working as consultants to public and private employers.*

A human resources associate may handle a broad range of human resources work. This type of employee is called a human resources generalist and is likely to be found in small organizations. Other associates may specialize in a particular area, such as benefit management, recruitment, or training. The job duties of a human resources associate vary depending on whether the position is that of a generalist or a specialist. For example, an employee may specialize in recruitment screens, interviews, or testing job applicants. Travel to college

campuses and job fairs and working with online job sites is typically part of the duties for this job.

Salaries for human resources associates vary by specific job, the size of the company, and the qualifications of the worker. Median annual earnings of employment, recruitment, and placement specialists were $41,190 in May 2004. Median annual earnings of compensation, benefits, and job analysis specialists were $47,490 in May 2004. Human resources associates may advance to managerial positions that offer higher salaries. For example, median annual earnings of compensation and benefits managers were $66,530 in May 2004.

Many colleges and universities have programs leading to a degree in personnel, human resources, or labor relations. This formal education as well as excellent communication, computer, and teamwork skills can help human resources associates be successful.

*"Human Resources, Training, and Labor Relations Managers and Specialists," Occupational Outlook Handbook, 2006-2007 Edition, accessed June 4, 2007, available from http://www.bls.gov/oco/ocos021.htm

Career Profiles have been added to the beginning of each part to provide students insight into various career opportunities available in the administrative field.

A new chapter entitled "Your Professional Image" teaches students the proper way to present and conduct themselves in a business environment.

Additional career planning tools provide even more resources to help students prepare for today's workplace.

A new chapter on customer service has been added to stress the significant role that customer service plays in the success of an organization.

chapter 4

Your Professional Ir

Learning Goals

1. Describe the personal characteristics and work characteristics that contribute to a positive professional image.

2. Identify the components of a professional appearance.

3. Understand the conventions of business etiquette.

Characteristics of a

You have probably heard the phra thousand words" and "you never ge a first impression." When it comes conduct yourself in a business envi that first interview or every day on th clients, these phrases ring far truer admit.

Appearance is only part of the ed maintaining your **professional ima** make on others, your attitude tow coworkers, your work ethic, your pre

chapter 9

02

Customer Service

Learning Goals

1. Describe the importance of effective customer service to an organization.

2. Identify characteristics of companies that value customer service.

3. Develop effective customer service skills.

Importance of C

Customer service is importa organizations. A **customer** is a or products that are offered **service** can be defined as t consistently give customers viding information to help p services best meet their need ery, installation, or service about product use after a se service.

In your career as an adm work for several types of org organizations, or governme types of organizations may nesses and other organization without effective customer se

A major goal of busines customer service is very in Customers who are not satis are likely to take their busine many customers take this act lower profits. However, cust service they have received a

210

Professional Pointers

Ask yourself the following questions if you are considering virtual work:

- Am I a good problem solver?
- Am I independent?
- Do I communicate well?
- Do I set regular break times for myself?
- Am I flexible?
- Am I able to cope with work-related stress?
- Do I exercise frequently?
- Do I set clear limits on my work?
- Do family members understand my job and my expectations of them?
- Do I hold regular meetings with my family to discuss issues?
- Do I allocate appropriate time for both my job and my family?

career *tip*

International Greetings

Keep in mind that although the handshake is an acceptable greeting in the United States, other countries have different greeting customs.

Country	Greeting
China	Give a slight nod and bow; if people applaud you should respond with applause.
Thailand	Place hands in a prayer position with your head slightly bowed (called the Wai); the higher your hands the more respect shown.
Poland	Men may greet women by kissing their hands; women greet other women with a slight embrace and kiss on the cheek.
Colombia	Women hold forearms instead of shaking hands.[10]

It is important to complete your research before

COMPREHENSIVE LEARNING SUPPORT

the **biases** (views based on background or experiences) of others. Such biases can cause **stereotyping** (holding perceptions or images of people or things that are derived from selective perception). Although you may think of stereotyping as negative, it can be positive. For example, stereotyping can help you learn the general characteristics of certain groups, people, or animals. As a small child, you learned that dogs are four-legged animals and are generally friendly to people. As you grew older, you could begin to distinguish among types of dogs and their natures and special characteristics.

Negative stereotyping can cause a premature end to communication and prejudicial behavior that leads to acts of rejection. For example, if an individual has a negative experience with an individual from another country and then decides that all individuals from that country have the same negative characteristics, **prejudice** (a system of negative beliefs and feelings) occurs. Other examples of prejudice are evident when **physically challenged** individuals (persons with a physical handicap) are judged and treated unfairly due to their physical handicaps.

None of this discussion is to imply that the ethical organization advocates a policy that ignores performance issues due to gender, physical challenge, race, ethnicity, or sexual orientation. All individuals must perform their jobs satisfactorily. What is important is giving all individuals the opportunity to do their job regardless of their minority status.

Here is the introductory statement concerning diversity from one of *Fortune* magazine's 2007 100 Best Companies to Work For, QUALCOMM Incorporated.

At QUALCOMM, we recognize that business success is driven by creativity and diversity. By valuing our differences and appreciating our similarities, we encourage the exchange of unique ideas and perspectives and build upon our individual, team and business strengths. Our diversity creates an energy that carries our global teams forward in developing new and superior products worldwide. At the heart of our global diversity and inclusion program is QUALCOMM's commitment to provide all employees, regardless of their backgrounds and

Key technology and vocabulary-building terms are highlighted in each chapter and included in the glossary for easy reference.

To reinforce learning, the accompanying student CD includes data files used in the end-of-chapter applications. This gives learners hands-on practice so they can learn what they will encounter in a real office.

An ethical organization affords equal treatment to all individuals, regardless of race or ethnicity.

Vocabulary Review

Open the *Microsoft® Word* file *CH01 Vocabulary* found on the Student CD. Complete the vocabulary review for Chapter 1.

The Reference Guide serves as a review of grammar and punctuation rules and basic formats for letters.

Reference Guide

This Reference Guide is a handy and easy-to-use reference to a variety of rules you will use frequently in preparing correspondence. You can use the guide to review grammar and punctuation rules. In addition, the guide includes basic formats for letters and reports. To assist you in using proper grammar and punctuation as you write and in using correct letter format, read this guide at the beginning of the course and refer to it as needed throughout the course. The parts of the Reference Guide are as follows:

Contents

Abbreviations 476
Adjectives and Adverbs 477
Bias-Free Language 477
Capitalization 478
Collective Nouns 479
Letters and Envelopes 480
Misused and Easily Confused Word and Phrases 483
Numbers 485
Parallelism 486
Plagiarism 486
Plurals and Possessives 487
Pronouns 487
Proofreaders' Marks 489
Punctuation 490
Reports 494
Spelling 501
Subject and Verb Agreement 501

Detailed *PowerPoint* slides from the Instructor Resource CD-ROM provide an overview of each chapter, outline major points of the chapter, and expand on selected concepts.

Leadership Traits

- Development of leadership poten
  - Providing mentoring, coaching, an
  - Having people accept assignment:
  - Providing positive and negative fe
  - Providing intensive training
  - Encouraging individuals to be lea communities
  - Making leadership development a the organization

Trait Development

- Serve
- Lead
- Build a shared vision
- Engender trust
  - Live by a stated set of values
  - Be reliable and predictable
  - Be fair
  - Contribute to an effective organizational culture

Women are assuming more positions of

Dr. Patsy J. Fulton-Calkins has extensive experience in the administrative professional field. Her experience in the workplace includes working as an administrative professional for large corporations. Early in her career she completed the CPS certification. Her teaching experience includes more than 17 years at the university, community college, and high school levels.

In addition to her teaching experience, she has extensive management experience in the following positions:

- Chancellor of Oakland Community College (the CEO), Oakland County, Michigan
- President of Brookhaven College, Dallas, Texas
- Vice President of Instruction, El Centro College, Dallas, Texas
- Vice President of Instruction, Cedar Valley College, Dallas, Texas
- Division Chairperson of Business and Social Science, Cedar Valley College, Dallas, Texas

Her educational credentials include a B.B.A., an M.B.Ed., and a Ph.D. Honors include Outstanding Alumnus, University of North Texas; Transformational Leader in Community Colleges; Who's Who in America, Outstanding Woman in Management; listee in *Michigan Women: Firsts and Founders*; Paul Harris Fellow of Rotary International; Beta Gamma Sigma, National Honorary Business Fraternity; and Piper Professor.

Karin Stulz has held a faculty position in the Walker L. Cisler College of Business at Northern Michigan University for the past 14 years. She has extensive experience in the administrative professional field. Her career at Northern Michigan University began with a variety of full-time administrative professional positions. While teaching primarily community college courses, her teaching responsibilities have included courses in office procedures, keyboarding, formatting, machine transcription, and business math, as well as a capstone evaluation course and internship program. In addition, she had taught a wide variety of software application courses, including beginning, intermediate, and advanced word processing, spreadsheets, database, presentation software, and software integrations. Karin is active in the College, the University, and the local community. She serves on a wide variety of academic and community committees.

Her educational credentials include a B.S., secondary teaching certification, and an M.A.E. degree. She has also earned specialized certifications through the Microsoft Office Specialist Certification program. Specialized certifications include core certification in *Access*, *Excel*, *PowerPoint*, and *Word* and expert certification in *Microsoft Word 2000*. Honors include the *Outstanding Teacher Award* in the Walker L. Cisler College of Business as well as the *Postsecondary Business Teacher of the Year Award* from the Michigan Business Education Association. Karin was awarded a 2007-2008 *Excellence in Teaching Award* from Northern Michigan University. She lives in Marquette, Michigan, with her husband Kevin and children Emily and Connor.

Contents

Part 1
The Dynamic Workplace 2

CHAPTER I

The Workplace—Constantly Changing   4

Labor Projections 4 • The Ever-Changing Workplace 4 • Organizational Structures 7 • Workplace Organization 8 • Organizational Strategies for Coping with Change 11 • Tomorrow's Workplace 15 • Administrative Professional Challenges 15 • Administrative Professional Workplace Requirements 17 • Career Plan 22

CHAPTER 2

Workplace Team and Environment   30

Teamwork 30 • Workplace Team Composition 34 • Diversity in the Workplace 40 • Productive Communication 42 • A Safe and Healthy Environment 45

CHAPTER 3

The Virtual Workforce   57

Telework and Virtual Assistants 57 • Virtual Workplace Considerations 65 • Creating an Effective Work Environment 71

Part 2
Workforce Behaviors 80

CHAPTER 4

Your Professional Image   82

Characteristics of a Professional 82 • Your Professional Look 88 • Understanding Business Etiquette 91

CHAPTER 5

Anger, Stress, and Time Management   103

> Understanding Stress 103 • Stress and Its Effects in the Workplace 104 • Factors Contributing to Workplace Stress 106 • Anger—Its Purpose and Its Resolution 108 • Administrative Professionals and Time Wasters 109 • Stress, Anger, and Time—The Relationship 111 • Techniques for Managing Stress, Anger, and Time 111

CHAPTER 6

Ethical Theories and Behaviors   126

> Business Ethics 126 • The Importance of Ethics 128 • Characteristics of Ethical Organizations 130 • Ethical Change 135 • Discrimination—Its Implications for the Organization 138 • Characteristics of Ethical Administrative Professionals 141 • Ethics—Your Call 145

Part 3

Communication Essentials 150

CHAPTER 7

Written Communications   152

> Written Messages 152 • Organizational Skills 154 • Characteristics of Effective Correspondence 160 • Planning and Writing Guidelines 162 • Collaborative Writing 179

CHAPTER 8

Verbal Communication and Presentations   185

> Verbal Communication 185 • Nonverbal Communication 190 • Verbal Presentations 193

CHAPTER 9

Customer Service   210

> Importance of Customer Service 210 • Commitment to Customer Service 211 • Future Customers 212 • Customer Service Skills 212 • Customer Service Call Centers 221 • Web Customer Service 222 • Inappropriate Customer Behavior 222

Part 4
Technology Basics 230

CHAPTER 10

Technology Update   232

Computer Hardware 232 • Computer Software 242 • Technology Issues 246

CHAPTER 11

Workplace Mail and Copying   256

United States Postal Service 256 • Private Mail Services 260 • Email 261 • Mail-Handling Responsibilities 261 • Office Copiers 267 • Shredders 272 • Fax Machines 273 • Recycling 274

CHAPTER 12

Telecommunications—Technology and Etiquette   280

Telecommunications Described 280 • Telephone Etiquette 287 • Messaging Services and Etiquette 294

Part 5
Records and Financial Management 306

CHAPTER 13

Managing Paper and Electronic Records   308

Importance of Records Management 308 • Managing Paper Records 310 • Alphabetic Indexing Rules 317 • Cross-Referencing Records 327 • Other Records Systems 327 • Managing Electronic and Microfilm Records 331 • Records Retention, Transfer, and Disposal 337

CHAPTER 14

Personal Finance and Investment Strategies   345

Financial Knowledge Is Important for Success 345 • Payroll Deductions 345 • Organizational Financial Statements 350 • Banking 355 • Personal Financial Security 357 • Benefits and Investments 360 • Education—Continual and Crucial 365

Part 6

Meetings and Travel 370

CHAPTER 15

Event Planning   372

Effective Meetings 372 • Meeting Roles and Responsibilities 380 • Conferences
and Conventions 391

CHAPTER 16

Travel Arrangements   399

Domestic Travel 399 • International Travel 405 • Organizational Travel
Procedures 409

Part 7

Career Advancement 422

CHAPTER 17

Job Search and Advancement   424

Understand Your Skills, Interests, and Abilities 424 • Determine Your Job Search
Plan 427 • Research Organizations of Interest 431 • Prepare a Resume 433 •
Prepare a Letter of Application 438 • Interview Successfully 438 • Evaluate a Job
Offer 445 • Develop Job Advancement Strategies 446 • Handle a Job Change
Appropriately 447

CHAPTER 18

Leadership and Management: Challenges and Characteristics   453

Leadership Traits 453 • Definition and Functions of Management 461 •
Administrative Professional Responsibilities 466

REFERENCE GUIDE   475

GLOSSARY   503

INDEX   511

part 1

The Dynamic Workplace

CHAPTER 1

**The Workplace—
Constantly Changing**

CHAPTER 2

**Workplace Team and
Environment**

CHAPTER 3

The Virtual Workforce

Career Profile

Administrative Assistant

Administrative assistant can be a challenging and rewarding career choice. Administrative assistants work in almost all industries and for small, medium, and large companies. About 4.1 million people worked as secretaries and administrative assistants in the United States in 2004.

An administrative assistant may work mainly with one or two executives or other employees or as part of a work group or team. The job duties of an administrative assistant typically include managing schedules and records, sharing information with others by telephone and through correspondence and reports, creating presentations, handling mail, making travel arrangements, conducting research, managing projects, and performing other tasks specific to the company.

Salaries for administrative assistants vary by geographic region, the size of the company, and the qualifications of the worker. The mean annual earnings of executive secretaries and administrative assistants was $34,970 in May 2004.* To be a successful administrative assistant, an individual must have formal education and skills in the areas listed below. According to

the *Occupational Outlook Handbook*, opportunities should be best for applicants with extensive knowledge of software applications.* One- and two-year programs in office administration offered by business schools, vocational-technical institutes, and community colleges provide needed training.

- Communication
- Interpersonal relations
- Time management
- Critical thinking
- Decision making
- Creative thinking
- Teamwork
- Technology
- Leadership
- Stress management

Possibilities for job advancement for administrative assistants include promotion to an office manager position or to other administrative positions with more responsibilities. These positions may involve supervising or training other administrative professionals.

---

*"Secretaries and Administrative Assistants," *Occupational Outlook Handbook*, 2006-2007 Edition, accessed April 23, 2007, available at http://www.bls.gov/oco/ocos151.htm.

chapter 1

The Workplace—Constantly Changing

Learning Goals

1. Identify changes that are occurring in the workplace.

2. Define common types of business organizational structures.

3. Determine major challenges confronting both management and administrative professionals.

4. Explain crucial skills and qualities for an administrative professional.

5. Determine how an effective administrative professional sets goals and makes decisions.

Labor Projections

A constantly changing world is a reality today, and all indications are that this change will continue in the future. The consistency of the change is evident by the technological innovations that confront you as you work and go about your daily life. In this changing world, medical breakthroughs will allow people to live considerably longer. Additionally, due to the growth of knowledge, continuous learning will be essential in meeting the needs of the job market.

By 2014, the number of persons working or looking for work is projected to reach 162.1 million, representing an increase of over 10 million from the 2006 workforce. The growth is due entirely to population growth within the United States. The young age group consisting of persons 16 to 24 years old is expected to be flat. The number of men in the labor force is expected to decrease from 53.6 percent to 53.2 percent in 2014. The number of women in the workforce is expected to increase to 46.8 percent in 2014.[1]

The Ever-Changing Workplace

You live in a world in which knowledge continues to increase dramatically. This knowledge increase means that you as a prospective administrative professional must be willing to

[1]"Labor Force Projections to 2014: Retiring Boomers," Monthly Labor Review Online, accessed March 6, 2007, available from http://www.bls.gov/opub/mlr/2005/11/art3exc.htm.

© Tetra Images / Getty Images

Lifelong learning is essential in our constantly changing world.

continue to learn and grow. Your success on the job hinges on your ability to continually learn and constantly seek to understand people of different races, ethnicities, and backgrounds. In this changing world, you cannot assume that you can develop a set of skills and then stop growing and learning.

Economic Globalization

The global nature of the United States economy is obvious to even the most casual of observers. You need only listen to the stock market news to understand the interrelatedness of the U.S. economy with the economies in Europe, Asia, and other countries around the world.

Global interdependence, the knowledge-based economy, and technological change have helped change the relationships between workers and employers. In the past, many workers spent a major portion of their careers with a single employer. Today, workers are less likely to stay with one employer throughout their career. Employers may not invest as much money in the training of their employees as in the past. Global

interdependence has increased pressure on companies to streamline their operations. Employers are moving operations to locations where they can operate with lower costs both within the United Stated and outside the United States. Additionally, immigrants to the United States help meet labor demands.[2]

Workplace Diversity

Whether you are preparing to enter the workplace after finishing your studies or you are presently employed either full- or part-time, the increased cultural diversity of the work environment is likely to be apparent to you. The number of immigrants entering the United States is expected to increase. From 2000 to 2050, white non-Hispanics in the labor force are expected to fall by approximately one-fourth of the population, while the share of Hispanics and Asians is expected to more than double within this same time frame.[3]

[2]"Workforce Challenges and Opportunities for the 21st Century: Changing Labor Force Dynamics and the Role of Government Policies," United States General Accounting Office, June 2004, accessed March 8, 2007, available from http://www.gao.gov/new.items/d04845sp.pdf.

[3]Ibid.

Older Workers

The United States labor force is projected to become older. As the **Baby Boom Generation** (individuals born between 1946 and 1964) ages, older workers are expected to become a larger share of the labor force. Individuals over 55 years old are expected to make up 20 percent of the labor force by 2020. Additionally, it is estimated that by 2050, this age group will make up 19 percent of the labor force.[4]

Women in the Workforce

For the past four decades, the number of women in the workplace has grown at a fast pace, increasing from 62.2 million in 1950 to 140.8 million in 2000. However, over the next 50 years, women's share of the workforce is expected to remain at around 48 percent. Without a major increase in productivity, low labor force growth will lead to slower growth in the economy and to slower growth of federal revenues.[5]

Changing Workweek

Although a number of organizations still adhere to the traditional five-day workweek and 8 a.m. or 9 a.m. to 5 p.m. hours, the tradition is changing. Some companies have begun to establish flexible hours to accommodate changing family structures and needs. Several alternatives to the traditional workweek are gaining in popularity. These alternatives include the **compressed workweek**, **flextime**, and **job sharing**.

COMPRESSED WORKWEEK

With a compressed workweek, employees work the usual number of hours (35 to 40) but work fewer than five days per week. For example, a 40-hour week may consist of four 10-hour days; a 36-hour week may be made up of three 12-hour days.

FLEXTIME

Flextime is another departure from the 8 a.m. to 5 p.m. workday. With flextime, working hours are staggered. Each employee must work the full quota of time but at periods convenient for the individual and the organization. Under this plan, all employees do not report to or leave work at the same time. For example, with a 40-hour week, one employee may come to work at 7:30 a.m. and work until 4 p.m. (with 30 minutes for lunch). Another employee may come to work at 9 a.m. and work until 5:30 p.m. Core hours (hours when everyone is in the office) may be from 9:30 a.m. until 2:30 p.m. Flextime helps reduce traffic congestion at the traditional peak hours and allows employees flexibility in their schedules.

JOB SHARING

Still another departure from the traditional work schedule is job sharing. Under this arrangement, two part-time employees perform a job that one full-time employee might hold. For example, job sharing might be two people working five half days or one person working two full days and another person working three full days. Such a plan can be suitable for parents with small children where one or both spouses want to work on a part-time basis. In addition, job sharing can be suitable for workers who want to ease into retirement by reducing the length of their workday or workweek. Both the employees and the organization can profit from job sharing. Because full-time benefits are generally not paid to part-time employees, the company saves on benefit costs.

Physical Workplace

Today the physical workplace has changed drastically from the traditional office located in an established structure, with the office staff working traditional hours of 8 a.m. or 9 a.m. to 5 p.m. The office exists in a number of different forms, with these forms being the virtual office, mobile office, or home office.

The virtual office has no physical form and allows you to perform work from a variety of locations—at home, in your car, at a coffee shop, or at an out-of-town location such as a hotel, to

---

[4]Ibid.

[5]Ibid.

name a few possibilities. Mobile offices generally are temporary offices set up at almost any location that has a workspace available, including airport terminals, hotels, and coffee shops. These offices are particularly convenient for people when they are traveling and need to communicate with people at their home work site. Home offices, as the name suggests, allow workers to work from their homes. Although a number of people who work at home are **self-employed**, a large number of home workers are employed by companies or organizations that allow employees to work full-time or even part-time from their homes. Additionally, with the continued growth of international businesses, workers have the potential for working at global sites owned and operated by U.S. businesses.

A growing number of administrative professionals today work from a home office.

© Blend Images / Jupiter Images

Future Workplace Sites

With the ever-increasing technological capacity of our world, the types of workplaces mentioned in this chapter will likely continue to expand and other types of workplaces that we do not anticipate today will emerge. If you are to be successful as an administrative professional, you must be able to adapt to continual changes in the workplace environment.

Organizational Structures

In your career as an administrative professional, you may work for several types of organizations. If you work in a business environment either now or when you complete your education goals, you will need to understand something about the type of business for which you work. The descriptions here are brief; however, they will provide you insights into various types of organizations. As you continue your studies, you will want to learn as much as you can about various business entities. The principal types of organizations are:

- Sole proprietorships
- Partnerships
- Limited liability companies
- Corporations
- Nonprofit organizations
- Governmental entities

Sole Proprietorships

A **sole proprietor** is a single owner of an unincorporated business called a sole proprietorship. A sole proprietor also may be referred to as an independent contractor, consultant, or freelancer. The business is owned and controlled by a single person. All responsibilities, profits, and losses belong to the owner.

Partnerships

A **partnership** consists of an association of two or more people as co-owners of a business. All profits and losses are distributed to the partners according to the terms of the partnership agreement. Partnerships are largely being replaced by limited liability companies.

Limited Liability Companies

A **limited liability company (LLC)** is a business form that combines the tax advantages of a partnership with the limited liability of a corporation. It must include two or more members. The rights of an LLC include conducting or promoting any lawful business or purpose that a partnership or individual may conduct or promote. The LLC can own property, borrow money, loan money, enter into contracts, and elect or appoint managers or agents. An advantage of an LLC is that members receive limited personal liability from business activities. Professionals such as medical doctors, accountants, and lawyers may operate as an LLC.

Corporations

Corporations are legal entities formed by following a formal process of incorporation set forth by state statutes. The corporation may be publicly or privately owned. Owners called **stockholders** own shares of stock in the company. S-corporations are a type of corporation that must have 75 or fewer stockholders. The purpose of an S-corporation is to avoid double taxation of dividends distributed to stockholders.

Nonprofit Corporations

Nonprofit corporations are those that are formed to promote a civic, charitable, or artistic purpose. These corporations are generally exempt from federal and state taxation on their income. However, they do have responsibilities for reporting their income, assets, and activities. They typically have fiduciary (holding in trust for another) responsibility to their members and contributors. They must be in compliance with federal and state laws governing nonprofit corporations. Numerous organizations, such as service organizations, performing arts groups, hospitals, faith-based organizations, charities, and private colleges are set up as nonprofit entities.

Governmental Entities

Governmental entities are organizations funded and managed by a local, state, or national government. Examples of governmental units include city services, county services, state services, and national services. There are numerous departments, commissions, bureaus, and boards in all governmental units. These entities may be profit or nonprofit entities.

Workplace Organization

An effective and productive administrative professional will learn as much as possible about how the entire organization functions. If the organization is publicly held, there are stockholders to consider in addition to the board of directors, the administrators, and employees of the organization. Although organizations operate differently, the major levels of an organization, along with an overview of the responsibilities of the individuals at this level, are discussed in the next sections.

Stockholders

Stockholders are investors in a business. A stockholder owns a portion or a share of a corporation. Stockholders may be affected by the actions, decisions, policies, or practices of the business. For example, if the business is poorly managed or has financial problems, the value of the company stock may decrease. Thus, the stockholder loses money on the investment.

Board of Directors

A **director** is an officer of a company who is charged with the management of its affairs and conduct. The number of board members varies based on the needs of the organization, with a board generally having approximately 12 to 15 members. Collectively, the group is referred to as a board of directors.

© Digital Vision / Getty Images

A board of directors establishes policies that guide the management of an organization.

Theoretically, the control of a company is divided between the board of directors and the shareholders. Large corporations have boards of directors who have the major responsibility of establishing policies that guide the management of the organization. Boards are composed of community, civic, and business leaders who meet monthly or every two or three months. A quorum must be present before any business may be conducted. In addition to making policy decisions, boards employ, evaluate, and dismiss (if necessary) the **chief executive officer (CEO)** of the corporation. Boards generally operate as a total board and also as committees of the board as a whole. Directors may not put themselves in a position where their interests and duties conflict with the duties that they owe to the company. For example, a director should not be in a position where there is a conflict of interest between the director's interests (e.g., making money for himself/herself) and the duties that the director owes the company.

Board members of corporations deal with a variety of issues such as the following:

- Creating a strategic vision or mission for the organization

- Employing the CEO
- Assisting the CEO in determining the direction of the organization
- Holding the CEO responsible for the profitability of the organization
- Insisting on organization accountability from the CEO

Management

Management refers to those individuals who are top or upper managers in a company, such as the CEO, chief operating officer, and vice presidents. Additionally, other administrators at lower levels are responsible for the day-to-day operations of the organization, with the individuals having titles such as Vice President of Marketing, Controller, Treasurer, Sales Representative, and so forth.

At the beginning of your career as an administrative professional, you are not likely to manage other personnel. However, as you become an experienced and respected member of the office team, you may manage one or two administrative professionals who report to you. As you continue to grow in your job, you may be asked to take on additional management responsibilities. Thus, you need some understanding of management challenges, the role of management, and characteristics of effective managers.

Major Management Challenges

If managers are to be successful in helping the organization to grow and employees to produce at their top level, they must face and overcome several challenges. A few of those challenges are discussed in the following sections.

GREATER WORKFORCE DIVERSITY

As you have already learned, the U.S. workforce will continue to become more ethnically diverse. White, non-Hispanic persons will become a decreasing share of the labor force, with Asians projected to account for 5.1 percent of the workforce by 2014 and Hispanics for 12 percent.[6]

INCREASED AGE DIFFERENCES

The number of women in the workforce is projected to grow at a faster rate than the number of men. Additionally, the youth labor force (persons 16 to 24 years old) is expected to decrease slightly, while the number of workers 55 and older is projected to increase. Changes in consumer demand, technology, and numerous other

Category	Date of Birth
Silent Generation	1925–1942
Baby Boomers	1946–1964
Generation X	1965–1975
Generation Y or Millennial Generation	1976–2003

FIGURE 1.1 Category Names

factors will provide additional challenges for management.[7]

Management employees can expect to work with individuals who are from 18 to 70 years old. Because of the age differences, management can expect workers to have vastly different values and goals. One way to develop an understanding of the differences in the workgroup of today and tomorrow is to look at studies that detail some of the differences. For example, demographers and writers in the field assign a name to groups of people according to their date of birth and then study their characteristics. Categories and the titles given to these groups are shown in Figure 1.1. Because generations are defined by demographers, the media, market researchers, and others rather than by a formal process, the dates of birth included in each category may vary depending on the source used.

---

[6]"Tomorrow's Jobs," U.S. Department of Labor, Bureau of Labor Statistics, accessed January 20, 2007, available from http://stats.bls.gov/oco/oco2003.htm.

---

[7]Ibid.

Each generation views the world through a different lens according to the events that were taking place during their formative years. Because people are staying in the workforce today longer than in the past, managers can expect to work with some individuals of the **Silent Generation**. Also, you as a prospective administrative professional may work for an employer who is a member of this generation. The Silent Generation grew up as children during World War II and the Great Depression. Although they grew up too late to be heroes of World War II, they may have fought in the Korean conflict. These people brought to our nation the civil rights movement, an unparalleled national wealth in the arts and commerce, and advances in science and technology.[8]

Baby Boomers make up a large part of the political, cultural, industrial, and academic leadership of the United States. The Boomers have had two U.S. presidents: Bill Clinton and George W. Bush. Leaders of this generation tend to reevaluate their lives in midlife; many focus on the successes and failures of their children. Baby Boomers will begin to reach age 65 by 2011 and will be about 25 percent of the total population.[9] Many people in this group will retire around age 65. However, many are expected to continue to work because they need to continue earning money or because they are still interested in their work and do not want to retire.

Members of **Generation X** were born between 1965 and 1975. They are described as persons who accept diversity, are practical and self-reliant, and reject rules and mistrust institutions.[10]

Generation Y, also called the Millennials, is the most diverse generation in U.S. history; only 61 percent of this generation identify themselves as Caucasian. This generation is considered more progressive on social issues than older generations. They have been described as individuals who have equal priorities on both career and family and are less work-centered in comparison to Baby Boomers. Characteristics of the generation include optimism, realism, and individualism.[11]

Organizational Strategies for Coping with Change

If an organization is going to be effective in a changing environment, management must focus on strategies for coping with change and assist employees with understanding their role in supporting the changes. Strategies that will assist both management and employees in meeting the needs of a changing organization are as follows:

- Become a learning organization
- Envision the future
- Clarify values
- Create a strategic vision
- Establish priorities
- Invite employees to participate in change
- Lead employees through change
- Continually evaluate organizational directions and needs

Become a Learning Organization

Organizations are not static; they change over time. Individuals also change. Organizations, along with individuals within the organization, must continually learn and grow. Earlier in this chapter, you learned how much the composition of our workforce is changing. U.S. businesses will continue to become more international in their operations, with more businesses establishing facilities in other countries. Additionally, companies will continue to market products all over the world, and other countries will continue to grow in their marketing ability. This fast-paced global

[8]"The Silent Generation," accessed January 20, 2007, available from http://www.univcon.com/SGen/index.htm.

[9]Jennifer Cheeseman Day, "National Population Projections," U.S. Census Bureau, accessed March 15, 2007, available from http://www.census.gov/population/www/pop-profile/natproj.html.

[10]Diane Thielfoldt and Devon Scheef, "Generation X and The Millennials: What You Need to Know About Mentoring the New Generations," Law Practice Today, accessed March 15, 2007, available from http://www.abanet.org/lpm/lpt/articles/mgt08044.html.

[11]Ibid.

Company managers establish dynamic strategic plans for a company.

market demands that companies become learning organizations. Characteristics of a learning organization are discussed in the following sections.

Envision the Future

You have learned that organizations do not stay the same. The business world moves at a fast pace and is constantly changing—becoming more global in scope and flat in nature, with products and services being available worldwide. The United States is no longer a country that merely provides for the needs of its population. Products are manufactured and sold for an international market.

Effective leaders of organizations help individuals within the organization to create a strategic vision for the organization. Leaders understand that the strategic vision is not static, but dynamic. The vision changes frequently during the life of the organization. An often-used model is one in which top management establishes the major directions and middle management, along with the individual employees, develop objectives for their units that support the directions established.

Clarify Values

The following story, related to values clarification, is told in a book entitled *Leadership the Challenge*.

> *Max DePree, former CEO of Herman Miller, tells the story of a granddaughter who was born prematurely, weighing only one pound and seven ounces. A nurse advised Mr. DePree and his wife to rub her arms and legs with the tip of their fingers and talk to her as they did so. The nurse stated that the child needed to be able to connect the voice and the touch. Max DePree comments that the nurse gave him one of the best possible descriptions of the work of a leader. A leader must always be able to connect one's voice to one's touch.*[12]

This story graphically portrays what a leader must do in clarifying values—the voice and the touch must be consistent. Leaders who are effective are clear about their own values and share their values with the people who work with and report to them. Their words and their

---

[12]James Kouzes and Barry Z. Posner, *Leadership the Challenge* (California: John Wiley & Sons, Inc., 2002).

© Digital Vision / Getty Images

Creating an ethical culture when working in organizations outside the United States is crucial.

actions must always be consistent—one should not contradict the other.

Establish Priorities

Leaders must help the organization to establish priorities. These priorities must reflect the strategic values and vision of the organization. If they are in conflict with the values and vision, the employees of the organization become confused about what is essential to the organization— what must be done in order for the organization to succeed.

Challenges outside an organization often impact the organization. You have already learned about two of these challenges: greater ethnic diversity and an older workforce. Additional challenges include the following:

- Top management of U.S. corporations understanding the global orientation of our world and setting organizational directions that meet the challenges presented
- Creating an ethical culture as corporations work across national, cultural, social, and economic boundaries
- Determining how to measure success when working in the global environment

- Learning from the business practices and values of countries such as China and India
- Raising the awareness of U.S. managers and employees concerning global issues

Create a Strategic Vision

Some of the best leaders in organizations are those who not only have a vision for where the organization and unit should go but who are also willing to help others understand and support that strategic vision. Effective leaders help their units to develop a strategic plan and then update that plan on an ongoing basis. Such a plan provides a clear path for people within the organization to follow. In addition to helping people understand where the organization is going, a strategic plan that is well done seeks the input of all people within the unit. Employees are more likely to become committed to the company goals if they have had a chance to help shape the goals. "Many organizations are like a long corridor with dozens of doors. If any of the doors are locked, the idea dies. Leaders must reduce the numbers of doors and ensure that people have keys to the ones that remain."[13]

---

[13]Perry M. Smith, *Rules & Tools for Leaders: A Down-to-Earth Guide to Effective Managing* (New York: The Berkley Publishing Group, 2002), p. 58.

© Digital Vision / Getty Images

Celebrate your successes.

Invite Employee Participation in Change

When individuals feel that they are a part of an organization, they want to participate. Successful organizations understand that involvement of employees within the organization is essential. Individuals may feel threatened when they are not involved in working through the change needed. "We have no choice but to invite people to rethink, redesign, restructure the organization. We ignore people's need to participate at our own peril. If they are involved, they will create a future that has them in it, one that they will work to make happen."[14]

Lead Employees through Change

Leaders of organizations have to be prepared for diverse and threatening emergencies. These emergencies may include stock market ups and downs, international incidents, airplane crashes, downsizing of the organization, and ineffective employees.

According to Smith, "Five major aspects of crisis leadership are decisiveness, flexibility, innovation, simplicity and empowerment.... A hallmark of crisis leadership is keeping things simple—asking associates to do things that they are already trained to do, and not asking them to do new things with which they are unfamiliar."[15]

Often employees need help in dealing with change. Good managers understand this need. They help employees understand the need for change and how the change will benefit individuals within the workgroup and the workgroup team as a whole.

Celebrate Victory

Too often people forget to celebrate their successes. In our fast-paced world, it is easy not to allow the time for congratulations on a job well done. However, such an approach is essential to both leaders and team members. Individuals must give themselves a chance to celebrate what

[14]Margaret J. Wheatley, *Finding Our Way: Leadership in an Uncertain Time* (San Francisco: Berrett-Koehler Publishers, Inc., 2004), pp. 88–89.

[15]Perry M. Smith, *Rules & Tools for Leaders: A Down-to-Earth Guide to Effective Managing* (New York: The Berkley Publishing Group, 2002), p. 105.

Challenge	Description
Language knowledge and proficiency	The ability to speak more than one language is becoming increasingly important in the global economy.
Cultural knowledge of the country or countries	A growing number of companies are establishing locations in more than one country; in this environment, understanding the culture of each country becomes crucial.
Information technology requirements	The explosion of information technology continues and promises to continue for generations to come.
Recognition of our flat world	Companies must recognize our flat world, as described by Thomas Friedman in *The World is Flat*, and realize that our world will not retreat to the world of our grandparents.[16]

FIGURE 1.2 Workplace Challenges

went well, while at the same time remembering that they are not infallible.

Look to the Future in Planning Efforts

Once plans have been accomplished and evaluated to see what can be learned from the accomplishment, it is time to move to the next planning effort. The global economy and explosion of knowledge demands that the future direction of the organization be considered at least once each year. If the company operates in a volatile market, it should consider future directions more often. Questions such as these should be asked:

- In what direction is the market moving?
- What direction should be taken by our company?
- Do we need to consider markets that we are not considering?
- Does our company need to be global in its mission?

Tomorrow's Workplace

As businesses in the United States and throughout the world continue to expand globally in product markets and in where they are physically located, numerous challenges must be satisfactorily met. Several of these challenges are listed in Figure 1.2.

---

[16]Thomas L. Friedman, *The World is Flat* (New York: Farrar Straus Giroux, 2006).

Administrative Professional Challenges

As an administrative professional, you will face numerous challenges. You live in a work world where change is constant, and change is not always easy to handle. If you are to be successful, you need to be clear about what is important to you and the directions you want to take.

Values Clarification

In the workplace, you make decisions daily. Many of these decisions will be affected by your values. **Values** are deeply held beliefs that come from many sources; some of these sources are your parents, your school experiences, your culture, and your friends. As you prepare to become an effective administrative professional, you

Professional Pointers

Some tips to help you take advantage of the possibilities available to you are as follows:

- **Practice creative dreaming of where you wish to be in your professional life 10 or 15 years from now.**

- **Know your own beliefs and personal goals; pay attention to what you value.**

- **Focus on your achievements and your strengths.**

- **Learn from your failures.**

- **Create a vision for your future.**

focus on *Electronic Portfolio*

In each chapter of this textbook, you will complete assignments that could become part of an **electronic portfolio**. An electronic portfolio is also known as an *e-portfolio* or a *digital portfolio*. An e-portfolio might be used as a developmental, reflective, or representational tool. A developmental portfolio allows the owner to keep a record of projects or assignments completed over a certain period of time. A reflective e-portfolio includes personal reflections on the owner's development. A representational e-portfolio lists the owner's achievements in relation to particular work or developmental goals.

You will develop and use an e-portfolio in all three ways. You will use it as a personal reflection tool of your development in this course. For example, you will be asked to examine your values (what is extremely important to you and why). In each chapter, you will also evaluate your professional and personal growth. You will use the e-portfolio as a representational tool in listing your career goals. You will use your e-portfolio as a developmental tool in keeping a record of what you have done over a period of time in meeting those goals. At the completion of the course, you will be asked to reread your e-portfolio and reflect on your achievements in this class, your professional goals, and the career directions that you want to pursue. When determining your career directions, you will carefully consider the type of businesses or organizations where you might maximize your existing strengths and continue to grow. You will select a company or organization where you would like to apply and write a letter of application and develop a resume.

Workplace applications and other assignments that you might want to include in your e-portfolio will be marked with an e-portfolio icon.

need to seriously consider your values. Almost daily you will face situations in the workplace that call into play your values. Understanding what you value and why is important. You will take time to consider your values in Workplace Application 1-4 at the end of this chapter.

Career Development

Due to office automation, the job responsibilities of administrative professionals continue to change. Core responsibilities typically include the following:

- Store, retrieve, and integrate information for dissemination to staff and clients.
- Serve as information and communication managers.
- Plan and schedule meetings and appointments.
- Organize and maintain paper and electronic files.
- Manage projects.
- Conduct research.
- Disseminate information through the telephone, email, regular mail, and Websites.

An administrative professional may also perform activities such as the following in addition to the core responsibilities.

- Provide training and orientation for new staff.
- Conduct research on the Internet.
- Troubleshoot problems with new office technologies.[17]

Continuing education is important for administrative professionals. The International Association of Administrative Professionals (IAAP) is a major professional organization for administrative professionals. This organization is the world's largest association for administrative support staff. IAAP administers two professional certification programs —CPS (Certified Professional Secretary) and CAP (Certified Administrative Professional). The letters *CPS* or *CAP* after an administrative professional's name are indicative of the achievement of the highest professional standard within the field.

---

[17]"Secretaries and Administrative Assistants," U.S. Department of Labor, Bureau of Labor Statistics, accessed January 20, 2007, available from http://www.bls.gov/oco/ocos151.htm.

Figure 1.3 gives information about who is eligible to become a CPS and other details. For additional information about IAAP, visit their Website. A link to the site is provided on the Website for this textbook.

Administrative professionals often conduct research on the Internet.

Administrative Professional Workplace Requirements

Postsecondary education and various professional skills and qualities are essential for success in administrative professional positions. This section identifies some of the major workplace requirements needed to be a successful and productive administrative professional.

Skills

Skills needed in all administrative professional positions include the following:

- Communication (listening, reading, verbal presentation, and writing)

THE CERTIFIED PROFESSIONAL SECRETARY	
Why certification?	Job Advancement—The CPS rating gives you a competitive edge for hiring and promotion. Professional skills—You will learn more about office operations and build your skills by studying for and taking the CPS exam. Salary—A recent IAAP membership profile study shows that CPS holders can earn an average of $2,228 more per year than those who do not have certification. Esteem—Attaining the CPS certification demonstrates to your employer and yourself that you are committed as a professional. College Credit—Many colleges and universities offer course credit for passing the CPS exam.
Who is eligible?	You may take the CPS exam if you are employed as an administrative professional or have at least two years of work experience as an administrative professional, varying according to your level of college education. Students or teachers in a college business education program also may qualify.
When and where is the exam given?	The CPS examination is a one-day exam, administered each May and November at over 250 locations across the United States, Canada, and other countries.
What are the parts of the exam?	The exam has three parts: • Finance and Business Law • Office Systems and Administration • Management

FIGURE 1.3 The International Association of Administrative Professionals administers the Certified Professional Secretary program.

Communication skills are a "must have" in the workplace.

- Interpersonal relations
- Time management
- Critical thinking
- Decision making
- Creative thinking
- Teamwork
- Technology
- Leadership
- Stress management

COMMUNICATION

Administrative professionals spend a major part of their time communicating with others. Communication takes the form of emails, letters, faxes, voice mail messages, telephone calls, written presentations, verbal presentations, and one-on-one conversations. As you assume greater responsibility on your job, you may be involved in presenting information to your peers and other groups of people both within and outside your organization. Regardless of the form communication takes, you must be extremely proficient in this area. You must express yourself accurately and concisely in written

correspondence, and you must be clear, tactful, and straightforward in verbal communications. Part 3 of this textbook, Communication Essentials, will help you improve your communication skills.

INTERPERSONAL RELATIONS

As an administrative professional, you will interact with many people. Within the company, you will work with coworkers, supervisors, and other executives. Contacts outside the company include customers and visitors to the workplace. The people you encounter will be of different cultures, races, ethnicities, and ages. Additionally, you will interact with individuals who have diverse educational and professional backgrounds. If you are to be successful in working with these individuals, you need to be sensitive and accepting of their needs, cultures, and diverse backgrounds. Throughout your life, you must continue to work on improving your human relations skills. This area is one in which you never completely master the skill but should always attempt to improve. Chapters 2, 5, and 8 will help you improve these skills.

TIME MANAGEMENT

As an efficient administrative professional, you will need to organize your time, paper records, electronic files, and calendar so work flows smoothly and tasks are finished on time. Chapter 5 will help you improve your time management skills.

CRITICAL THINKING

Critical thinking is a unique kind of purposeful thinking in which a person systematically chooses conscious and deliberate inquiry. *Critical* comes from the Greek word *krinein*, which means to separate or to choose. To think critically about an issue means to try to see it from all sides before coming to a conclusion.

As an administrative professional, you should think critically about the issues facing you. Doing so can save you time and make you more productive. These skills can also make you a valuable employee for your organization—one

CRITICAL-THINKING QUESTIONS

- What is the purpose of my thinking?

- What problem or question am I trying to answer?

- What facts do I need to address this problem or this question?

- How do I interpret the facts or information I receive?

- What conclusions can I make from the information I receive?

- Are my conclusions defensible?

- Have I dealt with the complexity of the situation?

- Have I avoided thinking in simple stereotypes?

FIGURE 1.4 Improving critical-thinking skills can help you be more productive.

CREATIVE-THINKING TIPS

- Have faith in your own creativity.

- Pay attention to everything around you.

- Ask questions constantly.

- Tackle tasks that are not easy and that require effort.

- Do one thing at a time.

- Stop worrying.

- Pay attention to your intuition.

FIGURE 1.5 Creative thinking may require considering several options for solving a problem.

who is recognized and promoted. As you are learning and practicing critical-thinking skills, a systematic process of asking appropriate questions will help you. Figure 1.4 lists several questions. Take a few moments to read them; then begin to practice and improve your critical-thinking skills.

DECISION MAKING

In your role as an administrative professional, you will make decisions daily. If you are to be effective in that process, you must understand and implement proper decision-making steps. A later section of this chapter gives these steps. Study them and practice these skills throughout this course so you make effective decisions in the workplace.

CREATIVE THINKING

Creativity means having the ability or the power to cause to exist. Creativity is a process. It is a way of thinking and doing. A creative person understands that multiple options exist in most situations and that he or she is free to choose from a wide variety of options. Creative individuals use more than one set of rules or one method for getting a job done. Consider the following situation.

You have decided to take advantage of your company's offer to become a teleworker five days a week. You are expected to be productive as you work from your home; you will have no support from your colleagues. You have two young children, Maria and Gloria, who are in the first and third grades. You will be the primary caregiver when they return from school each afternoon.

How do you think creatively in this situation in order to accomplish your job at the highest level of productivity while meeting your family obligations? How do you set up your home work space to provide for maximum efficiency? How do you provide for your children's needs after school and still get your work done? Take a few minutes to read and think about the tips given in Figure 1.5. Throughout this course, use these tips as you make decisions. Then, practice the tips on the job—at the one you have now or will have in the future.

TEAMWORK

The word *team* can be traced back to the Indo-European word *deuk*, meaning to pull. Successful teams in the work environment include groups of people who work together to accomplish a given task. Teamwork skills are similar to interpersonal skills in that they demand that you understand, accept, and respect the differences among your

Teamwork demands that you build strong relationships with team members.

team members. Teamwork also demands that you engage in the following behaviors:

- Treat all team members courteously.
- Build strong relationships with individual members of the team and the team as a whole.
- Learn collectively with the team. Start by developing self-knowledge and self-mastery; then look outward in developing knowledge and alignment with team members.
- Take responsibility for producing high-quality work as an individual team member and encouraging a high-quality team project.

TECHNOLOGY

If you are to succeed in the workplace, you must be competent and current in your knowledge and skills of technology as it applies to your job. You must develop the following:

- Proficiency with computers and current software
- Proficiency in telecommunications
- Capability in researching on the Internet
- Competency in using printers, copiers, and scanners

- Willingness to research and use new workplace technology

Later chapters of this textbook will help you develop these important skills.

LEADERSHIP

You can develop your leadership skills by seeking out and accepting opportunities that allow you to practice leadership. For example, you might accept a leadership position in one of your school's organizations or in your community. As you seek out and accept leadership opportunities, learn from each of them. Evaluate your performance or ask a close friend to evaluate your performance. What did you do well with the leadership opportunity? What did you not do well? How can you correct your mistakes? In Chapter 18 you will learn more about leadership and the application of leadership skills to your job.

STRESS MANAGEMENT

You live in a fast-paced world—one where you may find yourself dealing with work-related stress. Chronic stress can cause serious health problems and affect your work, not only in the way you perform when you are under stress, but also in the work you miss due to illness. Anger, stress, and time management are all closely related. If you experience deep-seated anger, you become stressed. In order to be effective in your work and personal life, you need to understand how to manage anger and your time so you do not become ill or chronically stressed. You will learn more about anger, time, and stress management in Chapter 5.

Success Qualities

In addition to the skills identified in the previous section, certain qualities are essential for the success of an administrative professional. These qualities include:

- Openness to change
- Creativity
- Initiative and motivation
- Integrity and honesty
- Dependability
- Confidentiality
- Commitment to observing and learning

OPENNESS TO CHANGE

Because change is constant in our society and all projections are that change will continue to be present in our world, you need to be able not only to cope with change but to embrace it. To help you cope with change, seek to understand your organization well. Read the strategic directions for your organization; discuss these directions with your employer. Consistently learn new technologies and how you may be more effective in using them. Try to predict the changes you will face and prepare yourself for them.

CREATIVITY

The dictionary definition of *creativity* is having the ability to produce new ideas and being original and imaginative. For example, when dealing with a new situation or a new technology, a creative person will have the ability to:

- Evaluate the situation.
- Determine what needs to be done.

- Establish guidelines for achieving objectives.
- Evaluate the effectiveness of the efforts.

INITIATIVE AND MOTIVATION

Initiative is the ability to not only begin but also to follow through on a project. You demonstrate initiative by taking the projects that are given to you and completing them successfully. Additionally, you seek out tasks beyond those that have been assigned to you. You consistently analyze what needs to be done and then follow through on doing it.

Motivation is defined as an inducement to act—to get a task done. Motivation and initiative are closely related, with motivation providing the incentive to act and initiative providing the ability to get the task accomplished. You may be motivated *extrinsically* (from outside) or *intrinsically* (from within). For example, you may be motivated to perform a task because it provides a monetary reward for you or because it provides external recognition from your supervisor. Additionally, you may be motivated to perform a task because you are committed to learning and growing. You understand that a new task provides you with an opportunity to learn and grow.

INTEGRITY AND HONESTY

In the workplace environment, *integrity* and *honesty* mean that you engage in the following behaviors:

- Adherence to a strict ethical code
- Truthfulness
- Sincerity

You do not engage in activities that provide an opportunity for others to question your values or your morals.

DEPENDABILITY

Dependability is defined as being trustworthy. In action, dependability means that you perform in the following manner in the workplace:

- You are productive and consistent in getting the tasks of your job done.
- You are thorough and timely in producing your work.

- You willingly put in additional time that is often needed for an important assignment.
- You do what you say you will do and when you say you will do it.

CONFIDENTIALITY

Confidentiality is defined as secrecy, privacy, or discretion. In the workplace, confidentiality means the ability to receive and keep private information that is secret. You may be made aware of information that, if exposed, may pose a threat to your organization or to people within the organization. You must have the ability to understand the importance of not leaking the information to others within or outside the organization. For example, if you work for a medical doctor, you will probably have access to highly personal and confidential information concerning health issues of various patients. You also may hear doctors discussing an illness of a particular patient. You are responsible for maintaining the confidentiality of this information. You must think carefully about what you say to others within and outside the organization about your job and the information that you have available to you because of your job. To give confidential information to others (except for the people who need to know in your organization) can cause irreparable harm to patients, clients, and customers.

COMMITMENT TO OBSERVING AND LEARNING

With the workplace constantly changing and new technologies being developed, your task as an administrative professional is to commit to continual learning. Several questions that you should continually ask yourself as you go about this process are as follows:

- Do I make an effort to understand the directions of my organization?
- Do I understand what my employer expects of me?
- Do I listen to others?
- Do I live by a set of ethics and values?
- Do I respect diversity of people and ideas?
- Do I commit to learning new technologies?
- Am I reliable?

career tip

Continuing Education

Throughout your career, continue to expand your knowledge and skills by:

- Attending seminars and workshops provided by your company or outside firms.
- Reading business periodicals.
- Participating in professional organizations.
- Constantly improving your communication, time management, and critical-thinking skills.
- Being a team player within your organization.
- Seeking out new learning opportunities by volunteering for assignments that you have not done in the past.

- Do I plan my daily and weekly schedule well?
- Am I flexible?
- Do I handle pressure well?
- Am I committed to continual learning?
- Am I productive on my job?

Career Plan

Where do you want to be in your education or career in three years? In five years? What steps do you need to take to accomplish your objectives? In order to get to your destination, you must set goals and make effective decisions about reaching your goals. Additionally, you must continue to evaluate whether you are reaching your goals.

Set Appropriate Goals

Personal goal setting involves setting both short- and long-range goals. In order to set goals, you need to determine what is important to you. Take an inventory of your needs, wants, interests, and abilities. Assume that in developing your master plan you decide you want your life to consist of career success, good health, financial security, and happiness. You must set some long-range goals that will help you realize these desires. Your goals, for example, may include becoming an administrative manager, having a family, and staying physically and mentally healthy. However, becoming a manager, having a family, and being healthy require hard work, and the accomplishment of many short-range goals.

How do you set short-range goals? You begin by considering the following areas:

- Your strengths and weaknesses
- Your motivation
- Your energy level
- Your ultimate desire to succeed in what you have planned for yourself

Consider the long-range goal of becoming an administrative manager. To do so will require experience, commitment, hard work, and time. Thus, a logical short-range goal may include getting a job that will allow you to use the skills and knowledge you have gained, in addition to providing you with work experience for future opportunities. Salary in your first job may not be your highest priority since you are seeking experience. Money may become a higher priority as you work toward your long-range goal.

Begin setting short- and long-range goals after asking yourself these questions:

- What are my strong points?
- What are my weak points?
- What are my achievements?
- What is my motivation?
- What do I enjoy doing?
- Where do I want to be in three years? In five years?

Keep in mind that your goals will change over time and that you may not always reach all of your short- and long-range goals. However, if you go through life never setting goals, you will never reach your maximum potential.

Make Effective Decisions

A **decision** is the outcome or product of a problem, a concern, or an issue that must be

STEPS IN MAKING A DECISION

1. Define the problem or the purpose.
2. Establish the criteria.
3. Generate alternatives or possible solutions.
4. Test the alternatives and make the decision.
5. Evaluate the decision.

FIGURE 1.6 Follow logical steps to make good decisions.

addressed and solved. In your role as an administrative professional, you will make decisions daily. It is important that you make good decisions. These decisions may range from recommending new technology to deciding how to handle a difficult client or customer. To make these decisions more effectively, you need an understanding of the decision-making process. Reaching a decision includes the five steps shown in Figure 1.6 and discussed in the following sections. You should follow these steps systematically when making a decision.

DEFINE THE PROBLEM OR THE PURPOSE

This step may sound simple, but it is usually the most difficult of the steps. When attempting to define the problem or purpose, ask yourself a series of questions:

- What problem am I trying to solve, or what purpose am I trying to achieve?
- Why is this decision necessary?
- What will be the outcome of this decision?

Assume you are completing your education and are ready to look for a position as an administrative professional. You know you want to enter the medical field. You have two job offers—one in a small medical office in the suburbs, approximately 15 minutes driving distance from your home. You have another offer for a job in a large city hospital, approximately 40 minutes driving distance from your home.

The medical office is small, and the advancement opportunities are limited. However, you understand you may have an opportunity to become an administrative manager, overseeing the operations. The office environment is informal, yet professional. The supervisor, Ms. Yung, seems helpful. People seem to care for one another. The workload of the position is heavy; however, the tasks are varied. The salary and benefits are fair.

The people in the hospital seem very nice, but the pace appears hectic. The workload of the position is heavy, but not varied. The personnel seem too busy to talk with each other. The promotional opportunities appear excellent and include a number of areas from which to choose. The benefits are excellent also. The salary for the hospital position is $50 more per month than the medical office.

In the situation described, your answers to the three questions might be as follows:

- What problem am I trying to solve, or what purpose am I trying to achieve?

    I am trying to solve the problem of finding a suitable position in the medical field. I want a job that provides good promotional opportunities and challenging work. Because I have a small child who will be staying with a babysitter, I do not want to drive long distances to work. I want to be able to spend as much time as possible with my child.
- Why is this decision necessary?

    The decision is necessary because (a) I am finishing my education, (b) I need money to help support my family, and (c) I want to be employed where the work is meaningful.
- What will be the outcome of this decision?

    The outcome of the decision is my employment in an administrative professional role where the position provides challenges and opportunities and an appropriate starting salary and benefits.

When you finish answering the questions, you should frame the problem in statement form. Your statement may be similar to the following:

My purpose is to find an administrative professional position in the medical field within reasonable proximity of my home. This position should be one that provides challenges and opportunities in addition to satisfying my financial needs.

ESTABLISH THE CRITERIA

The next step in the decision-making process is to determine criteria needed to make a sound decision. In setting criteria, here are three questions you may ask:

- What do I want to achieve?
- What do I want to preserve?
- What do I want to avoid?

Your answers to these questions in the situation given might be as follows:

- I want employment as an administrative professional in a medical office where promotions are possible.
- I want to use the skills that I have.
- I want to avoid traveling more than 30 minutes to and from work each day.

By asking and answering these questions, you can determine several criteria important to you as you look for a position.

GENERATE ALTERNATIVES OR POSSIBLE SOLUTIONS

The next step in the decision-making process is to begin generating alternatives or possible solutions. In the example discussed earlier, taking the job at the hospital is one possible solution. Taking the job at the medical office is another possible solution. You might identify other jobs that meet your criteria and could be possible solutions.

TEST THE ALTERNATIVES AND MAKE THE DECISION

The effective decision maker tests each alternative using this system:

- Eliminate alternatives that are unrealistic or incompatible with your needs or the criteria you listed.
- Give additional thought to alternatives appropriate in the situation.

- Select the alternative that appears most realistic, creative, challenging, or satisfying.

In the example discussed earlier, one position might have only one promotional opportunity offering a very small salary increase. The work environment in one position might be better than the other position. If neither position meets your needs, you may decide to decline both positions and continue your job search.

EVALUATE THE DECISION

The last step in the decision-making process is evaluating the decision. Evaluation serves two purposes:

- Evaluation helps you decide if you have made the right decision for the immediate situation.

- Evaluation helps you improve your decision-making skills for the future.

In evaluating your decision, ask yourself these questions:

- What was right about this decision? What was wrong?
- How did the decision-making process work?
- What improvements are necessary?
- What did I learn from the decision?
- What changes should I make for the future?

Setting appropriate goals and making effective decisions allow you to move in the direction you wish in your career. This decision-making model also helps you to deal realistically with your strengths and weaknesses and to minimize the latter as you reach your career goals.

Summary

To reinforce what you have learned in this chapter, study the summary.

- By 2014, the workforce is projected to grow to 162.1 million, an increase of over 10 million from the 2006 workforce.

- Several factors contribute to the changing workplace, including economic globalization, workforce diversity, changing workweek, and the physical workplace.

- Organizational structures include sole proprietors, partnerships, limited liability companies, corporations, nonprofit corporations, and governmental entities.

- Publicly held workplace organizations include stockholders and boards of directors.

- Management challenges include dealing with greater workforce diversity and older workers.

- Organizational strategies for coping with change include becoming a learning organization, envisioning the future, clarifying values, creating a strategic vision, and establishing priorities.

- Administrative professionals face challenges such as values clarification, career development, and learning new technological skills.

- The administrative professional's workplace requirements include skills such as communication, time and stress management, critical thinking, teamwork, openness to change, and commitment to observing and learning.

- The effectiveness of an administrative professional is enhanced by setting appropriate goals and making effective decisions.

What's the Problem?

Throughout this course, you will be working for United Pharmaceuticals. To learn more about this company, read the Your Organization section in Chapter 1 of the *Procedures and Theory for Administrative Professionals Applications Workbook*. As a part-time employee, you have had an opportunity to observe some of the human dynamics that occur in the organization. What is the problem in the following situation?

Josue Mendoza accepted his first job as an administrative professional in the Human Resources Department for United Pharmaceuticals. He was initially interviewed by a team of individuals. Several days after the interview, he was sent a letter welcoming him to the company and telling him to report to work in the Human Resources Department on Monday of the following week. The letter was signed by Roger Athens, Vice President. On Monday when Josue reported to work, he was introduced to Rebecca Masterson. He immediately extended his hand to her and stated that he was extremely pleased to work for United and was looking forward to meeting his boss. Rebecca smiled and said, "You have just met the boss; I am your supervisor." Josue was so embarrassed and confused that he simply said, "Well, I didn't expect to have a female boss; please forgive me for my assumption." Rebecca responded that he should not worry about what he had said and that she was looking forward to working with him.

Josue feels that he has made a major mistake and wonders if he should resign before he gets started. He has never reported to a woman before, and he wonders how the situation will work out. However, he is certainly willing to get to know her and understand what is expected of him.

What advice would you give Josue? Should he apologize to his new boss? Should he attempt to forget what he said and demonstrate to Ms. Masterson that he can be an asset to United? Should he quit immediately because he has made a major blunder?

Let's Discuss

1. Identify forces changing the workplace environment.
2. Describe two career opportunities available for the administrative professional.
3. List and explain six skills necessary for being a successful administrative professional.
4. Explain why flexibility and adaptability are essential for success in the workplace.
5. Explain the decision-making model.

Critical-Thinking Activity

Danxia Chan has completed her first year at Lincoln Hills Community College in Fort Worth, Texas. Danxia has always been an A student. However, when she started college, she was not certain of her career direction. She took general education classes. She enjoyed all of her classes, particularly her psychology and computer classes. She talked with one of the school counselors at the end of the year and completed the Myers-Briggs instrument which was suggested to her. According to the instrument, Danxia is an extrovert (likes working with people) and a thinker (makes decisions by logical reasoning). Danxia worked part-time in the president's office during the second semester. In this position, she answered the phone, made appointments, keyed reports, and handled complaints. She enjoyed every aspect of the job—especially the parts that dealt with people issues. The president's assistant complimented her several times on her decision-making ability. The president's assistant urged Danxia to take office systems courses in the fall, telling Danxia she thought the field could be rewarding.

How should Danxia go about deciding what to do? Danxia has never engaged in personal goal setting. In fact, she has no idea how to begin. However, Danxia is proud of her achievements this past year and is ready to make plans for the direction of her future. What advice would you give Danxia about how to set her personal goals? What should she consider? Develop a plan that you believe Danxia should follow, using the decision-making model presented in this chapter.

Vocabulary Review

Open the *Microsoft® Word* file *CH01 Vocabulary* found on the Student CD. Complete the vocabulary review for Chapter 1.

English and Word Usage Drill

Complete the English and Word Usage Drill for Chapter 1 found in the *Applications Workbook.*

Access the Website for This Textbook

The publisher of this textbook maintains a Website with information related to the textbook. The *Procedures and Theory for Administrative Professionals* Website contains data files, vocabulary flashcards, links, and other information that you will use as you complete the activities in this textbook. You will need to visit this site often. In this activity, you will explore the site and create a link to make visiting the site quick and easy.

internet

1. Access the Internet. Start your Web browser such as *Internet Explorer®*. In the Address box, enter **academic.cengage.com/officetech/fulton-calkins**.

2. A Website that contains Web pages related to your textbook should appear. Click a hyperlink. Quickly scan the new page to see the information that is provided. Click the **Back** button to return to the welcome page.

3. Locate and access the Links page on the Website. This page contains links to other sites that you can use as you complete activities. Whenever a Website is mentioned in an activity in the textbook, look for the link to that site on this page.

4. Return to the welcome page for this site. Add this Website to your Favorites or Bookmarks list. Use this Favorites or Bookmarks link whenever you need to access this site for later activities.

Workplace Applications

1-1 Conduct Research

internet

team building

(Goals 1 and 2)

1. Work with one of your classmates to complete this activity. Conduct research using the Internet or other sources on changes in the workplace and business structures. Identify at least five changes that are occurring today and three types of business organizational structures.

2. Prepare a short, unbound report to summarize your findings.

3. Use a program such as *Microsoft PowerPoint®* to create electronic slides that contain the main points of your findings. Use the slides as you present your findings to the class.

1-2 Interview a Manager

team building

e-portfolio

(Goal 3)

1. Work with three of your classmates on this assignment. As a team, identify a company and a manager that you will interview by telephone or in person. Before the interview, write six to eight questions that you will ask. You may use the following questions as examples.

   - What two or three challenges would you identify as major ones for your organization?

   - What is one major challenge facing you as a manager?

   - Do you anticipate additional challenges in the next two years? If so, what are they?

   - What skills and characteristics do you expect an administrative professional to have?

2. Conduct the interview and note the responses given to your questions.

3. Working as a team, prepare a memo to your instructor to report your findings. Use the *Word* file *Memo Form* found on the Student CD to create the memo.

1-3 Research Skills and Goal Setting

(Goals 4 and 5)

1. Visit the International Association of Administrative Professionals (IAAP) Website. You can access the site using the link provided on the Website for this

textbook or by entering the organization name in a search engine and following the appropriate link. Identify the career growth resources available for administrative professionals at this site.

internet

2. Using the Internet or other resources, research effective goal-setting techniques.

3. Write an unbound report to present your findings on these two topics. Label one section of your report "Career Growth Resources" and label the second section "Effective Goal Setting." Use at least four resources when preparing your report. Document the resources properly in the report.

e-portfolio

1-4 Consider Your Values

(Goal 5)

1. Think about your values. Values are deeply held beliefs that relate to people, things, or ideas that are important to you. Use the following list of topics to help you think about your values.

- Achievement
- Competence
- Creativity
- Excellence
- Family
- Freedom

- Friendship
- Integrity
- Knowledge
- Loyalty
- Recognition
- Security

2. Key a list of 15 values that are important to you. For example, one of your values might be "I believe I should do the best work I can on all assignments."

3. Select three of the values you have listed. For each of these three values, give an example of a work situation in which your actions or decisions would be affected by that value.

4. Keep your list of values throughout this course. After a few weeks, read your responses again. Add or remove items from the list if your values change.

Assessment of Chapter 1 Goals

Did you successfully complete the chapter goals? Evaluate yourself by filling out the form found in Chapter 1 of the *Applications Workbook*.

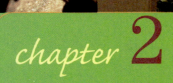

chapter 2

Workplace Team and Environment

Teamwork

If you are presently working, have you ever had a bad day at work? If so, have you stopped to analyze why that day was a bad one for you? Many bad days are the result of negative relationships with individuals in the workplace. These relationships affect not only your happiness on the job, but also your productivity. If you are unhappy, your work productivity drops significantly.

Another factor that contributes to happiness and productivity in the workplace is the physical environment in which you work. Is it safe? Can you work relatively free from physical harm? Is it a healthy place to work? Is the workplace clean and free from unhealthy factors, such as cigarette smoke? If the answer to any of these questions is no, the productivity of workers suffers. Employees cannot maintain maximum productivity if a threat of physical harm or a threat to long-term health exists. This chapter will help you understand how to work effectively with the workplace team and to contribute positively to a safe and healthy environment.

Teamwork is increasingly important as organizations continue to expand multinationally, adopt new technologies, and look for ways to decrease costs and improve profits. Employers rank teamwork as one of the most important skills for an employee to possess. In fact, studies show that effective teamwork increases worker productivity, decreases absenteeism, produces higher-quality products and services, and increases profits for organizations.

What does the word *team* mean? In the workplace, a team is a group of individuals who work together to achieve defined goals. Team effectiveness demands four behaviors from each team member:

- Understanding others
- Accepting different values
- Working together effectively
- Achieving goals

Seek to Understand Others

People who work together must understand and accept the differences that each individual brings to the team. These differences range from ethnicity, race, age, and gender to differences in values and backgrounds. You will encounter a workforce with greater ethnic diversity, an increased number of older workers, and larger numbers of women. As you learned in Chapter 1, diversity in the United States will continue to increase. (To remind yourself of the significance of the projected diversity, you may wish to re-read that portion of Chapter 1.) With this great diversity, understanding others can be difficult. Why? A major problem in understanding others is the value differences that are often present. The word *value* comes from the French verb *valoir*, meaning "to be worth." Values are your beliefs. You learn values at an early age from significant people in your environment, such as your parents and other family members. In addition, you learn values from educational, social, and religious structures, such as schools and places of worship.

Values are not inherently good or bad. However, the way in which you live your values may involve behaviors that are either acceptable or unacceptable in society. If you encounter someone who is not behaving appropriately for the values you hold, you may think that person has no values. Such thinking is incorrect; everyone has values. However, the values a person holds may not match your values or may not match the values of society. For example, one might say that Adolf Hitler was value-centered with one of his values being his desire to build a superior race. However, in his attempt to do so, he engaged in one of the greatest atrocities of history, killing over 6 million Jews.

Practice Acceptance of Different Values

Your job within the diverse workplace is to accept the different values that exist. Certainly you do not have to change your values to correspond to the values of others. However, remember that values are not static. As you grow and change, your values may change also. What is important to remember is that your effectiveness as part of a team depends on your acknowledgment and acceptance of different value structures.

Consider the following situation in which two individuals with different values clash in performing a task.

Benito grew up in Mexico. He is from a large family; he has five brothers and two sisters. As he was growing up, he was taught the value of the family unit. The family worked and played together. Every week a family meeting was held to discuss the activities of family members and the assignment of household chores for the upcoming week. If serious disagreements occurred during the week, a family council was held to settle the differences. Benito approaches his work life the same way. He believes that individuals within an organization should work together closely for the good of the organization.

Sarah grew up in a large city in the United States. Her family is small; she has one sister. Both of her parents worked outside the home while she was growing up. Sarah and her sister were taught to be totally independent. Family unity was not discussed. Her family rarely ate together; each person had his or her own schedule. Sarah's family stressed two main values—respect for the individual and the ability to operate independently.

Recently Sarah served as chair of a team; Benito was a member of the team. Sarah was an efficient chair, assigning each individual team member a task and expecting it to be done. Sarah never encouraged teamwork. Team members came to a meeting, received the assignment from Sarah, and reported to the group at the next meeting. After three team meetings, Benito voiced his concern that the group was not working as a team. Sarah did not seem to understand what he was saying. She suggested that the two of them discuss his concerns after the meeting. Benito became upset and told Sarah she was not listening to him. Sarah then responded angrily that he was not doing his assignments.

Value clashes such as this one are caused by differences in background and experience. Such incidents can cause misunderstandings among workplace team members and make it difficult for individuals to work together. As you work with others in the workplace, you must recognize and understand these differences. You do not need to adopt someone else's values or behaviors, but you cannot judge a person for behaving in ways that are consistent with his or her background, experiences, and values. When clashes occur, you need to find the solution to the problem, rather than lash out at the individual for his or her behavior.

Work Together Effectively

Members of a workplace team are a working unit. The design of almost all workplaces forces individuals into close physical proximity. Even as more and more people are engaged in telework, teams (although very different in composition) exist. When employed in a traditional workplace setting, you usually work on tasks with those people who are physically close to

It's important to accept differences that each individual brings to the team.

you. You are also generally part of a larger department or division of the organization. Each individual within the department works independently and interdependently to accomplish a variety of tasks. For example, you may be working on a marketing project. As a team, you work to determine the direction and content of the marketing project. As an individual, you prepare one piece of the project. If you are a teleworker or virtual assistant, your team may be your clients or customers.

Achieve Goals

Two sets of goals within an organization are generally important to you—your personal goals and the goals of the organization. For example,

A team must be committed to the goals of the organization.

© PureStock / Getty Images

you join an organization with certain personal goals. These goals are short-term and long-term. One of your short-term goals may be to learn your job as quickly as possible. One of your long-term goals may be to achieve a promotion to a higher-level position in the organization.

Although your personal goals are important, you must also be committed to the goals of the organization. If your personal goals are inconsistent with the organizational goals, you will not succeed. For example, assume the organization has a short-term goal of developing an employee recruitment plan. The timeline for development is three months. You are asked to be part of the team in charge of developing the first draft of the plan. You have a busy job, but one of your personal goals is to be promoted to a higher-level position. You decide, for career purposes, to be on the team. However, as the team begins its work, you find you must work overtime several hours each week to complete your regular job duties and finish your tasks on the recruitment plan. You have a small child at home, and one of your goals is to be a good parent. You do not believe you can work ten hours of overtime each week and still be a good parent to your child.

In this situation, your personal values and the organizational values are in conflict. These types of value conflicts often pose real dilemmas for people within the organization as well as the organization itself. Reconciling conflicting goals may require adjustments on your part and the part of the organization. If conflicting goals cannot be worked out, you may need to make personal sacrifices; if the sacrifice is too great, you may need to seek other alternatives. In the example above, you may decide to ask a relative to provide support for your child or you may decide to resign from the committee. If you decide to resign from the committee, you must recognize that you may jeopardize your plan for a promotion; however, you have decided that your child is your most important priority right now.

Workplace Team Composition

The administrative professional is often part of three basic types of teams:

- Project team
- Administrative professional and supervisor team
- Administrative professional and coworker team

Project Team

Project teams are brought together within an organization to accomplish an identified task. The teams are often responsible for a project from start to implementation. For example, the project team may be responsible for developing a diversity recruitment plan. The team must gather statistics on the diversity of the organization in the past and establish the type of diversity picture necessary for the future health of the organization. The next task for the team is to develop a plan to meet the diversity needs. The team may also be involved in evaluating the implementation of the plan after a period of six months or so.

Professional Pointers

Here are some tips for working successfully in teams.

- **Business is a team sport.** No one individual can be successful without the support of his or her fellow employees.

- Every member of a team must be involved; one way to get everyone involved is through appropriate communication.

- No one person has all the answers; all team members' opinions are valuable.

- There is no *I* in the word *team*.

- Teamwork is not about seeking credit for one's individual contributions; it is about the team succeeding.

When working in teams, worker **empowerment** is essential. Empowerment implies that individuals have access to the information they need to do the job and the authority and responsibility to do the job without constant checking from the supervisor. Supervisors trust the empowered worker to do the job well and to make decisions consistent with achieving the established goals.

If the project team is to be successful, certain essential criteria are necessary:

- Clarity of purpose
- Technical skills
- Administrative skills
- Interpersonal skills
- Commitment

CLARITY OF PURPOSE

The purpose and goals of the project team must be clearly established before the team begins its work. These questions need to be asked and satisfactorily answered:

- What is the team to accomplish?
- When is the team to complete its work?
- What standards will be used to determine whether a project has been completed successfully?
- Who will be evaluating the project?
- What additional resources does the team need outside the organization?
- What is the budget of the team?

As the project team operates, its membership must engage collectively in these behaviors:

- Ensure that team efforts are consistent with corporate-wide objectives.
- Ensure accountability of the team and each team member.
- Make certain that the team conforms to fiscal, legal, and other critical guidelines.

TECHNICAL SKILLS

If technical skills, such as telecommunication and writing skills, are important, careful selection of team members is crucial to ensure that they have the appropriate skills. Training sessions on certain new technologies can be made available to a team. However, there is usually not enough time to bring a neophyte (a beginner) in the field up to the level of expertise needed.

ADMINISTRATIVE SKILLS

Administrative skills include the ability to analyze financial data such as budgets, to process paperwork, and to set directions for a project. Since team members generally have various levels of proficiency in administrative tasks, the team should determine at the beginning of a project who is responsible for what particular administrative tasks. If several people need to be proficient in a task, the most proficient individual can provide short training sessions for other team members.

INTERPERSONAL SKILLS

Interpersonal skills are critical. Team members must be able to work together collaboratively, listen to each other effectively, and resolve conflicts that occur.

Suggestions for working together collaboratively include these:

- Define the purpose of the collaborative project at the first team meeting.
- Choose a chairperson or group leader.
- Determine each group member's skills and expertise.
- Assign tasks to each group member.
- Establish guidelines for completing the task.
- Determine a time for completion.
- Determine product evaluation standards.
- Determine evaluation standards for group members.

Although workers spend a large portion of their time listening to others, they may not know how to listen effectively. For example, people may spend their time being quietly critical of each other, rather than listening effectively to what others are saying. Listening effectively demands listening for the feelings and the words of the speaker. Listeners may disagree with what the speaker is saying, become angry, and block

the speaker's message. Figure 2.1 lists several suggestions for effective listening.

Another important interpersonal skill is conflict resolution. Even the most effective teams have certain areas of conflict. Understanding how to work through conflict is so important that team members may want to engage in a short session on conflict resolution at the beginning stages of a project. Here are several suggestions that can be effective in solving conflicts:

- Identify what is causing the conflict. Is it power, resources, recognition, or acceptance? Many times an individual's needs for these items are at the heart of the conflict.
- Determine what each person in the team needs or wants when a conflict occurs. Be willing to listen to the other person. If you do not understand what the other person is saying, paraphrase what you think you heard and ask

EFFECTIVE LISTENING TECHNIQUES

- Listen for facts.
- Listen for feelings.
- Withhold evaluation.
- Direct your attention to the speaker.
- Maintain eye contact with the speaker.
- Watch for nonverbal communication.
- Remove distractions.
- Ask questions if you do not understand what the speaker said.
- Paraphrase what the speaker said.
- Ask open questions.
- Do not anticipate the speaker.
- Organize what you hear.
- Try to understand the speaker's words.
- Do not get angry.
- Do not criticize.
- Take notes if appropriate.
- Set aside your own preconceptions about the topic being discussed.
- Use listening time productively. People speak at about 150 words per minute and think at about 500 words per minute. Use your thinking time effectively.

FIGURE 2.1 Effective Listening Techniques

for clarification. Be open to what the other person tells you.

- Identify points of agreement. Work from these points first, and then identify the points of disagreement.
- Create a safe environment. Establish a neutral location. Establish a tone that is accepting of the other person's views and feelings. Fear may be behind someone's anger. Let the other person tell you how he or she is feeling. Watch how you position yourself physically in the room. Remember, you have a more difficult time competing with someone who is sitting next to you than with someone who is across the table or room. A circular seating arrangement may be appropriate if you have several individuals involved in a conflict.
- Do not react. Many times individuals act too quickly when a conflict occurs. Step back, collect your thoughts, and try to see the situation as objectively as possible.
- Do not seek to win during a confrontation. Negotiate the issues and translate the negotiation into a lasting agreement.

- Listen actively. Watch the individual's eyes; notice his or her body language.
- Separate people from the issue. When the people and the problem are tangled together, the problem becomes difficult to solve. Talk in specific, rather than general, terms.

COMMITMENT

Each individual in the team must be committed to the accomplishment of the task and to the individuals within the team. People who are committed to the accomplishment of a task willingly engage in these behaviors:

- Sharing information with one another
- Taking risks
- Expressing their opinions
- Sharing accountability for the results

In demonstrating commitment, team members trust each other. They listen when another team member expresses ideas and opinions. Team members are committed to each other and to the task to be accomplished. By working together in an open and trusting environment, the contribution of each member can be maximized.

© StockByte / Getty Images

Team members must listen to one another and work together to solve conflict.

Administrative Professional and Supervisor Team

Another type of team in the workplace is the administrative professional and supervisor team. As an employee, you need to be clear about what you owe your immediate supervisor and what your supervisor owes you. Your relationship with your supervisor is of primary importance. Unless that relationship is satisfactory, you will not perform at your highest capacity. At the very least, you owe your supervisor respect, dependability, honesty, and loyalty.

RESPECT

Respect is showing regard and appreciation for your employer. You owe your employer respect simply because of the responsible position the person holds in the organization. You need to show respect for your employer's decision-making role although you may not always understand or agree with the decisions made. If for some reason you are unable to respect your employer, you need to find another position.

DEPENDABILITY

Dependability is defined in the dictionary as "trustworthiness." Dependability in practice means you observe the organization's rules regarding work hours, coffee breaks, sick leave, and vacation time. You are at work on time, and you consistently work all hours required. You do not abuse sick leave or vacation policies. You complete work assignments on time; or if on occasion you are not able to do so, you seek help. When you are in the workplace, you give the organizational goals top priority.

HONESTY

Honesty means that you are genuine; you are not deceptive or fraudulent. You are truthful, sincere, and fair. You do not play games on your computer or use the Internet for personal matters, such as making travel arrangements or shopping. You do not use email to send personal notes to friends.

LOYALTY

The definition of **loyalty** is "the quality of devoted attachment and affection." Loyalty between the administrative professional and the employer is essential. Actions that exhibit loyalty in the workplace include:

- Maintenance of confidentiality when necessary.
- Adherence to the chain of command. If a problem or an issue occurs with your supervisor, talk with him or her first. Your employer does not want to be surprised by concerns about which he or she had no inkling.
- Adherence to organizational values. Be honest with your employer and other employees.

Your employer also has certain obligations to you. Figure 2.2 lists several of these obligations.

Administrative Professional and Coworker Team

A third important team consists of your coworkers and you. What type of relationship should you have with your coworkers? Consider the following:

- Have you ever been in a situation where one employee who had nothing to do refused to

You owe your supervisor respect, dependability, honesty, and loyalty.

> ### SUPERVISOR'S OBLIGATIONS TO THE ADMINISTRATIVE PROFESSIONAL
>
> - Respect. Your employer should be aware of your needs and show respect for you and your abilities.
> - Feedback. Your employer should be honest and open with you concerning your work and how it is being evaluated.
> - Loyalty. Your employer should present you in a positive light to others. If your employer has a problem with your effectiveness, she or he should talk with you—not others—about the situation.
> - Ethical behavior. Your employer is responsible for managing ethically. You should expect your employer to uphold the values and ethics of the organization.

FIGURE 2.2 Supervisor's Obligations to the Administrative Professional

help another employee who was overloaded with work?

- Have you ever been in a situation in which workers spent break times and lunch hours gossiping about other employees?
- Have you ever worked in an environment where small cliques existed?

If you have worked at all, you probably answered yes to one or more of these questions. Uncomfortable situations with coworkers do occur from time to time. Although you cannot avoid these situations entirely, you can reduce such situations by applying effective human relations principles, such as acceptance, cooperation, tact, and fairness.

ACCEPTANCE

The dictionary definition of **acceptance** is "favorable reception; approval." You will come in contact with many different people in the workplace. Their backgrounds and interests may be quite different from yours. You may not understand many of these people at first. Because you do not understand them, you may dislike or disapprove of them. As a successful administrative professional, you need to accept other employees without judging them. You should recognize and respect people who are different

from you. If you sincerely listen to others, you will learn more about them and avoid conflicts that result from a lack of understanding.

COOPERATION

The dictionary definition of **cooperate** is "to work or act together toward a common end or purpose." In the workplace, cooperation means you are willing to work with coworkers for the common good. Since few jobs are performed in total isolation, cooperation is necessary in order to attain organizational goals. You should willingly assist other employees in meeting job deadlines when the situation demands. If one employee has a rush job that cannot be finished without help, you should offer that help, provided you have no top-priority work to complete.

TACT

Tact is defined as "acute sensitivity to what is proper and appropriate in dealing with others, including the ability to speak or act without offending." Tact demands sensitivity to the needs of others. You should consider the impact of what you say and avoid offensive statements. The tactful administrative professional emphasizes others' positive, rather than negative, traits. If you are tactful, you think before you speak. For example, if a fellow employee has just returned to the workplace after a serious illness, let the person know you are pleased that she is back. Avoid asking prying or possibly upsetting questions about her illness.

FAIRNESS

Fair is defined in the dictionary as "having or exhibiting a disposition that is free of favoritism." The fair person does not take advantage of others. You may get an idea from someone else; but if you are fair, you do not take credit for it. Instead, you give credit to the individual who gave you the idea. If you are fair, you also assume your share of responsibility without attempting to get coworkers to do your job.

Be tactful and sensitive to other people's needs.

Administrative Professional and External Team

Although the external team is not as closely constructed as the three previously mentioned teams, it nevertheless has some elements of a team. One or more individuals within an organization who work with individuals outside the company to achieve specified company goals compose the team.

Outsourcing (using outside firms to perform certain functions of an organization) provides a good example of an external team. For example, assume your organization is outsourcing the implementation of a new telecommunications system. As an administrative professional, you may be on a team that works with this organization. Working with the external team requires the same human relations skills as working with internal teams. Good communication skills and an understanding of the relationship between the outsourcing company and your organization are crucial.

POSITIVE PUBLIC RELATIONS

Working with an external team demands good **public relations**. Public relations is the technique of inducing individuals outside the organization to have understanding for and goodwill toward a person, a firm, or an institution. Favorable public relations are crucial to any organization.

The administrative professional must use good public relations when dealing with the external team as well as with visitors, clients, customers, and prospective customers of the organization. Through effective public relations, administrative professionals can increase the likelihood of a prospective customer becoming an established customer and an established customer becoming a repeat customer.

EFFECTIVE COMMUNICATION WITH WORKPLACE VISITORS

In many large organizations, a receptionist initially greets all workplace visitors. The receptionist may keep a register in which the name of the visitor, company affiliation, nature of the visit, person the visitor wishes to see, and date of the visit are recorded. After obtaining this information, the receptionist notifies the administrative professional of the caller's arrival. If the visitor is at the company for the first time, the administrative professional's job may include escorting the visitor to the executive's office.

Administrative professionals in small organizations may also serve as receptionists; that is, they have the responsibility of greeting all visitors to the company and directing them to the proper people.

Diversity in the Workplace

As the diversity of the U.S. workforce continues to grow, you must understand how to communicate with individuals coming from a wide range of diverse backgrounds.

Diversity—A Resource

Diversity can and should be a positive force in the workplace. However, understanding and acceptance is necessary. Think back for a minute on the history of the United States. People from different European countries and Africa helped build the United States. In fact, the term **melting pot**, coined by sociologists and meaning "the amalgamation of people of different ethnicities and races into one United States of America," describes the first few hundred years of the integration of people within this country. As the country's diversity continues to grow and people from Mexico, Asia, the Middle East, and other regions of the world seek residency here, the term *melting pot* has limited meaning. New terms, such as **salad bowl** and **quilt**, reflect the diversity more accurately. This country is no longer a group of people who become one big pot of sameness, but is a group of people who retain much of their identity from their homeland and much of their language. If you walk the streets of major U.S. cities, such as New York and Los Angeles, you hear a multitude of languages. In

other words, the *salad* has many ingredients, which remain intact even when mixed. The *quilt* has many different squares, maintaining their beauty even as the quilt is sewn together. In a number of places in the United States today (namely, California, Florida, and Texas), Spanish is the language spoken by many. If the United States is to be a strong country, everyone must practice acceptance and respect for people of diverse backgrounds and experiences.

Ethical and forward-thinking business organizations see diversity as a resource. How? Diverse groups of people bring to the workplace different perspectives, different values, and different ideas. The wise business organization uses these ideas to enrich its products and/or services so they appeal to a broad audience. Thus, the bottom line is that diversity treated with respect is good for the organization. In other words, diversity can make money for businesses.

© PhotoDisc / Getty Images

Diversity of ideas helps each individual grow and be more effective.

Additionally, diversity of ideas within an organization can help individuals grow and learn if they open their minds to hear what others are saying. Thus, diversity becomes a resource for individuals within the organization—a resource that helps each individual grow and be more effective in a highly diverse world.

Cultural Differences

Obviously, people from different countries and cultures bring a variety of thoughts and ideas to the workforce environment. Consider the following differences that exist among people of various countries.

Most people who speak English do not understand that the language and its nuances can be difficult for others to understand. For example:

- There is no egg in eggplant and no ham in hamburger.
- Are jumbo shrimp large or small?
- Is a working vacation relaxing or not?

How such terminology came into being is confusing. Imagine how puzzling it is for the person attempting to learn English.

Although the British speak English, a number of words have different meanings in Britain than they do in the United States. Consider these examples:

- An elevator is a *lift*.
- The bathroom is a *water closet* or a *loo*.
- The hood of a car is the *bonnet*.
- A cookie is a *biscuit*.
- The subway is the *underground*.

Figure 2.3 lists a few cultural differences that exist between people of different countries. If people are to be effective in dealing with one another, they must continue to learn and grow in their understanding of people from other cultures, races, and ethnicities.

Value and Attitude Clarification

You may not give much thought to how your values are different from other people's values.

CULTURAL DIFFERENCES

- In Korean culture, smiling can signal shallowness and thoughtfulness.
- Asians avoid eye contact as a sign of respect.
- In France and Mexico, being 30 minutes late to an appointment is perfectly acceptable.
- Latin Americans stand very close to each other when talking; the interaction distance is much less than in the United States.
- Open criticism should be avoided when dealing with Asian employees, as this may lead to loss of face.
- In Japan and China, yes does not always mean "yes." For example, if a person from Japan or China responds to a question in the affirmative, he or she may merely be demonstrating politeness—not acceptance of what you said.
- What is considered humor is not the same in all countries. One should be very cautious when attempting to be humorous; in fact, humor with people of other cultures should be avoided until the individuals know each other better.
- The types of food eaten vary greatly among cultures. For example, corn on the cob, grits, and sweet potatoes are not eaten as commonly in countries outside the United States. Muslims and Jews do not eat pork. Dog is considered a delicacy in some Asian cultures.
- Holidays are different; for example, other countries do not celebrate Thanksgiving, as is done in the United States.
- The colors of flowers have different meanings for different cultures. In China, white is the color of mourning; white flowers are sent only to people in mourning.

FIGURE 2.3 Cultural Differences

You may assume that everyone has the same values and then operate from this assumption. Obviously, that assumption is not true, and it can cause communication difficulties if it is not understood.

Also, you may not give much thought to the attitudes you demonstrate. The dictionary definition of **attitude** is "position, disposition, or manner with regard to a person or thing." Assume that as a North American, you value punctuality. One of your coworkers is from Mexico. Generally, people from Mexico do not consider punctuality to be as important as North Americans do. One of your coworkers is continually 30 minutes late for work. Although you do not have any supervisory responsibilities, you feel angry because she is consistently late. One day you grumble loudly as your tardy coworker sits down at her desk, "Some people are never on time." Obviously, she hears you and is less than friendly for the remainder of the day. Her interpretation of your remark is that you do not like people from Mexico—in fact, you are hateful toward them. You do value people from other cultures, but your attitude did not reflect your values. Just as you need to understand what you value, you also need to be clear about the attitudes you reflect to others.

Effective Communication Techniques for Diverse Environments

Communication in diverse environments can be improved if all individuals use good techniques. Put into practice these techniques:

BE RESPECTFUL

Be respectful of others' culture, background, experiences, and ethnicity. Attempt to remove your own cultural glasses to see the world in the way the person of a different cultural background sees it. Is this difficult? Of course it is. Is it possible? Yes, to a degree. You can never totally understand the world from another person's view, but you can try.

BE NONJUDGMENTAL

Do not be the "ugly American," always comparing others to your own culture and making value judgments when people from other cultures have different values and views. Remove your judging hat. Learn from other cultures, rather than judge them. When you adopt such an approach, you may be surprised to find yourself changing some of your views.

PLACE YOURSELF IN THE OTHER PERSON'S POSITION

When someone does something that you do not understand or that makes you angry, try to look beyond the action to the motivations and perspectives of that person. For example, if a person from China fails to make eye contact with you, the behavior is not disrespectful. In fact, just the opposite is true. Not making eye contact is a sign of respect.

BE FLEXIBLE

Learn to bend with the situation. If you ask a Japanese coworker his opinion on an issue and he does not respond, do not think he is being rude. Realize that cultures differ. In the Japanese culture, individuals are taught to withhold their personal opinions. An old Japanese proverb says, "Silence is a virtue."

PRACTICE GOOD LISTENING SKILLS

Listen and ask questions. Do not interrupt the speaker. Do not attempt to give your opinion on a particular subject at every opportunity.

Productive Communication

The previous section discussed several techniques to help you in communicating with people of other cultures. Certainly, the techniques are also effective in most communication venues. Additional information in this section discusses workplace communication; these techniques can be effective in many situations.

All organizations have formal and informal communication channels. Your goal as an employee is to be productive in both channels.

Formal Communication

Formal communication channels in an organization may be downward, upward, or horizontal. **Downward communication** consists of messages that flow from management to employees of the company. **Upward communication** includes those messages that travel from employees to management. **Horizontal communication** involves messages flowing from coworker to coworker or from manager to manager.

Informal Communication

In addition to formal communication in an organization, informal channels, often called the **grapevine**, are present. The origin of the term *grapevine* goes back to the time of the Civil War. Messages were transmitted by telegraph wires that were strung like a grapevine from tree to tree. These messages were often garbled. Today the grapevine has come to mean messages that may or may not be true and that originate from an unknown source.

The grapevine is a natural and normal outgrowth of people working together. The worst feature of the grapevine is untrue communication or rumors. Since rumors and untruths cannot be entirely squelched, the best way to reduce them is with open lines of formal communication. Management needs to give employees the information required to do their jobs. Employees also need to be kept informed about the direction of the organization.

Communication Techniques

This section presents several communication techniques applicable for workplace situations.

UNDERSTAND THE ORGANIZATIONAL STRUCTURE

When you join an organization, ask for an organizational chart if one is not made available to you. This chart will show you the organizational structure, the relationships between departments, and the levels of administrative authority.

The best way to reduce workplace rumors is with open lines of formal communication.

© Digital Vision / Getty Images

Certain portions of the chart may change from time to time, depending on projects of the company. These changes are usually reflected in dotted lines showing new relationships.

UNDERSTAND THE ORGANIZATIONAL MANAGEMENT STYLE

Management of an organization has considerable influence on the amount and type of communication within an organization. Management styles include the following:

- Management by coaching and development
- Management by consensus
- Management by information systems
- Management by objectives

Most managers use a variety of styles depending on the situation and needs of the organization. In fact, the word *manager* has come into question by those employed in the management field, as well as by theorists in the field. According to one widely accepted view, traditional management is too restrictive for the needs of today's organizations; the preferred term is *leader*. Here are a few of the differences between a manager and a leader.

- Managers see the world as relatively impersonal and static. Leaders see the world as full of color and constantly blending into new colors and shapes.
- Managers view work as an enabling process, involving a combination of ideas, skills, timing, and people. Leaders view work as developing fresh approaches to old problems or finding options for old issues.
- Managers focus on *how* things need to be done. Leaders focus on *what* needs to be done.

Proponents of the differences between management and leadership make the point that the skills necessary for individuals engaged in moving an organization forward include these:

- Empowering
- Restructuring
- Teaching
- Role modeling
- Questioning

As an administrative professional, you need to try to understand the philosophy of organizational leaders. Their philosophy becomes pervasive in an organization and impacts all decisions of the organization. You will learn more about leadership in Chapter 18.

WRITE AND SPEAK CLEARLY

As an administrative professional, you frequently engage in spoken and written communications. Be certain that your communications are as clear as possible. Keep your words simple; refrain from using difficult words to impress others. Express your thoughts, opinions, and ideas concisely. Tell others exactly what you mean. If you do not understand the speaker, repeat what you think the person said in your own words. Ask the speaker to confirm the accuracy or inaccuracy of your statements. If you think the listener has not understood you, tactfully ask the person to repeat what you said.

BE WORD CONSCIOUS

Words can mean different things to different people. You need to consider how the communicator interprets and uses words. The intended meaning of a supervisor may be misinterpreted by an employee unless both people are using the same point of reference. A good idea is to check your communication with the receiver of the message.

COMMUNICATE ETHICALLY

According to the National Communication Association, "ethical communication enhances human worth and dignity by fostering truthfulness, fairness, responsibility, personal integrity, and respect for self and others."[1] Here are several guidelines for helping you to communicate ethically.

- Be clear about your agenda when communicating with others. Do not subscribe to secret agendas; withholding information is dishonest.
- Consider the consequences of being unethical.

---

[1]NCA Credo for Ethical Communication, accessed January 31, 2007, available from http://www.natcom.org/policies/External/EthicalComm.htm.

- Make a commitment to yourself and others that you will reach resolution when conflict occurs.
- Be responsible and accountable for your words, actions, and judgments. Do not dump your problems and vent your anger on others.
- Use I statements and clear language.
- Go directly to the source of your concerns.
- Acknowledge the various levels of power within the organization.
- Let yourself be challenged by new ideas.
- Accept the consequences of your communication.
- Be accurate and truthful about your actions.
- Condemn communication that degrades individuals.
- Advocate sharing information, opinions, and feelings.
- Meet your commitments.

A Safe and Healthy Environment

Everyone prefers to work in a safe and healthy physical environment. If an environment is unsafe and unhealthy, productivity is affected. Employees are often sick and absent. Morale is low. For the employer, an unsafe and unhealthy environment results not only in lost productivity, but also in increased costs in the form of greater medical expenses and disability payments. The impact of the physical environment is great and affects the workplace team either positively or negatively.

As an administrative professional, what would you do if you developed these health problems?

- Your wrists hurt so badly that you could not key material.
- You had so much back pain that you could not sit at the computer for any length of time.
- You developed vision problems so serious that you could not read small print.

Health problems can result if you do not use proper techniques while working at your computer. This section will help you understand how to take good physical care of yourself.

Ergonomics—A Definition

Ergonomics, according to the dictionary, is "the study of the problems of people in adjusting to their environment; the science that seeks to adapt work or working conditions to fit the worker." Ergonomics comes from the Greek words *ergos* (work) and *nomos* (natural laws). Simply stated, ergonomics is the fit between people, the tools they use, and the physical setting in which they work. The health problems that can occur due to inattention to ergonomic factors demand that you take ergonomics seriously. You should adopt an ergonomic approach to the design of your work site.

Common Injuries

Due to the amount of time people sit at their computers, several common injuries can occur. The generic name given to these injuries is repetitive stress injuries (**RSIs**) or cumulative trauma disorders (**CTDs**). Thousands of workers annually have ergonomic-related injuries, and many of these workers miss some work as a result. Thus, RSIs impact workers' health and cost organizations dollars in lost work and insurance claims. The RSIs discussed here include the following:

- Carpal tunnel syndrome (**CTS**)
- Computer vision syndrome
- Back pain
- Headaches

CARPAL TUNNEL SYNDROME (CTS)

CTS is a condition that occurs due to the compression of a large nerve, the median nerve, as it passes through a tunnel composed of bone and ligaments in the wrist. Symptoms include a gradual onset of numbness, a tingling or burning in the thumb and fingers, pain that travels up the arm and shoulder, and weakness of hands causing difficulty in pinching or grasping objects.

COMPUTER VISION SYNDROME

Computer vision syndrome is a term coined by the American Optometric Association for eye complaints related to computer work. The symptoms of computer vision syndrome may include these:

- Inability to focus on distant objects after using the computer for several hours
- Dry or watery eyes
- Blurred vision
- Heaviness of the eyelids or forehead

A person's eyes can get extremely dry after using a computer for a long time. Individuals tend to blink less frequently when using a computer. Glare from a computer screen can also cause eye stress—as can glare from sunlight or from lighting in the workplace.

BACK PAIN

People who sit for long periods of time are at risk for back disorders. The two greatest problems are sitting upright or forward and not changing position.

HEADACHES

Headaches are frequently the body's way of saying something is wrong. Poor head and neck posture, as well as eye strain, can be causes of headaches. Stress is another cause.

Prevention—The Key

To avoid common injuries such as repetitive stress injuries, vision problems, back pain, and headaches, you must take certain precautions. Having the right equipment and furniture (keyboards, mouses, chairs, footrests, and so on), as well as maintaining proper posture and taking frequent breaks, are preventative measures that help you avoid serious work injuries.

KEYBOARDS

Using keyboards that are placed too high or low or that are not centered in front of the body can cause the user to bend the wrists sideways or upward while inputting data. Failure to use proper keying techniques and good posture can

© Digital Vision / Getty Images

People who sit for long periods of time are at risk for back disorders.

force the hands into awkward positions when keying. In addition, the smaller keyboards on laptop computers can contribute to increased stresses on the hands and arms when using these keyboards for long periods of time. Placing the keyboard in the proper position and using good posture and keying techniques can help prevent stress injuries related to keying. Taking regular breaks from keying is also important.

Some users prefer alternative keyboards that have been designed in an attempt to change the user's hand and body position when keying. These alternative keyboards may help users maintain more natural hand and arm positions. Some of the most common alternatives include split keyboards, tented keyboards, supportive keyboards, and negative-slope keyboards.

- Split keyboards allow a natural separation of the hands. The keyboard can be split into two separate pieces, or the keys of the board may be separated by a neutral space.
- Tented keyboards arrange the keys into two separate keyboarding areas and tilt them upward and toward the middle. This creates a two-sided tent, with half of the keyboard on each side. The intent of this design is to eliminate bent wrist (inward and upward) positions.
- Supportive keyboards have built-in wrist or palm rests that help prevent bending the hands up by providing support that straightens the wrists. Wrist supports are also sold separately.
- Negative-slope keyboards allow the user to raise the front edge of the keyboard, which helps to straighten out the wrist.

Although alternate keyboards are popular with some users, available research does not provide conclusive evidence that these keyboard designs prevent discomfort or injury with long-term use.[2]

---

[2]"Computer Workstations, Keyboards," U.S. Department of Labor, Occupational Safety & Health Administration, accessed March 5, 2007, available from http://www.osha.gov/SLTC/etools/computerworkstations/components_keyboards.html.

MOUSE ALTERNATIVES

Mouse alternatives include trackballs, mouse pens, mouses that use one finger, and touch tablets, plus a wide variety of mouse shapes and sizes. Additionally, a cordless mouse is now available that allows much greater freedom of movement than the traditional corded mouse. When choosing an alternative to a mouse, evaluate whether the alternative really uses different muscles.

HEIGHT-ADJUSTABLE WORK SURFACES

Desks should be at a height where you can easily key with straight wrists and read or write without slumping forward or without hunching your shoulders. One drawback to height-adjustable work surfaces is that they are more expensive than standard desks.

MONITOR ARMS

Monitor arms allow forward, back, or up-and-down movement of the monitor to accompany posture changes. Arms can be useful for people with neck, shoulder, or upper back discomfort.

© 2007 www.indexopen.com

Some users prefer alternative keyboards to the traditional computer keyboard.

© BananaStock / Jupiter Images

Mouse alternatives are preferred by some users.

DOCUMENT STANDS

Stands reduce distortion of print that occurs when a document is slanted away from the eyes. Stands also reduce neck twisting by bringing the document close to the monitor at a readable angle. Since they allow you to put the paper in front of you, document stands can be useful if most of your work involves looking at paper rather than the screen.

FOOTRESTS

Footrests allow different positions for the legs and feet. When using a footrest, you should change foot positions often. Footrests are available that exercise and massage the feet, which can be beneficial.

TASK LIGHTS

Task lights are used to reduce eyestrain by illuminating paperwork and reducing the need for bright light. Documents should be illuminated enough to be readable. However, too much light can cause a strong contrast between the brightness of the screen and the document, resulting in eyestrain rather than alleviating it.

CHAIRS

Adjustable chairs can help you avoid back pain by supporting multiple postures. The usual adjustments on the chairs include backrest, armrest, seat angle, and seat height.

Ergonomic Research

Ergonomic research counters some of the traditional wisdom of what was thought to be correct technique when sitting at the computer. Here are suggestions from the research findings shown on the Office Ergonomics Training Website posted by Ankrum Associates.

- Sit as far away from the monitor as you can while still being able to read it clearly.
- Conventional practice for mouse placement is to push it away from you. However, research shows that closer is usually better, with the mouse next to the keyboard.
- The chair should be low enough for your feet to be on the floor even when the legs are extended. This research is in opposition to the conventional wisdom of having the legs reach the floor at a 90-degree angle from the knees. Research shows that you should move your legs often; they should not stay in a fixed position.
- Conventional wisdom prescribes an upright posture, with the hips at 90 degrees. However, research supports a hip width of 130 degrees as optimal. This position reduces and evens out pressure on the intevertebral discs.
- Conventional practice recommends rest breaks about 15 minutes long, every 2 hours or so. Research supports very short breaks of 30 seconds every 10 minutes in addition to the normal 15-minute breaks.[3]

Figure 2.4 provides a checklist of ergonomic problems with possible solutions.

Smoking and Substance Abuse

For years, research has made people aware of the health dangers of smoking. Unfortunately, a large number of people continue to smoke. Additionally, substance abuse (alcohol and drugs) is a major problem in society.

SMOKING

With the public outcry to smoking, most organizations now have smoke-free environments or designated spaces for smokers. Service industries such as hotels and restaurants still allow smoking in designated areas. However, these areas are generally close to the nonsmoking area, so secondhand smoke can be a problem. Studies have shown that breathing secondhand smoke is unhealthy and that a link exists between secondhand smoke and emphysema and lung disease. Also, eye, nose, and throat irritations can result from secondhand smoke.

SUBSTANCE ABUSE

Substance abuse involves the use of alcohol or drugs to the extent that the habit is debilitating for the individual using the substance. It is a problem of monumental proportions in society. Employees who abuse drugs have high rates of absenteeism and illness. They may be absent more than other employees and may perform poorly when at work. Shoddy work and material waste can also be the result of individuals who abuse drugs. Substance abusers experience wide mood swings, anxiety, depression, and anger. Even small quantities of drugs in a person's system can cause deterioration of alertness, clear mindedness, and reaction speed.

Security

Employees must believe they are safe in the work environment. Effective organizations establish comprehensive safety plans that are made available to all employees. Each program should be designed to fit the needs of the company and the employees. According to the Occupational Safety & Health Adminstration (OSHA), there are four elements that every effective program should have: management leadership and employee involvement, workplace analysis, hazard prevention and control, and safety and health training and education.[4]

Organizations can use a variety of procedures to protect their employees. Security guards can be

[3]"Conventional Wisdom vs. Current Ergonomics," accessed January 31, 2007, available from Office Ergonomics Training by Ankrum Associates, http://office-ergo.com/conventi.htm.

[4]"Keeping Your Workplace Safe," U.S. Department of Labor, Occupational Safety & Health Administration, accessed February 2, 2007, available from http://www.osha.gov/Publications/98-40brochure.html.

ERGONOMIC PROBLEMS—POSSIBLE SOLUTIONS

Problem	Possible Solution
Elbows splayed out from body	Lower work surface Lower chair armrests
Twisting the head from side to side	Bring viewed item closer to centerline of view
Elbow or forearm resting for long periods on hard or sharp work surface	Pad surfaces, corners, and armrests
Rapid, sustained keying	Greater work variety Aggressive break schedule
Significant amounts of hand stapling, punching, lifting, opening mail	Mechanical aids, such as electric stapler or punch; reduce size of lifted load
Prolonged sitting, especially in only one position	Greater work variety Chair that supports posture changes through easy adjustability
Feet dangling, not well supported	Lower chair Lower work surface Footrest
Twisted torso	Rearrange work Provide more knee space Bring mouse and keyboard closer to body
Frequent or prolonged leaning or reaching	Rearrange work Bring mouse and keyboard closer to body
Light sources that can be seen by the worker	Cover or shield light sources Rearrange work area
Reflected glare on computer screen	Shield light sources Glare screen Move monitor so light comes from side angle, not back
Monitor image dim, fuzzy, small, or otherwise difficult to read	Upgrade monitor Use software to enlarge image
Eyestrain complaints	Check all aspects of visual environment Suggest consultation with vision specialist

Source: Adapted from "About Checklists," accessed February 1, 2007, available from Office Ergonomics Training by Ankrum Associates, http://office-ergo.com/a.htm.

FIGURE 2.4 Ergonomic Problems—Possible Solutions

© PhotoDisc / Getty Images

If you work late at the office, notify the security staff.

by use of a special card. Some organizations place television screens and cameras at various locations. Security personnel monitor these screens for suspicious individuals or behaviors.

Regardless of your organization's policies or procedures to ensure employees' safety, you should establish practices of your own. These are recommended:

- If you work late, notify the security staff. Also tell someone at home that you are working late. Call the person just before you leave to say that you are on your way home.
- If you drive to work, when possible, walk to your car with someone else. Someone from the security staff may be willing to accompany you if you work in a high crime area. Have your car keys ready to unlock your car; then lock it immediately after getting in.
- If possible, situate yourself near others who are working late.
- Work next to a telephone, and have emergency numbers handy.
- Keep all doors to your office locked while you are working.
- If you hear strange noises, call for help. Do not investigate on your own.

stationed at doors to monitor who enters and exits. Doors can have security locks that are opened only

Summary

To reinforce what you have learned in this chapter, study this summary.

- Team effectiveness demands that team members commit to understanding and accepting one another, being a productive team member, and achieving team goals.
- Within the diverse workplace, one must accept differing values.
- If a project team is to be successful, there must be clarity of purpose, appropriate technical skills, good administrative and interpersonal skills, and commitment to the task.
- For the administrative professional and supervisor team to be successful, the administrative professional must have respect for the supervisor and be dependable, honest, and loyal. The employer's obligations include respecting the administrative professional, providing appropriate feedback, and being a loyal and ethical manager.

- For the administrative professional and coworker team to be successful, there must be acceptance of the individuals within the team and cooperation among the members. Team members also must be tactful and fair with one another.

- To ensure success in working with external teams, administrative professionals must demonstrate positive public relations and effective communication.

- Diversity of ethnicity, race, gender, and age can be an excellent resource for organizations since diverse groups of people bring different perspectives, values, and ideas to the workplace.

- Effective communication techniques necessary for understanding people of different backgrounds include being respectful, being nonjudgmental, placing oneself in the other person's position, being flexible, and practicing good listening skills.

- To be effective in formal and informal communication channels, one must understand the organizational structure and management style, write and speak clearly, be word conscious, and communicate ethically.

- Common stress injuries that can occur in the workplace include carpal tunnel syndrome, computer vision syndrome, back pain, and headaches.

- To avoid repetitive stress injuries, one should have the right equipment and furniture, use proper posture, and take frequent breaks.

- Equipment possibilities that help reduce repetitive stress injuries include ergonomic keyboards, mouse alternatives, height-adjustable work surfaces, monitor arms, document stands, footrests, task lights, and chairs.

- Smoking and substance abuse in the workplace contribute to health problems, absenteeism, poor performance, and depression.

What's the Problem?

United Pharmaceuticals recently employed an individual from Saudi Arabia. You notice that the young man, a part-time employee, is having great difficulty understanding what his job is and how to accomplish it. You rarely see him chatting with anyone in the company and notice he is by himself on breaks and at lunch. You think this is because of the 9/11 tragedy, after which many of your coworkers voiced their fear and distrust of people from the Middle East.

You have been with the company on a part-time basis for almost a year and are successful at your job. You wonder whether you should try to help this young man. If you decide to help him, how would you go about doing so?

Let's Discuss

1. Explain the composition of the workforce teams of which administrative professionals may be a part.
2. List and explain criteria that make project teams successful.
3. List and explain five techniques for communicating with diverse groups.
4. List five techniques that enhance team communication.
5. Explain the meaning of ergonomics, and give at least three precautionary measures to prevent RSIs.

Critical-Thinking Activity

Reynolds & Reynolds is a 15-year-old company providing computer services in the United States and Canada. The company has been very successful over the last ten years. In this time period, its stock has increased an average of 15 percent each year. The company attributes part of its success to its emphasis on solving problems through a team-based approach. Employees serve on project teams.

Benjamin Toulous was asked by his supervisor to serve on an eight-member team to examine the company's employee evaluation procedures. Benjamin is pleased about serving on this team. He believes he has several good suggestions that will improve the evaluation procedures. After he accepted the invitation to serve, he learned that the team leader was Alice Wong, supervisor in the Accounting Department. Benjamin has little respect for Alice; he thinks she is a poor supervisor. He has heard stories from several of her employees about how unfair she is. Although Benjamin has not had direct experience with Alice as a supervisor, he believes she is an unacceptable team leader.

What should Benjamin do? Think through the choices he has. As you think about what he should do, use critical-thinking principles, which demand the following:

*   Intellectual curiosity
*   Willingness to entertain new ideas
*   Willingness to acquire new information
*   Willingness to evaluate assumptions and inferences

Vocabulary Review

Open the *Word* file *CH02 Vocabulary* found on the Student CD. Complete the vocabulary review for Chapter 2.

English and Word Usage Drill

Complete the English and Word Usage Drill for Chapter 2 found in the *Applications Workbook*.

Workplace Applications

2-1 Work as a Team to Create a Description

(Goals 1 and 3)

team building

e-portfolio

1. The local Chamber of Commerce asks you to create four Web pages about your college/university that it can link to its Website. The links will display on a page that targets new companies and individuals moving into the city. Work in a team with three other students to create the four pages as described below. The pages should have complete information and each should include at least one picture of the college and/or students, if possible.

   - A page presenting a brief history of the university

   - A page that highlights the academic programs in your department

   - A page with general information including costs, admission requirements, enrollments, and graduate information

   - A page that describes campus life including housing information, student activities, and student organizations

2. Each member of the team should fill out the team evaluation form found on the Student CD in the *Word* file *CH02 2-1 Evaluation*.

3. Discuss how the team process worked with the other team members. What were the team's strengths? What problems did it have? Did team members lack certain expertise? If so, what? As a group, write a memo to your instructor. Use the memo form found on the Student CD in the *Word* file *Memo Form*. Report on how the team process worked—the strengths of the team and its deficiencies, if any, and how they were handled.

2-2 Experience Communicating with a Diverse Audience

(Goals 2 and 3)

team building

1. Team up with two of your classmates. Attend a function in your community that attracts a diverse audience—an audience that differs from your own race/ethnicity. The function might be an activity at your college, a church service, a community function, or a musical/cultural event. While attending this function, make a point of talking with individuals who are of different races/ethnicities than you. Pay attention to your style of communication and to the communication of the person with whom you are talking.

2. As a team, write a short unbound report (no more than two pages). Include the following information in your report:

    - Name and date of the event

    - Description of the event

    - People with whom you communicated

    - Effectiveness (or lack of effectiveness) of your communication

    - What you learned from the event

3. Complete the team evaluation form found on the Student CD in the *Word* file *CH02 2-2 Evaluation*, as individual team members. Discuss your individual evaluations as a team, and compile one team evaluation.

2-3 Case Study: Workplace Diversity

(Goal 2)

The *Applications Workbook* contains a case study for Chapter 2. Read the case and respond to the questions.

2-4 Research Culture and History

(Goal 2)

internet

United Pharmaceuticals has several locations in the United States as well as locations in China and India. Your supervisor, Melody Hoover, has asked that you create electronic slides to be used in a presentation on business customs in China or India.

1. Choose a country (China or India) in which you are most interested. Using the Web, research business topics such as meetings, business cards, business social customs, business gifts, or professional attire.

2. Create seven to ten electronic slides on one or more of the topics you researched. Include a list of your sources on the last slide.

3. Prepare a handout on the same topics to give more detailed information or tips for business etiquette in that country.

2-5 Research Ergonomic Equipment and Furniture

(Goal 4)

internet

1. Using the Internet, research available ergonomic office equipment and furniture. Use at least three Web sources in gathering your information. Use the keywords

e-portfolio

ergonomic equipment and *ergonomic furniture* in an Internet search engine to help you find information.

2. Select two or three pieces of equipment or furniture on which to report. Include pictures of the ergonomic equipment or furniture you find, if possible, in your report. Format the report in unbound style and list your sources as endnotes.

Assessment of Chapter 2 Goals

Did you successfully complete the chapter goals? Evaluate yourself by filling out the form found in Chapter 2 of the *Applications Workbook*.

chapter 3

The Virtual Workforce

Learning Goals

1. Define *telework* and describe its benefits to teleworkers and organizations.

2. Define *virtual assistant* and describe benefits and concerns for virtual assistant clients.

3. Identify virtual workplace considerations including personal characteristics, virtual workforce skills, and challenges.

4. Describe an effective work environment for virtual workers.

Telework and Virtual Assistants

Not only is technology changing on a daily basis but it is also being quickly adopted by the generation that grew up with it. In fact, technology has become a part of all phases of daily life. You can electronically submit a shopping list to the local store and pick up your order at a specific time or even have it delivered. You can instant message your thoughts and watch them scroll across the bottom of the screen during your favorite television show, or you can play along with game show contestants from your home for a chance at cash and prizes.

With the use of technology at home becoming as common as it has been in the business world, it is only natural that the worlds of work and home have come together. The following statistics were released in 2007 as part of a report issued by WorldatWork:[1]

- The number of Americans who work remotely per month increased 63 percent from 7.6 million in 2004 to 12.4 million in 2006.
- The number of teleworkers (both employed and self-employed) working remotely has risen from 26.1 million in 2005 to 28.7 million in 2006.
- Roughly 8 percent of American workers have an employer that allows them to telecommute one day per month.

[1]"Telework Trendlines for 2006 from WorldatWork," accessed February 17, 2007, available from http://www.workingfromanywhere.org/news/Trendlines_2006.pdf.

- Roughly 20 percent of the workforce engages in telework.
- By 2010 it is estimated that 100 million U.S. workers will participate in some form of telework.

Consider the following reasons for an increased interest and participation in the virtual workforce:

- Businesses are increasing their investment in technology.
- Telecommunications costs have dropped.
- Computer use is widespread.
- Lawmakers are promoting alternate worksites to control transportation and pollution problems.
- E-business has flourished, leading many individuals to start their own Internet businesses.

Laptop computers, cell phones, high-speed Internet connectivity, satellite connectivity, e-business software, email, and instant messaging technologies continue to progress and provide more opportunities for both workers and employers. With advances in computing and telecommunications technology, and with the costs of these technologies falling, more individuals find themselves with the opportunity to complete at least some of their work away from a traditional office setting.

Telework is a broad term used to describe a variety of business situations where individuals use technology to work from somewhere other than a traditional workplace. This alternative work site can be a satellite business location, a hotel or motel room, an airport, a client's office, or a home office. A **teleworker** is an individual who uses telecommunications technology to work full- or part-time at home or at some other mobile work environment.

A **virtual assistant** is a self-employed person who uses telecommunications technology to provide administrative or technical services to clients for a fee. Although work is conducted on a contractual basis, many virtual assistants have long-term clients. Virtual assistants may work in a home office or a remote office location. Although they may serve clients in their immediate geographic location, these entrepreneurs are typically not limited to that area and may contract their services over a wide geographic range.

Telework

In addition to advances in technology, changes in the demands and expectations within the business world have created a need for more flexible working environments. Some companies now offer 24-hour customer support for their products, requiring people from around the globe to be available to answer consumer questions. Global business competition requires that businesses have representatives available to handle customers' and managers' work requests. In order to compete in these global markets, businesses are always looking for ways to reduce costs. Telework is a method that may help companies reduce costs.

The federal government has also increased its emphasis on telework by mandating telework opportunities for federal employees. Telework can help to reduce travel and commuting times, increase worker productivity, and ensure business operations in the event of a disaster. Telework also offers job opportunities to individuals regardless of geographical location or physical limitations.

TELEWORK DESCRIPTIONS

To better understand the concepts related to telework, you should be familiar with some general terms. Depending on the organization, telework may also be known by the following terms: telecommuting, **flexiwork**, and **flexiplace**. Regardless of the term used, this work arrangement allows people to conduct some or all of their work away from the organization's primary workplace. This alternate work location might be a residence, a satellite office closer to the employee's residence, a client's office, a telecenter, or other mutually acceptable location. The

U.S. Department of Health and Human Services uses the following definitions as part of its telework program:

- *Telecommuting* is described as performing work at a place other than the employee's official duty station in accordance with the terms of an employee and employer agreement.
- *Regular telecommuting* is when telecommuting occurs on a regularly scheduled basis for a period of several months or longer.
- *Non-regular* or *episodic telecommuting* occurs when work is performed at an alternate workstation without a regular schedule.
- **Hoteling** exists when offices or cubicles are set aside for the shared use of employees who spend the majority of their time telecommuting.
- **Alternate workstation** is a specific area at a telecommuting center, within an employee's residence, or at another approved location other than the official duty station.
- **Telecenter** is office space that is available for the use of telecommuters located in an area that will reduce commuting time.[2]

BENEFITS TO THE TELEWORKER

Many private organizations offer their employees the opportunity to participate in some form of telework. The increased accessibility of technology and the global economy has influenced the workplace considerably in the last few years. In addition to increased workforce flexibility, the federal government finds the following benefits to employees who participate in telework:

- Less, or no, commuting time
- Better work/life balance due to more time for family
- Less stress
- Increased productivity due to fewer interruptions and distractions
- More flexibility to work during most productive hours
- Increased ability to respond to unforeseen/unscheduled workload
- Ability to design and control work environment
- Increased job satisfaction
- Reduced commute-related costs—gas, tolls/tickets, parking, maintenance, and depreciation
- Reduced personal expenses, including clothing, grooming, and food costs
- Reduced child- and elder-care costs due to later drop-offs and/or earlier pick-ups, and ability for teenagers and elderly dependents to be at home pursuing their own activities
- Satisfaction of helping the environment[3]

Although many of the employee benefits of telework result in financial savings, there are also clear benefits on a personal level. Employees feel more empowered and more in control of their work environment and are often more satisfied with their jobs. Employees feel they are less stressed because of the decreased commuting time and fewer interruptions and that they have a better balance between work and life issues.

Some telework arrangements offer employees a flexible work schedule, which also increases job satisfaction. The ability to work a compressed workweek or to participate in flextime gives workers more autonomy. In addition, telework employees are typically more productive with their time because they have fewer interruptions and distractions. A flexible schedule is helpful when making daycare arrangements for children or medical appointments for other dependents. However, teleworkers should not assume that child or elder care will no longer be needed because the teleworker is working in a home office. In many cases, child or elder care will still be needed.

[2]"HSS Telecommuting Program Policy," U.S. Department of Health and Human Services, accessed February 17, 2007, available from http://www.hhs.gov/ohr/telework/policy.html#define.

[3]"Why Telecommuting Works," *It All Adds Up to Cleaner Air*, U.S. Department of Transportation, Federal Highway Administration, accessed February 17, 2007; available from http://www.italladdsup.gov/newsletter/winter06/why_telecommuting_works.pdf.

Teleworkers often feel less stressed and are more satisfied with their jobs.

BENEFITS TO THE EMPLOYER

In addition to individual benefits, telework can be advantageous to participating organizations. Some benefits to the employer include the following:

- Employees' increased productivity due to fewer interruptions and distractions and ability to work during most productive hours
- Fewer unscheduled absences resulting from unforeseen events
- Continuity of operations during weather-related or other emergency situations
- Improved planning ability
- Employees' ability to respond to unforeseen/unscheduled workload
- Reduced real estate costs due to less, or more flexible, need for office space
- Lower employee-relocation costs, because work is not location dependent
- Enhanced employee satisfaction and morale
- Less labor turnover and lower recruitment costs
- Better customer service as employees stay longer and become more proficient
- Access to larger labor pool—regional, national, international, military spouses, retired, physically challenged

- Enhanced compliance with Americans with Disabilities Act (ADA) and Family and Medical Leave Act (FMLA)
- Enhanced public relations and goodwill[4]

The September 11, 2001, terrorist attacks and the devastation from Hurricane Katrina in 2005 have served to increase emphasis on telework. Employers (and especially the federal government) are strengthening their **business continuity (BC) guides** or **continuity of operations plans (COOP)**. These plans provide for smooth business operations in the event of a disaster. Many of the federal government and private business COOP programs rely heavily on telework.

Although telework has existed in the federal government for many years, interest has been increasing in the last few years. In October 2000, Public Law 106-346, Section 359, established the mandate for federal agencies to establish policies for implementing teleworking opportunities and increasing the number of teleworkers. For

---

[4]Ibid.

federal agencies, telework is of particular interest for its benefits in the following areas:

- Recruiting and retaining the best possible workforce—particularly newer workers who have high expectations of a technologically forward-thinking workplace and any worker who values work/life balance
- Helping employees manage long commutes and other work/life issues that, if not addressed, can have a negative impact on their effectiveness or lead to employees leaving federal employment
- Reducing traffic congestion, emissions, and infrastructure impact in urban areas, thereby improving the environment
- Saving taxpayer dollars by decreasing government real estate costs
- Ensuring continuity of essential government functions in the event of national or local emergencies[5]

Telework also provides significant benefits to the community. Many counties and cities encourage organizations to allow employees to telework when appropriate. Some of the benefits of telework to the community are shown in Figure 3.1.

The Virtual Assistant

The virtual assistant is an administrative assistant who contracts her or his services to one or more clients. Many of the early virtual assistants were individuals who had spent several years performing administrative assistant duties within a traditional office setting. For a variety of reasons, these individuals decided they were ready to start businesses of their own. Through the rapid growth of computing technology, communications technology, and the Internet, this new career path has evolved and grown rapidly.

The virtual assistant profession is no longer limited to former administrative assistants. In

COMMUNITY BENEFITS OF TELEWORK

- Less air pollution, which improves human health and increases Clean Air Act compliance
- Less traffic congestion and fewer automobile crashes/deaths due to fewer people on the road
- Less wear and tear on transportation infrastructure, which postpones funding requirements
- Safer neighborhoods and less juvenile crime due to greater adult presence during the day
- Less dependence on imported oil, improving national security
- Smaller national budget deficit
- Less vehicle-related runoff from roads, ensuring cleaner water and improving ecosystem and human health

Source: "Why Telecommuting Works," *It All Adds Up to Cleaner Air*, U.S. Department of Transportation, Federal Highway Administration, accessed February 17, 2007, available from http://www.italladdsup.gov/newsletter/winter06/why_telecommuting_works.pdf.

FIGURE 3.1 Telework provides benefits to the community as well as to individuals and companies.

fact, this industry has developed to include several professional organizations, as well as training from several online universities. These professional organizations and universities provide an outlet to share information as well as serve as an advocate for the profession by establishing standard levels of competence. The online universities offer continuing education courses, certifications, and training. The professional organizations provide interested individuals with career tips, professional guidance, and professional recognition. Both provide members with a place to share information and network with others working in this unique field.

VIRTUAL ASSISTANT DESCRIBED
The majority of virtual assistants are self-employed. These entrepreneurs enjoy the freedom of being their own boss and usually work from a home office. They choose the types of work they would like to do, the amount of work they do, the number of clients they serve, and the

[5]"A Guide to Telework in the Federal Government," OPM-II-A-2, August 3, 2006; accessed February 17, 2007, available from https://www.opm.gov/pandemic/agency2a-guide.pdf.

A virtual assistant may provide services for both large and small businesses.

amount of time they wish to work. This flexibility, in part, is what drives the growth of the virtual assistant profession. Examples of the contracting, billing, and payment options that the virtual assistant can use are as follows:

- *Hourly*—Virtual assistants may contract their services based on an hourly rate. Typically, negotiation between the virtual assistant and the client takes place to discuss the type of work, the amount of work, and a reasonable

A virtual assistant may have an on-call agreement to do work for some clients.

time period in which to get the work done before the hourly wage is set.

- *Flat rate*—Virtual assistants who do not like to negotiate or who may have already developed a standard client base may offer their services at a flat-rate fee. That flat-rate fee may vary depending on the length of time the employer needs the services. For example, the rate for two days of work could be much different than the rate for two weeks of work or two months of work.

- *Per project*—A virtual assistant may contract a specific amount to be paid for a project. In this situation, the amount remains the same regardless of the time it takes to complete the project. A good deal of faith is required when agreeing upon a per-project payment schedule. The client has to have faith that the virtual assistant is working diligently to complete the project. The virtual assistant has to have faith that the client was honest in describing the amount of effort required to complete the project.

- *On-call*—When a virtual assistant has become comfortable with a specific set of clients and those clients can be counted on for steady business, they may enter into an *on-call* agreement where the virtual assistant agrees to accept assignments or projects from the employer when needed. Having an on-call agreement means the client will not have to continually shop for outside services. This type of agreement is also referred to as a *billable hours agreement*.

Virtual assistants can provide a wide variety of services to an organization. Since many virtual assistants were previously employed in a traditional office, they are well-versed in the duties and responsibilities of a typical administrative assistant. Depending on the needs of the organization, virtual assistants can take calls, prepare documents, manage databases, assist with marketing, make travel arrangements and appointments, and transcribe documents. Visit the Virtual Assistant Certification Website to learn more about skills needed by virtual assistants. A link to this Virtual Assistant Certification Website is provided on the Website for this textbook.

Most virtual assistants have the added dimension of being skilled in the use of the Internet, in Web page design, and in online product ordering and payment systems. They may also be skilled in the use of PDF documentation and document imaging, as these practices have become standard platforms for the handling of official business documentation.

BENEFITS TO THE CLIENT

Dramatic changes have occurred in today's workplace. Organizations are **downsizing**, outsourcing, and **off-loading**. Downsizing is reducing the number of full-time employees in an organization and may increase the need for outsourcing. Both outsourcing and off-loading occur when an organization contracts with individuals or companies outside the organization to complete part of the work of the organization. In today's global economy, organizations must be as flexible as possible, and outsourcing helps provide this flexibility. Much of a virtual assistant's work comes from this type of situation.

Other advantages to the business owner who wishes to contract with a virtual assistant include the following:

- Increased time to spend on other business-related issues or other activities not related to work
- Financial savings (elimination of associated payroll taxes, insurance, and possibly benefits)

- Real estate savings (no dedicated office space or parking issues)
- Equipment savings (no need to provide portable or home-office equipment or telecommunications connections)

A Web search for virtual assistant will provide thousands of hits. The employer that is looking for help with administrative duties, therefore, will have many options from which to choose.

CLIENT CONCERNS

The biggest drawback to clients when considering a partnership with a virtual assistant is general uneasiness. This is a relatively new and evolving field, and unlike the traditional administrative assistant who is right outside your door when needed, this work relationship will take some getting used to. The lack of face-to-face communication can increase the chances of miscommunication or misunderstandings early in the working relationship. Therefore, each party

Professional Pointers

Ask yourself the following questions if you are considering virtual work:

- Am I a good problem solver?
- Am I independent?
- Do I communicate well?
- Do I set regular break times for myself?
- Am I flexible?
- Am I able to cope with work-related stress?
- Do I exercise frequently?
- Do I set clear limits on my work?
- Do family members understand my job and my expectations of them?
- Do I hold regular meetings with my family to discuss issues?
- Do I allocate appropriate time for both my job and my family?

should ask clarifying questions and provide clear instructions to ensure that the appropriate messages are being sent and received.

Technical difficulties can also hinder communication and instructions. While one generally accepted communication tool should be agreed upon, there should always be a backup plan or an alternate way to contact the other party. Although many virtual assistants rely heavily on email for communication, they also use cell phones, personal home phones, or Web conferencing as alternatives. Because of the unique communication issues associated with email (lack of visual and verbal cues), some virtual assistants have increased their reliance on telephone communication.

Virtual Workplace Considerations

To be successful in an alternative work environment you need to review your personal goals. Spend some time reviewing the information presented in Chapter 1 on setting personal goals. You must also be sure you have the traits necessary to be a successful virtual employee. This section will help you determine whether you have the characteristics to be a successful virtual employee as well as review some of the challenges typically faced by the virtual employee. Before you consider working as a virtual assistant or ask your supervisor to pursue a telework arrangement, you should examine your personality traits, evaluate your skills, and consider some workplace challenges.

Personal Characteristics

In addition to understanding your goals, you need to be realistic about who you are. What personality traits do you have? How do you like to work? What characteristics do you have that contribute to your success? If you are interested in working as a virtual assistant or teleworker, the following characteristics will be important to your success.

- Disciplined
- Self-starter
- Independent
- Organized
- Self-confident
- Strong work ethic

DISCIPLINED

Working as a teleworker or in a home-based workplace means you will encounter a number of distractions. The telephone rings. The doorbell rings. The dog barks. The post office delivers a package. One of your customers or clients calls. Being disciplined means you know how to work with these distractions—because you generally cannot eliminate them.

When working from home, discipline involves the following activities:

- Set a routine, just as you would in a traditional workplace. Make a to-do list each afternoon and check it each morning. Check your email and voice mail several times a day.
- Establish times to communicate with your company or clients.
- Create a visual sign that lets your family know you are working and cannot be disturbed.
- Shut your office door at night. The virtual employee can overdo the work hours just as the traditional employee can. Determine the number of hours you will spend working, and then stick to that number.

Remember that the most productive worker is a balanced worker—one who knows how to balance work, family, and play.

SELF-STARTER

A self-starter is someone who begins a project or task without needing to be told or encouraged to do so. The self-starter knows what needs to be done and is eager to get it done. The self-starter shows initiative through an ability to begin and follow through on a plan or task without specific direction. The self-starter generally has a number of items on a to-do or task list. He or she not only accomplishes the tasks, but feels a sense of

The successful teleworker feels a sense of satisfaction when accomplishing items on a to-do list.

satisfaction at marking the items off the list. The self-starter is eager to begin the next task, enjoying a sense of pride and accomplishment from being able to do a number of tasks well.

A self-starter is the opposite of a procrastinator. **Procrastination** is trying to avoid a task by putting it aside with the intention of doing it later. A procrastinator is someone who always has an excuse as to why a project cannot be completed. Procrastinators are the people

- Who always have filing to be done.
- Whose desks are stacked with papers, but who cannot find a specific paper when needed.
- Who never accomplish the tasks on their to-do lists. In fact, they probably do not even have to-do lists.

A procrastinator is not likely to be successful in a telework environment. Good organization of resources and time are needed to be a successful teleworker.

INDEPENDENT

In the traditional workplace, you generally have someone, or several people, that you can go to for help in solving a problem. This is often not so in a telework or virtual assistant environment. In

these instances you must be a creative problem solver. If you are working on a Web page that includes graphics and you cannot get the graphics software to work properly, you cannot go to the computer expert in the next office for help. You must figure out the problem or find someone who can assist you.

ORGANIZED

Organization is important in any job, but particularly so in a nontraditional office environment. In order to juggle tasks and successfully manage interruptions, an individual must be organized. A teleworker or virtual assistant must be able to plan and organize activities well and to implement the time management techniques that will be described in Chapter 5 of this textbook. The organized individual participates in the following activities:

- Setting priorities
- Organizing the workstation
- Simplifying repetitive work
- Handling paperwork as few times as possible
- Using time management systems such as electronic calendaring and scheduling software

SELF-CONFIDENT

As a teleworker you need to know what you do well. Also, when you do something well, you need to take the time to congratulate yourself on your success. You may even set up your own reward system—however small. Maybe the reward is as simple as taking a 30-minute walk in the park when you successfully finish a particularly difficult project.

As a virtual assistant you do not have coworkers or a supervisor to tell you when you have done a good job. You must have the self-confidence to be your own support system. Additionally, you must have the self-confidence to admit when you cannot do something well. If a project involves a task that you are not confident you can do, find someone who can help you do that task, develop the necessary skills yourself, or decline the job.

STRONG WORK ETHIC

The teleworker must have a strong work ethic. No one is around to set the time clock or to determine the length of breaks or lunch. As a teleworker, you set and maintain a schedule that allows you to get your work done. Your supervisor or client is counting on you to do so.

The virtual assistant must also have a strong work ethic. Sometimes a project will take longer than planned. As a virtual assistant, you must be willing to work long hours if necessary, but you also need to have a balanced life. You should not routinely work late because you were undisciplined or disorganized; you should work late only occasionally so you can meet a deadline.

Virtual Workforce Skills

A virtual assistant or other teleworker must possess specific skills in order to be successful. What skills will be necessary to be effective in this type of position? A successful teleworker or virtual assistant will possess the following skills:

- Planning skills
- Communication skills
- Technology skills
- Commitment to lifelong learning

PLANNING SKILLS

A successful teleworker must be able to plan the workday and manage the workload to which he or she has committed. Teleworkers are also sometimes required to plan events for employers or clients. Planning requires the use of time management skills as well as organization skills.

To be successful as a teleworker, you must have an idea of what you are going to do and how you are going to accomplish it. You should not expect to get through the day without a plan. Planning the daily work routine provides the direction needed to keep projects on target. A daily plan will also reduce the possibility of getting sidetracked by events at home or by other projects with a lower priority. A successful plan begins each day with a list of the tasks you hope to accomplish and ends with an evaluation of how your work progressed.

COMMUNICATION SKILLS

Communication skills are crucial to both the teleworker and virtual assistant who must communicate with a variety of people (executives, co-workers, clients, business partners, and so on). As a teleworker you will periodically communicate with individuals in person, but when working outside the office your communication will take place electronically.

As a virtual assistant, you generally do not have the luxury of communicating with clients in face-to-face situations. Because your clients can be on the other side of the world, contact with clients usually happens through email, video-conferences, voice mail, or the telephone or fax; you may never see clients in person. These situations demand that you be a good communicator who strives to improve your skills as well as a person who cares about others. As you continue studying this text, you will learn how to develop and strengthen your written and verbal communication skills.

When communication goes poorly, you must step back and analyze what happened and why it happened. Realize that you can learn from your mistakes. When dealing with problems or conflicts, remember the Golden Rule: Treat others as you would have them treat you.

TECHNOLOGY SKILLS

Although technology skills are essential for all administrative professionals, they are even more vital for the virtual assistant and teleworker. Teleworkers and virtual assistants depend on both computing technology and communication technology to perform their daily duties. These technologies are the lifelines to maintaining productivity and staying in contact with their business partners. Because of this dependence on technology, they must become comfortable with troubleshooting equipment problems on their own, or they must make connections with

Comfort with technology is vital for teleworkers.

someone who can provide these equipment repair services in a timely manner.

Teleworkers and virtual assistants must also have the desire to stay current, or even ahead, of advances in computing and communication technologies. Continuing education at the local college or adult education center, online coursework, software certifications, and subscriptions to technology magazines are some options that the home office worker can pursue. Many software applications now have extensive help directories or built-in office assistants that help users fully explore the power of these software applications. Continuing to learn and to advance your skills will set you apart from those who do not and will enable you to work smarter as well.

COMMITMENT TO LIFELONG LEARNING

As a teleworker you must continue your professional growth. Because you are isolated from the busy workplace and from your coworkers, you may find you do not keep up to date about technological advances. In addition, the emphasis on technology skills for this type of worker will continue. A variety of options are available to help you stay current in your areas of expertise:

career tip

Virtual Workplace Organizations and Certifications

A variety of organizations exists to support and promote teleworkers and virtual assistants. The following list provides names of some of these organizations. Web addresses are given in the Links section of the Website for this textbook.

- ITAC (The Telework Advisory Group for WorldatWork)
- TelCoa (The Telework Coalition)
- IVAA (International Virtual Assistants Association)
- IAVOA (International Association of Virtual Office Assistants)

In addition, teleworkers and virtual assistants can now obtain certification through specialized programs. Web addresses for these programs are given in the Links section of the Website for this textbook.

- Virtual Assistant Certification includes two levels of certification: the MVA (Master Virtual Assistant) and the PVA (Professional Virtual Assistant)
- Virtual Office Temps, Virtual Assistant Certification includes a three-part test covering skills, ethics, and industry and technology knowledge and document practice
- InteleWorks Telework Certification offers telework program certification, teleworker certification, telemanager certification, and telework trainer certification

- Network with other teleworkers or virtual assistants. Attend seminars in your field. Make an effort to meet people at these seminars, get their business cards, and keep in touch with them. As you attend such training, update your resume as appropriate.

- Join professional organizations. Seek other organizations of interest to you. Stay involved in your community.
- Take classes. If opportunities do not exist in your local area, many opportunities to expand your knowledge are available online. Although online courses do not satisfy a need to see people face-to-face, many of the courses have discussion capabilities that allow you to interact with other students. A number of courses are available ranging from computer courses to liberal arts studies.
- Read. Read computer periodicals to keep informed of the changes in hardware, software, and telecommunications. Read periodicals relevant to your field. Visit your local bookstore or library for the latest books available.

Challenges

Effective virtual employees also face some challenges. For those who have transitioned from a traditional office setting, initially there may be feelings of isolation. Working in close proximity to family and household responsibilities presents its own unique set of challenges. There may be technological issues that need to be identified and handled. Supervisory issues must also be identified and discussed. The following sections will examine and provide suggestions for each of these challenges.

ISOLATION

The biggest challenge for many individuals not working in a typical office is the isolation. If you have been accustomed to working in a traditional workplace setting, you will recognize several differences when you become a remote worker. You cannot chat with a coworker on break. You do not encounter colleagues in the hallways or on the elevator. You have limited access to coworkers to discuss new ideas or problem situations.

As a full-time virtual assistant or teleworker, you must find ways to relieve these feelings of isolation. Suggestions include the following:

- Become involved in an activity outside of your home environment. Join a health club, volunteer with a local organization, or join a service organization. Find something that puts you in direct contact with others.
- Plan to have lunch occasionally with someone who is working in your field or has similar interests. It will help you feel connected and involved in the business world.
- Take advantage of professional development seminars or workshops that are offered in your area.
- Turn on a news program or radio during your lunch or break to keep you informed on what is happening in the outside world, just like you did when you were commuting to work.

As a part-time teleworker you must also develop strategies to deal with feelings of isolation. The following tips will help you stay in touch with your supervisors and coworkers.

- Arrange for daily contact with your supervisor or colleagues through telephone, email, or instant messaging. This is a great way to update a manager or supervisor on projects that you are working on or to get feedback from coworkers.
- Plan to have lunch with someone from the main office regularly to help you feel connected to your coworkers.
- Make sure you are accessible by telephone. Email is not always effective when brainstorming or working on team projects.
- Make sure to maintain personal friendships that have developed with colleagues. When visiting the office, stop to say hello to colleagues.
- Request that staff meeting notes or minutes be forwarded to you. This will enable you to remain informed about current workplace events.
- Continue to take advantage of email and voice mail technology to supplement telephone conversations. This technology can help maintain communication regardless of time zone differences.

FAMILY ISSUES

Maintaining an appropriate balance between job and home demands is often difficult for those working from home. If you are married, have a family, or live with other individuals, you must discuss your work arrangements with them. Unfortunately, many people will have misconceptions about you as a home-based worker. Some people may assume you are not really working or that you are available to take on additional responsibilities. Obviously, this is not true. Unless you can help these people understand what you are doing, you cannot be successful working at home.

To help deal with family issues, consider the following suggestions:

- Hold a meeting with your immediate family to explain how you will be working, what your work entails, and your work hours.
- Communicate with extended family and friends to discuss what your job entails and your work hours.
- Determine a clear division of household tasks. What are your spouse's responsibilities? What are your children's responsibilities?
- Determine whether you need someone to help care for children, either full time or after school. If you do, call a childcare referral service and ask friends for recommendations. Remember, a telework arrangement is not a substitute for daycare for children.
- Keep the lines of communication open. If you think someone is not doing his or her share, communicate your feelings.
- Do not expect perfection from your family as they perform tasks. Although they may not do tasks as well as you would, they are doing their part.

Make sure family and friends know your working hours and help them to understand when you cannot be disturbed. To assist in this effort, close your office door when you are working and post a sign on a bulletin board, indicating your work hours for the day or week. Refer to your home office as your workplace. Do not let family or friends think you can take on extra community and household projects because your workplace is in the home. Let them know you have business responsibilities that you must complete.

TECHNOLOGICAL CHALLENGES

As discussed previously, technology is vital if you choose to become a teleworker or virtual assistant. You may be working from your home, a client's office, a satellite office, or some other location. You will be using telecommunications technology to accomplish your job. The following suggestions can help you when dealing with technological challenges:

- Learn the telephone numbers of the technical support centers for your software programs, as well as hours of availability. Keep these in a file or on a contact list and handy at all times.
- Use Internet resources. A variety of Internet sites are available that allow you to post questions and/or problems.
- Make a listing of the telephone numbers of the manufacturer of your equipment (computer, printer, multifunction device, cell phone, and so on), and keep the warranty information in a safe and practical place.
- Know how to get assistance with Internet problems; for example, know the telephone number of your Internet service provider.
- Keep up to date as software changes. Take a short course from your local college or a workshop from your community education office. If taking a course is not practical, purchase books or manuals and schedule time to learn to use new equipment or software.
- If you are a virtual assistant, call a temporary agency for additional support if the job becomes too much for you to handle productively.

SUPERVISORY CONCERNS

Maintaining performance levels in a telework environment is sometimes a concern for both the employee and the supervisor. However, once a telework program has been implemented, the following suggestions can help to ease any concerns.[6]

---

[6]"Performance Management," U.S. Office of Personnel Management, accessed February 17, 2007, available from http://www.opm.gov/perform/articles/2001/win01-1.asp.

- Plan the work. In any work situation, planning work is the first step to managing performance. First, make sure employee assignments align with and support organizational goals. Second, determine employee accomplishments that support those goals.
- Set expectations. Not only do employees need to know *what* they are supposed to do, they need to know *how well* they are supposed to do it. Although supervisors can use the standards written in employee performance plans, they need to make sure they are verbally communicated as well. If employees know what they are supposed to do, and how well they are supposed to do it, the supervisor has set the stage for success.
- Monitor performance. Monitoring performance includes measuring performance and providing feedback. In a telecommuting situation (as in any work situation), measuring the results of employee efforts rather than their activities is more efficient and effective. Supervisors should review quantity, quality, timeliness, and cost-effectiveness. Once supervisors and employees establish performance measures, communicating performance on those measures should be frequent. Employees need feedback on their performance in order to maintain good performance and to improve overall. In addition, employees need to keep supervisors informed about work progress. Good communication between supervisors and employees is essential for successfully completing work and is especially necessary in a telecommuting environment.

Creating an Effective Work Environment

You need to consider a number of elements when setting up an effective work environment. What type of work are you going to be doing? What type of office will you require?

focus on — Create an Effective Telework Agreement

A successful telework arrangement requires that the employee and the employer reach agreement on a variety of issues. Regardless of the number of hours that are involved, a written agreement will remind everyone of what has been discussed. The agreement should address the following issues:

- Location of the telework office (home, telework center, other)
- Equipment required (what the employee is supplying, what the agency is providing, or what the telework center is providing)
- Job tasks to be performed while teleworking
- Telework schedule
- Telework contact information (the phone number to use on the telework day)

The employer and teleworker should evaluate the agreement periodically and make changes if necessary. Certainly the telework agreement should be revised as circumstances change. At least for the first year, however, the agreement should be reviewed every three or four months. Even without major changes, the employer and teleworker should review and re-sign the document on an annual basis.[7]

[7]"A Guide to Telework in the Federal Government," OPM-II-A-9 (page 9), August 3, 2006, accessed February 17, 2007, available from https://www.opm.gov/pandemic/agency2a-guide.pdf.

Types of Offices

The type of office you will need depends greatly on the type of work you will be doing. Although you may use a virtual office, mobile office, or work from a satellite or telework center, almost all teleworkers or virtual assistants will rely on a home office as well. A part-time teleworker may use a home office for a limited time, such as one day per week.

VIRTUAL OFFICE

For most people the virtual office has no physical form. Instead, the virtual office simulates a business location through the use of telecommunications and computer links. Therefore, a computer and network connection allow you to perform work from a variety of locations—at home, in your car, at a coffee shop, at an airport, or even at the beach. Technically, your office is wherever you are conducting business at the time.

The virtual office simulates a work environment through the use of telecommunications equipment.

© BrandX Pictures / Jupiter Images

MOBILE OFFICE

Mobile offices generally are described as a combination of portable electronic equipment, such as a computer, telephone, and fax, that duplicate the equipment of one's office. Mobile offices are used by salespeople or others who regularly work outside of their company office. A mobile office can exist in a specific location, such as airport terminals, hotels, or even restaurants. A mobile office can also be created at a client's office when a portable computer connects to the company network. Mobile offices are particularly convenient for employees when they are traveling and need to communicate with others at their home work site.

HOME OFFICE

A home office is a work or office space set up in a person's home. This specific area is used to conduct business on a regular basis. Although a number of people who work at home are self-employed, there are also millions of individuals who are employed by organizations who allow their employees to work from their homes on a part-time or full-time basis.

Workspace Considerations

Regardless of how you use your home office, a dedicated workspace is essential. A spare bedroom, a basement room, or even an unused dining room may be the answer. If you are hoping to claim a home-office deduction on your taxes, a specific space is essential. If clients, customers, and/or coworkers will be meeting with you, the space needs to be as close to an entrance as possible. You do not want these individuals walking through your entire house before reaching your office. Keep the following ideas in mind when choosing your location:

- Choose a quiet location. If a dedicated space with a door that closes is unavailable, choose an area away from the commotion of your home.
- Separate your work area from the rest of the house. If you have a door, close it. If you do

not have a door, find a way to put something between your office and the rest of the house.

- Minimize the distractions that are in your immediate workspace. Remove any and all items that will draw you away from the work at hand.
- Make sure it is comfortable. You will probably be spending a lot of time there. Choose a comfortable and ergonomically appropriate chair. Control the temperature. Working in an environment that is too hot or too cold lessens your productivity.
- Make sure the space will handle all the needed equipment. Choose an area that has sufficient electrical outlets and telephone jacks to accommodate your needs. Make sure the outlets and jacks are in close proximity to your equipment.
- Check the lighting. Make sure you have adequate lighting for using your equipment. Do not locate your computer so close to a window that the outside light causes a glare on the screen.

- Make the space your own. Create a space that nurtures and improves your state of mind. Choose a functional layout, but add personal touches such as pictures, artwork, plants, or even a fishbowl to make it a place you enjoy.

You must also consider the size of your workspace. Your space needs will be different if you are working full time from a home location versus one day a week or month. For example, if you are an occasional teleworker, you may need only a portion of a room. If you are working at home full time, you need a larger desk and additional space for a computer, copier, printer, and other workplace equipment. You may also need filing cabinets, storage units, and bookshelves. Overall, keep in mind that a productive teleworker needs a functional and safe workspace. Some safety guidelines are shown in Figure 3.2.

SAFETY GUIDELINES FOR THE HOME WORKSPACE

- Develop and practice a fire evacuation plan for use in the event of an emergency.
- Check your smoke detectors regularly and replace batteries once a year.
- Always have a working fire extinguisher conveniently located in your home, and check the charge regularly.
- Computers are heavy. Always place them on sturdy, level, well-maintained furniture.
- Arrange file cabinets so that opened drawers do not block aisles.
- Be sure to leave aisle space to reduce tripping hazards.
- Always make sure electrical equipment is connected to grounded outlets.
- Avoid fire hazards by never overloading electrical circuits.
- Inspect and repair carpeting with frayed edges or loose seams. Avoid using throw rugs that can cause tripping hazards in your workspace.
- Locate computers, phones, and other electrical equipment in a manner that keeps power cords out of walkways.
- Always power down computers after the workday is over.
- Keep your work area clean and avoid clutter, which can cause fire and tripping hazards.
- Always use proper lifting techniques when moving or lifting heavy equipment and furniture.

Source: "Safety Guidelines for the Home Workspace," Working for America, accessed February 15, 2007, available from http://www.telework.gov/documents/tw_man03/doc/appd_j.doc.

FIGURE 3.2 A home office workspace should be safe and functional.

Hardware and Software

Regardless of the type of office you have, you will certainly need a computer. For those individuals who work out of a home-based office a desktop computer will be suitable. However, if your work involves traveling to other locations, you should probably consider purchasing a notebook or laptop computer. If you are worried about working with the laptop, you can invest in a standard monitor, keyboard, and mouse to connect when you are at home. The following suggestions will help you select computer hardware to meet your needs.

- Read computer periodicals such as *Computer Shopper*, *PC World*, *Wired*, and *Maximum PC*.
- Conduct online research; many equipment and software manufacturers advertise their products on the Internet. Other Internet sites provide expert and customer reviews of products or compare prices.
- Shop at computer stores where you can try the equipment and talk with salespeople. Purchasing at a store may provide you with a resource for service or repair needs.
- Talk with people who use the technology. For example, discuss the best buys with other teleworkers, computer technicians, or friends who are computer users.

All home offices should include a printer. The type of printer you choose will depend upon your business needs. Printer quality varies greatly, so do your research before you buy. Ask yourself the following questions when selecting a printer:

- How much printing will I need to do?
- How important is document quality?
- Is printing speed an issue?
- Will I need to produce high-quality color illustrations, photos, or charts?
- How much money am I willing to spend on a printer and on replacement ink or toner cartridges?
- Will I use a print shop for some of my printing, or will I print all materials at my home?

Depending upon your workload, you may need other equipment. A scanner would be necessary if you need to scan documents or photos. A copier may be helpful. A fax machine might be necessary. If very high-quality printing is not a necessity, or if space is limited, you could consider a multifunction device. This type of unit will perform printing, copying, scanning, and faxing functions.

Software is also an important consideration. In addition to telecommunications software, you need a reliable email program and an Internet browser. You may choose to purchase a personal management program that includes an email program such as *Microsoft Outlook®*. You may choose an office suite that includes word processing, spreadsheet, database, and presentation software; or you may choose stand-alone programs. Virus protection software and system maintenance software should also be considered. If you are working with others and need to coordinate scheduling, maintain contact management, use an instant messenger (IM), or use chat rooms, there are software programs that you can purchase for these purposes. You may also choose to download instant messaging (IM) software for use in communicating with co-workers or clients. Making regular backups of your computer data is important and can be accomplished by using a variety of software and hardware combinations. You will learn more about backing up data in Chapter 10.

Keeping your employer's or clients' data confidential is important for virtual assistants and other teleworkers. You can use firewalls (consisting of both hardware and software) to help you protect electronic data. Data in paper form should also be stored in locked file cabinets or other containers when not in use. You will learn more about handling data in electronic and paper form in Chapter 13.

Other Equipment and Supplies

In order to maintain contact with your employer and/or your clients, you will need a reliable Internet service provider. Your local phone company, cable company, and cell phone provider may all offer these types of services. The fees charged and performance capabilities for these services can vary greatly. For additional information on telecommunications services, review the information contained in Chapter 12.

A landline phone and/or cell phone service should also be maintained. Although much of your actual work will be conducted online, there will be instances when telephone communication will be the easiest way to address a problem or complete a task. Also, the phone line will serve as an emergency backup when Internet service is interrupted or you are experiencing equipment problems.

Once you have selected a workspace and purchased your computer equipment, you need to determine the furniture you will need. At a minimum, you will need a desk and a chair. When selecting furniture, look for ergonomically designed furniture. For example, an ergonomic chair promotes healthy posture and more comfortable seating. Select a chair with adjustable armrests, seat, and back and a wheeled base with five coaster wheels to prevent tipping. Select a desk that suits your needs and fits your room. If your job is paperwork intensive, make sure you select a desk with a large work surface. Make sure your desk has ample space for your computer equipment as well.

If you are working at home on a part-time basis, your company likely furnishes you with letterhead, memorandum forms, envelopes, business cards, and other supplies. If you are a virtual assistant, you can design your own stationary and business cards. Most word processing and desktop publishing programs have the capability to create professional-looking documents. You can also use a local office supply store or printing business to assist in the design and to print these items relatively inexpensively and quickly.

Adequate storage is also important for a home office. Shelves, file cabinets, and storage cabinets will help you keep your materials organized. Make sure you have enough storage space for your supplies, files, customer information, specialized materials, and business records. Keeping frequently used supplies close at hand increases your productivity. Be sure you are able to keep supplies handy and still have an organized work area.

Summary

To reinforce what you have learned in this chapter, study this summary.

- Advances in telecommunications technology have increased opportunities for teleworkers and virtual assistants.

- Successful telework arrangements provide a variety of employee, employer, and community benefits.

- Virtual assistants are self-employed individuals who use telecommunications technology to provide administrative or technical services to clients. They contract their services on an hourly, flat rate, per project, or on-call basis.

- Business owners can realize several advantages through contracting with virtual assistants.

- The successful teleworker or virtual assistant must be disciplined, a self-starter, independent, organized, and self-confident and must possess a strong work ethic.

- The successful virtual worker must be skilled in planning, communication, and technology use and must have a commitment to lifelong learning.

- A virtual employee may face challenges including isolation, family issues, technological challenges, and supervisory concerns.

- Virtual workers may conduct their work at a virtual office, mobile office, or home office.

- When creating an effective home office, location, space requirements, hardware, software, other equipment, and supplies must all be considered.

What's the Problem?

In an effort to improve his work/life balance, Joe Park has teleworked two days a week from his home. His telework agreement requires that he be connected to an instant messaging system during working hours in case other employees or his supervisor need to contact him. While he is working during the day, friends and relatives frequently send him messages. He also finds other office employees sending him personal notes or bits of office gossip. Joe tries to ignore the messages. However, the messages automatically open on the computer screen, and he must close the message box before he can continue with work. Most of the time he finds it impossible to close the message without reading it. He often takes the time to send a note indicating he is working so as not to seem rude.

What suggestions do you have for Joe on handling messages to make him more productive during working hours?

Let's Discuss

1. Define *telework* and list benefits of telework to teleworkers.
2. List benefits of telework to businesses who allow employees to telework.
3. Define *virtual assistant* and describe benefits and concerns for virtual assistant clients.
4. List and explain personal characteristics that a successful teleworker must possess.
5. List the types of skills a successful teleworker should have.
6. Identify three challenges that face a teleworker.
7. Describe considerations for planning an effective home office workspace.

Critical-Thinking Activity

Carmen Perez has worked as an administrative assistant for several years. She has become accustomed to a daily routine that includes talking with coworkers and speaking informally with her supervisor. Two months ago the company offered Carmen the opportunity to work from home three days a week. Although she was hesitant, Carmen believed the extra time at home would enable her to be more productive in her workplace activities as well as her home activities.

One month into her teleworking experience, Carmen has begun staying up late and sleeping in the next morning on the days she does not have to commute. She moves from project to project and is beginning to accumulate several piles of paper on her desk. After she gets involved in a project, she often finds she has left important papers at the office and has to put the project aside until she goes back to the office.

On the two days that Carmen is at the office, she spends at least three hours each week in meetings. When she does have a few minutes in her office, her coworkers stop by to ask questions, discuss projects, and sometimes just to chat. Although some of the interruptions cannot be avoided, Carmen is becoming frustrated. She has three major projects due next week. Although she has begun all of the projects, none of them are complete. Carmen is overwhelmed because she does not seem to be getting any work done at home or in the office.

What suggestions can you give Carmen to help her complete her projects on time? What suggestions can you give Carmen to be more productive working at home? What suggestions can you give Carmen to be more productive working at the office?

Vocabulary Review

Open the *Word* file *CH03 Vocabulary* found on the Student CD. Complete the vocabulary review for Chapter 3.

English and Word Usage Drill

Complete the English and Word Usage Drill for Chapter 3 found in the *Applications Workbook*.

Workplace Applications

3-1 Conduct Research on Telework

(Goals 1, 2, and 3)

United Pharmaceuticals is considering expanding its telework opportunities to individuals within the administrative professional work group. Because telework is

internet

relatively new to United Pharmaceuticals, your supervisor has asked you to research two companies that have implemented successful telework programs. The research will be used to prepare a presentation for the department managers to help them understand how to implement a successful program.

1. Working with at least one of your classmates, conduct Internet research on teleworking. Use the following questions as a starting point for your research.

   - How long has the company participated in telework?

   - What types of positions are involved in telework?

   - What made the program successful?

   - What advantages have the company and teleworkers realized from the program?

   - What challenges have the company and teleworkers faced with the program?

2. Use a program such as *PowerPoint* to prepare a short presentation (four or five slides per telework program) with your findings. Be prepared to present this information to the class.

3-2 Plan Equipment and Supplies for a Home Office

(Goals 2 and 3)

You have decided to quit your job and work from home as a virtual assistant. You have identified a 10' by 10' room in your home that you can convert into your office. The room has adequate lighting and electrical outlets. It also has several small windows that will allow for some natural light. You purchased a laptop computer last month that has an Internet browser program and an office-suite software package. You have decided that in the beginning you will offer standard administrative assistant duties; however, you plan to expand into Web page design and graphic arts in the near future. You have received a $5,000 small business start-up loan to purchase the equipment and supplies that will be needed to get your business up and running.

1. Work with two of your classmates on this assignment. As a team, research and find descriptions and prices for all the furniture and equipment you will need to set up your office. Use the Internet and office supply catalogs, or visit a local retailer to identify specific items.

2. As part of the loan requirements, your team needs to provide the bank with a detailed list of the items you plan to purchase. Create a spreadsheet that includes the following information for each item:

   - Item name

   - Quantity of the item

   - Purchase price

- Total price for this item

- Model number

- Description

- Supplier name and address

- Tax (if applicable)

- Shipping and handling (if applicable)

3. Total the Total Price column. Make sure the total is equal to or less than the $5,000 loan amount. Provide an appropriate title for the spreadsheet and use an attractive, easy-to-read format.

4. Use graph paper or an appropriate design/drawing computer program to design a home office (10′ × 10′). Indicate where the individual pieces of furniture and equipment will be located to ensure an efficient working environment.

3-3 Interview a Virtual Assistant

(Goals 1, 2, and 3)

e-portfolio

1. Interview someone who is employed as a virtual assistant. If you are unable to locate a virtual assistant in your community, you may locate people to interview through Internet resources and interview them online or through email. Ask them to respond to the following items. Create two additional questions on your own.

- How did you become a virtual assistant?

- What type of education and experiences did you have that prepared you for this position?

- What personal qualities are necessary in order to be successful?

- Where is your workspace located? What equipment do you have? What software do you use?

- What do you find the most challenging about your work?

- What tips would you give a potential virtual assistant?

2. Write a short unbound report describing your findings, and present your findings to the class.

Assessment of Chapter 3 Goals

Did you successfully complete the chapter goals? Evaluate yourself by completing the form found in Chapter 3 of the *Applications Workbook*.

part *2*

Workforce Behaviors

CHAPTER 4

Your Professional Image

CHAPTER 5

Anger, Stress, and Time Management

CHAPTER 6

Ethical Theories and Behaviors

Career Profile

Human Resources Associate

Attracting, training, and retaining qualified workers is important to the success of organizations. Workers in Human Resources Departments handle these vital tasks. Human resources employees can be found in almost all industries and in small, medium, and large companies. Human resources, training, and labor relations managers and specialists held about 820,000 jobs in the United States in 2004. About 21,000 specialists were self-employed, working as consultants to public and private employers.*

A human resources associate may handle a broad range of human resources work. This type of employee is called a human resources generalist and is likely to be found in small organizations. Other associates may specialize in a particular area, such as benefit management, recruitment, or training. The job duties of a human resources associate vary depending on whether the position is that of a generalist or a specialist. For example, an employee may specialize in recruitment screens, interviews, or testing job applicants. Travel to college campuses and job fairs and working with online job sites is typically part of the duties for this job.

Salaries for human resources associates vary by specific job, the size of the company, and the qualifications of the worker. Median annual earnings of employment, recruitment, and placement specialists were $41,190 in May 2004. Median annual earnings of compensation, benefits, and job analysis specialists were $47,490 in May 2004. Human resources associates may advance to managerial positions that offer higher salaries. For example, median annual earnings of compensation and benefits managers were $66,530 in May 2004.

Many colleges and universities have programs leading to a degree in personnel, human resources, or labor relations. This formal education as well as excellent communication, computer, and teamwork skills can help human resources associates be successful.

_____

*"Human Resources, Training, and Labor Relations Managers and Specialists," *Occupational Outlook Handbook*, 2006-2007 Edition, accessed June 4, 2007, available from http://www.bls.gov/oco/ocos021.htm.

chapter 4

Your Professional Image

Learning Goals

1. **Describe the personal characteristics and work characteristics that contribute to a positive professional image.**

2. **Identify the components of a professional appearance.**

3. **Understand the conventions of business etiquette.**

Characteristics of a Professional

You have probably heard the phrases "a picture is worth a thousand words" and "you never get a second chance to make a first impression." When it comes to how you present and conduct yourself in a business environment, whether it is in that first interview or every day on the job with coworkers and clients, these phrases ring far truer than most would like to admit.

Appearance is only part of the equation when creating and maintaining your **professional image**. The impressions you make on others, your attitude toward your work and your coworkers, your work ethic, your professional dress, and your familiarity with business etiquette all work together to form your professional image. Your ability to get a job, keep a job, and move up the corporate ladder will all hinge on your professional image.

Successful business people are those that spend time cultivating their professional image. In survey after survey, business leaders are asked what they look for when seeking new employees, and the most common responses deal with their professional image. Although skills, education, and specialized certifications are important, employers are looking for successful individuals who possess a variety of professional characteristics as well. Successful individuals work hard to make a good first impression, present a positive attitude, and demonstrate their professionalism through their exceptional work ethic.

First Impressions

The power of a first impression is immeasurable. Think back to the day when you first set foot on your college campus. You are very likely to recall, no matter how long ago it was, exactly how you felt, even if you do not remember all of the details. Whether it was positive or negative, you remember the first impression that it made. Have you ever driven to a store or restaurant and decided not to enter because of the way it looked? Once again you made a decision based on the impression it made on you.

Business people also form a quick first impression of you, usually during the first 7 to 10 seconds of a meeting or interview. During that short period of time, you are being evaluated on your demeanor, mannerisms, **body language**, and grooming. The successful professional will not leave this first impression to chance. Instead, he or she will take the time to review his or her attitude, clothing, manners, and body language to ensure that the impression made is a positive one and one that will work to his or her advantage. What can you do to make a positive first impression?

- Be on time or arrive early. Arriving on time for an interview or meeting shows the person that the contact is important to you. When leaving for an appointment, allow extra time for traffic problems or other unforeseen delays. Although arriving early is always better than arriving late, do not arrive more than 15 minutes prior to your appointment time. If you have some extra time, get a cup of coffee, take a walk, or find a quiet place to review your notes. Timeliness is the first step in creating a positive first impression.

- Be comfortable and confident with your skills and abilities. If you are confident and comfortable with yourself, you will make the other person feel more at ease. This will help in presenting yourself in a positive light.

- Dress professionally. Whether you like it or not, people often make judgments based on the way you look. If the person you are meeting does not know you, your appearance is often their first clue to your personality. Pay careful attention to the section on professional dress and grooming that appears later in this chapter. What you wear and your personal hygiene make a strong statement about you.

- Smile. A warm and confident smile goes a long way toward making a good first impression. It will also put you and the other person at ease. Be careful not to seem insincere. Make sure your words and actions support the smile on your face.

- Be conscious of body language. You may have heard the phrase "your actions speak louder than words." Standing tall, making eye contact, and greeting people with a firm handshake all go a long way toward making a good first impression. Avoid fidgeting, twirling your hair, and playing with your jewelry. Crossing your arms may signal that you are angry. Crossing your legs may show you in more of a casual light.

- Be positive. Remember, your attitude shows through in everything you do.

- Be courteous. Good manners and polite, courteous behavior help make a good first impression. In fact anything less can ruin the one chance you have at making that first impression count. Give the person you are meeting with 100 percent of your attention. Turn off your cell phone and do not become distracted by what is going on around you. Focus all of your attention on the person with whom you are meeting.

Because you just have a few seconds to make a good first impression, it is important to always put your best foot forward. Whether you are meeting with prospective employers, colleagues, or other business associates, you must strive to make a positive first impression. Remember, it is almost impossible to change that first impression; so take the time and put forth the effort to make your first impression your best.

A confident smile will make a good first impression and put everyone at ease.

Positive Attitude

Attitude is defined as disposition, feelings, or moods toward things, circumstances, or people. Your attitude comes through in everything that you do, from answering the phone to working with others in the office. Although attitude can be positive or negative, it is something a person can control. Every day a person has a choice as to what attitude to have. Although there are things in life a person cannot change, individuals can change their attitudes and how they look at things.

How do you create a positive attitude? Positive attitudes attract positive results. One way to cultivate a positive attitude is to surround yourself with positive people who encourage you and believe in you. Spending time with positive people who make you feel good about yourself and your situation will help you to maintain a positive attitude. Everyone can possess a positive attitude. A positive attitude begins with a healthy self-image. If you choose to love the way you are, and are satisfied, confident, and self-assured, you

will also make others around you feel the same way. Focus on the positive things in life and you are more likely to exhibit a positive attitude.

Why is a positive attitude beneficial? Research in this area indicates that a positive attitude promotes better health. Studies have shown that such an attitude actually retards aging, makes you healthier, helps you develop a better stress-coping mechanism, and has a very positive effect on the people you meet every day.[1]

Many people in business say attitude is more important than education. When deciding between two equally qualified candidates, attitude is often the tiebreaker, and the person with the positive attitude comes out the winner. Although a person cannot change the past or how others act, individuals can change their reactions and

---

[1]Ros Oliveira, "Positive Attitude," Associate Programs.com, accessed March 25, 2007, available from http://www.associateprograms.com/articles/486/1/Positive-attitude.

A positive attitude is often contagious.

attitude. Everyone must also take responsibility for his or her attitude.

Our attitude, whether positive or negative, affects those around us as well. People like to spend time with someone who is positive; they do not like to spend time with someone who is negative. Also, a positive attitude is contagious. If you choose to project a confident, satisfied, positive image, those around you have a tendency to feel and act the same way.

Maintaining a positive attitude is not always easy. In fact, at times it is difficult to find a way of looking at things in a positive way. It helps to remember that not only is your positive attitude beneficial to you, but your positive attitude is also valued and appreciated by those around you. You may find that you can accomplish more, and it can be accomplished more effectively, if you take on the task with a positive attitude. You are more likely to be offered the opportunity to take on important responsibilities, or even be considered for a promotion, if your attitude is positive.

Work Ethic

What is work ethic? **Work ethic** is a set of values based on the merits of hard work and diligence. It is also a belief in the benefit of work and its ability to build a person's character. Coming to work on time, being prepared for meetings, and working cooperatively with others in your office says a lot about your work ethic. Exhibiting the right attitude, skills, and professional ethics is a positive start to developing an effective work ethic.

If you wish to be successful, you must develop a positive work ethic. Think about the type of work ethic you currently convey. Are you loyal to your employer? Do you take your job responsibilities seriously? Individuals with a strong work ethic typically display the following characteristics:

- Arrive at work on time and stay until their shift is over
- Meet all deadlines (both scheduled and unscheduled)
- Exhibit a sense of integrity and trustfulness
- Follow established rules and procedures
- Make productive use of work time

A person with a strong work ethic demonstrates responsibility and initiative, is reliable, and maintains appropriate social skills. Individuals with a strong work ethic demonstrate their integrity by using their sick days only when they are sick and by taking vacation days only as scheduled. If a worker's lunch hour is scheduled for noon and a customer needs assistance at that time, the individual with the strong work ethic will take care of the customer's needs first. Always putting forth your best effort and doing your best work demonstrates a strong work ethic.

Having a strong work ethic does not mean that you are a **workaholic**—a person who is addicted to work. Work ethic equates to putting in a full day's work for a full day's pay; it does not mean that you are working overtime for free. Instead, the successful professional will find balance between work and personal life. Remember, individuals who exhibit a strong work ethic are often those who get the job, are given additional responsibility and wages, or are considered for promotions.

Other Professional Characteristics

Possessing and demonstrating the workplace skills discussed in Chapter 1 and throughout this text are important to your professional image. Possessing the skills necessary to effectively complete your job responsibilities are vital, but the ability to effectively manage your time, anger, and stress or to make decisions is equally important. Demonstrating to your supervisor, coworkers, and clients your expertise in the following workplace skills contributes positively to your professional image.

- Communication (listening, reading, verbal presentation, and writing)
- Interpersonal relations
- Time management
- Critical thinking
- Decision making
- Creative thinking
- Teamwork
- Technology
- Leadership
- Stress management

As discussed in Chapter 1, the effective administrative professional possesses other personal characteristics. If you wish to be successful, review the personal qualities listed in Chapter 1. These qualities include:

- Openness to change
- Creativity
- Initiative and motivation
- Integrity and honesty
- Dependability
- Confidentiality
- Commitment to observing and learning

Remember, the personal qualities or job skills in isolation will not make you successful. If you wish to be a successful administrative professional, you must integrate these skills and qualities with other personal success qualities. They are not your complete professional image; they are only a part of it.

Work Characteristics

Your work area is another avenue for you to present a positive professional image because it is an extension of your professional appearance. Whether you work at a desk out in the open area of the office, a cubicle among many cubicles, or in a small, enclosed office, the appearance of that workplace says a lot to others about your professionalism and your attitude toward your work. Careful attention should be focused on both your workspace and your desk.

YOUR WORKSPACE

The area around your desk, or your workspace, says something about you. In most instances it is acceptable to personalize this area, but make sure to keep it professional. It is still a place of business, not an extension of your home. A few personal photos and a small plant demonstrate that you are an employee who takes pride in your home and family, but does not make visitors feel as if they are an uninvited guest into your living room.

To get a sense for how others view your workspace, periodically sit in the visitors' chair at your desk. Look around to see what they see. Things can look very different from the other side of the desk. Although it may be appropriate to display certificates or awards, do not overwhelm your space with these types of documents. A tasteful display of relevant certificates will enhance your professional image.

YOUR DESK

A professional has an organized desk. Your work supplies, including staplers, paper, envelopes, paperclips, and pens should be organized and easily accessible. Keep current projects and completed projects organized as well. Being able to locate material quickly and efficiently demonstrates your professionalism.

A neat, organized desk enhances your professional image.

Keep your desk clean. When something is no longer useful, move it from your desk to the garbage or the recycling bin. Keep food and drinks away from the papers on your desk. In addition to the potential for messes, assorted cans and bottles do not present a professional image. Eating at your desk does not give you the necessary break most professionals need. In fact, some workplace policies prohibit individuals from having food items at their desks at any time.

YOUR DAILY WORK

What does the quality of your work say about you? Are coworkers likely to come to you for assistance with a project or a problem? Their view of how you work is an excellent indicator of how customers and clients view the work that you have done. Attention to detail is very important. Documents that are proofread, names and titles that are spelled correctly and used correctly, and papers that are clean and folded evenly all indicate the level of professionalism that is appreciated by your employer and your clients. You have probably heard the phrase "don't sweat the small stuff." Although this may be good advice as a general rule, do not ignore the small details related to your work. In the business world, the "small stuff" should never be done haphazardly! The way you complete small or routine tasks says a great deal about your attention to detail.

If you make a mistake, it is imperative that you take responsibility for the error and do your best to correct it. Acknowledge the error, apologize to those the error affects, and develop a plan to avoid repeating the mistake in the future. Not only will your supervisor appreciate this approach, but so will your coworkers, as all too often people try to blame others for their errors.

Professional Organizations

Participating in professional organizations can help you improve your professional image. Through organizations such as the International Association of Administrative Professionals (IAAP) and ARMA International, administrative professionals can attain certifications that attest to their skills and knowledge in given areas. Professional organizations often provide Websites, articles, newsletters, and seminars that can help you improve your skills. Knowing that you take the time and effort to try to improve your skills and knowledge may give your superiors and coworkers a positive image of you.

Professional Business Cards

You work hard to present a professional image. Your business card says a great deal about you as well. Business cards should be displayed neatly on your desk so they are accessible to current and prospective clients. A professional business card will include the following information:

- Company name and logo
- Name and professional title
- Business address including city, state, and ZIP Code
- Office telephone number and fax number
- Email address and/or Web address

The professional always stores business cards in a professional holder. Nothing detracts from your professional image more than tattered, bent, and dirty business cards.

You might also belong to a professional organization related to the industry or organization in which you work. For example, suppose you work as an administrative professional for a school system and you deal largely with the system's adult education programs. You might join an organization such as the American Association for Adult and Continuing Education. Through the organization's publications and Website, you could learn about research and current issues in this field that could be helpful to you in your work. Being knowledgeable about issues related to your organization's work enhances your professional image.

Your Professional Look

People may think that the quality of a person's work will match the quality of the person's appearance. Your appearance may indicate your attention to detail, your level of motivation, and your sense of professionalism. What you wear and how you present yourself says a lot about you and can damage or even destroy your chances of success in business.

Dressing the Part

People often make judgments about others based on how they look. Remember that people establish their first impressions during the first 7 to 10 seconds of an initial meeting. Because not much is said in this short time, this early judgment is based strictly on appearance. According to an article in *Women in Business*, "a person's choice of clothing provides a critical first glimpse into who we are and what we believe is important or not important."[2] Although the person wearing jeans and a T-shirt may be both competent and intelligent, that person is often not taken as seriously as the person wearing a formal suit. In addition, your attitude and confidence level are also affected by the clothes you wear. If you dress more casually, you may tend to behave more casually as well.

Professional dress also affects an individual's chances for promotion. "The best advice is to dress for the next step—the job you want, not the job you have."[3] If you want to be respected as a professional and considered for promotion, dress the way that the individuals currently in that position dress. A good rule of thumb is to dress one step above your current level in the organization, or dress as well as the best-dressed person in the organization. A recent survey conducted by OfficeTeam investigated how style of dress influenced a person's chances of being promoted. When a group of executives were asked to what extent dress at work influences an individual's chances of being promoted, 33 percent felt that professional dress had a significant influence on promotion and 60 percent felt that it somewhat influenced his or her chances of being promoted.[4]

[2]Michele Compton, "Dress the Part," *Women in Business*, January/February 2007, p. 14.

[3]Martha McCarty, "Cracking the Dress Code: What to Wear to Work … and What Not to Wear," *OfficePro*, March 2006, p. 26.

[4]Michele Compton, "Dress the Part," *Women in Business*, January/February 2007, p. 14.

© Creatas / Jupiter Images

In much of the business world, a conservative suit is still the preferred professional attire.

It may seem unfair, but your clothes, including your shoes, say a lot about the person you are. For example, a person wearing scuffed loafers may be viewed as lacking discipline and attention to detail. Therefore, understanding what is and is not appropriate for business dress in today's work world is an important first step to getting and keeping the job you really want.

PROFESSIONAL BUSINESS ATTIRE

In the business world, professional business attire for women is typically a suit or tailored dress in a traditional color such as black, navy blue, brown, beige, or gray. The skirt should extend to the knee or below and should not have high slits or openings. A sleeved blouse in a light color that complements the color of the suit should be worn. Closed-toe, low-heeled, conservative pumps are also suggested. Women should avoid wearing spiked heels, sandals, and shoes with flashy beading or stitching. Hosiery should always be worn and should be neutral or skin-tone in color. Remember to make sure that your shoes and accessories are clean and polished.

Although pantsuits are becoming more acceptable in the business environment, do not assume that they are acceptable in all instances.

Many conservative businesses still adhere to a strict professional dress code. If you have questions about the appropriateness of something, check with someone in the organization or the Human Resources Department first. If you are not sure, a traditional skirted suit is always the safest bet. Keep in mind that professional dress is always the best choice for an interview.

Professional business attire for men is a two-piece matched suit in a conservative color such as navy, dark gray, or black. A long-sleeved dress shirt in white or a light color is also required. Ties are mandatory, and men are encouraged to select a conservative tie that matches the suit. Shoes should be either brown or black leather and polished. Socks should match the suit and should pull up over the calves so skin does not show when sitting down. A simple leather belt that matches the color of the shoes should also be worn.

BUSINESS CASUAL ATTIRE

In the last several years, a new category of business dress has emerged. This new category, often referred to as **business casual dress**, has relaxed some of the conservative standards of the past. Although the business casual code allows an individual to dress in a more relaxed manner, it still means dressing professionally. Business casual is not a license to be sloppy or dress inappropriately; individuals are still required to have a neat and coordinated appearance.

For women, business casual may consist of a business skirt or casual pants. As with the professional category, the skirt should be at least knee length. Anything shorter is never appropriate in a business setting. Although casual slacks may be acceptable, in some instances khakis may be viewed as too casual for women. Typically short-sleeved shirts or blouses are considered more casual than the long-sleeved blouses worn with suits. Knit sweaters or sweater sets are also considered business casual. Leather shoes with a low or flat heel fit into this category.

Business casual does not mean that anything goes. Short skirts and sundresses are never considered appropriate business attire. Regardless of sleeve length, shirts should not be tight or expose too much skin. Although tennis shoes and flip flops may be comfortable to wear during your leisure time, they are always considered too casual for a business setting.

In general, the best advice is to conduct research on the business before selecting your clothing. If you work for a company where there is no dress code, you will not be too far off if you study how those in senior management dress and emulate them. Also, do not be afraid to ask someone; it only shows that you care enough to get things right.

For men, business casual dress at a large corporation may mean a sport coat with a tie rather than a business suit. At a smaller company, business casual dress may mean khakis and a polo shirt. Once again, the best rule of thumb is not to make assumptions but rather watch what others are wearing before making your clothing selections. Athletic shoes, hiking boots, and sandals are never appropriate (even in the summer). Men should wear leather shoes, dark socks that pull up over the calf, and a belt that matches the

shoes. Research and find out exactly what business casual means for your organization.

OTHER DRESS CONSIDERATIONS

In addition to business standards or formalized dress codes, there are other variables that you may consider when deciding what to wear. Points to keep in mind when purchasing your business wardrobe may include the following:

- Climate. Wool suits may work well in the northern climates where the weather is cool but would not be as appropriate in the sunshine states.

- Regional variations. Wall Street brokers may dress more conservatively than those working in a more trendy city such as Los Angeles.

- Business environment. When choosing clothing, it is important to consider what type of company you work for and the kind of work you will do. For example, if you are a woman working in the construction field, you would not want to be walking around a construction site wearing high heels.

- Type of occasion. The function you are attending should always be considered. If you are attending an evening event, your jewelry may be more elaborate than what you would wear to a breakfast meeting. The polo shirt that would be acceptable when attending an outdoor event would certainly be out of place at an annual board meeting.

Appearance

Attention to personal appearance is just as important to your professional image as what you wear. In addition to selecting the right clothes, attention to personal hygiene is necessary. The checklist shown in Figure 4.1 will help you remember the important grooming issues that should be considered.

Remember, some individuals are allergic to fragrance. If you choose to wear perfume or cologne, make sure that it is never strong. In consideration of others, the best rule to follow is to use a little or do not use any at all.

APPEARANCE GUIDELINES	
Hair	Clean, trimmed, and neatly combed or styled
Facial hair (men)	Clean shaven; mustache or beard neatly trimmed
Fingernails	Neat, clean, trimmed; natural looking
Teeth	Brushed and clean
Breath	Fresh and clean; beware of food odors
Body	Freshly bathed; use deodorant
Makeup	Use sparingly; natural looking
Perfume/colognes	Use sparingly or not at all

Source: Dress and Grooming, Job Seeker Guides, Department of Workforce Services, Utah's Job Connection, accessed April 19, 2007, available from http://www.jobs.utah.gov/jobseeker/guides/07_33.pdf.

FIGURE 4.1 Paying careful attention to your appearance can help create a professional image.

Jewelry

For women, jewelry should not be gaudy or appear overpowering, and it should not be noisy. Some women are more relaxed when asked to shake hands if they don't have to worry about rings digging into someone's fingers. An easy guide for women suggests wearing no more than six or seven pieces of jewelry (earrings, a watch, two rings, a bracelet, and a necklace). For men, a conservative watch and wedding ring are appropriate. Even for business casual dress, jewelry should be minimal.

Although multiple body piercings are becoming more common in today's society, in the strict world of business, unconventional body piercing is not always accepted. Many companies address the issue of body piercing in their dress codes. It is not uncommon for company policies to indicate that the only visible body piercing acceptable for male and female employees is the conventional ear lobe piercing or piercing for cultural reasons. In fact, some business dress codes require employees to remove any visible jewelry for body piercing that does not fall into these categories.

Some dress codes also stipulate that employees cover any visible tattoos. If you wish to work in a conservative business setting, it is probably a good idea to remove jewelry from additional piercings on your ears or face during a job interview. If the issue of tattoos and piercings is important to you and it is not addressed during your interview, ask for a copy of the dress code from the Human Resources Department before you leave the interview.

Understanding Business Etiquette

Presenting a professional image also requires that individuals utilize appropriate etiquette. **Etiquette** is described as a code that governs acceptable behavior developed through customs and enforced by group pressure. Business etiquette is the special code of behavior required in employment situations. Although these standards of behavior may vary slightly from business to business, it is important to understand the main categories of business etiquette in order to enhance your professional image. Understanding appropriate business etiquette helps people become successful and productive employees.[5]

---

[5]"Etiquette," *Encyclopedia Britannica*, accessed March 23, 2007, available from http://www.britannica.com/eb/article-9033150.

General Courtesy and Manners

One of the most common ways we judge an individual's grasp of etiquette is through his or her display of manners. **Manners** are the standards of conduct that show us how to behave in a cultured, polite, or refined way. Although there are no laws governing manners, social judgments are made based on whether or not we include courtesy and manners in our behavior toward others. Manners, then, are the general rules by which we need to live. They are the rules that guide us in our treatment of others.

A **courteous** person is respectful and considerate of others. Courtesy is described as exhibiting excellent manners or polite behavior. Most of us learn about manners and courtesy when we are young. By the time children enter school, they are expected to behave politely in school and in other social settings. Much of what we learn can be summed up in the golden rule: Treat others as you would like to be treated.

Good manners are based on consideration for other people. Three phrases that are always important to remember are *please*, *thank you*, and *I'm sorry*. Use the word *please* freely and with

Professional Pointers

Getting the job is the first step, but keeping the job is the next step. The importance of getting started on the right foot cannot be overemphasized. A professional employee will learn what the employer expects from her or him and understand the company policies. Some pointers for helping you keep your job from the Kentucky Office of Employment are as follows:[6]

- Cooperate with others to get a task done.

- Be willing to compromise.

- Do your share of the work.

- Be willing to learn from others and consider suggestions.

- Be polite and friendly—good manners cost you nothing but will gain you a lot of respect.

- Be sensitive to feelings of others.

- Help make your workplace a pleasant environment.

- Avoid gossiping, taking sides, complaining, and questioning the way everything is done.

- Give help when needed.

- Be honest—if you make a mistake, admit it and try harder.

- Be flexible.

---

[6]"Keeping the Job," Kentucky Office of Employment, accessed March 23, 2007, available from http://www.oet.ky.gov/des/vws/general_job_search/keeping_the_job.asp.

© PhotoDisc / Getty Images

Greeting someone appropriately shows good manners.

sincerity. If you do, you will find others more willing to work with you and assist you. Thank people for what they do for you. Whether it is as simple as opening a door for you or helping you carry a heavy box, say thank you with a smile and genuine feeling. Thanking others for their efforts goes a long way to creating a positive working environment. If you know you have made a mistake, do not hesitate to apologize. Learn to say you are sorry for even the smallest mistake and take responsibility for your behaviors or actions.

Greeting people appropriately is also a function of good manners. As we pass individuals in the hall, it is appropriate to acknowledge them and to greet them. Acknowledging someone's presence with a polite "hello" shows good manners. Asking how someone is doing shows an interest in them. Acknowledging someone's existence shows that you care about them and their well-being.

If you are a smoker, good manners require that you do not smoke where you will cause discomfort to another person. In many public buildings, including workplaces, smoking is not allowed indoors. Smoking may be allowed outside the building in designated places. In some public buildings, smoking is allowed in designated areas. Be considerate of others who do not wish to be exposed to smoke by smoking only where you will not affect others.

Dining and Restaurant Etiquette

Much of today's business takes place during business meals. If you want to make a positive impression in a dining situation, you must use appropriate table manners. Regardless of whether you are having lunch with a business associate or dinner with a prospective client, your dining etiquette speaks volumes about you as a professional. There are different responsibilities you should assume if you are hosting the meal function or just attending as a guest. Review the following material to make sure you are presenting your best professional image during meal functions.

HOSTING A BUSINESS MEAL

If you are hosting a business meal, it is your responsibility to extend the invitation to your guests. You may offer your guests a few date or time alternatives and allow them to make the final selection of date, time, and restaurant. If it is possible, select a restaurant that will allow you to make reservations. As host, you should arrive 10 to 15 minutes early so you can greet your guests. Arriving early also gives you time to make arrangements as to how the bill will be paid.

As the host, you should be comfortable enough with the restaurant menu to make meal recommendations to your guests. If not, ask your server for suggestions. Allow your guests to order first and encourage them to feel comfortable to order whatever they wish. As the host, order something easy to eat so you can carry on a conversation during the meal. If this is a business meal, it is appropriate to discuss business but not until the major portion of the meal is over.

Table manners play an important part in presenting a professional image during dining. Regardless of whether dining with a business associate, a customer, or friends, manners say a lot about a person. Figure 4.2 lists table manners that should always be followed.

ATTENDING A BUSINESS MEAL

If you are the guest at a business meal, remember that the host should indicate the beginning of the meal by unfolding the napkin and placing it in his or her lap. The host should signal the end of the meal by placing the napkin back on the table. If the menu has not been preselected, the host will typically suggest that you order first. Avoid ordering the most expensive meal on the menu or making several changes to a menu item.

When eating, remember to use your utensils in the order they are placed from the outside moving inward toward the plate. When you are finished with your meal, do not push your plate away from you; instead, lay your fork and knife diagonally across your plate. If you are unsure about anything during the meal, watch your host

---

TABLE MANNERS

- The guest should always order first.

- Order items that are easy to eat.

- Leave your cell phone behind or turn it off.

- Sit up straight and keep your elbows off the table.

- Do not eat too quickly or too slowly. Try to keep pace with the others at the table.

- Never chew with your mouth open or try to speak with food in your mouth.

- If you use the wrong piece of flatware, do not panic. Continue using it and ask the server for a replacement when you need it.

- Once you pick up a piece of cutlery, it should never touch the table again. Put it on your dish, rather than leaning it half on and half off the dish.

FIGURE 4.2 Using proper table manners helps create a professional image.

or the others around you. When the host signals the end of the meal, place your napkin on the table and thank your host.

The two typical dining styles are continental and American. With the American style of dining, the knife is used only for cutting. When cutting, the knife is held in the right hand and the fork is held in the left hand to help control the object being cut. The knife is then put down on the edge of the plate (blade facing in), and the fork is switched to the right hand to lift the cut food to the mouth. Remember to keep your hands in your lap when not being used.

With the continental dining style the knife remains in the right hand and the fork in the left. After the food is cut, the knife is used to push the food onto the fork. The tines of the fork face downward when the cut food is lifted to the mouth. The hands remain above the table when they are not in use.

International Customs and Etiquette

In order to be successful in today's global economy, it is important to realize that appropriate

etiquette can vary greatly among cultures. It would be foolish to assume that the behaviors that are considered appropriate for a business function in the United States are the same for those in all countries. Instead, it's important to take a proactive approach and research the country you are visiting so you are aware of their special customs.

INTERNATIONAL DINING ETIQUETTE

Appropriate dining etiquette varies widely by culture. For example, appropriate table etiquette in Japan involves saying traditional phrases before and after a meal to signal the beginning and ending of a meal.[7] Also, when eating western food Japanese people use knives and forks. However, because chopsticks are the most frequently used utensils, be prepared to use them if traditional Japanese dishes are on the menu. If you wish to be a successful businessperson in Japan, learn how to use chopsticks and how to eat Japanese food.

When invited to dinner in China is it appropriate to sample every dish that is served. In order to indicate that you had enough to eat, you must leave some food on your plate or your host might think that you did not get enough to eat. However, when dining in Germany, it is considered wasteful to leave food on your plate.

As you can see, dining etiquette varies by culture and country. The best advice is to do your research so that you are prepared for whatever situation you may encounter.

INTERNATIONAL BUSINESS DRESS

The best suggestion for professional dress in countries outside the United States is to follow the most conservative professional standards found in the United States. Many countries expect this high level of formality in business dress.

In the Netherlands, conservative business attire is recommended at all times. Dark suits and

---

[7]Shizuko Mishima, "Japanese Table Manners," accessed March 23, 2007, available from http://gojapan.about.com/cs/tablemanners/a/tablemanner.htm.

ties for men and white blouses and dark suits or skirts for women are expected. Suits are required in Russia, and it is considered rude for men to remove their jackets during a business meeting. In Saudi Arabia men are expected to wear long-sleeved shirts that button up to the collar. For women, high necklines with skirts that fall well below the knee are required.

Accessories should also be carefully researched and selected. In Saudi Arabia men should avoid wearing any visible jewelry, especially around the neck. Although jewelry is acceptable in Germany, it should never be ostentatious or gaudy.[8] Women must display manicured nails in Brazil. Men should never wear anything on the lapel in Chile. Make sure to research the customs of the country you are visiting to avoid embarrassment.

OTHER INTERNATIONAL ISSUES

It is impossible to list and describe all of the cultural issues that may be relevant when conducting business in another country. Do not assume that every country is the same as all others. The best policy is to research the customs, culture, and etiquette of the country you are visiting so that you are prepared to act in a professional manner. Several items to consider when working with international colleagues, customers, or clients are listed here.

- Giving gifts may be an important ritual of business or gifts may be strictly off-limits.

- Religious and national holidays and their customs may affect how and when business can be conducted.

- Business hours are not always the same as the typical hours observed in the United States. Businesses in other countries may start later, stay open later, or close in the afternoon for a rest period.

- Greetings vary by culture. Know when it is appropriate to shake hands, hug, or kiss.

- Time has different connotations in different cultures and countries. In some cultures being late is expected while in other cultures tardiness is unacceptable.

- Be cognizant of your gestures and body language. It is possible to offend someone with a hand gesture that is acceptable in the United States but considered rude in other countries.

Visit your local library or bookstore to learn about the country you will visit. You may also conduct research using the Web. Several Web addresses that provide information on international business etiquette and customs are given on the Links section of the Website for this textbook.

Making Introductions

The way you meet and greet individuals in business situations creates lasting impressions. Making appropriate introductions will put you and the people you are introducing at ease. Introductions are the first encounter an individual will have with others so make sure to make it positive. Keep in mind that business introductions should be made based on professional rank, not gender. This means that the person of highest rank should be introduced first. Follow these guidelines when making introductions:

- Name the most important person first.
- Say each person's name clearly.
- Add interesting information (if you know something) about each person. "Terri Ruiz, please meet Robert Hailey, the vice president for Humber Electronics. Mr. Hailey transferred from Cleveland to the Detroit office. Mr. Hailey, Ms. Ruiz is the president of Great Lakes Electric."

The most important point to remember about introductions is to remember to make them. Failing to introduce a business customer to a colleague is embarrassing and rude. It may also cost your company business. Forgetting a person's name is not an acceptable excuse to skip an introduction. In fact, people would prefer you make an incorrect introduction than to

[8]"Kwintessential Language and Culture Specialists," accessed March 23, 2007, available from http://www.kwintessential.co.uk/resources/global-etiquette/germany-country-profile.html.

have them stand there unacknowledged and disregarded.[9]

At times, you will be the person who is being introduced. When this is the case, follow these guidelines:

- Stand up (both men and women) when meeting someone.
- Establish eye contact with the individual.
- Shake hands firmly. However, you do not want to shake hands so firmly that the other person feels as though his or her hand is being crushed. Neither do you want to shake hands so limply that the other person feels no expression of warmth from you.
- Repeat the other person's name.
- Establish conversation with the person. (It does not need to be a lengthy conversation; a brief exchange of words is acceptable.)
- After the conversation is over, let the person know you enjoyed meeting him or her. You might say, "I certainly enjoyed meeting you, and I look forward to seeing you in the future."

It is good manners and good etiquette to remember the names of work associates to whom you are introduced, even if you see them only occasionally. If you forget the name of a person, it is better to admit this than to guess and come up with the wrong name. Refer to Figure 4.3 to review how to introduce yourself.

Other Workplace Etiquette

Although proper etiquette in the workplace includes good manners, it does not stop there. Workplace etiquette includes learning how to behave around everyone you come in contact with including coworkers, superiors, and visitors in the office. It includes learning the appropriate behavior in a variety of business situations.

YOUR COWORKERS AND SUPERIORS

You must know how to establish cordial and respectful relationships with your coworkers.

INTRODUCING YOURSELF

- Stand.
- Smile and establish eye contact with the individual.
- Greet the other person; state your name and position.
- Shake hands firmly.
- Repeat the other person's name.

FIGURE 4.3 Acting appropriately during an introduction helps create a professional image.

International Greetings

Keep in mind that although the handshake is an acceptable greeting in the United States, other countries have different greeting customs.

Country	Greeting
China	Give a slight nod and bow; if people applaud you should respond with applause.
Thailand	Place hands in a prayer position with your head slightly bowed (called the Wai); the higher your hands the more respect shown.
Poland	Men may greet women by kissing their hands; women greet other women with a slight embrace and kiss on the cheek.
Colombia	Women hold forearms instead of shaking hands.[10]

It is important to complete your research before you conduct business in other countries. Learn the business customs and what constitutes an appropriate greeting or introduction.

---

[9]"Introductions," Etiquette International, accessed March 23, 2007, available from http://www.etiquetteinternational.com/Articles/Introductions.aspx.

[10]"The Handshake," *Operation STRIDE: Stopping Transmission of Respiratory Infectious Diseases Early*, accessed March 23, 2007, available from http://www.detrick.army.mil/stride/handshaking.cfm.

Not only do you need to work closely with them every day, but you often depend on them to get your job done. Do not use slang or inappropriate labels when speaking with a coworker. Words like "honey" or "dear" have no place in the workplace. Do not ask a coworker to do something you would be uncomfortable or unwilling to do yourself. The best advice is to follow the golden rule and treat you coworkers as you would like to be treated.

The tone of the workplace and the formality of the working relationships are typically determined by top management. This includes not only how people dress but how they address each other. Because this type of information is not written down anywhere, you will need to observe those around you. Typically, relationships in the business world are based on rank. A good rule of thumb is to address your superiors with a courtesy title such as Mr. or Ms. followed by a surname. Do not use first names unless or until you are specifically invited to do so.

There are also some behaviors that should be avoided. Swearing or using inappropriate language is never acceptable. Avoid telling gender, ethnic, or racial jokes. Hugging and kissing is never acceptable in a business situation. A good rule to follow is to refrain from doing anything that has the potential to make someone else uncomfortable.

GREETING VISITORS

When you receive a visitor in your office, remember that you are the host. Remember that how you treat a visitor says a lot about you and your company. Review Figure 4.4 to help you learn how to greet workplace visitors courteously and correctly.

Telephone Skills and Etiquette

Your use of the telephone and understanding appropriate telephone etiquette also affects the professional image that you project. Often in an office situation, your calls may be overheard by others. Because of this, be mindful of the volume and tone of your voice, the language that you use, and the content of your phone calls. You should avoid or limit personal calls while working. Telephone etiquette will be covered in greater detail in Chapter 12, Telecommunications—Technology and Etiquette.

Business Networking

Networking is the process of exchanging information and building positive business relationships. Although networking is often discussed in the context of a job search, networking has become an accepted part of everyday business. If

TIPS FOR RECEIVING OFFICE VISITORS

- When a visitor enters your office, greet the person graciously with a simple *Good Morning* or *Good Afternoon.*

- Learn the visitor's name, and address the person by name.

- Determine the purpose of an unscheduled visit. Avoid blunt questions such as "What do you want?" A more appropriate question is "Could you please tell me what company you represent and the purpose of your visit?"

- Be pleasant to a difficult visitor. Be wary of visitors who try to avoid your inquiries with evasive answers such as "It's a personal matter." An appropriate response to such a statement is "My employer sees visitors only by appointment. I will be happy to set one up for you."

- Handle interruptions well. If you need to interrupt your employer with a message when a visitor is in his or her office, do so as unobtrusively as possible. You may call your employer on the phone or knock on the door and hand him or her a note.

- Let angry or upset visitors talk for a little while. Listen and try to understand the visitor's viewpoint. Usually the anger will dissipate after you have listened. Then you can help the person with the concern. If the visitor continues with inappropriate behavior, ask him or her to leave or call security personnel for help.

FIGURE 4.4 Be courteous and professional when greeting office visitors.

you have ever recommended a business based on the quality of its work, a restaurant, a movie, or even a gas station, you have networked.

Networking is often a deliberate, planned process. It involves the open exchange of leads and introductions. People network in many different settings: on the telephone, in hallways, at professional conferences, company meetings, classrooms, elevators, airplanes, hotel lobbies, athletic events, symphonies, supermarkets, or just about anywhere. Some networking is carefully planned and some networking just happens. Regardless of how networking takes place,

the most effective networker shows a genuine interest in other people. The savvy professional uses networking skills to help develop a positive professional image.

As you progress through this textbook, you will continue to be reminded about professional etiquette as it relates to business. Appropriate email etiquette is discussed in Chapter 7, Written Communications; telephone and cell phone etiquette are covered in Chapter 12, Telecommunications—Technology and Etiquette; and behaviors and etiquette for meetings and events are discussed in Chapter 15, Event Planning.

Summary

To reinforce what you have learned in this chapter, study this summary.

* Successful businesspeople spend time cultivating their professional image through making positive first impressions, presenting a positive attitude, and exhibiting a strong work ethic.

* The successful administrative professional works hard to present a professional image through his or her work area, desk, and daily work.

* What you wear and how you present yourself can help or damage your chances of success in business.

* Professional business attire for women includes a suit or tailored dress in a conservative color. Professional business attire for men is a matched suit in a conservative color.

* If you have questions about appropriate business appearance, review the dress code, ask questions, or observe other individuals to help you decide what is appropriate in that environment.

* Presenting a professional appearance includes selecting appropriate clothing and considering other appearance issues such as hair, makeup, and jewelry.

* Understanding and using appropriate business etiquette is an integral part of your professional image.

* Administrative professionals should use appropriate manners and etiquette when dealing with coworkers, superiors, business associates, and office visitors.

* Because appropriate etiquette varies greatly among cultures, research the country you are planning to visit to make sure you are ready to make a positive impression.

* Because an introduction is often the first encounter an individual will have with others, make sure to conduct introductions in a positive manner.

* Networking is the process of exchanging information and building positive business relationships. Networking has become an accepted part of everyday business.

What's the Problem?

Last week Sydney Higgins took her roommate Emilio as her guest to a social event held by Sydney's employer. When Sydney and Emilio arrived, there were already several guests in attendance. Sydney immediately struck up a conversation with a group of people by the snack table. After a few minutes of conversation, Sydney moved to the next group of people. As Sydney moved around the room meeting and greeting her coworkers, Emilio patiently followed. After 30 minutes, Emilio left and went home. When Sydney returned to the apartment, Emilio would not speak to her. Sydney does not understand why Emilio left the party or why Emilio is angry.

What advice would you give to Sydney?

Let's Discuss

1. List and explain what you can do to make a positive first impression in a business situation.
2. Explain what is expected for professional dress for men and women in business.
3. Describe the appearance factors (other than clothing) that need to be considered when working in a conservative business environment.
4. Describe the responsibilities typically associated with the host of a business meal.
5. List four tips that will help you professionally greet office visitors.

Critical-Thinking Activity

Anna Chung has recently been hired to work with you at United Pharmaceuticals. You know Anna from school; she has been in a few classes with you. Although you think Anna has good skills, she is difficult to work with because of her negative attitude toward everything—her personal life, her relationships, her job, and her supervisor. In fact, Anna is rarely positive about anyone or anything. After a few weeks on the job, you are beginning to have negative feelings too. You like your work and your supervisor and you can see there will be opportunities for advancement in this job.

What can you do to overcome your negative feelings? What can you do to make working with Anna more productive?

Vocabulary Review

Open the *Word* file *CH04 Vocabulary* found on the Student CD. Complete the vocabulary review for Chapter 4.

English and Word Usage Drill

Complete the English and Word Usage Drill for Chapter 4 found in the *Applications Workbook*.

Workplace Applications

4-1 The Components of a Professional Image

(Goals 1, 2, and 3)

team building

e-portfolio

1. Work with a classmate to complete this application. Identify someone from a local business who works in the Human Resources Department or is responsible for hiring employees.

2. Interview this person, asking him or her to respond to three of the following questions. Create two additional questions on your own.

    - What personal qualities do you look for in an employee?

    - What types of things do you first notice about an applicant?

    - What do you look for when trying to determine an applicant's work ethic?

    - Does your business have a formal dress code or is it an unwritten policy?

    - What standards are included in your dress code?

    - How important is business etiquette?

3. Write a short unbound report describing your findings, and present your findings to the class.

4-2 Presenting a Professional Appearance

(Goal 2)

internet

team building

United Pharmaceuticals has decided to include a professional dress component in its new employee orientation program. You have been asked to prepare electronic slides that can be used in a presentation about the dress code.

1. Work with two of your classmates on this assignment.

2. Prepare eight to ten electronic slides that describe and illustrate examples of professional business attire for both women and men. Include information related to other appearance issues as well.

3. Include both text and graphics in the slides. Use the information included in this textbook as well as two additional resources to prepare your presentation.

4-3 Professional Image, Appearance, and International Etiquette

(Goals 1, 2, and 3)

internet

Your supervisor at United Pharmaceuticals, Amando Hinojosa, has been selected to make his first overseas business trip for the company. He will be part of a five-member team scheduled to attend a three-day meeting with the production team at the United Pharmaceuticals plant in New Delhi, India. During the visit Amando is scheduled to attend several meetings, a business luncheon, and a formal business dinner. Amando has never traveled to India, and he wants to make sure that he is prepared. He has asked that you research the business customs of that region (including professional dress and dining etiquette). Because the formal business dinner will be held at the president's home, Amando would like to bring flowers and a gift for the president's wife. Prepare a short memo that will help Amando be successful on his visit. Use the *Word* file *Memo Form* found on the Student CD to create the memo. Answer the following questions in your memo.

1.   What should Amando plan to wear to the business meetings?

2.   What should he wear to the formal business dinner?

3.   Are there etiquette suggestions you can give Amando so he feels more comfortable at the dinner?

4.   What suggestions can you give Amando so he can make appropriate flower and gift selections?

4-4 Plan a Professional Wardrobe

(Goal 2)

internet

You have interviewed for work as an administrative professional at three companies and hope to land a job soon. You have observed that employees at all three companies dress in a conservative and traditional manner. At your interviews at two of the companies, you were told that employees may wear business casual dress on Fridays. Prepare to begin working by planning your professional business dress and casual business dress wardrobes.

1.   Create a spreadsheet that lists the items you can use as part of your business professional and business casual wardrobes. List each item of clothing, shoes, and accessories that you already own that would be an appropriate part of your business professional wardrobe. Create a similar list for your business casual wardrobe. Include jewelry and accessories such as handbags and briefcases.

2.   List each item of clothing, shoes, and accessories that you need to purchase for your business professional wardrobe. Create a similar list for your business casual wardrobe. Again, include jewelry and accessories such as handbags and briefcases.

3.   For each item you need to purchase, enter an amount that you think will be enough to cover the cost of the item. Give this column the heading *Budget Amount*. Total the column. Adjust the items or amounts in this column so the total is an amount you can reasonably afford.

4.   Do research to find the actual cost of each item you need to purchase. Look for items in local stores, in mail-order catalogs, and on the Internet. List the actual cost of each item. Give this column the heading *Actual Cost*. Total the column.

5. Find the difference between the Budget Amount column total and the Actual Cost column total. If the total Budget Amount is less than the total Actual Cost, what can you change in your wardrobe to stay within the budget amount?

Assessment of Chapter 4 Goals

Did you successfully complete the chapter goals? Evaluate yourself by filling out the form found in Chapter 4 of the *Applications Workbook*.

chapter 5

Anger, Stress, and Time Management

Learning Goals

1. Determine the effects of stress in the workplace.

2. Identify factors that contribute to workplace stress.

3. Determine the purpose of anger and its resolution.

4. Determine how time may be wasted.

5. Describe the relationship among stress, anger, and time.

6. Apply appropriate techniques for managing stress, anger, and time.

Understanding Stress

Do you ever have any of these feelings?

- Anger
- Depression
- Anxiety
- Exhaustion
- Stress

Have you ever experienced any of these health problems?

- Headaches
- Backaches
- Muscular problems
- Sleeping problems
- Heartburn

If you answered yes to several of these questions, you are not alone. In the fast-paced, changing world in which you live, many people experience these feelings and health issues all too often. In fact, studies show that between 70 and 80 percent of Americans believe their jobs are stressful.

In addition to adding stress to your job, these factors can cause **negative stress** (factors that cause emotional and mental upset) in your personal life as well as your professional life. You may have one or more of the following responsibilities:

- Attending college and working 40 hours each week
- Assuming responsibility for elderly parents who live with you or who are in rest homes and demand your attention

- Assuming, as a single parent, total responsibility for small children

All of these situations can lead to negative stress. Additionally, you may be the sole wage earner in your household. If so, providing enough money to meet your family's needs is often stressful. Add these personal stressors to the stress of a job, and you may find yourself having difficulty performing successfully on the job and at home. For example, administrative professionals must accomplish a myriad of tasks quickly and accurately in the daily performance of their duties, while at the same time dealing with numerous interruptions. This is no easy task for anyone and can lead to negative stress. No matter how competent and capable you are, you will encounter workdays when nothing seems to go right. Everything you touch seems to fall apart in your hands. You make one error after another. Days like this can produce stress. When you add the demands of a family plus money worries, stress can become a negative factor that affects your health and relationships, causing increased work problems and issues.

Stress, however, is not always negative. In fact, stress can be a positive factor in your life and work. Part of lessening stress involves engaging in the following behaviors:

- Recognizing the difference between good stress and bad stress
- Understanding what bad stress can do to your body if it continues over a prolonged period of time

Stress and Its Effects in the Workplace

Stress is the response of the body to a demand made upon it. Wants, needs, and desires come from stress of some kind. Many positive accomplishments in life relate to feelings of stress.

- If you did not feel a need to achieve, you would not take a challenging job.

- If you did not feel a need to learn, you would not study.
- If you did not feel a need for friends, you would not join social groups.

All of these situations are examples of stress that can make a positive impact on your life. You feel pressure to satisfy needs, wants, or desires that you have; you respond in a positive way to obtain satisfaction. This type of stress is referred to as **eustress**, a beneficial stress that enables individuals to strive to meet challenges.

Now consider negative stress, often referred to as **distress** due to the negative impact it has on your life. For example, if someone you love is sick, you feel distress. If you are unable to keep up with new technology in your office, you feel distress. If you receive a negative performance review at your job, you feel distress. Even the stresses of driving to work in heavy traffic or getting you and your family ready for work each morning can cause negative stress.

If you are unable to cope with stresses, you can become physically, mentally, and/or emotionally ill. Therefore, you must achieve an appropriate balance between the distress in your life and the ability to cope with it. Figure 5.1 graphically illustrates appropriate and inappropriate balances.

Types of Negative Stress

There are two types of negative stress.

- **Acute stress**
- **Chronic stress**

ACUTE STRESS

Acute stress occurs when an individual must respond instantaneously to a crisis situation. For example, if your car goes into a skid on an icy road, you must react quickly. When you experience acute stress, two chemicals are produced in your body—adrenaline and noradrenaline. These chemicals have stimulated people to perform incredible acts in a crisis—from lifting extremely

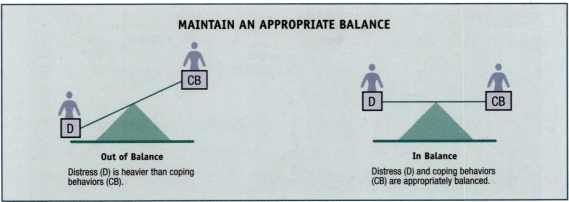

FIGURE 5.1 Maintain an Appropriate Balance

heavy objects off injured people (objects they would not be able to lift in an ordinary situation) to fighting off ferocious animals. Immediately after the crisis, however, these heroic people may become weak, their hands may shake, and their knees may quiver. They may even collapse. All of these aftereffects are the body's response to the acute stress event.

CHRONIC STRESS

Chronic stress occurs when a distressful situation is prolonged with no rest or recuperation for the body. Chronic stress triggers the production of different biochemicals in the body. While your body can break down adrenaline and noradrenaline, the chemicals produced by chronic stress cannot be broken down, and they remain in your system where they are capable of damaging your body. Chemicals produced by chronic stress can cause physical problems such as the ones listed here.

- High blood pressure
- Cardiovascular disease
- Migraine headaches
- Ulcers
- Elevated cholesterol
- Weakening of the immune system
- Shortness of breath
- Dizziness
- Chest pains
- Back pains

Chronic stress can also cause emotional problems such as the following:

- Depression
- Withdrawal
- Deep-seated anger
- Self-rejection
- Anxiety
- Loss of self-esteem

Cost of Stress

The cost of stress is high for both the organization and the individual. For the organization, the price can be absenteeism, loss of productivity, and poor work performance. For the individual, the price can be illness and temporary loss of work.

ORGANIZATIONAL COSTS

Workplace stress is estimated to cost American companies more than $300 billion a year in poor performance, absenteeism, and health costs.[1] In an attempt to reduce employee stress, many organizations offer stress-reduction programs in the workplace. These programs include exercise, diet, and stress-reduction techniques such as meditation, relaxation training, and a change in

---

[1]"Job Stress Management: Stress Causes & Effects: Tips for Workplace Stress Reduction," HelpGuide.org, accessed March 26, 2007, available from http://www.helpguide.org/mental/work_stress_management.htm.

Daily exercise increases mental and physical abilities.

lifestyle management. Some organizations even offer programs designed to increase fun in the workplace.

INDIVIDUAL COSTS

Stress can cause numerous health problems for individuals. High blood pressure, headaches, depression, and anxiety are some of the health problems to which stress may contribute. These problems may result in increased medical bills or lost wages. Individuals may not be able to participate in personal or community activities or may not be able to take advantage of work-related opportunities due to stress-related problems.

Factors Contributing to Workplace Stress

Some of the factors that contribute to stress on the job are these:

- Role ambiguity
- Job insecurity
- Working conditions and relationships
- Dual-career families, single parenthood, and extended families
- Anger

Many Americans work long hours on the job.

- Time
- Money

Role Ambiguity

Role ambiguity exists when individuals have inadequate information about their work roles—when there is lack of clarity about work objectives and expectations. As an administrative professional, you may experience role ambiguity. You may not understand exactly what is expected of you. When this situation occurs, you have the responsibility to find out what your job is. Many companies write **job descriptions** detailing the duties to be performed on the job. If a job description exists for your position, read it carefully. If there is no job description, ask your employer what he or she expects of you.

Job Insecurity

Another factor that contributes to stress on the job is job insecurity. In a volatile economy, organizations are often in the process of downsizing. If your organization is doing so, it is normal to wonder, *Will I be the next to go*? If you have these thoughts, you probably are not able to give your best efforts to the job. Your productivity may suffer.

Working Conditions and Relationships

A number of studies have shown a relationship between working conditions and an employee's physical and mental health. The following conditions impair health:

- A dehumanizing environment—one in which people are treated as objects rather than individuals
- A poor working relationship with a supervisor
- An unsatisfactory working relationship with colleagues
- Lack of trust among people who must work together
- Lack of support from coworkers
- Work overload

Dual-Career Families, Single Parenthood, and Extended Families

In the majority of two-parent families, both parents work. This means that the day-to-day pressures of the job must be balanced against spending time with children and juggling the

© PhotoDisc / Getty Images

The pressure of work and family can cause stress for both husband and wife.

demands of housework, grocery shopping, meal preparation, yard work, and so on.

In society, divorce is commonplace, which means numerous single parents must also juggle responsibilities of the job, home, and children. The pressures on these single parents can be tremendous.

Another factor that can cause negative stress is the need to take care of aging parents. People are living longer today than ever before, and due to advances in medical science, longevity is expected to increase. This phenomenon often means that both children and aging parents need care. Aging parents often live in their children's household, which can result in constant demands on the caregiver.

Anger

You live in a society in which the terms *road rage*, *desk rage*, and *phone rage* have become common terms. Although the overall violent crime rate has decreased in the United States from 2000 to 2005, the rate is still high.[2] The terrorists' attacks of September 11, 2001, were followed by the spread of the anthrax virus through the mail, resulting in postal workers and others becoming very sick, with some people dying. There has been violence in schools, with teenagers killing other teenagers and themselves. Many people find themselves yelling at someone over the phone for a perceived injustice or misunderstanding. The United States is an angry nation in many ways.

Time

People never seem to have enough time to satisfy the following needs and demands:

- Job demands of an employer
- Children's needs
- Spouse's needs
- Social needs
- Extended family's needs

People are stressed because *they think* they do not have enough time. They often make these or similar statements.

- *Stop the clock; I need more time.*
- *Stop the world; I need to get off for a while.*
- *There is never enough time in the day.*
- *If only I had more time, I could....*
- *Please slow down.* (to anyone who is in voice range)

Money

There is a very real relationship between time and money. The more money you spend, the more you need to work. The average person is in debt several thousand dollars, as reflected by national credit card statistics. Many people live from one paycheck to the next. Thus, individuals

Individuals often need to work long hours in order to pay their bills.

work more to have more money to pay their debts. They have less time to spend with family or on activities outside work. Their stress mounts higher, just as their debts do. It is a vicious cycle that millions in America have trouble breaking.

Anger—Its Purpose and Its Resolution

You have already learned that anger is prevalent in society. Administrative professionals may encounter anger or become angry on the job. Your role as an administrative professional is a complex one. You must have command of the very latest technology, be able to deal with all types of people (even the ones who are angry), and be able to satisfy your employer's needs for efficiency and effectiveness in turning out paperwork. You are expected to keep a stoic face and perform well when your employer is upset or angry—not an easy task, and one that requires you to grow and learn continually. You must learn how to deal with your anger and how to

[2]Reported Crime in the United States—Total, U.S. Department of Justice, Bureau of Justice Statistics, accessed March 26, 2007, available from http://bjsdata.ojp.usdoj.gov/dataonline/Search/Crime/State/RunCrimeStatebyState.cfm.

help diffuse the anger of coworkers, customers, and clients with whom you come in contact.

Its Purpose

To understand the purpose of anger, consider the following situation:

> *Regina has been working as an administrative assistant for Edwards Engineering for five years. Regina has attained the rating of CPS; she is very active in IAAP. Her employer, Mr. Wong, recently left Edwards Engineering; Cynthia Edwards, a recent graduate of a prestigious university, replaced Mr. Wong. Immediately, Ms. Edwards began making changes within the organization. Engineers within the organization have told Regina that the changes are hurting, not helping, the organization. They believe that Ms. Edwards is making decisions before she understands how the organization works. Regina finds herself in the middle of almost warring factions. A work environment that was challenging and rewarding has now become a place of discontent and bickering. Regina agrees with the engineers; she believes that there are too many changes in such a short period of time. Although Ms. Edwards has been very nice and supportive of Regina (even frequently complimenting her on the work that she does), Regina is experiencing a great deal of stress. Recently she called Mr. Wong and talked with him at length about the situation. He advised her to distance herself from the engineers and concentrate on her work. She knows he is probably right, but she finds it very difficult to do. How should Regina deal with the situation?*

Its Resolution

Rather than becoming stressed about something over which she has no control, Regina can take the steps detailed in the Problem-Solving Model shown in Figure 5.2.

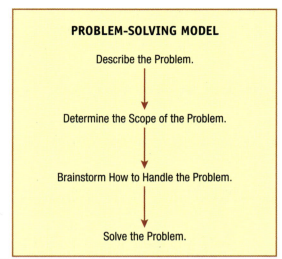

PROBLEM-SOLVING MODEL

Describe the Problem.

↓

Determine the Scope of the Problem.

↓

Brainstorm How to Handle the Problem.

↓

Solve the Problem.

FIGURE 5.2 Logical steps can be used to help solve a problem.

The problem seems to be that the new engineer is moving too fast for some of the employees. However, Regina has not had any trouble with her employer; her employer seems pleased with Regina's work. Thus, the problem should not be of concern to Regina. If the engineers have a problem, they need to confront it—not Regina. When Regina admits that it is not a problem for her, she should distance herself from talking with the engineers or even allowing them to bring up the situation with her. If she engages in such behavior, she possibly will remain upset. All issues within an organization do not need to be addressed by all employees.

Administrative Professionals and Time Wasters

Time is a precious commodity for most people. They never have enough time to get everything done they want or need to do. Administrative professionals are no exception. You, as a busy person in a world of change, will find yourself often lamenting the fact that you do not have enough time—not enough time to do all the tasks at your job, not enough time to handle all the stressors of your professional life and your personal life, and not enough time to relax and enjoy life.

Time—A Resource

In order to control time more effectively, you must understand something about time. You never seem to have the time you need; yet you have all the time there is. **Time** is a resource you cannot buy, sell, rent, borrow, save, or manufacture. You cannot change it, convert it, or control it. It can only be spent. Everyone receives an equal amount of time every day. You spend it even if you accomplish nothing. The term *managing time* is a misnomer. In actuality, managing time means managing yourself in relation to your time.

Time Wasters

Every day you waste time in a variety of ways. If you understand your own time wasters, you can become more effective in managing yourself in relation to your time. Listed here are several common time wasters.

CHATTER

If you presently have a job, do you go to work and get busy accomplishing the tasks of the day? Or do you report to work promptly and then spend the first 30 minutes of your workday talking to coworkers about what happened the night before? Certainly, it is important to have some time to talk about topics other than business, but socializing is more appropriate on breaks or at lunch. In most organizations, too much time is wasted in excessive socializing, when employees should be accomplishing the work of the organization.

DISORGANIZATION

I had that letter just a few minutes ago, but now I can't find it. It couldn't have disappeared into thin air. Have you ever made such a statement and then proceeded to rummage through the clutter on your desk for 30 minutes in an attempt to find the paper you never should have misplaced? A disorganized and cluttered desk can be a major time waster for administrative professionals. You should know what goes into your desk, what stays on top of your desk, and what goes into your file. Do not clutter your desk with papers that should be filed electronically or manually.

Part of organization is also organizing your day appropriately. For example, if you try to prepare a report, plan a meeting, and do a month's filing all at the most hectic part of the day (when the telephone is ringing constantly and callers are coming and going), the result will be wasted time, nothing accomplished, frayed nerves, and a stressed out or angry feeling. When you have a detailed task to accomplish, plan to do it during a time when interruptions are minimal.

INEFFECTIVE COMMUNICATION

As an administrative professional, you will communicate orally and in writing with people within and outside the workplace—your employer, coworkers, and customers or clients. It is important that the lines of communication between you and others be open and easily understood. Communication in today's workplace is complex, in part due to the various modes of communication that are available. The different modes of communication include email; fax; telephones (with cell phones being a constant companion for many people); voice mail; the Web; hard copy (paper) such as letters, reports, and organizational newsletters; in addition to face-to-face communication.

Lack of communication or misunderstood communication can cause confusion and loss of productivity. For example, think of the time you waste when you key and format a report incorrectly because you misunderstood instructions from your employer. Or think of the profits a company loses when customers become so unhappy due to ineffective communication that they take their business elsewhere.

© Digital Vision / Getty Images

A cluttered desk can be a major time waster.

PROCRASTINATION

Procrastination means trying to avoid a task by putting it aside with the intention of doing it later. Procrastination can be a big time waster. Procrastination takes many forms, but people who habitually procrastinate actually invite interruptions. They prolong telephone conversations, talk with coworkers, take long coffee breaks, or seek excuses to avoid doing their tasks.

Stress, Anger, and Time— The Relationship

Stress, anger, and time are closely related. For example, you get stressed out because you do not have enough time to do your job; you become angry with your husband or children because they are demanding your attention when you are already running as fast as you can in an attempt to keep up with all the demands made on you. In the next sections of this book, you will examine how you spend your time, what your stressors are, and what triggers your anger. You will learn techniques to help manage your stress, anger, and time. Notice that the word *manage* was used

since it is impossible to eliminate all stressors or all anger and equally impossible to add more time to the day. Your task is to learn how to manage these factors so you can live your life as productively and happily as possible.

Techniques for Managing Stress, Anger, and Time

The stress, anger, and time management cycle can become a vicious one. Figure 5.3 illustrates the cycle. Being aware of the relationship between stress, anger, and time and using the techniques listed here can help you lead a less stressful life. These techniques are geared to your professional life; however, they can be used successfully in your personal life as well. Practice them daily and you will reap the rewards.

Conduct Audits

To help manage stress, anger, and time, you need to know as much as you can about how you spend your time, what your major stressors are, and what makes you angry. An effective way to discover these factors is to take the time to do an audit. "What?" you may ask. "I don't have time to

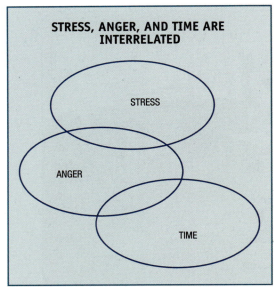

FIGURE 5.3 The Interrelationship of Stress, Anger, and Time

do these audits. I'm already too busy." Sometimes you need to get off the treadmill of life and take time to analyze what you are doing. In "Workplace Applications" at the end of this chapter, you will complete stress, anger, and time audits. To learn from these audits, you must do the following:

- Determine how often you are stressed and/or angry.
- Determine how much time you are spending in various activities each day.
- Determine positive steps you can take to decrease your stress and anger and to use your time more productively.
- Practice effective stress, anger, and time management techniques.

By looking closely at how often you are stressed, angry, and short of time, you can determine what is and what is not working for you. You will then be able to develop plans periodically to help you control the out-of-control factors.

Clarify Values

Even though you might not give it much thought, you live by a set of values. Generally, you developed these values at an early age. You acquired your values through the teachings of significant others in your life (parents, other relatives, and close friends) and through observing their behaviors. Values are principles that guide your life, such as honesty, fairness, love, security, and belief in a higher being. If you have not given much thought to your values recently, try answering these questions:

- What are the highest priorities in my life?
- Of these priorities, which are the most important?

Your thoughtful answers to these questions will help you identify your values. In people's hectic everyday lives, they often lose track of what is most important to them. They may find that their reality has little to do with their core values. However, psychologists say that when people bring together what they do or how they live with what they really value, they experience an inner peace and happiness that impacts every area of their life.

Set Priorities

Many times you will not be able to do everything you are asked to do in one day. You must be able to distinguish the most important items, tasks that should be done first, from less important items, tasks that can wait until a later date. If you are new to a job, you may need help from your employer to determine what items are most important. But once you learn more about the job and your employer, you should be able to establish priorities on your own.

Prepare Daily To-Do Lists

Each afternoon before you leave work, you should prepare a to-do list for the next day. List all tasks, activities, and projects you need to accomplish the next day. Then review your list. Mark the items in this manner:

- Most important matters—A
- Less important items—B
- Remaining items—C

Projects that have a deadline of the following day will be in Category A. In addition, you may have a very large project due next week. In order to get the project done on time, you must break it into parts. One part might be given a Category A priority to be completed tomorrow. On the following day, another part might be given a Category A priority to be completed. By breaking the project into parts and assigning priorities to those parts, the project becomes manageable. What once seemed overwhelming has been accomplished in an orderly and timely fashion.

Category B consists of those items that may be completed the next day, but no serious consequences will result if they are not. Category C consists of items that are fairly unimportant or that may be delegated. If you are going to delegate the items, be clear with the individual who will be doing the task exactly what is expected of him or her. If the project is a complex one, you may want to give the person written instructions.

If you have trouble setting priorities, try the procedure given in Figure 5.4.

Distinguish between Achievement and Perfection

Perfectionism is defined as "a propensity for setting extremely high standards and being displeased with anything else." Some people believe they must do everything perfectly. Certainly, they must achieve and perform well; however, no human being can be perfect. If you blame yourself continually for not doing everything perfectly, you are engaging in energy-draining behavior.

Use Down Time

If you have down time, you should use it productively. Accomplish those tasks you have been unable to do during your peak workload periods. These tasks may be cleaning out your desk, rearranging files, organizing supplies, or reading articles related to your business or to the technology you use on your job.

Handle Paperwork as Few Times as Possible

Handling paper over and over—putting it in piles on your desk, reshuffling, rehandling, rereading—can be the biggest paperwork time waster. The basic rule is this: *Handle paper once.* Read it, route it, file it, or answer it—but get it off your desk as quickly as possible without handling it repeatedly.

Complete Work Correctly the First Time

At times, as an administrative professional, you may need to redo work you should have done correctly the first time. How do you prevent the need to redo work? Here are several suggestions:

- Get appropriate instructions or procedures before beginning the work.
- Read the file on similar correspondence.
- Understand the scope of the task. What is the final product to be? What expectations does your supervisor have?
- If it is a new task for you, talk with the person (if possible) who did the task before you. Listen carefully to any pointers or suggestions that person gives you.

Organize Your Workstation

Organizing your workstation may not be an easy task, but it must be done if you are to make the most efficient use of your time. When you are working on a project, clear your desk of materials that relate to other projects. Put these materials in a file folder, label the folder with the name of the project, and place the folder in a drawer. Label in/out trays so you know what is incoming material and what is outgoing material. Keep the drawers of your desk organized so you have frequently used supplies in the top drawers.

Practice Speed-Reading

Numerous items that you must read will pass your desk. Before reading correspondence and other materials, organize the material in order of

SETTING PRIORITIES

This tool can be useful if you are having difficulty setting priorities. It is not intended to be used daily. However, if you are new to the process of setting priorities or are having difficulty, the steps help you break down the process into small increments. (*Note:* When keying your list, triple-space so you will have enough space to circle the numbers.)

Step 1

Make a list of ten things for which you must set priorities. Order is not important at this point. However, do give each item a number 1 through 10.

Step 2

Compare Number 1 with Number 2, and circle the number you believe is most important.

Step 3

Compare Number 2 with Number 3, and circle the number you believe is most important. (*Note:* You probably will be circling a number several times. When you circle a number a second time, make the circle bigger; this will help later when you must count the number of times you circled each item.)

Step 4

Compare Number 3 with Number 4. Circle the most important number of this pair. Compare Number 2 with Number 4; circle the number that is most important. Compare Number 1 with Number 4; circle the number that is most important.

Steps 5-10

Continue to go through the items on your list, comparing each item with every other item and circling the most important number of each set of two.

Last Step

Count the number of 1s, number of 2s, number of 3s, and so on. Your priority list will begin with the number you circled the most. The last item on your list (least important item) will be the number on the list that you circled the least number of times.

FIGURE 5.4 Setting Priorities

importance. Prepare folders, noting the dates when the materials must be read.

Practice speed-reading. Read for the main thought or idea. If you are reading periodicals or company literature, scan the table of contents first. Then selectively read the articles. Read carefully only the sections that will enhance your knowledge of your job and your organization.

Manage Large Projects

Most organizations have numerous large projects that must be managed. As an administrative professional, you may be responsible for assisting with the management of these projects. Generally, you will be working with a number of individuals. All team members need to understand not only the project but also the intended outcomes. Here are several suggestions that will help you be successful.

- Establish clarity as to the scope of the project with your employer.
- Set clear goals/outcomes for the project. The goal-setting step is generally done in conjunction with the administrator who is reponsible for the overall project.
- Determine what resources are needed; e.g., you may need to purchase a software system

to help you with the management of the project.

- Establish who will be involved in the project with you.
- Have a group discussion with the individuals involved. As a group, determine the responsibilities and expectations of each person.
- Break the project down into manageable components.
- Set deadlines for the small tasks/steps to be completed.
- Follow through on tasks to completion.

You may be responsible for monitoring the completion of the tasks. If so, you may choose to talk individually with the project members. If a member has not completed his/her task in the appropriate time allowed, determine what the problem is and help solve it. Additionally, having a group meeting on a regularly scheduled basis can be helpful. The progress of the project can be discussed so that all individuals will know if completion times are being met. If a project cannot be completed due to some other person not performing his/her task within the expected completion time, a group discussion of the cause and the solving of the problem is important.

Use Electronic Time Management Systems

Effective time management is critical in our fast-paced world. If you are to be an effective employee, you must not only be able to produce quality work, but also be able to produce this work quickly and efficiently. Computer software, such as personal information management programs, and electronic devices, such as PDAs and smartphones, can help you be an effective manager of your time.

PERSONAL INFORMATION MANAGEMENT SOFTWARE

The key to effective time management is finding a system that works for you. For example, you may need **personal information management (PIM)** software that works across different business units, such as the Sales and Marketing Departments. Before you search for a PIM, carefully consider what your needs are and then attempt to find the PIM that best fits your needs.

One effective PIM is *Microsoft Office Outlook. Outlook* allows you to schedule meetings electronically and prepare a calendar and to-do list by day, week, and month. This software allows you to prioritize tasks and set dates for their completion. You no longer have to remember dates and deadlines; instead, you can concentrate on the projects to be accomplished. You can manage information from multiple sources and stay connected to the appropriate people. You can easily share your calendar with others or subscribe to Internet calendars. If you are traveling, *Outlook* has the capacity to adjust your calendar to the time zone of your physical location. *Outlook* Contacts and To-Do items are shown in Figure 5.5.

PROJECT MANAGEMENT SOFTWARE

In your position as an administrative assistant, you may work on a number of projects. Project management software allows you to do so more effectively and efficiently. Several project management software packages are available. Two examples are *Microsoft Office Project 2007* and *Above & Beyond® 2007*.

Features of *Microsoft Office Project 2007* allow users to:

- Build a project plan, with all of the details needed
- Schedule tasks and assign resources
- Monitor costs
- Keep track of projects
- Develop charts to help communicate project data

Above & Beyond 2007 is software for planning, managing, and tracking both your business and personal life. This software allows you to manage your tasks and projects and to split large projects into definable tasks.

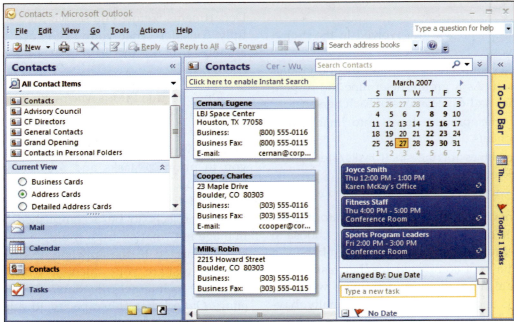

FIGURE 5.5 *Microsoft Office Outlook* is a popular PIM program.

PDAS AND SMARTPHONES

A **personal digital assistant (PDA)** is a handheld computer. PDAs can help you manage time and information. They provide programs that allow you to schedule appointments, take notes, manage contacts, and create tasks lists. Many PDAs also allow you to use application programs such as *Microsoft Word* and *Microsoft Excel*. Some PDAs have wireless transmission capabilities that make synchronizing data between your PDA and your desktop computer easy. The Start menu for a PDA is shown in Figure 5.6.

A **smartphone** is an electronic device that combines the features of a PDA and a mobile phone. A popular wireless handheld device is the BlackBerry®. This smartphone gives the user an always-on connection to email and data whether the user is across town or across the country. A BlackBerry can provide phone, email, instant messaging, GPS, organizer, browser, and media player features in one mobile device. Because

there are no time or space barriers with such devices, productivity can be improved dramatically. Some smartphones also have a speaker function that lets you communicate in a hands-free manner. Email, phone, and systems management applications come from a single integrated address book and inbox. Users can click on a telephone number or an email address in a message to make a call, compose an email, or check a Website. Many smartphones and PDAs include a digital camera. Pictures can be saved and sent to others via email.

Use Good Communication Techniques

Chapters 7 through 9 in this textbook are devoted to a discussion of effective communication techniques, including verbal, written, and presentation skills. You should study these chapters carefully and practice the techniques given to help you become a better communicator. Here are a few suggestions.

FIGURE 5.6 Menu Options for a PDA

Electronic equipment allows individuals to work from almost any place and at any time.

- Transmit ideas in simple, clear terms.
- Define terms if necessary.
- Listen carefully.
- Repeat what you think you heard, and ask for clarification if necessary.
- Be sensitive to the communicator's body language as well as to the words being spoken.
- Keep your mind open to new ideas.

Maintain a Proper Diet

What you eat or do not eat affects your overall health. Excessive intake of fat, sugar, salt, and caffeine contributes to poor health and to certain diseases such as hypertension and heart disease. The average cup of regular coffee contains 100 to 150 milligrams of caffeine. As little as 250 milligrams of caffeine can cause nervousness, insomnia, and headaches.

The average American consumes more than 126 pounds of sugar a year. Excessive sugar consumption can result in an increase in triglyceride levels in the blood, which can lead to cardiovascular disease. Too much salt can lead to an increase in blood pressure and the development of hypertension. The wisest course of action is to lower the intake of fat, sugar, salt, and caffeine in your diet.

Maintaining a diet rich in fruits and vegetables is also important. Eating fiber-rich vegetables, fruits, cereals, and legumes helps you maintain a high level of fiber in your diet.

Set Up an Exercise Program

Cardiovascular specialists have found that regular exercise can do the following:

- Lower blood pressure
- Decrease fats in the blood
- Reduce joint stiffness
- Lessen appetite
- Decrease fatigue

A few of the many exercises good for your body are swimming, bicycling, jogging, and walking. Participate in an exercise you enjoy. Determine a regular time of day to exercise and do it. When you begin exercising, go slowly. Train your body; do not strain it. If you have any medical problems, consult your doctor about the type of exercise that is best for you.

Get the Proper Amount of Sleep

The proper amount of sleep is essential to mental and physical health. Although the amount of sleep needed varies by individual, studies have shown that people who sleep seven to eight hours a night tend to live longer than people whose sleep is longer or shorter.[3] Yet a number of people have problems getting the proper amount of sleep due to busy schedules and stressful lives.

Even if you do go to bed at the proper hour, you may have difficulty falling asleep. You often have trouble turning off your mind. You rethink what went wrong in your day or begin to plan for the next day. Practicing the following techniques will help you fall asleep:

- Set aside the hour before bed for quiet activities such as reading.
- Take a hot bath.
- Turn off the TV in the bedroom and/or turn down the TV in an adjoining room.
- Practice deep-breathing exercises.
- Create a relaxing scene in your head—waves rolling up on a beach or a mountain stream.

- Be certain your mattress and pillow are right for you—the proper firmness or softness.
- Pay attention to the amount of coffee, tea, cola, and chocolate you are consuming. These items can lead to sleep deprivation.

Use Visualization

Visualization is the creation of a mental picture. Using visualization can help you relax. Through visualization, you block out unwanted thoughts. In order to achieve the maximum benefits from visualization, get into a comfortable position, relax any muscles that feel tense, and begin to visualize a pleasant scene. For example, you might imagine a sky of white fluffy clouds, ocean waves licking a golden beach, the sun glistening on a snow-covered mountain, or a beautiful sunset over your favorite lake. Focus on the scene for several minutes to block out the tensions of the day.

Professional Pointers

Try these anger, stress, and time management techniques to help you work more productively.

- Keep a journal of situations that make you feel angry or stressed. Writing in a journal and reviewing your thoughts periodically can be like talking to a trusted friend.
- Balance your professional life with a fulfilling personal life. Make time to pursue personal interests and to relax apart from your career.
- Do not allow yourself to lose sight of your vision and purpose in life. Take time to sit quietly and analyze whether you are living your values and being true to your purpose.
- Identify the time of day when you are at your peak. Plan to tackle your most difficult jobs during your peak periods.
- Do not overschedule yourself. Allow an hour or two of uncommitted time each day.

[3]Edward Claflin, ed., *Age Protectors* ((Pennsylvania: Rodale Press, Inc., 1998), 143.

Reduce Organizational Dependency

Do not depend totally on the organization for which you work for long-term employment. Educate and train yourself to be employable by a number of organizations. Engage in continuing education to keep yourself up to date on technology and other skills needed in the workplace. This education may be formal (from a college or university) or informal (from professional books and periodicals and attendance at workshops and seminars).

Understand Role Relationships

Be sensitive to the needs of your employer and your coworkers. Know what they expect of you. Know how you fit into the organizational structure. Be familiar with the organizational chart; know who reports to whom. Accept people; be tolerant. Strive to communicate openly and honestly.

Balance Work and Play

Many people comment with a sense of pride that they work a 50- or 60-hour week. Are these people producing a large amount of work? Maybe not. Do they have demanding and challenging jobs? Perhaps. Are they appreciated and respected for their work contributions? Not necessarily. A relationship does exist between hours worked and productivity. Of course, individuals differ in the number of productive hours they can work. However, studies show that productivity decreases after extended periods. Most people realize immediately when they are not being productive. When they become fatigued, the amount of work they produce goes down and their error rate goes up.

You actually can gain new energy by taking time to play. As an adult, you may have forgotten how to relax and, with complete abandon, enjoy the world around you. Some experts writing in the field of creative energy recommend *joy breaks* —stopping for a few minutes to play when feeling overtired or nonproductive. Another way to gain new energy is to take a short exercise break. You might keep athletic shoes at your desk for a short five- or ten-minute break to climb stairs or to take a brisk walk. Such physical activity allows you to release built-up tension, to open blocked thinking, and to trigger creative ideas.

© PhotoDisc / Getty Images

Effective employees know how to balance work and play.

Relax

Deep-breathing exercises are one of the quickest ways to relax your body. Begin by finding a comfortable position, sitting in a comfortable chair or lying down. You may close your eyes if that makes you feel more at ease. Then slowly inhale air through your nose until you feel your lungs fill with air. Next, exhale the air slowly, breathing out through your nose or mouth. Repeat the process until you begin to feel a sense of relaxation.

Use Positive Self-Talk

When you are angry or upset, negative self-talk can escalate your feelings; positive self-talk, on the other hand, can produce positive results. For example, assume you are playing a game of tennis with a skilled opponent. You want to play your best. You miss a ball and say to yourself, *That was terrible; I can't even get a ball over the net.* You are engaging in negative self-talk, and negative self-talk on the tennis court can cause you to miss even more shots. In other words, your negative self-talk is a self-fulfilling prophecy. You decide you are terrible, and you prove yourself right.

Now consider a positive self-talk response. When you miss a ball, you say to yourself, *No big deal; I'll get the next one.* And you do! You make a terrific shot that your opponent is unable to return. When you find yourself engaging in negative self-talk, turn it around by engaging in the following behaviors:

* Recognizing the negative self-talk
* Stopping it immediately
* Beginning positive self-talk

Walk Away

If you can, walk away physically from a situation that makes you angry. If you cannot walk away physically, walk away emotionally. Consider the following example, a common situation that often makes people angry.

You are waiting in line to pay for your groceries. The checker is slow. In addition, no sackers are available, so the checker must sack the items. The person in front of you has forgotten two items and asks the checker if he can go get them; the checker agrees. You have an important appointment, and you must be on time. You find yourself getting angry. You are ready to yell at the person in front of you and at the checker.

What are your choices? You can walk away mentally—count to 10, envision yourself at one of your favorite places having a wonderful time, or hum a song. Or if you really are going to be late for the appointment, you can walk away physically. You can come back to the grocery store at another time.

Talk to a Friend

If a situation at work makes you angry, talk to a trusted friend about what is bothering you. That person may be able to help you understand what is causing your anger and help you decide what you can do about the situation.

Solve the Problem

Chapter 1 presented several problem-solving steps. These steps are valuable in helping you manage your anger, stress, and time. When a situation is causing you to become angry, stressed, and overwhelmed because of the time you are wasting on it, stop! Ask yourself these questions:

* What is the problem?
* What are my alternatives?
* From the alternatives I have generated, what is the best alternative in this situation?

Once you have identified the problem and determined the best alternative in dealing with it, act and evaluate!

* Act on the best alternative—implement it.
* Evaluate the situation: Did the action I implemented solve the problem? If not, why not?

Did I choose the wrong alternative? If so, what other alternative can I try?

Success in managing your anger, stress, and time hinges on these behaviors:

• Constant evaluation of the situations that are causing you problems

• Thoughtful decisions that will lessen your stress and anger and help you use your time more effectively

A tough task? Certainly! However, the energy you spend in positive activities is well worth the effort for your mental and emotional health.

Summary

To reinforce what you have learned in this chapter, study this summary.

• Stress is the response of the body to a demand made upon it. Stress can be positive or negative.

• Positive stress prompts you to take beneficial actions. Negative stress can cause physical, mental, and emotional problems and must be managed to prevent these ill effects.

• Factors contributing to workplace stress include job insecurity, poor working conditions, poor relationships, frequent anger, and ineffective use of time.

• Time is a resource that cannot be bought, sold, rented, borrowed, saved, or manufactured. It can only be spent. Managing how you spend your time can help you avoid negative stress and anger.

• To help you manage your stress, anger, and time, you can conduct stress, anger, and time audits periodically.

• Dealing with your stressors, anger problems, and poor time management will help you be a more productive and effective individual.

What's the Problem?

Last week, Baysan had a problem with her employer, Helena Edwards. Ms. Edwards yelled at Baysan about an error she thought Baysan had made. Actually, Baysan did not make an error; the accounting office gave her the numbers that she reported to her employer. However, Baysan's culture has always taught her that you do not counter your employer. Baysan was most upset when her employer yelled at her. She is thinking about quitting her job.

What advice would you give Baysan?

Let's Discuss

1. Explain the differences between acute stress and chronic stress.
2. List and describe five factors that contribute to workplace stress.

3. List and explain four time wasters for an administrative professional.

4. List five suggestions for improving communication in the workplace.

5. Explain the meaning of positive self-talk; describe how you might use it in the workplace.

6. Explain how stress, anger, and time management are interrelated.

Critical-Thinking Activity

On Monday, Kim Chang had a problem with Joleen March, the administrative assistant who works in the office next to her. They have been friends for several months and usually take their morning and afternoon breaks together. On Monday, Kim was extremely busy and could not take a break at either time because her employer had an emergency situation occur. Kim needed to get several documents ready for her employer's supervisor. As Kim was leaving her workstation at five in the afternoon, she saw Joleen. Kim smiled and said, "I have had a terrible day; nothing seemed to go well." Joleen replied in an angry voice, "Well, apparently you forgot about our coffee breaks and my birthday also." Kim started apologizing to her; however, Joleen walked away. Kim does care about their friendship; however, she believes that Joleen has definitely overreacted to the situation. After all, she had to get the work done for her employer.

How should Kim handle the situation? What steps can she take to cope with the stress and communicate clearly with Joleen?

Vocabulary Review

Open the *Word* file *CH05 Vocabulary* found on the Student CD. Complete the vocabulary review for Chapter 5.

English and Word Usage Drill

Complete the English and Word Usage Drill for Chapter 5 found in the *Applications Workbook*.

Workplace Applications

5-1 Interview an Administrator

(Goals 1 and 2)

team building

1. Work with a classmate to complete this activity. As a team, interview an administrator concerning stress in the workplace. Ask these questions:

   • What factors contribute to stress in the workplace?

   • What is the cost of negative stress to the organization?

- Does your organization offer workshops for employees on stress management?

2. Write a short unbound report to summarize the interview. Use an appropriate title for the report and include the name of the person interviewed and the name of the organization.

e-portfolio

5-2 Complete Stress and Anger Audits

(Goal 3)

1. Chapter 5 in your *Applications Workbook* contains an anger audit. Respond to the items on the audit. Save the audit to use in Application 5-4.

2. Several Internet sites provide free stress audits. Links to sites that have stress audits are provided on the Links page of the Website for this textbook. You can also find sites by accessing an Internet search engine and searching for *free stress test* or *free stress audit*. Access a Website that has a stress audit or test.

3. Complete the stress audit or test. Save or print the results or evaluation of the test to use in Application 5-4.

internet

5-3 Consider How to Cope with Stress and Anger

(Goal 6)

You recently joined United Pharmaceuticals as a part-time administrative assistant. You are attending college for the first time, taking 15 hours. Your classes require much more of your time than you anticipated. You average 25 hours per week on class work and 20 hours per week on your job. You have an apartment, which you share with two roommates; the three of you share the cooking and cleaning responsibilities. You have little time for fun and relaxation. The job is demanding, your classes are time-consuming, and you feel overwhelmed. You find yourself becoming irritable with your roommates.

How can you get the situation under control? Using the techniques suggested in this chapter, key a list of the steps to take to cope with your stress and anger.

5-4 Prepare an Action Plan

(Goal 6)

1. In this activity, you will prepare an action plan for managing stress, anger, and time this semester. To help you in this task, review the stress and anger audits you prepared in Application 5-2.

2. Using the forms provided in the *Applications Workbook*, log the time you spend in various activities for the next five days. Then complete the time management analysis using the form provided in the *Applications Workbook*.

team building

e-portfolio

3. Work with two classmates to complete this step of the activity. As a team, offer suggestions to each other on how each person may improve her or his management of stress, anger, and time.

4. Individually, prepare an action plan following the directions provided in the *Applications Workbook*. Submit one copy of your action plan to your instructor, identifying the team members with whom you worked. Keep another copy of your plan for your e-portfolio. At the end of the course, assess whether you have met your objectives for managing stress, anger, and time.

5-5 Manage Appointments and Contacts

(Goal 6)

In your work with United Pharmaceuticals, Melody Hoover asks that you input some information for Teresa Winwright, the vice president of marketing. Use *Outlook* or another PIM program to complete this activity.

1. Ms. Winwright has a few business cards that were given to her by people at a recent meeting. Enter the names and contact information into the contacts section of the PIM program. To view the business cards, open and print the file *CH05 Cards* found on the student CD.

2. Enter the following appointments for Ms. Winwright. Assume all the appointments are for the current year if the current month is August or earlier. If the current month is later, enter the appointments in the following year. Set ending times for meetings when known. If conflicts arise, use your judgment to suggest possible solutions. Compose email messages to the appropriate persons to offer solutions. Assume that the changes you suggest are accepted. Send an email to Teresa Winwright noting the changes. (Send the email messages to an address provided by your instructor.)

   - Appointment with Maxwell Edwards from 2 p.m. to approximately 3:30 p.m. on the third Wednesday in September.

   - Appointment with Tomas Mendoza at 9 a.m. on the second Tuesday in September; she anticipates the appointment will last approximately an hour.

   - Luncheon meeting with Rodney Rodriquez at noon on the third Tuesday in September; Teresa will meet Mr. Rodriquez at the Palm Restaurant.

   - Appointment with John O'Malley at 2 p.m. on the third Wednesday in September to discuss a new drug that United Pharmaceuticals is developing. This appointment is extremely important and the time cannot be changed.

   - Mr. Mendoza calls to say that he is unable to make the 9 a.m. meeting previously scheduled. He needs to change the appointment to 2 p.m. on the third Wednesday in September.

   - Appointment with David Anderson each Monday morning from 9 a.m. to 11 a.m. This appointment should be scheduled for the next two months. (Enter this as a recurring appointment during September and October.)

   - Meeting with Ray Gonzales in Los Angeles to discuss new products that are being developed for United Pharmaceuticals. The meeting is scheduled for the fourth Monday through Wednesday in September. Ms. Winwright will fly back on

Wednesday afternoon at approximately 5 p.m. (If using *Outlook*, enter this as an event.)

3. Print a copy of Ms. Winwright's calendar for September and the names and addresses of the new contacts.

Assessment of Chapter 5 Goals

Did you successfully complete the chapter goals? Evaluate yourself by filling out the form in Chapter 5 of the *Applications Workbook*.

chapter 6

Ethical Theories and Behaviors

Learning Goals

1. **Explain the importance of ethical behavior in the workplace.**

2. **Identify characteristics of an ethical organization.**

3. **Determine how to achieve ethical change.**

4. **Determine implications of discrimination in an organization.**

5. **Identify characteristics of an ethical employee.**

6. **Determine your commitment to ethical behavior.**

Business Ethics

Ethics (the systematic study of moral conduct, duty, and judgment) plays an important role in the effectiveness and the long-term viability of an organization. If you wonder about the efficacy of such a statement, pause for a few minutes to think about the ethics (or lack thereof) of two major organizations.

Ethical mismanagement of Enron, a major energy trading company with headquarters in Houston, Texas, caused an organization to go from a firm that was listed in 2000 by *Fortune* as one of the most admired companies to a bankrupt corporation. Enron's debacle was of such significance to the U.S. economy that Congress led a major investigation through a series of hearings with employees and leaders of Enron. Enron's mismanagement impacted thousands of employees and shareholders who lost significant dollars, with some people losing their life savings. Another major corporation involved in the scandal was Arthur Andersen, employed by Enron as an accounting consultant. The government filed a suit against Arthur Andersen, charging the company with destruction of tons of paper and thousands of computer files in an attempt to thwart federal regulators investigating Enron. A jury found Arthur Andersen guilty of the charges. A federal judge gave the defunct Arthur Andersen the maximum sentence for its part in the Enron scandal, calling it a warning to the auditing profession.

126

Unfortunately, these are only two of any number of examples of organizations whose ethics are in question. A writer from *The New York Times* expressed these sentiments:

> *The term* **business ethics** *[the study of just and unjust behavior in business] does not have to be an oxymoron [the combining of incongruous or contradictory terms]. But in today's scandal-a-minute atmosphere, it has surely become one. Public trust in corporate America has been undeniably shattered.*[1]

However, in contrast are those many organizations that hold ethics sacred in their day-to-day operations. For example, contrast the lack of ethical behavior with some of the ethical statements and policies of three companies listed on *Fortune* magazine's 2007 100 Best Companies to Work for—The Container Store[SM], Wegmans Food Markets, and Genetech.[2]

- The Container Store provides these value-driven benefits for its employees:

  — An environment that ensures open communication
  — Extensive training programs
  — Individual and team-based incentive programs

  The cofounders, Kip Tindell and Garrett Boone, state that their goal is not growth for growth's sake. Rather, it is to adhere to a fundamental set of business values, centered around deliberate merchandising, superior customer service, and constant employee input.[3]

- The mission of Wegmans Food Markets includes these statements: "We believe that good people, working toward a common goal, can accomplish anything they set out to do. In this spirit, we set our goal to be the very best at serving the needs of our customers. Every action we take should be made with this in mind."[4]

- Genetech's Diversity Value Statement reads as follows: Diversity is integral to our culture and how we conduct our business. It is evident in who we are, the patients we serve, the physicians with whom we partner, the vendors we rely upon, and the communities in which we work. It strengthens our organization and contributes to our competitiveness. We are inclusive; we demonstrate respect and appreciation for diversity and encourage the richness of ideas, approaches and points of view that it enables."[5]

Ethical and unethical behaviors by organizations make a difference in society. People managing organizations and employees of organizations must adhere to some standard of ethics. Business is a cooperative activity, with its existence hinging on ethical behavior. For example, organizations will collapse if their managers, employers, and customers believe it is morally permissible to steal from the organization.

Conversely, ethical behavior by organizations, in addition to being the right thing to do, often pays off on the financial bottom line. The fact that good corporate citizenship and good business go hand in hand is evident when reading about companies found on Business Ethics' 100 Best Corporate Citizens list.[6]

As you study this chapter, take the tenets presented seriously. If you are working presently or will be working when you finish your schooling, you want to be associated with an organization that upholds ethical standards. Ethical behaviors contribute to making the world a better place in which to live and work. Unethical behaviors impact people who are working for the organization as well as the economy.

[1]Gretchen Morgenson, "The Big Board Is Standing Up for Independence," *The New York Times*, June 2, 2002.

[2]CNNMoney.com, "100 Best Companies to Work For," accessed April 16, 2007, available from http://money.cnn.com/magazines/fortune/bestcompanies/2007/full_list/.

[3]The Container Store, accessed April 16, 2007, available from http://www.containerstore.com/learn/index.jhtml.

[4]Wegmans, accessed April 17, 2007, available from http://www.wegmans.com/about/pressRoom/overview.asp#whatwebelieve.

[5]Genetech, accessed April 17, 2007, available from http://www.gene.com/gene/about/diversity/index.jsp.

[6]Corporate Responsibility Officer, "100 Best Corporate Citizens 2007," accessed April 17, 2007, available from http://www.thecro.com/?q=node/304.

In this chapter, ethics is a **pragmatic** topic—one to be understood conceptually and practiced in the day-to-day operations of organizations and in the lives of employees within organizations. This chapter provides you with a framework for understanding the importance of ethics and the characteristics of ethical organizations. Additionally, it provides suggestions for practical ethical behavior for administrative professionals.

The Importance of Ethics

As you learned earlier in this chapter, ethics is the systematic study of moral conduct (a set of ideas of right and wrong), duty, and judgment. Practically, business ethics is the study of just and unjust behaviors in business. Business ethics requires that judgment be exercised about a proposed act and the anticipated consequences of the act. Business ethics means that individuals within an organization, collectively and singularly, are socially responsible for their conduct.

Ethics—The Roots

So you can understand what religion and some of the great philosophers of history have contributed to ethical thinking, look briefly at both. The major roots of today's ethical principles stem from religion and philosophy. For example, many of the major religions of the world are in basic agreement on the fundamental principles of ethical doctrine. Buddhism, Christianity, Confucianism, Hinduism, Islam, and Judaism teach the importance of acting responsibly toward all people and contributing to the general welfare of the world. In fact, the work ethic still practiced by many in the United States came from what was called the **Protestant ethic**. The Protestant ethic began as a religious teaching in Europe in the fourteenth century and was carried to the American colonies. It encouraged hard work, thrift, and dedication to the task. This philosophy still holds true for millions of Americans.

The great philosophers in history added to the body of knowledge concerning ethics. Here are a few examples of their influence:

- Socrates taught that virtue and ethical behavior are associated with wisdom.
- Plato taught that justice might be discovered through intellectual effort.
- Jeremy Bentham and John Mills taught that morality resides in its consequences and one must maximize the greatest benefit for the greatest number of people.
- Immanuel Kant taught that one must behave in such a way that one's actions can become a universal law.
- Saint Thomas Aquinas taught that ethical behavior in business is necessary to achieve salvation.

In addition to the religious and philosophical roots of ethical behavior, cultures and systems of government teach ethical behavior. For example, the Golden Rule—*Do unto others as you would have them do unto you*—came from many ancient cultures. The Declaration of Independence emphasizes that there are certain *inalienable rights: life, liberty, and the pursuit of happiness.*

© PhotoDisc / Getty Images

The Golden Rule—Do unto others as you would have them do unto you—continues to be an important concept to uphold in the day-to-day actions of an organization.

The study of ethics began in the classroom in the 1970s. In the 1980s, ethics became a part of the business curriculum, where it progressed from religious and philosophical theory into the pragmatic study of ethical behavior and decision making within organizations.

The Why

Why be ethical? This question is debated in academic materials and classrooms. However, it is more than an academic question. At some point, individuals and organizations must answer it. There are numerous ways to do so. You might answer it from a religious or philosophical point of view. You might also answer it from your own value perspective. However, from whatever view you take, the questions and possible answers around ethical dilemmas are not easy. Consider the issue of stem cell research that burst on the scientific scene in November 1998, when researchers first reported the isolation of human embryonic stem cells. This discovery continues to offer great promise for new ways of treating disease, but the ethical issues surrounding this research continue to be debated.

Opponents of stem cell research believe that human life begins as soon as an egg is fertilized, and they consider a human embryo to be a human being. Therefore, any research that necessitates the destruction of a human embryo is morally abhorrent. Proponents of stem cell research point out that in the natural reproductive process, the fertilization of human eggs can occur, but the eggs sometimes fail to implant in the uterus. They argue that a fertilized egg, while it may have the potential for human life, is not the equivalent of a human being until it has at least achieved successful implementation in a woman's uterus.

In 2001, President Bush decided to allow federal funding of stem cell research, but only on cells already in existence. He decided that for a cell line (isolated stem cells from a human embryo that often replicate themselves) already in existence, research is permissible because destruction of an embryo has already taken place. To prevent the federal government from acting in a way that encourages the destruction of human embryos, he refused to allow federal funding for research on any cell line created in the future. This research continues to offer great promise for new ways of treating disease, but the ethical issues surrounding this research continue to be debated.[7]

Overcoming the ethical dilemmas you face now and will face in the future requires great wisdom. An understanding of your own principles of **morality** (a set of ideas of right and wrong) is vitally important. You must do whatever you can to strengthen your ethical understandings and **moral integrity** (consistent adherence to a set of ideas of right and wrong) within and outside the workplace.

Stem cell research continues to raise issues that demand ethical answers.

[7]National Institutes of Health, U.S. Department of Health and Human Services, Federal Policy "Stem Cell Information," accessed April 19, 2007, available from http://stemcells.nih.gov/policy.

© PhotoDisc / Getty Images

The How

How can you, as an administrative professional, make a difference on important ethical issues? As a professional employed in the workplace and as a contributing member of society, you must grapple with answers to this question. However, here are partial answers:

- You can recognize the importance of behaving ethically and how ethical and unethical behavior impact the nation.
- You can constantly seek to understand the corporate culture in which you work and the philosophies of the leaders within the organization.
- You can understand how to achieve ethical change from within.
- You can behave ethically when dealing with your supervisor; your peers; and the customers, clients, and vendors of your organization.
- You can regularly examine your own ethical standards to determine whether you are behaving in ethical ways.

Characteristics of Ethical Organizations

The characteristics of ethical organizations are many. Here are a few important ones.

Environmentally Responsible

An environmentally responsible organization is aware of the possible dangers in business and takes necessary precautions to keep the environment free from pollution. The organization pays attention to **OSHA (Occupational Safety & Health Administration)** regulations regarding careful disposal of waste products. The organization makes it a top priority when constructing new buildings to cut down as few trees as possible and to protect wetland areas, as well as other areas that are important ecologically.

Internationally Aware

The ethical organization is aware that ethical behavior has different meanings in different countries. Different countries interpret human rights in different ways. In some countries, there is no consideration of gender equity. Even harassment and discrimination are not ethically wrong. Such awareness on the part of U.S. businesses operating in other countries does not mean they adopt the ethical standards of that country. It does mean that U.S. businesses must be knowledgeable about the practices that occur and carefully formulate their own practices and behaviors. Ethical organizations understand the

Ethical behavior has different meanings in different cultures.

© PhotoDisc / Getty Images

importance of learning the cultures and business customs of the countries in which they operate.

Culturally Committed to Ethical Behavior

Organizational culture is defined as "the ideas, customs, values, and skills of a particular organization." All organizations have a culture. The organizational culture may be one of the following:

- Commitment to behaving ethically
- Verbal commitment with little follow-through
- No commitment to ethics

Employees in ethical organizations are aware of the ethical stance of the organization and realize they are accountable for upholding the ethics espoused by the organization. Preparation and dissemination of mission/value statements are communication vehicles that organizations use to inform employees and customers of their ethics.

Consider the following statements made by two companies on *Fortune* magazine's 2007 100 Best Companies to Work For.

- SC Johnson. The guiding philosophies of SC Johnson include these:

  Employees: We believe our fundamental strength lies in our people.

  Consumers: We believe in earning the enduring goodwill of the people who use and sell our products and services.

  General Public: We believe in being a responsible leader in the free market economy.

  Neighbors and Hosts: We believe in contributing to the well-being of the countries and communities where we conduct business.

  World Community: We believe in improving international understanding.[8]

- Starbucks Coffee. Starbucks' mission statement: Establish Starbucks as the premier purveyor of the finest coffee in the world while maintaining our uncompromising principles while we grow. The following six guiding principles will help us measure the appropriateness of our decisions:

  — Provide a great work environment and treat each other with respect and dignity.
  — Embrace diversity as an essential component in the way we do business.
  — Apply the highest standards of excellence to the purchasing, roasting, and fresh delivery of our coffee.
  — Develop enthusiastically satisfied customers all of the time.
  — Contribute positively to our communities and our environment.
  — Recognize that profitability is essential to our future success.[9]

Honest

An ethical organization is honest when dealing with employees and other organizations and individuals. For example, the company makes its personnel policies clear to all employees. Employees understand salary and promotion policies. In a sales organization, product specifications and pricing structures are clear to external organizations and individuals. An ethical organization holds employees accountable for honesty. Honest employees do not falsify expense reports, time reports, or personnel records.

Committed to Diversity

The ethical organization believes in providing equal treatment to all individuals, regardless of race, ethnicity, age, gender, sexual orientation, or physical challenge. For example, women sometimes face obstacles in the workplace that occur not because of their performance, but because of their gender and how others perceive them. Gays and lesbians often face discrimination based not on who they are or how they perform on the job, but on their sexual orientation. Often minority group members encounter problems based on

[8]SC Johnson, "Our Philosophy," accessed April 19, 2007, available from http://www.scjohnson.com/family/fam_com_phi.asp.

[9]Starbucks Coffee, "Starbucks Mission Statement," accessed April 19, 2007, available from http://www.starbucks.com/aboutus/environment.asp.

the **biases** (views based on background or experiences) of others. Such biases can cause **stereotyping** (holding perceptions or images of people or things that are derived from selective perception). Although you may think of stereotyping as negative, it can be positive. For example, stereotyping can help you learn the general characteristics of certain groups, people, or animals. As a small child, you learned that dogs are four-legged animals and are generally friendly to people. As you grew older, you could begin to distinguish among types of dogs and their natures and special characteristics.

Negative stereotyping can cause a premature end to communication and prejudicial behavior that leads to acts of rejection. For example, if an individual has a negative experience with an individual from another country and then decides that all individuals from that country have the same negative characteristics, **prejudice** (a system of negative beliefs and feelings) occurs. Other examples of prejudice are evident when **physically challenged** individuals (persons with a physical handicap) are judged and treated unfairly due to their physical handicaps.

None of this discussion is to imply that the ethical organization advocates a policy that ignores performance issues due to gender, physical challenge, race, ethnicity, or sexual orientation. All individuals must perform their jobs satisfactorily. What is important is giving all individuals the opportunity to do their job regardless of their minority status.

Here is the introductory statement concerning diversity from one of *Fortune* magazine's 2007 100 Best Companies to Work For, QUAL-COMM Incorporated.

At QUALCOMM, we recognize that business success is driven by creativity and diversity. By valuing our differences and appreciating our similarities, we encourage the exchange of unique ideas and perspectives and build upon our individual, team and business strengths. Our diversity creates an energy that carries our global teams forward in developing new and superior products worldwide. At the heart of our global diversity and inclusion program is QUALCOMM's commitment to provide all employees, regardless of their backgrounds and

© Digital Vision / Getty Images

An ethical organization affords equal treatment to all individuals, regardless of race or ethnicity.

perspectives on the world, the opportunity to achieve their personal and professional goals.[10]

Because of their commitment to diversity, QUALCOMM has received several prestigious awards including the "Secretary of Labor's Opportunity Award" from the Department of Labor, "Best Employers for Workers over 50" from the American Association of Retired Persons (AARP) and the "Top 100 Employers" from *Black Collegian Magazine*. Figure 6.1 explains in greater detail QUALCOMM's stance on diversity.

In dealing with diversity issues, ethical organizations should engage in the following behaviors:

- Ensure that initial employment practices support diversity
- Ensure that promotional opportunities provide for equal treatment of all individuals
- Hold managers accountable for supporting and implementing nondiscriminatory policies
- Assist individuals who have English language deficiencies by allowing them to enroll in onsite or off-site courses at a college or university
- Provide access for the physically challenged to all facilities and provide proper equipment and work space
- Ensure that age differences are not used as an evaluation measure

---

QUALCOMM'S DIVERSITY COMMITMENT

QUALCOMM is committed to encouraging an environment of inclusion where employees see their differences as an asset and a strength. We will continue to make global diversity and inclusion an essential part of our business strategy, central to how we interact with each other and how we approach each other in our communities. At its core, global diversity and inclusion is about people, communication and technology.

People

- Employees: innovation, determination, perspective, interdependence, health, wellness and balance are a few qualities that make QUALCOMM employees special
- Lifestyles: embracing each others' ways of life enriches us and bolsters our business success
- Communities: our sustained commitment to supporting our local and regional initiatives allows us to enrich and give back to our communities

Communication

- Engaging Perspectives: our success is driven by open discussions at all levels resulting in improvements, new ideas and growth
- Boundless Connection: the technologies we develop allow communication without boundaries
- Global Networking: QUALCOMM is changing the way we interact by connecting people around the world

Technology

- Pushing the Limits: recognized globally as a leader in advanced digital wireless communications, we continually strive to exceed expectations
- Superior Quality: our business strategies and processes are closely aligned with our values to exceed expectations
- Continuous Learning: leveraging state-of-the-art training techniques and tools assists employees in expanding talents and meeting individual goals

---

Source: QUALCOMM, Diversity, "Our Commitment," accessed April 17, 2007, available from http://www.qualcomm.com/diversity/commitment.html.

FIGURE 6.1 QUALCOMM'S Diversity Commitment

---

[10]QUALCOMM, Diversity, "Our Commitment," accessed April 17, 2007, available from http://www.qualcomm.com/diversity/index.html.

QUALCOMM'S VOLUNTEER PROGRAM

QUALCOMM's corporate volunteerism program, QUALCOMM Cares, encourages employee involvement in the community, and is our way of connecting our diverse employee base to local volunteer opportunities.

From walkathons to holiday drives, QUALCOMM Cares creates many opportunities for its employees, friends, and families to participate in charitable events. Serving a wide range of needs, our employees are helping people with disabilities, improving the environment, feeding and clothing the homeless, and caring for animals. QUALCOMM Cares organizes volunteer team building projects as special opportunities for internal departments to foster teamwork and celebrate accomplishments, while simultaneously contributing to the improvement of our communities.

In addition to the volunteer opportunities offered through QUALCOMM Cares, many QUALCOMM employees are contributing their management experience and talents though leadership positions at various non-profit organizations. Through both board governance and committee involvement, QUALCOMM's managers provide such services as strategic planning, public relations, marketing, information technology, accounting, and financial management to a variety of non-profit organizations.

Source: QUALCOMM, Community, "Volunteerism," accessed April 17, 2007, available from http://www.qualcomm.com/community/volunteerism. html.

FIGURE 6.2 QUALCOMM'S Volunteer Program

- Raise the diversity awareness of other managers and individuals by providing seminars on diversity

Committed to the Community

Ethical organizations understand that they have a social responsibility to contribute to the community. In fulfilling this responsibility, the organizations may engage in any of the following activities:

- Contributing to charities
- Participating in the local Chamber of Commerce and other service organizations
- Working with youth groups
- Supporting the inner city in its crime reduction programs
- Assisting schools and colleges with internship programs
- Encouraging employees to participate in their local communities by recognizing and rewarding employees' endeavors

Notice Figure 6.2, which spells out QUALCOMM's commitment to the communities it serves.

Committed to Employees

Promoting employee productivity is important to ethical organizations. Although fear about job performance and security exists at some level in most organizations, the ethical organization takes steps to reduce such fears. Here are some ways companies can reduce employee fear:

- Establish realistic job descriptions
- Help employees set achievable goals
- Administer performance evaluations fairly
- Support employees in learning new skills
- Encourage employees to cooperate with each other
- Reward employee creativity
- Provide personnel policies in writing to all employees
- Establish teams to work on significant company issues

Committed to Standards

When carrying out ethical behavior, organizations establish standards that support ethical decision making and quality delivery of products and services. In addition to individual organizational standards, standards are set for entire industries. For example, the **FDA (Food and Drug Administration)** establishes standards for food and drug products manufactured in the United States. OSHA establishes standards for workforce safety. Figure 6.3 shows a portion of the standards established by OSHA.

INTRODUCTION TO THE EMERGENCY ACTION PLAN EXPERT SYSTEM

An emergency action plan (EAP) is usually a written document required by particular OSHA standards. For smaller organizations, the plan does not need to be written and may be communicated orally if there are 10 or fewer employees [29 CFR 1910.38(b)]. The purpose of an EAP is to facilitate and organize employer and employee actions during workplace emergencies. The elements of the plan must include, but are not limited to:

- Means of reporting fires and other emergencies

- Evacuation procedures and emergency escape route assignments

- Procedures to be followed by employees who remain to operate critical plant operations before they evacuate

- Procedures to account for all employees after an emergency evacuation has been completed

- Rescue and medical duties for those employees who are to perform them

- Names or job titles of persons who can be contacted for further information or explanation of duties under the plan

Source: U.S. Department of Labor, Occupational Safety & Health Administration, "Introduction to the Emergency Action Plan Expert System," accessed April 20, 2007, available from http://www.osha.gov/SLTC/etools/evacuation/expertsystem/default.htm#.

FIGURE 6.3 Portion of OSHA Standards

Ethical Change

You do not live in a perfect world. Thus, you do not live in a world where all individuals and organizations are ethical. However, many people and organizations strive to make their corner of the world a better place in which to live and work. Assuring that ethical change takes place in an organization is partly the responsibility of management. Management cannot dictate ethical change; they can only provide an environment that encourages ethical change. Although you will not be in a management position when you first begin your career, you may find yourself, at some point, supervising one or more individuals. Figure 6.4 gives several steps management can take to produce ethical change within an organization.

Employees of an organization must take whatever steps are necessary to change their individual behaviors. No one employee can dictate to another how he or she should behave; ethical change for each employee becomes a matter of personal consideration and commitment. In the next section, you will examine factors that can impede ethical change for you as an individual. Additionally, you will consider pragmatic steps you can take to produce ethical change within yourself.

Factors Impeding Ethical Change

A person's background and beliefs often stand in the way of ethical change. As you read the following negative beliefs, ask yourself if you believe any of them.

- Values cannot be changed.
- Organizations are amoral.
- Labels accurately describe individuals.
- Leaders do not behave ethically.

Now examine each of these statements individually.

VALUES CANNOT BE CHANGED

Clearly, values can be difficult to change since they are generally adopted at an early age. However, change is possible. Consider this example:

Harold's father (who was divorced from Harold's mother when Harold was two) taught his son that women are inferior to men. Harold's father reared him and sent him to an all-male school from first grade through high school. As a result of his rearing and his lack of exposure to women in significant leadership roles, Harold does not value women in management roles. He believes they are incapable of making good decisions for an organization and of being strong leaders. Harold went to work for

> ## ETHICAL CHANGE STEPS FOR MANAGEMENT
>
> - Take into consideration the interests of all individuals within the organization. For example, sometimes the welfare of an individual must be preserved (as is the case when unfounded accusations could end a career). Sometimes the welfare of many must be weighed over the good of a few (as in the closing of a plant to sustain the long-term viability of the company).
> - Measure the acts of an organization against a variety of ethical yardsticks. For example, the acts of an organization must be balanced against such values as justice, honesty, the good of the stakeholders of the corporation, and the external community.
> - Be alert to the pressures and counterpressures of the internal and external environment. Evaluate those pressures in light of the goals of the organization.
> - Establish a framework by which to consider the ethical implications of an act and how to achieve the greatest good for the organization and its stakeholders.
> - Appoint senior-level management to monitor the actions of the organization as compared to the established organizational ethics.
> - Develop an internal mechanism that employees can use to report ethical violations.
> - Consistently reinforce ethical standards.
> - Establish a training program to allow managers to understand how to bring about ethical change within an organization.

FIGURE 6.4 Ethical Change Steps for Management

a male department manager in a large company. Six months after Harold began his job, his supervisor left for a position in another company. His supervisor was replaced by a woman, Jessica Alvarez. Harold decided he should start looking for another job immediately. However, after one month of reporting to his female supervisor, he began to second-guess his long-held assumption that women cannot make good decisions. He also began to question his lack of valuing women in management roles.

Even though you may have established certain values early in life and held on to them into adulthood, you can change these values if you are open to honestly evaluating situations that suggest a need to change long-held beliefs.

ORGANIZATIONS ARE AMORAL

Amoral is defined as "lacking moral judgment or sensibility, neither moral nor immoral." History has shown that amoral organizations do not achieve long-term success. If an organization is to achieve long-term success, its values must be clearly defined by management and upheld by everyone in the organization. Employees do not have the authority to establish organizational values even though they, no doubt, are living by their own set of values. The leadership within an organization must be willing to establish the organizational values, live by the established values, make employees aware of the values, and hold employees accountable for living by them.

LABELS ACCURATELY DESCRIBE INDIVIDUALS

Generally, when you attach a label to someone, you are not describing that individual accurately. For example, to describe someone by his or her job title clearly leaves out much of who the person is. Or to describe a person as a *team player*, a *bore*, or any other term is restrictive of the whole person's qualities and traits. The point to keep in mind is that labeling hinders, rather than helps, the change process. Labeling individuals affects your view of individuals and often affects the view of significant others in your life. The process of making ethical change within an organization can be harmed by the labeling of individuals.

More women are successfully assuming positions of leadership in organizations.

LEADERS DO NOT BEHAVE ETHICALLY

Clearly, organizations exist in which individual members of the leadership team do not behave ethically. However, to assume that all management is bad suggests that you are negatively stereotyping management. If you do not want to behave ethically yourself, you can easily shift the blame for your lack of performance to management. The following comments are often made:

- All managers are unethical. Why should I be ethical if my supervisor is not?
- You cannot trust your supervisor.
- Presidents of corporations do not care about the workers; they only care about making huge salaries and pleasing the board to whom they report.

If you find that management within your organization is unethical, you need to leave the organization. When organizational ethics are not adopted by management, the organization is not a good place to work.

Steps Producing Ethical Change

Now that you have looked at factors that hinder ethical change, consider these steps that can help produce ethical change:

- Determine the ethical change required.
- Determine the steps required to achieve the objective.
- Practice the new behaviors.
- Seek feedback.
- Reward yourself and the individuals involved.
- Evaluate the effects of ethical change.

To help you understand how to apply these steps, consider the following situation involving an employee (Theresa), along with examples of the appropriate handling of each step.

DETERMINE THE ETHICAL CHANGE REQUIRED

Consider this situation:

You are chairing a task force charged with improving the organization's sexual harassment policy. Theresa is a member of the task force. She attends the meetings and seems to listen attentively, but she does not say anything during the meetings. Once outside the meetings, Theresa attempts to sabotage the decisions.

When determining the ethical change required, the specific behavior must be considered. What is that behavior?

Not: Theresa is unprofessional in her conduct. Such an analysis is too broad. What does un-professional behavior mean?

Rather: Theresa does not express her feelings and thoughts in meetings.

DETERMINE THE STEPS REQUIRED TO ACHIEVE THE OBJECTIVE

The objective in this situation is to get Theresa to express her thoughts during the meeting—not after the meeting is over. The process you use here is similar to the decision-making process you learned in Chapter 1. You may want to go back and review the process now. After you define the problem, you establish the criteria and generate possible alternatives. In this case, you decide to take the following steps:

- Talk with Theresa in private before the next meeting. Tell her you have noticed she is very quiet in meetings, you value her opinions, and you would like to hear her opinions on issues. Tell her you believe the entire group can benefit from her opinions and suggestions.

- At the next meeting, if Theresa is not forthcoming with comments, ask for her comments. Then thank her when she does express her viewpoints.

PRACTICE THE NEW BEHAVIORS

At each meeting, use the same behavior with Theresa and with any others in the group who are not participating.

SEEK FEEDBACK

After a group meeting, talk with a trusted member of the group. Ask that person to evaluate your leadership abilities with the group. Listen openly to the positive and negative comments the person shares. Do not become defensive about negative comments. If you think you are not being successful with the group, you might seek the help of an outside consultant. Invite the consultant to several group meetings to observe you and the group together. Listen to what the consultant has to say, and implement any suggestions made.

REWARD YOURSELF AND THE INDIVIDUALS INVOLVED

Once you see a change in Theresa's behavior, reward yourself for bringing about the positive change. Mentally add this success to your list of strengths. Reward Theresa for the change in her behavior by praising her in a one-on-one session. Thank the entire group for its work if the situation warrants it.

EVALUATE THE EFFECTS OF ETHICAL CHANGE

Is the group more effective in making decisions now that Theresa is voicing her concerns in the meetings? Is the group working together as a cohesive team? Is there a sense of cohesiveness and camaraderie in the group? No doubt, the answer to each of these questions is a resounding yes.

Discrimination—Its Implications for the Organization

You learned earlier in this chapter that the ethical organization does not discriminate due to race, ethnicity, gender, age, sexual orientation, or physical challenge. In fact, in the United States, discrimination is taken so seriously that laws have been enacted to protect citizens against discrimination. These laws are listed in Figure 6.5. Unfortunately, even with laws in place, discrimination continues to occur. The U.S. **EEOC (Equal Employment Opportunity Commission)** reports that in 1997, 80,680 charges of discrimination were filed by employees against their employers, while in 2006, 75,768 employees filed discrimination lawsuits.[11] Headlines such as the following attest to the fact that discrimination happens and it can be costly to an organization.

[11]The U.S. Equal Employment Opportunity Commission, "Charge Statistics," accessed April 19, 2007, available from http://www.eeoc.gov/stats/charges.html.

FEDERAL LAWS PROHIBITING JOB DISCRIMINATION

- Title VII of the Civil Rights Act of 1964 (Title VII), which prohibits employment discrimination based on race, color, religion, sex, or national origin
- Equal Pay Act of 1963 (EPA), which protects men and women who perform substantially equal work in the same establishment from sex-based wage discrimination
- Age Discrimination in Employment Act of 1967 (ADEA), which protects individuals who are 40 years of age or older
- Title I and Title V of the Americans with Disabilities Act of 1990 (ADA), which prohibits employment discrimination against qualified individuals with disabilities in the private sector and in state and local governments
- Sections 501 and 505 of the Rehabilitation Act of 1973, which prohibits discrimination against qualified individuals with disabilities who work in the federal government
- The Civil Rights Act of 1991, which, among other things, provides monetary damages in cases of intentional employment discrimination

Source: The U.S. Equal Employment Opportunity Commission, "Federal Equal Employment Opportunity (EEO) Laws," accessed April 20, 2007, available from http://www.eeoc.gov/abouteeo/overview_laws.html.

FIGURE 6.5 Federal Laws Prohibiting Job Discrimination

Tax Shelter Leaders Get Jail Time, Must Pay Restitution

Analyst Fired for Personal Trading

Adelphia, U.S. Settle for $415 Million

FBR Nears Settlement with SEC

Although discrimination may take many forms, only sexual harassment and racial discrimination are considered here.

Sexual Harassment

According to statistics maintained by the EEOC, thousands of sexual harassment charges are filed each year. Of the 12,025 charges reported in 2006, 15.4 percent or 1,851 charges were reported by men.[12]

What is **sexual harassment**? It is defined by the EEOC as "harassment arising from sexual conduct that is unwelcome by the recipient and that may be either physical or verbal in nature." Three criteria for sexual harassment are set forth:

- Submission to the sexual conduct is made either implicitly or explicitly as a condition of employment.
- Employment decisions affecting the recipient are made on the basis of the recipient's acceptance or rejection of the sexual conduct.
- The conduct has the intent or effect of substantially interfering with an individual's work performance or creates an intimidating, hostile, or offensive work environment.

When sexual harassment is based on the first two criteria, it is referred to as quid pro quo (Latin meaning "this for that") sexual harassment. When sexual activity is presented as a prerequisite for getting a job, a promotion, or some type of benefit in the workplace, the behavior is illegal.

The third criterion is referred to as hostile environment sexual harassment. In this situation, the employer, supervisor, or coworker does or says things that make victims feel uncomfortable because of their gender. Hostile environment sexual harassment does not need to include a demand for sex. It can be the creation of an uncomfortable working environment.

The courts have found that suggestive comments, jokes, leering, unwanted requests for a date, and touching can be sexual harassment.

[12]The U.S. Equal Employment Opportunity Commission, "Sexual Harassment Charges," accessed May 9, 2007, available from http://www.eeoc.gov/stats/harass.html.

SEXUAL HARASSMENT POLICY STATEMENT

It is against the policy of the company to discriminate against and/or exclude an employee from participation in any benefits or activities based on national origin, gender, age, sexual orientation, or handicap. Harassment on the basis of sex is a violation of the law and a violation of company policy.

FIGURE 6.6 Sexual Harassment Policy Statement

Sexual harassment can occur between people of the same sex; it can also be a woman harassing a man or a man harassing a woman. Victims of sexual harassment can sue and recover for lost wages, future lost wages, emotional distress, punitive damages, and attorneys' fees. EEOC guidelines state that harassment on the basis of sex is a violation of Title VII of the Civil Rights Act and that the organization has a duty to prevent and eliminate sexual harassment. A federal appeals court ruled that an organization is liable for the behavior of its employees even if management is unaware the sexual harassment is taking place. Management is also responsible for the behavior of nonemployees on the company's premises.

For example, if a visiting representative or salesperson harasses a company's receptionist, the receptionist's company is responsible. As a result of these responsibilities, many companies have published policy statements on sexual harassment. A sample policy statement is shown in Figure 6.6.

Once the policy statement is established, it must be communicated to all supervisors and employees, along with a grievance procedure. If you are not made aware of the organization's sexual harassment policy and grievance procedure when you are employed, you should ask for a copy. A sample grievance procedure follows.

Any employee who believes he or she is being sexually harassed on the job shall file a written grievance with the director of Human Resources within 24 hours after the alleged sexual harassment takes place. The grievance is reviewed by the supervisor, and appropriate action is taken. If the employee believes the grievance is not handled satisfactorily, he or she has the right to appeal to the next-level supervisor, with appeal going through the line of authority to the president.

To prevent sexual harassment in the workplace, management has the responsibility of educating its supervisors and employees concerning procedures. If you, as an employee, are faced with sexual harassment, you can seek help or handle the situation yourself, whichever you believe is more appropriate.

Racial Discrimination

In addition to sexual harassment in the workplace, **racial discrimination** also exists. Why? It is based mainly on prejudice, and prejudice is often the result of ignorance, fear, and/or cultural patterns. As past generations viewed groups of people in certain roles and with certain characteristics, those generations learned certain attitudes, passing their beliefs on to the next generation. Changing learned attitudes is a slow process. Strides toward reducing racial prejudice are being made, but even greater strides must be made in the future.

What can be done about racial discrimination? Just as policies must exist to deal with sexual harassment, so must they exist for racial discrimination. Employees who experience discrimination should first seek to correct the problem within the organization by making their concerns known to their supervisor or to the Human Resources Department. If help is not forthcoming, relief can be sought through the EEOC. The local EEOC office should be listed in your area telephone book. Figure 6.7 gives several steps for handling sexual and racial/ethnic discrimination.

STEPS FOR HANDLING SEXUAL AND RACIAL/ETHNIC DISCRIMINATION

- Know your rights. Know your organization's position on racial discrimination and sexual harassment, what is legal under the EEOC guidelines, and what your employer's responsibility is. Know what redress is provided by Federal Laws.
- Keep a record of all harassment infractions, noting the dates, incidents, and witnesses (if any).
- File a formal grievance with your organization. Check your organization's policy and procedures manual or talk with the director of Human Resources as to the grievance procedure. If no formal grievance procedure exists, file a formal complaint with your employer in the form of a memorandum describing the incidents, identifying the individuals involved in the harassment or discrimination, and requesting disciplinary action.
- If your employer is not responsive to your complaint, file charges of discrimination with the federal and state agencies that enforce civil rights laws, such as the EEOC.
- Talk to friends, coworkers, and relatives. Avoid isolation and self-blame. You are not alone; sexual harassment and racial discrimination do occur in the work sector.
- Consult an attorney to investigate legal alternatives to discriminatory or sexual harassment behavior.

FIGURE 6.7 Steps for Handling Sexual and Racial/Ethnic Discrimination

Characteristics of Ethical Administrative Professionals

If you are to be an ethical administrative professional, you need to understand the importance of ethics, ethical leadership, corporate culture, and ethical change. You also need to address your own ethical behavior. Pay careful attention to the following characteristics of ethical administrative professionals.

Make Ethical Decisions

The following people and beliefs influence your personal ethics:

- Your parents
- Significant individuals in your life
- Your peer group
- The culture in which you grew up
- Your religious beliefs

Your personal ethics plus the culture and expectations of the organization for which you work have the potential of making it difficult for you to determine what is right and wrong in a particular situation. Asking these questions can help you decide what is ethical:

- What are the facts of the situation?
- What are the ethical issues involved?
- Who are the **stakeholders** (people who have an interest in the outcome)?
- Who will be affected by my decision?
- Are there different ways of looking at this issue? If so, what are they?
- What are the practical constraints?
- What actions should I take?
- Are these actions practical?

If you are still unclear about what you should do, ask yourself these questions:

- If my actions appeared in the newspaper, would I feel comfortable knowing everyone was reading about what I did?
- Is what I anticipate doing legal?
- Could I proudly tell my spouse, my parents, or my children about my actions?
- Will I be proud of my actions one day, one week, and one year from now?
- Do my actions fit with the person I think I am?

Support Ethical Behavior

Whenever you, as an administrative professional, encounter someone whose words or deeds indicate that the person is not responding to the ethics of the organization, take a stand. Be

Significant others in your life influence your personal ethics.

© PhotoDisc / Getty Images

sensitive and direct. Let people who are cynical about ethical organizations know that you believe strongly in the concept. Let them know that you believe honesty, concern for society, concern for the future health of the world, and respect for the rights of others are values that belong in the organization.

Refuse to Engage in Negative Workplace Politics

What does the term **workplace politics** mean? It means that the people you know within an organization can be important. It means that networks can exist in which favors are done for people based on the networks. Workplace politics can be good or bad. Consider this example of positive workplace politics.

Assume that you believe your department records management system is inadequate. You begin to talk with your employer and your coworkers about a more effective system. You also talk with coworkers in other departments, *express your concerns, and suggest possible solutions. You are able to garner support, and your employer goes to bat with upper management for the money to get the system. You have used people in the workplace positively to get support for an idea that will benefit the organization.*

Workplace politics becomes bad when it is used as a quid pro quo. That is, if you do something for me, I will do something for you, with no consideration of whether that something is good for the organization. It is merely good for you. In other words, you are furthering your own personal interests.

In a perfect world, negative workplace politics do not exist. But the reality is that they do exist. So what do you do about workplace politics? How do you handle them? First of all, you become aware of their existence. When you begin a new job, notice what is happening around you. Become aware of the power bases. Become aware of who knows whom and what the relationships are. Next, hold on to your own value system. Be respectful and polite to everyone. Do not gossip about people in the workplace. Use your awareness of the workplace politics to help yourself do your job. Generally, if you live your values and do your job well, you will be recognized and respected.

Professional Pointers

Here are some tips for helping you to behave ethically in the workplace.

- **Critique ideas, not people.**

- **Do not publicly criticize your supervisor or your coworkers.**

- **Do not listen to or pass along gossip about other individuals.**

- **Check out information you hear from the grapevine. If you know the information is false, say so without becoming emotional. Feed accurate information into the grapevine.**

- **Communicate in person when appropriate. Even though the majority of communication is through electronic means, face-to-face communication is valuable. It allows you to see a person's reaction to the message and to clarify any misunderstandings quickly.**

- **Be a good listener, but do not pass on everything you hear. Remember that you must behave professionally; professionalism carries with it lack of pettiness and rumormongering.**

- **When you have a problem, go directly to the source of the problem in an attempt to correct the situation.**

- **Appreciate diversity. Understand that people have different values, abilities, and priorities.**

- **Practice empathy. Putting yourself in the situation of others (figuratively) allows you to relate more closely to the barriers they face or the feelings they have.**

Accept Constructive Criticism

If your supervisor recommends that you do something differently, do not take his or her remarks personally. For example, assume you recently set up a meeting for your employer at a hotel where lunch was served. It was the first time you planned such a meeting, and you thought you did a fair job. After the meeting, your employer called you in and told you the room arrangement was not satisfactory and the food choice was poor. How should you respond? First, you deal with the issues at hand. You might ask, "Can we talk about it more? What type of room arrangement would have been better? What type of meal would you suggest?"

Realize that you have much to learn and that everyone makes mistakes. You might also

© Digital Vision / Getty Images

Would you be comfortable if your actions concerning an ethical issue were printed in the newspaper?

suggest to your supervisor that you would like to review the arrangements with her before the next meeting takes place. With any type of criticism, you want to learn from your mistakes and not make the same mistake twice.

Keep Confidential Information Confidential

Administrative assistants are often privy to information of a confidential nature. For example, they key reports containing confidential information and they are told information by their supervisor that is confidential. The technological age has exacerbated the issues around confidential information in that more and more information is available to all employees in the organization—often with merely a touch of the keyboard. Sharing confidential information, even though it may be divulged innocently to a coworker, can cause irreparable harm to an organization. For example, the divulgence of information concerning a pending lawsuit can cause an organization to lose an important case. As an administrative professional, you must understand the importance of not discussing confidential information with anyone in the organization who does not have the right of access to that information. Even if a longtime friend in the organization asks about a confidential matter, you must not give out the information. A true friend will respect your ethical stance in not answering the question.

Accept Responsibilities

Ethical administrative professionals understand and accept the responsibilities of their jobs. They perform all tasks to the best of their ability. They do not attempt to pass the blame for incomplete or subpar work on to another individual; they accept responsibility. Also, you may at times be required to assist someone else in doing a task or to work overtime to get your job done. Ethical administrative professionals accept these responsibilities.

Ethical behavior does make a difference in an organization.

© PhotoDisc / Getty Images

Are Honest

Honest administrative professionals avoid hypocrisy. They do not tell white lies to supervisors or coworkers. Even the smallest white lie can cause major damage to one's professional reputation. Honest employees do not blame someone else for their errors or break rules and then claim ignorance of the rules. Honest employees do not take organizational supplies or equipment for their own personal use. For example, understanding that workplace copiers are used for the business of the organization, employees do not make personal copies.

Are Loyal

The ethical employee is loyal to the organization, but not in an unquestioning sense. The important issue for the employee and the company is not blind loyalty, but commitment to company directions that support the values. Employees must be allowed to disagree constructively with directions, to speak out on issues, and to be heard by management in the process. However, once a direction is decided, employees must be loyal and productive members of the team. Ethical employees understand and live by this type of loyalty.

Keep the Faith

The ethical employee keeps the faith. The employee understands that changing behaviors is a slow process, but that the commitment to ethics must be upheld even when the organization seems to be mired in behaviors that do not support the stated ethical policies. Certainly, the ethical administrative professional may become discouraged at times. Nevertheless, the ethical employee continues to behave ethically, keeping the faith that others in the organization will eventually adopt appropriate behaviors. A total commitment by all employees to upholding ethical standards makes a company not only a great place to work, but also a success with its clients and customers.

Ethics—Your Call

Although you cannot impact the ethics of an entire organization unless you are in upper management, you can check out an organization's ethics before you accept a position. Here are a few suggestions as to how to evaluate an

organization's ethics in the job application process.

- Read the organization's Web page. Are the ethics of the organization mentioned? Is a commitment to diversity mentioned? Is a commitment to the external community mentioned? Is integrity mentioned? Does the organization have professional growth programs for employees?
- Check the history of the organization. Has the company ever made newspaper headlines for behaving unethically?
- Talk with acquaintances who work for the organization. Ask them to describe the ethical environment of the company.

In addition to checking out an organization's stated ethics before accepting a position, you can promise yourself that if for some reason your organization ever begins engaging in grossly unethical behaviors, you will seek employment elsewhere.

Beware, however, of becoming complacent about ethical issues. Unless you are completely committed ethically, you may stay in an organization that becomes unethical and find yourself supporting the unethical behaviors to the detriment of your own value system and career growth. Commit now to making ethical behavior an important part of your professional life.

Summary

To reinforce what you have learned in this chapter, study this summary.

- Ethics is the systematic study of moral conduct, duty, and judgment—what is right and what is wrong. Business ethics is the study of just and unjust behaviors in business.
- Ethics has its roots in religion and in the philosophies of some of the great philosophers, such as Socrates, Plato, and Saint Thomas Aquinas.
- The ethical organization is environmentally responsible; is internationally aware; is culturally committed to ethical behavior; is honest; and is committed to diversity, to the community, to employees, and to standards.

- Factors impeding ethical change include the beliefs that values cannot be changed, organizations are amoral, labels accurately describe individuals, and leaders do not behave ethically.

- Steps producing ethical change include determining the ethical change required, determining the steps required to achieve the objective, practicing the new behaviors, seeking feedback, rewarding yourself and the individuals involved, and evaluating the effects of ethical change.

- Two forms of discrimination include sexual harassment and racial discrimination. Laws protect individuals from racial and sexual discrimination, with one of the most important laws being Title VII of the Civil Rights Act of 1964.

- Characteristics of ethical administrative professionals include making ethical decisions, supporting ethical behavior, refusing to engage in negative workplace politics, accepting constructive criticism, keeping confidential information confidential, accepting responsibilities, being honest, and being loyal.

- The decision to act ethically and to seek employment in an ethical organization is a personal one. A person must believe strongly in the concept in order to live his or her beliefs on a daily basis.

What's the Problem?

Isabella was recently hired in her first full-time position as an administrative professional. She has been working for the company for six months. She is not happy in her position. She does not like her supervisor because she believes he is unethical. Isabella talked with Dao, one of her friends in the company, and asked her advice about quitting her job. Yesterday Isabella's supervisor called her in and told her she was being disloyal to him. He explained that he was told she had been spreading vicious rumors about him throughout the company.

What is the problem? How should Isabella handle the problem?

Let's Discuss

1. Why is ethical behavior important in the workplace?
2. List and explain six characteristics of an ethical organization.
3. Explain how ethical change is achieved.
4. Explain how sexual harassment can be reduced in the workplace.
5. Identify six characteristics of an ethical employee.

Critical-Thinking Activity

Inez Ramos has been working as an administrative professional at United Pharmaceuticals for one year. One of her employer's male friends from another company, Timothy Madeley, visits the office three or four times a month. Inez has a pleasant relationship with him, and they usually chat for a few minutes each time he comes to the office. Mr. Madeley is married, and he frequently talks about his wife and their three children. On his last visit to the company, Mr. Madeley stopped by to chat with Inez. At the end of the conversation, he said, "Let's have lunch some time." Inez, thinking she would enjoy a casual meal out, replied, "Sounds good to me." Today as he came to her office after his visit with her supervisor, he said "I really want to have lunch with you. How about next Tuesday? I have the afternoon free. Maybe you can take the afternoon off so we can enjoy a pleasant outing." Inez was surprised and concerned when he suggested they spend the afternoon together. She did not know how to respond. She merely said, "Let me think about it."

How should Inez handle the situation?

Vocabulary Review

Open the *Word* file *CH06 Vocabulary* found on the Student CD. Complete the vocabulary review for Chapter 6.

English and Word Usage Drill

Complete the English and Word Usage Drill for Chapter 6 found in the *Applications Workbook*.

Workplace Applications

6-1 Review Company Ethics Statements

(Goals 1, 2, and 6)

1. Access *Fortune* magazine on the CNNMoney Website. A link to the site is provided on the Website for this textbook.

2. Search to find *Fortune's* list of 100 Best Companies to Work For in the current year.

3. Select three companies from the list and indicate their ranking out of 100.

4. Access the Website for each of the three companies you selected. Find the company's mission and vision/value/diversity statement. (Your instructor may ask you to print a copy of this information to attach to your report.)

internet

e-portfolio

5. Prepare a memo report to your instructor. Use the *Word* file *Memo Form* found on the Student CD to prepare the report. In the report, include the following information about each company:

   - Do these statements adequately reflect the importance of ethical behavior in the workplace? Why or why not?

   - Do these statements adequately address the company's ethical responsibility to society? Why or why not?

   - Choose four of the eight characteristics of an ethical organization that are described in the chapter and explain how the company's mission and vision/value/diversity statement addresses those characteristics.

   - Would you like to work for this organization? Why or why not?

6-2 Understand Ethics within an Organization

team building

(Goals 2, 3, 4, and 5)

1. Work with three classmates to complete this application.

2. As a team, interview two managers and two administrative professionals about the ethics of their organizations. Ask the following questions plus two additional questions your team creates.

   - Does your organization have a vision/value statement? If yes, what is the statement?

   - Does your organization have a grievance procedure for dealing with discrimination and sexual harassment? If yes, what is the policy?

   - How does your organization achieve ethical change?

3. Create eight to ten electronic slides that describe your findings. As a team, present your findings to the class. Provide printouts of the slides to your instructor.

6-3 Research Current Ethical Cases

internet

(Goals 1, 2, 3, 4, and 6)

1. The U.S. Equal Employment Opportunity Commission (EEOC) Website contains a vast news archive. This archive contains EEOC press releases that cover a variety of suits, cases, and settlements relating to disability, harassment, ethics, and bias cases. Visit the EEOC site and browse through the news archive. A link to the site is found on the Website for this textbook. Select a recent case that interests you based on subject matter or employer.

2. Research journal or newspaper articles to find at least two additional news articles related to the case you have selected.

3. Prepare an unbound report of your findings. The report should include the following information:

   - A description of the case and the related ethical issue(s)

- Facts of the case

- How the case was resolved (was the case settled, was the case dismissed)

- If there were judgments against the violating individual or company, the consequences that were given

- Documentation of your sources

6-4 Research Sexual Harassment Statistics

(Goal 4)

The U.S. Equal Employment Opportunity Commission (EEOC) maintains statistics on the number of discrimination charges that have been filed. Review the information provided below and on the EEOC Website to complete this project. A link to the EEOC site is provided on the Website for this textbook.

internet

1. Using your spreadsheet software, prepare a chart that shows trends in the total number of sexual harassment cases reported to the EEOC for the last five years. Use the information given below and additional information from the EEOC Website to find the number of cases that have been filed for each of the last five years.

Year	Number of Cases
2002	14,396 cases
2003	13,566 cases
2004	13,136 cases
2005	12,679 cases
2006	12,025 cases

2. Create a memo to your instructor that defines sexual harassment and describes the types of circumstances where sexual harassment can occur. Discuss how the number of reported cases is changing and include the chart you created in the memo.

Assessment of Chapter 6 Goals

Did you successfully complete the chapter goals? Evaluate yourself by filling out the form found in Chapter 6 of the *Applications Workbook*.

part 3

Communication
Essentials

CHAPTER 7

Written Communications

CHAPTER 8

**Verbal Communication
and Presentations**

CHAPTER 9

Customer Service

Career Profile

Customer Service Representative

Effective customer service is vital to the success of organizations. Customer service representatives serve as a direct point of contact for customers. The impression they make on customers can lead to increased sales or lost business for the company. Customer service representatives work in almost all industries and for small, medium, and large companies. About 2.1 million people worked as customer service representatives in the United States in 2004.*

Customer service representatives communicate with customers in person or by telephone or written communications (letters, email, or live chat). They provide answers to inquiries about products or services and handle complaints. Because the customers they deal with are often reporting problems, effective communication skills are essential to success. They must also be very familiar with company policies and the products they handle. Some customer service representatives specialize in a particular product or service area. Others handle general questions and complaints.

Salaries for customer service representatives vary by the skill, experience, and training of the worker and by the size and location of the company. The mean annual earnings of customer service representatives were $27,020 in May 2004. Because many customer service call centers are open 24 hours a day, workers may have the benefit of working flexible hours and may receive additional pay for working at night.

Some customer service jobs require only a high school diploma and training on company policies and products or services. Other companies require that customer service representatives have an associate or bachelor's degree. Some jobs, such as for handling problems with computers or software, require specialized education and experience. Good interpersonal, communication, and problem-solving skills are important for all customer service representatives.

Job prospects for customer service representatives are expected to be good for the next several years. Possibilities for job advancement include promotion to a managerial position in customer service or to other areas in the company such as product development.

---

*"Customer Service Representatives," *Occupational Outlook Handbook*, 2006-2007 Edition, accessed June 25, 2007, available from http://www.bls.gov/oco/ocos280.htm.

Written Communications

Written Messages

Written communications can spell success or failure for a writer and the organization. Consider for a moment the correspondence you receive from organizations. Have these letters ever contained incorrect information? Have any letters ever made you angry? Have you, after reading a letter, decided that you will never do business with the company again?

Have you ever received an email from an individual inviting you to a meeting, with the following information missing from the message?

- Purpose of meeting
- Location of meeting
- Time meeting begins
- Projected ending time

Have you picked up an organizational report and read only the first two pages because it was too technical or too poorly organized?

No doubt you answered yes to several of these questions. There is no surer way to make someone upset than to send that person correspondence that is poorly composed, does not contain all necessary information, demeans the reader through its tone, or is so poorly organized that the reader does not understand its purpose.

As an administrative professional, your job often demands that you compose correspondence. When you begin working for an organization, you may compose draft copies of correspondence. As you learn your position and the needs of the organization, you may send out correspondence under your own signature or write final copy for your employer to sign. Being a competent and careful writer is important to your success. This chapter will help you develop techniques for writing effectively.

The administrative professional produces four basic types of written messages—email, memorandums, letters, and reports.

Email

Throughout the United States, organizations send billions of email messages each day. Additionally, email access is readily available on home computers, and individuals, including children, frequently send email messages to friends and family members. Text messaging is also available via cell phones and is widely used to communicate with others. We have become an instant messaging society, and the increased use of technology by both businesses and individuals throughout the world promises to continue to provide fast and efficient communication. This chapter will help you learn to use an excellent communication tool without abusing it.

Email has a number of advantages for businesses, with these advantages being the ability to:

- Compose and send messages to destinations all over the world in a matter of minutes.
- Send messages at the convenience of the sender that can be read at the convenience of the recipient.
- Save messages as permanent records of business activity.
- Provide quick answers for questions.
- Transfer files from one organization to another or within organizations as an email attachment.
- Communicate nationally or worldwide at a minimum cost.
- Make appointments quickly and efficiently.

Although there are numerous advantages, there are disadvantages, with a few of the disadvantages being:

- Email is not the best medium for answering complicated questions.
- Security problems can result if an organization transfers sensitive information via email.
- Communication misunderstandings can occur if clear and precise language is not used.
- International communication can be misunderstood due to language differences.

focus on *Writing Effective Email*

As an administrative professional, you will write numerous emails each day to people both within and outside your organization. When writing an email, follow these guidelines:

- Use a subject line.
- Keep the message short.
- Use standard spelling and capitalization.
- Use standard typeface.
- Proofread carefully.

Individuals within organizations send billions of email messages each day.

Memorandums

Although email is the tool of choice for internal correspondence in most organizations, memorandums continue to have a place in the work world. For example, a memorandum is more appropriate in these situations:

- When the correspondence is relatively lengthy (longer than one-half page)
- When a signed document is needed

As an administrative professional, you may write a number of memorandums. You must pay careful attention to writing a clear, effective memorandum—one in which the reader receives all the necessary information. For example, if you are writing a memorandum to invite coworkers to a meeting, you must let them know the purpose of the meeting, the date and time of the meeting, how long the meeting is expected to last, who will be attending, what participants are expected to do to prepare for the meeting, what participants should bring to the meeting, and so on. Other elements of effective memorandums appear later in this chapter.

Letters

Although organizations communicate extensively with their customers, clients, and employees via telephones, memorandums, and emails, letters remain an important part of organizational communication. Letters are more formal and are the preferred method of communication when writing to current and prospective clients and customers. Letters provide formal documentation that you and your client or customer may want for future reference. This chapter provides the opportunity to improve your letter-writing skills.

Reports

In addition to email, memorandums, and letters, numerous reports are prepared in the workplace. These reports may be informal ones of two or three pages, or they may be formal reports containing a table of contents, body (with footnotes or endnotes), appendices, and references.

Organizational Skills

If you are to be successful in writing, you must develop your organizational skills. A large part of writing effectively is determining the readers' needs, gathering the appropriate information, drafting, editing, and preparing the final product. Additionally, you must be able to organize your time so you can produce the correspondence in a timely manner.

Determine the Goal or Purpose

Many times people start the writing process before they understand clearly what their purpose or goal is. As you begin, ask yourself these questions:

- What is my purpose in writing?
- What do I hope to accomplish?

Before you begin writing the first draft of the correspondence, write a purpose statement. This statement should be short—only a sentence or two. It should state clearly and concisely what you intend to accomplish with the correspondence. If writing the purpose statement is difficult for you, begin by merely putting down what you want to accomplish. For example, you might write these rather rambling thoughts when presented with the task of writing a letter to a colleague.

I must write a letter to Rhea Melrose in our Baton Rouge, Louisiana, office, inviting her to speak to administrative professionals in the Dallas office. We want her to speak sometime in January on a topic that is interesting to administrative professionals. Our group is interested in several areas, including conflict resolution, anger management, and time management. No one knows her, but we have heard she is a good speaker. We have also heard she speaks frequently on anger management and conflict resolution. We do not know if she speaks on time management.

Those thoughts result in this purpose statement:

The purpose of this letter is to persuade Rhea Melrose to speak to administrative professionals in the Dallas office on conflict resolution.

However, before writing the letter, you must be clear about the exact date or suggest two or three possible dates for the presentation. You also need to give Rhea information about who will attend the session.

Analyze the Reader/Audience

An important consideration in the writing process is determining the reader(s). The strongest communications focus on the readers and their needs. You can understand this more clearly if you think about your own personal communications. Do you write the same type of letter to your 80-year-old grandmother as you do to your 10-year-old son? The answer, of course, is no. These two people are quite different in what they need and understand.

Here are some basic questions to ask yourself about the reader/audience.

- What are the values and beliefs of the reader/audience?
- How does the reader typically communicate—with facts or with feelings?
- How old is the reader?
- What is the reader's level of education?
- What attitudes does the reader have? Will the reader be receptive or resistant to the message?
- Does the reader come from a different background? If so, what is that background?
- Is the reader local or international?
- What will the reader do with the document? Will the reader read only a portion of it? Study it carefully? Skim it?
- How much does the reader know about the topic?
- Will the reader resist the message? Will the reader have concerns about the message?
- What will the reader expect from the communication?

PROFESSIONAL AUDIENCE

If you are writing to a professional audience (engineers, physicists, lawyers, and so on), you can use technical vocabulary common in the particular field without defining the terms. Additionally, you can deal with the subject immediately, without spending time explaining the background of the material.

GENERAL AUDIENCE

If you are writing to a general audience, you need to use simple vocabulary and explain any concepts that may be confusing. Additionally, if a concept is complex, you may want to use examples. You should concentrate on what your communication will mean to the readers and what you expect the readers to do with the information.

INTERNATIONAL AUDIENCE

Words do not have the same meaning for all audiences. This statement is particularly true for international audiences. Consider these examples of business bloopers.

© Tetra Images / Jupiter Images

Is the reader local or international?

- In Belgium, General Motors used a tagline *Body by Fisher*. When translated into Flemish, it said *Corpse by Fisher*.

- An American maker of T-shirts in Miami printed shirts for the Spanish market promoting the Pope's visit. Instead of the desired *I saw the Pope*, the shirts proclaimed in Spanish, *I saw the potato*.

- Gerber introduced its line of baby food in African markets using the same packaging graphics as were used in the United States (a picture of a baby on the container). Gerber soon learned that African companies routinely put pictures on the label of what is actually inside the container.

When writing for an international audience, make certain that words do not offend or translate into incorrect meanings. Figure 7.1 lists a

number of general principles to keep in mind when writing for international audiences.

Gather the Appropriate Information

Once you know the purpose or goal you are trying to achieve with your correspondence, gather the information necessary to begin writing. In gathering the information, you may do the following:

- Peruse the organization's files on the subject if such files exist.

- Talk with your employer (if he or she has any background information).

- Research the topic through the Internet, periodicals, or books.

Organize the Content

Did you ever read a piece of correspondence and, once you finished, realize you did not understand what the writer was trying to convey? Why? There could be a number of reasons.

- The writer was verbose.

- The writer failed to clarify the message; the purpose was not discernible.

- The content jumped from one topic to another with no apparent pattern.

Brainstorm (a sudden clever idea; a group problem-solving technique) by yourself or with others if the project is a collaborative one. Brainstorming is a good way to begin to organize content. Write down everything that comes to mind. Then group your ideas. Determine what ideas are related and, thus, should be in the same paragraph. You might label the ideas as Idea 1, Idea 2, Idea 3, and so on. At this point, the ideas do not need to be in order of presentation. Your purpose is to get all similar ideas in the same paragraph. The next step is to determine which idea goes first, which goes second, and so on. For example, Idea 3 might be the first paragraph; Idea 1, the second; and Idea 2, the third.

Do not bury the purpose of the document in the middle of the correspondence. The basic

GENERAL PRINCIPLES FOR INTERNATIONAL CORRESPONDENCE

- Use the title of the individual with whom you are corresponding. Do not use first names.
- Use relatively formal language. In the United States, people pride themselves on informality, but people from most other countries do not. Informality often means disrespect.
- Be certain that you understand the order of first and last names. In many Asian countries, the last name appears first.
- Do not use expressions unique to the United States. Do not refer to events that are common only to the United States.
- Use the dictionary meanings of words; do not use slang.
- Be courteous; use *thank you* and *please* often.
- Be complimentary when appropriate but do not be excessive in your comments. Such outpourings may be seen as insincere.
- Avoid asking questions that can be answered with *yes* or *no*. For a number of other countries, these two words do not have the same meaning as they do in the United States.
- Ask questions tactfully.
- Do not use humor; it may be misunderstood.
- Respect all customs of the country (social, religious, and so on).
- Learn all you can about particular countries; read extensively.
- Translate correspondence into the native language of the country.
- Send business cards that are printed in the native language of the country.

FIGURE 7.1 General Principles for International Correspondence

organizational structure uses a three-pronged approach. The first part of the document conveys the purpose of the correspondence. The second part supports, informs, and/or convinces the reader. The last part states the desired results, the action, or a summary of the findings.

Draft the Correspondence

Your goal when drafting correspondence is to write down everything you want to say in rough-draft form. Do not spend time agonizing over each word and mark of punctuation. Get your ideas down.

Edit

Your next step is to edit the correspondence. Now that you have completed the draft document, you need to pay careful attention that the document is grammatically correct, the language is clear, the sentence structure is appropriate, the readability level matches the audience, and so on.

During the editing process, you are precise—you address the writing mechanics.

ENSURE EFFECTIVE PARAGRAPHS

Effective paragraphs possess unity, coherence, and parallel structure.

- Unity. A paragraph has unity when its sentences clarify or support the main idea. The sentence that contains the main idea of a paragraph is the **topic sentence**. For example, in this paragraph, the topic sentence is at the beginning. However, it may also be at the end of the paragraph. The point to remember is that the topic sentence helps the writer stay focused on the main idea of the paragraph.

- Coherence. A paragraph has coherence when its sentences relate to each other in content, grammatical construction, and choice of words. One method of achieving coherence is to repeat key words in a paragraph or to use certain words for emphasis. Consider the following use of repetitive words.

The anthropologist described life in a squalid district of New York by telling how much people know about each other—who is to be trusted and who is not, who is defiant of the law and who upholds it, who is competent and well informed, and who is inept and ignorant.

- Parallel. Parallel structure also helps you achieve coherence. When grammatically equivalent forms are used, **parallelism** exists. Consider the following illustration of nonparallel and parallel constructions.

    Nonparallel: The position is prestigious, challenging, and *also the money is not bad.*

    Parallel: The position offers prestige, challenge, and money.

USE APPROPRIATE SENTENCE STRUCTURE

Sentences should be simple but varied. Use a combination of sentence structures to keep your reader's attention. There is no formula for determining sentence length, but shorter sentences help keep the reader's attention. Generally, short sentences are also easier to understand. Consider this sentence.

Edit your documents for clarity, correct grammar, sentence structure, and readability level.

© BananaStock / Jupiter Images

January reports indicate that sales in the pharmaceutical market increased by more than 40 percent, which serves to support the proposed plan presented at last week's board meeting for 20 additional positions.

Did you get lost? The sentence has 32 words. A reader generally loses attention when a sentence is more than 20 words in length. You do not need to count the words in each sentence or limit sentences needlessly. However, you should be aware that readability is generally increased when sentences are short.

ELIMINATE PASSIVE VOICE

Passive voice is present when the subject of the sentence receives the action or is acted upon. It has three characteristics:

- A form of the verb *to be* (*is, am, are, was, were, be, been, being*)
- A past participle (a verb ending in *ed* or *en*)
- A prepositional phrase beginning with *by*

    Notice these examples of passive voice.

- The document was written by Mylien.
- The results of the meeting will be sent to you on Monday.

    In contrast, **active voice** is present when the subject performs the action. Read the sentences rewritten in active voice.

- Mylien wrote the document.
- You will receive the results of the meeting on Monday.

    Do you see the difference? The active voice is clearer and stronger than the passive voice. Is use of the passive voice wrong? No, it does have its uses. For example, the person performing the action may not be known. Additionally, sometimes the writer uses passive voice to obscure who was responsible for the action. For example, in the sentence below, the reader does not know who made the decision.

The decision was made to downsize the organization by 20 percent.

The writer intended to be ambiguous about the decision; the writer did not want the reader to know who made the decision. Although the writer can use passive voice intentionally, if it is overused, it can result in wordy, dull writing. Use passive voice when necessary, but do not overuse it.

DETERMINE READABILITY LEVEL

Readability is defined as the degree of difficulty of the message. These items contribute to greater reading difficulty:

- Long sentences
- Words with several syllables
- Technical terms

Readability formulas, such as the Gunning Fog Index and the Flesch-Kincaid Index, provide readability indices. The higher the readability index, the less readable the message. As a rule, the writer should achieve a readability index of between seventh- and eleventh-grade levels for the average business reader. However, there are exceptions. If you are writing a highly technical report for an expert audience, you may write at the fourteenth or higher grade level. Writers must understand the background and educational level of their audience.

You can check the readability level of your document by activating the software writing aid on your computer. You also can obtain word counts, average words per sentence, sentences per paragraph, characters per word, and passive sentences from this software. Figure 7.2 provides readability statistics.

Prepare the Final Correspondence

Your next step is to prepare the final correspondence. In doing so, you should do the following:

- Check to be certain that the format is appropriate. For example, if it is a letter, did you use an acceptable letter style? If it is a report, is your document formatted correctly? Have you sized your headings appropriately? Have you used boldface and italics to emphasize important points and headings? Do the type sizes and font styles provide for easy readability?

- Run the grammar and spelling feature of your software to help you locate errors.

- Proofread the document on the screen before you print it. Figure 7.3 lists several proofreading tips.

- Print a copy and proofread again.

Evaluate—Process and Time Usage

When you are new at the writing process, take some time at the end of each project to analyze how you spent your time. Were you able to produce the document in a reasonable amount of time? Did you use good organizational skills? Were you able to gather the appropriate information in a reasonable time period? Did you effectively organize the content before beginning to write? Did you use software aids to assist you in editing your writing? What are your

Readability Statistics	
Counts	
Words	786
Characters	4251
Paragraphs	106
Sentences	41
Averages	
Sentences per Paragraph	1.4
Words per Sentence	10.3
Characters per Word	4.7
Readability	
Passive Sentences	9%
Flesch Reading Ease	67.2
Flesch-Kincaid Grade Level	8.2
	OK

FIGURE 7.2 Readability Statistics

writing weaknesses? How can you correct these weaknesses?

Characteristics of Effective Correspondence

Certain characteristics of effective correspondence are common to letters, emails, memorandums, and reports. As you write, you must pay careful attention to each of the elements given here.

Complete

Correspondence is complete when it gives the reader all the information he or she needs to accomplish the results the writer intended. To help you achieve completeness, ask the *W questions:*

- *Why* is the correspondence being written?
- *What* is the goal of the correspondence? What do I hope to accomplish?

- *What* information is needed before writing the correspondence?
- *Who* needs to receive the correspondence?
- *What* information needs to be included in the correspondence?

Refer to Figure 7.4 for examples of ineffective writing when *W* questions were not asked and corresponding examples of effective writing when *W* questions were asked.

Clear

After reading a message, the reader should be able to determine (without a doubt) the purpose of the correspondence. Clear messages reflect clear thinking. Writing clearly requires good organization and simple expression. Each sentence should have one thought; each paragraph, one purpose. Business correspondence is not the place to impress a person with your vocabulary. Your aim is to get your purpose across in a

---

PROOFREADING TIPS

- Proofread your document on the screen before you print it. Scroll to the beginning of the document, and use the top of the screen as a guide for your eyes in reading each line.
- Proofread a document in three steps:
  - General appearance and format
  - Spelling and keyboarding errors
  - Punctuation, word usage, and content
- Read from right to left for spelling and keyboarding errors.
- Use a spell checker.
- If possible, do not proofread a document right after keying it; let the document sit while you perform another task.
- Pay attention to dates. Do not assume they are correct. For example, check to determine that Thursday, November 15, is actually a Thursday. Check the spelling of months; check the correctness of the year.
- Do not overlook proofreading the date, subject, enclosure notation, and names and addresses of the recipients.
- Use the thesaurus if you are not certain a word is appropriate.
- Watch closely for omissions of *-ed*, *-ing*, or *-s* at the ends of words.
- If punctuation causes you problems, check a grammatical source after you have completed all other proofreading.
- Be consistent in the use of commas.
- Be consistent in the use of capital letters.
- Check numerals.
- Be consistent in format.
- Keep a current reference manual at your desk to look up grammar or punctuation rules you question.

FIGURE 7.3 Proofreading Tips

simple, concise manner. If a short, easily under-stood word is available, use it. Your words should *express* rather than *impress*.

Accurate

Get the facts before you start to write. Check your information carefully. If you are quoting prices, be certain you have the correct price list. If you are presenting dates, confirm them.

When you are writing, keep your biases out of the correspondence as much as possible. Your task is to write objectively. Do not slant the in-formation or overstate its significance. Deal with the facts—simply and accurately.

Prompt

A conscientious business correspondent is prompt. Prompt answers to messages say to readers that the writer or organization cares about them. Con-versely, late messages often give the following impressions:

- The writer or organization is indifferent to the needs of the readers.
- The writer is grossly inefficient.

The result in either instance is a negative message. The basic promptness rule is this:

- Reply to email on the same day of receipt.
- Reply to memorandums within one day.
- Reply to letters within three to five days.
- Respond to reports within the timeline estab-lished by the cover letter or memorandum.

Concise

Conciseness in writing means expressing the necessary information in as few words as possi-ble. Say what you need to say without cluttering your communication with irrelevant information or needless words. As a checklist for conciseness, ask yourself these questions.

- Are my sentences short?
- Are my paragraphs short?
- Have I used simple, easy-to-understand words?
- Have I used bullets or numbered lists when-ever possible?
- Have I avoided unnecessary repetition?
- Have I eliminated excessive information?
- Have I avoided clichés?

Figure 7.5 lists several clichés to avoid.

Courteous

Courteousness in correspondence means using good human relations skills as you write. Treat the reader with respect. Demonstrate that you

---

ASKING THE *W* QUESTIONS

Notice the following examples of ineffective writing when the *W* questions were not asked and the corresponding examples of effective writing when the *W* questions were asked.

Ineffective	Effective
Your recent order will be mailed soon. (WHEN?)	Your order of November 15 will be mailed on November 21.
The seminar will be on November 3. (WHERE and WHAT kind of conference?)	The letter-writing seminar will be held in the Green Room at 2 p.m., November 3.
The planning meeting was canceled. (WHAT planning meeting and WHY was it canceled?)	The planning meeting scheduled for November 3 at 2 p.m. has been canceled due to a conflict with the letter-writing seminar scheduled at the same time. The planning meeting has been rescheduled for November 15 at 2 p.m. in the Executive Conference Room.

FIGURE 7.4 Asking the *W* Questions

AVOID CLICHÉS

You have probably read such phrases as *according to our records*, *at your earliest convenience*, and *under separate cover*. These phrases are clichés; they are overused. Notice the following clichés and the improved wording.

Cliché	According to our files…
Improved	Our files indicate…
Cliché	At the present time…
Improved	Now…
Cliché	In view of the fact that…
Improved	Now…
Cliché	May I take the liberty…
Improved	Omit the phrase and make your statement.
Cliché	Your kind letter…
Improved	Omit kind—people, not correspondence, are kind.
Cliché	May I request a copy.
Improved	Please send me a copy.

FIGURE 7.5 Avoid Clichés

care about the reader as you write. Keep in mind that writing is similar to talking. When talking with people face-to-face, courtesy and consideration are necessary in order to develop and maintain goodwill. The same or perhaps even greater concern must be evident in written correspondence since only the written word conveys the message; a smile or a friendly gesture cannot be observed.

Do not show your anger in a communication. You may be extremely unhappy about a situation, but showing your anger merely compounds the problem. Angry words make angry readers. Both parties may end up yelling at each other through the written word, accomplishing little. Remember, anger and courtesy are not logical partners.

Courtesy also means being considerate. If a person is asking you something, respond. If you are unable to give a positive response, explain why. Explanations let others know you are sincere.

Positive

People hear the word *yes* easier than the word *no*. Certainly, you will not always be able to say yes to someone or something. However, if you use a positive tone when saying no, the reader will respond in a more favorable manner. You set a positive tone by the words you choose and the way you use them. Some words and phrases possess positive qualities, whereas others possess negative qualities. Consider the following negative expressions and their positive equivalents.

Negative
Sorry
Whenever possible
Displeasure
Unsatisfactory
You failed to let us know.
You neglected to send your check.
I hate to inform you that your order has not been shipped.
The difficulties are …
Do not throw trash on the grounds.

Positive
Glad
Immediately
Pleasure
Satisfactory
Please let us know.
Please send your check.
Your order will be shipped on October 11.
To help you avoid further problems …
Please put your trash in the receptacles.

Planning and Writing Guidelines

You must adhere to a number of guidelines when writing emails, memorandums, letters, and reports. These guidelines include determining the appropriate format, establishing the basic

Angry words make angry readers.

purpose, conducting research (if necessary), and observing appropriate ethics and etiquette.

Email

Due to its speed and ease of use, email is a major form of communication for organizations and individuals today. Workers spend hours at their place of employment sending and receiving emails. Additionally, people may spend a considerable amount of time at home sending emails to family and friends. In fact, people are so obsessed with email reaching the recipient quickly that they now use a derivation of email called **instant messaging (IM)**. If a person's computer is turned on, a message flashes on the screen telling the person that he or she has an IM. In other words, IM lets people know immediately that an email is waiting for them; they do not have to check the email screen to determine whether they have received messages.

Since email is such an important communication tool, you must adhere to certain guidelines, etiquette, and ethics as you use it.

GUIDELINES

The basic characteristics of effective correspondence presented earlier in this chapter are applicable to email as well:

- Completeness
- Clarity
- Accurateness
- Promptness
- Conciseness
- Courteousness
- Positivism

Several general guidelines, as well as guidelines for etiquette and ethics, apply to email specifically.

- Be appropriately formal when writing email. The rule of thumb is to be almost as formal as you are in standard memorandums. Notice the two messages here. One message is too informal, while the other message is appropriately formal.

Too Informal

Ramon, we need to have a meeting soon—can you arrange? I'm free next mon. thks.

Tony

Appropriate

Ramon,

We need to meet soon to discuss our division's projected budget for the next six months. Are you available on Tuesday, December 15, from 9 a.m. until 11 a.m.? If so, let me know by this afternoon. We can meet in my office.

Tony

- Avoid using emoticons (faces produced by the Internet counterculture in answer to email being devoid of body language). Here are a few emoticons.

  <G>   I'm grinning as I write this sentence.

  <LOL>   I'm laughing out loud.

  ☺   Denotes a smile

  ;-)   Denotes a wink

  :")   Embarrassed

  :-!   Foot in mouth

  X-(Mad

- Use the subject line provided on the email form. This line should be concise yet give enough information so the receiver knows the purpose of the message at a glance.

- Think through the purpose of your email before you begin writing.

- Organize the message. Email should not be longer than one screen. If you are writing a memo longer than one screen, send a traditional hard-copy memorandum. People become frustrated when they must scroll from screen to screen and then scroll back to reread something.

- Edit and proofread carefully. Check your spelling. Do not send an email that contains inaccuracies or incorrect grammar. Most email programs allow for checking spelling and grammar. Set the preferences so spelling and grammar are checked.

- Use complete sentences.

- Capitalize and punctuate properly.

- Do not run sentences together.

- Insert a blank line after each paragraph.

- Include your name and title (if appropriate) when replying to an email. Often you can add a signature in your preferences, which will automatically include this information at the end of every email you send.

- Assume that any message you send is permanent.

- Do not double-space your entire message; it takes up too much space and makes the message more difficult to read.

- Be wary of humor or sarcasm. Electronic communication is devoid of body language; thus, the slightest hint of sarcasm could be badly misinterpreted.

- Avoid using all uppercase or all lowercase letters.

Figure 7.6 demonstrates an appropriate format for email.

ETIQUETTE

Use appropriate etiquette when sending email.

- Do not use different types of fonts, colors, clip art, and other graphics in email. Such an approach merely clutters your message and takes longer to send and receive, particularly if you include numerous graphics.

- Do not key the message in all uppercase letters. You may emphasize a word or phrase in all capital letters, but use the Caps Lock button sparingly.

- Avoid sending messages when you are angry. Give yourself time to cool down and think about the situation before you send or reply to an email in anger. Take a walk around the office, drink a cup of hot tea to soothe your nerves, or wait 24 hours to respond. In some cases, you may want to make a telephone call or have a personal conversation with the person. You have a more difficult time being angry when you see the person face-to-face or when you hear the person's voice.

- Answer email promptly. The general rule is to read and respond to email once or twice a day (depending on volume).

- Do not send large attached files unless you know the person can receive them. When sending an attachment, ask the receiver to acknowledge receipt.

ETHICS

Ethical behavior is important. Ethics in regard to email means you do not misuse the organization's email system.

- Do not send personal email from your office computer.

- When people send you inappropriate email, let them know politely that you cannot receive it. You might say, "I would love to hear from you, but please send any personal email to my home. I cannot receive it at the office."

- Do not use email to berate or reprimand an employee. Do not use email to terminate someone's employment.

- Do not use email to send information that might involve legal action.

- Remember that even if you delete email, it may not actually be deleted. Some organizations make backup tapes of all electronic files. Think carefully before putting something on email.

- Do not respond to unsolicited email.

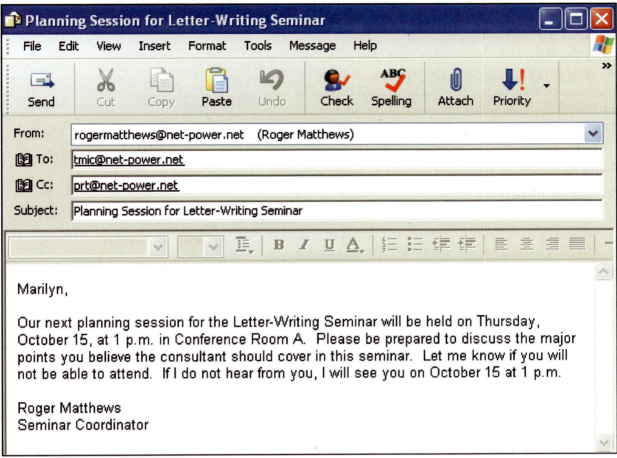

FIGURE 7.6 Email Format

- Do not forward junk mail or chain letters to a mailing list. This practice is **spamming**, and some organizations have email policies that result in loss of computer privileges for individuals who engage in spamming. Many email providers allow users to report spam and have it blocked from the user's email address.

- Do not forward an email unless you know the message is true. For example, you may think you are being helpful forwarding a message about a computer virus. However, when you receive ten email messages concerning misinformation about viruses, you understand the importance of being certain that an email is true before forwarding it.

- Do not include credit card numbers in email messages. It is possible to intercept email in transit; thus, an unscrupulous individual can steal and use someone else's credit card number.

Memorandums

Although email messages have become the preferred vehicle for communicating within the company and short messages sent outside the company, at times, a memorandum is more appropriate. For example, when the message is longer than one computer screen or a hard copy with a signature is necessary, a memorandum is the better choice.

The characteristics of effective correspondence hold true for memorandums also. Memorandums must be complete, clear, accurate, prompt, concise, courteous, and positive. In style, they are slightly more formal than email, but less formal than letters. A memorandum form contains *To, From, Date*, and *Subject* lines. The word *memorandum* or an organizational name or logo may also be included. A copy notation, indicated by the letter *c*, may follow the body of the memorandum.

General guidelines for writing memorandums include the following:

- Use the first name (or initials) and last name of the individual(s) to whom you are sending the memo.
- Use the job title of the individual if company policy dictates doing so; many organizations do not use titles in memorandums.
- Do not use *Ms.* or *Mr.*
- If you are sending a memorandum to more than one individual, list the names in alphabetical order or by hierarchical order within the company.
- List *c* recipients alphabetically or hierarchically.
- If you are addressing a memo to ten or more people, use a generic classification, such as *Strategic Planning Team*.
- If the memorandum is more than one page, key the additional pages on plain paper. Include an appropriate header on additional pages.

Figure 7.7 presents an appropriate format for a memorandum.

Letters

Letters represent the company to the public—customers, clients, and prospective customers and clients. A well-written letter can win friends and customers. Conversely, a poorly written letter can lose customers and make enemies of prospective customers.

Your task as an administrative professional is to assist your employer with writing effective letters. The characteristics of effective correspondence outlined in the sections on email and

memorandums hold true for letters as well. Letters must be:

- Complete
- Clear
- Accurate
- Prompt
- Concise
- Courteous
- Positive

DETERMINE THE BASIC PURPOSE
Before you begin to write a letter, you must determine the basic purpose for writing. Generally, letters fall into six types:

- Requesting information or seeking a routine action
- Providing information
- Acknowledging information
- Conveying negative information
- Demanding action
- Persuading

The first three types of letters (requesting information, providing information, and acknowledging information) are letters in which the reader's reaction to the message will be favorable or neutral. The next two types of letters (conveying negative information and demanding action) are letters in which the reader's reaction may be unfavorable. Use the **direct approach** in the first three types of letters and the **indirect approach** in the others.

As you write, you want to keep the reader uppermost in your mind and attempt to put yourself in the place of the reader. The approach, called the *you approach*, demands empathy (identification with and understanding of another's situation, feelings, and motives) on the part of the writer. You must place yourself in the reader's shoes and try to understand the situation from the reader's perspective. If you are trying to sell a product or a service, you must look at the benefits it will offer to the reader. If you are trying to persuade someone to speak at a conference, you must highlight the contributions

Begin at 2"
Default side margins 1"

TO: Madelyn Ice
            Liam Nelson
            Rico Osbourne

FROM: Ruth Shank

DATE: November 15, 200-

SUBJECT: Budget Session

Please be prepared to discuss your budget actuals for the past three months and any changes on your proposed budget (with justification) for the next six months. The budget session will be held in my office on November 23, 200-, from 1 p.m. to 3 p.m.

c   Darius Hamilton
       Miguel Quinones

FIGURE 7.7 Memorandum Format

the proposed speaker can make—his or her unique gifts and skills. When carrying out the *you approach*, adhere to two words of caution: Be sincere. Your goal is not to flatter the reader, but to see the situation from the reader's point of view. The *you approach* is important when writing all types of letters; however, it is essential in the persuasive approach, which is discussed below.

Direct Approach.   Direct correspondence begins with the reason for the correspondence. If you are making a request or an inquiry, state it. Continue with whatever explanation is necessary so the reader will understand the message. Close the letter with a courteous thank you for action taken or with a request for action by a specific time.

Figure 7.8 is an illustration of a letter requesting information in which the direct approach is used. Notice the format of the letter is block style with open punctuation. The document examples in this chapter use a format that takes advantage of *Microsoft Office Word 2007* default settings. They vary slightly from traditional document formats. Refer to the Reference Guide in this textbook to see traditional and new document formats.

Indirect Approach.   When writing indirect correspondence, use this format:

- Begin with an opening statement that is pleasant but neutral.
- Review the circumstances and give the negative information.
- Close the correspondence on a pleasant and positive note.

Figure 7.9 is an illustration of a letter using the indirect approach. Notice the format of the letter is modified block style with blocked paragraphs and mixed punctuation.

Persuasive Approach.   Use the **persuasive approach** when you want to convince someone to do something or you want to change an indifferent or negative reader's reaction. Your goal is to turn a negative or indifferent attitude into a

positive one. When writing a persuasive letter, use the following approach:

- Get the reader's attention quickly; open with the you approach.
- Continue by creating interest and desire.
- Close by asking for the desired action.

Figure 7.10 illustrates the persuasive approach.

EDIT, PROOFREAD, AND FORMAT

Once you have written a letter, you are responsible for editing and proofreading the document. The grammar and spelling software on your computer can aid you in this job. However, the software will not catch all errors, and certain errors noted by the software may not in fact be errors. Therefore, you must have a good command of grammar and proofread carefully. You also might ask someone else to proofread the document. Remember to follow standard formats when keying a letter.

Professional Pointers

In written communication, the message is affected by the way it is presented. As you strive to prepare professional messages, keep these points in mind:

- Be critical of the documents you prepare. Make certain your work is accurate and has a professional appearance.

- Use reference guides for punctuation, grammar, and word usage.

- Continually strive to improve your writing skills. Take a writing seminar if possible.

- Develop a manual of preferred document styles and formats for your office if one does not exist.

- Use technology to create interesting and professionally prepared documents. Today's readers are accustomed to documents that are visually appealing and that include graphics.

Begin at 2" or center vertically

Default side margins 1"

United Pharmaceuticals

1211 East Eighth Street
Fort Worth, TX 76102-5201
817-555-0122

October 9, 200-

Dr. Leonard Montgomery
3418 Melrose Street
Dallas, TX 75201-9702

Dear Dr. Montgomery

Thank you for talking with me last Monday concerning our new cancer drug. At your request, I am enclosing a copy of the research studies.

You will notice that United Pharmaceuticals conducted these studies over a five-year period, using a sample group of 1,500 people. The results were excellent, and we are pleased to offer a drug that has such potential for significantly dropping the cancer mortality rate.

I will call your administrative assistant within the next few days to schedule a follow-up meeting after you have had a chance to review the studies. I look forward to discussing any questions you may have.

Sincerely

Katalina Komanie

Katalina Komanie
Sales Representative

lc

Enclosure

FIGURE 7.8 Letter Using the Direct Approach

United Pharmaceuticals

1211 East Eighth Street
Fort Worth, TX 76102-5201
817-555-0122

November 11, 200-

Ms. Grace Edwardson
2345 Shady Bend Lane
Dallas, TX 75209-3456

Dear Grace:

Thank you for asking me to speak at your conference in December. I greatly enjoy my association with your group; you truly provide an excellent growth opportunity for managers.

The demands on my time for the next several months are extremely heavy. In addition to a new planning process that I must implement, we have recently employed two new managers who are looking to me for assistance in learning their jobs. As you might expect, I am extremely busy. I must say no to your request as the time. However, if you need a speaker in the future, please contact me again. I always enjoy talking with your group.

Best wishes for success with the conference.

Sincerely,

Sandra L. Portales

Sandra L. Portales
Executive Vice President

lc

FIGURE 7.9 Letter Using the Indirect Approach

1211 East Eighth Street
Fort Worth, TX 76102-5201
817-555-0122

December 8, 200-

Dr. Consuelo Soto
5121 Valley View
Dallas, TX 75301-7802

Dear Dr. Soto

Your expertise is needed! Our administrative professionals need your assistance in developing their letter-writing skills. Some of them have several years of writing experience, yet they have not perfected their skills to the level needed. Others are relatively new employees and have had little experience writing letters.

Your work with our employees in the past helped tremendously. They not only learned from your presentation but also enjoyed the experience. We want to offer the workshop during February. Our preferred dates are February 5-6 or February 23-24.

I will call your office next week to talk with your further. I am hopeful that your answer to our request will be an affirmative one. We know you can make a difference in the quality of letters sent out by our company.

Sincerely

Wanda Foster

Wanda Foster
Human Resources Manager

dr

FIGURE 7.10 Letter Using the Persuasive Approach

Reports

The administrative professional's role in preparing reports varies. You may have the responsibility of keying the report, producing the final copies, and distributing the report to the appropriate individuals. Or you may assist with the creation of visuals for the report (charts, graphs, and so on), do research, and draft some or all portions of the report.

Technology has opened up new opportunities for administrative professionals, one possibility being virtual assistants (work-at-home professionals who provide numerous business support services, including making appointments, laying out reports, organizing files, and so on). If you are an administrative professional who plans to set up your own business and work independently from a home office, you may find yourself writing a business plan, a plan that provides the strategic direction for your company's ongoing activities. Such a plan describes what you want to do, how you want to get there, and how you plan to achieve your goals. As a virtual assistant, you also may be responsible for formatting and keying a client's business plan or even assisting the client in writing the plan.

PLANNING STEPS

Whether you are writing a basic report or a business plan, the planning steps should include the following:

- Determine the purpose of the report.
- Analyze the audience who will receive the report.
- Prepare a summary of what should be included in the report.
- Gather information for the report.
- Prepare an outline of the report.
- Draft the report.
- Prepare any necessary graphics, charts, and tables.
- Read and edit the report.

- Prepare the executive summary.
- Print and distribute the report.

A business plan includes these unique elements:

- Strategic directions
- Vision and mission
- Potential investors (if appropriate)
- Target audience
- Opportunities, market strategy, and business strategy
- Proposed organization and operations, management structure, and core competencies
- Financial projections

Most reports involve some type of research. This research may be **primary research**—collecting original data through surveys, observations, or experiments. The research also may be **secondary research**—data or material that other people have discovered and reported via the Internet, books, periodicals, and various other publications. In addition, the research may be a combination of both primary and secondary.

PRIMARY RESEARCH

If you are conducting primary research, you must decide how you are going to gather the information. You may decide to take these steps:

- Observe situations and individuals.
- Survey or interview groups of individuals.
- Perform an experiment.

Observational research involves collecting data by observing events or actions. Survey research involves collecting data through some type of survey or interview. An interview is usually done in person; however, it may be done over the telephone. Sometimes **focus groups** (people brought together to talk with an interviewer about their opinions of certain events or issues) are used. Acceptable methods of administering surveys include mailing them or giving them in person. For example, you may decide to assemble several people, pass out a survey, and ask them to complete it immediately. Generally, there is a much better **response rate** (the number of people responding to a survey or questionnaire) on surveys administered in person than those done by mail.

Scientific researchers have used experimental research for years; however, business researchers are now using it more and more. Such research may involve selecting two or more sample groups and exposing them to certain treatments. For example, a business may decide to test a marketing strategy before implementing a marketing campaign. Researchers select experimental groups and implement the marketing strategy. Based on the outcome of the research, the business proceeds with the marketing strategy, modifies it, or selects another one.

SECONDARY RESEARCH

Secondary research involves using printed information available from sources such as books, periodicals, and the Web. In the not-too-distant past (1992 or so), research was associated with libraries and librarians helping you find what you needed. You may still go to a brick-and-mortar library to do research. Certainly, these libraries have advantages:

- Libraries carry a huge collection of materials that may offer considerable depth in the subject matter you are interested in researching.
- Libraries have materials that may not be on the Web, including historical, highly specialized, and often quite rare materials.
- Libraries employ librarians to assist you in finding what you need. These people have degrees in Library Science or another equivalent field and can assist you in finding information in their own libraries as well as libraries in other U.S. or world cities.

Visiting Online Libraries.   Most libraries have some type of presence on the Web; it may include only their location, hours, and other general information. However, many libraries provide much more information:

- You can search for everything published by a particular author. This type of search is beneficial when you find an article on the Web and want to verify the credentials of the author.
- You can access special collections of the library.
- You can search for documents by subject; libraries offer a more sophisticated subject index than is available on the Web.
- You can verify author names, book titles, publishers, and dates of publication.
- You can borrow books, order photocopies of articles, and make copies from home if the library offers this service.
- You can access a virtual librarian at the **Library of Congress** (U.S. national library that carries more than 17 million books, plus over 100 million other items, such as maps and manuscripts). A link to the Library of Congress Website is provided on the Website for this textbook.

Clarifying Your Web Search.   One of the most difficult parts of searching the Web for information is clarifying your search so you can get information you need. If you do not clarify your search sufficiently, you may find yourself looking

career tip

Writing Ethics

- Do not take credit for something that you did not write.
- Do not make negative comments about people or events.
- Do use positive or neutral statements when writing.
- Use appropriate language; do not use clichés.
- When writing to an international audience, recognize and respect the culture.

© ImageSource / Jupiter Images

Give credit for information you receive from printed sources.

at hundreds of articles that do not match what you need. Ask yourself these questions to assist you in clarifying your search:

- Is the Web the best place to look? If you know very little about a topic and believe you are going to need help in narrowing the field to something that fits your needs, you may decide that the library is the best place for you to do your research. There you can get the help of professionals in the field.

- What information do I want? For example, assume you are interested in finding information on ethics. Do you want a history of ethics in the United States? Do you want a history that goes back to early philosophers? Are you interested in business ethics? Are you interested in societal ethics? In other words, you need to narrow your search so you can obtain information that is helpful for the project in which you are engaged.

- When keying in your search words, enter the most clarifying word first.

- Click *Help* or *Search Tips* on the search engine to learn more about what the search engine can do.

Using Web Search Engines.   Several search engines are available. Google™ has an extremely large database of Web pages, including many types of Web documents. For example, PDFs, *Word, Excel,* and *PowerPoint* files are all available on Google. Two other Web search engines that have a large database include Ask.com™ and Yahoo!® Search. The Web addresses for these search engines are provided on the Links section of the Website for this textbook.

Evaluating the Information.   Since anyone can place information on the Web, you must determine the credibility of the company or individual hosting the information and the currentness of the data. Ask yourself these questions:

- How do I know if the information is reliable? First, look for current information unless you are interested in the history of a topic. Check the dates given on the Websites. Obsolete information may be worthless to you, even if it does have some historical value.

- What organization or person is hosting the information? Is that person or company credible?

If you are looking for company information, the company itself is a good resource. Check the date on the Website. Is it current? If you have information written by a particular individual, try to find out something about that individual. Is the person representing a respected organization? Has the person written in the field previously? What education does the person have? The Website may provide some information about the author. If not, you can do a search of the author's name on the Web or visit the library for credentials on the individual.

Handling Copyrighted Information.   Some individuals assume they do not need to credit the source of Web information. This is not true! Just as you must credit the source when quoting information from a textbook or periodical, you also must give credit when you are using a reference you found on the Web. In addition, you cannot print multiple copies of a copyrighted work on the Web and send it to other people. You can probably print one copy as long as it is for your own personal, noncommercial use. Some Websites spell out their copyright policies; others do not. Some Websites invite you to distribute freely the information on the site. However, the general rule is to give credit for all information. If no author is listed, which is often the case, list the name of the article or the name of the Website and the date you accessed it. If an author is given, list the author's name first, followed by the title of the article and the name of the Website. Then give the exact Website address where the material was accessed and the date the material was accessed.

Jennifer Cheeseman Day, "National Population Projections," U.S. Census Bureau, http://www.census.gov/population/www/pop-profile/natproj.html (accessed March 15, 2007).

REPORT PARTS

An informal report may have only one or two parts—the body and/or an executive summary. Formal reports and business plans contain several parts.

Formal reports usually contain the parts listed below. You can eliminate certain parts, such as the list of tables and illustrations, documentation, bibliography, and appendix, if the report is relatively short and you have done no external research. The following is a list of parts for formal reports:

- Executive Summary
- Title Page
- Table of Contents
- List of Tables and Illustrations
- Body
- Documentation (endnotes/footnotes)
- Bibliography or Reference Section
- Appendix

Executive Summary.   The **executive summary** is a one- or two-page summary of the document. It is written for the busy executive who:

- Wishes to preview the report to determine whether he or she wants to read a portion in its entirety.
- Does not need a detailed understanding of all aspects of the report, but does need to know the background, major findings, and recommendations.

The executive summary provides the following information:

- Background—establishes why the report was written; identifies the problem or issues
- Major findings—explains what was discovered
- Recommendations

Title Page.   The title page contains the title of the report; the writer's name, title, and department or division; and the date the report is submitted. Refer to the Reference Guide in this textbook for an example format for a report title page.

Table of Contents.   The table of contents lists each major section of the report and the page number of the first page of each section. A table of contents is not required; however, when a report is long, the table of contents helps the reader find particular parts of the report. Refer to the Reference Guide in this textbook for an example format for a report table of contents.

List of Tables and Illustrations.   If a report contains numerous tables and illustrations, it is appropriate to list each title with the respective page number. This page helps the reader quickly locate and scan the data presented.

BODY OF REPORT

The body of a report should present information in a logical order. For example, a report dealing with a business problem or issue might be organized into the following sections:

- Introduction
- Research
- Findings
- Conclusions and Recommendations

Begin the body of a report with the report title. Use the Title style of your word processing program if one is available. If not, use a font style and size such as Arial, 16 point for the report title. So the reader may easily distinguish between sections of the report, use headings throughout the report body. Your word processing software may have heading styles that you can use for this purpose. If heading styles are not available, use the same font as for the report body but in a larger size or choose a compatible style. Arial and Times New Roman fonts are compatible, so you might use Arial for headings and Times New Roman for the body. Be consistent throughout the report with whatever heading styles you choose. If the report is long, you may use two or three levels of headings to organize information.

Lists, used effectively in a report, call attention to important information and contribute positively to the readability level of the report. Software packages contain a variety of bullet styles. Choose an appropriate bullet style, and use it consistently throughout the report.

If you are not binding a report, side margins of 1 inch are acceptable. However, if you intend to bind the report (and most reports of more than five pages should be bound), change the left margin to at least 1.5 inches. Before making the final decision on the left margin, determine what type of binding you will use and the extra space it requires. Use a top margin of 2 inches on the Table of Contents page, the first page of the body, and the first page of a section such as References. Use a bottom margin of 1 inch for all pages.

Most pages of a report should be numbered. Use the header and footer options of your word processing software to insert the page numbers. The title page comes first and does not have a page number. If the report has an executive summary, it follows the title page and is numbered with a lowercase Roman numeral (ii). The table of contents comes next and has a lowercase Roman numeral (ii or iii) as a page number. The first page of the body of the report does not have a page number. The remaining pages of the body are numbered in the upper-right corner. If the report has a References page, it comes at the end and is also numbered in the upper right corner of the page. Figure 7.11 shows the first page of an unbound report. Examples of other report pages are shown in the Reference Guide.

Tables and graphics can sometimes be used in reports to convey information more effectively than text in a paragraph. For example, a table could be used to list sales figures by region by year. A pie chart could be used to show the sales contributed by one sales region. Use consistent formatting for all tables within a report. Introduce the table or chart in the paragraph above where it is placed in the report (or on the page before if the graphic requires a full page). Include titles and other labels in tables and charts so that the data is easy to understand. Figure 7.12 shows a pie chart in a report.

Documentation.   Documentation is the process of giving credit to the sources used in a report. If you quote a source directly, use quotation marks around the quote within the body of the report. If you paraphrase a source, no quotes are

Verbal Presentations

Verbal presentations are often used in the workplace to convey information to a group of people. These presentations may be informal ones to a small group or formal ones to a large group. Individuals also may have occasion to speak at professional organization or civic group meetings.

Presenting is challenging for some people. For most people, becoming an effective presenter is a learned skill. This skill is so important to individuals and organizations that some businesses develop training to help people become effective verbal presenters. Like all skill development, one must practice presentation skills to improve them.

Plan the Presentation

Preparing a good presentation takes time and may require research or development of visual aids or handouts. The presenter may also need to learn about the audience and the setting for the presentation. Beginning preparation three weeks before the presentation is not too soon.

Determine the Purpose

The first step in planning a presentation is to define clearly the purpose of the presentation. Ask these questions to begin planning a presentation:

- Why am I giving this presentation?
- What do I want the audience to know as a result of my presentation?
- What, if anything, do I want the audience to do as a result of my presentation?

Consider the Audience

Consider the characteristics of the people who will hear the presentation. Try to determine areas of common interest to which you can relate points of information. For example, if your audience is a group of administrative professionals, you know some of their interests. You can use anecdotes or stories that have meaning for them. If you are speaking to a group of colleagues from your workplace, again you know some of their interests. You can tailor your message to meet their needs. If you are speaking to a general audience, keep these questions in mind as you begin to plan your remarks.

- What are the ages and genders of the people who will be in the audience?
- What is the education level attained by the audience members? Are they high school graduates, college graduates, or a mixture of both?
- What knowledge does the audience have about the subject of the presentation?

FIGURE 7.11 Unbound Report, Page 1

2

Sales for the Dallas region and the Columbus region increased 12 percent from last year. Sales from the Seattle region were down significantly—20 percent below last year. The pie chart below shows the percent of sales contributed by each region.

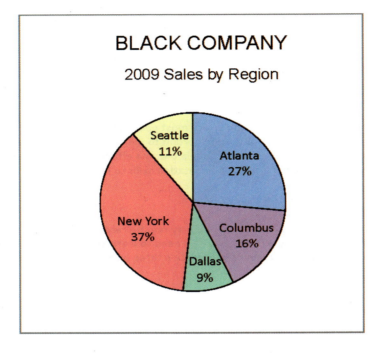

BLACK COMPANY

2009 Sales by Region

Seattle 11%
Atlanta 27%
New York 37%
Columbus 16%
Dallas 9%

FIGURE 7.12 Report with Pie Chart

necessary but you should credit the source. Documentation may follow several different styles using footnotes or internal citations.

Footnotes are the traditional method of documentation. As the name suggests, you place a footnote at the bottom of the page that cites the information. Your word processing software may allow you to easily add the superscript number within the body of the report and the footnote at the bottom of the page. Footnotes for print items should include the name of the author(s), title of the work, publication city,

publishing company, date, and page number of the quote. The following example shows a footnote that references a quote from a book.

[1]Gary McClain and Deborah S. Romaine, *The Everything Managing People Book* (Massachusetts: Adams Media Corporation, 2002), p. 85.

On Web sources, many articles or pages do not give an author, merely a title. Some articles give only a company name, with no title or author name. When documenting your research, use whatever information is available. The example footnote below includes an author name, article name, Website name, Web address, and access date.

[1]Jennifer Cheeseman Day, "National Population Projections," U.S. Census Bureau, http://www. census.gov/population/www/pop-profile/ natproj.html (accessed March 15, 2007).

Another method of referring to a source of information within the text of a document is to use an internal citation. This citation gives the last name of the author (or authors) and the date of publication in parentheses in the sentence. Page numbers can also be used if needed for clarity. If the author's name is mentioned in the sentence, only the year and possibly page numbers should be shown in the internal citation. Examples of this style are shown below. The full details of the source are given on a References page at the end of the report.

> *If you want people to act responsibly, you have to give them responsibility—and hold them accountable for meeting the objective (McClain and Romaine, 2002).*

> *According to McClain and Romaine (2002), if you want people to act responsibly, you have to give them responsibility—and hold them accountable for meeting the objective.*

The internal citation style provides the full details of the sources on a References page at the end of the report. The reference notes appear in alphabetical order according to the authors' names. Hanging indent format is used. Examples are shown below.

Chopra, Deepak. *Grow Younger, Live Longer.* (New York: Harmony Books, 2001).

Day, Jennifer Cheeseman. "National Population Projections." U.S. Census Bureau. http://www. census.gov/population/www/pop-profile/natproj.html (15 March 2007).

Bibliography or Reference Section. All references used in a report should be included in a bibliography or reference section. This section includes the complete name of the author(s), the title of the book or periodical, the date of

publication, the publishing company, and page numbers. A title, Bibliography or References, is placed at the top of the page using Title style. Refer to the Reference Guide for an example format for a References page.

Appendix. A formal report may contain an appendix that includes supporting information such as tables, statistics, and other pertinent material. Items in an appendix are lettered *Appendix A, Appendix B,* and so on. The appendix is the last part of the report.

Business Plans

Although business plans are widely used in the business world, only cursory information on writing them appears in this textbook. If you need to write a business plan, refer to other sources for information about content and format. The parts of a business plan are as follows:

- Title Page
- Table of Contents
- Executive Summary
- Vision and Mission
- Opportunity
- Market Strategy
- Business Strategy
- Organization and Operations
- Management
- Challenges
- Financials
- Appendices and Attachments

Collaborative Writing

Today the workplace uses project teams extensively. These teams gather the appropriate information and write the report. To be an effective member of a writing team, you need to use standard communication skills such as the following:

- Listening actively
- Being nonjudgmental
- Coping with criticism
- Using language appropriately
- Resolving conflict
- Observing body language

- Understanding and accepting cultural differences

In addition to these positive communication skills, your team can produce a better product by following these suggestions.

- Determine the purpose of the writing assignment. What are you to produce? What is the deadline? Are there certain stipulations?

- Determine the audience. Who is to receive the final report? What is their background? How much do they know about the subject matter? In other words, you need to determine at what level you should write the report and how much information you need to give the recipients.

- Select a team leader. The team leader is responsible for the following:

  — Setting the procedures for the team writing meetings

  — Facilitating the meetings

  — Helping the group meet deadlines

  — Solving problems

  — Seeing that the group produces the report in a timely manner

- Set a work schedule. Decide when and where you are going to meet. Set timelines and stick to them.

- Allocate the work. Define the tasks of each team member. Determine each team member's writing strengths, and use these strengths when assigning tasks.

- Monitor the progress. The group must stay focused and produce the written product by the deadline established.

- Reduce the chance of conflict by:

  — Actively listening to each member of the group.

  — Paying attention to cultural differences that may exist.

  — Acknowledging the worth of the other group members and their points of view.

© PhotoDisc / Getty Images

The team leader should facilitate the team writing meetings.

Summary

To reinforce what you have learned in this chapter, study this summary.

- Written communications can spell success or failure for a writer and the organization.

- Email is used extensively in the workplace today due to its ease, speed, and relative low cost.

- When an interoffice communication larger than one-half page needs to be written, a memorandum is the preferred vehicle.

- Letters are the preferred method of communication when writing to current and prospective clients and customers.

- Reports prepared in the workplace may be informal reports of two or three pages, or formal reports containing a table of contents, body, appendices, and references.

- For successful writing, determine the goal or purpose, consider the readers, gather the appropriate information, organize the content, draft the document, edit, prepare the final draft, and evaluate your work.

- The characteristics of effective correspondence include completeness, clarity, accurateness, promptness, conciseness, courteousness, and positivism.

- When writing email, you should use the basic characteristics of effective correspondence in addition to proper formatting, etiquette, and ethics.

- Use the direct approach when writing letters requesting information, providing information, and acknowledging information.

- Use the indirect approach when writing letters conveying negative information, demanding action, and persuading.

- Use the persuasive approach when attempting to convince someone to do something or change an indifferent or negative reader's reaction.

- Primary or secondary research is usually required when writing formal reports.

- The parts of a formal report may include the executive summary, title page, table of contents, list of tables and illustrations, body, documentation, references, and appendix.

- Collaborative writing has become an important skill for use in team projects.

What's the Problem?

Melody Hoover and Amando Hinojosa, the two people to whom you report, asked you to compose a draft memorandum for their joint signatures. Recently, there has been a flurry of emails in the company. Many of them are very negative and even use inappropriate language.

Melody and Amando are working on an ethics policy that will be disseminated with the email. Before you begin to write the email, think through what should be said and how the message should be worded.

What should you consider as you draft the memorandum? What should the tone of the memo be? Write a draft memo for Melody Hoover and Amando Hinojosa to review.

Let's Discuss

1. List the organizational skills necessary in composing written messages.
2. Explain what is meant by effective paragraphs.
3. List and explain the characteristics of effective correspondence.
4. List six ethical behaviors you must consider when writing email messages.
5. List and explain the different types of approaches that may be used in writing letters.
6. What is the purpose of documentation in a report? List two styles of documentation that may be used.
7. Why might a writer use tables, charts, or other graphics in a report?

Critical-Thinking Activity

Eduardo Mendez began his career five years ago as an administrative professional with United Pharmaceuticals. He has excellent administrative assistant skills. He writes well, has outstanding computer skills, and has superior human relations skills. Two months ago, Eduardo's supervisor left United Pharmaceuticals for another position. Janelle Duderstadt has been promoted to Vice President of Research, the position that Eduardo's supervisor held. Ms. Duderstadt seems to be a nice person and capable; however, she almost ignores Eduardo. In the two months since Janelle took the position, Eduardo rarely sees her; she is out of the office approximately 50 percent of the time. When she is in, she stays busy in her office. She does give Eduardo correspondence that she has written in a rough draft format on the computer to redo. Eduardo has always been told that he has excellent writing skills. He believes that he can help his new employer with the writing. If she would verbally tell him what the correspondence should include, he believes he can write it satisfactorily. Also, she spends a considerable amount of time preparing internal reports. Again, Eduardo believes he could be of help to her in at least doing a rough draft of certain reports.

What advice would you give Eduardo? Should he suggest to her that he can assist her? If so, should he ask for a meeting with her and call her attention to the fact that he has time to assist her? Should he inform her that he did most of the written correspondence for his previous supervisor?

Vocabulary Review

Open the *Word* file *CH07 Vocabulary* found on the Student CD. Complete the vocabulary review for Chapter 7.

English and Word Usage Drill

Complete the English and Word Usage Drill for Chapter 7 found in the *Applications Workbook.*

Workplace Applications

7-1 Write an Email Message

(Goals 1, 2, and 3)

1. Write an email message to Fujio Komuro, Ray Edwards, and Edward Wilson. Use an appropriate subject line. (Use your own email address or addresses provided by your instructor.)

2. In the body of the message, inform the recipients of a meeting on next Wednesday to discuss progress on the goals for their department. The meeting will be in Room A304 beginning at 10 a.m. It will last approximately one hour. The meeting is being called by Teresa Winwright, Vice President of Marketing.

7-2 Write a Memorandum

(Goal 1)

e-portfolio

During your first week on the job, Melody Hoover asked you to write a letter. You had little experience writing letters, and you felt very uncomfortable with her request. However, you were too afraid to ask any questions, so you wrote the letter to the best of your ability. When you gave the draft to Ms. Hoover, she quickly read it and said you needed to work on your organizational skills. You did not understand what she meant, and you were embarrassed to ask. You merely said, "Certainly, I will do that." Then you returned to your desk frustrated. You have now learned that organizational skills pay a major role in writing effectively.

1. What advice would you give a novice letter writer in how to write letters effectively?

2. Prepare a memorandum to your instructor stating the advice you would give. Use the *Word* file *Memo Form* found on the Student CD to prepare the memo.

7-3 Write Business Letters

(Goals 1, 2, 3, and 4)

1. Locate the letter-writing situations that appear in Chapter 7 of the *Applications Workbook.*

2. Work with two of your classmates to compose letters for all three situations.

team building

e-portfolio

3. Create a letterhead for United Pharmaceuticals. Use the company name, address, logo, and telephone number. The address is shown below. The company logo is provided on the Student CD in the file *CH07 Logo*.

Address: 1211 East Eighth Street
              Fort Worth, TX 76102-5201
Telephone: 817-555-0122

4. Using the letterhead you created, print copies of your letters.

5. Print four copies of the forms *CH07 Writing Process* and *CH07 Organizational Skills* found on the Student CD (one for each of you and one to submit to your instructor). Using the Collaborative Writing Process Evaluation form, evaluate the collaborative writing process. Using the Organizational Skills Evaluation form, evaluate your organizational skills. Submit your letters and one copy of each evaluation form to your instructor.

7-4 Conduct Research and Write a Report

(Goals 1, 2, 3, and 4)

team building

internet

1. Choose two classmates to work with on this project.

2. Conduct primary research by surveying eight to ten students in your college/university on the characteristics of an effective leader. Ask the following three questions and determine three other questions that you will ask.

   • What are the characteristics of an effective leader?

   • What, in your opinion, makes a leader ineffective?

   • What are the characteristics of effective communication?

3. Review one book and three Web sources on effective leadership.

4. Write a report of your findings. Include the following parts in the report: title page, table of contents, body, references page. Use headings in the body to identify information. Use footnotes or internal citations in the body.

Assessment of Chapter 7 Goals

Did you successfully complete the chapter goals? Evaluate yourself by filling out the form found in Chapter 7 of the *Applications Workbook*.

chapter 8

Verbal Communication and Presentations

Verbal Communication

To be an effective administrative professional, you must develop your verbal and nonverbal communication skills. You will use your verbal and nonverbal communication skills daily as you communicate with your employer and others in your organization. You may also talk with customers or clients in person or by telephone. You may have to deal with a person who is frustrated about a problem. Such a situation will test your communication skills.

Developing verbal and nonverbal communication skills is an ongoing process. No matter how long you have been a student of communication, you can continue to learn more about becoming an effective communicator. As you study this chapter, commit to continually improving and expanding your skills.

Verbal communication is the process of exchanging information through the use of words. As with all communication, verbal communication involves a sender, a receiver, and a message. Successful communication occurs when a listener (receiver) has heard and understood the message of the speaker (sender). Initially, the concept of verbal communication seems simple. Everyone understands words and knows what they mean. In actuality, verbal communication is not simple at all. Words can have different meanings for different people. In a diverse workforce, communication can be complex and

© PhotoDisc / Getty Images

Effective verbal communication is important for business success.

challenging. This section offers several techniques to help you become a more effective verbal communicator.

Listen and Understand

An important step in effective verbal communication is to listen. Hearing alone does not constitute listening. A person can hear words and yet not try to understand them. To listen means to make a conscious effort to hear and understand information. Many individuals spend about 70 percent of their day communicating, with about 45 percent of this time spent listening. Being an effective listener can improve your productivity.[1]

LISTEN ACTIVELY

Listening actively requires that you listen for the meaning as well as the words of the speaker. Using these techniques will help you improve your active listening skills.

- Prepare to listen. Drive distracting thoughts from your mind, and direct your full attention to the speaker. Remove distracting noises from the listening environment if possible.

- Listen for facts. Mentally register the key words the speaker is using, and mentally repeat key ideas or related points. Relate what the speaker is saying to your experiences.

- Do not let your mind wander. People speak at approximately 150 to 200 words a minute, although they can understand spoken information at about 300 words a minute or more. Unless you are actively listening to the speaker, your mind will probably wander.[2]

- Listen for feelings. Search beneath the surface. Listen to what is and is not being said.

- Minimize mental blocks and filters by being aware of them. Know your biases and prejudices that may lead to false assumptions. Do not let them keep you from hearing what the speaker is saying.

- Question and paraphrase. Ask questions (at the appropriate time) when you do not understand what you have heard. Paraphrase by

[1]"Listening," ACT WorkKeys, accessed April 4, 2007, available from http://www.act.org/workkeys/assess/listen/index.html.

[2]"Speech and Listening," Wikipedia, accessed April 4, 2007, available from http://en.wikipedia.org/wiki/Words_per_minute#Speech_and_listening.

putting the speaker's message in your own words and asking the speaker if you have understood correctly.

- Summarize. Clarify a discussion by summarizing it. By doing so, you set the framework for examining what has been said. Individuals can then either agree with your summary or point out areas that are incorrect according to their understanding so the group agrees on the message being communicated.

UNDERSTAND FACTORS THAT AFFECT COMMUNICATION

The way people understand messages is influenced by their backgrounds and experiences. Based on their backgrounds and experiences, they interpret the meaning of information they receive. They may make assumptions based on their interpretation of the information. They may also draw conclusions, adopt beliefs, or take action.

Assumptions can help or hinder communication. Suppose you attend a professional development seminar. The presenter is a speaker you have heard in the past. You found the information she presented to be accurate and her suggestions helpful. You may assume that the information she presents today will also be accurate and helpful. You are likely to listen actively during the presentation and accept her suggestions as worthy of consideration. Your assumption will make communicating the message easier for the speaker.

Now consider a situation where an assumption can hinder communication. Suppose you tell a coworker about a new device you have used to back up files from your computer. You mention the brand name of the device and describe how it works. Further assume that the person with whom you are speaking has bought other computer equipment of this brand and has found the devices to be defective, of poor quality, or difficult to use. The listener may assume that all products of this brand are similarly of poor quality or difficult to use. As soon as you mention the brand name of the device, the listener may

assume that the product is not worth consideration. Your coworker may politely listen as you relate your success with using the product; however, your message will likely not be accepted.

A person's **self-esteem** can also affect the way he or she communicates. Self-esteem is the way a person feels about himself or herself. Your self-esteem affects the way you send and receive messages. People who have low self-esteem may think that others have a low opinion of their skills or abilities. This idea can affect how messages are interpreted or stated. People with low self-esteem are more likely to focus on their failures than on their successes. When asked to express their thoughts, they may start their answers with statements such as the following:

I'm probably wrong, but....

I never was very good at doing this, but....

You don't really want my opinion; I have never done well in that area.

When you think that another person's low self-esteem may be hindering communication, let the person know that you value his or her thoughts and skills. Encourage the person to take part in the communication process by asking questions and commenting on his or her responses.

COPE WITH CRITICISM

A **criticism** is a value judgment or statement about the worth of something. In common usage, a criticism is often assumed to be a negative remark or judgment. Such criticism is not easy for anyone to hear; however, no one can escape it. Not only will you be on the receiving end of criticism at times, but you may also find yourself criticizing others. When you are on the receiving end of negative comments, engage in the following behaviors:

- Listen! Hear the person making the criticism. Give the person time to make his or her critical comments without interrupting.

- Make no excuses for your behavior if you are in the wrong.

- If you do not understand why you are being criticized, ask for specific examples of the behavior or work being criticized.

- Accept the criticism if it is valid. Be positive about your ability to change your behavior. Stress the positive—not the negative.

- If the person delivering the criticism is very agitated (perhaps screaming at you), you do not have to listen. Tell the person you will be happy to discuss the problem when he or she is calmer; then leave. You have the right to walk away from an out-of-control situation.

- End the dialogue on a positive note if possible. For example, you might tell the person that you appreciated hearing the comments.

BE NONJUDGMENTAL

The tendency to judge other people often gets in the way of communication. When a person is speaking, you may spend your time judging the person rather than listening to what he or she is saying. That judgment can be as superficial as judging the way the person looks (hair style or dress), pronounces words, or uses language. The judgment can be more substantive in nature (but just as dangerous) when you judge the person's beliefs and value system. Judgment comes from the listener's frame of reference and experiences. If what is said is in agreement with the listener's experiences, the listener tends to receive the message in a positive way. If what is said is not in agreement with the listener's experiences, the listener may reject the message.

In order to prevent or reduce the tendency to judge other people, listen with understanding. Attempt to understand the other person's point of view and try to sense how the other person feels. If you have the courage to listen with understanding, communication will improve greatly. You may even find that you have learned and grown in the process.

WILLINGLY ACCEPT CHANGE

In our fast-paced and changing world, you must accept and grow with change if you want to

Professional Pointers

Practice these tips when communicating with others.

- **Respect cultures and traditions that are different from your own.**

- **Avoid stereotyping or generalizing.**

- **Assume that people can always be trusted until proven otherwise.**

- **Always seek to understand others and their behaviors.**

- **Encourage cooperation rather than competition.**

- **Be willing to compromise.**

- **Listen to an associate's point of view without interrupting.**

- **Respond calmly to a loud or angry voice. An angry response only generates anger.**

- **If you disagree with someone's ideas, deal with the disagreement calmly and rationally—not angrily and emotionally.**

© PhotoDisc / Getty Images

Listening to constructive criticism can help you improve your work performance.

be a contributing member of an organization. Forward-thinking individuals are not fearful of change; they do not view change as bad. They look for the positives that occur because of change and decide how they can contribute to helping change occur. In fact, these people are often called **change agents** (individuals who facilitate change and help others accept change).

Speak and Be Understood

In addition to listening and attempting to understand what others are saying, good verbal communicators seek to speak so they are understood. They concentrate on using language appropriately. They also understand that communicating effectively can help resolve conflict when it arises.

USE LANGUAGE APPROPRIATELY

The language people use often prevents clear communication. Words in isolation have no meaning. They have meaning only because people have agreed on a particular meaning. The dictionary contains the correct meaning of words. However, cultural differences impact the meaning certain words have for individuals. For example, even though Americans and the British speak the same language, they use words in different ways. In America, waiting in line at a theater for tickets is referred to as *standing in line;* in Britain, it is referred to as *queuing up*.

Meanings of words also change with time. New words come into existence, and other words become obsolete because of lack of use. The computer era has generated different meanings for a number of words and terms. For example, a *chat room* in computer terminology is not a room at all in the sense of the standard dictionary definition of the word. A chat room in computer terminology is a place in cyberspace where individuals from various locations (even worldwide) come together to talk (share computer messages) through Web connections.

When speaking to be understood, you should engage in the following behaviors:

- Pay attention to the different meanings words can have. Clarify your meaning when necessary.

- Use an appropriate tone and the proper degree of formality for the situation and the message you want to share.

- Be sensitive to whether the individual or group seems to understand what you are saying. **Paraphrase** (restate the concept in different terms) when appropriate.

COMMUNICATE TO RESOLVE CONFLICT

Conflict is a state of opposition or disagreement between persons, ideas, or interests. Effective communication can help resolve conflicts. When a conflict arises at work, listen and talk with your coworkers or others involved in the situation. Although the situation seems straightforward, you may find that different people have different ideas about the cause of the conflict. In attempting to understand another person's perception of a situation, you should withhold judgment while you attempt to think from that person's point of view. Attempting to understand another person's view is not the same as agreeing with it. You may never agree with the person. Attempting to understand allows you to consider another perspective, which may or may not modify some of your own perceptions. However, you are listening to a different point of view and giving yourself a chance to learn from it.

After listening and talking with others, analyze the situation and try to determine the real cause of the conflict. Define the conflict issues objectively in terms that are separate from the people involved.

Once the conflict issues are clearly understood, work collaboratively to resolve the conflict. Concentrate on solving the problem and not on assigning blame. Brainstorm ideas for solving the problem, allowing everyone to express ideas freely. Be tactful in expressing ideas and show concern for the feelings of others. When discussing sensitive issues, remember that people's

---

RESOLVING CONFLICT

- Identify the issues causing the conflict. Is it power, resources, recognition, or acceptance? Many times the need for these items is at the heart of the conflict.

- Be willing to listen to the other person. Ask questions to determine what the other person wants or needs. By understanding the needs of the other person, you may be able to find ways to resolve the conflict.

- Identify points of agreement. Work from these points first. Then identify points of disagreement.

- Create a safe environment for discussion. Meet in a neutral location and use a tone that is accepting of the other person's views and feelings. Let the other person tell you how he or she is feeling. Share your feelings with the other person.

- Be objective. Many times individuals act too quickly when a conflict occurs. Step back, collect your thoughts, and try to see the situation as objectively as possible.

- Do not seek to win during a confrontation. Negotiate the issues and translate the negotiation into a lasting agreement.

- Listen actively. Watch the individual's eyes and notice body language to help you determine whether you are communicating effectively.

FIGURE 8.1 Resolving Conflict

feelings or emotions may affect their behavior. Do not react to an emotional outburst with an outburst of your own. If the discussion becomes too emotional or heated, delay the discussion until the participants have a chance to bring their emotions under control and can discuss the issues in an objective manner.

Compromises are often required to resolve conflicts. Remember to examine your role in the situation. Is your position reasonable and appropriate? What can you do to help resolve the conflict? Be willing to compromise when appropriate. Figure 8.1 lists several additional suggestions for resolving conflicts.

Nonverbal Communication

Nonverbal communication is sharing information with another through the use of body language, gestures, voice quality, or proximity to another rather than by using words. The nonverbal elements of a message can enhance or even change its meaning. For example, the words "We're so glad you could join us this morning" can convey a different meaning when delivered with a cheerful tone and a pleasant expression

than when delivered with a sarcastic tone and a scowl.

Elements of nonverbal communication can have different meanings to people of different backgrounds or cultures. As you study this section, know that the statements made here apply primarily to natives of North America. Do not assume that nonverbal behavior in other cultures has the same meanings as in North America. Costly and embarrassing mistakes can occur if you make such an assumption. You must study the individual cultures to understand their nonverbal communication.

Body Language

Body language is extremely important in face-to-face communication. Assume you are involved in this situation:

As an administrative professional, you have one part-time employee reporting to you. This person generally does a good job; however, today she has made a major error. You call her in to discuss it. When she enters your office, you have a very stern look on your face. You say, "Sit down. I have something very important to discuss with you." When you tell her to sit, you point to the chair on the opposite side of your desk. (This behavior is contrary to your usual behavior of asking employees to sit at a table in your office where chairs are close to each other.) She immediately sits, but does so on the edge of her chair while crossing and uncrossing her arms throughout the conversation. She also alternately bites her lip and stares at the ceiling. At one point, she begins biting her nails.

What does your body language say? First, you let the employee know you have a real problem by the look on your face and the tone of your voice. You do not offer her a chair at the table; you place yourself behind the desk. You place more distance between you and the employee than you usually do. What does the employee's body language say? By sitting on the edge of her chair and biting her nails, the employee lets you know she is concerned. By crossing and then uncrossing her arms, she also lets you know she may not be open to some of what you say. She lets you know she is passively absorbing or ignoring the message by staring at the ceiling. Both of you start the meeting operating at a disadvantage. The conversation may not be a good one unless you modify your behaviors significantly.

People transmit body language through their eyes, face, hands, arms, legs, and posture. However, you must be careful not to judge a person based on one gesture alone. You must consider all the gestures a person makes, along with what he or she says. Eye contact is extremely important for North Americans. They tend to believe that people who do not make eye contact with them have low self-esteem, are shy, or are uninterested in what they are saying.

In becoming a student of body language, you should observe the eyes, face, hands, arms, legs, and posture of others.

EYES AND FACE
Raising one eyebrow is seen as a gesture showing disbelief; raising both eyebrows shows surprise.

Winking may mean that a person agrees with you. When a person looks upward and blinks the eyes, he or she may be considering carefully what you are saying. Wide-open eyes may mean fear. Avoidance of eye contact in North America may be seen as lack of respect, insincerity, disinterest, or dishonesty. In North America, adults have a tendency to say to a child who is looking down while answering a question, "Are you telling me the truth? Look at me when you talk."

Facial expressions often betray a person's feelings. Common facial expressions include frowns (anger or unhappiness), smiles (happiness), sneers (dislike, disgust), clenched jaws (tension, anger), and pouting lips (sadness). A smile is probably the gesture most recognized and favorably received in all cultures.

HANDS, ARMS, AND LEGS
Tightly clenched hands or wringing hands usually indicate that a person is under some pressure. Authority and superiority are often indicated when a person stands with his or her hands joined behind the back. Hands that are flat on a table usually indicate a readiness to agree. Hands on hips may indicate aggression, readiness, or even defiance. Boredom or tiredness is indicated by a person resting his or her head in the hands. Tapping or drumming the fingers means impatience.

Crossed arms tend to indicate defensiveness. They seemingly act as a protective guard against an attack by someone, whether that attack is verbal or physical. People who tightly cross their legs seem to be saying they disagree with others. People who have tightly crossed legs and tightly crossed arms usually are feeling negatively about what is being said or what is happening around them. People who cross their legs tightly and kick their feet may be bored. Foot tapping also indicates boredom.

POSTURE
People with arms folded, legs crossed, and bodies turned away are seen as rejecting people and messages. When a person leans back, looks at the

A smile is a nonverbal communication that can help ease tensions in many situations.

ceiling, writes on a pad, and so on, he or she is either passively absorbing or ignoring the message.

People with open hands, bodies facing the speaker, and both feet planted on the ground are seen as accepting of people and messages. When a person leans forward and nods as the speaker makes points, he or she is seem as actively listening or accepting the message. Figure 8.2 indicates other meanings for various body positions.

Voice Quality

The loudness or softness and the pitch of the voice are nonverbal behaviors that can affect communication. A loud tone of voice usually is associated with anger; a soft tone, with calmness. When two people are talking softly with each other, they are probably at ease. Higher-pitched voices tend to mean that people are tense, anxious, or nervous. People often talk faster when they are angry or tense. In contrast, a low pitch and a slow pace indicate an intimate or relaxed tone. Other forms of nonverbal voice communication include a nervous giggle, a quivering

emotional voice, and a breaking stressful voice. These voice characteristics can affect the message shared with others.

Space

Proxemics is the study of personal and cultural use of space. Proxemics is also sometimes referred to as *social space*. People in various cultures perceive and use space in relationship to others differently. Individuals also often perceive distances between others differently depending on various relationships with individuals. Edward T. Hall, who pioneered the study of proxemics, identified four ranges of distance based on the nature of the relationship between individuals: 0–18 inches is intimate distance, 18 inches–4 feet is personal distance, 4–12 feet is social distance, and 12–25 feet is public distance.[3] For example, 6 to 18 inches is considered appropriate for whispering to another. The distance for talking with

[3]Dean H. Krikorian, Jae-Shin Lee, T. Makana Chock, and Chad Harms, "Isn't That Spatial?: Distance and Communication in a 2-D Virtual Environment," accessed April 4, 2007, available from http://jcmc.indiana.edu/vol5/issue4/krikorian.html.

INTERPRETATION OF BODY LANGUAGE

Listening	Tilts head, makes eye contact, nods
Evaluating	Chews on pencil/glasses, strokes chin, looks up and right
Eager	Leans forward with feet under chair
Bored	Stares into space, doodles
Aggressive	Leans forward with fists clenched
Rejection	Moves back with arms folded and head down, walks with hands in pocket
Defensive	Clenches hands, stands, crosses arms on chest
Lying	Looks down, shifts in seat, glances at you
Anger	Clasps hands behind back
Disbelief, doubt	Rubs eye
Sincerity, openness	Offers open palm
Confidence	Walks briskly with upright posture
Authoritative	Steeples fingers
Indecision	Pulls or tugs at ear

FIGURE 8.2 Interpretation of Body Language

good friends may be 2 to 4 feet. The distance for conversations among acquaintances may be greater, 4 to 8 feet.

Being too close or far from others can have adverse effects on communication. If you think someone is too close to you, you may be uncomfortable or distracted and unable to concentrate on the message being shared. If someone is too far away, you feel left out of the conversation or have trouble focusing on what is being said.

Territoriality is an expression of ownership and control over a particular area or space. Having someone occupy a space that you have identified as yours can also affect communication. For example, do you have a certain desk or chair in a classroom that you consider yours? Do you feel displaced when someone else occupies that space? If you are working, have you ever arrived at the workplace to find someone else at your desk? If so, what was your reaction? You

may have felt violated. You may have wondered or even said, "What are you doing at my desk?" When you think that someone is "in your space" you may have trouble concentrating on what the message says to you or even feel hostile toward that person.

Verbal Presentations

In the workplace, information is often presented verbally to a small or large group of people. With the team approach commonly used in organizations today, administrative professionals sometimes give presentations. These presentations may be informal ones to a small group or formal ones to a large group. You also may have occasion to speak at professional organization meetings. Because presenting can be an important part of your professional life, the remainder of this chapter focuses on proper presentation techniques.

Presenting is challenging for some people. For most people, becoming an effective presenter is a learned skill. This skill is so important to individuals and organizations that some businesses develop training to help people become effective verbal presenters. Like all skill development, you must practice the skill. The next sections will help you develop your presentation skills. The workplace activities will give you the opportunity to practice these skills by presenting to your instructor and classmates.

Plan the Presentation

Preparing a good presentation takes time and may require research or development of visual aids or handouts. You may also need to learn about the audience and the setting for the presentation. Beginning preparation three weeks before the presentation is not too soon.

DETERMINE THE PURPOSE

The first step in planning a presentation is to define clearly the purpose of the presentation. Ask yourself these questions as you begin to plan your presentation:

- Why am I giving this presentation?
- What do I want the audience to know as a result of my presentation?
- What, if anything, do I want the audience to do as a result of my presentation?

CONSIDER THE AUDIENCE

Consider the characteristics of the people who will hear the presentation. Try to determine areas of common interest to which you can relate points of information. For example, if your audience is a group of administrative professionals, you know some of their interests. You can use anecdotes or stories that have meaning for them. If you are speaking to a group of colleagues from your workplace, again you know some of their interests. You can tailor your message to meet their needs. If you are speaking to a general audience, keep these questions in mind as you begin to plan your remarks:

- What are the ages and genders of the people who will be in the audience?
- What is the education level attained by the audience members? Are they high school graduates, college graduates, or a mixture of both?
- What knowledge does the audience have about the subject of the presentation?
- What ideas or biases may the audience members have about the subject of the presentation?
- What will be the size of the audience? Will there be 15 or 50? Numbers make a difference. A small audience allows greater interaction. Questions can be used effectively. With a large audience, there is little chance for interaction other than a question-and-answer period at the end of the presentation.

CONSIDER THE SETTING

The time and location of your presentation and any other activities that will occur around the same time are important to know. Ask these questions about the setting:

- What time is your presentation? In the morning? Right before lunch? Immediately after lunch? In the evening (before or after a meal)?
- Is there entertainment before or after your presentation, such as a musical group?
- Is there other business occurring before or after your presentation?
- Is the presentation being held in the workplace, a hotel, a conference center, or a school?
- What is the size of the room? What is the configuration of the seating? Is the room a theater-type setting? If the audience is small, are they sitting around a table? Are the chairs to be set up in a circle?

If you have an opportunity to influence the setting, do so. Be certain the size of the room is appropriate. You do not want to give a presentation to 12 people in a room designed for 100 people. It will look as though you gave a party

© Digital Vision / Getty Images

Profiling the audience will help you prepare an effective presentation.

and no one came. Nor do you want to give a presentation to 50 people in a room designed for 25. People are not comfortable when they are crowded. As far as possible, be sure the chairs are comfortable, the temperature is pleasant, the room is clean, the lighting is appropriate, and the acoustics are good.

Research and Write the Presentation

Research the topic, if necessary, using resources from your company, a library, or the Internet. If you are researching on the Web, use several search engines to help you find material. Google™, Yahoo!®, Lycos®, and Ask.com™ are examples of comprehensive search engines. Figure 8.3 shows a screen from a search engine. Take notes on the relevant material you find and record the source of each resource used.

Conduct original research if needed. For example, you may be developing a presentation for the local chapter of the International Association of Administrative Professionals (IAAP) on email ethics. Therefore, you decide to do primary research with the IAAP members on ethical and/or

unethical email practices they observe in their own organizations.

Individuals usually gather more information during research than they can use during a presentation. An audience can absorb only so much information. You do not want to burden your audience by giving them more information than they can comprehend and remember. Your next step is to select the most relevant material appropriate to the subject and audience for the presentation.

ORGANIZE THE MATERIAL

Organize the main points of the material for effective communication and to accomplish the purpose of the presentation. Make an outline or a numbered list of the main points you want to include. For example, you may have four or five points that you want to cover. Figure 8.4 shows part of a presentation outline. Begin by listing these points and then deciding on the best order in which to present them. Remember that you should not attempt to cover too many points in one presentation. You will lose your audience

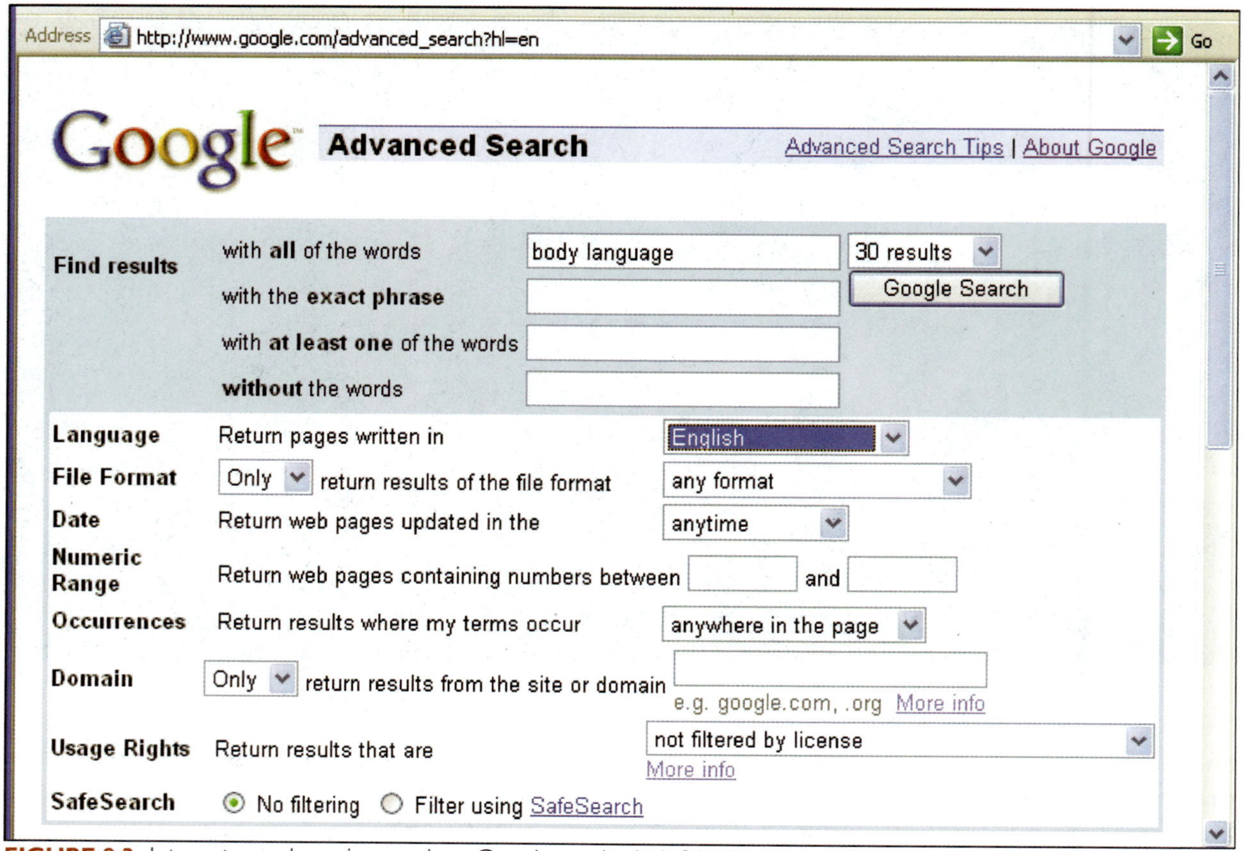

FIGURE 8.3 Internet search engines such as Google can be helpful when researching materials for a presentation.

quickly if you attempt to do so. If you have an audience who is knowledgeable about the topic you are presenting, you may be able to cover as many as ten main points; however, that number is too many for most audiences. Generally, with fewer points that are more developed, you will retain the audience's attention to a greater degree.

DEVELOP AN OPENING

The opening for a presentation should get the audience's attention immediately. For example, you may do one of the following:

- Tell a story.
- Use a quotation.
- Ask a question.
- Refer to a current event.

Knowing what *you* do best is important. If you can never remember the punch line of a

joke, do not try to tell a joke. Nothing is worse than beginning with an opening that flops. If you do tell jokes well and decide to do so, make sure the joke is not in poor taste. Humor that is never appropriate includes the following:

- Jokes based on an individual's ethnicity and race are taboo. Even if you are Irish and are presenting to an all-Irish audience, do not tell a joke about the Irish. An ethnic or racist joke is not acceptable, even if the audience is of one race or ethnicity. People may be able to laugh at themselves, but they do not feel good about a speaker calling attention to their weaknesses or inadequacies through humor.

- Gender jokes about males or females are not appropriate; nor are jokes about homosexuals. AIDS jokes are also inappropriate. Jokes are

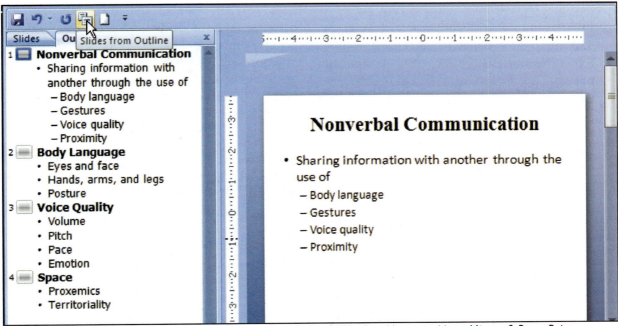

FIGURE 8.4 A presentation outline can be created in *Microsoft Word* and imported into *Microsoft PowerPoint*.

not funny when they belittle a particular group of people.

- Off-color jokes that have sexual connotations should not be told, even if they are told to a male-only or female-only audience. Someone will be offended. Off-color jokes are not appropriate, regardless of the audience makeup.

When you are determining how to open your presentation, ask yourself these questions:

- Is there a link between the story and the presentation?

- Is it a new story or joke? You do not want to relay one that the audience has heard numerous times.

- Am I telling the story as succinctly as possible? You do not want to spend one-third of your time on your opening story.

- If it is a joke, am I timing the punch line well?

WRITE THE BODY

Look at the main points for the presentation that you identified earlier. Expand on each point, including appropriate details. Make a note of visuals you can use to emphasize various points. The visuals can be developed later. Use language creatively to help you keep the listeners' attention and convey your points. The following techniques can help you in writing the body of the presentation.

- Establish a link with your audience. For example, if your audience is a group of administrative professionals, what concerns do the audience members have in common? Make your major points and relate those points to experiences common to both you and the audience.

- Use interesting facts, figures, and quotations. If you are giving a motivational talk on the importance of service, for example, you might remind the audience of the years of service that Mother Teresa gave to the world and use a quote from her. When using a quotation, relate the quote to a point in your presentation. Figure 8.5 shows a quote used in a presentation.

- Use direct language. Do not use long words when simpler words would be just as powerful.

- Personalize your talk. Address your audience directly; use *you* frequently.

- Talk in a conversational tone. Use the active rather than the passive voice. For example, do not say "It is believed …;" say "I believe …."

- Use analogies (comparisons made of two different things by stressing their similarities) to help explain your ideas. For example: *Stress is like a roller-coaster ride; it has numerous highs and lows.* Tie the analogy directly to the subject matter of the presentation.

DEVELOP A STRONG CLOSING

The closing must tie together the opening and the overall purpose of your presentation. The conclusion is your destination. It is the part of your presentation that should take your audience where you want them to be—to what you want them to learn or what you want them to do. A good conclusion gets the audience's attention. It helps them see the relationship between each part of your presentation—between the opening and the body and the body and the conclusion. The closing puts the pieces of your presentation together in a creative and interesting way so the audience leaves thinking you have helped them learn and/or have motivated them.

Let the audience know you are ready to conclude by stating simply "In conclusion" or "My final point is …." Make the conclusion short (about 5 to 10 percent of your talk) and powerful. The conclusion can be a moving statement, a story, a call to action, or a challenge. For example, if you are delivering a presentation on human potential, you might end by saying, "I leave you with three challenges—to be the best person you can be, to constantly grow and learn, and to reach the unreachable star." The last few lines of your conclusion should be memorable. Connect with the audience for one final moment—make them laugh and/or make them think.

Veterans Day

Through the generations, America's men and women in uniform have defeated tyrants, liberated continents, and set a standard of courage and idealism for the entire world. On Veterans Day, our Nation pays tribute to those who have proudly served in our Armed Forces.

President George W. Bush
Veterans Day 2006

Source: The White House, Honoring Our Veterans, accessed April 10, 2007, available from http://www.whitehouse.gov/infocus/veterans.

FIGURE 8.5 Use quotes in presentations to add interest and build credibility.

Prepare Visual Aids

A **visual aid** is an object or an image that a person can see to help understand a spoken or written message. Posters, transparencies, and slides are examples of visual aids that might be used during a presentation. Visual aids, if used properly, can be very effective. According to research studies, on average, people retain about 20 percent of what they hear, about 30 percent of what they see, and about 50 percent of what they see and hear. If you want your audience to remember what you said, show them effective visuals during your presentation.

The media you choose for the visuals will depend on the equipment you have available for use during the presentation and the size of the audience. Flip charts are effective for small, informal group meetings. Overhead transparencies are effective for small or large groups and for formal or informal presentations. Transparencies are easy to produce and use. They can be created in black and white or using a wide range of colors. You can also write on them as you give a presentation.

Presentations that use electronic slides and a projection system are appropriate for both large and small groups. Programs such as *Microsoft PowerPoint* allow you to create slides quickly and easily. Electronic slides offer the following features that help make a visual presentation a powerful one.

- Color. Presentation software typically has many color schemes that can be used to make professional-looking slides.

- Clip art and photos. Clip art and photos can be used on electronic slides to add interest or illustrate points you wish to make. Some clip art and photos may come with the presentation program. Additional images can be purchased. Some images can be downloaded from the Internet without charge. Be sure to understand and follow the copyright restrictions on any clip art or photos you use.

- Sound clips and movies can be accessed from electronic slides to enhance a presentation. For example, you might have soft music playing as the audience gathers for the presentation. You might include a short video from the company president to introduce a presentation to co-workers. Sound can be used effectively to build excitement or emphasize transitions in a presentation. Be careful, however, to ensure that the sound does not compete with your voice. Use sound only to serve a specific purpose.

Although visual aids can be effective, they can also lessen your effectiveness if you do not use them well. Have you ever seen a presentation where the speaker used ineffective visuals? If so, did the visuals have some of the following flaws?

- The visuals were not clear or were too small to be read easily.

- The visuals did not relate to the presentation.

- The visuals were so ineffectively presented that they distracted from the speaker's message.

Have you seen a presentation in which the speaker seemed to talk to the visual aids rather than the audience or where the equipment for presenting the visuals did not work properly? If you have observed these events, you understand that although visuals can add interest, they can also detract from a presentation. The Focus On

© PhotoDisc / Getty Images

Overhead transparencies can be used for presentations to small or large groups.

focus on   *Visual Aids*

Visual aids, such as transparencies or electronic slides, can enhance a presentation when they are prepared and used effectively. Follow the suggestions below to improve your use of visual aids.

- Prepare a visual for each of the main points of your presentation.

- For transparencies or electronic slides, keep the text to a minimum on each one. Include only the main points—not everything you intend to say about the point.

- Include only one graphic on each slide or transparency. Use only graphics relevant to the point.

- Use the same font styles for all major points on a slide or transparency. You may use a different font style for minor points; however, do not use more than two font styles. A visual looks cluttered when you use too many different fonts.

- Make sure the visuals can be seen and read from all parts of the room. If your audience is large,

you may need two screens on opposite sides of the room.

- Proofread the visuals carefully. Check for spelling and content errors. Errors are embarrassing and they detract from a presentation, making the audience wonder about your attention to detail.

- Practice using the transparencies or slides before the presentation.

- Make sure all equipment is in good working order and that you know how to operate the equipment.

- Introduce visuals when appropriate. Glance at the visual when it is first displayed to make sure it is the correct one and that it can be seen clearly. Then face the audience as you discuss points of the presentation.

- Stand to the side of the screen or other visual display when presenting. Adjust the light level in the room so that both you and the visuals can be seen.

Visual Aids feature gives several tips for preparing and presenting visuals.

Practice and Prepare to Present

Rehearse the presentation exactly as you plan to give it. If you will stand at a lectern during the presentation, stand at one during the rehearsal. If you will use a microphone during the presentation, use one during the rehearsal. If you plan to use visuals during the presentation, use them in the rehearsal. Also, you might ask a trusted colleague to listen to and critique your rehearsal presentation. Ask the person to be totally honest with you. You want to be able to correct your errors before you make your presentation. Figure 8.6 lists ten common mistakes people make in presentations. You can avoid these mistakes by planning and rehearsing.

CHECK THE PRESENTATION ROOM

Be sure to visit the room where you will make your presentation. Know how the room will be set up. Find out where the lectern is going to be if you are using one. Be certain you have the visuals in order. Check your visuals on the actual equipment you will be using. Be certain you know how to use the equipment. If you are at all uncomfortable using the equipment, ask a colleague to assist you by operating the equipment. Learn how to control the temperature and lighting in the room.

CONSIDER YOUR ATTIRE

Decide what you will wear several days before the presentation. The usual attire for women is a suit or dress; for men, a suit and tie. Wear something you are comfortable in and that looks good on you. Bright colors are perfectly acceptable.

> ## MISTAKES PEOPLE OFTEN MAKE WHEN GIVING PRESENTATIONS
>
> - Failing to prepare with the audience's interests and needs in mind
> - Failing to rehearse
> - Failing to practice using visual aids
> - Failing to check the room setup, temperature, and lighting
> - Making the presentation too long
> - Beginning with an inappropriate opening, such as a joke or story
> - Ignoring the body language of the audience during the presentation
> - Failing to modify the message when listeners seem not to understand it
> - Trying to appear knowledgeable about a subject for which you are not knowledgeable
> - Failing to use a short, powerful conclusion that challenges the listeners or calls for action

FIGURE 8.6 Common Mistakes in Presentations

Women should avoid necklaces and earrings that are large and distracting. Rings and bracelets are appropriate, but women should not wear noisy bracelets; they may distract audience members. Men may wear colored shirts and bright ties. The color of the suit should be one that looks good on the man. Men should not wear gold bracelets and a number of rings; they are distracting to the audience. Hair for both men and women should be well groomed and away from the face.

WRITE YOUR INTRODUCTION

You have already learned that you need to build credibility with the audience. One way to do this is to tell the audience your credentials. How do you do this? First, find out who will be introducing you. Then write a succinct statement (that will take no more than two minutes to deliver) highlighting your major accomplishments, and give it to the person who will introduce you. Do not send a packet with pages of information about you and leave it up to the introducer to determine the important points to make. Do not write a long introduction; the audience will become bored, and you lose time that could be used for your message. Taking a copy of the introduction you wrote with you is a good idea (in case the introducer has misplaced the copy you sent).

CONTROL NERVOUSNESS

Remember that nervousness is normal. Even professionals experience it. You have already learned how to help control nervousness—prepare and rehearse. You know who your audience is, what you intend to say, and how you will say it. A well-prepared and well-rehearsed presentation can eliminate many of your fears. Try not to push yourself to the limit with work responsibilities in the few days before a presentation. When you are overly tired, you increase your chances of being nervous.

Deliver the Presentation

Arrive early enough to check out the microphone, the equipment, and the layout of the room. If changes need to be made, find someone who can assist you in making them. In the 10 or 15 minutes before your presentation begins, find a private place (maybe a small room away from the gathering audience) and sit quietly to relax.

Pay attention to your body language as you are being introduced. Look at the person who is speaking and then look slowly at the audience. As you approach the lectern, walk with confidence. As you reach the lectern, slow down and collect yourself. Place your notes (paper or

Make eye contact to help you connect with listeners.

electronic) where you can refer to them easily. Respond to the introduction, but make your response brief. You might say, "Thank you very much," and exchange a handshake with the person who introduces you.

CONNECT WITH THE AUDIENCE

As you begin your presentation, pause for just a moment before beginning. Let your eyes sweep the room. Realize that the audience is much less aware of your nervousness than you are. Do not draw attention to your hands, which may be shaking as you begin. For example, instead of holding a microphone, leave it on a stand.

Remember these points to help you deliver a successful presentation:

- Maintain eye contact with the audience. As you speak, focus on one side of the room and then (after a period of time) on the other side of the room. Make eye contact with as many people as you can.

- Watch for nonverbal feedback from the audience. For example, puzzled looks or blank stares are cues the audience does not understand what you

are saying. Modify your presentation as quickly as possible to help your audience understand.

- Focus on the positive body language (smiles, nodding heads, and so on) coming from the audience. Let yourself feel good about positive reactions.

Speak with Credibility

Credibility (being perceived as reliable or believable) is important for a successful presentation. When your audience thinks you are credible, they will be more likely to accept your message or take the action you want them to take. One obvious way to appear credible is to be very knowledgeable about the topic of your presentation. Use examples from your own experience. Be able to answer questions or provide more details about the topic when asked. If you make contradictory statements or give incorrect information, the audience will not find you credible. State the source of facts and figures that you present. This will lend credibility to your presentation.

- Use natural gestures. You may use your arms and hands to emphasize points. However, do not use constant arm and hand motions. Use these motions sparingly and for emphasis only.

- Be natural; do not perform. Speak in a normal tone of voice and at an appropriate rate—not too fast and not too slow.

- Speak loud enough that everyone can hear you. Indicate emphasis through variations in tone. Do not speak in a **monotone** (a succession of sounds or words uttered in a single tone of voice).

CONDUCT A QUESTION-AND-ANSWER SESSION

Allow time for a question-and-answer session at the end of your talk. Anticipate questions that the listeners may have and prepare answers ahead of time. Learn as much about the topic of the presentation as you can so that you may be able to answer other questions that you did not anticipate ahead of time. If you do not know the answer to a question, admit that you do not know the answer. Offer to find the answer and provide it later, if appropriate, or suggest another source for the information. Unless the audience is a very small group in which everyone can be heard easily, repeat each question before answering it. This procedure allows you to have a minute to think about the answer. It also ensures that everyone can hear the question as well as your answer.

Critique Your Presentation

Within a day after the presentation, critique your performance. Evaluate yourself using these guidelines:

- Think objectively about your performance. List what you did well and what you need to improve in future presentations.

- Do not try to solve too many problems at once. Identify one or two things to improve each time you give a presentation.

- Realize evaluation is an ongoing process.

- Congratulate yourself by recognizing the improvements you have made.

- Make notes to help you improve the next time you give a presentation.

Additionally, get feedback from other people. You can ask a respected colleague to evaluate you. You or the individuals who asked you to speak may provide evaluation forms for the people in the audience. A sample evaluation form is shown in Figure 8.7. Ask to see copies of the completed forms and review them carefully. Do not let yourself become upset over a few negative comments. Know that there will always be some negative feedback.

Team Presentations

You have learned in previous chapters that project teams are used extensively in business today. These project teams often report on their activities or findings in a team verbal presentation. Team members work together to prepare and deliver the presentation. The techniques presented in the previous section also apply to team presentations. Some additional suggestions for team planning are given below.

- Discuss as a team the goal or purpose of the presentation, the main points it will include, and how best to present the information.

- Decide who will deliver each part of the presentation.

- Determine how you will make the transition from one speaker to another. One way is for the speaker who is finishing to introduce the next speaker.

- Practice your presentation as a group. If visual aids or handouts are part of the presentation, determine who will prepare them.

- Determine appropriate dress. Speakers should dress in a similar fashion. For example, they may all wear suits.

- Determine how the group will be seated before and after each person's presentation. Will the speakers be on a stage? In what order will they be seated? The first speaker should be closest to the podium.

PRESENTATION EVALUATION FORM

Presenter Name _____ **Date** _____

Title of Presentation _____

Please indicate the appropriate response for each statement. Thank you for your feedback.

	No	Yes	Somewhat
1. The presenter seemed professional and knowledgeable about the topic.			
2. The content of the presentation will be helpful to me.			
3. The visual aids were helpful and appropriate.			
4. The handouts were helpful and appropriate.			
5. Enough time was allowed for questions and answers.			
6. The overall time allowed for the presentation was appropriate.			
7. The room was comfortable.			
8. I would recommend this presentation to others.			

Comments:

FIGURE 8.7 Presentation Evaluation Form

Summary

To reinforce what you have learned in this chapter, study this summary.

- Developing verbal and nonverbal communication skills is an ongoing process. You can always learn more about effective communication with others.
- When listening and understanding, engage in these behaviors: listen actively; understand the relationship between past experiences, self-esteem, and communication; cope with criticism; be nonjudgmental; and willingly accept change.
- Use language appropriately by paying attention to the different meanings words can have and the way tone and degree of formality can affect a message.
- Effective communication can help resolve conflicts. When a conflict arises, listen and talk with others involved in the situation as a first step toward conflict resolution.
- Nonverbal communication can be just as important as verbal communication.
- People use a variety of nonverbal communication methods, including body language, voice quality, and space. Body language differs from country to country.
- In the workplace, information is often presented verbally to a small or large group of people. With the team approach commonly used today, administrative professionals sometimes give presentations.
- Steps in planning a verbal presentation include determining the purpose, considering the audience, and considering the setting.
- Steps in researching and writing a presentation include researching and selecting relevant material, organizing the material, developing an opening, writing the body, identifying visual aids, and developing a strong closing.
- Posters, transparencies, and electronic slides are examples of visual aids that might be used during a presentation.
- Before the presentation, check the setup of the presentation room, determine what you will wear, and write a brief introduction for yourself.
- As you speak, make eye contact with listeners and modify the message if listeners do not seem to understand your message. Be aware of your body language and try to control nervousness.
- Conduct a question-and-answer session at the end of the presentation if appropriate.
- After a presentation, critique your performance. Also, ask for feedback from the audience using an evaluation form.
- When presenting as a team, work together to decide what the presentation will include and who will prepare each part of the message and the visual aids.

What's the Problem?

Gloria Delgado is an administrative professional in the Human Resources Department of her company. Gloria's supervisor asked her to give a presentation to 20 employees regarding employee benefits that will take effect in the coming year. Gloria reviewed a report that summarizes changes to the employee benefits and prepared her comments using information from the report. Gloria assumed that the employees who would hear her presentation would be other administrative assistants. She prepared opening comments and examples to which other administrative assistants would relate. On the day of the presentation, Gloria was surprised to see that the audience contained people from several different departments and job positions. Gloria's presentation addressed the changes that would take place in employee benefits. During the question-and-answer session, several people asked about aspects of the benefit plan other than changes. Some listeners seem annoyed when Gloria was not prepared to answer these questions.

What went wrong? What should Gloria have done differently in preparing for the presentation? What could she have done during the presentation when she realized that some of her assumptions had been incorrect?

Let's Discuss

1. What constitutes a successful verbal communication?
2. How is listening different from hearing?
3. How do people's background and experiences affect their communication?
4. How can you use effective communication to help resolve conflicts?
5. Why is knowing people's culture and background important to understanding how they interpret nonverbal communication?
6. What activities should be completed when planning a presentation?
7. What activities should be completed when researching and writing a presentation?
8. What factors will determine the visual aids that you choose for use in a presentation?
9. What strategies can you use to help you connect with the audience during a presentation?
10. How should you prepare for the question-and-answer session of a presentation?

Critical-Thinking Activity

As a part-time administrative assistant reporting to Kurt Woo you have been given an excellent opportunity to be part of a workplace team. Kurt will chair the team; he has told you that your role will be more of an observer than a participant. However, he has also told you to feel free to make occasional suggestions. The team is composed of seven administrative professionals (with you being the eighth one). Its task is to establish a mentoring program for new administrative professionals joining the company. At the first meeting, Kurt delivers the charge to the group—establish a mentoring program for new administrative professionals. The mentoring program is to be ready for implementation in six months. Kurt asks the group to come to the next meeting with suggestions as to what should be included in the mentoring program and how it should be implemented.

At the second meeting, a major conflict arises. Three individuals in the group suggest that the administrative professionals within the company be used as trainers for the new employees. Two members of the group strongly disagree with this suggestion, stating that the administrative professionals in the company have a biased view and that outside consultants should do the training. Two administrative professionals try to act as mediators in the dispute but have no success. At one point, two people begin screaming at each other, making the following statements:

- You are totally out of touch with reality. Our internal people do not have the skills to conduct the training. Why in the world would you make such a stupid suggestion?

- You are so wrong, but I should have known you would conduct yourself this way. When I discovered you were going to be on the team, I should have declined the invitation to be a part of it. You are always "off the wall" in your suggestions. Do you ever think about what you are going to say before you say it? Your mouth always seems to overload your brain.

Kurt suggests to the group that the meeting be adjourned, stating that tempers need to cool. He asks the team members to come to the next meeting prepared to discuss what happened and how the conflict can be resolved.

After the meeting, Kurt asks you to share with him your impressions of what happened. What do you say to Kurt? What should Kurt do as team leader to help resolve the conflict?

Vocabulary Review

Open the *Word* file *CH08 Vocabulary* found on the Student CD. Complete the vocabulary review for Chapter 8.

English and Word Usage Drill

Complete the English and Word Usage Drill for Chapter 8 found in the *Applications Workbook*.

Workplace Applications

8-1 Complete a Listening Assessment

(Goals 1 and 2)

1. Open and print two copies of the Listening Assessment provided in the *Word* data file *CH08 8-1 Listening*.

2. Rate your listening skills and tally your score.

3. Give one copy of the Listening Assessment to a trusted friend or family member. Ask that person to rate you. Compare the ratings and discuss them with the friend or family member.

4. Write a memo to your instructor discussing your listening skills. Discuss the skills that are your strengths. Identify areas that need improvement and explain how you will try to improve in these areas. Use the data file *Memo Form* to prepare the memo.

8-2 Research Nonverbal Communication

team building

(Goal 2)

Several employees of United Pharmaceuticals in the United States are of Hispanic or Asian heritage and culture. The company has offices in China and India as well as in the United States. Employees in these countries have their own unique customs and ways of communicating. In this activity, you will explore the nonverbal communication of a culture. Work with a classmate to complete this activity.

internet

1. Select a culture (Hispanic, Chinese, or Indian) that is different from yours. Search the Internet and/or other resources for information on nonverbal communication used in this culture. Use at least three sources and document the sources.

2. Prepare a handout that could be shared with coworkers that highlights the nonverbal communication of the culture you selected. Note any nonverbal communication common to North Americans that would be inappropriate if used in the culture you researched.

3. List the complete sources for your information on a separate page.

8-3 Research and Write a Presentation

e-portfolio

(Goal 4)

1. Choose a topic for a presentation that you will give to your classmates. You may select one of the topics below or another business-related topic approved by your instructor. Some of the topics listed are broad. You may need to select one or two aspects of the topic to cover.

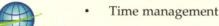

internet

- Time management

- Stress management

- Resolving conflicts

- Globalization of business

- Business etiquette

- Business professional and business casual dress

- Telephone etiquette

- Appropriate use of email

- Characteristics of the diverse workforce of the United States

- Population dynamics of the United States now and in projections for the future

- New version of a software program (advantages, disadvantages, reasons to upgrade or not)

- Design principles for documents such as newsletters and advertising brochures

- Items needed and design/layout for a home office for a teleworker

2. The purpose of the presentation is to inform your classmates about the topic chosen. Profile your audience (your classmates). Think about their ages, genders, backgrounds, career interests, and other characteristics that they may have in common. Write a brief paragraph or list that describes the audience.

3. Research the topic you have chosen. Note the source information for all reference material.

4. Select five or six main points to cover in the presentation. Create an outline that organizes these points in the order you will present them.

5. Develop each point further. Write details that you want to mention in your presentation. Your presentation should last about 10 to 12 minutes, including a short question-and-answer period.

6. Develop visual aids for the presentation. Create electronic slides that contain the main points you will present. Include clip art, photos, or other graphics on at least two of the slides. Use sound on one slide if appropriate. Use the Notes area of each slide to key reminders of details you want to mention related to the points on that slide.

7. Use color, animation, transitions, or other design elements to create an attractive slide show that will hold the listeners' attention.

8-4 Deliver a Presentation

(Goal 4)

1. Create a presentation evaluation form to use in getting feedback on a presentation you will deliver. Figure 8.7 shows an example evaluation form. Make enough copies for each member of the audience.

2. Practice the presentation you created in Application 8-3. Review the strategies for rehearsing a presentation, controlling nervousness, and connecting with the audience given in the chapter.

3. Deliver the presentation to a group of your classmates. Ask the audience members to complete an evaluation form.

4. Write a memo to your instructor giving a critique of your presentation content and delivery. Mention points on which the audience gave you a high rating and points on which you need to improve in future presentations.

Assessment of Chapter 8 Goals

Did you successfully complete the chapter goals? Evaluate yourself by filling out the form found in Chapter 8 of the *Applications Workbook*.

For additional resources, access the Website for this textbook at academic.cengage.com/officetech/fulton-calkins.

chapter 9

Customer Service

Learning Goals

1. Describe the importance of effective customer service to an organization.

2. Identify characteristics of companies that value customer service.

3. Develop effective customer service skills.

Importance of Customer Service

Customer service is important to businesses and many other organizations. A **customer** is a person who receives the services or products that are offered by an organization. **Customer service** can be defined as the ability of an organization to consistently give customers what they want and need. Providing information to help people decide which products or services best meet their needs; offering options such as delivery, installation, or service plans; and answering questions about product use after a sale are all examples of customer service.

In your career as an administrative professional, you may work for several types of organizations—businesses, nonprofit organizations, or government entities. Although different types of organizations may have different goals, many businesses and other organizations cannot fully achieve their goals without effective customer service.

A major goal of businesses is to make a profit. Effective customer service is very important in achieving this goal. Customers who are not satisfied with the service they receive are likely to take their business elsewhere in the future. When many customers take this action, the lower sales may result in lower profits. However, customers who are pleased with the service they have received are more likely to buy from the company again. Increased sales and profits can be a major benefit of providing effective customer service.

Nonprofit organizations and government entities seek to provide products or services to certain groups of people. Even though these organizations may not be trying to make a profit, effective customer service is important for achieving their goals. Consider public schools as an example. The goal of an elementary school may be to provide quality instruction in a safe, friendly environment that is conducive to learning. School staff members must consider the students' needs and wants (provide effective customer service) if they are to accomplish their goal.

Customer service is important in organizations such as schools that provide services as well as in those that sell products.

Commitment to Customer Service

Organizations with effective customer service are committed at all levels of the organization to serving customers. The leaders and employees of these organizations understand that effective customer service is essential for achieving their goals.

Mission Statement

Organizations dedicated to customer service take time to ask and answer the question: What is our mission? A **mission statement** addresses an organization's goals. It is a statement of purpose that can be used to initiate, evaluate, and refine an organization's directions. A mission statement for a company that provides an Internet search engine is shown in Figure 9.1. Notice that this company's mission statement focuses on what it will do for customers. Mission statements should not be static but dynamic. Each year the mission statement should be reviewed and modified or changed according to the new directions of the organization that may have emerged.

Vision Statement

In addition to a mission statement, many organizations develop a vision statement. A vision statement addresses what the organization wants to become; it is a picture of the future. The vision statement for an Internet search engine company might be: "We seek to become the world's largest search engine and to offer a service that gives users highly relevant results in only a few seconds." This vision statement

---

MISSION STATEMENT

Our mission is to make the information that is available on the Internet accessible to all users by providing a free service that is fast and easy to use.

FIGURE 9.1 Mission Statement

focuses on growth for the future and continued service to customers.

Leadership

Management must help employees understand the values and mission of the organization through written statements. They must provide training in areas that affect customer service. Most importantly, they must show constant adherence to the organization's values and mission in their actions.

Leadership as it relates to customer service does not mean only the officers and management of an organization. It means all employees who take any kind of leadership roles in the organization. These leaders must have a strong commitment to serving customers. They must understand that quality customer service will help the organization achieve its goals. They must be receptive to new ideas and have a genuine interest in continuing to improve customer service.

Employees

Employees must understand the importance of customer service to the success of the organization. They must be committed to providing excellent customer service to both external and internal customers. **External customers** are the companies or people outside the organization who buy or use the products or services provided by the organization. For example, a consumer who buys a new car is an external customer of an automobile dealership. **Internal customers** are departments or employees within an organization who use the services or products provided by others within the organization. For example, employees in the Technical Support Department of a company serve the needs of other company employees. These employees are the internal customers of the workers in the Technical Support Department. Without the services this department provides, others in the company would not be able to do their work, and service to

external customers would suffer. Employees who have no direct contact with external customers can make important contributions that help the organization provide quality customer service.

Future Customers

As you learned in Chapter 1, the demographics of the population are changing significantly. The population of the United States is already more diverse than it has ever been in age, race, and ethnicity. Thus, the future customers of any organization will be diverse. If you are dealing directly with external customers of your organization, you may deal with people who are very different from you. These people may come from various cultures and be of various ages. They may be recent immigrants to the United States or they may be of a different race. Figure 9.2 shows the U.S. population figures by race for the year 2000 and projections for 2010 and 2020.

Customers may live in the United States or outside the country. They may communicate with you from China, Brazil, New Zealand, or from a multitude of other locations. In many cases, you may never talk with the customer. Many office employees receive numerous messages each day, with a large number of messages being electronic ones. When you cannot see or sometimes even hear your customers, communicating effectively is more difficult. Written messages can be misinterpreted. You will need to rely on the communication skills you studied in Chapter 7 and Chapter 8 to help you communicate effectively with customers.

Customer Service Skills

Your role as an administrative professional may include the first contact a customer has with your organization. If so, you play an extremely important part in customer service. What you do or say may determine whether the customer

U.S. POPULATION BY RACE

POPULATION	2000	PROJECTED 2010	PROJECTED 2020
Total	282,125,000 (100.0%)	308,936,000 (100.0%)	335,805,000 (100.0%)
White alone	228,548,000 (81.0%)	244,995,000 (79.3%)	260,629,000 (77.6%)
Black alone	35,818,000 (12.7%)	40,454,000 (13.1%)	45,365,000 (13.5%)
Asian alone	10,684,000 (3.8%)	14,241,000 (4.6%)	17,988,000 (5.4%)
All other races	7,075,000 (2.5%)	9,246,000 (3.0%)	11,822,000 (3.5%)

Source: "U.S. Interim Projections by Age, Sex, Race, and Hispanic Origin," U.S. Census Bureau, accessed May 15, 2007, available from http://www.census.gov/ipc/www/usinterimproj/.

FIGURE 9.2 Projected U.S. Population by Race

will do business with your organization. You may not always be able to satisfy a customer's need. However, you can listen to the customer and offer appropriate alternatives for the customer.

The Customer Is Always Right

Most of us have heard the statement, "The customer is always right," numerous times. Is it true? No, it isn't. A customer is a person, and no person is always right. Customers make unreasonable requests at times; sometimes their requests cannot or should not be fulfilled by an organization. Consider this simple but realistic situation:

Assume you have recently taken a test. When you get your test back, you think you answered a question correctly for which you were given no credit. You talk with your instructor, Ms. Waters. She explains that your answer is not correct and refers you to a source for the correct answer.

In this situation, you are the customer—you receive the services of your school and instructor. If the instructor had agreed that you were right when you were not, you would have gone away with incorrect information, which would not

Professional Pointers

Keep these points in mind to help you deliver effective customer service.

- A customer is anyone who receives the services or products offered by your organization. Not all customers pay for the product or service received.

- Customers may be of diverse ages, races, and cultures.

- All customers should be treated with respect and courtesy, even when they are at fault or do not have a legitimate complaint.

- Delivering effective customer service can help your organization achieve its goals.

- Employees can contribute to the success of an organization by serving internal customers as well as external customers.

help you to learn and grow. Even when the customer is not right, the customer still deserves to be treated well and have his or her complaint or question heard by a representative of the organization. In the example just given, the instructor listened to your question. She then referred you to a source where you could get the correct answer, which helps you learn. The instructor also did so without insulting you. Customers should be treated with respect. They should be given an explanation if there is a question about the product or service.

Preparing Yourself

What basics do you need to know before you can begin to deliver excellent customer service? Finding answers to the following questions will give you the basic information you need about your organization to be prepared to deal with customers.

- What are your organization's values?
- What is its mission and goals?
- What is its vision for the future?
- Who is it attempting to serve?
- What is the philosophy of its leadership?

The previous sections have emphasized some of the crucial organizational elements necessary in effective organizations—ones that consider their customers' needs and help their employees grow and learn. This section is devoted to giving you a number of practical suggestions for effectively dealing with customers.

VISUALIZE SUCCESS

Know who you are and what your strengths are. Be honest about your weaknesses. However, do not let your weaknesses define you. You can learn and grow by recognizing what you know and deciding to do something about what you do not know. In visualizing success, you might say, "I have much to learn about being effective in a customer service environment. However, I am willing to learn and I know I can." Visualizing your success is the first step to achieving it.

Make a commitment to learn and improve your customer service skills.

© PhotosIndia / Getty Images

TAKE RESPONSIBILITY

Everyone makes mistakes in the workplace at least occasionally. However, the mature individual willingly takes responsibility for his or her mistakes and learns from them. In a customer service environment, it is important to take time at the end of the day to think through what went right and what went wrong, both with internal customers and external customers. Ask yourself, "What can I learn from each experience?" Then, do so—learn from the positives and negatives. Reinforce the positives and move on. Peak performers know what they need to do, and they stay focused on their goals.

ADMIT MISTAKES

When you make a mistake in your personal life, do you admit it or try to hide the fact that you have made a mistake? If you answered honestly, you probably had to say that there have been times in your life when you did not admit a personal mistake. If so, have you ever been found out? If your answer to this question is yes, did it hurt your relationship with the other person?

Does that person now think of you as a dishonest person? When such a situation occurs, you have to work almost twice as hard to get back the person's trust.

If you as a business employee fail to admit a mistake to a customer, you run the risk of being seen as dishonest. The customer may see your entire company as dishonest; and thus the company may lose the customer and thousands of dollars in sales. When you make a mistake or your company makes a mistake, apologize quickly for the error and then solve the problem.

GO THE EXTRA MILE

Have you ever complained about a product you received while the customer service representative listened intently to your concerns and then said, "Our company is so sorry that we caused you this inconvenience; we will reduce the cost of your next order 5 percent"? If something similar has happened to you, how did you feel? Did you decide that everyone makes an error occasionally and that the company is not as incompetent as you had originally thought? Did you decide that you would give the company a second chance? Most of us would probably answer in the affirmative to the last two questions. By going the extra mile, the company has maintained a valued customer for a small cost. According to the popular book *Exceptional Customer Service*, "It costs between five and six times more to attract a new customer than to keep an existing one."[1]

Although keeping customers happy is important, never do anything that violates company ethics or standards just to keep a customer happy. A good question to ask yourself is: Would I be comfortable explaining what I did to my supervisor the next day? Know the actions you can take to keep customers, such as giving discounts on orders, by talking with your supervisor ahead of time.

---

[1]Lisa Ford, David McNair, and Bill Perry, *Exceptional Customer Service* (Massachusetts: Adams Media Corporation, 2001), p. 7.

Face-to-Face Customer Service Skills

Many times in a customer service organization, you encounter the customer on a face-to-face basis. The skills that you use in face-to-face contacts are somewhat different from the skills that you need to use when talking with a customer over the telephone or in cyberspace. Listed here are several skills you will need when working with the customer in person.

MAKE EYE CONTACT

Body language is an extremely important element in verbal communication. Body language can be divided into five forms—eye contact, facial expressions, posture, gestures, and space. Eye contact is an extremely powerful form of body language. It lets customers know that you are interested and attentive to what they are saying. You should make immediate eye contact with a customer. However, you should also look away from time to time. Staring at a person for a prolonged time may make the person feel uncomfortable.

SMILE

Generally a warm smile is extremely valuable. It signals that you care about the customer and are eager to help her or him. However, if the customer is extremely upset, a smile can signal that you are laughing at the individual, suggesting to the customer that you are not taking his or her issue seriously or possibly laughing at her or him.

MAINTAIN AN APPROPRIATE DISTANCE

Interpersonal space boundaries are cultural and individual. Some cultures, such as the Hispanic culture, tend to have small interpersonal space zones; people get close together to talk. However, most Americans will back away if you get too close to them; again, personal space is a cultural issue.

When you are working with customers, respect their personal space requirements. If you get too close, you will notice that people will back away. Honor their need for you to not violate

A warm smile and cheerful greeting let the customer know you are pleased to help.

their personal space. Sometimes people will use space as an intimidation factor; they will get "in your face" and possibly even yell if they are angry enough or shake their finger at you. Such an approach is never an acceptable way to deal with customers; it only makes people angrier and nothing is accomplished.

CALL THE CUSTOMER BY NAME

When a company representative whom you have just met immediately calls you by name, how do you feel? Do you feel as if the representative is interested in you and your concerns? Most of us would answer with a "yes." When someone takes the time to actually hear your name and then uses it, you tend to think that the representative and the company care about you.

LISTEN TO THE CUSTOMER

Have you ever had the experience, when you called a company to report lack of receipt of all items that you ordered, of being interrupted by the company employee before you could finish your statement? If you have, you understand the importance of letting a customer tell you the

story. Do not interrupt midway into the story. Even though it is time-consuming to hear a customer's entire story when you think you understood all that was necessary to solve the problem at the first of the conversation, it is important to let the customer finish her or his statement. You may be wrong; you may not have understood the real problem. Let the customer talk freely without your interruption.

Individuals spend much of their waking hours in some form of communication, with a large part of the communication time spent listening. You might wish to review the listening strategies given in Chapter 8, Verbal Communication and Presentations, now. Also read carefully the information in Figure 9.3; observing these tips will help you listen well to customers.

Listening cannot be overemphasized when you are dealing with customers. Listening says to the customer that you believe she or he is important, that you are paying attention to the customer's concerns, and that you care about the individual. One effective listening technique is to repeat back

- Listen actively, focusing all your attention on the customer.
- Listen for facts. Mentally register the key words the speaker is using and mentally repeat key ideas or related points.
- Notice the body language of the speaker for clues to the real meaning of what is being said.
- Let the customer finish the entire complaint or description of the problem. Do not interrupt.
- Repeat in concise terms the problem as you understand it. Ask the customer to verify that you have understood.
- Listen carefully to the customer's responses as you ask questions to further clarify the issues.

FIGURE 9.3 Listening Tips

to the customer what you believe the customer said. Even though you think you are listening effectively you can misunderstand, particularly when the customer is upset. For example, you might say to the customer, "I understand that our shipment to you included eight laptops and you had ordered ten. Did I understand you correctly?"

Occasionally, you might have a customer who swears or yells at you. You need to continue to listen in such a situation; if you get mad, the situation only gets worse. Try to find a neutral place where the two of you can meet; also try empathy statements. Consider the following conversation.

> *Customer: Your organization is totally incompetent. I bought this (bleep) printer in here two days ago, and I have had nothing but (bleep) problems. I expect your (bleep) organization to do something about it immediately.*

> *Employee: It's frustrating, isn't it, when something does not work properly, particularly when you are under a deadline to get work completed. I understand; I've been in situations such as this myself. Let's see what we can do.*

Generally such an approach will help diffuse the person's anger. The next step is to see what is wrong (if anything) with the printer. It could merely be that the person does not know how to

set it up. Remember to treat the customer with respect, even when the complaint is not valid.

USE LANGUAGE EFFECTIVELY

Difficulties in communication may be due to a lack of understanding of the language being used. When you or the customer have English as a second language or do not speak English, you may need to use an interpreter. If you routinely deal with customers who speak another language, learn a few basic phrases in that language to help you establish communication and determine whether an interpreter is needed.

The tone you use can be as important as your words. Voice tone is extremely important when talking with customers. You can convey friendliness and empathy or anger and disbelief simply by the tone of voice you use. Remember that you should remain calm and courteous even when talking with customers who are not.

Pay attention to the rate of speech you use when talking with customers. Speaking too quickly may make it difficult for a customer to understand what you are saying. Talking too fast may also make the customer think that you do not want to take time to talk about a problem or answer a question.

USE EMPATHY STATEMENTS

Empathy means showing an understanding or concern for someone's feelings or position. It is the ability to imagine yourself in the other person's situation. Showing empathy is a skill that must be practiced; you must listen to what the person is saying without evaluation. Empathy does not involve agreeing or disagreeing; it does involve respecting the other person's right to express a point of view. It also involves attempting to understand the other person's point of view. Being able to show genuine empathy for a customer who is describing a problem will help you gain or keep the customer's trust. An empathy statement such as "I can imagine it is frustrating when equipment does not operate as expected" acknowledges how the customer is feeling without admitting or denying fault. Using empathy statements can help diffuse feelings of anger or frustration.

EXPLAIN THE SITUATION

Have you ever been in a situation in which you spoke clearly, articulated well, and used empathy, and yet the individual to whom you were talking still did not understand you? Most of us would answer in the affirmative to such a question. Why? The basic reason is that the person is not using the same frame of reference that you use. Consider this story. Two individuals were talking and one said, "My new car is a lemon." The other person responds, "I did not know that you bought a yellow car." You almost laugh out loud, because you are so surprised. However, you restrain yourself and try to clear up the matter. You explain you have had one mechanical problem after another with the car. What you thought was a simple statement turned into a communication problem. However, at least the person let you know what she was thinking. Often, you do not know; thus, it is important for you to explain clearly what you mean. Then, you might give the person a chance to let you know if she or he understands by asking, "Does this make sense to you?" With such a statement, you are giving the individual a chance to tell you whether or not you have been clear in your communication.

ASSIST DIFFICULT PEOPLE

Some people are going to be difficult no matter how helpful and professional you are. Do not take it personally. Take a deep breath and tell yourself you will do the best you can. Use positive self-talk. Here are some statements you can make to yourself:

- I will not get angry.
- I have been successful in situations such as this one in the past, and I will be successful again.
- I care about people, and I know that most people are not difficult to deal with.

Telephone Customer Service Skills

Although email and instant messaging are used extensively, the telephone remains an important tool of the workplace environment. As an administrative professional, you must be effective in your telephone communications. Without appropriate telephone customer service skills, you may not only make customers angry but also lose customers for your organization.

Communicating with Customers

Practice these tips when communicating with customers in person or by telephone.

- Use a pleasant and friendly tone of voice.
- Use correct English.
- Speak at an appropriate volume and speed for your speech.
- Listen carefully.
- Ask questions tactfully.
- Respond calmly to a loud or angry voice.

ANSWER THE PHONE PROFESSIONALLY

When your telephone rings, answer quickly, between the first and second ring if possible, and certainly by the third ring. You may lose a potential customer if you are slow in answering the telephone.

Answer the phone with the appropriate information. Greet the caller, give the name or department of your organization, give your name, and ask how you can help the caller. For example, you might say:

Hello, Green Corporation, Maria Perez speaking. How may I help you?

Answer the phone using a pleasant and friendly tone. Have you ever made a call and the person who answered the phone sounded as if she or he wished you had not called? Most of us have. The voice of a tired or unhappy person is readily discernible over the telephone and is not appealing to the caller.

Transfer the call when you cannot help the caller. If the caller has dialed your number by mistake or has inadvertently chosen the wrong department, tell the caller immediately. Ask the caller if you may transfer the call to the appropriate person. For example, you might say:

Jacqueline Edwards in our Customer Service Department can assist you. Her number is 555-388-0234; may I transfer you?

Close the call courteously. As you finish the call, thank the caller and state again that you will take the appropriate action. For example, you might say:

Thank you for calling, Ms. Wong. I will have the missing item from your order shipped to you right away.

LISTEN INTENTLY

As you are speaking with the caller, visualize the person. Listen politely to what the person is saying; do not interrupt. If the caller is unhappy about an experience with the organization, listen to the person's complaint. Use good listening skills, such as:

- Listen for facts.
- Search for subtle meanings.
- Be patient.
- Do not evaluate.
- Act on what the caller is saying.

If there is a problem, respond with empathy. Make statements such as "I'm sorry these items were not included in your order. Let me make a list of what is missing so I can have the items sent to you right away." Make notes of what the customer tells you. Then, repeat the complaint in concise terms to be sure you have understood it correctly.

Determine how you can help the customer. If you must find needed information, you may

© Blend Images / Jupiter Images

Greet callers professionally and courteously.

focus on — *Effective Email Messages*

Even though email messages are seen as more informal than letters, you need to be certain the customer has all the information she or he needs to buy your product or handle a problem. Follow these suggestions for writing effective email messages.

- Use an appropriate subject line so the reader will know at a glance why the email is being written.

- Do not use acronyms when writing to customers, such as FYI (for your information) and IMO (in my opinion). You will have some customers who do not understand the acronyms, and it is also very informal. You may use acronyms internally within the organization, but not for customers.

- As you would when writing letters, be clear and concise. Good email messages give the customer the necessary information but do not belabor the points covered.

- Read each email message carefully before you send it; it is extremely important to give the customer clear, correct, and complete information. Your email message should also be free of grammatical or typographical errors, errors that can say to the customer that your organization is sloppy and thus your product or service may be inferior.

- Check the email address of the individual. You do not want to send an email message to the wrong individual.

need to put the customer on hold. Explain why you need to put the caller on hold. Do not leave a caller on hold for several minutes. If finding the information will take more than a few minutes, take the caller's name and telephone number. Call the customer back when you have the needed information. Give the customer your name and number for reference.

DEAL WITH AN ABUSIVE CUSTOMER

Usually, you cannot help an abusive customer until she or he calms down. Do not let yourself become angry; this behavior merely escalates the situation. Look for points of agreement with the customer and voice those points. These techniques generally work well, and you can then begin to help solve the problem with the customer. If the customer continues to be abusive, you may have to ask the customer to call back later when he or she can discuss the issue calmly.

Many organizations have a policy concerning difficult or abusive telephone situations. Find out what the policy is and observe it. Some companies have a recorded announcement telling customers that the call may be recorded for

customer service quality or training purposes. Customers may be less likely to make threats or inappropriate comments if they know the call might be recorded.

Email Customer Service Skills

Because email is less expensive and faster than regular mail, its use is widespread in business. Effectively managing the amount of email that is received by businesses is a major issue. You should answer your work email messages as soon as possible. The messages should not sit in your in-box for days before you open them. However, neither can you be expected to answer each email message within five minutes of receiving it.

One way to handle email effectively and still be productive at the other work you must do is to schedule specific times when you will write and respond to email. You will need to determine the scheduling times based on the volume of messages you receive. For example, if most of your job requires handling email customers, then you will need to check your email every hour or every half hour (depending on the volume of email).

© Digital Vision / Getty Images

A call center may have dozens of customer service representatives to answer questions or provide product information.

However, if only a portion of your job requires handling email customers, you may want to check your email only three or four times a day. Keep in mind that the customer should be served in a timely, caring, and efficient manner.

Customer Service Call Centers

Many organizations deal with customers through call centers. A **call center** is a centralized customer contact office in an organization. Calls are answered and handled by employees who are trained to handle customer questions and issues. Staff of the call center may handle customer contacts made through written messages, email, fax, telephone, or the company Website. Some call centers respond only to incoming communications from customers such as product inquiries or requests for help. Other centers also place calls for telemarketing purposes. **Telemarketing** is selling, soliciting, or promoting a product or service on the telephone.

As an administrative professional, you may not be employed by a call center. However, the organization for which you work may use a call center to handle some of its customer service functions. You need to be knowledgeable concerning these centers. The customer service skills that have been stressed in this chapter are applicable to call centers. Call centers often become the public face of the company. The customer's call center experience can become a key driver of a company's success. Research has shown that 96 percent of unhappy customers will not report their frustration to the company. Of those unhappy customers, over 90 percent will simply not come back. An unhappy customer will tell nine others about the bad experience.[2] This is a type of word-of-mouth advertising the organization does not need. In contrast, customers that have a good experience are more likely to purchase or use services from the organization again.

---

[2]Anthony Mullins, "8 Critical Steps to Establish a Customer Service Culture," Ezine Articles, accessed May 16, 2007, available from http://ezinearticles.com/?8-Critical-Steps-to-Establish-a-Customer-Service-Culture&id=37272.

Call centers exist in many types of businesses and organizations. Call centers continue to grow in number, with centers located all over the world. Several U.S. companies have located their call centers in other countries in an attempt to lower costs. However, some customers express frustration when talking with call center staff members located in other countries. Customers complain that they cannot understand the call center staff members or that the staff members are not knowledgeable about the company or products and only respond with scripted messages. Companies must decide whether the decreased cost of using offshore call centers outweighs the cost of having dissatisfied customers. "Despite all of the concern about call center jobs going offshore to India or nearshore to Canada, the United States is still the center for call center positions, according to David Butler, executive director of the National Association of Call Centers." Data gathered from a variety of sources shows that approximately 62 percent of call center jobs are located in the U.S.[3]

Web Customer Service

Millions of people in countries all over the world use the Internet. For example, there were over 200 million Internet users in North America as of March 2007 (69.7 percent population penetration).[4] People use the Web for activities such as booking travel reservations, banking, and shopping for products.

Businesses today see the Web as an avenue for sales and customer service. Some companies offer customers the option of searching for answers to their questions on the company Website as an alternative to contacting customer service by telephone. This option is called Web self-service. For example, many of Dell Computer's customers who need help choose Web self-service. This service lets them tap into the same

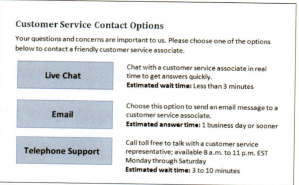

FIGURE 9.4 Many companies offer several customer service options on their Websites.

tools and knowledge bases that Dell agents use to help customers. Customers can get answers quickly using this service, and Dell agents can focus on handling other customers who may have more complex problems.[5]

Some companies offer a **live chat** feature as part of their Web-based customer service. Customers can exchange text messages with a staff member in real time. This option offers a personalized service that may be less expensive for the company than telephone support. Figure 9.4 shows an example Web screen for a company that offers live chat as a support option.

As an administrative professional, your work may not directly involve customer service via the Web. However, the organization for which you work may offer Web self-service or live chat as options for customers. Review the Web self-service if your organization offers this option so you can be knowledgeable about what it offers when talking with customers.

Inappropriate Customer Behavior

You learned earlier in this chapter that the customer is not always right. However, the premise is an extremely good one. As you work in

[3]Phillip Britt, "Call Center Jobs: The U.S. Is Still Number One," CRM Magazine, accessed May 16, 2007, available from http://www.destinationcrm.com/articles/default.asp?ArticleID=6267.

[4]"Internet Usage Statistics—The Big Picture," Internet World Stats, accessed May 16, 2007, available from http://www.internetworldstats.com/stats.htm.

[5]Alice Dragoon, "Put Your Money Where Your Mouthpiece Is," CIO, accessed May 16, 2007, available from http://www.cio.com.au/index.php/id;401260420.

organizations that value customer service, treat each customer with respect and follow the suggestions that have been given in this chapter in regard to working with customers. However, there are times when you encounter individuals who behave in threatening, racist, or sexist ways. You need to understand your options when such situations arise.

Handling Threats of Bodily Harm

Workplace violence is a serious issue. According to the National Institute for Occupational Safety and Health (NOISH), "On average, 1.7 million workers are injured each year, and more than 800 die as a result of workplace violence."[6] Although all verbal threats of bodily harm are just that—threats—you do not know which threats are serious and which threats are not. Thus you must behave in a way that protects not only you, but also other workers within the organization. In order to contribute to a safe workplace, report all threats to management. If the threat puts you or others in serious danger, also report it to the police.

If you are in a threatening situation, try to remain as calm as possible. You may need to call security officers to escort the customer from the premises. If the organization does not have security officers, you may need to call the police emergency assistance number (911 in many areas) for immediate assistance. Record details about the situation as soon as the immediate danger is over. Know and follow your organization's policies and guidelines regarding dangerous situations in the workplace.

Handling Inappropriate Comments

When a customer uses foul language or makes racist and/or sexist comments to you, try not to let yourself be drawn into the situation. It may be best to ignore a passing remark and focus the

conversation on the business needs of the customer. If the foul language or inappropriate comments continue, tactfully let the customer know that the language or comments are not considered appropriate. Stress that you want to focus on helping the customer and not be distracted by these issues.

Always report incidents that may be considered sexual or **racial harassment** to your supervisor in writing. Know your organization's policy on dealing with sexual or racial harassment, including instances involving customers. According to the U.S. Equal Employment Opportunity Commission (EEOC):

> *Examples of harassing conduct include: offensive jokes, slurs, epithets or name calling, physical assaults or threats, intimidation, ridicule or mockery, insults or put-downs, offensive objects or pictures, and interference with work performance. An employer may be held liable for the harassing conduct of supervisors, coworkers, or non-employees (such as customers or business associates) over whom the employer has control. An isolated incident would not normally create a hostile work environment, unless it is extremely serious. On the other hand, an incident of harassment that is not severe standing alone may create a hostile environment when frequently repeated.[7]*

If you report repeated harassment and your organization does not deal with the issue, you may wish to file charges with federal or state agencies that deal with civil rights issues such as the EEOC. You may want to look for employment with another organization that values employees and strives to create a positive work environment.

[6]"Workplace Violence Prevention Strategies and Research Needs," National Institute for Occupational Safety and Health, accessed May 16, 2007, available from http://www.cdc.gov/niosh/docs/2006-144/.

[7]"Questions and Answers About Race and Color Discrimination in Employment," U.S. Equal Employment Opportunity Commission, accessed May 16, 2007, available from http://www.eeoc.gov/policy/docs/qanda_race_color.html.

Summary

To reinforce what you have learned in this chapter, study this summary.

- Many businesses and other organizations cannot fully achieve their goals without effective customer service.

- Organizations that have a commitment to customer service reflect this commitment in their mission and vision statements and in the actions of their leaders and employees.

- The future customers of any organization will likely be diverse and of various cultures, ages, and race. They may be from a different country than the organization's workers.

- Customers should be treated with respect, even when they are at fault or incorrect about an assumption. They should be given an explanation if they have a question about the product or service.

- Customer service includes listening with empathy to customers when they have a problem and providing options and alternatives when you cannot give the customer exactly what she or he wants.

- To prepare to give good customer service, learn about the goals of your company, visualize success, take responsibility, and admit mistakes. Go the extra mile when solving customer problems.

- When serving customers face-to-face, make eye contact, smile, maintain appropriate interpersonal distance, call the customer by name, listen to the customer, use language effectively, use empathy statements, explain the situation, and assist difficult people in a patient and professional manner.

- When serving telephone customers, answer the phone professionally and quickly, answer with appropriate information, listen intently, deal with an abusive customer tactfully, and close the call courteously.

- Answer email messages in a timely fashion. Schedule specific times of the day when you will write and respond to email if you receive a large number of messages.

- A call center is a centralized customer contact office in an organization. Staff of the call center may handle customer contacts made through written messages, email, fax, telephone, or the company Website.

- Some companies offer customers the option of searching for answers to their questions on a Website as an alternative to telephone service. Some companies offer a live chat feature as part of their Web-based customer service.

- When customers threaten bodily harm or engage in inappropriate racist and/or sexist behaviors, you have the responsibility to deal appropriately with such incidences.

What's the Problem?

Susie Chang works as an administrative assistant in the Human Resources Department. Recently she answered a telephone call on the second ring:

Susie:	This is Susie Chang in HR. How may I help you?
Customer:	Hello. Is this the Jackson Corporation? I am trying to reach Tom Cushner.
Susie:	Yes, this is Jackson Corporation, but as I said, I am Susie Chang. You must have dialed the wrong number. I think someone named Tom works in the Accounting Department, but I am not sure. Please hang up and try your call again.
Customer:	Well, could you transfer me to Mr. Cushner?
Susie:	Sorry. I do not have that number. Goodbye.

Did Susie handle this customer contact effectively? What did Susie do that was positive? What could she have done differently to improve customer service?

Let's Discuss

1. Why is effective customer service important to businesses and other organizations?
2. Describe characteristics of companies that value effective customer service.
3. "The customer is always right" is not a true statement. What implications does this have for the way customers should be treated?
4. Give an example of "going the extra mile" to resolve a customer problem.
5. List five tips for improving face-to-face customer service.
6. What information should you provide when answering the phone in a business setting?
7. What is a call center? What types of communications do call center staff members handle?
8. Describe two ways that customers may find answers to questions on a company Website.

Critical-Thinking Activity

You have been dealing with a customer over the telephone for several months. He continues to buy telecommunications equipment from your organization. At this point, he has spent approximately $100,000 with the organization. You have never had any problems with him; he has been very professional in his conduct with you, as you have with him. When he calls, he always asks for you by name. He has been extremely polite and businesslike. However, on two recent occasions, he has told you that you sound so nice over the telephone that he would like to meet you. You have made statements such as, "Thanks for the compliments; I do care about customers." You have evaded the suggestion that you meet him, thinking that he would not insist. The last time he called to place an order, he repeated his interest in meeting you, making a threatening statement (you believe) that he will stop ordering from the company unless you are willing to meet him. He did laugh after he made the statement, but you believe he is serious.

You know your employer values his business. He has mentioned to you that he appreciates your help with this valuable customer. You are single, but you do not think that it would be wise to meet the customer.

How should you handle this difficult situation? Should you talk with your employer?

Vocabulary Review

Open the *Word* file *CH09 Vocabulary* found on the Student CD. Complete the vocabulary review for Chapter 9.

English and Word Usage Drill

Complete the English and Word Usage Drill for Chapter 9 found in the *Applications Workbook.*

Workplace Applications

9-1 Customer Service Situations

(Goals 1 and 2)

**team
building**

1. Work with two or three classmates to complete this activity. Each team member should share with the group at least one incident from personal experience that involves customer service.

2. As a group, discuss each incident. Discuss how you think the incident made the customer feel. For example, good customer service may make the customer feel loyal to the company. Poor customer service may make the customer feel angry or frustrated.

3. For incidents involving poor customer service, discuss what the company might have done differently to improve customer service.

4. Choose one of the incidents discussed to share with the class. As a group, write a summary of the incident, the outcome, and recommendations for improving customer service in that situation.

9-2 Customer Service Tips

(Goal 3)

internet

Your company is launching a program to improve customer service. As part of this effort, you have been asked to create a Web page to be posted on the new section of the company Website devoted to improving customer service.

1. Review the tips for improving customer service given in this chapter. Using the Internet or other sources, find and read at least three articles about improving customer service. Note the source information for these articles.

e-portfolio

2. Create a Web page to be posted on the company Website. Only employees (not customers) will have access to this page.

   - Use *Customer Service* as the main heading for the page.

   - Use *Tips for Improving Customer Service* as the subheading for this page.

   - Under the heading, key a bulleted list of ten tips for improving customer service.

   - Place footnotes at the bottom of the page for any material lifted from articles you read.

   - Use an attractive design and color scheme for the page. Add appropriate artwork if desired.

3. Save the document as a single file Web page using an appropriate name. View the page in a browser. Make changes or corrections as needed for a page that is attractive and easy to read.

9-3 Call Center Statistics

(Goal 3)

You work for Carson Company, a small business that uses a call center to answer customer inquiries. The call center is open from 8 a.m. to 8 p.m. Monday through Friday. Callers that contact the center on Saturday and Sunday are invited to leave a message. Those calls are returned on Monday. In the call center, Ramon handles calls from 8 a.m. to 1 p.m. and 2 p.m. to 4 p.m. Janice starts work at 1 p.m. and answers calls until 2 p.m. when Ramon returns from lunch. Janice has other duties until she begins answering calls again at 4 p.m. She answers calls until 8 p.m. when the center closes. Calls typically last at least 5 minutes and may last as long as 20 minutes. You have been asked to examine the number of calls the call center receives during certain periods of the day and recommend whether additional staff members are needed in the call center.

1. Open the *Excel* file *CH09 Call Statistics* found on the Student CD. This worksheet shows the number of calls received by the call center during three periods during the day. Data are given for the month of June.

2. Enter a formula to find the total number of calls for each time period.

3. Enter formulas to find the average number of calls for each time period and the maximum number of calls for each time period. Round numbers to the nearest whole number (0 decimal places).

4. Create a pie chart to show the average calls received in each time period. Title the chart *AVERAGE CALLS BY TIME PERIOD*. Use *June* and the current year as the chart subtitle. Show the category name and percentage in the data labels.

5. Enter a formula to find the total number of calls made on each day in June.

6. Enter a formula to find the average number of calls made on each day of the week (Sunday through Saturday). Round numbers to the nearest whole number (0 decimal places).

7. Create a column chart to compare the average number of calls made on each day of the week (Sunday through Saturday). Title the chart *AVERAGE CALLS PER DAY*. Use *June* and the current year as the chart subtitle. Show data labels for each column.

8. Write a memo to your supervisor (your instructor). Use the file *CH09 Carson Memo* found on the Student CD to create the memo. Use the current date and an appropriate subject line. Summarize your findings regarding the number of calls made on different days of the week and during different time periods each day. Include the two charts you created in the memo. Recommend whether or not the company should hire additional workers for the call center. If you recommend that workers be added, discuss when the workers are needed (day of week and time period).

Assessment of Chapter 9 Goals

Did you successfully complete the chapter goals? Evaluate yourself by filling out the form found in Chapter 9 of the *Applications Workbook*.

part 4

Technology Basics

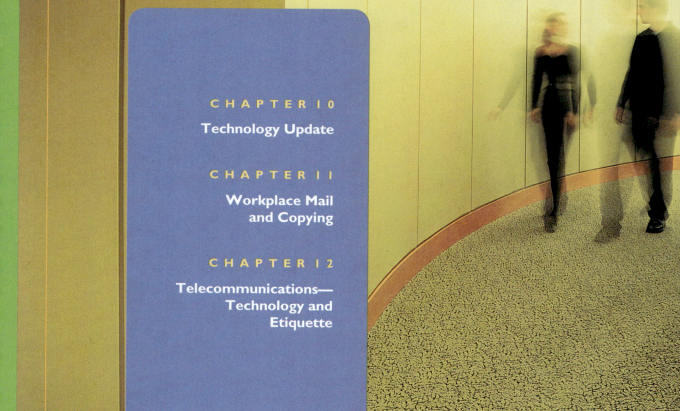

CHAPTER 10

Technology Update

CHAPTER 11

Workplace Mail and Copying

CHAPTER 12

Telecommunications— Technology and Etiquette

Career Profile

Network Administrator

For many organizations, computer technology plays a vital role in sharing information within the organization and with customers and partners. Network administrators design, install, and support an organization's computer networks and Internet connections. Network administrators work in almost all industries and for small, medium, and large companies. About 278,000 people worked as network and computer systems administrators in the United States in 2004.*

Network administrators manage an organization's computer networks, including intranet systems and Internet use. They monitor the performance of existing systems and plan for improvements and future needs of the organization. They oversee care of network hardware and software. They may also be responsible for the security of computers and networks, a role with increasing importance in this era of cyber crime. Network administrators typically work about 40 hours per week during regular business hours; however, they may be on call to handle problems after hours.

Salaries for network administrators vary by the education, training, and experience of the worker. The mean annual earnings of network administrators were $58,190 in May 2004. Strong problem-solving, analytical, and communication skills are important for success as a network administrator. Because these workers often interact with other company personnel and customers, they must be able to communicate effectively. A bachelor's degree in computer science or information systems is required for many jobs; however, for some entry-level jobs only a computer-related associate's degree is required. The completion of a certification training program, offered by a variety of vendors and product makers, may help some people to qualify for entry-level positions.

Rapid job growth is projected for computer specialists and network administrators over the 2004–2014 period. Job prospects should be best for college graduates who are up to date with the latest skills and technologies.

---

*"Computer Support Specialists and Systems Administrators," *Occupational Outlook Handbook*, 2006-07 Edition, accessed June 25, 2007, available from http://www.bls.gov/oco/ocos268.htm.

chapter 10

Technology Update

Learning Goals

1. **Describe types of computers, input devices, storage devices, and networks commonly found in businesses.**

2. **Describe the function of applications software and systems software.**

3. **Understand threats and solutions related to computer security and privacy.**

Computer Hardware

Computers impact our lives on a daily basis. People use computers to order food at a restaurant, to make airline reservations, to file income taxes, and even to purchase groceries. Wireless technologies enable people to work and play from nearly anywhere in the world with notebook computers, PDAs, and cell phones. Computer technologies continue to progress, enabling people to stay connected and to work faster and with greater portability.

Computer Types

Computers in business come in all shapes and sizes. While the traditional computer was a machine on a desk in an office, computers are now found in police cars, the hands of package delivery personnel, at the grocery checkout, and in the pockets and handbags of millions of people. Some of the most common computer types are described in the following sections.

MICROCOMPUTERS

The most common type of personal computer is the microcomputer. This type of computer system is designed to be used by one person at a time and is often called a desktop computer because the complete system fits on or next to a desk in an office or home. Microcomputers are used extensively in businesses and home offices to prepare correspondence, maintain accounting files, create and respond to customer email, access and update Web pages, and to complete other office-related tasks. These computers are affordable for both business and home use. These computer systems are also considered modular equipment because they are equipped with components that can be replaced or upgraded easily.

NOTEBOOK COMPUTERS

A notebook computer is a portable microcomputer that is specifically designed to be moved from one place to another. These systems are similar to the desktop computers in speed, performance, and usage. They are sometimes referred to as laptop**s** because they were originally developed to be used when no desk was available and the computer rested on the user's lap. Notebook computers perform the same functions and contain components that are similar to those found on a desktop computer, but they are made smaller for ease in transporting. Because of their portability, notebook computers are used by many workers who need to use their computers at remote locations.

Notebook computers typically weigh between 2 and 5 pounds and are about the size of a standard paper notebook. Because these computers are equipped with long-life rechargeable lithium batteries, notebook users can typically work or play remotely for three or four hours at a time. Notebooks usually have a built-in keyboard, a touchpad, or a pointing stick for input as well as the capability of attaching an external keyboard or mouse. A notebook computer may be a little more expensive than its desktop equivalent, but it provides a great advantage to users who require portability. Notebook computers are popular with salespeople, real estate agents, students, and others whose work requires them to be on the move. Figure 10.1 gives some tips on proper computer hardware care.

© PhotoDisc / Getty Images

Notebook computers allow users to conduct their work in a variety of locations.

HARDWARE CARE TIPS

Follow these tips to keep your hardware working properly.

- Do not physically harm your hardware by dropping a notebook computer, knocking a piece of hardware off a desk, or jostling the system unit. If you need a more durable computer, you can purchase one that will withstand much more physical abuse than a conventional computer.

- Use a surge suppressor to protect hardware from damage due to power fluctuations. For a desktop computer, use the surge suppressor with all of the powered computer components (including the system unit, monitor, printer, and scanner).

- Safeguard your computer from dust, heat, static, and moisture. All of these can be dangerous to a computer. Remove the dust from your computer with a small handheld vacuum. To protect your computer from heat, do not leave it in the direct sunlight and use it in an area that has plenty of ventilation.

FIGURE 10.1 Proper care of hardware can help to prevent serious damage to a computer system.

TABLET PCS

A **tablet PC** is also a portable or mobile computer. It is smaller and thinner than a notebook computer. The screen can be turned or rotated to allow the user to write or select items using a **digital pen** designed for the tablet. Although a tablet PC may include a traditional keyboard, more often the user will use handwriting, drawing, or speech recognition tools for data input. Tablet PCs without a dedicated keyboard are often called slates.

Many users find the tablet PC more portable than the traditional notebook computer. The slim and lightweight design makes it easy to carry under your arm like a book. Individuals who lack keyboarding skills find the ability to take handwritten notes and diagrams with a digital pen or stylus more functional. Tablet PCs are used for data entry by hospital staff, home inspectors, engineers, salespeople, and students.

Some users find tablet computers cumbersome. Individuals with excellent keyboarding skills may be unable to input data as quickly when relying on handwriting. Tablet PCs have a higher risk of screen damage because the screen is typically used for input. However, for many users, the mobility and flexibility of the tablet PC outweigh any potential disadvantages.

HANDHELD COMPUTERS

A handheld computer is a computing device about the size of a deck of cards. Typically, handheld computers have a small display screen as well as a small keyboard or touchpad that is used for data input. Because they were originally created to provide personal organizer functions, handheld computers are sometimes called personal digital assistants or PDAs. The original PDA functions included a calendar, appointment book, and address book as well as access to email and Internet services. The capabilities of handheld computers have broadened to include global positioning services, video recording, and use of many programs formerly reserved for traditional desktop computers such as word processing and spreadsheets.

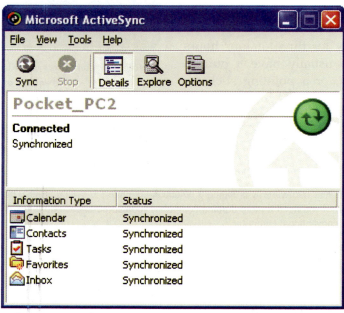

FIGURE 10.2 Data such as Contacts and Calendar entries can be updated by synchronizing a handheld computer and a notebook computer.

Although handheld computers are used by mobile workers in a variety of business occupations, they are often used in other fields including medicine, forestry, meter reading, asset management, surveying, and parking enforcement. Handheld computers for business use have evolved to include full keyboards or the ability to connect the handheld to a full-size keyboard. Many of the handheld devices use wireless technologies to connect to the Internet, GPS services, or a computer network. For those individuals who use both a handheld and a desktop or portable computer, the ability to share data between the computers is an important feature. For the business user, the ability to synchronize a handheld computer with a personal computer is an important feature so that data is up-to-date on both. Figure 10.2 shows the *Microsoft ActiveSync*® screen that indicates two computers have been synchronized.

SMARTPHONES

A smartphone is a full-featured mobile phone that includes many of the functions of a handheld computer. In addition to the typical telephone features and a built-in camera, smartphone features include a complete email system, Internet access, scheduling software, and contact management capabilities. Additional features such as navigation software and the ability to read business documents may also be available. Some of the newer models of phones include video recording capability and electronic music file downloading and storage capabilities. A variety of accessories are also available for phones, including detachable speakers, printers, and even projectors.

Input Devices

Information is input to a computer in a variety of ways. The basic and most recognized computer input device is the keyboard. Although new input technologies continue to be developed, the keyboard continues to serve as the most widely used input device. Today, most computers are equipped with a keyboard and mouse. Other input devices that may also be used are discussed in the following sections.

POINTING DEVICES

A **pointing device** is a computer hardware component that allows a user to input data or give commands to a computer. The most common pointing device by far is the mouse. Another commonly used pointing device is the trackball. A **trackball** is a stationary ball that can be rolled in place to move the cursor on the screen. Trackball rollers are often installed within a keyboard. They may also be attached to the side of a keyboard as a removable accessory.

The digital pen, also called a stylus or electronic pen, is another pointing device that can be used to select objects, draw, give commands, or write electronically on the screen. This pointing device is used with a touchpad or a touch screen. A touchpad or touch screen senses motion and pressure by the digital pen to control the motion of the on-screen pointer or to enter handwriting. With some touch screens, the individual can use

© Image100 / Jupiter Images

Smartphones combine the features of a digital phone and a handheld computer.

his or her finger to select commands or provide input to the computer.

The most recognizable use of an electronic pen is in retail businesses where it is used to electronically record signatures used to authorize credit card purchases. Touch screens are found in a variety of applications including airports (used as a self-check-in system), restaurants (used as an order entry system), gas stations (used to select fuel and method of payment), and banking (used to complete banking and financial transactions).

The digital pen is also used with a **graphics tablet**, which is an input device that allows users to draw images and graphics in much the same way as with a pencil and paper. Using a digital pen, the user creates the image on the tablet and the image is displayed on a computer monitor. Graphics tablets are available in a variety of formats and price ranges and typically connect to a computer through a USB connection.

SCANNERS

Scanners are commonly used computer input devices. A **scanner** is used to capture an image in digital form and transfer that information to a computer. Original images can be in the form of a printed document, handwritten document, photograph, drawing, or other graphic image. Once the information is scanned, it can be resized, inserted into other documents, posted on a Web page, sent as an email attachment, printed, or treated like any other digital image.

Some scanners are equipped to work with software programs to perform optical character recognition (OCR). This technology recognizes handwritten or typed characters and converts them to an electronic form as text rather than images. The text can be edited in a word processing program. OCR technology has been used by the United States Postal Service to sort mail since the late 1960s. OCR technology is used by businesses to scan printed documents that need

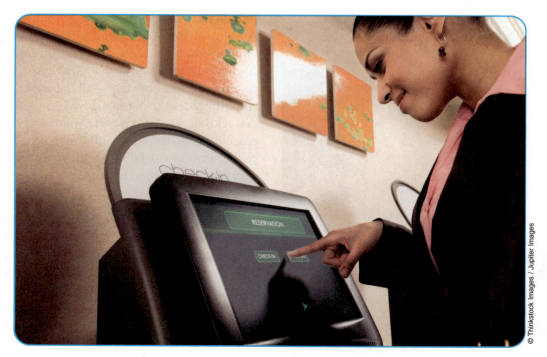

© Thinkstock Images / Jupiter Images

Touch screens are a common self-service technology.

to be edited and revised. Because handwritten text varies widely from individual to individual, it is difficult to accurately translate handwritten information.

DIGITAL CAMERAS

Digital cameras allow users to take pictures that are automatically captured as digital files. The software that comes with the camera then takes the pictures from the camera and transfers the files directly to the computer. Most digital cameras are multifunctional in that they allow users to record sound and or video as well as photographs.

When a digital camera is used in conjunction with a computer, users can insert pictures into a variety of software applications where they can be edited, printed, faxed, or included with email messages. In addition, photographs can be incorporated into electronic presentations; posted on Websites; or included in newsletters, reports, or memos. There are also many electronic devices that include digital cameras as a component. For example, many mobile telephones and PDAs contain an internal digital camera. Pictures taken with these devices can be transferred to notebook or personal computers through a USB or wireless connection or sent as an email.

Professional Pointers

To be successful as an administrative professional, you must stay current with technological advances. Follow these pointers to learn about current technology.

- Read articles in computer journals and magazines.

- Enroll in continuing education courses or workshops to learn about new technology.

- Learn from others about the software programs they use.

- Visit computer retail stores to observe demonstrations of available hardware and software.

- Look for online software tutorials.

SPEECH RECOGNITION

Speech recognition is the process of converting spoken words into digital form. You may have heard of these systems by other names, such as voice input system, voice recognition system, or computer speech recognition. Regardless of the name used, these systems require the use of a microphone or headset as well as an appropriate software package. Although speech recognition technology was originally developed for people who found it difficult to use a keyboard or mouse, it has evolved into a system that is used in a variety of business situations. Some computer operating system programs, such as *Windows Vista*™, include speech recognition. Application programs, such as *Dragon Naturally Speaking*®, are also popular with speech recognition users.

Advances in speech recognition continue to make the technology easier to use and more accurate. Programs for recognizing a few isolated words, such as telephone voice navigation systems, work for almost every user. As the accuracy and ease of use have increased, speech recognition systems have increasingly been incorporated into portable PCs, mobile devices, cell phones, and GPS systems to allow hands-free operation. Other similar systems are used to control machines, robots, and other electronic equipment such as that used by doctors during surgical procedures.

Medical and legal transcriptions are the most frequently used speech recognition applications; however, speech recognition technology is also used for querying databases and giving commands to computer-based systems. When using continuous speech programs (such as a dictation program) the user must take the time to train the software to recognize his or her speech patterns. Training involves the user reading aloud samples of text as indicated in Figure 10.3. With the growing power of personal computers, the accuracy of speech recognition has improved markedly, making it an important input method.

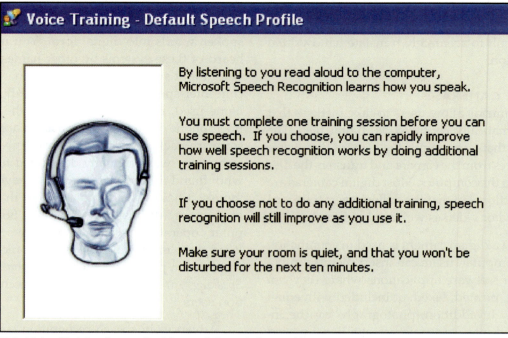

FIGURE 10.3 Voice Training Screen for Microsoft Speech Recognition

Data Storage

As information is created on a computer, it is often saved for future reference or as part of a permanent record of a completed project. Today, a wide variety of computer storage options exist, and there continue to be great advances in this area. Currently the most popular storage systems are:

- Hard drives
- Optical disk systems
- Flash memory systems

HARD DRIVES

A **hard drive** is a device that stores data magnetically on metal disks that are permanently sealed. On many computers, the hard drive continues to serve the two functions for which it was created—storing program information and storing user data. Internal hard drives hold between 80 to 500 GB, and that storage capacity is expected to grow.

Although hard drives are typically located inside the computer, external hard drives are also available. These devices are storage mechanisms that operate like an internal hard drive but connect to a computer using a USB port, a FireWire port, or a wireless networking connection. External hard drives can be used to move a large amount of data from one computer to another, as a backup hard drive, or as additional information storage. Because hard drives use magnetic recording, they are susceptible to the effects of minor bumps or careless handling that can affect the integrity of the stored data.

Portable hard drives are small devices used to move information from one computer to another. Typically, these small devices are designed to be used with handheld computers, digital music players, and other portable devices. Hard drives today come with built-in security features, such as fingerprint readers that allow only authorized users to access the information on the drive.

OPTICAL DISK SYSTEMS

An **optical disk** is a thin, lightweight plastic disk that can be used to store and retrieve data with a low-powered laser beam. Many people are familiar with the first generation of optical disk storage, the compact disk (CD). Although CDs were originally created to store music and software, there has been a constant succession of optical disk formats. Second generation optical disk storage includes digital versatile disks (DVDs). This storage medium was created to store large amounts of data, including TV-quality digital video. The main enhancements from the CD to the DVD are that the DVD can be used to store high-quality video and sound data. DVDs resemble CDs in the way they look; however, they are encoded in a different format and at a much higher density.

CDs and DVDs come in a variety of formats. CD-ROMs (compact disk read-only memory) and DVD-ROMs (digital versatile disk read-only memory) are read-only storage media. This means that they can be read but no data can be added, changed, or erased. This media form typically comes prerecorded with software programs, clip art, product demos, or music. Most CD-ROM drives can play data and audio CDs; DVD-ROM drives can play data and audio CDs and DVDs.

Recordable disks include CD-R, DVD-R, DVD+R, and DVD+R DL. A recordable disk is one that can be written to but the disk cannot be erased and reused. Recordable CDs are commonly used for backing up files, sending large files to others, and creating custom music CDs. Recordable DVDs are used for similar purposes or when more storage space is needed such as for large backups or for storing home movies or video files. Rewritable disks are also available. These disks can be recorded on, erased, and overwritten. The most common types of rewritable optical media include CD-RW, DVD-RW, and DVD+RW disks.

A variety of third generation **blue laser disks (BDs)** are currently in development. Using a blue laser instead of infrared lasers (CDs) or red lasers (DVDs), the new optical disks are designed for storing high-definition video and support larger storage capacities. Although there are a variety of third generation disks still in development, the Blu-ray Disc (BD) and HD- (high density) DVD are two examples of third generation disks currently on the market.

Optical disks offer a number of advantages over traditional magnetic storage media. First, an optical disk holds much more data. Because there is greater control and focus possible with laser beams, much more data can be written into a smaller space. Also, storage capacity increases with each new generation of optical media. For example, a BD can store five to six times the amount of data than can currently be stored on a DVD; the HD-DVD can store three times the data of a standard DVD. Optical disks are also inexpensive to manufacture, and data stored on them is safe from most environmental threats such as magnetic disturbances and power surges.

FLASH MEMORY SYSTEMS

Flash memory is a type of nonvolatile memory where data can be electrically stored, retrieved, and erased. Nonvolatile memory can retain stored information even when there is no power. What makes flash memory systems different from hard drives and optical disk technology is that they are a solid-state storage system, meaning they have no moving parts. Because of this, flash memory systems require much less power than conventional drives and are resistant to shocks and vibrations.

Flash memory usually takes on one of two forms: cards or drives. Flash memory cards are small cards that are inserted into computers or other portable devices for storage purposes. Flash cards come in a variety of formats. A flash drive is a portable storage device that typically connects to the USB port on a computer. A flash drive, also known as a mini drive, jump drive, keychain drive, pen drive, or thumb drive, is typically the size of a package of gum or smaller.

The small size of flash memory devices make them an excellent storage medium for digital cameras, digital music players, handheld

Flash memory has become a very popular and stylish data storage option.

computers, notebook computers, smartphones, and other portable devices. This small size also makes them an excellent method for transporting data from one place to another in a briefcase or pocket. Flash memory media are rewritable and have a longer expected life than other removable media.

Networks

In the workplace and in the home office, computers and other devices are commonly linked together to form a computer network. A **computer network** is two or more computers and other hardware devices connected together for the purpose of communicating and sharing resources. There are several advantages to using networks.

- Networks assist in communications. Using a network, individuals can quickly communicate using email, instant messaging, chat rooms, and videoconferencing. Sometimes these communications occur within an organization's network; other times they occur globally over the Internet.

- Networks facilitate sharing information. When using a network, any authorized user can access data and information stored on other computers connected to the network. For example, a university may store student records on a network so that a variety of individuals within the organization could access this information.

- Networks facilitate sharing hardware. Each computer linked to a network can access and use hardware on the network. Many organizations use a network so users can share a printer, scanner, or other device.

- Networks facilitate sharing software. Users can often access software from a network. Many software vendors offer a site license agreement which allows an organization to provide access to software from multiple computers.

Computer networks exist in a variety of sizes and configurations. The following sections will describe the most common network types, the Internet, and the World Wide Web.

COMMON NETWORK TYPES

A personal area network (PAN) is a network of personal computing devices for one individual. The devices in a PAN must be physically located close together and connected to share data, hardware, and/or an Internet connection. For example, a person traveling with a notebook, a personal digital assistant, and a portable printer could connect them and create a PAN. If the devices are connected through the use of wireless technology, the network is called a WPAN (wireless personal area network). WPANs have the added benefit of enabling a group of devices to communicate with each other whenever they are within a certain physical distance of one another without making a physical connection. For example, a PDA would automatically synchronize with a desktop computer when it is within a certain range.

A local area network (LAN) links various types of computer devices within a small geographic area. This area could be a single office, a home office, a building, or several nearby buildings. Today, LANs are common in the workplace and many home offices. One of the main benefits of using a LAN is the ability to share equipment. For example, one or two printers can accommodate everyone on the network. Also, a LAN typically has storage space and software applications that are shared by users. A local area network may serve as few as two or three users or thousands of users.

A metropolitan area network (MAN) links LANs and equipment over a distance equal to the size of a city and its surroundings. A college or university that links more than one LAN or several city or regional campuses is an example of a MAN.

A network that connects computing equipment over an area that can include hundreds of thousands of miles is called a wide area network (WAN). WANs are used to connect LANS and other types of networks together so that users and computers in one location can use the computers and systems in other locations. Many WANs are built for one particular organization and are therefore private. However, there are examples of public WANs as well. In fact, the largest and most widely known example of a WAN is the Internet.

THE INTERNET

The Internet is the largest and most well known network linking millions of computers throughout the world. Both individuals and businesses have found uses for this network. Individuals use the Internet to access information, communicate with family and friends, and purchase products and services. Businesses use the Internet to communicate with customers and vendors, sell their products and services, and provide customer support.

The Internet is a vast WAN that connects computers and computer networks through a series of routers. The routers direct Internet traffic in the same way that routers direct phone calls. When you request a Website on the Internet by typing a URL or when you click through to a new site, you are essentially dialing a new number and connecting to another computer or server. Thinking of it in this way will help to visualize how the system works.

The Internet of today grew from seeds planted by the United States government. On December 6, 1967, the Defense Department issued a $19,800 contract for the purpose of studying the design and specification of a computer network. From that study grew a network called the ARPANET, and from ARPANET emerged the Internet.[1] The original goal of the network was to link the top researchers at universities around the country through their computers. The goal was to increase the ability to share ideas and discoveries. Because of the way the information was transmitted, a side benefit was that this communication network could

---

[1]"Something to Share," Communications History, Federal Communications Commission, accessed July 30, 2007, available from http://www.fcc.gov/omd/history/internet/something2share.html.

continue to operate even if a part of it was not working. In the 1990s this network was turned over to commercial providers, and the Internet was created.

How you access the Internet depends on the Internet service provider (ISP) that you select. An ISP is a business or organization that sells access to the Internet and related services. As the Internet has grown, the number of ISPs has grown as well. A variety of technologies are available to connect to the Internet. Cable television companies, phone companies, cell phone companies, and even local computer businesses all sell access to their Internet connection service. You should research the fees, the type of connections that are offered, and the services that are included before deciding on an ISP. Specific telecommunications technologies will be discussed in Chapter 12, Telecommunications—Technology and Etiquette.

Since the 1990s, the number of individuals using the Internet has grown phenomenally. According to Internet World Stats, 1.114 billion people were using the Internet in March 2007.[2] Individuals are using the Internet for a variety of purposes such as exchanging email and instant messages; participating in discussion groups, chat sessions, and videoconferences; downloading software and music; purchasing goods and services; accessing computers remotely; and transferring files between Internet users.

THE WORLD WIDE WEB

The most widely used component of the Internet is the World Wide Web (WWW or Web)—a large collection of interlinked pages. Although many people use the terms Internet and WWW interchangeably, they are not the same thing. The Internet is the physical network, and the WWW is one resource available through the Internet. The Web consists of computers called Web servers that can be accessed with an Internet connection. A Web server stores multimedia documents that

can contain text, graphics, video, and audio. These documents, called Web pages, are located on a Web server and linked to other multimedia documents. A group of related Web pages is called a Website. Web page links are called hyperlinks or just links.

Although the Internet became open to the public in the 1980s, the variety of programming languages that were being used and the varied and complicated login sequences made the Internet difficult to use. In 1989, Tim Berners-Lee, a computer consultant and researcher at the Swiss research laboratory CERN, set out to create a common set of computer commands that would help physicists at the laboratory share their research information. To assist in this, Mr. Berners-Lee adapted a technology called **hypertext** (text linked to other text). Mr. Berners-Lee is credited with using this technology in May 1990 to create the first Web server, the first Web browser, and the first Web pages.

Today individuals and businesses use Web browsers (a program used to view Web pages) for communications, research, entertainment, and shopping. In addition to being used to display Web pages, most Web browsers offer the ability to search the Web based on keywords, allow users to bookmark favorite sites for later use, and block Web sites identified by the user. Browsers can also be used to perform other Internet tasks such as downloading files, exchanging email, accessing discussion groups, and participating in chat sessions.

Computer Software

As hardware capabilities have continued to evolve, so have software programs. In addition to selecting appropriate hardware, being able to select the most efficient software program is equally important. The ability to understand software and its ability to accomplish desired results has become a key responsibility of the administrative professional. Although your role as an administrative professional does not require

[2]"World Internet Usage and Population Statistics," Internet World Stats, accessed May 22, 2007, available from http://www.internetworldstats.com/stats.htm.

that you have an in-depth understanding of the inner workings of a computer, it does require that you know the particular software packages you will use in the workplace. You may also be expected to select software packages for use in your organization. The intent of this section is not to provide detailed information on a specific brand of software; the intent is to give you an overview of the various types of software packages available. Additionally, you will learn how to care for and maintain software and learn ways to use software to maintain the efficient operation of computer hardware.

Applications Software

Applications software consists of programs that perform a specific function or specific tasks for users. This type of software is sometimes called productivity software because it allows people to become more efficient and productive while performing daily activities. Applications software allows the user to tell the computer how to perform a desired function. For example, you can produce a report through the use of word processing software, or a brochure through the use of a publishing program. You can take photographs with a digital camera and, using photo-editing software, add the photos to the report or brochure. Figure 10.4 describes common types of applications software.

Selecting software may be one of your duties as an administrative assistant. Ask yourself the following questions when making a software purchase.

- Do you have the hardware, memory, and storage requirements needed for the software? Will the program run on your existing operating system? Do you have the memory capacity to support the software?
- Does the program offer the features you need?
- What software support is available? Support may be in the form of tutorials, telephone support, or Web support.

APPLICATIONS SOFTWARE	
Program Type	**Description**
Word processing	Allows the user to produce (create, edit, format, and print) text-intensive documents
Spreadsheet	Allows users to enter data into rows and columns and perform mathematical calculations on that data
Database management system	Allows users to collect records or data that is used to answer queries and make decisions
Presentation	Allows users to present ideas, messages, or reports to a group of individuals through the creation of electronic slides that contain text, images, video clips, or sound clips
Graphics	Allows users to create or edit visual images, drawings, or photographs
Communications	Allows users to communicate with other users through email, Web browsers, newsgroups, and instant messaging
Personal information manager	Functions as a personal organizer that allows users to track information such as appointments, notes, lists, and significant calendar events; it may also include email and instant messaging capabilities
Accounting	Allows users to maintain financial data by automating the recording and processing of traditional accounting transactions
Publishing	Allows users to combine text and images to create documents that look like they were created by a professional printer

FIGURE 10.4 Administrative professionals typically use several types of applications software.

- Does the vendor have a reputation for providing good service? Is the vendor reliable? How long has the vendor been in business? Will the vendor assist you during package implementation?

- What is the reputation of the software? You can check with individuals who have used the software or read reviews in computer periodicals such as *PC World* and *PC Magazine*.

- Will there be conversion costs? When investing in software, you may have more to consider than the initial purchase. Do you have old files that must be converted to the new software? If so, how long will the conversion take?

- Is the software compatible with other programs you use?

- How much does the software cost? Will there be productivity improvements as a result of using the software?

- Will others in the company be using the software? If so, talk with those individuals and agree on a package that will serve everyone's needs.

Multiple applications bundled together as a package are referred to as an application suite or productivity suite. These multiple programs typically include word processing, spreadsheet, and presentation software. They may also include database and information management applications and communications software. The components in a suite typically have a consistent user interface and share some of the same concepts and functions. For instance, documents in a software suite are commonly opened, saved, printed, and edited in a similar manner. Documents created using a software suite may also work together better than those created with separate software packages. For example, it is quite easy to transfer information created with the spreadsheet component of an application suite into a word processing document of the same suite.

Systems Software

Systems software includes any instructions or programs that are used to manage and control

Avoiding Illegal Software

Software piracy is the illegal reproduction and distribution of software applications. Because software is protected by the federal software copyright laws, making unauthorized copies is an act of copyright infringement. Individuals (or businesses) that violate copyright laws are subject to civil and criminal penalties.

Review the following guidelines to make sure you meet the requirements of the law.

- Read and comply with the license agreement on all software.

- Install and use the software on the appropriate number of machines. Do not give copies to others or allow them to make copies for themselves.

- Register all software with the producer.

- Limit access to the original software.

- Do not copy or allow copying of software manuals.

- Remove all software from hard drives when disposing of equipment.

- Secure, return, or destroy old software versions when you receive upgrades.

computer functions. Systems software is an essential part of the computer system because it manages and controls the hardware so that the application software can perform a task. These programs enable the computer to start operation, launch application programs, and facilitate important jobs, such as transferring files, configuring the system to work with a specific brand of printer or monitor, managing files on the hard drive, and protecting the computer system from unauthorized use. Systems software is usually divided into two categories: operating system software and utility programs.

UTILITY PROGRAMS

Program Type	Description
File management	Allows users to format a disk; look at the contents of a storage medium; and copy, move, delete, and rename folders and files
Search tools	Allow users to search for files that meet a particular pattern, such as having certain characters in the filename, being of a particular type (database, song, photo), or having a specific date of creation or modification
Diagnostic and disk management	Evaluates the system by looking for problems and making recommendations for fixing any errors or problems that are discovered
Disk defragmenter	Reorganizes information on a hard drive to optimize data placement
Uninstall utility	Removes computer programs and all small pieces of programs that are left behind when program files are deleted
File compression	Reduces the size of files so they take up less storage space or can be transmitted faster over the Internet

FIGURE 10.5 Utility programs are essential to the operation of computer systems.

OPERATING SYSTEM SOFTWARE

A computer's **operating system** is a collection of programs that manage and coordinate the activities taking place within a computer system. The operating system is the software that provides the connection between the user and the computer's hardware and applications software. The operating system starts the computer, launches application and software programs, manages system resources, and facilitates connections to networks.

The most important role of an operating system is to translate user instructions into a form the computer can understand. Although operating systems continue to be upgraded and redesigned, all of the newest operating systems feature a **graphical user interface (GUI)**. This feature of the software uses visual images such as icons and buttons that are selected with a mouse to issue commands to the computer. Both the *Microsoft Windows®* family of operating systems (*Windows 2003* and *Windows Vista*) and the *Mac OS®* X system use a graphical user interface. The newest *Windows* release, *Windows Vista*, includes more visual features, improved search

capabilities and file sharing, and increased security measures.

UTILITY PROGRAMS

A **utility program** is a type of system software that performs a specific task, usually related to managing or maintaining the computer system, its devices, or its programs. Many utility programs are built into operating systems. Some of these programs are described in Figure 10.5.

Other utility programs can be purchased separately or as a part of a utility suite of related programs. Utility suites combine several utility programs into a single package. Purchasing additional utilities may offer improvements or additions to the programs that are included with the operating system. In addition, utility program vendors offer Web-based utility services. To use a Web-based service you pay an annual fee, which allows you to access the vendor's programs and updates on the Web.

One of the most widely used utility programs is the antivirus program. A **computer virus** is a computer program that can copy itself and infect a computer without the knowledge or permission of the user. Some computer viruses can erase or alter data stored on the machine; steal data and send it to someone else; waste computer resources; or interfere with the user's ability to do work by randomly presenting text, video, or music.

Antivirus software can be used to combat the threats and annoyances caused by computer viruses. Antivirus software is a utility program that protects, detects, and removes viruses from a computer's memory or storage devices. Antivirus software will typically scan incoming email messages for hidden threats and alert users to attempts to infect the computer when surfing the Web. Many computers are sold with an antivirus program already installed. Additionally, there are several antivirus programs available for purchase. Figure 10.6 shows a screen from a popular security program *Norton Internet Security*™. Because these viruses and computer threats are continually being developed, it is important to keep antivirus software up-to-date. Usually these updates can be completed online

by visiting a Website maintained by the software company.

Technology Issues

As more individuals and organizations rely on computers to create, store, and manage critical information, keeping that information secure is also important. Users need to make sure the information is accessible when needed. Users also need to protect that information from loss or misuse. Because several computer threats have emerged, a variety of software products have been developed. These products help ensure the privacy of individuals and the security of computer systems and data.

Security

It is important to make the information on your computer secure. There are a variety of ways you can accomplish this. The first step is to recognize what computer security threats exist. Then you

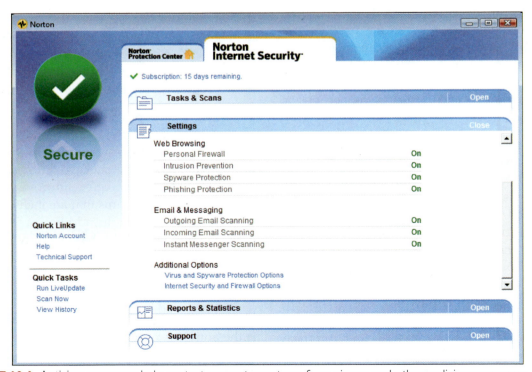

FIGURE 10.6 Antivirus programs help protect computer systems from viruses and other malicious programs.

can take the steps necessary to protect your hardware and software.

SECURITY THREATS

As discussed previously, computer viruses are a security issue that users need to recognize and attempt to avoid. A computer virus is a program that infects data files or software programs with which it comes in contact. Because of this, viruses are often transmitted when you retrieve an infected file from secondary storage or by sharing infected files across a network. Other threats exist that can wreak havoc on your computer system or data.

A **worm** is a malicious, self-replicating program specifically designed to cause damage. Unlike a computer virus, however, a computer worm does not infect computer files to spread. In other words, worms affect the network whereas viruses typically affect computer files and data. A worm makes copies of itself and sends those copies to other computers through a network. The first worms were sent as email attachments. When an infected attachment was opened, the worm inflicted its damage and then sent copies of itself to other computers. Newer worms do not require any action by the users. Instead, the worm is activated when an email message is read or spreads itself automatically through the Internet. Unfortunately, worms are not limited to email programs alone. Worms can also be acquired though instant messaging programs, chat rooms, and shared network folders. Worms can delete files, transmit data, overload primary storage, or create a secret electronic entrance into a network.

Another computer threat is the **Trojan horse**. A Trojan horse is malicious software designed to look like something useful. Trojan horses may appear to be useful or interesting programs (or at the very least harmless) to an unsuspecting user, but they are harmful when executed. Like viruses, Trojan horses are most often spread through email attachments. Trojan horses can erase, corrupt, or overwrite data on a computer, upload and download files, log keystrokes for the purpose of stealing information (such as passwords), or allow remote access to a computer.

An additional computer security threat appears in the form of unauthorized access. Although unauthorized access can take place in several ways, the most common type is perpetrated by a computer hacker. A **hacker** is an individual who uses his or her computer knowledge to break into personal or business computer systems to delete, steal, or alter files. The motivation for hacking is to steal information, sabotage a computer, or perform some other type of illegal act. Hacking is a crime in the United States, and the 2001 USA Patriot Act gives the government authority to prosecute individuals participating in hacking activities and increases the penalties for this crime.[3]

SECURITY SOLUTIONS

Because so much information is created and stored on a computer or network, it is important to have a system that will maintain the security and confidentiality of that data. This can be accomplished in a variety of ways.

- Back up and carefully store important information. A backup of information may help protect data from the threat of computer viruses, worms, or Trojan horses.

- Protect hardware and data by assigning effective passwords. Figure 10.7 offers some tips for creating effective passwords.

- Log off the computer or network when away from your desk. This prevents unauthorized users from accessing information inappropriately.

Because individual passwords are not always as secure as they should be, many organizations use other forms of verification in addition to passwords. One method used is **two-factor authentication**, where an individual is required

[3]"USA Patriot Act Information," Financial Crimes Enforcement Network, accessed June 5, 2007, available from http://www.fincen.gov/pa_main.html.

CREATING EFFECTIVE PASSWORDS

- Create passwords that are at least eight characters in length.

- Use both lowercase and capital letters.

- Use a combination of letters, numbers, and special characters.

- Use different passwords on different systems.

- Do not use passwords that are based on personal information that can be easily accessed or guessed.

- Do not use words that can be found in any dictionary of any language.

- Develop a mnemonic for remembering complex passwords.

Source: "Choosing and Protecting Passwords," *Cyber Security Tip ST04-002,* accessed May 22, 2007, available from http://www.us-cert.gov/cas/tips/ST04-002.html.

FIGURE 10.7 Using effective passwords can help protect valuable data.

to provide a password and an additional item such as a smart card, security badge, fingerprint, or retinal scan for identification purposes.

To protect your computer from threats including viruses, worms, and Trojan horses, adhere to the following guidelines:

- Protect yourself against malicious email attachments. Do not open attachments from people you do not know.

- Make sure the settings on your email program do not open attachments automatically.

- Be cautious even when opening attachments from people you do know because worms can automatically send to individuals listed in an address book.

- Install an antivirus program on all computers and run virus scans regularly.

- Obtain virus software updates regularly to protect equipment from new threats.

- Check downloaded programs for viruses, worms, or Trojan horses. New threats come out every day and equipment is vulnerable when security software is not up-to-date.

- Back up files regularly. Scan the backup program before archiving disks and files.

Another way to protect your computer and data from security threats is to install and maintain a firewall. A **firewall** is a software

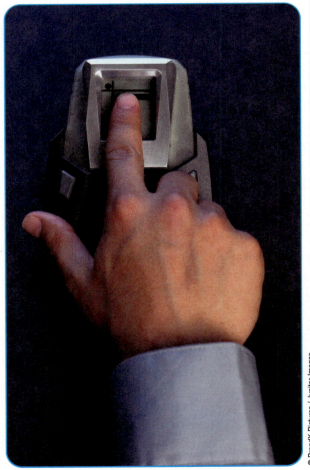

© BrandX Pictures / Jupiter Images

Many organizations require employees to provide a password and an additional identification item such as a fingerprint scan.

focus on *Protecting Data on Portable Devices*

When traveling with portable devices it is imperative to make sure that data is secure. The following suggestions will help you protect the information stored on your portable devices.

- Use passwords correctly. Do not choose options that allow your equipment to remember passwords. Do not choose passwords that can easily be guessed, and do not use the same password for multiple devices.

- Store important data separately. Use removable storage media and store this media in a different place than your notebook computer bag.

- Encrypt files. If you encrypt files, unauthorized individuals cannot view the data even if they have physical access to it.

- Install and maintain antivirus software. Make sure to keep virus definitions up-to-date for your notebook and handheld computers.

- Install and maintain a firewall. Although firewalls are always important, they are vital when traveling and using several different networks.

- Back up your data. This will ensure that you still have access to data if your equipment is stolen.[4]

program that monitors information as it enters and leaves a computer. A firewall provides protection from outside attackers by shielding your computer or network from malicious or unnecessary Internet traffic. Firewalls can be configured to prevent random attacks by outsiders on your computer while still allowing relevant and necessary data through. For example, a firewall allows individuals to access the Internet, but blocks other computers from accessing any information that is stored on your system. Firewall software operates in a manner similar to a two-way mirror: You can see out, but no one else can see in! Firewall software is especially important to businesses that maintain personal and private information, such as physicians, police agencies, and universities.

Privacy

Although the most widely recognized computer privacy threat is identity theft, there are other privacy issues that need to be addressed. Because personal information on your computer can be mined and used by unethical persons in an inappropriate manner, it is important to understand how to protect yourself from privacy threats.

PRIVACY THREAT

Today, more and more information about a person's daily computer activities is collected and stored in databases. Data is collected about items purchased online. When someone uses a credit card or membership card, information about the purchase may be collected as well. The fact that the information is being collected is not necessarily a concern, but what happens to that collected information does present some unique questions.

When you browse the Internet and visit a Website, a small text file (or cookie) may be installed on your computer. A **cookie** will store information about how you use the site. This information might be general information about

---

[4]"Protecting Portable Devices: Data Security," National Cyber Alert System, US-CERT, accessed May 22, 2007, available from http://www.us-cert.gov/cas/tips/ST04-020.html.

your computer, such as the IP address, or it might be more specific information, such as the last time you visited a particular Website. Most cookies are harmless and are used to remember information so that your next visit to the site will be more productive or tailored to your needs. For example, if you visit a Website for a book seller, information about the type of books you view or purchase may be recorded. The next time you visit that site, a list of recommended books that relate to the same topics may be presented to you.

Unfortunately, there are programs similar to a cookie that work in a malicious way. **Spyware** is a software program that runs on a computer without the permission of its user to gather personal information, often through an Internet connection. Unlike viruses and worms, spyware does not self-replicate. Instead, the goal of spyware is to exploit infected computers for commercial gain. Most spyware is installed without the user's knowledge. It can be hidden in a piece of desirable software (such as shareware or music CDs), installed through trickery (like a Trojan horse), or installed through security holes in a Web browser or other software. The information gathered by spyware, such as email addresses or credit card numbers, is transmitted in the background to someone who may use it for illegal purposes.

Adware is also software that runs on a computer without the owner's consent. However, instead of taking information from the user, this software typically runs in the background and displays random or targeted pop-up advertisements. In many cases, the ad slows the computer down, and it may also cause software conflicts.

PRIVACY SOLUTIONS

With increased use of the Internet, email, instant messaging, and e-commerce, a new category of software has evolved. Privacy software was developed to protect the privacy of its users. One way to protect information is through **encryption**, which is a method of scrambling data or email messages so that they are unreadable if intercepted by an unauthorized user. An encrypted document is scrambled and remains unreadable until received and decrypted or unscrambled. Data, files, instant messages, and email can all be encrypted before they are sent over the Internet. Websites also use encryption so that sensitive data (such as Social Security numbers or credit card numbers) are protected as they travel over the Internet.

As described under security solutions, a firewall can protect information stored on a computer. Firewalls can protect the security and

---

PROTECTION AGAINST SPYWARE

To avoid unintentionally installing spyware on your computer, follow these security practices.

- Do not click on links within pop-up windows or within the window itself. To close a pop-up window click the Close button for the window.

- Choose *No* or *Cancel* when asked any unexpected questions while browsing.

- Be wary of free downloadable software. You may be exposing your computer to spyware by downloading free programs.

- Do not follow email links claiming to offer anti-spyware software. Like email viruses, the links may serve the opposite purpose and actually install the spyware they claim to be eliminating.

Source: "Recognizing and Avoiding Spyware," Cyber Security Tip ST04-016, US-CERT, accessed May 22, 2007, available from http://www.us-cert.gov/cas/tips/ST04-016.html.

FIGURE 10.8 Following security procedures can help prevent spyware from being installed on your computer.

privacy of personal information. A firewall, however, does not protect against the installation of malicious programs like spyware. Nor does it prevent security threats such as viruses, worms, or Trojan horses from infecting your computer. The best way to avoid the threats of spyware is to prevent it from being installed on your computer. The guidelines in Figure 10.8 will help you avoid the installation of unwanted spyware.

Even with diligent efforts, spyware can be installed without your knowledge. When that happens, you need to find ways to remove it. Because some antivirus programs are able to locate and remove spyware programs, running antivirus programs on a regular basis is important. However, antivirus programs do not find all instances of spyware. Therefore, you should install anti-spyware software and use it regularly to scan your computer. This software may be more effective than your antivirus program in finding and deleting spyware.

Conducting business online and connecting to networks can improve productivity. However, the benefits of working online come with risks. Do research to make sure that the Websites you are visiting are secure. Secure Websites use firewalls, incorporate data encryption software, and may also use password protection.

Summary

To reinforce what you have learned in this chapter, study this summary.

- Personal computers come in a wide variety of shapes and sizes including microcomputers, notebook computers, tablet PCs, handheld computers, and smartphones.

- A variety of pointing devices can be used for computer input including a trackball, touchpad, touch screen, electronic pen, and graphics tablet.

- Other input devices include scanners, digital cameras, and speech recognition technology.

- Although hard drives continue to be used, computer data is also stored on optical disks and flash memory systems.

- Networks assist users in communicating and sharing resources. Types of networks include personal area networks, local area networks, metropolitan area networks, and wide area networks.

- The Internet is a network of networks linking millions of computers throughout the world.

- The World Wide Web, the most widely used component of the Internet, is a large collection of interlinked pages.

- Applications software consists of programs that perform a specific function such as word processing, spreadsheet, database management, presentations, graphics, communication, and other functions.

- Systems software includes programs that are used to manage and control computer functions including the operating system and utility programs.

- To combat computer viruses, worms, Trojan horses, and hackers it is important to protect your equipment by creating appropriate passwords, making backups of your data, and installing and maintaining firewalls.

- Using encryption software and maintaining computer firewalls is important in order to protect private information.

What's the Problem?

Alex Torres works in the IT Department at United Pharmaceuticals. Every day his job takes him out of his office and around the corporate office building to troubleshoot computer hardware and software issues. Alex works with many people during his day and has developed a passing friendship with some of the individuals because of the frequency of visits to these departments. One of these people is Sheila Ogrodnick. Alex and Sheila usually chat for a few minutes when Alex is working in her department, and they always greet one another when passing in the hall or in the cafeteria. Sheila has recently purchased a home computer system that operates quite differently than the system she uses at work. She has been asking Alex a lot of questions about this new system when she sees him, and Alex has very politely answered all of her questions. Now, however, Sheila is sending Alex email messages asking questions almost every day. Alex is finding that answering Sheila's questions is taking almost 30 minutes a day.

Is Sheila's behavior appropriate? How should Alex handle the situation?

Let's Discuss

1. Describe four types of computers that are found in business.
2. Explain how optical storage media work and describe the three types.
3. List four network types and describe the advantages of using a network.
4. List five types of applications software and describe how they would be used in business.
5. Explain the difference between computer viruses, worms, and Trojan horses.
6. Give five suggestions that should be followed to create a secure password.

Critical-Thinking Activity

Your supervisor, Mr. Black, has asked you and a team of administrative professionals to recommend an updated office suite package for use in the company. The team has completed its assignment. Your supervisor was asked to attend the last team meeting to hear the recommendation from the group. As chair of the committee, you made the recommendation to your supervisor along with the rationale. He congratulated you on doing a fine job and stated that the package would be purchased. He also asked that as soon as the software was received, the committee act as trainers for other employees in the company. He asked that you continue to chair the training group and that you make 20 copies of the software so that everyone in your division can have a copy.

Because you only purchased one copy of the software, you were surprised when Mr. Black asked that you make 20 copies. However, you were so shocked that you did not say anything. The team made no comment. As soon as everyone left the room, you became upset. Now you wonder how you are going to handle the situation.

Is there an ethical issue? If so, what is it? Is there a legal problem? If so, what is it? How should you handle the situation? Should you discuss the situation with the team?

Vocabulary Review

Open the *Word* file *CH10 Vocabulary* found on the Student CD. Complete the vocabulary review for Chapter 10.

English and Word Usage Drill

Complete the English and Word Usage Drill for Chapter 10 found in the *Applications Workbook*.

Workplace Applications

10-1 Create a Newsletter

(Goals 1, 2, 3)

1. Work with two classmates to complete this application.

2. Use your word processing software or desktop publishing software to create a newsletter. The newsletter should include all of the following items and two additional articles or features of your choice.

    - A title for the newsletter and a date

    - A spotlight article on the program that you are using to create the newsletter

    - An article that compares two computer storage methods and recommends at least one storage media or item to purchase

    - An article that discusses three computer input methods and how they are used in business settings

e-portfolio

team building

- A feature box that lists five to eight facts about computer viruses
- Three graphics (at least one should be a photograph)

10-2 Create a Flyer about Password Security

(Goals 2 and 3)

internet

United Pharmaceuticals has recently become concerned because employees have become careless with data security and in the creation of passwords. Your supervisor, Amanda Hinojosa, has asked for your help.

1. Create a one-page flyer to distribute to all employees that stresses the importance of password security. The flyer should contain at least four strategies for creating a secure password.

2. Include font enhancements (bold, italic), a bulleted list, at least one graphic, and a page border.

3. Print the flyer to submit to your instructor.

10-3 Create a Speech Recognition Presentation

(Goals 1 and 2)

internet

e-portfolio

Your supervisor, Melody Hoover, has asked for your help in the following situation. United Pharmaceutical employees have had access to speech recognition technology for the last few years; however, many executives continue to dictate correspondence and reports on microcassettes. Although this system has been effective in the past, Melody thinks implementing speech recognition technology would be beneficial. Melody knows that you have studied speech recognition at school. The office is using the most current version of *Microsoft Office*.

1. Use your knowledge and conduct additional research on the Internet to prepare an electronic presentation that addresses the following issues:

   - How speech recognition technology functions
   - The advantages of using speech recognition technology
   - Potential drawbacks to using speech recognition
   - Ways any potential problems could be avoided
   - Suggestions that will encourage employees to incorporate this technology in their work

2. Include a title slide and at least seven additional slides in the presentation. Apply text animation to the slides. Include at least two appropriate graphics.

3.   Deliver the presentation to the class or a small group from the class.

Assessment of Chapter 10 Goals

Did you successfully complete the chapter goals? Evaluate yourself by filling out the form found in Chapter 10 of the *Applications Workbook*.

Workplace Mail and Copying

Learning Goals

1. **Identify United States Postal Service mail classifications and services.**

2. **Identify mail services available through private mail carriers.**

3. **Process incoming and outgoing mail.**

4. **Identify uses and features of copiers.**

5. **Discuss the importance of ethical and legal considerations when copying and shredding materials.**

United States Postal Service

Mail is delivered by a variety of methods including email, fax, private delivery companies, and the United States Postal Service® (USPS). This chapter focuses on USPS, along with private mail services. Copying, shredding, and faxing documents are often a part of managing mail. Use and features of copiers, shredders, and fax machines, along with related ethical and legal considerations, are presented later in this chapter.

The Post Office Department, the predecessor of the United States Postal Service, was created in Philadelphia in 1775 through a decree of the second Continental Congress. From 1837 to 1970, a running pony was used as the logo. That logo was changed to a full eagle logo; and in the 1990s, the eagle was redesigned. Today an eagle head is the logo. The USPS is one of the largest employers in the United States, employing thousands of people. It is an independent establishment of the executive branch of the government of the United States.

The processing of mail by the USPS is highly automated, including the reading of handwritten addresses. Mail that has a keyed address goes to a multiline optical character reader (OCR). The OCR reads the ZIP Code information and prints the appropriate bar code on an envelope. Mail with handwritten addresses goes to an advanced scanning system that has the ability to read addresses and prints the appropriate bar code on the envelope regardless of poor handwriting. If a customer has

Mail reaches individuals and businesses today through a variety of carriers.

filed a change of address card, the mail is sent to a machine that connects to a computerized database to determine the new address. Once the address is found, the machine pastes a label with the current address over the former address.

U.S. Mail Classifications

The USPS offers several standard classifications for mailing materials. Choosing the appropriate mail classification helps ensure that the materials are delivered in a timely manner and at the most cost-effective rates. Some of the classifications used by the USPS are discussed in the following sections.

EXPRESS MAIL

Express Mail® is delivered 365 days a year to most locations with no extra charge for Saturday, Sunday, or holiday delivery. It is the fastest delivery available from the USPS, offering delivery by 3 p.m. the following day to many destinations. Proof of delivery and tracking information are available if requested.

FIRST-CLASS MAIL

First-Class Mail® is appropriate for sending letters, greeting cards, large envelopes, and packages. The maximum weight for First-Class Mail is 13 ounces. Delivery time is typically one to three days. For materials weighing more than 13 ounces, Priority Mail® should be used. Examples of items that may be sent by First-Class Mail include:

- Cards—the least expensive item that can be sent via First-Class Mail
- Letters—the everyday letter mail
- Large envelopes—materials in large envelopes
- Packages—small packages weighing 13 ounces or less
- Presorted mail—used for high-volume business mail

PRIORITY MAIL

All first-class mail exceeding 13 ounces is designated **Priority Mail**. The words *Priority Mail* should be prominently displayed on the envelope or package to ensure proper handling.

Delivery of documents and packages is typically made in two to three days. Low flat-rate shipping is also available with Priority Mail for any destination and any weight up to a 70-pound maximum when using either Flat Rate Envelopes or Flat Rate Boxes.

No shipment weighing over 13 ounces should be sent by Priority Mail until it has been determined that Priority Mail is the most cost-effective method. For large and/or irregularly shaped items, a private delivery company should be considered along with the USPS to see which carrier would be more cost effective.

STANDARD MAIL

Standard Mail® offers a lower price on postage because of the work that is performed by the sender. The sender does some of the preparing, sorting, and entering of the mail. An annual mailing fee of $175 is required. The mail piece must weigh less than 16 ounces. A minimum of 200 pieces or 50 pounds per mailing is required for the use of Standard Mail. Standard Mail cannot be used for sending personal correspondence, handwritten or typewritten letters, bills, or statements of account. Rates are based on weight, shape, preparation, and entry. Advertising flyers, newsletters, and catalogs are examples of items that can be sent by Standard Mail.

PACKAGE SERVICES

The Package Services class is used for mailing merchandise, books, circulars, catalogs, and other printed material. Four classes of package services are described in the following list.

- **Parcel Post**® is used for mailing gifts, merchandise, books, and other printed matter. Bulk rates are available, in addition to a discount for items with bar codes. Packages can weigh up to 70 pounds and measure up to 130 inches in combined length and width around the thickest part. Delivery time is typically two to nine days.
- Bound Printed Matter is used to mail small and large packages containing bound sheets such as catalogs and phone books. Packages can weigh up to 15 pounds and measure up to 108 inches in combined length and width around the thickest part. Discount rates are available for 300 or more pieces.
- Media Mail® is generally used for items such as books, film, printed music, printed test materials, sound recordings, play scripts, and computer media. Presorted rates are available for bulk quantities of mail (300 pieces or more).
- **Library Mail** is used by qualifying institutions, such as schools, libraries, and museums, to mail books, sound recordings, and educational/research material. Packages should show the name of the school or nonprofit organization in the address or return address.

International Delivery Services

The USPS offers several options for sending mail and packages to international destinations. The principal categories of international delivery services are described below.

- Global Express Guaranteed® offers shipping to more than 190 countries and territories worldwide. It is guaranteed to meet date-certain delivery standards (usually one to three days) or postage will be refunded.
- Express Mail International® is used for mailing time-sensitive material to numerous countries. Date-certain delivery is guaranteed to select destinations, usually within three to five business days.
- First Class Mail International® is an economical way to send cards, letters, printed matter, and small packages (4 pounds or less) worldwide. Delivery time varies by destination.
- Priority Mail International® provides customers with a reliable and economical means of sending correspondence and merchandise up to 70 pounds to more than 190 countries and territories worldwide. Typical delivery time is six to ten business days. Flat rate boxes and envelopes are available. It is important to check with the USPS for specific information

International mail can be sent to many countries around the world.

about mail services in the receiving country or countries when planning to send items internationally.

Online Services

The USPS has many online services available at its Website. These services make preparing and mailing items more convenient for customers. Some of these services are in the following list:

Numerous online services from USPS are available to businesses and individuals.

- Calculating domestic, international, and business postage
- Obtaining the guaranteed delivery time for Express Mail
- Confirming delivery of an item
- Finding a ZIP Code for a business or residential address
- Ordering stamps and mailing supplies
- Printing shipping labels
- Requesting a free carrier pickup
- Shipping packages worldwide
- Creating Direct Mail
- Tracking packages

Additional USPS Services

The USPS offers other services such as **Registered Mail™**, **Collect on Delivery (COD)**, and **Delivery Confirmation™** that can be important for ensuring safe and prompt delivery of items. Some of the services available are described in Figure 11.1.

Private Mail Services

Several private companies offer fast and effective mail services. Three of these companies are FedEx, United Parcel Service (UPS), and DHL Express. Similar services are provided by all these companies. You can find detailed information about the services offered by these companies on their Internet sites. Web addresses for these companies are provided on the Links page on the Website for this textbook. A few of the services provided by FedEx are listed below.

- Guaranteed time and day-definite delivery of goods
- Delivery to residences in the United States
- Delivery of freight throughout the United States and Canada
- Delivery services between the U.S. mainland and Puerto Rico, the Dominican Republic, and other Caribbean islands

FedEx acquired Kinko's Inc. in February 2004 and changed the name to FedEx Kinko's Office

SERVICES OFFERED BY THE U.S. POSTAL SERVICE	
Service	**Description**
Certified Mail™	This service provides proof of mailing and delivery and is available for First-Class Mail and Priority Mail.
Delivery Confirmation	This service provides the date and time a First-Class Mail, Priority Mail, or package services parcel was delivered. If the item could not be delivered, the date and time of the delivery attempt is provided to the mailer.
Return Receipt	This service provides proof of delivery. A mailer purchasing return receipt service at the time of mailing may choose to receive the return receipt by mail or email. Mailers receive a postcard with the recipient's actual signature or an email message with a PDF attachment that includes an image of the recipient's signature.
Signature Confirmation™	This service provides proof of delivery and requires a signature from the person accepting the item. It is available for many classes of mail.
Insured Mail	This service provides up to $500 indemnity coverage for a lost, rifled, or damaged article. It is available on domestic mail and some Global Express Guaranteed mailings.
Registered Mail	This service provides security from the point of mailing to delivery and up to $25,000 insurance against loss or damage. It provides a receipt showing an item was mailed and the delivery date and time. It is available for First-Class and Priority Mail. An International Registered Mail service is also available.
Carrier Pickup	This service provides pickup of packages being mailed. Pickup is free and is available for Overnight Guaranteed, Priority Mail, and international packages. Pickup occurs on the scheduled day when regular mail is delivered.
Collect on Delivery (COD)	This service allows the mailer to collect the price of goods and/or postage on the item(s) ordered by the addressee when delivered. The amount to be collected from the recipient may not exceed $1,000. A delivery record is maintained by the USPS.
Money Orders	This service allows customers to send money orders to numerous locations throughout the world. They can be purchased from any Post Office™ in the United States and are available for up to $1,000 each.

FIGURE 11.1 The U.S. Postal Service offers many options and services for mailing items.

and Print Services. A few of the services provided by FedEx Kinko's are listed here:

- Wide range of business services, including printing, copying, and Internet access
- Central location for FedEx customers to deposit packages for shipping
- Delivery of urgent, valuable, or hazardous items

Email

You learned in Chapter 7 about the importance of email in society. You may use email many times each day just as millions of people across the world do for a variety of reasons. Email is fast, easy to use, and can reach many people. You can write and send an email at any time of the day or night to many places in the world.

The use of email has grown exponentially since its invention in the early 1970s, and email use continues to grow throughout the world. Email has many advantages and also some disadvantages. In many cases, messages are delivered almost instantly. Users may send a message written in haste or anger and wish that they could take back the message a few minutes later. Some individuals seem to assume that there are no inappropriate emails—whatever one wants to say at that particular time is appropriate to say. However, even though you can say anything at any time on email, it certainly is not always a good idea to do so. You must consider to whom you are writing and the intended message that you want the individual to receive. Sarcasm is always inappropriate in email. Another disadvantage of using email is that you may receive spam, which is unwanted and unsolicited messages. You must use your valuable time to sort through many messages and delete unwanted messages.

In addition to email, a growing number of text messages are sent each day using phones or computers. The use of instant messages, in which users communicate in real time with an online contact, are also increasing. Before communicating in writing with anyone, you should carefully consider the most appropriate way to deliver your message. Is it through email, a written letter, or a report?

Mail-Handling Responsibilities

Although many large organizations outsource the handling of mail, small companies generally do not. Thus, it is important that you as an administrative professional understand how mail should be handled. You cannot assume that all mail will be outsourced or automated to the extent that an administrative professional will have no responsibilities for handling mail.

Outgoing Mail

An administrative professional in a large company may be responsible for preparing the mail for processing by mailroom employees. Several important steps that will help you handle outgoing mail properly are listed here:

1. Place all interoffice correspondence in appropriate envelopes with the name and department of the addressee listed on the envelope.
2. Use the notations *Attachment* and *Enclosure* appropriately. Use *Attachment* when an item is attached to the document. Use *Enclosure* when the item is placed behind the document without being attached.
3. Key the address on the envelope carefully; check the letter address against the envelope address. You may want to keep a list of frequently used addresses. Before placing a letter in an envelope, check to see that it is signed.
4. Use the appropriate feature of your word processing software to insert the address from a letter automatically on an envelope. Using this feature saves time and reduces the chance of error because the address is keyed only once. Figure 11.2 shows a correctly addressed envelope created using the Envelope feature of *Microsoft Word*.

```
United Pharmaceuticals
1211 East Eighth Street
Fort Worth, TX 76102-5201




                              Mr. William Anderson
                              Ludington International
                              2857 Washington Street
                              Grand Rapids, MI 49509-2857
```

FIGURE 11.2 Correctly Addressed Envelope

5. Seal and stamp the envelope. If you work in a medium or large organization, the outgoing mail may be sent to a mailroom or outsourced. If you work in a small office, you may seal and stamp envelopes using stamps or a postage meter.

Most organizations have correspondence they send to certain groups of individuals on a regular basis. As an administrative professional, your responsibility is to maintain a current mailing list on your computer. From this compu-terized list, you can print envelopes and address labels with bar codes. It is important to check the mailing list often to see that the appropriate companies, individuals, and organizations are on the list and that the names and addresses are accurate and spelled correctly.

Incoming Mail

Responsibilities for handling incoming mail depend largely on the size of the company. One of your responsibilities as an administrative professional in a small firm may be to receive and process the mail. In large companies, a large percentage of mail functions are often outsourced to independent companies. If mail is not outsourced, however, large companies have a centralized mail department that receives and distributes the mail. Mail is typically delivered twice each day.

As an administrative professional, you need to establish a schedule for handling mail. Know when to expect the mail and how it is delivered to you. Mail may be delivered by one of the following means:

- The mail carrier (USPS or private carrier)
- The company's mailroom attendant

Professional Pointers

Follow these suggestions to handle outgoing mail effectively:

- **Always double-check addresses on letters and envelopes to be certain they are correct.**

- **Check the spelling of the names of organizations and individuals.**

- **Double check the ZIP Code for accuracy.**

- **Maintain updated mailing lists for both individuals within the organization and external clients or customers.**

- An electronic cart, which is self-powered, un-attended, and robot-like that uses a photo-electric guidance system to follow paths painted on floor surfaces

SORT MAIL

Once you receive the mail in your organization or department, you must do a preliminary mail sort. If several individuals are in the department, sort the mail according to the addressee. An alphabetic sorter is handy if you are sorting for a number of individuals. After completing the sorting, place the mail for each individual into separate stacks. When this preliminary sort is complete, sort each person's mail in the following order:

1. Personal and confidential items. Do not open mail that is marked *Personal* or *Confidential* on the outside of the envelope. Place this mail to one side so you do not inadvertently open it.
2. Special delivery, registered, or certified mail. This mail is important and should be placed so the individual to whom it is addressed sees it first.
3. Regular business mail (First-Class Mail). Mail from customers, clients, and suppliers is also considered important and should be sorted so it receives priority handling.
4. Interoffice communications. Email has become pervasive in the workplace; however, there are still times when an interoffice memoran-dum is more appropriate, particularly when the correspondence is relatively long—more than one-third to one-half page in length. In-teroffice memorandums are generally sent in a distinctive interoffice envelope. Reports of various kinds are also often sent in interoffice mail.
5. Advertisements and circulars. Advertisements and circulars are considered relatively unim-portant and can be handled after the other correspondence is answered.
6. Newspapers, magazines, and catalogs. These materials should be placed at the bottom of the mail stack because they may be read at the recipient's convenience.

OPEN MAIL

You can open mail in the mailroom (using a machine to slit the envelope) or at your desk. When opening mail at your desk, you will usu-ally use an envelope opener. Even if you have used a machine to open the envelope, you need to follow most of the procedures listed here.

- Have necessary supplies readily available. These supplies include an envelope opener, a date and time stamp, routing and action slips, a stapler, paper clips, and a pen or pencil.
- Before opening an envelope, tap the lower edge of the envelope on the desk so the con-tents fall to the bottom and will not be cut when the envelope is opened.
- Place envelopes face down with all flaps in the same direction.
- Open the correspondence by using an enve-lope opener or running the envelope through a mail-opening machine.
- Empty each envelope. Carefully check to see that everything has been removed.
- Stamp each item in the upper right-hand cor-ner to show the date and time received. You can use a machine that automatically dates and time-stamps or a manual stamp that prints the date and/or time.
- Fasten any enclosures to the letter. Attach small enclosures to the front of the corre-spondence. Attach enclosures larger than the correspondence to the back.
- Mend any torn paper with tape.
- Stack the envelopes on the desk in the same order as the opened mail in case it is necessary to refer to the envelopes. Save all envelopes for at least one day in case they are needed for reference.

If you open an item marked *Personal* or *Confidential* by mistake, do not remove it from the envelope. Write *Opened by Mistake* on the front of the envelope, add your initials, and reseal the envelope with tape.

The envelopes for some mail items may be discarded. The envelopes for some items should be retained. Retain envelopes in the following situations:

- An envelope has an incorrect address. You or your supervisor may want to call attention to this fact when answering the correspondence.
- A letter has no return address. The envelope usually contains the return address.
- A letter written on letterhead has a different return address than that written on the envelope. For example, a person may write a letter on hotel letterhead and write his or her business address on the envelope.
- A letter has no signature. The envelope may contain the writer's name.
- An envelope has a postmark that differs significantly from the date on the document. The document date can be compared with the postmark date to determine how much of a delay there was in receiving the document.
- A letter specifies an enclosure that is not enclosed. Write *No Enclosure* on the letter and attach the envelope.
- A letter contains a bid, an offer, or an acceptance of a contract. The postmark date may be needed as legal evidence.

The administrative professional often has the responsibility of handling both outgoing and incoming mail.

© Image Source Ltd.

READ AND ANNOTATE MAIL

Busy executives need help with the large amount of mail that crosses their desks each day. As an administrative professional, you can help by scanning the mail and noting important parts of the correspondence. For example, you might underline important elements with a colored pen or pencil. You should also check mathematical calculations and verify dates that appear in the correspondence.

The next step is to **annotate**, which means to underline important elements or place repositionable paper notes on a document. The advantage of using notes is that they can be peeled off and destroyed when you and the executive are finished with them. Here are some examples of when to make annotations:

- The enclosure is missing from the letter. Call the person who sent the letter and inform the person that the enclosure is missing. Request that the enclosure be sent. After making the call, put a note on the letter as to when the enclosure is expected.
- A discrepancy exists between the amount of a bill and the check received.
- The correspondence refers to a previous piece of correspondence written from your office. Retrieve the previous correspondence and attach it to the new correspondence, noting the attachment of the previous document.
- A meeting is suggested at a time when the executive is already committed.
- Periodicals can be annotated by checking the table of contents for items that might be of interest to your employer. Place a check mark by the title of the article in the table of contents or place a note on the page where the article begins. You can also read articles of interest and highlight the key points in the article or write a short summary of the article.

focus on *Mail Organization*

After you have completed the preliminary mail sort and other processing steps, organize the mail by doing a final sort. Here is one method that you may use to organize mail into categories:

- Immediate action. This category consists of mail that must be handled on the day of receipt or shortly thereafter.

- Routine correspondence. This mail includes interoffice memorandums and other correspondence that are not urgent in nature.

- Informational mail. Periodicals, newspapers, and other types of mail that do not require answering, but are merely for the executive to read, are included here.

Generally, you will not be asked to print the executive's email. Many times the executive will carry a portable computer with her or him and answer the correspondence while out of the office. However, if the executive does not carry a computer, she or he may call and ask that you organize and relay email messages and answer (if needed) according to his or her direction.

© Image Source Ltd.

Mail may be presented one or two times per day, depending on the volume.

PRESENT OR ROUTE MAIL

The executive may ask that you present the mail two times a day. For example, if external mail is received in the morning and afternoon, the executive may ask that you organize and present it approximately 30 minutes after you receive the mail. If you have been with the company and the executive for a period of time, she or he may not want to see all mail; you may handle a large portion of it.

More than one person may need to read a piece of correspondence. If so, you can make copies of the correspondence and send a copy to each individual on the list or you can route the correspondence to all individuals by using a routing slip. The basic question to ask when determining whether to make copies is this: *Is it urgent that all individuals receive the information immediately?* If the answer is *yes*, make a photocopy. If the answer is *no*, use a routing slip, particularly if the correspondence is lengthy.

A routing slip also provides a reference so you know when and to whom you sent the correspondence in case a question arises about who received the document. When each person on the routing slip receives and reads the copy, she or he initials next to his or her name before sending the copy to the next individual on the list. The last person to receive the correspondence generally returns it to the individual who sent it. A routing slip is shown in Figure 11.3. Notice the initials placed next to the individuals' names to indicate that they have read the copy. Notice also that the sender is requesting that the correspondence be returned to him or her.

Handle Mail When the Executive Is Away

To handle the mail when the executive is away from the workplace, follow these general guidelines:

- Before the executive leaves, discuss how the mail should be handled. Be specific in your questions so you understand your responsibilities. Mistakes in handling mail can be costly to the organization.
- When urgent mail comes in, handle it immediately. If you cannot answer the mail, send it to the appropriate person in your organization. Usually your employer will have designated someone who is in charge in her or his absence. See that this person receives the urgent correspondence quickly.
- Answer mail that falls within your area of responsibility in a timely manner.
- Maintain mail that has been answered (with the answer attached) in a separate folder. The executive may want to review it upon her or his return.
- In a separate folder, maintain mail that can wait for the executive's return. Retrieve any previously written correspondence that the executive will need when reviewing the mail; place it in the folder also.

Handle Email

To handle email effectively, you should establish a logical filing system on your computer for storing email messages. One effective method is to mirror your paper filing system (assuming it is an effective one) on your computer. A good

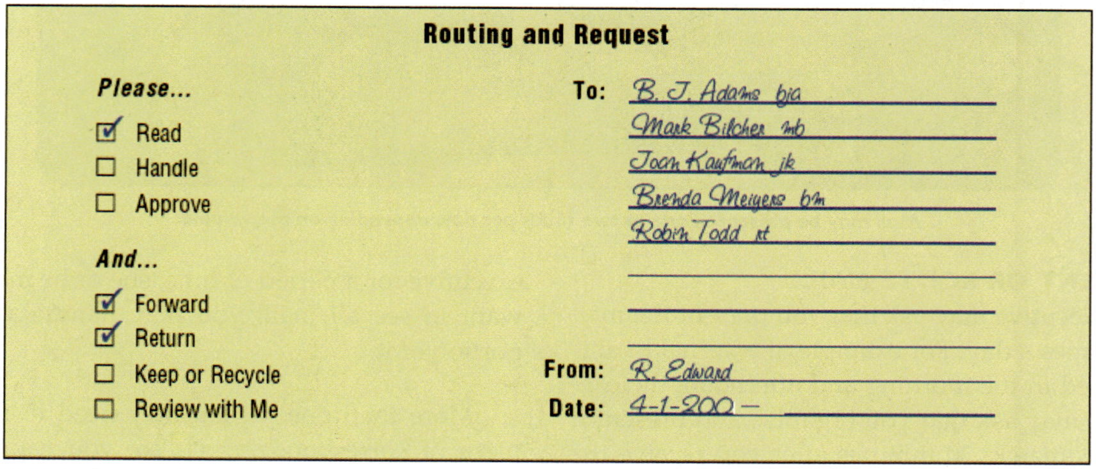
Routing and Request

Please...
☑ Read
☐ Handle
☐ Approve

And...
☑ Forward
☑ Return
☐ Keep or Recycle
☐ Review with Me

To: B. J. Adams bja
Mark Bilcher mb
Joan Kaufman jk
Brenda Meyers bm
Robin Todd rt

From: R. Edward
Date: 4-1-200–

FIGURE 11.3 Routing Slip

system that is consistent for both paper and computer filing makes it easier to find documents. For example, if you generally reference your work by client or customer, then set up your email folders by client or customer name or number.

When email messages are received, do not let them stay in your inbox. Read the messages at regularly scheduled times (probably at least twice each day). Reply, forward the message if needed, and file the message in an appropriate folder. If you clearly do not need to save the message, delete it. Delete any spam (also called junk email) that may be received. If your email system allows, indicate that the message is spam. This may help prevent receiving spam messages from that sender in the future. Figure 11.4 shows

a *Windows Mail* dialog box that allows you to set options related to junk email.

Office Copiers

Today people have the ability in business and home offices to do less copying due to the information available on computers. In fact, the term *paperless office* sprang up as a concept due to the ability to store information on computers rather than in file drawers. However, many offices have not been effective in producing less paper than in the past. In fact, the opposite is often correct; offices produce more paper today than in the past. A number of businesses provide copying services to the public. You may have visited one

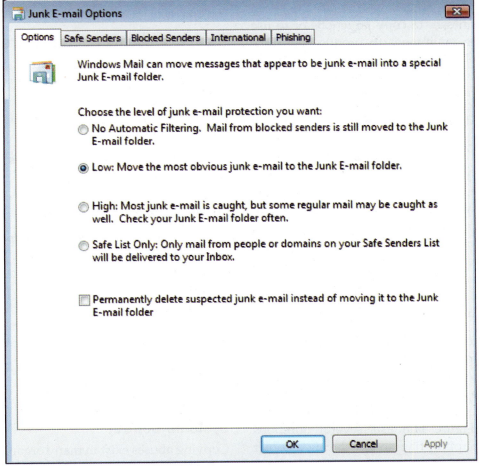

FIGURE 11.4 *Windows Mail* provides options for handling spam.

CONSIDERING COPIER NEEDS

- How many people will be using the copier?

- How many copies will be made per month?

- Is there a projected increase or decrease in copy volume during the next three years?

- What features are necessary? You may want to survey potential users to determine their needs.

- Will color copying be needed?

- What space limitations exist for the copier?

- Should a maintenance contract be purchased?

- What amount of money is available for purchasing the copier?

FIGURE 11.5 Several questions should be considered when selecting a copier.

QUESTIONS TO ASK DURING A COPIER DEMONSTRATION

- What is the quality of the copy?

- If it is a color copier, are the colors clear?

- Is the copier easy to operate?

- Does the copier have the features that you need?

- How long has the vendor been in business?

- Does the vendor offer service agreements? If so, what are the costs?

- If service contracts are provided, what is the response time on a typical service request?

- Does the price of the copier compare favorably with a similar copier from another dealer?

FIGURE 11.6 Asking questions during a copier demonstration can help you learn about copier features and operation.

of these businesses to copy large jobs or to use their binding equipment to produce booklets. Many people (with the number constantly growing) work from their homes, and they have established home offices that often have a copier.

As an administrative professional, you will use copiers extensively. Because you could be involved in helping to select a copier for your business or your home office, you need to understand the types of copiers available and their features. If you are working with several individuals in an office, a task force may be formed to recommend the appropriate copier. You and the task force need to ask and answer several questions as you consider the copier needs of your group. Some appropriate questions are listed in Figure 11.5.

After the task force has identified several copiers that may meet the group's needs, a sales representative may be invited to demonstrate one or more copiers. The task force might also visit an office machine or supply store to look at copiers. Figure 11.6 lists several questions that may be appropriate to ask during a copier demonstration.

Copier Capacities and Features

Copiers are generally categorized according to the volume of copies that can be produced and the features that they provide. For example, high-volume and multifunctional machines typically have the ability to:

- Produce 50 to 100 or more pages per minute
- Print, scan, and fax
- Sort, fold, staple, punch holes, and saddle stitch pages

High-volume copiers produce approximately 50 to 100 or more pages per minute. Mid-volume copiers produce approximately 16 to 40 pages per minute, and low-volume copiers produce approximately 15 pages per minute. However, due to advances in technology, copiers continue to improve in speed and services offered.

Common features of copiers are described in Figure 11.7.

Systems Control

Copying abuses exist in many organizations. For example, employees may make ten copies of a

COPIER FEATURES

Feature	Description
Reduction and enlargement	This feature allows users to change the size of copy from that of the original document. For example, reduced copies can be made of large documents so all filed copies are uniform in size. The enlargement feature allows a copy of a document to be produced in a larger size than the original. For example, fine details on an original can be made more legible by using the enlargement feature.
Automatic document feeder	This device feeds a stack of original documents to be copied into the machine one by one. This feature allows users to copy multipage documents without having to lift and lower the platen cover for every sheet.
Trayless duplexing	This feature provides automatic copying, printing, or faxing of two-sided originals. This feature is available on some copiers.
Fax and scanning kit	These optional kits transform a copier into a powerful, multifunctional device that has the ability to scan to email and scan to file.
Editing	Features such as border erasing, centering, color adjusting, marker editing, and masking are provided on some copiers. Marker editing allows users to change the color of specific sections of a document to highlight these areas. Masking allows users to block out areas of sensitive or confidential information.

FIGURE 11.7 Copier features vary by brand and model.

document when only six are needed. The additional copies are made "just in case." More often than not, the extra copies are thrown away. Unfortunately, another widespread abuse is the copying of materials for personal use. Such behavior is clearly unethical.

To curb copying abuses, many organizations use copy control devices. For example, the user may enter an account number on a keypad or insert a card to gain access to the copier. Each department or division is able to check copy costs against specific accounts. If abuses seem to be occurring, appropriate fact gathering can be done by the department. If there is an abuse, appropriate action can be taken.

Ethical Considerations

Each employee in a company should be ethical in the use of copying machines. Additionally, each employee should be aware of the legal restrictions on the copying of certain documents.

© Keith Brofsky / Photodisc / Getty Images

Due to advances in technology, copiers can produce more copies per minute today than in the past.

The administrative professional must not waste paper by making more copies of a document than are needed.

Behaving ethically when copying means that you do not engage in the following activities:

- You do not copy documents for your own personal use.
- You do not copy cartoons and jokes for distribution to coworkers.
- You do not make copies of documents that you need for an outside professional group unless you have approval from your organization to do so.
- You do not copy materials restricted by copyright.

Copyright is a form of protection provided by the laws of the United States (title 17, U. S. Code) to the authors of "original works of authorship," including literary, dramatic, musical, artistic, and certain other intellectual works. This protection is available to both published and unpublished works.[1] If you have questions about what is legal to copy, check with your organization's attorney or check the U.S. Copyright Law. The U.S.

Copyright office maintains a Website with information about the U.S. Copyright Law. A link to this site is provided on the Website for this textbook. Figure 11.8 shows a list of frequently asked questions relating to copyrights.

Etiquette Considerations

You will generally be sharing a copier with a number of other people in your office. Always observe basic courtesies. No one enjoys going into a copying room and finding that the copier is not working, no copy paper is available, or the room is completely disorganized. When sharing a copier with several people, be considerate of their time. Observe the basic courtesies listed here.

- If you are involved in an extensive copying job, let your colleagues interrupt if they have only a few pages to copy.
- If the machine malfunctions while you are copying, try to fix the problem. If you cannot do so, call the key operator in your organization or call a service repairperson.
- When toner runs out, refill it.

---

[1]"What Is Copyright," U.S. Copyright Office, accessed July 31, 2007, available from http://www.copyright.gov/help/faq/.

Source: "Frequently Asked Questions about Copyright," U.S. Copyright Office, accessed July 31, 2007, available from http://www.copyright.gov/help/faq/.

FIGURE 11.8 Frequently Asked Questions about Copyright

- When paper jams, remove it.
- If you are using additional supplies, such as paper clips or scissors, return them to their proper location before leaving the copier.
- If you have made copies that are not usable, destroy them. Put them in a shredder or a recycle bin. Do not leave a messy work area for the next person to clean up.
- Return the copier to its standard settings.

Copier Maintenance

The copy machine is an integral component in today's business world. Workers have become dependent on the many specialized functions that these machines offer. To maximize a copier's usefulness in the workplace, careful consideration must be given to the maintenance of the copier, selection of the correct type of copier for the needs of the business, and correct placement of the machine for single or multiple users.

As an administrative professional, you may be responsible for making a variety of copies. In addition, you may be responsible for certain areas of copier maintenance. Keep the following suggestions in mind so that maintenance costs are minimal.

- Store paper properly. It should be stored in a dry area, away from extreme hot or cold temperatures. Keep the paper flat and, if possible, on a shelf or a pallet above the floor. Because paper is affected by humidity, keep it wrapped and boxed until it is needed. Reseal or box partially used reams of paper.
- Check the paper before you load it into the machine. Paper that is wrinkled, curled, or damp can cause repeated paper jams and will eventually harm the internal components of the copier. Paper that has been packaged has very little air in it. It is wise to fan the paper prior to loading it to increase the amount of air between the sheets, which in turn allows the paper to feed through the copier one sheet at a time. Fanning the paper also helps get rid of static in the paper and lessens the possibility of a paper jam.
- Be cautious. Copiers have moving parts and areas that become hot during operation. If you attempt to make a minor repair or adjustment, such as removing a paper jam or changing a

toner cartridge, be very careful. Jewelry, scarves, ties, or loose-fitting clothes can become caught in the equipment.

- Trust the control panel warning. When the control panel instructs you to add toner, do so. If you do not, the quality of the copy is affected.

- Look for consistency. When a particular problem appears consistently, you should inform the technician of the malfunction. If you make a list of the types of problems or how the machine reacts in certain situations, you can save repair time and cost.

- Designate a **key operator**, a person who is responsible for making simple repairs. One person who is located near the copier should be responsible for removing paper jams, fixing malfunctions, replenishing supplies, and determining when a repair call is justified. Consistent care adds to the operating life of the equipment.

Management should designate a key operator for each copier and determine how the key operators will be trained. The vendor usually has personnel who can provide initial training. Information is also usually provided in a copier manual. A schedule should be established for the key operator to train all individuals who will use the copier. Proper training of all personnel using the copier will enhance productivity.

Copier Procedures

If you are asked to be the key operator for a copier, request a meeting of all administrative professionals in the area to discuss their copier needs. Ask the group for suggestions on appropriate ways for dealing with problems that may occur when using the copier. Once procedures have been developed, post them on a bulletin board in the copying room. Meet with others that use the copying machine on a periodic basis to discuss any problems that may occur.

Although management will most likely make the decisions about maintenance contracts and where the copier is located, an administrative assistant may be asked for input. Some issues that you may be asked to consider are listed below.

- Choose an appropriate location. A copier needs proper ventilation and adequate temperature control. The user also needs sufficient space to place paper and other supplies so the top of a copier is not abused. Paper clips and staples that fall into a machine can cause major repair bills.

- Determine how often preventative maintenance is needed. Preventative maintenance increases the productivity of a copier in the long run by decreasing the number of copier breakdowns. Preventative maintenance typically should occur every three months. Maintenance can be scheduled by independent contractors, through a maintenance agreement purchased from a dealer, or by the manufacturer.

- Consider whether to lease or buy the copier. Leased copiers may include preventative maintenance checks by the leasing company's technicians. However, leases may also have restrictive copy count plateaus that result in the copier being underutilized so extra use charges are not accrued.

- Investigate remote diagnostic systems availability. These systems can detect copier problems before they occur; these problems can be corrected remotely by using an off-site computer.

Shredders

For those times when a machine malfunctions and copies must be destroyed, businesses often place a **shredder** in proximity to the copier. A shredder is a machine that cuts paper into strips of confetti-like material. Shredded paper is recycled by many businesses as packing material. Because mailrooms process a large amount of paper and often pack materials for shipping, they use shredders also. Shredders are being used more extensively due to the increase in identity theft.

FAX MACHINE FEATURES

Feature	Description
FoIP (Fax over Internet Protocol)	FoIP uses an IP-based network to transmit fax data. FoIP can transmit and receive documents at very fast speeds. The most basic fax mode transfers black and white only; however, color fax is possible when a color printer is used.
Multifunction machines	Multifunction machines allow users to perform a variety of functions including sending a fax, enlarging or reducing documents, collating, and making copies.
Automatic fax/phone switching	With this service, the user can distinguish between incoming fax and voice calls, thus eliminating the need for an extra phone line.
Fax broadcasting	Fax broadcasting is the ability to personalize faxes and transmit to multiple locations simultaneously. Broadcasting often can be accomplished at a fraction of the cost of direct mail or overnight services.

FIGURE 11.9 Fax machines have features designed to increase productivity.

Fax Machines

A **fax machine** electronically sends a facsimile (images and text) of an original document from one location to another via a communications network. A fax usually consists of an image scanner, a modem, and a printer. Some fax machines can be connected to a computer, with the scanner and the printer used independently. In the business world, many standalone fax machines have been replaced by systems capable of receiving and storing incoming faxes electronically and routing them to their destination on paper or through secure email.

Fax Features and Services

Numerous features are available on fax machines. Some of the features are listed in Figure 11.9.

Services are available that will allow the use of the Internet to send and receive faxes. Some of these services are free, and some are pay services. You can send and receive faxes via email or a Website. Individuals and corporations may also subscribe to an Internet fax service. This service allows users to receive faxes from their personal computers using an email account. No software, fax server, or fax machine is needed.

Elimination of Junk Fax

Businesses have had problems with junk mail clogging their fax machines. With a special device attached to a fax machine, users can eliminate the receipt of junk faxes. The device requires that the sender know the receiver's security code and fax number. If the sender does not know the security

To help ensure confidentially of materials, shred documents that are no longer needed by the organization.

© Tetra Images / Jupiterimages

Recycling paper can help reduce the need for landfills.

© Rob Melnychuk / Corbis / Image100 / Jupiterimages

code, the machine blocks the message. Another way to control junk fax is to purchase a fax machine that allows communication only with user-selected numbers stored in the machine memory.

Recycling

The recycling of paper and other materials is extremely important and is often part of an organization's plan for green operations. *Green* (or *greening*) is a term used to indicate that a practice is environmentally friendly. Valuable forests are being lost due to the millions of tons of paper that are used each year in the United States. Additionally, many landfills are reaching capacity. Recycling has many benefits; a number of these benefits are listed here.

- Save money. Recycling services can be cheaper than trash disposal services.

- Divert material from disposal. Keeping paper out of the waste stream saves landfill space and reduces pollution through avoided incineration.

- Conserve natural resources. By using recycled paper, fewer trees have to be cut down.

- Save energy. Less energy is used in recycling products than in processing virgin materials.

RECYCLING COORDINATOR RESPONSIBILITIES

- Develop a plan of action with measurable goals and a realistic timetable for reaching the goals.

- Obtain authorization from management to purchase equipment and supplies and to implement the program.

- Conduct a waste audit to find out what is in the organization's trash containers.

- Determine the types of materials that are to be included in the waste reduction program.

- Obtain the support of the organization. Promote the program through talks, posters, and programs.

- Coordinate the purchase of products with the purchasing office. Recycled paper products should be used if at all possible.

- Encourage the use of more emails to save paper.

- Monitor the program carefully. Develop a system for determining whether the efforts devoted to recycling are effective. Attempt to correct problems with the system.

- Listen to and evaluate feedback from both management and employees.

- Publicize the success of the program on a consistent basis—perhaps a monthly email to all individuals within the company.

- Celebrate the success of the program through an event, such as an afternoon gathering with food and drink provided.

FIGURE 11.10 A recycling program coordinator has many responsibilities.

- Reduce greenhouse gas emissions. Recycling reduces greenhouse gas emissions that may lead to global warming.

Although it is not the responsibility of the administrative professional to manage recycling, you can suggest to your manager that you believe that the organization should begin a recycling program if it does not have one. Management must support a recycling program for it to be successful. A recycling coordinator may be appointed. This person is responsible for designing, implementing, and managing the program. Some of the responsibilities of a recycling program coordinator are listed in Figure 11.10.

In addition to recycling, organizations can take other steps to reduce the paper used.

Some suggestions are provided in the following list.

- Ask employees to write or print on both sides of the page.
- Convert scratch paper into memo pads and telephone answering slips.
- Print or copy only the number of copies needed.
- Increase the use of email to save paper used for printed memos.
- Shred used paper to use in packing materials instead of using plastic pellets.
- Use recycled paper.
- Use a single-space format for the text of a document.
- Store information on computer disks or other memory devices rather than on paper.

Summary

To reinforce what you have learned in this chapter, study this summary.

- The processing of mail by the USPS is highly automated. The USPS provides several mail classifications such as Express Mail, First-Class Mail, Priority Mail, Standard Mail, and package services. International delivery services are also provided.

- The USPS provides numerous online services such as calculating postage, confirming delivery, ordering supplies, requesting carrier pickup, and tracking packages.

- The USPS provides additional services such as money orders, Delivery Confirmation, Registered Mail, and Collect on Delivery (COD).

- Private companies, such as FedEx, United Parcel Service (UPS), and DHL Express, offer fast and effective mail services.

- Business messages are often transmitted by email or instant messaging systems. These files should be organized and managed in an effective manner.

- The administrative professional often has responsibilities for handling outgoing and incoming mail. Outgoing mail should be checked carefully for correct addresses and inclusion of attachments or enclosures.

- Incoming mail duties include sorting, opening, reading, annotating, organizing, presenting, and routing mail. The administrative assistant may have additional duties related to handling mail when the executive is away.

- Copiers are used extensively in business offices. Copiers are available for low-, medium-, and high-volume needs and provide a variety of useful features.

- Administrative professionals may be asked to help select a copier and to serve as the key operator.

- Office employees should use copiers efficiently to avoid wasting time and resources and should follow copyright restrictions.

- Shredders are used in offices to cut paper into strips of confetti-like material that can be recycled or used as packing material.

- Fax machines are used by businesses to electronically send a facsimile (images and text) of an original document from one location to another via communications networks.

- Recycling and other green practices have become a major initiative as many organizations seek to conserve natural resources, save energy, and reduce gas emissions. Many organizations appoint a recycling coordinator who is responsible for developing and implementing an effective recycling program.

What's the Problem?

Josue Mendoza is angry. He has been working for United Pharmaceuticals for one year, and he prides himself on doing good work on each job he is given. He also thinks that he has grown tremendously in his skills, both human relations and technical, during his time with United. Because the company is growing, Josue has asked his employer, Rebecca Masterson, if it would be possible to employ another student from one of the local community colleges for 20 hours a week. Josue mentioned that he could suggest two or three people for her to interview. She agreed, and Gloria Romero was employed. Josue has spent numerous hours helping Gloria learn her job.

Recently Ms. Masterson was out for two weeks, and Josue gave Gloria the task of opening, sorting, and annotating her mail. Ms. Masterson returned this morning. In the afternoon, Ms. Masterson asked Josue to come to her office. She was going through her mail, and she was furious. She could not find several enclosures for various letters which indicated that enclosures were included. The mail was not presented to her in any logical order; for example, the top piece of correspondence was written on April 1, and the next piece of correspondence was written on March 3. One piece of correspondence had no date on it. There was no way to check the approximate date of writing because the envelope had been thrown away. There was also an urgent request for material; she asked Josue if the material had been sent. Her comments to Josue were: "What in the world happened here? You know that I expect my mail to be presented in an appropriate order and that all necessary material is available so that I might respond appropriately!"

How should Josue respond to Ms. Masterson? How can he provide more training for Gloria to prevent problems with handling the mail in the future?

Let's Discuss

1. Identify five commonly used classifications of USPS mail.
2. Identify five online services offered by the USPS.
3. List four USPS options for sending mail and packages to international destinations.
4. In what order should incoming mail be sorted?
5. Give three examples of annotations to a document.
6. Identify four features of copiers.
7. List four reasons why an organization might have a recycling program.

Critical-Thinking Activity

You have worked part-time for United Pharmaceuticals for two years. During this time, you have always received outstanding evaluations, with significant increases in salary. You have consistently been told that you do excellent work; you enjoy your job.

Eight months ago you were designated the key operator for the copying room. One of the new administrative assistants, Tomas Alvarez, apparently left a mess after using the copying room. Additionally, he seems to be copying a number of items for his personal use. You have not confronted him about his behavior because you could not prove that the copying jobs were personal. However, you are beginning to think that you must deal with the situation since you have recently seen several copies that he has left behind. It is clear that these copies have nothing to do with United Pharmaceuticals. Also, you have found the copy machine not working several times after his use. He has not reported any problems. Another administrative professional, Alice Wong, complained to you about a mess left in the copying room by Tomas. Copies were scattered all over the room and paper supplies were not left in the appropriate place. Alice remarked that she knew Tomas had used the copying machine immediately before she used it.

How should you handle this situation? With whom should you discuss the problem first? What should you say to Tomas?

Vocabulary Review

Open the *Word* file *CH11 Vocabulary* on the Student CD. Complete the vocabulary review for Chapter 11.

English and Word Usage Drill

Complete the English and Word Usage Drill for Chapter 11 found in the *Applications Workbook*.

Workplace Applications

11-1 Research Mail Services

internet

team building

(Goals 1 and 2)

1. Work with two classmates on this project. Use your text and the Internet to research the various USPS mail services and classifications.

2. Identify and describe services offered through two private mail companies.

3. Prepare an electronic presentation that highlights the information you found. Present your findings to the class, using the electronic slides.

11-2 Process Incoming Mail

(Goal 3)

Melody Hoover and Amando Hinojosa have asked you to open and sort (by importance) all incoming mail.

1. The incoming mail listed below was received today. All items are addressed to Teresa Winwright. Ms. Winwright is out of town, and she does not respond to her email when she is away.

   - Report
   - Catalog
   - Three first-class letters
   - Two newsletters
   - Letter marked *Personal and Confidential*
   - Special delivery letter
   - Magazine
   - Two circulars
   - Email message confirming an appointment for next week

2. List the items in the order they should be presented to Amando, who will later give the items to Ms. Winwright.

11-3 Handle Outgoing Mail

(Goal 3)

Melody Hoover has given you several pieces of outgoing mail to process. Key a list of the items; then explain how you will process each piece of mail (private mailing or shipping services or USPS mail). If it is USPS mail, identify the mail classification of the item.

1. A letter addressed to Sunil Vettickal in New Deli, India. It is to be delivered as quickly as possible.

2.   A letter addressed to Edwardo Sanchez in New York. There is no urgency.

3.   A package to be delivered to John Hamilton, Vice President of Marketing, Grand Rapids. It needs to reach him tomorrow and signature confirmation is needed.

4.   First-Class Mail that is over 15 ounces—a book to be sent to Yao Chen in Guangzhou, China. The book must reach him within two weeks.

11-4 Identify Copier Types and Features

(Goal 4)

1.   Work with two of your classmates to complete this activity.

internet

2.   Do research on the Internet to find information about three copiers that are intended for business use. Find copiers with different features or ones intended for different levels of use (high volume, low volume).

3.   Review the Yellow Pages of your local directory for office equipment businesses. From the research that you have done on the Web, determine three types of copiers that you want to see at the business.

team building

4.   Visit the businesses and talk with a salesperson about the advantages of each copier. If handouts are available on the copier features, ask for one for each of the copiers that you have reviewed.

5.   Write a report (working with teammates) to report your findings. The report should include the following:

e-portfolio

   • A description of the copiers reviewed

   • Advantages and disadvantages of each copier

   • The copier you would recommend (from among the ones reviewed) for a small United Pharmaceuticals branch office

11-5 Research Ethical and Legal Considerations

(Goal 5)

1.   Use the Internet or other resources to find an article about ethical or legal considerations related to copying or shredding documents.

internet

2.   Key a short report to summarize the main points of the article. Include source information for the article.

Assessment of Chapter 11 Goals

Did you successfully complete the chapter goals? Evaluate yourself by completing the form in Chapter 11 of the *Applications Workbook*.

For additional resources, access the Website for this textbook at academic.cengage.com/officetech/fulton-calkins.

Telecommunications—Technology and Etiquette

Telecommunications Described

Telecommunications once described the telephone system that carried local and long-distance phone calls. Making connections with friends and family throughout the United States was very costly, and calling overseas was impossible. Landline phones were used to transmit all calls, and it was not until the mid-1800s, when the first trans-Atlantic cable was installed, that people were able to send telegraph messages overseas. Today telecommunications refers to a worldwide industry that links the far corners of the earth via fax machines, mobile phones, satellite phones, GPS navigational systems, and the World Wide Web.

Telecommunications is the transmission of text, data, voice, video, and images (graphics and pictures) from one location to another. Initially phones could only "talk" with phones, and computers with computers. Today these strict lines of communication no longer exist. Standard telephones can link with computers via modems, mobile phones and personal digital assistants can play videos, email and the Internet can be accessed in real time on smartphones or PDAs, and the Internet can be used as a long-distance tool for standard phone calls.

With these technologies and other communications tools at our disposal, new communication etiquettes have evolved. The technologies that drive email, instant messaging, and text messaging have allowed users to create their own languages and communication tools to keep information flowing in a timely manner. Unfortunately, there are drawbacks to these tools if they are not used appropriately. Perhaps you have heard mobile phones and pagers ring during weddings, musical performances, and public lectures. You may have also watched as family or friends compulsively check their email and instant messaging accounts on their PDAs. With the ability to communicate so freely comes the responsibility to do so in an appropriate manner. Old, new, and evolving telecommunications technologies, and the personal and business communication etiquette that should accompany the use of these technologies, will be discussed in this chapter.

Telecommunications Pipelines

The information that is transmitted by today's telecommunications systems travels through a variety of electronic pipelines. Depending on whom you are calling, the location of the Website you are visiting, or who is on the receiving end of your email and instant messages, the route that this information travels can vary widely. This information revolution has transformed the role of traditional telephone companies from delivering a service that connects people via standard telephone lines to connecting people to people and people to machines through traditional telephone lines as well as through analog dial-up, cable, digital subscriber lines, satellites, wireless communication, and fiber optic cable.

ANALOG DIAL-UP

The original telecommunications connection was created through **analog dial-up** (connecting devices to a network via a modem and a public telephone network) and has been around for many years. A **modem** is a device that converts the digital signal from a computer to an analog signal that can be transmitted along an ordinary phone line. This type of connection is commonly used to access the Internet. The name comes from the terms modulation and demodulation because the original analog modem *modulates* data so it can be transmitted over telephone lines in analog form and *demodulates* incoming signals so the computer's processor can understand them. Of the pipelines available for transmitting information today, analog dial-up is the slowest. With the large number of people using the Internet and the continued growth of telecommunications users, faster connections continue to be developed and expanded.

CABLE

Cable is a pipeline that connects computers to a coaxial cable line to provide voice and data transmission. Nearly everyone is familiar with the coaxial cable that provides access to hundreds of different channels on a television set. Because the data-carrying capacity of this network is much higher than what is required to provide a television signal, the excess capacity is now commonly used to access the Internet. A cable modem allows you to hook up your computer to a local cable television line and receive data similar to the way cable boxes are used to obtain cable television service. Although a cable modem modulates between analog and digital signals, it is a much more complex device than an analog modem. The Internet service provided by a cable modem is often referred to as broadband access. **Broadband** is a form of digital data transmission that uses a wide range of frequencies to achieve added bandwidth. The broadband technology provides opportunities for high speed and high capacity.

There are several advantages to using a cable modem. Because much of the population has access to cable television, a vast network of coaxial cable is already in place. This makes cable a convenient method for connecting to the Internet. When compared to dial-up connections, cable provides faster access to data. Another advantage is that a cable modem provides a continuous connection.

The greatest drawback to a cable connection is the limited amount of bandwidth that is provided by each cable line. If large numbers of users are accessing the cable simultaneously, Internet connection speeds can be affected. For example, a subscriber in a rural area with few users is likely to have faster download speeds than a subscriber in a metropolitan area that has more users. Also, cable services are not available in some rural areas.

DIGITAL SUBSCRIBER LINE (DSL)

A **digital subscriber line (DSL)** is a technology that transmits and receives digital data over existing telephone lines. Because DSL systems use broadband access, the download and access times are similar to those of a cable modem. Although conventional dial-up modems also make their connection through phone lines, DSL connections allow information to transfer in its original digital format, which allows the user to access the Internet and make voice calls at the same time. This is accomplished by electronically separating the phone line into two lines or bands. One band carries the standard low frequency voice phone call, and one band carries the higher frequency digital computer calls. Phone line filters are used to separate the phone line into the two frequencies. Once the filter is in place, the Internet signal and the phone signal will not interfere with each other.

DSL modems provide subscribers with a continuous connection. Because DSL subscribers do not share bandwidth, access speed remains constant and is not affected by the number of users. However, DSL is available only to those users who are within three miles of a telephone switching station and who have telephone lines capable of handling DSL. As the distance to the switching station increases, access speed may be compromised. As with cable systems, DSL is not available in some areas.

SATELLITE

Much of today's communications is transmitted around the globe by satellite. A **satellite** is a device that orbits the Earth and relays signals between telecommunications stations. Satellite communication has been around for many years, but it has recently become a high-speed Internet solution available to almost everyone in the United States. Satellite modems are used to transmit and receive data through a satellite dish.

One of the disadvantages of cable and DSL is that broadband pipelines are not available in certain areas of the country, particularly in rural areas. Satellite transmissions are a little slower than either DSL or cable transmissions, but they have the advantage of being available for use in rural areas. Broadband by satellite allows users to access to the Internet, download files in seconds, enjoy Web music and video, and free up the phone line so users can receive calls. However, because installation requires an unobstructed view of the southern sky, performance might degrade or stop during very heavy rain or snowstorms.

WIRELESS COMMUNICATION

Wireless communication is the transfer of information over a given distance without the use of a

Wireless technology makes it possible for a user to access computer data remotely.

physical connection. Wireless technology enables communication to take place through radio wave or microwave transmissions. Wireless technologies such as Bluetooth and Wi-Fi make it possible for a user to stay connected to a LAN or the Internet and share information with coworkers without having his or her computer physically connected to a network.

Bluetooth is the name given to a technology that uses short-range radio signals to connect and exchange information between devices such as mobile phones, laptops, printers, digital cameras, and other handheld devices. Because Bluetooth technology has the ability to simultaneously handle both data and voice transmissions, it allows users to eliminate the cords associated with keyboards or other computer peripherals, connect a smartphone to an earpiece, or send a print job from a notebook computer to a printer. Although Bluetooth is not a line-of-sight technology, it does have a limited transmission range of between 3 to 300 feet.

Wi-Fi, or wireless fidelity, is medium-range radio transmission technology. Wi-Fi uses the same radio frequencies as Bluetooth, but with a higher power output resulting in a stronger connection. Wi-Fi can be used to create an entirely wireless network in the home as well as to add wireless capabilities to an existing wired network. Wi-Fi is designed for medium-range data transfers, which typically are described as 300 feet away indoors or 1,000 feet outdoors.

Wi-Fi technology is most often used to connect wireless LANs at home or to connect portable computer users to the Internet at public hotspots. A **hotspot** is a public location that offers a Wi-Fi access point. For example, a home wireless user can use Wi-Fi to connect to a home network or the Internet anywhere in the house or yard. A business may wish to add wireless capabilities to the company network and the Internet in common areas such as meeting rooms, lobbies, or cafeterias. Other businesses, such as hotels, offer wireless capabilities through hotspots

in common areas. Colleges typically have hotspots on campus to allow students to connect wirelessly to the campus network. If you have recently been in an airport, a coffee shop, a library, or a hotel, you probably have been in the middle of a public hotspot. Some public hotspots can be accessed for free while others charge by the minute or the hour.

Wireless technologies continue to be developed and enhanced. For example, municipal wireless networks are being developed by cities to allow fire and police departments to do parts of their jobs remotely. Other cities are creating a municipal network to provide high-speed Internet access free or for substantially less than the price of other broadband services. Other technologies including **WiMax** (long-range wireless broadband) have been designed to provide faster speeds and service for distances up to 30 miles. An advantage of WiMax is that it does not require line of sight; it works in areas containing buildings and trees. A version of WiMax has also been developed to be used with mobile technologies.

FIBER OPTIC CABLE

Standard telephone lines and coaxial cable transmit signals via electronic pulses through copper wire, but many newly installed telephone lines are equipped with fiber optic cables. A **fiber optic cable** consists of hundreds or thousands of glass threads or fibers with each thread about the diameter of a human hair. Each glass fiber is capable of transmitting information for several television stations or thousands of two-way voice conversations. Data is transferred though the glass fiber as light pulses. Because light does not weaken as it travels through the cable and it is less susceptible to interference than other types of cable, fiber optics is an excellent fit with telecommunications.

Fiber optic technology has several advantages over other transmission methods. Fiber optic cables are thinner and lighter than metal wires and are less susceptible to interference. Fiber optic cables have a much greater bandwidth

Hotspots are public locations that offer Wi-Fi access free or for a small fee.

than cable, DSL, or satellite can provide. Also, data can be transmitted digitally (the natural form for computer data), which makes it a perfect technology for telecommunications. Although it will take time before fiber optic cables are available everywhere, telephone companies are steadily replacing traditional telephone lines with fiber optic cables, and in the future almost all lines will use fiber optics.

Telecommunications Devices

The tools used to communicate with customers and clients, access files, send and receive email, and access the Internet have changed a great deal in only a few short years. The standard phone and desktop computer in an office have been transformed into a handheld device that includes a phone, computer, camera, and personal organizer. Users are no longer tied to a desk in an office; instead they can carry equipment in a pocket or in a purse. These cellular phones, smartphones, and personal digital assistants work equally as well when sitting in the coffee shop down the street and in the airport as the

standard phone and computer did on a desk at work, and sometimes even better! The following sections will highlight a few of the devices that are used in today's high-volume, fast-paced telecommunications environment.

STANDARD TELEPHONES

Standard telephones have been used to conduct business and to maintain contact with family and friends since their development in 1876. The standard telephone remains a key component of the telecommunications system. Though standard fixed line telephones are somewhat limited in their capabilities in comparison to other telecommunications tools, a simple phone call to an associate is sometimes the best way to pose a question, solicit advice, or just check in to say hello. When you place a telephone call and that call is answered, the communication is instantaneous, just as if you were standing face-to-face with the person who is on the other end of the line. The standard telephone continues to be an important telecommunications device used in business today.

MOBILE PHONES

In less than a decade, the mobile or cellular telephone has completely changed how the world communicates. The mobile telephone is a long-range, portable device that enables users to be in constant communication with clients, customers, and coworkers. Calls can be sent and received from nearly every corner of the globe, with the sound quality and clarity equivalent to the sound you hear when someone is standing right next to you. Depending on where your mobile call originates, it can travel by cell tower, by microwave transmission, or via satellites. Phone conversations and text messages are relayed back and forth using any or all of these technologies.

The most common mobile telephones today include more than just the voice function of a telephone. Mobile phones now include digital cameras, radios, and small video screens. They also have the ability to access the Internet and to send and receive text messages and email.

An electronic device that combines the features of a PDA and a mobile phone is called a smartphone. These mobile phones support email capabilities, Internet access, and personal organizer and contact management capabilities. They may also include navigation software and the ability to read business documents. Smartphones usually include interfaces such as a miniature keyboard or a touch screen.

Satellite telephones are mobile phones that are able to directly access communications satellites. Satellite phones serve a unique purpose because they enable communication from those areas where cell phones cannot reliably function, such as mountainous regions or aboard ships far out to sea. The size and shape of satellite phones can vary a great deal depending on the satellites a particular phone is programmed to access. A satellite phone handset is quite a bit larger than today's mobile phones, and it usually has a large retractable antenna. Portable satellite phones typically require a stationary base to be set up; this base acts as the relay to and from the satellite.

© Photos.com / Jupiterimages

Mobile phones come in a wide variety of shapes and sizes and have a wide variety of capabilities.

Every time the base is set up it must be aligned with the track of the satellite in order to transmit and receive its signals effectively. A fixed installation, which might be used aboard a ship, may include large mounted electronics and an antenna that automatically tracks the position of overhead satellites. One major disadvantage of satellite phones is that the handheld units need a clear view of the sky. They will not work inside buildings, cars, or boats unless external antennas are adapted to the phone.

PERSONAL DIGITAL ASSISTANTS (PDAs)

The personal digital assistant is an electronic device that was originally designed as a portable electronic calendar and data organizer. Electronic phone books, address lists, and to-do lists were the primary functions of the first PDAs. Today, these devices are also commonly called handheld computers. The functions of handheld computers are described in Chapter 10, Technology Update.

In addition to their computer-like functions, the PDA has evolved into a widely used tele-communications device. Some PDAs are mobile phone hybrids that are capable of accessing and sending email, others have instant messaging and text messaging options, and still others have global positioning capabilities. Newer PDAs have color screens and audio capabilities, enabling them to be used as Web browsers or portable media players. Also, the telecommunications abilities of PDAs have been expanded so that they can access the Internet or company networks via Wi-Fi or wireless wide-area networks.

Many businesspeople find a PDA an extremely helpful business tool. While waiting for a meeting or an appointment, a businessperson can use a PDA to review or make adjustments to a task list or calendar entries. He or she may browse the Internet for articles related to the business or review current headlines in business periodicals. A PDA can be used to record notes for a business meeting or article, respond to email, record business expenses in a spreadsheet, or even listen to a recorded book.

VOICE OVER INTERNET PROTOCOL (VoIP)

Voice over Internet Protocol (VoIP), also called Internet telephony, is a technology that allows a user to make voice telephone calls using an Internet connection instead of a regular phone line. Internet telephony can currently take place in one of three ways: computer-to-computer connections, computer-to-telephone connections, or telephone-to-telephone connections.

A VoIP user is able to send voice messages from his or her computer to the recipient's computer using the computer's speakers and microphone. VoIP technology converts the analog signal from the telephone to a digital signal that can be received by a computer. The digital signal is transmitted via the network to a second computer that is also connected to the network. The receiving computer, also using VoIP, receives the digital signal and converts it back into an analog signal. The phone call is then transmitted from computer to computer via a computer network instead of using the standard telephone channels. Some free Internet telephony is available for computer-to-computer voice calls. Users can download a variety of free software programs that will enable them to use this system.

Newer VoIP applications involve placing telephone-to-telephone calls over the Internet. In this system, telephone calls are routed over the Internet to and from the user's regular telephone system via an Internet connection. VoIP is currently available from a number of telephone, cable, and VoIP companies. Although VoIP users can make computer-to-computer calls for the cost of their monthly Internet connection fees, telephone-to-telephone connections are usually assessed a small fee or accomplished through a monthly service agreement. Businesses with their own private internal networks (LANS or WANS) can also adopt this technology to communicate without the costs of using the standard telephone connections. VoIP phones can integrate with other network services, including video conversation, data file exchange, and audio conferencing.

Using VoIP technology can be as easy as buying a VoIP phone and plugging it into the USB port of your computer, or buying a VoIP converter that connects your existing phone through the USB port of your computer. Another method is the softphone, which is application software that enables VoIP from a computer, a smartphone, or a PDA.

There are some disadvantages, however, to using VoIP technology. Because the technology is still evolving, the clarity and the quality of the message are not always as consistently clear as they are when using standard telephone technology. In addition, the information flowing from your VoIP connection is dependent on the speed of your computer, the type of connection to the Internet that you have (broadband connectivity is required), and the reliability of your Internet service provider (ISP). Softphone software may also be vulnerable to worms, viruses, and Trojan horses. Encryption technology is not always available with VoIP connections, and as a result it is relatively easy to eavesdrop on VoIP calls. As the technology continues to evolve, VoIP access will evolve as well.

Telephone Etiquette

Although the use of email and other communications methods have increased in business, the telephone is still the most commonly used telecommunications device. Although the first phones were developed to transmit and receive sound or voice, newer telephone technologies allow the user to send and receive voice as well as text, video, and images. In addition to landline phones, a wide variety of mobile phones have been introduced on the market. Regardless of whether you use landline or mobile telephone technology, as an administrative professional you will spend countless hours on the phone. If you are to be effective in your telephone communications, you must use proper etiquette. Study and apply the suggestions given in the following sections as you use the telephone.

Answering the Telephone

As discussed in Chapter 4, etiquette is an important component of your professional image. In addition, using appropriate etiquette is important for promoting a positive professional image of your organization. Using phrases such as *please* and *thank you* are essential professional components. The suggestions in the following sections will help you present yourself and your organization in a positive and professional manner.

ANSWER PROMPTLY
When your telephone rings, answer promptly— between the first and second ring if possible and certainly before the third ring. You may lose a potential customer if you are slow in answering the telephone. Even if you do not lose a customer, you may not make a good impression on the person calling. Have you ever been on the receiving end of a telephone that rings five or six times before someone answers? If so, you understand how irritating it can be when the person does not answer the phone promptly.

DEVELOP A PLEASANT VOICE
Always answer the telephone with a smile. Have you ever noticed how happiness shows through in the tone of your voice? A smile on your face has the same effect. If you are smiling, the caller can hear your friendly attitude reflected in your voice. Treat the caller the same as you would a person sitting across from you requesting information or assistance. Make your voice positive and full of energy and enthusiasm. Let all callers know you want to help with whatever needs they have.

SPEAK DISTINCTLY
Your voice carries clearly when you speak directly into the mouthpiece with your lips about an inch away from the transmitter. You cannot speak distinctly with something in your mouth. Do not have gum, food, or a pencil in your mouth when you answer the telephone. Speak in a normal tone of voice; do not shout or mumble. Callers may become irritated if they must ask you continually to repeat what you said or if they need to hold the telephone one or two inches away from their ear.

If your job involves considerable telephone work, you may use a hands-free headset. If this is the case, make sure you hold your conversations in office areas where outside noise will not interfere with your conversations. In addition, do not bring your conversations into parts of the office where they do not belong or where they may be overheard by other employees.

IDENTIFY YOURSELF AND THE ORGANIZATION
Your employer will usually instruct you in how to answer the telephone. Many large organizations have voice messaging systems that identify the

© BananaStock / Jupiterimages

Answer the telephone with a friendly tone of voice.

organization and give callers the available options. Other large companies have individuals who personally answer the phone with the name of the organization and route the incoming call. When your telephone rings, identify your office or organization and yourself. For example, you might say, "Thank you for calling United

An Effective Voice Message

If you are using a voice messaging system when you are away from your desk, the message should include the appropriate information. For example, "This is Melody Hoover. I am away from my desk now. Please leave your name, number, time of your call, and any necessary information. I will return your call as soon as possible. Thank you."

Pharmaceuticals, this is Melody Hoover," or "Administrative Services, Julaine speaking."

Handing Calls Effectively

Your professional telephone image needs to continue beyond the initial contact with the caller. People make business calls for specific reasons. Usually they are not calling to chat, but rather they are calling to conduct business. Remember, you may be the first and only contact a person may have with your organization, and that first impression will stay with the caller long after the call is completed. The suggestions in the following sections will help you handle calls in an effective and professional manner.

SCREEN CALLS

Many executives have two telephone numbers—one that is published and one that is not. The executive uses the inside unpublished number to make outgoing calls; the executive may also give the number to close friends or family members who can then dial the office directly. The administrative professional may be asked to screen calls that come from the published number. For example, when the executive receives a call, the administrative professional must determine who is calling and why.

The executive may choose not to take certain calls. If someone else in your company can handle the call, transfer it to that person after requesting permission from the caller. If no one is available to take the call or if no one is interested in taking it, let the person know courteously that your employer is not interested. One response might be this: "I appreciate the information; however, Ms. Winwright is not interested in pursuing the matter."

ASK QUESTIONS TACTFULLY

It is your responsibility to learn the caller's name. Usually a caller identifies herself or himself. If not, ask for a name tactfully. Do not say, "Who is this? Say, "May I tell Ms. Winwright who is calling, please?" Being courteous and using *may* and *please* completely change the approach. The caller usually understands that you are responsible for finding out who is calling and does not resent your asking. Try to put yourself in the other person's place, and ask questions the way you would want to be asked.

PLACE CALLS ON HOLD EFFECTIVELY

You may be responsible for answering your supervisor's phone when he or she is away from the office or handling another call. A call may come in when you are on another line. In these instances, you may need to put a caller on hold. If that is the case, first ask whether the caller is willing to be placed on hold, and wait for the answer. It may be appropriate to provide an explanation for the inconvenience. For example, you may say, "She's on another call. Would you like to hold?" Remember to keep the person on hold updated on the status of his or her call every 30 seconds and ask if he or she would like to continue to stay on hold. When checking with the caller, you may offer to take a message. For

© Comstock Images / Jupiterimages

Ask permission before placing callers on hold.

example you may say, "Ms. Hoover is still on another call. May I take a message or would you like to continue to hold?"

A caller may request information that you do not have at your fingertips. You may need to check with someone else or find the information in your records. When this happens, do not place the caller on hold without his or her permission and make sure to indicate how long it will take to locate the information. You may say, "I need to locate the information in my files. Would you like to hold for a minute while I get it or shall I call you back?" If the caller agrees to hold, get back to the person as soon as possible. If you are taking longer than you anticipated to locate the material, check with the caller within a minute to ask whether he or she would like to continue to hold. When you return to the line, let the caller know you are back by saying "Thank you for waiting."

Be honest about the time it will take you to locate the information. If you know it will take you an hour to find the necessary material, tell the caller and indicate when you will call with the information. If you are having trouble locating the material, return the call and indicate how much more time you will need. Follow through on your promise and be honest with the caller.

TRANSFER CALLS PROPERLY

You may need to transfer a call to another person. Before you transfer a call, explain to the caller why it is necessary to do so. Make certain the caller is willing. You may say, "Ms. Winwright is out of the office now, but I believe Mr. Sanchez can help you. May I transfer you to Mr. Sanchez?" Additionally, give the caller the complete number or the extension number in case you are disconnected. Stay on the line until the person picks up the phone and announce the transfer. If the person to whom you are transferring the call is not in, ask if the caller would like to leave a voice message. If the caller does not want to do so, take a number from the caller and have someone return the call.

RECORD MESSAGES CAREFULLY

Although many organizations have voice mail systems to handle messages, some supervisors prefer messages written on paper. Make sure you understand your supervisor's preferences when answering the phone for your organization. Also, do not automatically transfer clients or customers to a voice mail system. Instead, ask a customer "Would you like me to transfer you to Mr. Sanchez's voice mail?"

When taking messages, you are responsible for getting all necessary information from the caller and recording it accurately. Be prepared with a pen and message slip or paper when you answer the phone. When taking messages, you need to get the following information.

- Person's name (spelled correctly). If you do not know how to spell the name, ask the caller to spell it and then repeat the spelling to the caller to be certain you recorded it correctly.

- Organization of the person calling. If you are unfamiliar with the business name, ask the caller for the correct spelling.

- Telephone number, including the area code. Repeat the number to be certain you heard it correctly.

- The message. If the person leaves a message, get the necessary details. For example, if the caller says he will call your employer tomorrow, you may respond "May I tell him when to expect the call?" This approach helps avoid delays if your employer is going to be out of the workplace. Your task is to get the two individuals connected as quickly as possible and to eliminate numerous repeat calls when your employer is not in.

- Date and time. This information gives the recipient a point of reference for the message. The message "Mr. Wong will call you tomorrow" has no meaning if you do not know the date of the original call.

- Your initials or name. If the recipient has questions, your initials or name identifies who took the message.

Organizations usually have a procedure for recording and delivering messages. They may provide message pads or have a form that can be completed on the computer. Another possibility is to send an email to your supervisor or coworker containing the telephone message.

TERMINATE CALLS COURTEOUSLY

When closing a call, thank the person with whom you are speaking when appropriate. Do not make promises you cannot keep. For example, do not promise that your supervisor will call someone back. Instead, let the caller know that you will give your supervisor the message. Say *good-bye* pleasantly. Let the person who called hang up first. Treat the handset gently; do not slam it down in the caller's ear.

REMEMBER TIME DIFFERENCES

You need to remember time zone differences when placing calls. There are four standard time zones in the continental United States—Eastern,

Central, Mountain, and Pacific. Most of Alaska is in the Alaskan Time Zone. A portion of the Aleutian Islands and St. Lawrence Island are in the Hawaii-Aleutian Standard Time Zone as is Hawaii.

There is a one-hour difference between neighboring zones. For example, when it is 10 a.m. in New York City (Eastern Standard Time), it is 9 a.m. in Dallas (Central Standard Time). If you call from New York to Los Angeles, you do not want to call at 9 a.m. Eastern Standard Time; it would be only 6 a.m. in Los Angeles (Pacific Standard Time). You might note on your telephone list time differences for frequent callers. Websites are also available that provide time zone information. Figure 12.1 shows a Website that gives time information provided as a public service by the National Institute of Standards and Technology (NIST) and the U.S. Naval Observatory (USNO).

There are also international time zones. For example, the person who places a call from New York to London must remember that when it is 11 a.m. in New York, it is 4 p.m. in London. If you are placing many international calls, you need to become familiar with the international time zones.

Placing Effective Calls

As an administrative professional, you may be responsible for making business calls or placing calls for your supervisor. Professional handling is just as important whether a call is incoming or outgoing. A good strategy to follow is to treat the

FIGURE 12.1 The Official U.S. Time Website

call as if it were a meeting. Take a few minutes to plan your call before you make it. Know the purpose of your call and plan what you intend to say. Always identify yourself and your company as soon as the call is answered. For example, you may say, "This is Susan Wilson of United Pharmaceuticals. I am calling to confirm your appointment with Ms. Winwright on June 13 at 3:30 p.m."

If your business will take several minutes, be sure to state that and ask if you are calling at a convenient time. This allows the person an opportunity to call you back at a more appropriate time. Also, make sure to follow through with promises you have made. If you told a person you would call at a certain time, call when promised. If you need to delay the conversation, call to postpone it; but do not make the other person wait for your call. Leave your name and number if you expect someone to call you back.

Developing Your Telephone Personality

Whether answering the telephone or making calls, using proper etiquette is a must. The way you handle telephone calls from customers and clients goes a long way toward creating a positive impression of you and your organization. You will project a positive telephone personality when you use the caller's name, use language effectively, are helpful and discreet, and are attentive to the caller.

USE THE CALLER'S NAME

Individuals like to be recognized and called by name. Use the person's name frequently. For example, say, "Yes, Mr. Jordan. I will be happy to get the information." End the conversation with a comment such as "It was nice to talk with you, Mr. Jordan."

USE LANGUAGE EFFECTIVELY

Use correct English and pronunciation. People who have a good grasp of the English language develop a negative impression of your organization when they hear *this is her* or some other grammatically incorrect statement.

Using slang is neither businesslike nor in good taste. Figure 12.2 provides several slang

expressions that are incorrect, followed by more appropriate expressions.

BE HELPFUL AND DISCREET

When someone calls and your employer is not available, tell the caller approximately how long your employer will be gone or ask if someone else can help. Let the person know you are trying to help. Here are two examples of how to handle such a call—the wrong way and the right way.

Incorrect Handling of Call

Pablo Rodriguez:	This is Pablo Rodriguez. May I speak with Shareen Edwards?
Administrative Professional:	Ms. Edwards is out of the office.
Pablo Rodriquez:	When will she be back?
Administrative Professional:	I expect her back sometime this afternoon.
Pablo Rodriquez:	Will she be back in an hour?
Administrative Professional:	She might.
Pablo Rodriquez:	Ask her to call me when she comes in.
Administrative Professional:	Okay.

What is wrong with the conversation? Perhaps you do not see any glaring errors. The assistant

AVOID SLANG EXPRESSIONS

Avoid	Say
Yeah	Certainly
Okay	Yes
Uh-huh	Of course
Bye-bye	Good-bye
Huh?	I beg your pardon. I did not understand.

FIGURE 12.2 Avoid slang expressions and speak professionally when talking on the phone.

answered Pablo Rodriquez's questions—which is precisely the point. Mr. Rodriquez had to ask all the questions; he probably thought the assistant was uncooperative. The closing "okay" by the administrative professional was too informal. Additionally, the administrative professional did not get a phone number. Notice the improvement in this conversation.

Correct Handling of Call

Pablo Rodriquez: This is Pablo Rodriquez. May I speak with Shareen Edwards?

Administrative Professional: Ms. Edwards is out of the office now; however, I expect her back in about two hours. Please give me your telephone number, and I will ask her to call you when she returns.

Pablo Rodriquez: That would be helpful. My number is 555-0129.

Administrative Professional: Thank you, Mr. Rodriquez. I will give her the message.

The administrative professional has saved time for Mr. Rodriquez and Ms. Edwards and has probably left a positive impression with Mr. Rodriquez.

Another important point to remember in such a situation is to be discreet. In other words, do not give unnecessary information to the caller. Consider the same situation.

Pablo Rodriquez: This is Pablo Rodriquez. May I speak with Shareen Edwards?

Administrative Professional: Ms. Edwards went to see Bill Chung at IPI about an advertising matter. She should be back in two hours. Please give me your telephone number and I will ask her to call you when she returns.

Although it was a good idea to tell Mr. Rodriquez that Ms. Edwards will be asked to return his call, there was a problem in the conversation. What went wrong? The administrative professional gave out entirely too much information. It was not necessary to tell Mr. Rodriquez where Ms. Edwards was, who she went to see, and why. The assistant could be revealing confidential information or information that would hurt the business relationship. You want to help the caller, but you also must protect your employer by not revealing too much information. Figure 12.3 provides examples of appropriate telephone responses.

APPROPRIATE TELEPHONE RESPONSES	
Avoid	**Say**
She is out.	She is not in the office at the moment. May I take a message or would you prefer to leave a message on her voice mail?
I don't know where he is.	He has stepped out of the office. Would you like to leave a message?
She is busy.	She is unavailable right now. Would you like to leave a message?
He hasn't come in yet.	I expect him shortly. Would you like to leave a message?
She took the day off.	She is out of the office for the day. Can someone else help you or would you like to leave a message?
He's in the men's room.	He has stepped out of the office. Would you like to leave a message?

FIGURE 12.3 An appropriate response is courteous but does not reveal too much information.

BE ATTENTIVE

As you are talking with the caller, visualize the person. Speak *with* the person, not *at* the phone. Listen politely to what the person is saying. Do not interrupt or continue to key. If the caller is unhappy about an experience with the company, listen to the person's complaint. You will have an easier time dealing with a disgruntled caller after you hear what the caller has to say. Use good listening skills.

- Listen for facts.
- Search for hidden or subtle meanings.
- Be patient.
- Do not evaluate.
- Try to understand the words the caller is using.
- Act on what the caller is saying.

Take notes during a long or involved conversation so you will remember all the information. Courtesy is always important. Use words such as *please* and *thank you* often. Let the caller know you care about her or him and the situation.

Messaging Services and Etiquette

Telecommunications messaging systems presented in this textbook include standard telephones, instant messaging, text messaging, email (presented in Chapter 7), voice messaging, and mobile phones. Each of these messaging systems has a prominent place in business and home offices. Additionally, individuals use these systems for personal communications. If these messaging services are to be effective business tools, you must use them effectively and efficiently. In addition, you should use proper etiquette when communicating with messaging services.

Instant Messaging Services

Instant messaging (IM) is a software program that allows a user to send and receive messages over the Internet instantly in real time. Although IM systems were originally designed for text conversations over the Internet, IM is now accessible through cell phones, PDAs, or other handheld devices as well as on a computer. In addition to text messaging, IM features include voice chat, videophoning, file sharing, and gaming. In fact, instant messaging has promoted Internet telephony because the IM software makes it easy to switch from text chat to voice chat, providing the user has a headset or microphone and speakers.

Although originally designed for personal use, IM has become a widely used tool in business. Typically, IM is used when the response time of email is not fast enough. With email, you do not have any way of knowing if the person you are sending email to is online at that moment. Also, if you are exchanging multiple emails with the same person, you normally have to click through a few steps to read, reply, and send the message. While there are many types of IM clients, they all function in a similar manner.

Figure 12.4 shows a screen from *Windows Live™ Messenger*, a popular IM program.

BENEFITS OF INSTANT MESSAGING

The use of instant messaging in the corporate world has continued to increase. Why is corporate instant messaging increasing in popularity? Businesses find IM a very productive use of time to communicate internally as well as with other businesses and clients all around the world.

FIGURE 12.4 Instant Messaging Screen

Business IM services have been developed with features that include online voice, text, and video-conferences and meetings to both online and offline users and clients. IM provides these benefits for coworkers, clients, customers, vendors, and other business associates:

- IM facilitates real-time communication. IM allows you to communicate with colleagues and customers in real time. IM is considered faster than email because the questions and answers are sent and received instantly. IM eliminates the delays associated with unanswered email or voice mail and provides the ability to send and receive important documents and files without having them get lost in an email inbox. With IM, there is little waiting required.

- IM encourages collaboration. Employees have quick and easy access to one another. IM encourages people to work together because the delays associated with email and voice mail are eliminated.

- IM facilitates group communication and messaging. IM programs allow you to broadcast messages to groups of people. This function is similar to sending a group email except that with IM the message immediately appears on the user's screen. Important meeting announcements or reminders can be sent to all participants quickly and efficiently.

- IM provides quicker and more complete answers to customer questions. With IM systems, the user can be connected to more than one person at a time. For example, if a service representative does not have complete answers for a customer's telephone question, he or she may send an IM to a colleague for assistance. This also eliminates the necessity to research the answer and return the call at a later time.

- IM eases communication with off-site employees. Because IM is considered more personal than email and less intrusive than the telephone, IM works especially well when communicating with mobile employees or freelance workers.

- IM facilitates quick exchanges of lengthy text or technical information. Exchanging lengthy URLs or sections of documents is often difficult through phone conversations. The text and attachment features provide an easy way to share these types of information in real time.

INSTANT MESSAGING ETIQUETTE

Although the original forms of instant messaging relied on communicating through text information only, many IM systems now offer video conferencing features, VoIP, and Web conferencing services. Web conferencing services integrate video conferencing and instant messaging capabilities simultaneously. In order to present a professional image, it is important to follow some basic rules of etiquette when using IM for business purposes.

- Pay attention to status indicators (busy and away indicators). Sometimes people will use an away message if they are trying to avoid interruptions while working on an important project. As a user, respect their busy message by not interrupting them. Also, make sure to update your status indicators appropriately. If you are not available for IM messages, let others know by setting the appropriate status settings offered on the system.

- Make your message concise. State your request or point as succinctly as possible. Remember that the basic purpose of an IM message is to get a quick response. A longer and more technical message should be reserved for the telephone, email, a memorandum, or a letter, depending on the length and subject.

- Watch what you write. Do not write anything in an IM that you would not write in an email or a printed letter. Remember, whatever you say in instant messages can be saved and distributed to others. Do not assume that once your IM leaves your computer screen, it is gone. If you would not want to see your words on a postcard or in a newspaper, do not put them in an instant message.

- Allow the individual to answer. Do not continue to ask question after question without waiting for a response. Also, do not expect instantaneous

focus on   *Using Messaging Systems Safely*

When using messaging systems, it is imperative to make sure that your data is secure. The following suggestions from the US-CERT Website will help protect you and your information when using messaging systems.

- Evaluate your security settings. The default software settings are typically more permissive to make the software more usable; however, this also makes you more vulnerable to attacks. Protect your systems by checking your default settings, disabling automatic downloads, and limiting your interactions to certain users if possible.

- Be conscious of what information you reveal. Be careful about discussing sensitive business information over public IM or chat services. If you are using a free commercial service, the exchange may be archived on a server.

- Verify the identity of the individual you are talking to if it matters. In some situations, the identity of the individual you are talking to is not important. However, if you are sharing certain types of information or being asked to take action (like running a program), make sure to verify that person's identity.

- Do not believe everything you read. Try to verify information or instructions you receive from outside sources before taking any action. Information you receive by IM could be false, or worse, malicious.

- Keep software up to date. When using messaging programs it is important to keep the chat software, your browser, your operating system, your email system, and especially your antivirus software current.[1]

replies. You may or may not be the only person that individual is working with at the time or your question may require a few minutes of research. Give the person an opportunity to reply to your message before you ask for additional assistance.

- Use correct capitalization and spelling; avoid jargon. When using instant messaging in business, use professional writing conventions. Do not use language that others will not understand. Avoid abbreviations, acronyms, and emoticons.

- Be considerate in public places. If you are using an IM system in a public place, let others know that you are in a public place and that your messages may be viewed by others around you. When in a public area, turn off system sound effects out of consideration for others.

- Consider cultural differences. It is important to remember the global nature of business when dealing with IM. You may encounter different

spelling of words, words that are specific to a geographical or regional area, or individuals who do not have a good grasp of your native language. Consider what you are saying as well as how it might impact the other person. If you do not understand something that has been said, politely ask the sender to repeat it.

- Recognize time zone differences. Keep in mind the time zones of the persons with whom you are communicating.

- Be courteous. In an effort to be concise, do not be curt or rude. Remember your manners; use *please* and *thank you* as appropriate.

- Focus on what is important. Most individuals believe they can multitask: talk to a colleague, handle a phone call, and use IM at the same time. Trying to do it all at once may distract you from the task at hand. Focus on the

---

[1]"Using Instant Messaging and Chat Rooms Safely," National Cyber Alert System, US-CERT, accessed June 22, 2007, available from http://www.us-cert.gov/cas/tips/ST04-011.html.

immediate task, and then get back to where you were in IM.

- Send only appropriate messages. Instant messages are not replacements for serious, face-to-face communications. Do not use instant messages to be confrontational, criticize a colleague, or reprimand an employee.

Short Message Service (SMS)

Short Message Service (SMS), also known as text messaging, is the ability to send and receive short text messages through telecommunications channels. Most messages are limited to 160 alphabetic and numeric characters and cannot contain images or graphics. SMS was originally designed for use with mobile phones and PDAs. However, SMS is now used with other computer devices including handheld computers, notebook and desktop computers, and some landline or fixed phones. Although SMS is similar to paging, SMS messages do not require the mobile phone to be active when sent. Messages will be held for a number of days until the phone is active and within range.

Although the most common application of SMS is still person-to-person messaging, SMS has been expanded to include business uses as well. Text messages are often used to interact with automated business systems, such as ordering products and services. In fact, text messaging has become so popular that advertising agencies and advertisers are using text messages to promote their products. Services that provide bulk text message sending are also becoming a popular way for clubs, associations, and advertisers to quickly reach a group of individuals. Typical business uses of SMS can include notifying:

- A mobile phone user of a voice mail message
- A salesperson of an inquiry and contact to call
- A doctor of a patient with an emergency problem
- A service person of the time and place of the next call
- A driver of the address of the next pickup

Email

The ability to compose and send messages to destinations all over the world in a matter of minutes as well as the convenience of email continue to make it a widely used telecommunications tool in business. In fact, throughout the United States, organizations send billions of e-mail messages each day. Clearly, email is an important part of business today. The information provided in Chapter 7, Written Communications, and the following suggestions will help you create effective email messages.

- Plan your message before you begin.
- Include an appropriate subject.
- Be concise with your message.
- Use correct capitalization, spelling, and punctuation and avoid jargon.
- Send messages related only to topics that are appropriate to be discussed by email.
- Remember that email messages may be saved and may be seen by people other than the intended recipient.

Email etiquette and ethics are also important when using email systems. Review the following suggestions and the material in Chapter 7 to make sure your messages are ethical and appropriate.

- Check email regularly and answer email promptly.
- Do not use email to avoid speaking to someone in person.
- Be professional when speaking of others. Email is easily forwarded.
- Reply only to those individuals who need to be included. Do not use the Reply to All feature or automatically send a message to all individuals on your address list.
- Avoid sending messages when you are angry.
- Remember that email can be monitored and that it is a permanent record of an organization.
- Separate your business and personal email.
- Do not forward junk mail or chain letters.

Voice Messaging

In its simplest form, voice messaging functions as an answering machine. It uses a standard telephone handset and a centralized computer system to compile and store messages rather than messaging equipment at the individual telephone. Voice messaging systems are more complex than answering machines because they can provide some or all of the following functions:

- Answer many phones at the same time
- Store incoming voice messages in personalized mailboxes
- Enable users to forward messages to another voice mailbox
- Send messages to one or more voice mailboxes
- Add a voice introduction to a forwarded message
- Store voice messages for future delivery
- Make calls to a mobile phone or messaging service to notify the user a message has arrived in his or her mailbox
- Transfer calls to another phone number for personal assistance

When voice messaging is set up with an effective routing system and a pleasant voice giving directions, the system can be very efficient. However, some voice systems are not well constructed. You may find yourself in a loop that never allows you to connect with the office or person to whom you want to talk. You may find yourself unable to speak with an operator. Additionally, some systems attempt to give too much information, resulting in confusion for the caller. The following information will help you use voice messaging systems in an efficient manner.

ADVANTAGES OF VOICE MESSAGING

Although there are some problems associated with inappropriate voice messaging systems, organizations do not need to eliminate the technology. It can be an extremely effective business tool when used appropriately. Review the following advantages to voice messaging.

- Greater productivity of workers by eliminating repeated telephone calls when the individual being called is not available
- Greater productivity due to calls being routed to the appropriate individuals and the elimination of calls being transferred
- Less extraneous conversation, with voice messages averaging 30 seconds as compared to regular phone conversations averaging 4 to 5 minutes
- Faster delivery of communications by messages getting through even with time zone changes

VOICE MESSAGING ETIQUETTE

If voice messaging is to be effective, system designers must pay attention to the message content, length, and branching system. If you, as an administrative professional, are involved in helping to design a voice messaging system, you will want to help make the system both effective and efficient. Carefully consider the ability of the system to respond to the needs of clients and

Professional Pointers

When using telecommunications devices, adhere to these rules of etiquette.

- **Ask for information rather than demand that you receive it. Use** *please* **and** *thank you* **often.**
- **Plan carefully before you make a call, write an email, or send a message covering complicated issues. Be certain you include necessary details.**
- **When sending messages to fellow employees, use proper language, just as you would when writing to a client or customer. Be polite.**
- **Do not attempt to be clever or cute when writing messages. Be professional.**
- **When talking on the phone in a public place, remember to be courteous to those around you.**
- **Do not discuss confidential information in a public place. You never know who might hear and use what you say to the detriment of your organization.**

customers. Some suggestions for making a voice messaging system effective are given below:

- A voice message may be too long and complex. Make the voice message succinct and clearly stated. Do not give the caller superfluous information.

- A voice message may not allow the caller to talk with a person. No one likes to be lost in a voice messaging system that does not allow the caller to talk to a person. Be certain your system allows for exits to a person at appropriate intervals.

- The voice on a voice message may not sound pleasant. Create a favorable impression with a voice message not only with what you say, but also with the tone of your voice. Do not talk in a monotone; vary your vocal tone. Also be careful not to record any unpleasant or inappropriate background noise with your message.

A voice message may have a poorly designed routing system. To create an effective system, incorporate the following suggestions:

- With each step of the routing system, give callers no more than four options.

- Instructions should be short, under 15 seconds if possible.

- Give the most important information or answer the most frequently asked questions first.

- Tell the callers what they need to do first; then tell them the key to press. For example, a message might be as follows: *To transfer to the operator, press zero.* If you give the number first, the caller may forget what number to press.

In addition to a voice messaging system that routes outside calls to the appropriate department or person, organizations may use voice messaging systems on individual phones. Such systems allow employees to receive messages while they are away from their desks so they can return calls later. Unfortunately, sometimes these systems are misused by employees who regularly put their phones on voice mail, even when they are available. At times, you may need to use voice messaging while in the workplace, particularly if you are working on a project where interruptions cause problems. However, make certain that these situations are rare. Do not use a voice messaging system as an excuse for not answering your phone. You can save yourself and the caller time by answering the phone when you are at your workstation. Courteousness to callers demands that you consider their needs and time constraints.

Mobile Phones

Mobile phones have become standard equipment for many individuals. In many areas, mobile phones outnumber landline phones. Mobile phones are no longer used only by businesspeople; many adults and children rely on their personal mobile phones. Individuals carry their mobile phones with them constantly and enjoy the ability to send and receive calls from any location at any time. Mobile phone technology has made great advances in the last few years.

ADVANTAGES OF MOBILE PHONES

Mobile phones have become extremely popular as a business and personal tool. Some individuals are eliminating their landline phones in the home and switching to a mobile phone for their personal use. There are a several advantages that can be realized from using a mobile phone.

- Mobile phones allow communication in many places outside the home or office.

- Mobile phones often support the use of other messaging technologies including SMS, IM, and voice messaging.

- Mobile phones may include organization tools such as calendaring functions, task lists, and personal organizers.

- Mobile phones may provide access to email, information on the Internet, or mobile news services through SMS.

MOBILE PHONE ETIQUETTE

Have you ever been in a crowded airport where the person seated next to you was talking on a mobile phone while you were attempting to hear boarding instructions for your flight? Have you ever been out for a quiet dinner with family or friends

Many mobile phones allow users to access the Internet and send and receive email.

and had to contend with a constantly ringing mobile phone at the table next to you? If so, you understand that people are often less than courteous when using their mobile phones. Individuals seem to forget that others around them have needs also. Consider the following suggestions when using your mobile phone in a public place.

- Turn your cell phone off when attending church functions, musical or theater performances, seminars, or other events. At the very least, use the silent or vibrate setting. Leaving your ringer on when it will disturb others is unacceptable.

- Make calls only when absolutely necessary in public places like restaurants, elevators, and public restrooms. Whenever possible, move to a more private location before you place or answer a call.

- If an expected call cannot be postponed, alert your companions ahead of time and excuse yourself when the call comes.

- Keep your phone voice as low as possible so as not to disturb those around you.

- Keep your calls short. Out of respect for those around you, take care of your business and end the call as quickly as possible.

- Use discretion when discussing private matters or sensitive topics in front of others.

- When walking and talking on your mobile phone, be aware of your surroundings and respect the rights of others.

Remember, no one needs or wants to hear your private conversations. Respect others by following the suggestions given.

Summary

To reinforce what you have learned in this chapter, study this summary.

- Telecommunications is the transmission of text, data, voice, video, and images from one location to another.

- Telecommunications pipelines include traditional analog dial-up, cable, digital subscriber lines (DSL), satellites, wireless transmission, and fiber optic cable.

- A variety of devices are used for telecommunications including standard telephones, mobile phones, PDAs, and VoIP.

- Answer your telephone promptly. Use a pleasant tone of voice, speak distinctly, and identify yourself and the organization.

- You can handle incoming calls effectively by screening calls, asking questions tactfully, placing calls on hold effectively, transferring calls properly, recording messages carefully, terminating calls courteously, and remembering time differences.

- Establishing an effective telephone personality includes using the caller's name, using language effectively, being helpful and discreet, and being attentive.
- An instant messaging service offers many advantages to business, and it is important to follow basic etiquette rules when using this system.
- Email can be an important business tool if users create effective messages and remember to use appropriate etiquette and ethical principles.
- Because organizations use voice messaging extensively, using proper voice messaging etiquette is essential.
- Appropriate etiquette is also essential when using mobile phones.

What's the Problem?

Estelle was hired two months ago as a receptionist for a busy real estate firm where you work. You are the administrative assistant to one of the major partners in the business, and your office is just around the corner from Estelle. It seems that Estelle is having trouble dealing with callers. She is often chewing gum or candy when talking on the phone and is not listening attentively to phone callers. She uses incorrect English and, even though she has been corrected several times, she mispronounces the names of the real estate partners. Her questions often leave the callers defensive and cause major miscommunication and confusion.

What suggestions can you give Estelle to help her handle calls more effectively?

Let's Discuss

1. List and describe four of the most commonly used telecommunications pipelines.
2. Describe how to maintain a professional image when answering the telephone.
3. Identify the information that should be included when recording a telephone message.
4. List four benefits businesses can realize from using instant messaging software.
5. Identify three advantages to using a voice messaging system.

Critical-Thinking Activity

Ricardo Gonzales was excited when United Pharmaceuticals installed an automated voice messaging system. Ricardo hoped that this system would enable customers to quickly find and self-direct their calls to the correct department. However, he is finding that callers are getting lost in the menus and sometimes end up in a loop leading back to the main menu. Frustrated, the callers are then selecting the last option, which is to speak to a customer service representative. All of these calls lead to the desk of Ricardo. Ricardo is taking the heat from these frustrated callers, so much so that he is beginning to lose sleep. For the first time

Ricardo is dreading going to work in the mornings. Although he has talked to his supervisor about the problems, nothing seems to have changed since the implementation of the system.

What can Ricardo do to make his days less stressful? What changes could be made to the voice messaging system to make it more effective?

Vocabulary Review

Open the *Word* file *CH12 Vocabulary* found on the Student CD. Complete the vocabulary review for Chapter 12.

English and Word Usage Drill

Complete the English and Word Usage Drill for Chapter 12 found in the *Applications Workbook*.

Workplace Applications

12-1 Select a Telecommunications Pipeline

internet

(Goal 1)

Your supervisor, Melody Hoover, is considering working from home one day each week. In order to facilitate this request, United Pharmaceuticals will provide a laptop computer equipped with a network card. However, in order to complete her assignments, Melody will need access to the Internet as well as access to the company network. Melody has asked you to research the costs associated with setting up a telecommunications link.

1. Select at least three telecommunications pipelines available in your area. For each pipeline, determine the following:

    *   What are the costs associated with this pipeline? What is the monthly connection fee? Is there a start-up fee? What is the total annual cost?

    *   What specialized equipment do you need to purchase to access the pipeline?

    *   What are the contractual obligations? For example, are you required to keep the system for a minimum number of months or years?

2. Use a spreadsheet to calculate costs for the pipeline you think Melody should use. Include monthly or other regular fees associated with the pipeline for one year, setup costs, and the cost of any specialized equipment. Find the total costs for one year.

3. Write a memo to Melody Hoover describing your findings and giving a recommendation of the pipeline you think she should use. Include data from the

spreadsheet in the memo. Use the *Word* file *Memo Form* found on the Student CD to prepare the memo.

4.   Be prepared to briefly discuss the information with the class.

12-2 Create a Presentation on Telephone Etiquette

(Goal 2)

United Pharmaceutical employees have recently noticed that not all employees are answering the telephone in a positive manner. Melody has asked that you and a coworker create a presentation that reminds employees of the importance of using appropriate telephone etiquette.

team building

1.   Work with a classmate to complete this project. Use your knowledge and conduct additional research on the Internet to prepare an electronic slide presentation that addresses at least three of the following issues:

internet

*   Answering the phone effectively

*   Creating appropriate voice messages

*   Handling incoming calls appropriately

*   Placing effective calls

*   Tips for telephone success

2.   Include a title slide and at least seven additional slides in the presentation. Apply text animation to the slides. Include at least two appropriate graphics.

3.   Deliver the presentation to the class, working with your classmate. Submit printouts of the slides to your instructor.

12-3 Create a Newsletter

(Goals 2 and 3)

1.   Work with two classmates to create a newsletter using your word processing or desktop publishing software.

internet

2.   The newsletter should include all of the following items and two additional articles or features of your choice.

*   A newsletter title and the current date

*   A spotlight article on a telecommunications pipeline

*   A product review of a telecommunications device

*   An article that discusses the business benefits of instant messaging

team building

*   An article that reviews etiquette for a telecommunications device

*   A feature box that reviews commonly used IM jargon and their English equivalents (example: u for you; brb for be right back)

e-portfolio

*   Three graphics (at least one should be a photograph)

12-4 Create a Flyer on Telecommunications Etiquette

e-portfolio

(Goal 3)

United Pharmaceuticals has recently become concerned because employees have become careless with their instant messaging etiquette. Your supervisor, Amando Hinojosa, has asked for your help.

1. Create a one-page flyer to distribute to all employees that stresses the importance of professional behavior when using instant messaging software. The flyer should contain at least five etiquette suggestions.

2. Format the flyer attractively. Include a title, a bulleted list, at least one graphic, and a page border.

3. Print the flyer and submit it to your instructor.

4. Save the flyer as a Web page file that could be posted on the company intranet.

Assessment of Chapter 12 Goals

Did you successfully complete the chapter goals? Evaluate yourself by filling out the form found in Chapter 12 of the *Applications Workbook.*

part **5**

Records and Financial Management

CHAPTER 13

Managing Paper and Electronic Records

CHAPTER 14

Personal Finance and Investment Strategies

Career Profile

Database Administrator

Many businesses and other organizations generate large volumes of data. Database administrators help organizations manage and use their data. Database administrators work in almost all industries, but many are employed by Internet service providers; Web search portals; and data processing, hosting, and related services firms. Others work for government or organizations such as insurance companies, financial institutions, and universities. About 104,000 people worked as database administrators in the United States in 2004.*

To be successful, businesses need to store, manage, and extract data effectively. Managing data effectively is especially important for e-commerce. Database administrators work with database management software and determine ways to organize and store data. They identify user requirements, set up computer databases, and test changes to ensure the performance of the system. Database administrators often plan and coordinate backup systems and security measures for the database system.

Salaries for database administrators vary by geographic region, the size of the company, and the qualifications of the worker. The mean annual earnings of database administrators were $60,650 in May 2004. Database administrators must be able to think logically, work on teams, and have good communication skills. A bachelor's degree in computer science, information science, or management information systems is required for many database administrator positions. Employers increasingly seek individuals with a master's degree in business administration, with a concentration in information systems, as more firms move their business to the Internet. Employers, hardware and software vendors, colleges and universities, and private training institutions offer continuing education and training needed to keep skills up to date.

Computer scientists and database administrators are expected to be among the fastest growing occupations through 2014. Database administrators may advance into managerial positions, such as chief technology officer, on the basis of their experience managing data and enforcing security.

---

*"Computer Scientists and Database Administrators," *Occupational Outlook Handbook*, 2006-2007 Edition, accessed June 26, 2007, available from http://www.bls.gov/oco/ocos042.htm.

chapter 13

Managing Paper and Electronic Records

Learning Goals

1. **Understand the importance of records management.**

2. **Describe the considerations in managing paper records.**

3. **Describe the considerations in managing electronic records.**

4. **Identify the factors associated with records retention, transfer, and disposal.**

Importance of Records Management

The paperless workplace, touted by early computer manufacturers and business consultants, has proven to be a myth. In truth, technology has increased the ability to manipulate so much data that organizations are using more paper than at any time in history. The administrative professional in today's work environment is responsible for taking care of many of the organization's records. The responsibility for managing and maintaining records continues to increase in complexity. Technologies will continue to change, but the reliance on both paper and electronic files will continue to be important. A sound understanding of records management and the indexing rules associated with records storage will continue to be an essential skill for the administrative professional. Because both electronic and paper systems are used in many organizations, this chapter will emphasize management systems that address both systems.

Records Management Defined

Records management is the systematic control of records from creation to final disposition (through the life cycle for the record). This life cycle has five distinct phases:

1. Creation or receipt of the record.
2. Distribution of the record to internal or external users.

3. Use of the record (information gleaned from the record for making decisions, determining directions, and so on).
4. Maintenance of the record (filing and retrieving).
5. Disposition (retaining or destroying the record after a period of time).

A **record** is stored information on any media created or received by an organization that is evidence of its operations or that has value requiring its retention for a period of time. For example, information may be:

- Written and recorded on paper
- Written and recorded on some type of electronic form or microform (any medium containing miniaturized or microimages)
- An oral record that captures the human voice and is stored on DVD or other electronic storage media
- Email, spreadsheets, databases, word processing documents, or other computer files stored in an electronic folder
- Movies or digital photographs stored on DVDs or other media

Records Are Assets

Records are assets to a business just as products and services, management expertise, and a good reputation are assets. Records are important because they provide a history of the business. Successful organizations use the information contained in records to make decisions and plans. The additional value of records to business includes:

- Legal value by providing evidence of business transactions, such as articles of incorporation, real estate transactions, and contracts
- Financial value through records needed in audits and for tax purposes
- Historical value through items such as employee evaluations, payroll records, and employment termination records
- Day-to-day operational value through such records as policy and procedures manuals, organizational charts, minutes of meetings, information sent to clients and customers, and sales reports

Considerations for Effective Systems

The administrative assistant's records management responsibilities may go beyond maintaining existing files to include the design and installation of records systems. In planning an effective records system, three factors must always be considered: findability, confidentiality, and safety.

FINDABILITY

An important criterion for judging a records management system is findability. Whether the records are in paper, microfilm, or electronic form, the ability to find records in a timely manner is crucial. Think of file folders as places to find materials, not just places to put materials. Before

© Bob Llewellyn / Image State / Jupiterimages

The ability to find records quickly is the most important criterion of any records system.

determining where to file an item, consider these questions:

- How will this information be requested?
- How can I most efficiently locate the information when it is needed later?

CONFIDENTIALITY

Confidentiality of records is an important aspect of a records management system. Great care must be exercised to maintain the security of highly confidential information. Reasonable protection must also be exercised over less sensitive materials. When working with highly sensitive records, users are required to follow company policies that have been designed specifically for handling confidential information. In some offices, a written request bearing the signature of a designated officer of the organization is required for release of certain classified or confidential records. In an electronic system, access to confidential records is limited to those users who know the password or have been given access through a security system. In other instances, confidentiality of records may preclude users from removing the records from the storage room.

SAFETY

The administrative professional is often responsible for the safety of records in the workplace. Because many records are irreplaceable, administrative professionals should pay careful attention to security. Security measures protect records from improper access, accidental loss, theft, damage, and unwanted destruction. Losing records as a result of a natural or human disaster can result in a large monetary loss. Detectors that can perceive changes in levels of light, heat, and air conditioning can be installed. These units can send electronic messages to notify staff when changes in the environment occur. Other sensors can recognize heat from fire and activate sprinkler systems as needed.

Organizations can improve the safety of their paper and electronic files by installing security systems. Traditional key and lock systems can be installed on important file cabinets, file shelves, or records storage rooms. Electronic access security devices including magnetic cards or electronic keys can be installed to control and monitor access to storage areas. Many of these devices will also record an employee's name and date and time of access. Biometric devices such as a fingerprint scanner or iris pattern recognizer could also be used. Organizations can also keep backup copies of their most important records in a different, safe location. These records can be used when onsite records are lost, as when a fire or flood occurs.

Managing Paper Records

Records, whether handled electronically or manually, are the memory of a business. Depending on the size of the organization, records may be centralized (stored in one central location) or decentralized (stored in various departments or branches). Many administrative professionals maintain decentralized files as well as send materials to, and retrieve materials from, large central files.

Records storage systems are the manner in which records are classified for storage. The four basic storage categories are alphabetic, subject, numeric, and geographic. Records in a paper filing system may be stored in any of these ways. Alphabetic systems will be discussed first. Other systems will be discussed later in this chapter.

Alphabetic Storage Systems

An alphabetic storage system uses letters of the alphabet to determine the order in which the names of individuals, businesses, and organizations are filed. This method is the most commonly used storage method and is found in one form or another in almost every organization. With an alphabetic storage system, records placement is based on the alphabetic indexing rules detailed later in this chapter.

An alphabetic system has several advantages over other types of systems. It is a direct access system. There is no need to refer to anything except the file to find the name, which saves time. The dictionary arrangement is simple to understand. Misfiling is easily checked by alphabetic sequence. An alphabetic system also has some disadvantages. Confidentiality of files is difficult to maintain because the file folders bearing names are seen by anyone who happens to glance at a folder. Related records may be filed in more than one place, and misfiling may result when rules are not followed.

Basic Equipment and Supplies

Basic supplies for filing paper documents and records include storage cabinets, file guides, file folders, and labels.

STORAGE CABINETS

The conventional storage cabinet for paper records is a vertical file cabinet. In a vertical file system, the arrangement of folders in the file drawers is from front to back because the cabinet is deeper than it is wide. Vertical cabinets are available in one- to five-drawer designs. Although they are most commonly found in standard letter size (8½″ × 11″), they are also available in sizes to accommodate legal-sized records (8½″ × 14″).

Other types of storage systems used in businesses include lateral file cabinets, shelf systems, and mobile filing systems. Lateral filing cabinets are similar to vertical units except they are wider than they are deep. In a lateral file the drawer rolls out sideways, exposing the entire contents of the file drawer at once. Less aisle space is needed for a lateral file than a vertical file because the drawers extend sideways.

Open shelf filing systems are used in some organizations because they can store many records in a minimal amount of space. In fact, open shelf files typically occupy 50 percent less floor space than drawer files having the same capacity. Open shelf files are simple shelving equipped with dividers where file folders are shelved like books, therefore records can be accessed quickly and easily. However, open shelf files are exposed

Open shelf files typically occupy 50 percent less floor space than drawer files having the same capacity.

to potential fire and water damage and should be kept in a fireproof room.

Other organizations use mobile banks of shelves that can be moved as needed for storage and retrieval. Mobile file systems consist of a series of shelving units that move on tracks attached to the floor. Mobile systems are popular in instances where floor space is expensive or scarce.

FILE GUIDES

A guide is a rigid divider used to separate a file drawer into various sections. Guides are typically made of heavy materials such as pressboard, manila, or plastic. A guide typically has a tab with a caption that contains a name, number, or letter representing a section in the file drawer. Depending on the storage system used, the tab may appear at the top or side edge of the guide. Some guides have metal or acetate tabs to give

added strength for extended use. Because of their sturdy construction, guides can also serve to keep the contents of a container upright. Keeping records upright promotes efficient storage and retrieval of records. Guides for sections A and B of an alphabetic file are shown in Figure 13.1.

FILE FOLDERS

A file folder is a container used to hold and protect the records in a file. The most popular types of folders are manila folders and hanging folders. File folders are typically made of manila and are available in a variety of colors. Most folders are also equipped with a tab that is used to hold a caption which identifies the folder's contents. The tab is at the top of the folder when used in filing cabinets and at the side of the folder for open shelf filing. The width of the tab is referred to as its *cut*. Folders are available in a variety of cuts including straight cut, one-half

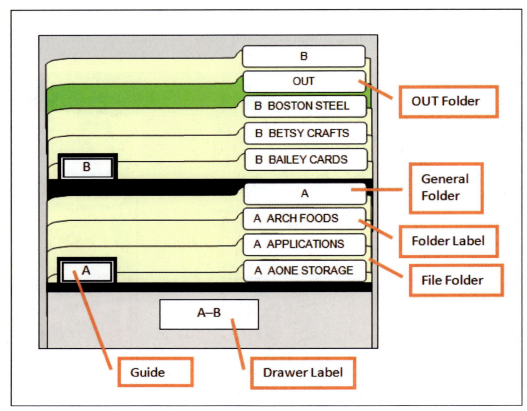

FIGURE 13.1 Section of an Alphabetic File

cut, one-third cut, and one-fifth cut. If the tab is one-fifth as wide as the folder, it is called a one-fifth cut tab. If the tab is half as wide as the folder, it is called a one-half cut tab.

Another type of folder that may be used for storing business documents is a suspension folder, or hanging folder. Generally hanging folders have metal extensions that enable them to hang on file drawer frames. The main advantage of having suspension folders over conventional folders is their added support for holding records in a neat, upright position. The frame serves to support both the front and back of the folder with hooks on the drawer rails. Suspension folders are available in an assortment of colors. They have up to ten slots across the upper edge for placement of plastic tabs to identify the folder content. Suspension folders are often used to hold several interior file folders to subdivide a file.

LABELS

Guides and folders that help filers store records efficiently must be labeled to guide the eye to the appropriate storage location. A label is a piece of material, usually paper or plastic, that has a caption with the name, subject, or number assigned to the file folder or section contents. A caption is a title, heading, short explanation, or description of documents or records. A label may also be color-coded to denote its place in an overall filing system or have a bar code.

Labels can be purchased as pressure-sensitive adhesive paper in continuous folded strips or on sheets. Labels can be white, colored, or white with a colored stripe across the top of the label. Labels can be prepared with computer software and affixed to folders or guides. Most word processing software has settings for different label sizes that match common label product numbers. Also, packaging that comes with the labels often has instructions for required software settings. In an alphabetic system, the section of the file (A, B, etc.) is keyed at the left of the folder label followed by the filing segment. Label captions are keyed in all capital letters with no punctuation as shown in Figure 13.1.

Paper Storage Procedures

Storing records is an important job that must be taken seriously. Replacing or locating a missing record can be costly to an organization in both time and money. Therefore, certain procedures should be followed before placing a record in the file. These steps include inspecting, indexing, coding, cross-referencing, and sorting documents.

INSPECTING

Incoming records must not be stored until the record has been reviewed and acted upon. The process of checking a record to determine whether it is ready to be filed is called **inspecting**. The copy of an outgoing document is usually ready to be stored when it is received by the filer. However, before storing any incoming record, the filer should check for a release mark. A release mark is an agreed-upon mark such as initials, a stamp, or other symbol to show that the record is ready for storage. The person who handled the document (prepared the reply or made a calendar notation) usually puts the release mark on the document. The initials GM serve as the release mark on the letter shown in Figure 13.2. Sometimes records will be placed in the

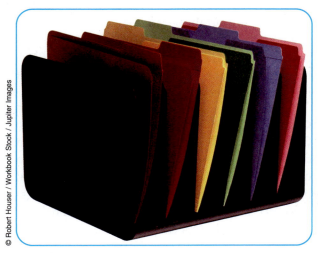

Folders are available in a variety of cuts including straight cut, one-half cut, one-third cut (as shown here), and one-fifth cut.

© Robert Houser / Workbook Stock / Jupiter Images

filing area by mistake. If there is no release mark, check to see if the record is ready to be stored.

INDEXING

Indexing refers to the mental process of determining the filing segment (or name) to be used in storing. The filing segment is the name by which a record is stored and requested. Although the rules for indexing may vary slightly from organization to organization, most organizations file information based on the indexing rules established by ARMA International, an association for information management professionals. Those rules are described in detail later in this chapter. Indexing is extremely important because accurate indexing is necessary for quick retrieval of information.

When selecting a filing segment, choose the name most likely to be used in asking for the record. Use the following guidelines when indexing incoming correspondence in an alphabetic system:

- The name for storage purposes is usually on the letterhead.
- If a letterhead has no relationship with the contents of the letter, the writer's name or the writer's business connection is used. In this instance, the letterhead name is disregarded for filing purposes. An example is a letter written on hotel stationery or plain paper when an executive is traveling.
- Incoming correspondence on plain paper (paper without a letterhead) is usually personal and will be called for by the name in the signature line.
- When both the company name and the name of the writer seem to be of equal importance, the company name is used.

When indexing outgoing correspondence in an alphabetic system, follow these guidelines:

- The most important name on a file copy of an outgoing letter is usually the one contained in the letter address.
- When both a company name and the name of an individual are contained in the letter address, the company name is used for filing

unless the letter is personal or unless a name in the body is the correct name to index.

- On a copy of a personal letter, the writer's name is usually the most important and should be used for storage.

CODING

For paper records, coding is the process of marking a record to indicate the filing segment and indexing units of a record. The first step in coding paper records usually includes placing diagonals (/) between the parts of the filing segment. The next step is to underline the key unit. The following steps are to number each succeeding unit that you mentally identified in the indexing process. For example, the coded personal name Raymond Thomas Johnson would appear as shown below.

The company name, L & M Advertising Agency, is coded on the letter shown in Figure 13.2. A name to be used as the cross-reference, Kirkman Products, Inc., is also coded. You will learn about cross-references later in this chapter. Coding is important because it saves time in the filing and refiling process. When a document has been removed from the files and must be refiled, the user does not need to reread the document if it has been coded.

CROSS-REFERENCING

Cross-referencing should be completed when a document may be called for under more than one name. A variety of examples when personal names and business names should be cross-referenced are presented after the alphabetic indexing rules in this chapter.

SORTING

Sorting is arranging records in the order in which they are to be stored (placed in filing cabinets or other storage containers). The records

L&M Advertising Agency
80 Second Avenue
New York, NY 10022-1421
Telephone: 212.555-0146   Fax: 212.555-0187

September 24, 20--

SEP 25, 20-- 11:03 A.M.

Ms. Graciella Melena
Melena & Daughters, Inc.   *GM*
600 E. 52 Street
New York, NY 10022-2844

Dear Ms. Melena

Your ad with Kirkman Products, Inc. is well under way. Executives at Kirkman   X
are more than a little excited about the advertising tie-in with your company. We
have a two-page ad for spring distribution we would like to share with you and
Juan Ramos, Advertising Director at Kirkman.

Juan is eager to complete the work on this campaign. By the way, Kirkman is
also willing to supply a personal appearance of one of its product designers for
your spring exhibition. Kirkman has agreed to pay $47,000 for the first spring ad
if you will handle all production costs. We can work out these arrangements in
more detail at our joint meeting.

Melena & Daughters and Kirkman Products are uniquely compatible, Graciella.
This cooperative effort creates a far more dynamic campaign for today's market
than we could have developed from an independent effort. We are eager to show
you what we have done.

I will call you next week to arrange a convenient time for a joint ad presentation.

Sincerely

J. R. McGuire

J. R. McGuire, Advertising Coordinator

kac

FIGURE 13.2 This letter has a release mark and is coded for filing.

should be sorted as soon as possible after coding and cross-referencing, especially if storage must be delayed. Typically records are sorted into a few groups and then into the final arrangement. The records are often sorted more than once. For example, in an alphabetic system items may be arranged into groups of A to C, D to H, I to M, N to S, and T to Z. The last sorting consists of arranging the items in exact alphabetic order. When the last sort is complete, the materials are ready to be filed.

STORING

Storing is the process of placing the record into storage containers. Storing records correctly is very important. The time at which records are actually stored depends on the workload during the day. In some offices, storing is the job performed first in the morning; in other instances, storing is done when a lull in other work occurs. As you are accumulating documents for storage, keep them in order at your desk in case someone needs to refer to a record.

Before placing a document in a storage location, remove any paper clips used to keep pages together. Staple the pages together in the upper left corner. Paper clips often fall off in the files; if records that need to be kept together are not stapled, other records may be inserted between them by mistake. Steps in storing records will vary somewhat depending on the type of records storage system used. Follow these general steps to store records in an alphabetic filing system:

1. Locate the proper file drawer by reading the drawer labels.

2. Search through the guides in the drawer to find the needed alphabetic section of the file.

3. Individual folders are used when several records with the same name are placed in the file. If an individual folder has been prepared for records with this name, place the record in the individual folder. Place the front of the record facing the front of the folder and the top of the record at the left side. Place records in the folder by date, with the most recent date in front.

4. If no individual folder is has been prepared for this name, file the record in the general folder for that section. For example, if a coded name

begins with *A* and there is no individual folder for the name, file the record in the A general folder. Arrange records in a general folder alphabetically by name. If there are two or more records with the same name, they are arranged by date with the most recent date in front.

Records Retrieval

In all records management systems, whether they are paper, electronic, or image, it is important to be able to retrieve records, retain them for their useful life, and transfer them to other locations to reduce the size of the active files. Retrieval of records in paper systems is discussed here.

If a record is taken from a file, it is necessary to indicate what was taken, who has possession of the record, and when it was removed. It may also be helpful to indicate when the record will be returned. Procedures using requisition forms and OUT guides and OUT folders provide a system for tracking records when they are taken from the files.

A requisition form includes a space for identifying the record borrowed, the name and location of the borrower, data about the borrowed record, and the date the record is to be returned to the files. This form may be prepared on a computer or handwritten in duplicate. One copy is typically kept in a tickler file and the other copy is inserted in an OUT guide or an OUT folder.

An *OUT guide* is usually a pressboard or plastic guide with the word *OUT* printed on the tab; it is used to replace a record that has been removed from the files. The guide may have a pocket in which information regarding the removed items can be recorded. When an entire folder is taken from the files, papers for that folder cannot be filed until the folder has been returned. For continuity in filing, you may choose to use an *OUT folder* to take the place of the file that has been borrowed. An OUT folder can hold papers that will need to be placed in the file when it is returned to the file drawer. The OUT guide or folder remains in the file until the borrowed record or folder is returned. An OUT folder is shown in Figure 13.1 on page 312.

Alphabetic Indexing Rules

The rules for filing may vary slightly from business to business based on the specific needs of the organization. However, most organizations base their systems on the rules generated by ARMA International, an association for information management professionals. The rules presented in this chapter are compatible with ARMA International filing rules.

Rule 1: Indexing Order of Units

A. PERSONAL NAMES

A personal name is indexed in this order: (1) the surname (last name) is the first (key) unit, (2) the given name (first name) or initial is the second unit, and (3) the middle name or initial is the third unit. If it is difficult to determine the surname, consider the last name written as the surname. A unit consisting of just an initial precedes a unit that consists of a complete name beginning with the same letter—*nothing before something*. When indexing, punctuation is omitted.

Filing Segment / **Indexing Order of Units**

Name	Key Unit	Unit 2	Unit 3
Francine Sanderson	Sanderson	Francine	
Martha J. Sanderson	Sanderson	Martha	J
F. Joseph Severson	Severson	F	Joseph
Franklin J. Severson	Severson	Franklin	J
Frederick L. Severson	Severson	Frederick	L
Frederick Lionel Severson	Severson	Frederick	Lionel

B. BUSINESS NAMES

Business names are indexed as written using letterheads or trademarks as guides. Each word in a business name is considered a separate unit. Business names containing personal names are indexed as written.

Filing Segment / **Indexing Order of Units**

Name	Key Unit	Unit 2	Unit 3
Herman Franklin Paving	Herman	Franklin	Paving
Herman Franks Photography	Herman	Franks	Photography
Howard Ogea Excavating	Howard	Ogea	Excavating
Howard Oil Company	Howard	Oil	Company
Huron Mountain Bread	Huron	Mountain	Bread
Huron Waters Realty	Huron	Waters	Realty

Rule 2: Minor Words and Symbols in Business Names

Articles, prepositions, conjunctions, and symbols are considered separate indexing units. Symbols are considered as spelled in full. When the word *The* appears as the first word of a business name, it is considered the last indexing unit. Examples include:

Articles: a, an, the

Prepositions: at, in, out, on, off, by, to, with, for, of, over

Conjunctions: and, but, or, nor

Symbols: &, ¢, $, #, % (and, cent *or* cents, dollar *or* dollars, number *or* pound, percent)

Filing Segment	Indexing Order of Units			
Name	Key Unit	Unit 2	Unit 3	Unit 4
A & A Drilling	A	and	A	Drilling
Dollar and Cents Store	Dollar	and	Cents	Store
The $ Shop	Dollar	Shop	The	
The Gingerbread House	Gingerbread	House	The	
Lawton & Lawton Shoes	Lawton	and	Lawton	Shoes
Lawton Interiors by Design	Lawton	Interiors	by	Design

Rule 3: Punctuation and Possessives

All punctuation is disregarded when indexing personal and business names. Commas, periods, hyphens, apostrophes, dashes, exclamation points, question marks, quotation marks, underscores, and diagonals (/) are disregarded.

Filing Segment	Indexing Order of Units		
Name	Key Unit	Unit 2	Unit 3
Alger-Marquette Community Foundation	AlgerMarquette	Community	Foundation
Bob's Septic Service	Bobs	Septic	Service
E-Z Storage Co.	EZ	Storage	Co
North/South Collection Agency	NorthSouth	Collection	Agency
Irene B. Oakley-Peters	OakleyPeters	Irene	B

Rule 4: Single Letters and Abbreviations

A. PERSONAL NAMES

Initials in personal names are considered separate indexing units. Abbreviations of personal names (Wm., Jas., Jos., Thos.) and nicknames (Liz, Bill) are indexed as written.

Filing Segment	*Indexing Order of Units*		
Name	**Key Unit**	**Unit 2**	**Unit 3**
J. T. Hung	Hung	J	T
Jas. T. Hung	Hung	Jas	T
L. Pauline Hung	Hung	L	Pauline
Liz P. Hung	Hung	Liz	P

B. BUSINESS NAMES

Single letters in business and organization names are indexed as written. If single letters are separated by spaces, index each letter as a separate unit. Index acronyms (words formed from the first few letters of several words, such as ARCO and NASDAQ) as one unit regardless of punctuation or spacing. Abbreviated words (Corp., Inc.) and names (IBM, GE) are indexed as one unit regardless of punctuation or spacing. Radio and television station call letters are indexed as one unit.

Filing Segment	*Indexing Order of Units*			
Name	**Key Unit**	**Unit 2**	**Unit 3**	**Unit 4**
E C I Inc.	E	C	I	Inc
EG Environmental	EG	Environmental		
F A D Mfgs.	F	A	D	Mfgs
K & L Enterprises	K	and	L	Enterprises
KBER Radio	KBER	Radio		

Rule 5: Titles and Suffixes

A. PERSONAL NAMES

A title before a name (Dr., Miss, Mr., Mrs., Ms., Professor, Sir, Sister), a seniority suffix (II, III, Jr., Sr.), or a professional suffix (CRM, DDS, Mayor, M.D., Ph.D., Senator) after a name is the last indexing unit.

Numeric suffixes (II, III) are filed before alphabetic suffixes (Jr., Mayor, Senator, Sr.). If a name contains a title and a suffix (Ms. Emily Pagel, Ph.D.), the title (*Ms*) is the last unit.

Royal and religious titles followed by either a given name or a surname *only* (Princess Anne, Father Mark) are indexed and filed as written.

Filing Segment	Indexing Order of Units			
Name	**Key Unit**	**Unit 2**	**Unit 3**	**Unit 4**
Gary J. Estevant	Estevant	Gary	J	
Gary J. Estevant, II	Estevant	Gary	J	II
Gary J. Estevant, Jr.	Estevant	Gary	J	Jr
Mr. Gary J. Estevant	Estevant	Gary	J	Mr
Father Paul	Father	Paul		
Gaynelle D. Hawkins, M.D.	Hawkins	Gaynelle	D	MD
Miss Gaynelle D. Hawkins	Hawkins	Gaynelle	D	Miss
Sister Gaynelle Hawkins	Hawkins	Gaynelle	Sister	
Sister Gaynelle	Sister	Gaynelle		

B. BUSINESS NAMES

Titles in business names are indexed as written. Exception: The word *The* that begins a business name is considered the last indexing unit.

Filing Segment	Indexing Order of Units			
Name	**Key Unit**	**Unit 2**	**Unit 3**	**Unit 4**
Aunt Joan's Fudge	Aunt	Joans	Fudge	
Doctor Frank's Greenhouse	Doctor	Franks	Greenhouse	
Dr. Phil's Counseling	Dr	Phils	Counseling	
The Dr. Store	Dr	Store	The	
Mr. Tom's Bait Shop	Mr	Toms	Bait	Shop
Sister Suzy's Shrimp Shack	Sister	Suzys	Shrimp	Shack

Rule 6: Prefixes, Articles, and Particles

A foreign article or particle in a personal or business name is combined with the part of the name following it to form a single indexing unit. The indexing order is not affected by a space between a prefix and the rest of the name (Amber La Cruz), and the space is disregarded when indexing.

Examples of articles and particles are: a la, D', Da, De, Del, De La, Della, Den, Des, Di, Dos, Du, E', El, Fitz, Il, L', La, Las, Le, Les, Lo, Los, M', Mac, Mc, O', Per, Saint, San, Santa, Santo, St., Ste., Te, Ten, Ter, Van, Van de, Van der, Von, Von der.

Filing Segment	Indexing Order of Units			
Name	**Key Unit**	**Unit 2**	**Unit 3**	**Unit 4**
Mrs. Francis R. De Gabriele	DeGabriele	Francis	R	Mrs
Le May's Fine Foods	LeMays	Fine	Foods	
Dr. Marsha P. O'Connell	OConnell	Marsha	P	Dr
St. Germain and McDougal, CPAs	StGermain	and	McDougal	CPAs
Mr. Alexis P. Von der Grieff	VonderGrieff	Alexis	P	Mr

Rule 7: Numbers in Business Names

Numbers spelled out in a business name (Sixth Street Grocery) are considered as written and filed alphabetically. Numbers written in digits are filed before alphabetic letters or words (3 Day Cleaners is filed before Adams Cleaners).

Names with numbers written in digits in the first units are filed in ascending order (lowest to highest number) before alphabetic names (229 Boutique, 534 Grocers, First National Bank of Marquette). Arabic numerals (2, 3) are filed before Roman numerals (II, III).

Names with inclusive numbers (33-37 Fence Court) are arranged by the first digit(s) only (33). Names with numbers appearing in places other than the first position (Pier 36 Cafe) are filed immediately before a similar name without a number (Pier 36 Cafe comes before Pier and Port Cafe).

When indexing names with numbers written in digit form that contain *st*, *d*, and *th* (1st Mortgage Co., 2d Avenue Cinemas), ignore the letter endings and consider only the digits (1, 2, 3).

When indexing names with a number (in figures or words) linked by a hyphen to a letter or word (A-1 Laundry, Fifty-Eight Auto Body, 10-Minute Photo), ignore the hyphen and treat it as a single unit (A1, FiftyEight, 10Minute).

When indexing names with a number plus a symbol (55+ Social Center), treat it as a single unit (55Plus).

Filing Segment	*Indexing Order of Units*			
Name	**Key Unit**	**Unit 2**	**Unit 3**	**Unit 4**
5 Step Cleaners	5	Step	Cleaners	
5th Street Bakery	5	Street	Bakery	
50% Discounters	50Percent	Discounters		
65 Ice Cream Treats	65	Ice	Cream	Treats
65+ Senior Center	65Plus	Senior	Center	
400-700 Rustic Way	400	Rustic	Way	
The 500 Princess Shop	500	Princess	Shop	The
XXI Club	XXI	Club		
Fifth Street News Shoppe	Fifth	Street	News	Shoppe
Finally 21 Club	Finally	21	Club	
Finally Free Club	Finally	Free	Club	
I-275 Garage	I275	Garage		
#1 TV Deals	Number1	TV	Deals	
Sixty-Six Highway Deli	SixtySix	Highway	Deli	

Rule 8: Organizations and Institutions

Banks and other financial institutions, clubs, colleges, hospitals, hotels, lodges, magazines, motels, museums, newspapers, religious institutions, schools, unions, universities, and other organizations and institutions are indexed and filed according to the names written on their letterheads. Exception: The word *The* that begins an organization name is considered the last indexing unit.

Filing Segment	*Indexing Order of Units*			
Name	**Key Unit**	**Unit 2**	**Unit 3**	**Unit 4**
1st National Bank	1	National	Bank	
Assembly of God Church	Assembly	of	God	Church
Bay de Noc High School	BaydeNoc	High	School	
Disabled American Veterans	Disabled	American	Veterans	
Grace United Christian Church	Grace	United	Christian	Church
The Marquette Exchange Club	Marquette	Exchange	Club	The
Northern Michigan University	Northern	Michigan	University	
University of Michigan	University	of	Michigan	

Rule 9: Identical Names

When personal names and names of businesses, institutions, and organizations are identical, filing order is determined by the addresses. Compare the addresses in the following order.

1. City names

2. State or province names (if city names are identical)

3. Street names, including *Avenue, Boulevard, Drive,* and *Street* (if city and state names are identical)

    a. When the first units of street names are written in digits (18th Street) the names are considered in ascending numeric order (1, 2, 3) and placed together before alphabetic street names (18th Street, 24th Avenue, Academy Circle).

    b. Street names written as digits are filed before street names written as words (22nd Street, 34th Avenue, First Street, Second Avenue).

    c. Street names with compass directions (North, South, East, and West) are considered as written (SE Park Avenue, South Park Avenue).

    d. Street names with numbers written as digits after compass directions are considered before alphabetic names (East 8th Street, East Main Street, South Eighth Avenue).

4. House or building numbers (if city, state, and street names are identical)

    a. House and building numbers written as digits are considered in ascending numeric order (8 Riverside Terrace, 912 Riverside Terrace) and placed together before spelled-out building names (The Riverside Terrace).

    b. House and building numbers written as words are filed after house and building numbers written as digits (11 Franklin Avenue South, One Franklin Avenue).

    c. If a street address and a building name are included in an address, disregard the building name.

    d. ZIP Codes are not considered in filing order.

Names of Cities Used to Determine Filing Order

Filing Segment	Indexing Order of Units			
Name	Key Unit	Unit 2	Unit 3	Unit 4
Lakeside Books Oceanside, CA	Lakeside	Books	Oceanside	CA
Lakeside Books Oceanview, NJ	Lakeside	Books	Oceanview	NJ
Lakeside Books Sacramento, CA	Lakeside	Books	Sacramento	CA

Names of States and Provinces Used to Determine Filing Order

Filing Segment	Indexing Order of Units				
Name	Key Unit	Unit 2	Unit 3	Unit 4	Unit 5
Spencer J. Higgins Fenwick, ON (Ontario)	Higgins	Spencer	J	Fenwick	ON
Spencer J. Higgins Fenwick, WV	Higgins	Spencer	J	Fenwick	WV
Ricki's Antiques Clifton, AZ	Rickis	Antiques	Clifton	AZ	
Ricki's Antiques Clifton, TN	Rickis	Antiques	Clifton	TN	
Ricki's Antiques Clifton, TX	Rickis	Antiques	Clifton	TX	

Names of Streets and Building Numbers Used to Determine Filing Order

Filing Segment	Indexing Order of Units					
Name	Key Unit	Unit 2	Unit 3	Unit 4	Unit 5	Unit 6
Take-N-Bake 6490 6th St. Houston, TX	TakeNBake	Houston	TX	6	St	
Take-N-Bake 1493 28th St. Houston, TX	TakeNBake	Houston	TX	28	St	
Take-N-Bake 1692 Birch Ave. Houston, TX	TakeNBake	Houston	TX	Birch	Ave	
Take-N-Bake 21500 Birch St. Houston, TX	TakeNBake	Houston	TX	Birch	St	21500
Take-N-Bake 32890 Birch St. Houston, TX	TakeNBake	Houston	TX	Birch	St	32890
Take-N-Bake 255 SW 15th St. Houston, TX	TakeNBake	Houston	TX	SW	15	St
Take-N-Bake 572 SW Eighth St. Houston, TX	TakeNBake	Houston	TX	SW	Eighth	St
Take-N-Bake 159 Tamarack Way Houston, TX	TakeNBake	Houston	TX	Tamarack	Way	159
Take-N-Bake 253 Tamarack Way Houston, TX	TakeNBake	Houston	TX	Tamarack	Way	253

Rule 10: Government Names

Government names are indexed first by the name of the governmental unit—city, county, state, or country. Next, index the distinctive name of the department, bureau, office or board. A discussion of local and regional, state, federal, and foreign government names is provided in this section.

A. LOCAL AND REGIONAL GOVERNMENT NAMES

The first indexing unit is the name of the county, city, town, township, or village. *Negaunee Sanitation Department* is an example. *Negaunee* (a city) would be the first indexing unit. Next, index the most distinctive name of the department, board, bureau, office, or government/political division. In this case, *Sanitation* would be the most distinctive name of the department. The words *County of, City of, Department of, Office of*, etc., are retained for clarity and are considered separate indexing units. If *of* is not a part of the official name as written, it is not added as an indexing unit.

Filing Segment	Indexing Order of Units				
Name	**Key Unit**	**Unit 2**	**Unit 3**	**Unit 4**	**Unit 5**
City of Arlington Public Library	Arlington	City	of	Public	Library
City of Arlington Senior Center	Arlington	City	of	Senior	Center
Arlington County Highway Patrol	Arlington	County	Highway	Patrol	
Ashley County Department of Elections	Ashley	County	Elections	Department	of
Augusta City Water Works	Augusta	City	Water	Works	
Baker County Bureau of Licenses	Baker	County	Licenses	Bureau	of
Barstow Municipal Court	Barstow	Municipal	Court		
Benton City Hall Benton, GA	Benton	City	Hall	Benton	GA
Mayor's Office Benton, GA	Benton	Mayors	Office	Benton	GA

B. STATE GOVERNMENT NAMES

Similar to local and regional political/governmental agencies, the first indexing unit is the name of the state or province. Then index the most distinctive name of the department, board, bureau, office, or government/political division. The words *State of, Province of, Department of*, etc., are retained for clarity and considered separate indexing units. If *of* is not a part of the official name as written, it is not added as an indexing unit.

Filing Segment	Indexing Order of Units					
Name	Key Unit	Unit 2	Unit 3	Unit 4	Unit 5	Unit 6
Michigan Department of Community Health	Michigan	Community	Health	Department	of	
Michigan Department of Education	Michigan	Education	Department	of		
Michigan Natural Resources	Michigan	Natural	Resources			
Michigan State Attorney General	Michigan	State	Attorney	General		
State of Michigan Department of Aging	Michigan	State	of	Aging	Department	of
Secretary of Education, State of Michigan	Michigan	State	of	Education	Secretary	of
Michigan State Police	Michigan	State	Police			

C. FEDERAL GOVERNMENT NAMES

Use three indexing "levels" (rather than units) for the United States federal government. Consider *United States Government* as the first level. The second level is the name of a department; for example, *Department of Agriculture*. Level three is the next most distinctive name; for example, *Forest Service*. The words *of* and *of the* are extraneous and should <u>not</u> be considered when indexing. In the following examples, note that *United States Government* is the first level in all cases.

Filing Segment	Level 1	
	United States Government	
Name	Level 2	Level 3
1. National Weather Service, Department of Commerce	Commerce Department (of)	National Weather Service
2. Office of Civil Rights, Department of Education	Education Department (of)	Civil Rights Office (of)
3. Department of Health and Human Services	Health and Human Services Department (of)	
4. Federal Emergency Management Agency Department of Homeland Security	Homeland Security Department (of)	Federal Emergency Management Agency
5. Bureau of Reclamation, Department of the Interior	Interior Department (of the)	Reclamation Bureau (of)
6. Federal Bureau of Investigation, Department of Justice	Justice Department (of)	Investigation Federal Bureau (of)
7. Federal Bureau of Prisons, Department of Justice	Justice Department (of)	Prisons Federal Bureau (of)
8. Democracy and Global Affairs, Department of State	State Department (of)	Democracy and Global Affairs

D. FOREIGN GOVERNMENT NAMES

The name of a foreign government and its agencies is often written in a foreign language. When indexing foreign names, begin by writing the English translation of the government name on the document. The English name is the first indexing unit. Then index the balance of the formal name of the government (China Republic of). Branches, departments, and divisions follow in order by their distinctive names. States, colonies, provinces, cities, and other divisions of foreign governments are followed by their distinctive or official names as spelled in English.

Filing Segment	English Translation in Indexed Order			
Name	Unit 1	Unit 2	Unit 3	Unit 4
Govern d'Andorra	Andorra	Government		
Republik of Osterreich	Austria	Republic	of	
Druk Yul	Bhutan	Kingdom	of	
Bundesrepublik Deutschland	Germany	Federal	Republic	Of
Jamhuri ya Kenya	Kenya	Republic	of	

Cross-Referencing Records

Some records of persons and businesses may be requested by a name that is different from the one by which it was stored. This is particularly true if the key unit is difficult to determine. When a record is likely to be requested by more than one name, a cross-reference is prepared. A cross-reference shows the name in a form other than that used on the original record (by which it is likely to be requested), and it indicates the storage location of the original record. Cross-referencing will save time when there may be confusion about where a record is stored.

On the original document, the name for the cross-reference should be underlined with a wavy line and the filing segments numbered. An X should be placed in the margin of the document near the cross-reference name as shown in Figure 13.2. The cross-reference may be prepared using a cross-reference sheet as shown in Figure 13.3. The cross-reference sheet shows the name under which the item is cross-referenced, and the sheet is filed under that name. The sheet also shows the name under which the record is filed. As an alternate to preparing a cross-reference sheet, a copy of the document may be made and filed under the cross-reference name.

When indexing personal names and business or organization names, cross-referencing should be used for any name that may likely be requested under a different name. Similar names that sound the same but have different spellings should also be cross-referenced. Examples of names that should be cross-referenced are shown in Figure 13.4.

Other Records Systems

Earlier in this chapter, you learned about alphabetic records storage systems. Three other types of storage systems commonly used in organizations are subject, numeric, and geo-graphic systems. Records in a paper or electronic filing system may be stored in any of these ways.

Subject Storage Systems

In a subject storage system records are coded, stored, and retrieved by their subject or topic.

CROSS-REFERENCE SHEET

Name or Subject: Kirkman|Products| Inc.
                          2   3

Date of Item: September 24, 20--

Regarding: Two-page ad for spring distribution

SEE

Name or Subject: L|& M|Advertising| Agency
                 2 3   4   5

Authorized by: G. Melena   Date: September 29, 20--

FIGURE 13.3 This cross-reference sheet was prepared for the letter shown in Figure 13.2

Subject filing is recommended when the range of topics used within an organization is broad and may include a variety of materials including correspondence, reports, news clippings, and other items.

Subject filing systems have some advantages over other types of systems. Subjects are easier to remember than names. Related records are stored in the same location. Files can be expanded easily by adding subdivisions of topics. Confidentiality is maintained because individual names are not visible on file folder labels. Subject filing systems also have disadvantages. Indexing, coding, and cross-referencing take more time because each record must be read carefully to determine the subject to use for filing. Users must be careful to file records under established topics and sub-topics; otherwise, finding records will be difficult.

A necessary component of a subject file is a master index. The index is a list of all subjects under which a record may be filed. Without an index, it is almost impossible for the subject filing system to function satisfactorily. The index should be kept up to date as new subjects are added or obsolete subjects are eliminated. Although the subject index is often stored as a word processing or database file, a printed copy should always be available in the front of the first file drawer or shelf.

The following suggestions will help users avoid some of the disadvantages associated with subject filing systems.

- Select subject titles that best reflect stored records, are meaningful to users, and are easy to remember.
- Use one-word subject titles whenever possible.
- Designate one person to select the subjects and add new categories as needed.
- Combine filing methods when subdividing records in a large subject filing system. For

Name Type	Original	Cross-Reference
Easily Confused Name	Thomas / <u>Joseph</u>	Joseph / <u>Thomas</u> SEE Thomas / <u>Joseph</u>
Hyphenated Personal Name	Francine / <u>Haslitt-Higgins</u>	Francine / <u>Higgins</u> SEE Francine / <u>HaslittHiggins</u>
Hyphenated Business Name	<u>Trenton-Harding</u> / Excavating	<u>HardingTrenton</u> / Excavating SEE <u>TrentonHarding</u> / Excavating
Compound Name	<u>Kendricks</u> / and / Adamini / Cleaners	<u>Adamini</u> / and / Kendricks / Cleaners SEE <u>Kendricks</u> / and / Adamini / Cleaners
Alternate Name	Isabel / <u>Rodriguez</u>	Isabel / <u>Perez</u> SEE Isabel / <u>Rodriguez</u>
Popular or Coined Name	<u>Tom</u> / Chung's / Asian / Garden	<u>Tommys</u> SEE <u>Tom</u> Chungs Asian Garden
Name with Acronym	<u>MADD</u>	<u>Mothers</u> / Against / Drunk / Driving SEE <u>MADD</u>
Changed Name	<u>Harris</u> / Distribution / Inc.	<u>Harris</u> / Supply SEE <u>Harris</u> / Distribution / Inc
Similar Name	<u>Allstate</u> / Insurance / Co.	<u>All</u> / State / Insurance / Co SEE <u>Allstate</u> / Insurance / Co

FIGURE 13.4 Cross-Reference Examples

example, records can be sorted alphabetically within a subject category.

Numeric Storage Systems

A numeric storage system arranges records based on a number classification system. Numeric records management is particularly useful for organizations that must maintain confidentiality of their records. Examples of organizations that might use a numeric system include insurance companies that maintain records according to policy numbers, social welfare agencies or law firms that maintain records according to case numbers, and physician offices that maintain records by patient ID numbers.

A numeric filing system has four components, including:

1. Numeric files storage, which includes numbered guides and folders to house the records

2. Alphabetic general file for miscellaneous records

3. Database software (or a lined book) for an **accession log** to maintain a record of the numbers that have been assigned

4. Database or word processing software for an alphabetic index that shows the number assigned to each name or subject in the file

The basic procedures to file records in a numeric filing system are as follows:

- When a document is received for storage, the alphabetic index is consulted to see if the correspondent or subject has been assigned a number.

- If a number has already been assigned, the number is placed on the document; the document is placed in the folder labeled with that number in the numeric file. Records within the folder are arranged by date with the most recent date in front.

- If the name or subject is new and no number has been assigned, the record is placed in the general alphabetic file. No number is assigned when there is only one record for a name or subject.

- When several records for the same name or subject have been accumulated in the general alphabetic file, the accession log is consulted. The records are assigned the next available number, a folder is prepared and labeled with the assigned number, and the folder is placed in the numeric file.

Although the records are filed in numeric sequence, the alphabetic rules are still a major part of a numeric system. Information in the alphabetic index is organized according to the ARMA rules previously described. If the index is kept in an electronic database, the same file can serve as an accession log. The records are sorted by name or number as needed.

Numeric systems have several advantages. Expansion is easy and unlimited. Confidentiality is maintained because names do not appear on guides or folders. All records for one name are located in the same place. Numeric systems also have disadvantages. Because more supplies are necessary, the cost of this system is usually higher than for other systems. Filing is more time consuming because records must first be sorted alphabetically and then numerically. The accession log and alphabetic index must be consulted often.

Variations of the numeric storage system are also used in businesses. In consecutive number storage (also called serial, sequential, and straight numeric filing), numbered records are arranged in ascending order (lowest number to highest number). In chronologic storage systems, records are filed in date sequence.

In a terminal digit storage system, the assigned numbers are divided into groups. The groups of numbers are read from right to left. For example, in the caption 125 784 773, 773 is the first indexing unit, 784 is the second indexing unit, and 125 is the third indexing unit. The first (primary) unit indicates the file drawer or shelf number; the secondary unit indicates the guide number, and the third (tertiary) unit indicates the folder number. The following numbers are in proper order for terminal digit filing.

Reading from the front of file drawer:

Tertiary (Folder)	Secondary (Guide)	Primary (Drawer)
268	449	105
489	982	105
557	982	166
115	449	289
782	482	289

In a middle digit storage system, the assigned numbers are divided into groups. The groups of numbers are read from middle to left to right. For example, in the caption 125 784 773, 784 is the first indexing unit, 125 is the second indexing unit, and 773 is the third indexing unit. The primary unit indicates the file drawer or shelf number; the secondary unit indicates the guide number, and the tertiary unit indicates the folder number. The following numbers are in proper order for middle digit filing.

Reading from the front of file drawer:

Secondary (Guide)	Primary (Drawer)	Tertiary (Folder)
115	449	289
268	449	105
782	482	289
489	982	105
557	982	166

Geographic Storage Systems

A geographic system is used when records are requested by location rather than by name. The geographic method is based first on the location of the originators and second on their business or company names. It is useful for organizations in situations such as the following:

- Utility companies where street names and numbers are of primary importance in troubleshooting
- Real estate firms that have listings according to land areas
- Sales organizations that are concerned with the geographic location of their customers
- Government agencies that file records by state, county, or other geographic divisions

To function correctly, the breakdown into geographic divisions must fit the type of business, its organization, and its need for specific kinds of information. Also, an alphabetic index is required for a geographic system. This index lists all correspondents or subjects in geographic storage. The index can be a computer database index or a list printed from a word processing program. However the index is kept, it must be easy to update and a copy should be stored in the first file drawer.

The main advantage of a geographic system is that records relating to a specific location are filed together. This can be very important for some businesses, as previously noted. Because each geographic area is a unit or group, moving records is easily accomplished, which can be another advantage. A disadvantage of geographic storage is that several cross-references may be necessary for organizations having more than one address or more than one business in the same location. Because this is an indirect filing method, the user must check the alphabetic index often to ensure accurate placement of files.

Managing Electronic and Microfilm Records

Management of paper records has always been important; however, with the explosion of electronic records in business, managing electronic records and image records has become an important priority. An **electronic record** is a record stored on electronic storage media (hard drive, flash memory) that can be accessed or changed. An **image record** is a digital or photographic representation of a record on any media such as microfilm or CD. The same information found in many paper records is also stored as electronic files. In many instances, records move from computer to computer and are never printed to paper. Therefore, administrative professionals must be able to name, file, distribute, and otherwise manage electronic and image records.

Managing Electronic Files

Because many electronic records are stored on a computer or removable storage media such as a

---

Professional Pointers

As an administrative professional, you may have the opportunity to be involved in recommending, implementing, or expanding a records management system. If so, keep these pointers in mind.

- Define the needs of the organization— department, division, or entire company. Know the types of records used, how long they are to be retained, who can have access, and the capacity needed for storage.

- Conduct research and seek information. Based on your identified needs, collect recommendations from representatives of records supplies and systems firms. Solicit input on systems used in other organizations similar to yours.

- Ensure that everyone has adequate training on the system that is chosen.

- Provide a list of the filing procedures/ rules as a reference source for all individuals who have access to the files.

- Implement a method for ongoing evaluation of the records management system. Efficiency and cost effectiveness are vital to the success of the system and the business.

flash memory drive, sorting data and records in electronic files and organizing electronic files and folders are important aspects of managing electronic records. Electronic files are created using programs such as word processing, spreadsheet, presentation, and email software. To best understand how to organize electronic files, users must understand the following phases of the life cycle for an electronic record:

- Creation and Storage
- Distribution and Use
- Maintenance
- Disposition

CREATION AND STORAGE

Electronic records contain data that is created, distributed, or received from others using computer software. Just like paper files, electronic records must be managed properly to ensure that only information that is useful or required is maintained and that all other information is deleted. As electronic information is created or received, it is stored as a file on a network, a hard disk, or another storage device such as a CD, DVD, or flash memory drive. (Computer storage devices are presented in Chapter 10, Technology Update). Whatever type of storage device is used, the data should be stored using meaningful filenames and in a logical structure of folders or directories to facilitate retrieving the information.

A saved document is any stored information that requires a user to give it a filename. A filename is a unique name given to a computer file that must follow the computer's operating system rules. For example, the operating system may limit the filename to a certain number of characters. Using meaningful filenames is an important part of managing electronic files. An organization may have procedures in place for naming files. If no procedures or guidelines exist, think about how the data might be requested when you need to retrieve it.

Because computers can store millions of files, organization is essential. Users should store

electronic files in folders. A folder (also called a directory) is a subdivision of storage space created by the operating system of a computer. Users can create new folders as needed. Each folder is given a name. Also, just like a folder in a file drawer, a computer folder can contain files and other folders, sometimes called subfolders.

Files on computer storage devices are organized using the operating system's filing system.

Electronic files can be stored on a network, a computer hard drive, or another computer storage device.

The electronic filing system maintains a list of all files and their location. Information that shows the location of a computer file is called a file path. A typical path contains the computer drive designation, the folders and subfolders in which the file is located, and the filename. For example, in the path *C:\Documents\Applications\JWGreen.doc*, C is the drive designation. *Documents* is the main folder. *Applications* is a subfolder within the main folder. *JWGreen.doc* is the filename. Depending on the settings that have been selected for the operating system, the filename extension *.doc* may or may not display. By understanding how these filing systems work, you can manage the files stored on a computer logically and consistently.

The folders and subfolders where documents are saved should be structured in a manner that is similar to the filing system created for paper documents. This is true regardless of whether you create the documents or receive them. For example, if you would file a paper memo, note, or letter relating to budgets in the administrative section of your file cabinet designated for budget correspondence, an electronic memo, note, or letter relating to budgets might be filed in a folder structure similar to the example shown in Figure 13.5. If the information is filed by year, you could have a correspondence folder for each year.

Once a logical structure for storing files has been established, all members of an organization will be able to save or retrieve documents efficiently. The most important rule to remember in organizing electronic files is that the same methods that work with paper also apply to computers. For example, if your organization files paper records using a geographic filing system, then the electronic folders should be set up using a geographic system. If the organization typically files information according to subjects, the electronic folders should be subject names.

USE AND DISTRIBUTION

The next phase of the record cycle is using and distributing the information contained in the electronic files. Distribution can take place through electronic channels such as email or shared folders on a LAN. Files can be copied and distributed on DVDs. Electronic files can also be printed and the page sent by regular mail or facsimile. When email systems are used to distribute electronic files, an additional records management opportunity exists. Most email programs allow the user to create and manage folders to store and organize messages.

career *tip*

Electronic Files

When naming electronic files, use names that will make sense to users over time. The following guidelines will help you name files effectively:

- Each filename should be unique and independent from its location so that if the file is moved the name will not conflict with names already in the new location.

- When more than one version of a record (file) is kept, the version should be indicated. Determine how to indicate the version of the record in the filename. For example, if you have several drafts of committee bylaws and must retain all of them, each name should include information about the version.

- Filenames must make sense to others once the file creators are no longer available.[1]

[1]"Electronic Records Management Guidelines," Minnesota State Archives, accessed July 15. 2007, available from http://www.mnhs.org/preserve/records/electronicrecords/erfnaming.html.

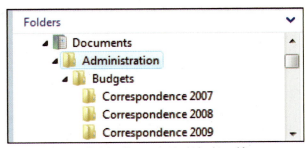

FIGURE 13.5 Folder Structure in *Windows Vista*

As with paper records, electronic records can sometimes be difficult to locate. The record may have been saved in an incorrect folder or accidently moved to an incorrect folder. A filename may have been used for the record that is inconsistent with the naming scheme used for other records. The search feature of an operating system such as *Windows Vista* can help locate electronic records. The user can enter a filename for which to search and other details about the file. For example, the date the file was created can be specified as shown in Figure 13.6.

MAINTENANCE

Files and folders can be moved from one location to another as part of managing records. Moving electronic files that are more than a year old, to a CD for example, can free storage space on a computer's internal hard drive. Moving older files that are accessed infrequently can make finding active files easier as there will be fewer files in a folder to look through. As with paper records, copies of electronic records can be useful. For example, an employee can copy a file to a removable storage device and then edit the file using another computer while away from the office. When the employee returns to the office, the updated file is copied to the office computer. The earlier version of the file may be retained or deleted, depending upon its usefulness.

DISPOSITION

Users must be aware of hardware and software upgrades that may affect the ability to retrieve and read electronic records. Data migration is used to copy electronic files and folders onto new media and in new formats as they become available. The media on which the information is stored has a useful life span that may depend on how many times the media is accessed. Also, as discussed in Chapter 10, the storage media that is available continues to change. Users must anticipate and follow through with the migration of electronic records to new media as they are developed. Upgrades of hardware and software must be monitored to ensure the electronic records will continue to be available and readable as long as they are needed. When electronic records are no longer needed, they should be deleted or the storage medium, such as a CD, should be destroyed. A discussion of how long records should be retained is presented later in this chapter.

Managing Database Files

Although many electronic records are stored as files created with other software programs, much of the information used in business today is stored in electronic databases. An electronic database is a collection of related data stored on a computer system. When using a database, data

FIGURE 13.6 Advanced Search in *Windows Vista*

can be created, modified, reorganized, sorted, selected, and accessed in a variety of ways to carry out administrative tasks and to help solve business problems. Businesses use databases to store information about customers, inventory, products, and employees. Many organizations use a database to create an index of their paper and other records. For example, all personnel information for a company could be stored in a database rather than in paper files. In this way, it is easy to locate information as well as to create letters and mailing labels from the data.

Although desktop databases are useful for smaller organizations or for departments within larger organizations, most large companies use network databases. These databases can work similar to a desktop database or can be accessed through the company's network or the Web. An advantage to using a network database is that a network database enables many different people to access the information in the database at one time.

UNDERSTANDING DATABASE FILES

The information stored in a database is organized into tables that hold the data. Data in a table is organized into fields and records. A field contains a single fact or piece of information, for example, an employee's last name. A database record includes all the fields related to one entity. This could be a customer, employee, company, organization, product, or other entity. Records related to one subject or topic (customers, students, orders) are usually stored in one or more related tables. A database can also contain several other objects such as forms and reports.

WORKING WITH DATABASE INFORMATION

Locating a specific piece of information in a database is relatively easy using the search or find feature. A database query can be used to retrieve data that meet specific criteria set by the user. For example, you can search a database for employees who are making less than $75,000 or all females in the Accounting Department. The design of the database allows the user to ask for information efficiently and retrieve it in a useful format.

Managing Image Files

Document imaging is the process of scanning paper documents and converting them to digital images. These images can be stored on media such as a CD or DVD. Images of records may also be stored on microform media. **Microform** is a collective term for several types of microimages such as roll microfilm, microfiche, and aperture cards. To view information in electronic image files, you must use a computer. To view information on microfilm, you must use a machine called a reader or a viewer. These machines magnify the miniature images and display them on a screen. A reader/printer displays images on a screen and can also print full-size documents on paper.

Not all microforms are created from printed documents. **Computer output to microfilm (COM)** is the process of converting computer data to a microform without first printing the records. This process conserves the use of paper. COM is particularly useful when multiple copies of output from the computer are needed. COM output can be in either roll or flat form.

ADVANTAGES AND DISADVANTAGES

Using image records greatly reduces the amount and cost of storage space that is required for records. A CD or a single roll of microfilm can hold the same amount of information as several boxes of paper files containing hundreds of documents. Image records also offer other advantages. Duplicates are inexpensive to produce and can be mailed at lower rates than paper. Security is improved because original disks or microforms are kept and copies are loaned out for use. This practice also helps preserve the original records.

Using image records has some disadvantages. A computer or a reader is needed to view images. Creating the images can be costly and quality of the images must be monitored as they are prepared. Electronic media and microforms are more sensitive to variations in temperature

A microform is a storage medium containing images too small to be read without magnification.

focus on   *Microforms*

A variety of microforms are used in business. Some of these include the following:

*   Roll microfilm contains a series of frames or images much like a movie film. This is the most widely used and least expensive microform to create.

*   Microfiche is a rectangular sheet of film containing a series of images arranged in a grid pattern. Microfiche sheets are easy to use, handle, and identify.

*   A microfilm jacket is a flat, transparent, plastic carrier with single or multiple film channels created to hold single or multiple film strips. Jackets are often used for medical records because they can be updated by inserting new records into a channel and because they keep related records together. The jacket also protects the microfilm from surface abrasion.

*   An aperture card is a data processing card with a rectangular hole (or aperture) into which a piece of microfilm can be inserted. These cards are typically used to store engineering and architectural drawings or blueprints.

and humidity, so a carefully monitored storage environment is required.[2]

FILING IMAGE RECORDS

Image records can be organized and filed using the same system (alphabetic, numeric, or subject) as the organization's other types of records. Electronic image files are stored in electronic folders as are other electronic records. Electronic storage media (CDs, DVDs) and microforms are organized and stored in cabinets or other containers designed for each type of media.

The process of recording information to serve as a location directory for microforms or electronic records is an important step in managing image records. An index attaches identification data, called an address, to microforms or electronic image records. Having an index is crucial for retrieving digital images. A computer-assisted retrieval (CAR) system can speed up the retrieval of imaged documents through the use of a computer. Drawing on a combination of microform and computer technology, CAR can result in more effective and economical approaches to document storage and retrieval.

Records Retention, Transfer, and Disposal

The major error in handling records is to assume that every paper or electronic document is a record worth keeping. To be classified as a record, a document must have value to the organization. Many paper documents do not meet these requirements. Much incoming paperwork should be kept only temporarily or discarded immediately. The administrative professional must recognize the difference between information that is of no value to the organization (and is discarded) and information that is of value (and is kept as a record to be managed).

Records Retention

A **retention period** is the time that records must be kept according to operational, legal, regulatory, and fiscal requirements. As an administrative professional, you will probably not make decisions about how long important documents should be kept. If you work for a large organization, you will be responsible for adhering to a records retention schedule that has been created. A records retention schedule is a plan for the management of records. It lists the types of records and how long they should be kept. If the company does not have a records retention schedule, the administrative professional should check with his or her supervisor before making any decisions about how documents should be transferred or destroyed.

A records retention schedule determines when records should be sent to a storage facility.

[2]"Records Management Publications," Texas State Library and Archive Commission, accessed July 10, 2007, available from http://www.tsl.state.tx.us/slrm/recordspubs/di.html.

Whether the records are in paper or electronic form, decisions need to be made regarding retention. The decisions will be based on how important the record is to the organization. Four categories of records used to determine records retention times are described in Figure 13.7.

When developing a retention schedule, the following issues should be considered.

- *Use.* How long does the organization require the use of the records?
- *Inactivity.* At what point should records be declared inactive? Should inactive records be transferred to low-cost storage or should they be destroyed?
- *Laws and regulations.* What federal, state, and local requirements for keeping records must be followed?
- *Cost.* What is the cost of keeping records versus the cost of not keeping them?

- *Off-site storage.* Which records should be transferred to a less expensive or more secure storage location away from the central offices?
- *Integrity and security.* Will transferred records maintain their integrity so specific records can be located when needed? Will transferred records be protected properly from destruction and unauthorized use?

Records retention schedules are based on the value of the information contained in the records. By closely following an approved records retention schedule, an organization can reduce the costs associated with the storage of unnecessary records.

Records Transfer

At some point in the life cycle of a record, the decision is made to destroy the record, retain it permanently, or transfer it to inactive storage.

RECORDS CATEGORIES

Vital records
- Necessary for the continuing operation of the organization
- Cannot be replaced and should never be destroyed
- Highest degree of protection is necessary
- Examples include corporate charters, titles to property, and reports to shareholders

Important records
- Necessary to an orderly continuation of a business
- Usually replaceable but at great cost
- High degree of protection is necessary
- Examples include personnel records, financial statements, operating and statistical records, and board minutes

Useful records
- Contribute to the smooth and effective operation of an organization
- Usually replaceable at a slight cost
- Moderate degree of protection is necessary
- Examples include general correspondence and bank records

Nonessential records
- Have no future value to an organization
- Lowest degree of protection is necessary
- Examples include newsletters, employee announcements, periodicals, and routine email and phone messages

FIGURE 13.7 Records are retained according to their continuing value.

Records transfer is the act of changing the physical location of records. Two common methods of records transfer are perpetual transfer and periodic transfer.

PERPETUAL TRANSFER

With **perpetual transfer**, materials are continuously transferred from the active to the inactive storage when they are no longer needed for frequent reference. The advantage of this method is that all files are kept current because inactive files are immediately transferred to storage. The perpetual transfer method works well in organizations where jobs are completed by units. Examples include medical cases that no longer need attention, student records after graduation, construction jobs that are completed, and research projects when results are finalized.

Perpetual transfer should also be applied to electronic records. Keep in mind that not all electronic records need to be retained. Electronic documents can remain on the local or network hard drive until they can be deleted, or until they are no longer active. Electronic documents can be transferred to storage media such as CDs or DVDs or converted to microfilm.

PERIODIC TRANSFER

With **periodic transfer**, active records are transferred to inactive status at the end of a stated period. For example, you may transfer records that are over six months old to the inactive file and maintain records that are less than six months old in the active file. This procedure is repeated every six months. This method of transfer works well and is used by many businesses. Periodic transfer should also be used for electronic files. For example, electronic records that no longer need to be retained should be deleted; electronic records that need to be kept can be transferred to magnetic or microfilm storage.

Records are transferred either to inactive or archive (permanent) storage. Inactive storage indicates that the record will be referenced infrequently. **Archive records** have historical value to an organization and should be preserved permanently. At the end of the retention period, inactive records are destroyed. Records stored in archives must be kept permanently.

Records Disposal

Records that are no longer of use should be destroyed. Paper records that are not confidential can be disposed of by simply dropping the paper in a basket for trash or recycling. Electronic records that are not confidential are simply deleted or erased from the storage medium.

When information is confidential, the information should be destroyed beyond any possible reconstruction. Confidential paper records should be destroyed by shredding, burning, or pulping. Some organizations will contract with an outside organization for destruction of paper records. Once you have identified electronic records that need to be removed, the files can be deleted from the computer or storage media. Next, the user must perform the process to clean the unused portions of the media. This can be completed with a special software program that will overwri[te] those areas of the disk that are no longer us[ed.] This will prohibit sophisticated users from storing deleted files whose space has not [been] overwritten. This will help ensure tha[t elec]tronic information that is no longer u[sed or] required is not inadvertently retained.

Summary

To reinforce what you have learned in this chapter, study this summary.

- Business records can include paper documents, computer files, microforms, movies, digital photographs, and oral records.

- Records are assets to businesses and provide legal, financial, historical, and operational value to organizations.

- When designing storage systems, it is important to consider findability, confidentiality, and safety of records.

- Paper records storage procedures include inspecting, indexing, coding, cross-referencing, sorting, and storing documents.

- Basic manual filing supplies and equipment include storage cabinets, file guides, file folders, and labels.

- ARMA International has developed alphabetic indexing rules designed to assist the administrative professional in indexing records for filing.

- Records storage systems include alphabetic, subject, numeric, and geographic.

- Managing the creation and storage of networked electronic records includes creating appropriate filenames and understanding the computer operating system for folder creation.

- Maintenance of electronic information requires that users manage the storage media as well as the computer hardware and software necessary for retrieval.

- Document imaging is the process of scanning paper documents and converting them to digital images. Image records, including electronic files and microforms, are appropriate for long-term storage of many types of records.

- A records retention policy that takes into account the classifications of records should be created and followed.

- Records can be transferred to storage using perpetual or periodic transfer methods. Records that have no continuing value to the organization should be destroyed using an appropriate method.

What's the Problem?

Alice Dao is a clerk in the medical records department at a large hospital. Solomon Keyes, a patient services advocate, routinely uses patient files to update billing information for patients and insurance companies as new tests and procedures are completed. Alice and Solomon have been working together for several years, and they have become somewhat informal in their handling of patient records. Rather than fill out the paperwork to request a file, Solomon has become accustomed to going directly to the file room and retrieving the files as he needs them. He is so familiar with the system that he also puts the files back when he is done. Recently other employees have been unable to locate several patient files. Alice and Solomon have come under scrutiny because of the way they have handled files in the past. Although they know they are not responsible for the missing files, they are facing serious questions from their department managers.

What could Alice and Solomon have done differently to avoid their present situation?

Let's Discuss

1. Describe the life cycle of a record.
2. Describe the steps followed to effectively store paper records.
3. Describe three instances when a name should be cross-referenced and provide an example of each instance.
4. Define *terminal digit storage* and explain how it is used to store numeric files.
5. Explain the importance of maintenance of electronic files.
6. Describe three types of microforms that are used in business.
7. List and describe the four categories of records used to make retention decisions.

Critical-Thinking Activity

The organization you are working for recently purchased a new document imaging system. Although the system won't be up and running for several months and many training seminars must still be conducted, the staff has been instructed to get an early start on this program. All of the paper files from the last fiscal year need to be pulled and prepared for scanning. This processing includes batching all work orders by company or client name. (The current paper filing system was organized by subject.) The records need to be batched in groups of 50 files, and each batch must include a cover sheet listing the client names that are included in the batch. The employees who must prepare the files for imaging are not happy with this change; they believe their old system worked fine. They have no idea how the new document imaging system works and do not like the fact that they had no input into the purchase of the system.

1. What needs to be done to prepare the files for imaging?
2. How could the department managers have made this transition less intimidating?
3. What steps can be taken to give the employees an understanding of how the new system will affect their work and the company's overall operations?

Vocabulary Review

Open the *Word* file *CH13 Vocabulary* found on the Student CD. Complete the vocabulary review for Chapter 13.

English and Word Usage Drill

Complete the English and Word Usage Drill for Chapter 13 found in the *Applications Workbook*.

Workplace Applications

13-1 Organize Records for Alphabetic Filing

(Goals 1 and 2)

Correspondence has been received from several individuals. Their names are stored in a *Word* file named *CH13 Names*. The correspondence must be indexed and coded for the alphabetic file.

1. Open the *Word* file *CH13 Names* found on the student CD.

2. Use the alphabetic indexing rules found in this chapter to determine the indexing order for each name. Key each name in indexing order under the name that already appears in the file. Do not key punctuation in the indexed name. Code the name by underlining the key unit and keying diagonals (/) between the units.

3. In the same file, copy and paste the coded names to create a list of names in alphabetic filing order. Print the file.

4. Open the *Word* file *CH13 Names Key* found on the student CD. Check your work against the key. Identify on your list any names that you indexed or placed in order incorrectly. Review the filing rules to see why your work is not correct.

13-2 Organize Records for Numeric Filing

(Goal 2)

Your department has been filing records using an alphabetic records system. Recently your supervisor, Estelle Lombardini, has decided that a more confidential records system is needed. Estelle has asked that you help convert the records to a consecutive numeric system. Client numbers will be assigned in ascending order starting with 100.

1. Open the *Word* file *CH13 Data* found on the student CD. Numbers have been assigned to five names as shown in the file.

2. Create a database to serve as an accession log. Name the database file *13-2 Accession Log*. Create a table named Accession Log to include the fields shown in the following table. Make the File Number field the primary key.

FIELD NAME	DATA TYPE	DESCRIPTION
File Number	Number	Unique number assigned to a name
Indexing Order	Text	Name or subject in indexing order in all capitals with no punctuation
As Written	Text	Name as written
Date Assigned	Date	Date the number is assigned

3. Enter data for the five names for which numbers have already been assigned into the database. Use the current date in the Date Assigned field.

4. Index and code the correspondence that is received. Assign a number and create a database record for new names.

5. Print the Accession Log database table.

13-3 Recommend Filing Supplies

(Goals 2 and 4)

internet

Amando Hinjosa has determined that your department needs to expand its paper filing system. Amando has asked that you research two office supply companies for information on filing supplies and equipment. Amando anticipates the following needs:

team building

- An additional file cabinet. The cabinet will hold confidential records and needs to be secure.

- Suspension (hanging) folders. You need at least 500 hanging folders, tabs, and insertable labels. The current folders use one-third cut tabs.

- File folders. You need at least 1,500 colored file folders. The current system includes an assortment of primary colors with one-third cut tabs.

- OUT guides or folders. You will need at least 200 OUT guides or folders.

- Amando has also asked that you include at least one new, innovative supply that would be helpful in this system.

1. Work with two classmates to complete this application.

2. Research vertical and lateral file cabinets, hanging folders, file folders, and OUT folders or guides on the Internet or at office supply stores. Identify and research a new, innovative supply as Amando suggested. Links to the Web sites for two companies, TAB and Smead Manufacturing, that provide filing supplies and equipment are provided on the Links section of the Website for this textbook. Find other companies by searching for *filing systems, filing equipment* , or *filing supplies.*

3. Prepare a spreadsheet that shows individual and total costs for each item at each of the two companies. Prepare a memo to Amando recommending the supplies

you think the company should purchase and why. Discuss prices and include the spreadsheet with the memo. Use the *Word* file *Memo Form* found on the student CD to prepare the memo.

13-4 Organize Electronic Files

e-portfolio

(Goal 3)

You have been instructed to save several of the documents and presentations you have created in this course to place in an electronic portfolio. You will use these files you have been collecting for this activity.

1. Organize the files according to the skills demonstrated. For example, create a folder for those activities that demonstrate communication skills; create a second folder for those activities that demonstrate teamwork skills. Follow this procedure to create other folders and organize all your electronic portfolio files.

2. Rename the files using a system that describes the content of the file.

3. Create a one-page handout that describes your naming and storage procedures so that others could easily retrieve files if necessary. Include a list of the folders you created and the names of the files you placed in each folder.

Assessment of Chapter 13 Goals

Did you successfully complete the chapter goals? Evaluate yourself by filling out the form found in Chapter 13 of the *Applications Workbook*.

chapter 14

Personal Finance and Investment Strategies

Financial Knowledge Is Important for Success

If you are to be successful in your career, you must learn to effectively manage your current income. You must also begin to establish a long-range financial plan so that you may have the financial resources to sustain the lifestyle you wish to live. As you finish your program of study and begin to look for a position, you should have a cursory knowledge of financial statements. This knowledge will help you make an informed decision about the financial stability of the company or organization for which you choose to work. This chapter will help you fulfill those goals.

Payroll Deductions

Whether you are working for an organization or are self-employed, a portion of your salary goes to the federal government in the form of payroll taxes. These taxes include federal income, Social Security, and Medicare taxes. Some states and cities tax personal income. If so, this tax is also withheld from your check.

You may have optional deductions taken from your ch‑ for items such as a retirement plan or health insurance. you receive a payroll check, examine it to see what de have been made for taxes and other items.

Contributing monthly to a savings account is important for financial security.

- Check the amount of federal income tax that is taken out of each check.
- Determine if there are state and city taxes deducted and if so, how much.
- Check the amounts deducted for Social Security tax and Medicare tax.
- If you are enrolled in a retirement or health care plan with your company or have other optional deductions, determine how much is taken out of your check each month for these items.

Figure 14.1 shows the Taxes and Deductions section of a payroll check stub. In this example, deductions are made for Social Security, Medicare, and federal, state, and city income taxes. Pre-tax deductions are made for an optional 401(k) retirement plan and for medical insurance payments.

Federal Income Tax

Federal income tax is a mandatory deduction under federal law. Taxes are withheld from each payroll check on the basis of information

TAXES AND DEDUCTIONS		
Description	Current Amount	Year-to-Date Amount
Taxes Withheld		
Social Security Tax	214.71	1,924.40
Medicare Tax	50.21	450.06
Federal Income Tax	386.66	3,512.98
State Tax	110.57	1,005.81
City Tax	73.50	658.00
Total Taxes	835.65	7,551.25
Pre-Tax Deductions		
401(k)	350.00	2,800.00
Medical Insurance	36.83	294.64
Total Pre-Tax Deductions	386.83	3,094.64

FIGURE 14.1 Payroll Check Deductions

furnished by the employee on a **Form W-4** (Employee's Withholding Allowance Certificate). The number of exemptions claimed on the Form W-4 in addition to the amount of money you earn determines the deduction to be

TAXABLE INCOME AND TAX AMOUNT
2007 SINGLE TAXPAYERS

If Taxable Income Is Over—	But Not Over—	The Tax Is:
$0	$7,825	10% of the amount over $0
$7,825	$31,850	$782.50 plus 15% of the amount over 7,825
$31,850	$77,100	$4,386.25 plus 25% of the amount over 31,850
$77,100	$160,850	$15,698.75 plus 28% of the amount over 77,100
$160,850	$349,700	$39,148.75 plus 33% of the amount over 160,850
$349,700	No limit	$101,469.25 plus 35% of the amount over 349,700

Source: "2007 Federal Tax Rate Schedules," Internal Revenue Service, accessed August 17, 2007, available from http://www.irs.gov/formspubs/article/0,,id=164272,00.html.

FIGURE 14.2 Tax rates vary according to income and other factors.

withheld. The Internal Revenue Service (IRS) administers the federal income tax program. Tax rates change periodically. Taxes from the federal government are determined for each of the following categories of people:

- Single
- Married Filing Jointly or Qualifying Widow or Widower
- Married Filing Separately
- Head of Household

Cities may levy taxes to improve parks.

INCOME TAX RATES JANUARY 1, 2007			
HIGHEST INCOME TAX RATES		**LOWEST INCOME TAX RATES**	
State or District	**Percent**	**State**	**Percent**
Vermont	9.5	Illinois	3.0
California	9.3	Pennsylvania	3.07
Iowa	8.98	Indiana	3.4
District of Columbia	8.7	Michigan	3.9
Hawaii	8.25	Arizona	4.57
North Carolina	8.0	Colorado	4.63

Source: "State Individual Income Taxes," Federation of Tax Administrators, accessed August 17, 2007, available from http://www.taxadmin.org/FTA/rate/ind_inc.html.

FIGURE 14.3 Income tax rates vary widely by state.

Figure 14.2 gives the taxable income and tax amount of federal income tax for 2007 for single taxpayers. Separate schedules are available for married persons filing jointly or qualifying widows, married persons filing separately, and heads of households. As of 2007, the federal income tax rate is a maximum of 35 percent. However, this federal tax rate is subject to change.

State Income Tax

The majority of states within the United States have mandatory state income taxes. At the time of the writing of this textbook, the following states have no state income tax:

- Alaska
- Florida
- Nevada
- South Dakota
- Texas
- Washington
- Wyoming

Additionally, New Hampshire and Tennessee limit their state income tax to dividends and interest income only. State income tax rates vary but are lower than federal rates. For example, the highest state income tax rate currently is 9.5 percent, which is for Vermont. Other states with high income tax rates and states with low tax income rates are shown in Figure 14.3. Just as federal tax rates can change, so can state tax rates.

City or Local Taxes

A number of cities within the United States have city income tax. For example, Michigan cities are authorized to levy a city income tax upon passing a tax ordinance. Tax rates vary depending on whether you are a resident, non-resident, or a corporation. Non-residents are people who earn income in the city but do not live there. For example, the income tax rates for the City of Detroit for the calendar year 2005 and subsequent years are 2.5 percent for resident individuals, 1.25 percent for non-resident individuals, and 1 percent for corporations.[1] Some counties also have income taxes. The deduction on a payroll check may say *local* instead of *city* or *county*.

---

[1]"City of Detroit 2005 Income Tax Rates," City of Detroit, Finance Department, accessed August 17, 2007, available from http://www.ci.detroit.mi.us/finincometax/incometax_rates.htm.

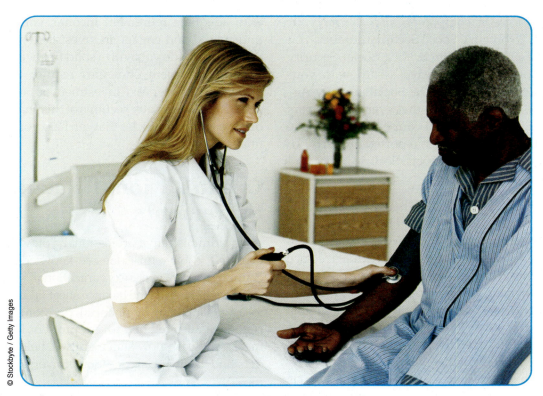

Medicare is available for individuals who are 65 and older.

Additionally, cities and counties may levy taxes to improve parks, fund schools, pay for police and fire departments, build and repair local roads, and pay for other services.

Social Security and Medicare

Social Security is a social insurance program with its beneficiaries being retired individuals, widows and survivors, and the disabled. Social Security benefits are paid when a person retires or becomes disabled. The program may also pay benefits to the survivors and/or dependents of an insured person in the event of the person's death.

Medicare is a health insurance program for people age 65 or older. Certain people younger than age 65 can qualify for Medicare, such as those who have disabilities and certain other medical conditions. The program helps with the cost of health care, but it does not cover all medical expenses or the cost of most long-term care.

Social Security's Old-Age, Survivors, and Disability Insurance (OASDI) program and Medicare's Hospital Insurance (HI) program are financed primarily by employment taxes. Tax rates for Social Security apply to earnings up to a maximum amount. In 2007 the maximum amount is $97,500. Medicare is also financed in part by monthly premiums deducted from Social Security checks. The 2007 Social Security tax rate is 6.2 percent for an individual employee and 12.4 percent for a self-employed individual. The 2007 Medicare tax rate is 1.45 percent for an individual employee and 2.9 percent for a self-employed individual.[2]

Having a Social Security number is important because you need it to get a job, collect Social Security benefits, and receive some other government services. Many businesses, such as

---

[2]"Social Security and Medicare Tax Rates," Social Security, accessed August 22, 2007, available from http://www.ssa.^r ProgData/taxRates.html.

banks and credit companies, also ask for your number. To obtain a Social Security number, you must file an application with a Social Security office. You will then receive a card with your Social Security number. The Social Security Administration recommends that every three years you request a statement of your earnings to make certain that they have been reported properly. To get this statement, call a Social Security office and ask for details.

The earliest age at which benefits are payable through Social Security is 62. However, if an individual elects to take early retirement, Social Security benefits are reduced. Individuals receive full benefits at varying ages depending on date of birth. However, the retirement age is gradually increasing to 67. A worker under 70 and eligible for retirement can delay receiving benefits past full retirement age. By doing so, the worker's eventual retirement benefit and the surviving spouse's benefit is increased due to a credit that is applied to the account for each month's delay in receiving retirement benefits, up to age 70. A current spouse is eligible for benefits and divorced or former spouses are generally eligible if the marriage lasts for at least ten years. Maximum benefits for individuals who retired in 2007 are $2,116 per month.[3]

In the past, Social Security has been a benefit that provided a measure of security after retirement. However, future Social Security benefits are in question. If you listen to senators and representatives discuss Social Security, you hear an ongoing debate about what should happen to ensure its viability for the future. Although no unanimity exists on how Social Security funds should be handled, there is widespread belief that if something is not done to ensure financial stability, the funds will be bankrupt in the not-too-distant future. Since the dollars provided by Social Security are not enough to provide you

with adequate retirement income, you need to understand and engage in investment strategies that will provide you with a solid financial future. Sound investment strategies require that you understand the types of investment opportunities available to you. Later sections of this chapter will discuss various vehicles that can help you achieve financial security.

Organizational Financial Statements

As an administrative professional, you will not be expected to have an extensive knowledge of accounting. However, organizational financial statements, such as the balance sheet (also referred to as a statement of financial position), income statement (also referred to as a profit or loss statement), and cash flow statement will help you understand the financial condition of an organization.

Who uses financial statements? Internal users consist of owners, managers, and employees of the organization. External users include potential investors, banks, government agencies, and other individuals who need financial information concerning the business.

Balance Sheet

A **balance sheet** shows a company's assets, liabilities, and owners' equity at a given point in time—how much the company owns and how much it owes. Assets are resources owned by the company. Current assets consist of cash and other assets that are expected to be turned into cash or consumed within a year. Liabilities are debts that must be paid. Short-term liabilities must be paid within one year. Long-term liabilities are debts that are not due for a comparatively long period (more than one year). Owners' equity is the owners' financial claims to the assets of the company. If the company is a corporation, this part of the balance sheet is called *stockholders' equity* or *capital*. The balance sheet shown in Figure 14.4 has a Stockholders' Equity section.

---

[3]"Frequently Asked Questions, Benefits," Social Security Online, accessed August 22, 2007, available from http://www.ssa.gov/.

This section reports the amount of each of the two sources of stockholders' equity. The first source is capital contributed to the company by stockholders, which is called paid-in capital. The second source is the accumulated, undistributed net income of the company, which is called retained earnings. These two sources equal the total stockholders' equity.

United Pharmaceuticals
Balance Sheet
As of December 31, 20--
(dollars in thousands)

ASSETS

Current Assets	
Cash and Cash Equivalents	$ 200,012
Accounts Receivable	276,282
Inventories	399,026
Prepaid Expenses	52,380
Total Current Assets	927,700
Property and Equipment, Net	1,354,151
Investments in Affiliates	55,000
Total Assets	$ 2,336,851

LIABILITIES AND STOCKHOLDERS' EQUITY

Current Liabilities	
Current Portion of Notes Payable	$ 9,559
Accounts Payable	246,920
Accrued Expenses	225,009
Total Current Liabilities	481,488
Notes Payable	658,697
Total Liabilities	$ 1,140,185
Stockholders' Equity	
Common Stock ($1 Par Value, Authorized Shares	
100,000,000, Issued Shares 56,587,129)	$ 56,587
Additional Paid-in Capital	520,989
Retained Earnings	619,090
Total Stockholders' Equity	1,196,666
Total Liabilities and Stockholders' Equity	$ 2,336,851

FIGURE 14.4 Balance Sheet

Income Statement

An **income statement** reports the company's financial results over a period of time. An income statement shows the total amount of money earned and the total amount of expenses incurred in earning the money for the period designated. The excess of revenue over expenses is called net income or net profit. If expenses exceed revenue, the results are a net loss. A simple income statement is shown in Figure 14.5.

Cash Flow Statement

A **cash flow statement** reports an organization's cash flow activities, for example, the operating, investing, and financing activities. This statement shows the sources of cash received and the uses of cash for a given period. The time period for a cash flow statement is adjusted to meet the organization's needs. For example, the time period may be one month or one quarter.

Financial Statement Analysis

Numerous financial statements provide needed data for decision makers within a company and individuals investing in the company. Only a few of the statements are discussed in this textbook. Additionally, there are several ratios that are used to compare the organization's financial picture over a period of time. A number of methods of analysis are used; five methods are discussed in this chapter.

HORIZONTAL ANALYSIS

A **horizontal analysis** is a side-by-side comparison of two or more years of financial statements. It compares increases and decreases in items for particular periods of time. For example, sales and profits or losses may be compared for the current year and for the previous year. If sales are increasing, this may indicate that the company is growing. If sales are decreasing, this may indicate that the company is losing customers or having other problems.

VERTICAL ANALYSIS

A **vertical analysis** shows the relationship of each component to the total within a single statement. Each category on the balance sheet is treated as a percent of the total of its section. Figure 14.6 on page 354 illustrates a portion of a comparative balance sheet. Notice that cash and cash equivalents for the current year are 21.56 percent of the total current assets of $927,700. (Cash equivalents are short-term investments such as money market funds and Treasury bills.) This analysis can provide information to help better manage the business. For example, if the percentage of Accounts Receivable is very high, the company may need to do a better job of collecting amounts owed by customers. It may also need to review its credit policies. If the percentage for Inventories is very high, the company may not have enough cash on hand to meet current obligations such as payroll and taxes.

CURRENT RATIO

The **current ratio** is an indication of an organization's ability to pay its current obligations from current assets. The ratio is calculated by dividing current assets by current liabilities. In the balance sheet shown in Figure 14.4, the current assets are $927,700. The current liabilities are $481,488. The current ratio is 1.9.

When the current ratio is 1.0 or higher, the company should be able to pay its current obligations. If the ratio drops below 1, the company may not be able to pay its current obligations. If the ratio is much higher than 1.0, the company may not be using its assets to its best advantage.

QUICK RATIO

The **quick ratio** (also called an acid-test ratio) is another measure of a company's ability to meet current obligations. This ratio is a more conservative measure of liquidity and expresses a company's ability to cover its current liabilities by its most liquid assets (without selling inventory). This ratio is often used to evaluate creditworthiness.

United Pharmaceuticals
Income Statement
For the Year Ended December 31, 20--
(dollars in thousands, except per share data)

Net Sales	$ 3,113,843
Cost of Sales	1,523,989
Gross Profit	1,589,854
Operating Expenses	1,154,628
Operating Income	435,226
Other Income (Expense)	
Interest Income	5,289
Interest Expense	(14,569)
Restructuring Costs	(5,589)
Income Before Taxes	420,357
Income Taxes	168,143
Net Income	$ 252,214
Net Income Per Common Share	$ 4.46

FIGURE 14.5 Income Statement

The quick ratio is determined by subtracting inventory from total current assets and dividing by current liabilities. In the balance sheet shown in Figure 14.4, the current assets are $927,700 and the inventories are $399,026. The current liabilities are $481,488. The quick ratio is 1.1. A value of 1.0 of higher for this ratio is consider acceptable.

United Pharmaceuticals
Comparative Balance Sheet
As of December 31, 20-- and December 31, 20--
(dollars in thousands)

| | Current Year 20-- | | Previous Year 20-- | |
	Amount	Percent	Amount	Percent
Current Assets				
Cash and Cash Equivalents	$200,012	21.56%	$194,367	25.45%
Accounts Receivable	276,282	29.78%	237,401	31.09%
Inventories	399,026	43.01%	286,401	37.51%
Prepaid Expenses	52,380	5.65%	45,450	5.95%
Total Current Assets	$927,700	100.00%	$763,619	100.00%

Note: Percentages have been rounded to the nearest one-hundredth of a percent

FIGURE 14.6 Comparative Balance Sheet

P/E RATIO

The **P/E ratio** (price/earnings) compares the profit per share earned by a company to the current price per share of the company's stock. It is often used by investors to gauge the relative value of a stock in the current market. The P/E ratio is calculated by dividing the current market price of a stock by the last 12-month earnings per share. For example, suppose the current market price of a stock is $20 and the earnings per share of the stock for the last 12 months are $4.50. The P/E ratio would be 4.4.

P/E ratios are useful to investors in comparing one company to another and evaluating how a company has performed over time. For example, if Company A has a P/E ratio of 30 and Company B has a P/E ratio of 10 (and they are similar in all other important respects), Company

Professional Pointers

Follow these tips to help you work with financial records and information:

- Review statements from the files to see an acceptable format to use for company financial statements.

- Double-check figures on all reports or statements that you prepare.

- Proofread figures by having someone read all the figures to you and by checking all calculated numbers.

- Read the financial section of a newspaper or business magazine regularly.

- Watch television programs dealing with the economy and investments.

- Read at least one book about investing each year.

Understanding your organization's financial statements is important.

share and the stock price has stayed the same or fallen. However, suppose this company recently announced a product recall. The recall will not immediately affect earnings per share. However, the stock price may fall quickly because investors lose confidence in the company. The lower stock price will result in a lower P/E ratio. In this situation, the low P/E ratio may not indicate that the company is a good investment.

Banking

Changes in banking in the last few years have been dramatic. In past years, payments of bills were made using paper checks. Deposits were made by filling out a deposit form and personally taking or mailing it to the bank. Your paycheck was given to you or mailed to you. It was not possible for your employer to automatically send it to a bank. Today banking is very different. Automation is a major part of banking operations. The following changes are a few that have been made possible through computer technology.

- You may use an ATM (automated teller machine) to get cash from your account. If your payroll check is not deposited automatically, you can deposit the check using an ATM. Most banks also allow you the option of getting your bank balance after each ATM transaction.

- You can pay many of your bills electronically by giving the organizations where you pay monthly bills the authority to deduct money from your bank account. Utility companies, credit card companies, mortgage companies, and numerous other companies offer this option. Due to automatic deduction, the number of checks that individuals write each month has dropped considerably.

- You can use your banking card as a debit card to pay for purchases at retail stores such as grocery stores and clothing stores.

B is a more attractive investment. If the two companies continue to perform as they have in the recent past, you are likely to earn more money from an investment in Company B than from an investment in Company A.

In another example, assume that you track a stock for a period of time. The P/E ratio presently is 13. This ratio means that the stock is selling at 13 times the amount of earnings per share. The P/E ratio for the stock a year ago was 25, and it has a historical low of 10 for the P/E ratio. What can you conclude from this analysis? The P/E ratio has fallen significantly from a year ago. The stock may present a good buying opportunity if the drop in P/E is due to increased earnings per

Today many individuals rarely go in⁺ bank. Both **online banking** and Internet b⁺

are terms that mean handling banking transactions over the Internet. There are numerous advantages to this type of banking, some of which are:

- Banking may be done at the convenience of the individual, with transactions occurring at hours outside of bank hours and from anywhere there is access to the Internet.
- Bank statements may be accessed and printed at the bank's Website.
- Account balances may be checked at the bank's Website.
- Fund transfers may be made from a customer's checking and savings accounts to another person's account.
- Other activities, such as stopping payment on a check, may also be accomplished online.

You may be a good candidate for online banking if you:

- Have several bills (more than two or three) to pay each month.
- Travel extensively and need access to banking facilities quite frequently.
- Have a limited amount of time due to extremely heavy job assignments.
- Need to access your account frequently.

The customer's account security is maintained through password authentication. Online banking interfaces are secure sites and all information is encrypted, which makes it almost impossible to obtain or modify information after it is sent. However, it is possible for hackers to gain access to personal computers and intercept the password. Thus, all individuals who do online banking should be extremely careful in maintaining the security of their password; for example, not keeping it in your wallet or purse. There is always the possibility of losing your wallet or purse, leaving you vulnerable for bank fraud. Safe online banking involves taking precautions. Some steps recommended by the Federal Deposit Insurance Corporation (FDIC) are given in Figure 14.7.

Due to ongoing technological inventions and a changing population (with greater diversity and technological expertise), projections are that bank owners and administrators will continue to

---

TIPS FOR SAFE BANKING OVER THE INTERNET

- Confirm that an online bank is legitimate. Watch out for copycat Websites that look like the site of a real bank.

- Verify that the bank is a member of the FDIC and that your deposits are insured.

- Be aware that only deposits offered by FDIC-insured institutions are protected by the FDIC. Investments and insurance products, such as mutual funds and stocks, that may be sold through Websites or at the bank itself are not FDIC-insured, are not guaranteed by the bank, and may lose value.

- Keep your personal information private and secure. Read the bank's privacy policy to see how your personal information may be used or shared with other companies.

- Be concerned about the security of online transactions. Learn how the bank uses passwords, ID words or numbers, encryption, and other measures to keep transactions secure.

- Understand your rights as a consumer. Many regulations provide consumer protection for both traditional and online transactions. If you have any questions or concerns, first try to get answers from your bank. If you are still not satisfied, seek help from a federal agency such as the FDIC or a Federal Reserve office.

Source: "Safe Internet Banking," FDIC, accessed August 23, 2007, available from http://www.fdic.gov/bank/individual/online/safe.html.

FIGURE 14.7 The FDIC recommends several safety precautions for online banking.

revise structures and technology to increase the bank's efficiency. Some projections related to the future of banking are:

- Discerning customers will redefine the rules by demanding more control in their banking relationships and seeking banks that can fulfill their ever-changing needs.
- Banks will simplify their fee structures and implement processes that help customers avoid unnecessary fees.
- There will be a strong emphasis on people empowerment.
- Banks will be extremely responsive to changing market conditions and a more empowered customer base.

A young, computer-literate population will demand increased financial services provided in an easily accessible manner.

- Advances in global connectivity and computer power will create market conditions that foster greater specialization.

Personal Financial Security

Most individuals have some picture in their minds of the lifestyle that they want to live, but often not enough thought has been given to how they will be able to afford this lifestyle. Do you know the type of lifestyle that you wish to live? Have you determined or even given any thought to how you will be able to afford your desired lifestyle? If you plan to marry or are already married, have you and your spouse developed financial goals that you want to achieve? If you have children or plan to have children, have you determined how much money it will take to support your children and provide for their education? These questions are important ones for you to answer at an early age so that you can obtain the education that you need and be able to acquire the necessary financial resources to support your desired lifestyle.

Understand Your Investment Philosophy

Just as individuals are different in their willingness to take physical risks, they are also different in their willingness to take financial risks. You may be an individual who is willing to take significant financial risks in developing an investment portfolio, or you may be extremely conservative in your financial approach and always want to play it safe. The important point is for you to understand your financial risk-taking ability. How much risk or how little risk meets your tolerance level? Do you spend sleepless nights when you lose even a small amount of money? On the other hand, if you lose money in investments, do you merely tell yourself you are in for the long haul and refuse to let minor loses upset you?

If you are married, understand that your investment philosophy and risk tolerance may be

Families should discuss and agree on their financial goals.

different from that of your spouse. Many people do not like to talk about money even with family members. However, to be successful in providing financially for a family, spouses should discuss money and investment issues.

Consider Needs and Expenses

You and your family will have many needs that require money. You must have food, clothing, and a place to live. You may need a car or other means of transportation. Medicine and health care are major expenses for many people. You have already been asked to think about whether or not you plan to have children. Raising children and paying for their higher education requires financial planning. You can probably think of many other items that you need or want on a regular basis that require money. You need to start early and plan to meet your goals. If you plan and save for the needs of a family, the chances of your being able to afford all that you need are greatly increased.

Establish Financial Goals

Create a list of your personal financial goals. For example, you may write financial goals for the next six months or a year and also write long-term financial goals to be accomplished in five or ten years. File your goals away so that you remember where they are, and then evaluate your achievement of them every six months or every year.

As you intelligently and thoughtfully invest your money, take the long view in planning your financial future. When you face troubled times with your investments, analyze where you have invested your money and the returns you are receiving. You may want to get the help of a financial adviser. However, even if you take this step, you need to be consistently involved in evaluating your own financial investments and how you are doing in meeting your long-term financial goals. Realize that you will make investment mistakes occasionally; even the best financial advisers make mistakes. No one has a crystal ball with which to predict the future of investments. Appropriate questions to ask as you make investment decisions and monitor your investments are:

- Am I consistently putting a certain amount of money aside for my retirement years?
- Do I save the appropriate amount for my financial situation? Only you can answer that question. However, you do need to achieve a balance between saving money and spending money. You want to live a full and successful life; you do not want to deny yourself and your family the lifestyle that you can afford. You do want to consistently question the balance between your lifestyle and your long-term savings plan.
- Do I carefully research a company's success before making an investment in it?
- Do I evaluate my investment portfolio on a set time schedule—perhaps every six months?
- Do I seek financial advice from professionals in the field if I have a number of questions about my investment strategies?

Make Realistic Choices

Think for a moment about a financial decision that you made that did not turn out to be the right decision. Here is an example. Sue bought a car that she thought was the perfect one for her even though it was very expensive. At first, Sue thought she probably could not afford the car, but she discussed it with her best friend, Jose. He suggested that Sue should go ahead and get the car since she liked it so much. Sue told herself (even though she knew better) that he was right, and bought the car. Within two months, Sue discovered that she could not possibly make the payments, and had to sell the car.

If you are to be financially successful, you must trust yourself and make appropriate, realistic choices and decisions. You must not ignore the voice of reality; if you cannot afford an item, do not buy it.

Seek Advice When Needed

If you would like to improve your understanding of money management, you might consider

Reviewing Financial Goals

Reviewing your financial goals periodically is important for achieving financial security.

1. Establish a timetable as to how often you will review your financial goals, for example, every six months, every year, or every two years.

2. Invite your immediate family to participate in this review.

3. If you are not meeting your goals, discuss behaviors that you need to change to meet these goals.

4. If you are exceeding your goals, discuss whether you are being too materialistic and not taking care of your higher level of needs, such as the quality of life that you want to live.

taking a short course on money management. Many community colleges have programs that offer short-term courses or seminars on topics such as personal money management and understanding investing.

In addition to learning all you can about money management and investing, you may want to consult a financial planner. A financial planner is a person who provides financial advice to individuals. The planner will discuss your goals with you and provide advice on how you can meet your goals. Be careful to use a financial planner who has your best interests in mind. Some financial planners work for commission income. They make money when they sell products to the people they advise. Other planners are paid a fee for their advice that is not related to investments people buy or sell.

Practice Effective Money Management

Understanding how to invest and beginning to invest early in your career are important for your long-term financial security. In order to have money to invest, you may need to forgo buying some goods or services that you would like to have now. To help ensure that you have money for saving and investing as well as for current living expenses, create and follow a budget. A **budget** is a spending and saving plan based on expected income and expenses. A budget should list all your sources of income for a certain length of time, such as a month, and all the expenses you anticipate. Money for saving or investing should be one of the items you list under expenses. At the end of the budget period, compare your actual income and expenses with the amounts on your budget. Did you allow enough money for expenses? Did you make the income you expected? Did you restrict your buying of nonessential items to stay within the budgeted amount? Adjust your budget for the coming period to be realistic. However, resist the temptation to overspend for items such as movies, clothes, or vacations that you can do without that result in failing to save or invest the planned amounts.

Benefits and Investments

The essence of investing is deciding to forego spending now in exchange for future income and security. In an era when individuals cannot expect to be employed by one organization for their entire careers and when organizations are continuing to limit fringe benefits (employment benefits given in addition to wages), individuals must be concerned about their financial security. Several types of employer-sponsored retirement plans exist. Some are tax-deferred plans, meaning you do not pay taxes on the money when you put it into the plan. You do pay taxes on the money when you start withdrawing it for retirement.

Defined Benefit Plans

Some employers offer retirement accounts that are paid for by the employer. These accounts are called **defined benefit plans** or simply pensions. Defined benefit plans usually require that you work a minimum number of years (usually five)

before you are qualified for the plan. The amount contributed to the plan on your behalf increases as you continue to work for the organization. However, there is not a guaranteed benefit amount when you retire. Your benefits depend on the number of years worked, your salary, and other factors. Defined benefit plans are offered by fewer companies now than in the past. Employees do not choose how the funds are invested. When retired employees receive payments, they must pay taxes on the money received.

Employee Stock Purchase Plans

Some companies offer their employees an opportunity to buy stock through payroll deduction. A **stock** is a share of ownership in a corporation. Money can be withheld from your paycheck and then used to buy stock over a particular offering period of time. The benefits of buying stock in this manner are the following:

- You can save money with which to purchase stock through automatic deduction from your paycheck.
- The company may provide a discount on the price over what you would pay on the open market.
- You do not have to pay for the services of a stockbroker.

Such a plan also gives you a chance to have a stake in the company's financial growth. Such an investment can give you the satisfaction of knowing that your dedication to the company and the job that you hold help the company grow and also increases your financial security.

401(k) and 403(b) Accounts

Many companies and organizations offer employees an option to enroll in a 401(k) or 403(b) plan. A **401(k) account** is a tax-deferred retirement plan for employees of private companies and corporations. The employee sets aside money each month through a pre-tax payroll deduction. Employer contributions are optional. Sometimes employers match a certain

focus on *Planning for Retirement*

Begin planning for your retirement early in life. Saving and investing money now will help ensure that you have the resources you need to live comfortably after you retire. Follow these suggestions:

1. Examine your present finances. Determine how much you can save or invest toward retirement at the present time.

2. Determine the type of lifestyle you want to have in retirement; for example, do you want to live in a house that you own? Do you want to travel?

3. Look at your current living expenses and estimate an amount for living expenses after retirement. Resources are available online to help you do this.

4. Establish a saving and investing plan for your working years to generate the income you will need in retirement.

5. Write your plan down and live by it.

6. Evaluate your plan every six months to determine if it is still financially sound.

7. Revise your plan every year or two as your circumstances and goals change.

---

percentage of employee deposits. Employees choose investments for their 401(k) fund, based on their willingness to take risks. A **403(b) account** is a retirement plan for employees of nonprofit organizations or educational institutions. Teachers, nurses, professors, and ministers are examples of people who might qualify for a 403(b) account. The employee sets aside money each month through a pre-tax payroll deduction and chooses investments for the fund. Contributions are not matched by the employer. When you consider the tax savings on original earnings due to tax deferment, 401(k) and 403(b) plans generally are sound investment vehicles.

Individual Retirement Arrangement (IRA)

An **individual retirement arrangement (IRA)** is a plan that permits individuals to save and invest for retirement (as opposed to employers setting up the plan). The money deposited is not taxed until you start to withdraw the money, usually at retirement or after. You decide how to invest the funds; however, the types of investments that can be purchased through an IRA are restricted.

Money can be invested in items such as stocks, bonds, mutual funds, and certificates of deposit. Money cannot be invested in collectibles such as artwork, antiques, gems, and coins. Money set aside for a traditional IRA can be deducted from gross income if you meet certain requirements. This lowers your income tax. The contribution amount is limited; for example, for 2007, the contribution amount for a traditional IRA is $5,000 or your taxable compensation for 2007, whichever is smaller.[4]

A Roth IRA is a variation of the plan. With a Roth IRA, you cannot make pre-tax contributions. However, if you meet certain requirements, the earnings on a Roth IRA are tax free. Thus, when you withdraw money at retirement, you do not have to pay taxes on that money. A Spousal IRA is set up to benefit a spouse who does not work outside the home. To qualify, the couple must file a joint tax return.

---

[4]"Tax Law Changes for IRAs and Other Retirement Plans," Internal Revenue Service, accessed August 23, 2007, available from http://www.irs.gov/formspubs/article/0,,id=117542,00.html#trad_2007.

With all types of IRAs, there may be limits on the amount invested and restrictions on when the money can be withdrawn. If you are interested in opening an IRA, research all the requirements and restrictions before opening the account.

Stocks

Stocks are shares of ownership in a company. Stockholders become partial owners of a company through buying stock. If the price of stock you own increases due to its growth and profitability, your personal assets increase. You may also be entitled to a share of the company's profits that may be paid as **dividends**. However, if the stock goes down in price due to the company's poor performance or poor economic conditions in the world, your personal assets also go down. As a stock owner, you are vulnerable to the volatility of stocks.

Most stocks are common stocks; however, some companies also sell preferred stocks. As an investor, you need to understand the major differences in common and preferred stocks.

- Owners of common stock have voting rights in decisions made by the shareholders.
- In many companies, owners of preferred stock have a guaranteed dividend rate.
- When dividends are declared, preferred stockholders are paid in full before common stockholders are paid any dividends.
- The market value of common stock may fluctuate more than the market value of preferred stock.

The stock market has shown us that stocks as a totality go up in value over a period of time. However, the price for an individual stock may rise or fall regardless of how the overall stock market is changing. The smart investor carefully researches a company before buying its stock. You need to look at how the company has done over a period of time. Earlier in this chapter you learned about reading financial statements and calculating ratios to help you evaluate a company. Some additional questions you need to ask and answer are these:

- What is the present selling price of the stock?
- How long has the company been in business?
- What was the stock price when the company was initially formed?
- What is the outlook for the company—is it a good investment?

You can also compare an individual company to an index of stocks. The Dow Jones Industrial Average (often called *the Dow*) is the best known U.S. index of stocks. It contains 30 stocks that trade on the New York Stock Exchange. It is considered an indicator of what is happening in the stock market. Even though the Dow represents only 30 stocks, these stocks have been a mainstay in the United States economy for years. If they are down as a group, it is likely that the majority of stocks are down. The Standard & Poor's 500 (S&P 500) index is derived from the price of common stocks of 500 publicly traded companies. The S&P 500, like the Dow, is also an indicator of trends in the stock market.

As you develop your stock portfolio and monitor prices of the stocks over a period of time, you may need to buy more of a stock or sell some of a stock. Investing in the stock market demands time on your part in researching and modifying your portfolio when needed. Stockbrokers are professionals who can help you make investment decisions; however, there is a charge for their services.

STOCK EXCHANGES

The stock market in the United States consists of a number of exchanges, where traders physically stand on the floor of the exchange and buy and sell stocks. The largest stock exchange is the New York Stock Exchange. Other stock exchanges in the United States include the following:

- Boston Stock Exchange
- Chicago Stock Exchange

The New York Stock Exchange is the largest stock exchange in the United States.

- Cincinnati Stock Exchange
- Pacific Stock Exchange
- Philadelphia Stock Exchange

NASDAQ

NASDAQ, established by the National Association of Securities Dealers, is an over-the-counter market for trading stocks. It does not have a physical location like the New York Stock Exchange. It consists of an automated information network that provides quotes on stocks for brokers registered with NASDAQ. Trades are made via phone or computer.

Bonds

A **bond** is basically a loan that a buyer makes to a bond issuer. The bond issuer may be a government or a corporation. Bonds are designed to be long-term investments. They represent a bond issuer's promise to pay a definite sum of money at a specified time to the holder of the bond. Thus, bonds do not represent a share of ownership in a company (as stocks do), but are evidence of a debt owed by the issuer. In times when the stock market is bearish (at a low), bonds generally yield a greater return to the investor than stocks. However, when the stock market is bullish (stock prices are increasing), stocks may yield a greater return to the investor than bonds.

Types of bonds include corporate, government, and municipal bonds. Corporate bonds are issued by corporations to raise money. The interest from corporate bonds is taxable. Some corporate bonds are considered low-risk investments; others are not. The risk depends on the issuing company's ability to make interest payments and repay the bond. Investment-grade bonds are considered fairly low-risk investments. Speculative-grade bonds (also called junk bonds) are not considered low-risk.

Government bonds are issued by the United States Treasury or other federal government

We committed early in our careers to be informed investors; we developed a financial plan and implemented it well.

agencies. These bonds are low-risk when held to maturity. You do not have to pay state and local taxes on the income from some government bonds. Municipal bonds are issued by states, counties, cities, and towns. You do not have to pay federal, state, or local tax on the income from many municipal bonds. Municipal bonds are relatively safe investments.

Mutual Funds

A **mutual fund** is an investment fund that consists of stocks, bonds, and other investments focused on an investment strategy such as balance or growth. A mutual fund is operated by a professional investment company. The company sells shares in the mutual fund and invests the money in stocks and bonds. Mutual fund companies employ investment advisers who select, buy, and sell investments based on a fund's investment objective. Mutual funds provide one of the simplest ways for the small investor to buy stocks and bonds. The individual investor in a

mutual fund owns a small fraction of each share of stock or bond that is purchased. Through mutual funds, the investor is able to achieve diversification within his or her account and also to have a professional manager who is buying and selling the investments.

Portfolio Evaluation

As you develop your investment portfolio, you need to pay continued attention to the balance between stocks and bonds. For example, you might have set a goal for yourself to have a portfolio of 60 percent stocks and 40 percent bonds. If the value of stock falls, you might find yourself in a position where the portfolio is 50 percent stocks and 50 percent bonds. If you have additional money that you can invest, you might want to invest more in stocks to get back to your initial position of 60 percent stocks and 40 percent bonds. If you do not have more money that you can invest, you may want to sell some of your bonds and add some money to stock. The important investment point here is that you need to watch your portfolio balance. If the balance changes significantly, you will want to make adjustments to return to your target goal.

Education—Continual and Crucial

When investing in stocks and bonds, you must be committed to continually educating yourself about the investment world. You should never blindly accept a *tip of the week* from a friend or even a financial adviser. When you purchase a car, a house, or make any other major investment, you should first do research. You should also do your research when investing in stocks and bonds. Even if you work with a stockbroker when investing, you should be an educated investor who understands:

- Your long-term investment goals

- Your level of acceptable risk
- Your financial needs in 5, 10, 20, or even 30 years

When using the services of a stockbroker, be a participant with her or him in determining what stocks, mutual funds, or bonds best meet your needs. Wise investors do not blindly follow anyone's advice. They chart their investment course with qualified assistance from financial professionals.

Establish a financial goal that you want to achieve. It does not have to be an exact amount, but it is good to have an approximate amount of money in mind that you want to have when you retire. You also do not want to let yourself be so miserly that you save every penny for the future and do not enjoy the present. Then exercise commitment and control in taking the financial steps that help you to satisfy your long-term financial position.

Summary

To reinforce what you have learned in this chapter, study this summary.

- Effective money management is crucial for present and long-term success and happiness.

- Mandatory payroll deductions include federal income tax, Social Security tax, and Medicare tax. State income tax and local (city or county) income tax may be mandatory deductions in some areas. Optional payroll deductions may be made for items such as a health care plan, retirement plan, or life insurance plan.

- A majority of states within the United States have mandatory state income taxes.

- Social Security is a social insurance program with its beneficiaries being retired individuals, widows and survivors, and the disabled. Medicare is a health insurance program primarily for people age 65 or older.

- Social Security's Old-Age, Survivors, and Disability Insurance (OASDI) program and Medicare's Hospital Insurance (HI) program are financed primarily by employment taxes.

- Organizational financial statements, such as a balance sheet, income statement, and cash flow statement, provide important information about the financial condition of an organization.

- Doing a horizontal analysis and a vertical analysis and finding the current ratio, quick ratio, and P/E ratio can help investors understand the financial condition of an organization.

- Automation is a major part of modern banking operations. ATMs make getting cash and checking balances convenient. Bank cards can be used as debit cards to pay for purchases at retail stores and online. Computers allow users the luxury of banking online; however, safety precautions should be followed when banking online.

- Individuals should develop their own personal financial goals. In order to do this successfully, a person must know his or her investment philosophy and tolerance for risk. Individuals must also practice good money management and seek advice when needed.

- Some employers offer retirement accounts called defined benefit plans that are paid for by the employer. An employee stock purchase plan is another fringe benefit offered by some companies.

- Many organizations offer employees an option to enroll in a 401(k) or 403(b) plan. These are tax-deferred retirement plans for employees.

- An individual retirement account (IRA) is a plan that permits individuals to save and invest for retirement (as opposed to employers setting up the plan).

- Investment possibilities that can help provide funds for retirement include stocks, bonds, and mutual funds.

What's the Problem?

When Joe Chin went to work for his company, he filled out a Form W-4 and listed no dependents. Several months ago, Joe married Alice. She is going to school full-time and does not have a job. Joe asked the HR department for a new Form W-4 and changed the dependent status from zero to one. Joe's check is automatically deposited by his employer each month. Four months have passed, and Joe is attempting to reconcile his bank statements. Joe notices that the amount of money deposited to his account for his pay is considerably more than he had expected. Joes thinks an error may have been made; however, he is embarrassed that he did not report it earlier. He is tempted to just forget about it. After all, isn't it the responsibility of the company or the federal government to find such an error?

What is the problem? How should Joe handle it?

Let's Discuss

1. Define and give examples of mandatory and optional payroll deductions.
2. What is the purpose of an income statement? of a balance sheet?

3. What types of information are compared in a horizontal analysis of financial statements? in a vertical analysis?

4. List four considerations that will help you identify your financial goals.

5. What is a defined benefit plan?

6. How does an IRA differ from a 401(k) plan?

7. Identify three investment possibilities (other than a retirement account) that can help you prepare for retirement.

Critical-Thinking Activity

You are in a two-year program at your local college. Once you complete your program, you plan to go to work as an administrative professional. You are 22 years of age and have recently become engaged to a person who is finishing the last year of a degree in accounting. Both of you believe that you have a good understanding of financial investments, but neither of you have established an investment program. The two of you do not have any savings. However, both of you understand that it is crucial to become good money managers if you are to have the standard of living that you both want. You have not discussed a family to any degree; however, the two of you have agreed that you would like to have children. Both of you plan to continue your education (with you graduating in the next year). Your fiancé plans to go on to get a master's degree in business.

What steps should you take as a couple to begin planning for financial success?

Vocabulary Review

Open the *Word* file *CH14 Vocabulary* on the Student CD. Complete the vocabulary review for Chapter 14.

English and Word Usage Drill

Complete the English and Word Usage Drill for Chapter 14 found in the *Applications Workbook*.

Workplace Applications

14-1 Interview an Employee

(Goal 1)

1. Work with two classmates to complete this application.

2. As a team, interview an individual who is presently employed full time. Ask this person to explain the mandatory and optional payroll deductions taken from his or her pay and other optional deductions that could be requested. (Do not ask the

team
building

individual to be specific about the deduction amounts.) Your objective is to understand more concerning mandatory and optional payroll deductions.

3. Prepare a written report of your findings and present the report to the class. Give the written report to your instructor.

14-2 Analyze Financial Statements

(Goal 2)

internet

1. Find a balance sheet and income statement for a corporation. You may find these statements on the Web or in your school library. When searching online, use the company name as the search term. After you reach the company Website, look for links such as *Financial Statements* or *Annual Reports.*

2. Read and evaluate the balance sheet and income statement for the corporation. Using spreadsheet software, prepare a vertical analysis of the balance sheet. For each item listed under Assets, find its percentage of Total Assets. For each item listed under Liabilities, find its percentage of Total Liabilities.

3. Using the data on the balance sheet, find the current ratio and the quick ratio for the company.

4. Find the price per share earnings for the last 12 months for the company. Find the current selling price of the company's stock. Calculate the P/E ratio for the company. (To find earnings per share and stock prices online, search using the term *stock quotes* or visit a site such as *Yahoo! Finance.* Enter the company name or stock symbol on the Website.)

5. Prepare a short report to include the vertical analysis and the ratios you calculated. What can you infer about the company from this analysis? Include your answer in the report.

14-3 Research Banking Services

(Goal 3)

1. Visit the bank you use or do research online to answer the following questions:

   • What banking services does the institution provide for consumers? (If the bank has handouts, ask for a copy of each one that is discussed.)

   • Are there new banking services that the bank plans to provide in the future? If so, what are they and what advantages do these services have for customers?

   • Are there any services that the bank now provides that are projected to change in the future? For example, are there additional online services that may be provided in the future?

2. Create electronic slides to summarize your findings. Use the slides in an oral presentation of your findings to the class.

14-4 Develop an Investment Plan

(Goal 4)

e-portfolio

Determine your own personal investment strategies. You may have already started an investment plan. If you have, consider what additional strategies you will add to that plan in the future.

1. Begin by writing a statement that tells the level of risk-taking (low, medium, or high) you are comfortable with for investments.

2. Write your financial goals, both short-term and long-term, that you want to achieve at least partially through investing. If you have educational loans to pay off in the future, address how you will take care of your obligations.

3. List the types of investments you will choose based on your risk tolerance and your goals. For example, you might list stocks, mutual funds, bonds, or certificates of deposit.

4. Do research and identify at least one option in each type of investment identified in step 3 that you think will be a wise investment. Explain your strategy for buying/acquiring these investments.

5. Submit a copy of your plan to your instructor if requested. Keep your plan and modify it as your goals change.

Assessment of Chapter 14 Goals

Did you successfully complete the chapter goals? Evaluate yourself by filling out the form in Chapter 14 of the *Applications Workbook*.

part 6

Meetings and Travel

CHAPTER 15
Event Planning

CHAPTER 16
Travel Arrangements

Career Profile

Meeting Planner

Meetings bring people together to share information. Whether the purpose of the meeting is to inform, persuade, instruct, or entertain, meeting planners manage all the details that make a meeting successful. Meeting planners work for both small and large organizations, and some work as independent consultants. About 43,000 people worked as meeting planners in the United States in 2004.*

Meeting planners work for a variety of organizations—businesses, nonprofit groups, professional associations, hotels, and government. They coordinate every detail of meetings, such as meeting location, lodging, speakers, meals, entertainment, printed materials, and communication equipment. Planners may negotiate contracts with facilities and suppliers. Planners may also oversee the finances of meetings and conventions. They may be given an overall budget by their organization and asked to create a detailed budget, showing what each aspect of the event will cost. Determining how well a meeting achieves set goals is also an important duty for many meeting planners.

Salaries for meeting planners vary by the qualifications of the worker and the job duties. The mean annual earnings of meeting and convention planners in May 2004 were $39,620. Meeting planners need strong analytical, communication, and interpersonal skills. They must be detail-oriented with good organizational skills, and they must be able to meet tight deadlines and work with composure under pressure. The ability to speak multiple languages is a plus. Planners also need computer skills, such as the ability to use financial and registration software and the Internet. Many employers prefer that a meeting planner have a bachelor's degree, but this is not always required. Although there are some certification programs and college and university courses in meeting and convention planning available, a large proportion of the skills needed is learned on the job and through experience.

Employment of meeting and convention planners is expected to grow over the 2004–2014 period. As meeting planners prove themselves, they may be given greater responsibilities. For example, a planner may be promoted from conference coordinator, with responsibility for meeting logistics, to program coordinator, with responsibility for booking speakers and formatting the meeting's program. The next step up may be meeting manager, with responsibility for supervising all parts of the meeting, and then director of meetings, and then possibly department director of meetings and education. Another path for promotion is to move from a small organization to a larger one, taking on responsibility for larger meetings and conventions.

---

*"Meeting and Convention Planners," *Occupational Outlook Handbook*, 2006-2007 Edition, accessed June 26, 2007, available from http://www.bls.gov/oco/ocos298.htm.

chapter 15

Event Planning

Learning Goals

1. **Describe the characteristics of effective meetings and the wide variety of meeting formats.**

2. **Describe the roles and responsibilities of individuals associated with a meeting.**

3. **Plan meetings and prepare materials related to meetings.**

4. **Participate in effective meetings and evaluate meetings.**

Effective Meetings

Meetings are an important component of the workplace; therefore, a great deal of time is spent in meetings. As organizations increase their use of teams to solve problems and make decisions, the occurrence of meetings for all employees increases. With such an investment of time (and money) in meetings, they must be effective. This chapter will give you the knowledge and skills you need to assist your supervisor in holding meetings that are productive for all participants—and thus, an efficient use of organizational time. In addition, this chapter will help you develop skills as a meeting planner, leader, and attendee.

Why are meetings held? Effective meetings make you and your organization function more efficiently. Many money-wasting activities occur in business because of poor workplace communication. Much of this ineffectiveness could be changed through productive meetings. Voice mail has made phone tag a familiar game. If you are trying to reach someone, you can save time by simply scheduling a quick in-person or audio meeting. Email is another useful technology tool that can be used in place of a meeting at certain times. When you are communicating over long distances or need to send information to more than one person, email is effective. However, do not use email when a face-to-face meeting would be more effective. Do not spend a great deal of time writing an email when you can

Face-to-face meetings continue to be an important part of business.

discuss the issue in person. If you need to discuss an issue in depth, a meeting is the best alternative.[1] The effective meeting is one in which:

- There is a definite need for the meeting.
- The purpose is stated and clearly understood by all participants.
- The appropriate people are in attendance at the meeting.
- An agenda is prepared and followed.
- All members participate.
- Outcomes are achieved because of the meeting.

Although these criteria seem relatively straightforward, few meetings satisfy all of them.

Face-to-face meetings will continue to be a necessary part of the workplace even though electronic meetings are another option. As an administrative professional, you should understand when it is necessary to hold a meeting, the types of meetings that are held, and the types of electronic meeting opportunities available.

Necessary Meetings

Calling a meeting is appropriate when:

- A group needs to be involved in solving a problem or making a decision.
- An issue arises that needs clarification.
- Information needs to be shared with a group.
- Communication needs to occur quickly with a large number of people.

Notice that each situation includes a purpose for the meeting. Once a purpose is identified, considerable planning needs to occur before the meeting takes place. The meeting leader has a role to play if the meeting is to be effective; he or she must understand that role and be well prepared for the meeting. Meeting participants also have a role to play. They must understand the need and purpose of the meeting, prepare before the meeting, and participate actively during the meeting.

Unnecessary Meetings

Unfortunately, many meetings are either unnecessary or ineffective. In fact, a great deal of time and money is wasted by businesses in these instances. Meetings are often called that are not

[1]"Meeting Basics, So Why Do We Still Have Meetings?" EffectiveMeetings. com, accessed September 7, 2007, available from http://www. effectivemeetings.com/meetingbasics/meetings.asp.

> ## SIX RULES OF MEETING MANAGEMENT
>
> The following rules of meeting management will help make meetings more productive and less frustrating.
>
> - Run your meetings as you would have others run the meetings that you attend.
>
> - Be prepared and ensure that all the participants can be prepared as well.
>
> - Stick to a schedule.
>
> - Stay on topic.
>
> - Do not hold unnecessary meetings.
>
> - Wrap up meetings with a clear statement of the next steps and who is to take them.

Source: "The 6 Golden Rules of Meeting Management," GovLeaders.org, accessed August 15, 2007, available from http://www.govleaders.org/meetings_print.htm.

FIGURE 15.1 An effective meeting requires planning and focus.

appropriate and should not be held. Meetings are not a good idea when:

- There is no clearly defined purpose for the meeting.
- No consideration has been given to people who need to attend.
- Confidential or sensitive personnel matters must be addressed.
- There are inadequate data for the meeting.
- There is insufficient time to prepare for the meeting.
- There is considerable anger and hostility in the group, and people need time to calm down before coming together.
- The same information could be covered in a memo, an email, or a brief report.

One of the ways to ensure that meetings are effective is to differentiate between the need for one-way information dissemination and two-way information sharing. To distribute information, you can use a variety of other avenues, such as sending an email or posting the information on your organization's Website or intranet. Figure 15.1 lists six rules of meeting management.

Types of Meetings

The traditional face-to-face meetings where people gather to discuss an issue or a problem continue to be used in organizations.

Typical business meetings include staff meetings, committee meetings, project team meetings, customer/client meetings, board of directors meetings, conventions, and conferences. These meetings may be held face-to-face or through electronic means.

STAFF MEETINGS

Staff meetings are common within organizations. Staff meetings are scheduled on a regular basis when an executive meets with members of his or her staff. For example, an executive may meet with his or her six direct reports as a group every week. The purpose of staff meetings is to review directions, plans, and assignments and to handle routine problems.

COMMITTEE MEETINGS

In most organizations, committees or task forces have been created. A **task force** is formed to deal with a specific issue or problem. Once the problem has been handled or solved, the task force is disbanded. In other words, the task force has a specific beginning and ending. It is organized for a purpose; once the purpose is accomplished, it no longer exists. A **committee** is established for an ongoing purpose. For example, your workplace may have a safety committee that meets regularly (perhaps every month) to identify and address safety concerns. Since safety is an ongoing concern, the committee functions from year to year.

© Stockbyte / Getty Images

Board meetings usually follow strict procedures.

PROJECT TEAM MEETINGS

Project teams are frequently used in organizations to accomplish a specific project. For example, a project team may be organized to determine the type of document imaging software that will be used in an organization or to implement quality control policies within a company. Once the project has been completed, the team is disbanded or it takes on another project.

CUSTOMER/CLIENT MEETINGS

Most employers hold meetings with customers and clients. These meetings are generally small, including only two or three people. For example, a lawyer may meet with a client to discuss the evidence in a case. An engineer may meet with a customer to discuss the design of a product.

BOARD OF DIRECTORS MEETINGS

Most large corporations and organizations operate with a board of directors. There are usually **bylaws**, written policies and procedures that clearly define how board meetings are to be conducted. Boards may meet once a month or less. The chairperson of the board conducts the meeting, and strict procedures are usually followed. An agenda is distributed before the meeting, indicating the items to be discussed. If the organization is a public entity in which the open meetings rule applies, notice of the meeting is posted according to legal procedures. Participants generally follow parliamentary procedures as set forth in *Robert's Rules of Order Newly Revised*.

CONVENTIONS AND CONFERENCES

Conventions are formal annual meetings of the members of a professional group. A convention can involve hundreds or thousands of people. Planning and executing a convention are so complicated that meeting consultants are often hired to assist in carrying out the details.

A **conference** is a meeting where discussion on certain issues or topics takes place. For example, a conference or seminar may be held on topics such as conflict management, written communications, and union negotiations.

Face-to-Face Meetings

While technology can allow people to communicate almost instantly 24 hours a day, nothing can replace the need for people to meet face-to-face. Traditional meetings have not gone away; instead, they continue to be essential to the success of organizations. The traditional meeting, where people gather for face-to-face discussion of an issue or problem in one location, has a number of advantages.

- All individuals have a chance to talk informally with other participants before, during, and after the meeting.
- Participants can closely observe others' body language.
- People generally feel more relaxed with the informal setting.
- If the issue to be discussed is a difficult one, the atmosphere allows attendees to deal with the issue effectively.
- A creative, interactive group discussion is more likely.
- Widespread participation among group members is more likely.

Electronic Meetings

The increased emphasis on teamwork and the development of telecommunications technology has contributed to the need and ability to communicate with individuals in remote locations. These electronic options are often referred to as **teleconferencing**. Teleconferencing is a general term applied to a variety of technology-assisted two-way (interactive) communications via telephone, DSL, cable modems, and other high-bandwidth connections. Will electronic meetings eventually replace all traditional meetings? Probably not. If the meeting is collaborative in nature and its purpose is to exchange information, audioconferencing, videoconferencing, and Web conferencing are ideal venues.

The use of teleconferencing continues to increase in business. An increasing number of businesses are using teleconference technology to supplement the traditional face-to-face meetings. This allows them to reach remote areas and save time and costs because of decreased travel.

These services are not designed to replace face-to-face meetings. Instead, they provide reliable opportunities for businesses to supplement traditional meetings with virtual meetings. Advances in virtual conference technology have made teleconferencing easier to use and more cost effective than in the past.

AUDIOCONFERENCING

An **audioconference** is a type of conference in which three or more participants use a voice input unit to participate in a meeting. An audioconference differs from a telephone conversation in that it involves more than two people in at least two locations. This technology may be as simple as a speakerphone or as elaborate as meeting room microphones, speakers, and other technology. Audioconferencing is also called conference calling. Common applications include team meetings, project update meetings, job interviews, and communication with employees who work in different locations.

Today's telephones come with speakerphone technology that has high reception and sound quality, allowing people to participate in the conference from almost any part of a room. Many telephone companies now offer three-way calling as an option for business and home phone lines for a small fee. Also, audioconferencing can take place over the Internet. If you wish to include more than three individuals in the audioconference, a number of communications companies can assist you. Figure 15.2 provides tips for an effective audioconference. Advantages of an audioconference include:

- The ability to assemble individuals on short notice, assuming their schedules allow.
- The ability to connect individuals at any location, nationally or internationally.
- The use of telephone technology, which is readily available to almost everyone.
- The availability of special technology for supporting large groups and rooms.
- Decreased time and expense associated with travel.

AUDIOCONFERENCE TIPS

- Identify yourself whenever you speak.

- If there are materials everyone needs to use during the conference, distribute them ahead of time.

- Take turns speaking one at a time.

- Move the speakerphone as close as possible to the speaker.

- Avoid side conversations; they compete with the speaker and distract other participants.

- Mute the phone when your site is not actively participating.

- If you need to leave the meeting before it is over, say goodbye.

Source: "Tips for Participating in a Telephone Conference Call," The South Carolina Enterprise Information System, accessed August 15, 2007, available from http://www.sceis.sc.gov/content/implement/conf-call-tips.htm.

FIGURE 15.2 Tips for Participating Effectively in an Audioconference

One of the primary disadvantages of audioconferencing is the lack of visual input. However, distributing basic information or confirming the details of previous communication can be handled effectively by email, or a fax can be used to distribute detailed information that includes graphics and text. Other disadvantages to audioconferencing include these:

- Participants cannot see others' body language.
- Without visual cues, it is difficult to manage turn-taking when people are speaking.
- Identifying the speaker can also be a problem. Successful audioconferencing requires participants to follow protocols such as announcing who is speaking, and asking if anyone else has something to say.
- The potential exists for participants to feel excluded. When many people are in the same room conferencing with individuals in other places, those in the same room have the advantage of being able to see each other. Unless this imbalance is carefully monitored, remote participants may feel left out of the group.

VIDEOCONFERENCING

As business becomes more global, communication between individuals at distant locations becomes more prevalent. Videoconferencing is an important alternative to audioconferencing when body language is an important element of a meeting. **Videoconferencing** is a system of transmitting audio and video between individuals at two or more locations. Videoconferencing can range from a simple conversation between two individuals in two locations to a more complex endeavor involving several individuals located at several sites.

Although the equipment for audioconferencing is minimal, videoconferencing equipment can vary from the basic to a more complex system. When videoconferencing is transmitted from a computer-based application it is called desktop videoconferencing. Desktop videoconferencing typically uses an inexpensive camera and microphone that is attached to a USB connection on a computer. In fact, many newer laptop computers come with a tiny camera built into the computer screen. This basic equipment combined with the video capabilities of instant messaging software provides users with the ability to use desktop videoconferencing in a very simple format. Many organizations will invest in a more complex videoconference system that involves numerous pieces of equipment that are set up in a specially designed room. The cost of videoconferencing increases as more complex equipment becomes involved.

Although the capabilities for videoconferencing have been around for over 35 years, the technologies associated with it have continued to develop. Advances in telecommunications have increased videoconferencing opportunities. A basic form of videoconferencing is available on

Teleconferencing continues to be an important way to conduct business.

handheld computers and mobile phones. Advanced communications and video collaboration have become important tools in business today. The faster and more effectively a corporation makes decisions, the more competitive it can be in the marketplace. Companies today are beginning to realize that videoconferencing is a necessary tool for driving business forward and obtaining a competitive advantage. Figure 15.3 provides tips for setting up effective videoconferences.

ONLINE CONFERENCING

Online meetings link individual participants through a computer. Other terms used to describe online meetings include computer conferencing, data conferencing, and Web conferencing. **Data conferencing**, which enables two or more people to communicate and collaborate as a group in real time using the computer, is an example of an online meeting in its simplest form. Data conferencing software allows participants to:

- Share a program running on one computer with other participants in the conference. Participants can review the same information and see the work of the person sharing the application.

- Exchange information between shared applications through a clipboard, transfer files, and collaborate on a shared whiteboard.

- Send files to conference participants.

- Chat with other conference participants by keying text messages or record meeting notes and action items as part of the collaborative process.

The technologies for online conferencing continue to develop. Nearly all Web conferencing providers offer a common set of features that enable increased productivity and collaboration. Current features include the ability to integrate data, audio, and video functions during an online meeting. In addition, Web conferencing provides participants with the following capabilities:

- Instant messaging and chat functions for private chats or for creating conversation among all participants.

- Document sharing features to encourage audience participation, attention, and retention.

VIDEOCONFERENCE TIPS

- Designate a central contact person who is responsible for organizing the videoconference.

- Research videoconference providers. Compare prices, accommodations, and technical expertise.

- Prepare and distribute an agenda prior to the conference.

- Develop a plan to handle technical issues if they arise.

- Allow for a transmission delay when speaking. Pause after the end of your comments to allow time for remote sites to respond to a question or comment.

- Practice appropriate meeting etiquette; be on time and avoid side conversations.

- Dress appropriately; avoid loud jewelry or busy or boldly patterned clothing.

FIGURE 15.3 Videoconferences can be an effective tool for competitive businesses.

- Polling and survey software to determine consensus of ideas or acceptance of suggestions.
- Quizzing software to determine participant understanding of meeting content.
- Whiteboard features to encourage and record brainstorming sessions or discussions.
- Archival abilities so content can be saved for absent participants or reference at a later time.
- Security features to help determine who is logged on at any given time.

ADVANTAGES AND DISADVANTAGES OF ELECTRONIC MEETINGS

Just as face-to-face meetings have advantages and disadvantages, so do electronic meetings. Advantages include:

- Savings in travel time, costs, meals, and hotel rooms.
- Presentation of a considerable amount of information concisely through sophisticated audio and video technology.
- Bringing together people with expertise in a number of different areas to discuss problems of mutual concern with a minimum of effort.
- Providing conference information to individuals who are not in attendance.
- Increased availability of software packages and service providers.

Disadvantages to electronic meetings include:

- Less spontaneity between individuals due to a structured environment.

- The tendency to be more formal in nature.
- Inability to see body language of all participants at one time.
- Inability to pick up small nuances of body language over the monitor.
- Little or no socializing time between participants.
- Less chance for effective brainstorming on issues.

International Meetings

In today's global business environment, international business meetings are quite common. These meetings may be face-to-face or electronic. In either situation, you cannot forget that cultural differences exist. If the meeting is to be successful, such differences must be understood and respected. Otherwise, you might have an international incident rather than resolution to a problem. International meetings are more formal in nature. Hierarchical considerations must be considered and dealt with appropriately.

Being prepared for cultural differences is crucial. For example, language has different meanings in different cultures. Consider the following examples.

- Even though the British speak English, they do not speak American English and vice versa. For example, in the United States, *tabling* means postponing a discussion. In England, to

International meetings are common in today's global business environment.

table a subject means to put it on the table for present discussion.

- Values in other countries are different from values held in the United States. Americans value honesty and directness. However, Asians are more concerned with the quality of an interaction; they do not expect and do not want your complete candor.

- Silence is a form of speech in some cultures. For example, the Swedes value silence, whereas Americans are often uncomfortable with silence.

- In Thailand, it is customary to exchange gifts during the second business meeting. In China, however, gift giving is considered a form of bribery and is actually illegal.

When you are assisting with an international meeting, prior to the meeting you need to research carefully the culture of participating countries. Your local bookstore or library has resources that can assist you. You can also conduct your research on the Internet.

International etiquette is also essential if you are meeting over the Internet. Virtual meetings also need to reflect the customs and traditions of the individuals involved. Virtual meetings have the added difficulty of participants not physically being with the people they are meeting. A misinterpreted sentence could lead to a major misunderstanding with no chance for rebuttal.

Meeting Roles and Responsibilities

When organizing a meeting, several individuals play an important part in planning and implementing effective meetings. These individuals include the executive who calls the meeting, the administrative professional who assists in planning and preparing for the meeting, the leader who facilitates the meeting, and the attendees. Each individual or group of individuals has specific roles and responsibilities for the creation of an effective meeting environment.

The Executive's Role and Responsibilities

The executive has a variety of responsibilities when planning a meeting, including determining

Every meeting must have a purpose.

the purpose of the meeting, setting objectives, determining who should attend, determining the number of attendees, planning the agenda, and establishing the time and place.

DETERMINING THE PURPOSE

Every meeting must have a purpose; without it, there is no need for a meeting. Generally, the executive calls the meeting, so it is his or her role to determine the purpose. When meeting notices are sent out, the purpose should be stated clearly so all participants understand why the meeting is occurring. Although the administrative professional is not responsible for calling the meeting or determining the purpose, he or she must understand the purpose. Understanding the purpose is necessary so that the administrative professional can make appropriate arrangements.

SETTING THE OBJECTIVES

Every meeting should have specific written objectives. Objectives more clearly define the purpose and delineate what is to be accomplished. For example, if the general purpose is to determine

the training needs of the organization, the objectives might be to:

- Establish training needs for each department.
- Determine whether the training needs are to be done by internal staff or by an outside consultant.
- Determine the amount of time necessary for training.
- Determine the budget for training.

Meeting objectives should be shared with attendees before the meeting. This will provide them with an understanding of the purpose and objectives and allow them to clarify any questions they may have.

DETERMINING WHO SHOULD ATTEND

The individual who is calling the meeting is generally responsible for determining who should be included. Attendees should be selected based on the type of meeting and the meeting topic. Attendees may include individuals with knowledge, resources, or decision-making authority. In some instances, the individuals who will be impacted by potential outcomes or decisions should be included. The people who should be invited to the meeting are those who:

- Have knowledge that can contribute to meeting the objectives.
- Will be responsible for implementing the decisions.
- Represent a group that will be affected by the decisions.

In addition, you need to consider the backgrounds of the people who are attending. For example, a **heterogeneous group** (a group having dissimilar backgrounds and experiences) can often solve problems more satisfactorily than a **homogeneous group** (a group with similar backgrounds and experiences). A heterogeneous group can bring varying views to the problem and encourage creative thinking through the diversity that is present. However, a heterogeneous group demands a skilled facilitator to make the meeting productive.

DETERMINING THE NUMBER OF ATTENDEES

The ideal number of attendees is based on the purpose of the meeting and the number of people who can best achieve the purpose. The best size for a problem-solving and decision-making group is from seven to ten people. This size group allows for creative **synergy** (the ideas and products of a group of people developed through interaction with each other). This size group provides enough people to generate divergent points of view and to challenge what each person is thinking.

Small groups of seven or fewer people are necessary at times. For example, if the purpose of a meeting is to discuss a personnel issue, the employee, supervisor, and human resources director may be the only individuals in attendance. If the purpose of a meeting is to discuss a faulty product design, the product engineer, the manager of the Engineering Department, and the line technician may be the only people in attendance.

PLANNING THE AGENDA

The executive's role is to plan the agenda. The agenda, which should be distributed before the meeting, provides participants with the purpose and objectives of the meeting. Make sure the agenda includes the following information:

- Name of the group, department, or committee
- Date of the meeting
- Start and end times
- Location of the meeting

An agenda is an outline of what will occur at a meeting and helps to ensure that all participants are prepared for the meeting, that each agenda item achieves the desired outcome, and that no time is wasted during the meeting. In addition, an agenda should provide:

- The order in which the objectives of the meeting will be presented.
- The individual responsible for presenting the agenda item.
- The amount of time allocated for each agenda item (optional).
- The action expected on agenda items.
- Background materials (if necessary).

A well-planned agenda saves time and increases productivity in a meeting. By providing attendees with review information before a meeting, the leader can use the meeting time effectively.

ESTABLISHING THE TIME AND PLACE

The executive is responsible for establishing the approximate time of the meeting and the general location for the meeting. For example, the executive may tell the administrative professional that the meeting should take place on Tuesday morning. The administrative professional must then check with other attendees (or their administrative professionals) to determine the most appropriate time on Tuesday morning. The administrative professional may have access to an online calendar or scheduling program, which assists in determining an appropriate meeting time. The executive decides whether the meeting should be held on-site at the organization or held at an off-site location such as a hotel conference room.

The Administrative Professional's Role and Responsibilities

As an administrative professional, you have a number of responsibilities when planning face-to-face or electronic meetings. In addition to attending meetings, you must work closely with the supervisor to clarify the meeting's purpose and expectations. Although many of the responsibilities of the administrative professional can be handled independently, you should understand your supervisor's preferences in a variety of areas. When you first join an organization or begin to work with a supervisor, take time before each meeting to understand his or her needs and preferences. Once you have spent some time with a supervisor, you will have less need to discuss details. However, you should continue to discuss the purpose of the meeting, the objectives, and the general expectations. Otherwise, you may make decisions about details that lessen the effectiveness of a meeting.

CONFIRMING THE DATE AND TIME

At times, the executive will request to hold a meeting on a specific date and at a specific time. At other times, one or both of these decisions will be left up to the administrative professional. When selecting a date, consider the expected attendees' other commitments. If you know several attendees have a standing monthly meeting on the second Tuesday of the month, try to avoid that day. In addition, you may want to avoid scheduling meetings for Monday mornings and late Friday afternoons. Many employees use Monday mornings to get an overview of the week and to handle pressing items that occurred over the weekend; Friday afternoons are often used to tie up loose ends and to complete projects.

The time of the meeting is also an important consideration. When selecting a time, avoid meetings immediately after lunch and near the end of the day. Keep in mind that meetings should last no longer than two hours; when people must sit longer than two hours, they get restless and lose interest in the topic. If a meeting will go longer than two hours, the leader should schedule short five- to ten-minute breaks for participants, after which the attendees will be better able to focus on the task at hand.

SELECTING AND PREPARING THE MEETING ROOM

When you know the date and time of the meeting and number of attendees, you should select the meeting room. Most businesses have several conference rooms of varying sizes. Be certain to reserve a room that is appropriate for the size of the group. If you choose a room that is too large, participants may feel "lost" in the room. Conversely, if you choose a room that is too small, participants will feel crowded.

Check the temperature controls before the meeting. Remember that bodies give off heat, so the room will be warmer with people in it. A standard rule is to aim for about 68 degrees. Know what to do if the temperature gets too hot or cold during the meeting. A hot stuffy room or a room that is icy cold is a big distraction for people who are trying to make important decisions. Check the ventilation. Is the airflow adequate? Make sure the lighting is adequate and you have enough space and an electrical outlet for whatever equipment is needed.

DETERMINING THE SEATING ARRANGEMENT

The seating arrangement of the room depends on the objectives of the meeting. The five basic seating arrangements are rectangular, circular, oval, u-shaped, and semicircular. Figure 15.4 depicts these seating arrangements.

The rectangular arrangement allows the leader to maintain control since she or he sits at the head of the table. This arrangement is also effective when particpants will be talking in groups of two or three. Individuals seated next to or opposite each other have a chance to discuss issues as they arise. However, if discussion is

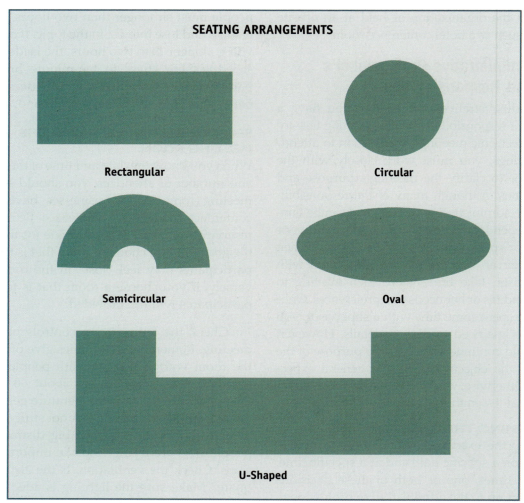

SEATING ARRANGEMENTS

Rectangular

Circular

Semicircular

Oval

U-Shaped

FIGURE 15.4 Seating Arrangements

important, the table should not be too long. A long table may make communication difficult because people cannot see the nonverbal behavior of other participants. A long table may also prevent the leader from taking part in discussions if he or she is seated away from other participants. The rectangular arrangement is most effective in formal meetings.

The circular and oval arrangements work best when the purpose of the meeting is to generate ideas and discussion and the meeting is relatively informal. These arrangements encourage togetherness, shared communication, and participation. Attendees can make direct eye contact with

everyone else in the group. Communication channels are considered equal among all participants since no one person is in a dominant position.

The u-shaped and semicircular arrangements work well for small groups of six to eight people. The leader retains moderate control since he or she is in a dominant position. The two arrangements are also good for showing visuals because the visual can be positioned at the front of the configuration.

Make certain you have enough chairs for the number of participants who are scheduled to attend. You do not want to have extra chairs;

they just get in the way, and it appears as though some people failed to attend. You also do not want to have too few chairs; it appears as though you did not plan properly.

PREPARING THE MEETING AGENDA

All meeting participants should know the purpose and plan of action before coming to a meeting. An **agenda** is an outline of the procedures or the order of business to be followed during a meeting. Participants should receive a detailed agenda at least a day (preferably a week) before the scheduled meeting. It is a good idea to send out the agenda with the meeting notice. The agenda should include the following information:

- Name of the meeting or group
- Date of the meeting
- Start and end times
- Location of the meeting
- Order of agenda items
- Individual responsible for presenting the agenda item
- Expected action on agenda items
- Background materials (if necessary)

You can also allocate a particular time for each item on the agenda. Although doing this is not essential, it does remind people of the importance of time and of adhering to a schedule. The order of the agenda items can vary. Some people believe the most difficult items should be presented first; others think they should be presented last. Check with your supervisor to determine the order that he or she prefers.

The action that is expected on the agenda items should be noted. Notice in Figure 15.5 that the word ACTION is listed after specific agenda items. This word denotes that a decision will be made on the item. This approach helps participants know that they should come to the meeting prepared to make a decision.

PREPARING MEETING NOTICES

If the meeting is scheduled within the organization, notify participants by email or through an interoffice memorandum. If you have access to employees' individual online calendars, you can check the schedules of meeting participants to determine whether they are free at the time of the meeting. Be certain the meeting notification includes the following information:

- Purpose and objectives of the meeting
- Meeting agenda
- Location, date, and time
- Background information
- Assigned materials for preparation

You may be responsible for following up on meeting notices. Although you have asked people to let you know if they cannot attend, not everyone will respond. Email or telephone the people who have not responded to determine if they will be present. You also need to let your supervisor know who will be attending the meeting and who will be late. If a number of people are unable to attend, inform your supervisor. He or she may choose to change the meeting time and/or date.

PREPARING MATERIALS FOR THE LEADER

Materials for the leader should include:

- The meeting notice with a list of the people who will attend.
- Materials that have been sent out before the meeting.
- Notes that are needed at the meeting.
- Visuals or handouts.

If the leader is a participant in an off-site meeting, you may need to include directions to the meeting location. A variety of Internet sites are available that provide maps, driving directions, and traffic reports.

PREPARING MATERIALS FOR ATTENDEES

Background materials should be sent to attendees with the meeting notice and agenda. If handouts are to be distributed during the meeting, prepare them well in advance of the meeting. If the handouts are made up of several pages, place them in individual folders. Sometimes attendees

MEETING AGENDA

PLANNING MEETING
CONFERENCE ROOM C

April 20, 20--

1. Review of accomplishments on department objectives
    for the last six month (30 minutes) .... All Managers

2. Proposed budget for next year (20 minutes).. Juan Menendez

3. Goals for the next six months (1 hour) ACTION.. All Managers

4. Objective planning timelines (15 minutes) ACTION .... Juan Menendez

FIGURE 15.5 Meeting Agenda

Make sure all necessary equipment is provided for a meeting.

are expected to take notes. If so, you might provide a pad of paper in the folder. Extra pencils and pens should be made available for attendees.

ORDERING EQUIPMENT

Determine what equipment, if any, is needed for the meeting. Follow through to make sure the equipment is available. It is a good idea to make a list of the necessary equipment and note on the list the arrangements that have been made. List the person responsible for obtaining each item. If it is your responsibility, note that. Before the meeting begins, take your list to the room and check it against the equipment there.

ORDERING FOOD AND BEVERAGES

For a morning meeting, coffee, tea, and juice can be provided for participants. Water should also be available. If it is an afternoon meeting, you may want to provide coffee and/or soft drinks. It is not necessary to provide beverages. Check with your supervisor to see what he or she prefers.

For a luncheon meeting, you may have the responsibility of selecting the menu, calling the caterer, and arranging for the meal to be delivered. The lunch should be light if you expect the participants to work afterward; a heavy meal often makes people sleepy. If you are aware of participants who have special dietary needs, make special accommodations for them. The caterer can usually recommend a substitute meal.

For a dinner meeting, you may work with an outside caterer or with hotel staff. You are usually responsible for selecting the menu. If you know the attendees, consider their preferences when selecting the food.

DUTIES DURING THE MEETING

The administrative professional's responsibilities during the meeting are varied. You may be expected to greet guests and introduce them to other participants. Your role is to make them feel comfortable and welcome.

Your main responsibility during the meeting is to take the **minutes** (a written record of a meeting). Sit near the leader so you can clearly hear what is being said. You need to note the

A laptop is an efficient way to record the minutes of a meeting.

names of the people in attendance and those who are absent. A laptop computer can be an efficient way for you to record the proceedings of a meeting. With a laptop, the minutes are almost ready to print (with minor editing) and distribute once you leave the meeting.

If you are taking the minutes of an organizational meeting, such as a board meeting or a professional group, the proceedings are recorded in a formal manner. Minutes contain a record of important matters that are presented in the meeting. Although you do not need to record the entire minutes verbatim, you must record motions verbatim and all other pertinent information. Items that should be included in the minutes are as follows:

- Date, time, and place of the meeting
- Name of the group
- Name of the presiding officer
- Members present and absent

- Approval or correction of the minutes from the previous meeting
- Reports of committees, officers, or individuals
- Motions made, including the name of the person who made the motion, the name of the person who seconded it, and an indication of whether it passed or failed
- Items on which action needs to be taken and the person responsible for taking the action
- A concise summary of the important points of discussion
- The date and time of the next meeting (if one is scheduled)
- The name and title of the person who will be signing the minutes (the secretary) along with a signature line

Minutes should be prepared in a timely manner, usually 24 to 48 hours after the meeting. Although there is no set format for minutes, some general guidelines should be followed.

- Minutes are generally single-spaced. Margins should be at least 1 inch. If the minutes are to be placed in a bound book, the left margin should be 1½ inches.
- Capitalize and center the heading.
- Subject captions (the agenda's subject captions may be used) should be used for ease in locating various sections of the minutes.
- Use businesslike language. Do not include personal opinions or comments.
- List verbatim any motions made.
- Minutes may or may not be signed. Minutes of board meetings and professional organizations are generally signed. However, routine minutes of meetings within a business may not be signed. If minutes are to be signed, a signature line should be provided.

Professional Pointers

You may be asked to present at meetings within your organizations and at meetings of professional organizations. The following pointers can help you present effectively.

- Thoroughly research the topic you are presenting well in advance of the meeting.

- Secure supporting data and documents you can use to clarify the information you are presenting.

- Anticipate the kinds of questions that may be asked about the subject. Write the questions down and outline your answers. This approach will help you remember the issues and be better prepared when you are asked a question.

- Explain your topics in terms the group can understand.

- Be familiar with parliamentary procedure so you do not breach a rule.

- Be concise; do not ramble.

- Exhibit confidence in yourself and your topic.

ROUTINE FOLLOW-UP TASKS

Some routine tasks should be performed after a meeting, including these:

- Check the meeting room to see that it is left in good order. Return all equipment. See that additional chairs or tables are removed from the room. Clean up any papers and materials left in the room. If the room needs to be cleaned, notify the cleaning staff.
- Notify individuals who were not present at the meeting but were given duties or assignments.
- Note on your calendar items that require future attention.
- Note on the next meeting agenda any items that need to be considered at that meeting.
- Evaluate the meeting. Consider how you might improve the arrangements for the next meeting. Make notes for your files so you can review them before the next meeting.

The Leader's Responsibilities

To conduct an effective meeting, a leader who is skilled in running a meeting should be put in charge. She or he must understand the purpose of the meeting and be able to engage people in effective conversation around the issues. The leader must also be able to bring closure to the agreed-upon objectives.

MAKE THE PURPOSE AND OBJECTIVES CLEAR

As you have already learned, the purpose of the meeting must be clearly established. The leader of the meeting does not necessarily establish the purpose. For example, assume that an executive of a company calls a meeting. He or she determines what the purpose is before the meeting and makes that purpose clear in writing. Although the executive is the leader of the meeting, he or she may choose to have someone else preside over the meeting. Once the purpose of the meeting is established and sent out in writing to the participants by the executive, the leader's responsibility is to reiterate the purpose at the beginning of the meeting. The leader should also let the participants know the objectives of the meeting—what must be accomplished at the meeting and what must be completed after the meeting.

ADHERE TO THE AGENDA

The leader is responsible for keeping the participants focused on the agenda. If the attendees stray from the agenda, the leader must sensitively but firmly bring them back to the agenda. The leader might say, "Thank you for your comments about that issue. We can put that issue on the agenda for a future meeting. Now let's continue with the agenda for today."

MANAGE TIME

The leader must begin the meeting on time, even if several people are not present. Waiting for others to arrive is not fair to the individuals who have made an effort to be on time. Just as important as starting on time is ending on time. The leader must be sensitive to other commitments of participants. Time frames, both beginning and ending, should be established when the notice of the meeting is sent out. The leader is responsible for maintaining these time commitments.

ENCOURAGE PARTICIPATION

Before participants are invited to a meeting, considerable thought must be given to who should attend. The leader should guide, mediate, probe, and stimulate discussion. He or she should allow time for thoughts to emerge. Any group discussion is strengthened by diversity of thinking. The leader should encourage participation from those who may not otherwise express their views during meetings. The leader can use well-placed questions to draw out less-talkative participants.

The leader is also responsible for making sure that one or two attendees do not dominate the discussion. The leader can guide a balanced and controlled discussion by adhering to the following suggestions.

- Keep the participants focused on the agenda.
- Encourage participation from everyone even if the opinions being expressed are about highly volatile issues.

- Limit the domination of any one person in the meeting.
- Positively reinforce all individuals for their contributions.
- Keep the discussions moving toward the objectives and outcomes that have been determined.

REACH DECISIONS

The leader is responsible for helping the participants reach a decision about the issue, problem, or direction. Remember that every effective meeting has a purpose and objectives, from which outcomes occur. For example, assume you are setting goals for your department for the next year. One of your goals is to increase the number of customers by 5 percent. How are you going to meet this objective? What steps will you take? Merely saying that a goal is to increase the number of customers does not help the objective get accomplished. Detailed steps as to how, when, and by whom it will be done bring closure to the objective.

EVALUATE THE MEETING

It is not necessary to complete a formal evaluation for informal meetings within an organization. However, an informal evaluation by the leader (and possibly by the participants) should be completed. The attendees are usually very forthright. They may even tell the leader they found the meeting a waste of time. If an attendee makes such a statement, the leader should seek clarification about what the person meant. Regardless of the method of evaluation, after the meeting, the leader should ask himself or herself the following questions.

- Were the attendees participatory?
- Was the nonverbal behavior positive?
- Were the participants creative problem solvers?
- Did the participants exhibit a high energy level?
- Was the purpose of the meeting satisfied?
- Were appropriate decisions made?
- Can I improve on how I handled the issues, the people, or the meeting in general?

```
                    MEETING EVALUATION FORM

                                                        Yes      No

    1.  Were the purpose and objectives of the meeting accomplished?    ☐       ☐
    2.  Was the agenda received in time to prepare for the meeting?     ☐       ☐
    3.  Did the leader adhere to the agenda?                            ☐       ☐
    4.  Were the appropriate people included in the meeting?            ☐       ☐
    5.  Did the leader encourage participation by all members?          ☐       ☐
    6.  Did participants listen to one another?                         ☐       ☐
    7.  Did the meeting start on time?                                  ☐       ☐
    8.  Did the meeting end on time?                                    ☐       ☐
    9.  Did the leader help bring closure to the objectives?            ☐       ☐
   10.  Were decisions consistent with the purpose and objectives of the meeting?  ☐   ☐
```

FIGURE 15.6 Meeting Evaluation Form

If the meeting is relatively formal, the leader may ask participants to fill out an evaluation form, as shown in Figure 15.6.

Participants' Responsibilities

As a leader has responsibilities, so do the participants. Their roles are much broader than just attending the meeting. Their responsibilities begin before the meeting and continue after the meeting.

BEFORE THE MEETING

Before the meeting, participants are responsible for responding to the meeting notice in a timely manner. In addition, they are responsible for reading any materials that were distributed before the meeting. Participants should make sure they understand the purpose of the meeting and evaluate the meeting materials in relation to the purpose of the meeting. Participants must understand that they have been included in the meeting because the executive or leader believes they have something to contribute. Therefore, they must take their role seriously. If participants have questions before the meeting, they should contact the leader for clarification.

DURING THE MEETING

Participants also have the following responsibilities during the meeting.

- Arrive on time.
- Adhere to the agenda.
- Make contributions.
- Listen to other participants' contributions and respond if they have additional information.
- Respect the leader's role.
- Avoid dominating the discussion.
- Avoid being judgmental of others' comments.
- Be courteous to each individual in the meeting.
- Take notes, if necessary.

AFTER THE MEETING

Once the meeting is over, a participant's responsibilities do not end. The participant may be responsible for research, study, or action before the next meeting. The participant may also be asked to work with a small group of people to bring back a recommendation to the next meeting. Whatever follow-up is necessary by the participant, he or she must be committed to carrying out those responsibilities in a timely manner.

Conferences and Conventions

A conference is much larger in scope and has many more participants than a meeting. For example, a company or companies may hold a national sales

Conferences and conventions have many more participants than typical business meetings.

conference each year to introduce and market the company's new products. Executives may belong to professional organizations in their field of expertise, such as accounting, financial management, or human resources. Many professional organizations hold at least one conference a year, and executives are encouraged to participate as a means of staying current in their field. As an administrative professional, you may belong to a professional organization such as the International Association of Administrative Professionals (IAAP) or NALS, the association for legal professionals. Your role as an administrative professional may be to plan or help plan a national conference.

Before the Event

Preparing for a regional or national conference takes months of work, and the planning is extremely important. Good planning will ensure a smooth, successful conference; poor planning will result in a disorganized, ineffective conference. Two of the most important considerations are to determine the location and to arrange for

meeting facilities. Once the location has been determined, you can contact a variety of agencies to obtain information that will assist you in your planning.

- Contact the chamber of commerce in the city under consideration. Ask for information about the city and appropriate conference facilities. You can use the Internet to do this.
- Request conference planning guides from hotels and conference centers that will provide you with floor plans of the facilities, dining and catering services, price lists of rooms, and layouts of meeting rooms.

It is important to know how many people are expected to attend overall and approximately how many people will attend each session so rooms large enough to accommodate the attendees can be reserved.

If outside presenters will be speaking at the conference, you may be asked to make their travel arrangements. You should determine the type of accommodations required—room arrangements (single, double, queen- or king-size bed), flight preferences, arrival and departure times, rental car needs, and so on. If an individual is expected to arrive late at a hotel, the hotel should be notified to hold the reservation for late arrival. Find out if someone from the organization will pick up the guests when they arrive in town. If so, the designated person should be given the name(s), times of arrival, flight numbers, hotel accommodations, and other relevant information.

A preregistration period usually takes place during which people can register for the conference (sometimes at a reduced cost). As an administrative professional, you may be responsible for designing the registration form, sending it out, and handling the completed registration forms. You should create a database of registrants if you are responsible for the preparation of name tags, folders, or envelopes containing tickets for special events. You may also be asked to assist with registration at the conference. If the conference is a large one, several individuals may be needed to staff the registration tables.

During the Event

Your responsibilities during the conference may include running errands, delivering messages to participants, and solving problems that arise. Other responsibilities may include checking room arrangements, equipment needs, meal arrangements, and so on. At a conference, you are a representative of the company or organization for which you work. You must present a positive image at all times. Keep a smile on your face, and handle even the most difficult situations with poise and confidence.

After the Event

After the conference, your basic duties involve cleaning up and following up. You may need to assist speakers and guests with transportation to the airport, write letters of appreciation to presenters, and process expense reports.

You may also be responsible for making sure that the proceedings of the conference are published and mailed to the participants. Generally, you are not responsible for the actual writing of the conference proceedings, but you may be asked to work with the conference reporters in producing a comprehensive report based on taped conference sessions. If papers are presented at a conference, each presenter is usually asked to submit his or her paper before the conference. Copies of the papers may then be provided for the participants at the meeting. As a final responsibility, you may be asked to keep a record of problems that occurred and make recommendations for future conferences.

Summary

To reinforce what you have learned in this chapter, study this summary.

- An effective meeting is one in which there is a definite need for the meeting, the purpose is stated and understood by all participants, the appropriate people are in attendance, an agenda is prepared and followed, all members participate, and outcomes are achieved as a result of the meeting.

- Typical business meetings include staff meetings, committee meetings, project team meetings, customer/client meetings, board of directors meetings, conventions, and conferences.

- Face-to-face meetings continue to exist and are more productive than electronic meetings in some situations.

- Teleconferencing opportunities continue to increase because of ongoing globalization of corporations and the increased availability of conferencing and integration tools.

- International meetings are quite common and leaders and participants must give considerable attention to the cultural differences that exist.

- The executive's role in meetings is to determine the purpose of the meeting, set the objectives, determine who should attend, plan the agenda, and establish the time and place.

- The administrative professional has a variety of roles to fulfill when preparing for a meeting. The administrative professional may also be requested to take minutes of the meeting and to perform routine follow-up tasks.

- The leader's meeting responsibilities include making the purpose and objectives clear, adhering to the agenda, managing time, encouraging participation, helping the group reach decisions, and evaluating the meeting.

- Participants' responsibilities include preparing for the meeting, contributing appropriately during the meeting, and completing assigned tasks after the meeting.

- A conference or convention is much larger in scope and has many more participants than a meeting.

- The administrative professional's responsibilities for conferences and conventions may include responsibilities before, during, and after the event.

What's the Problem?

Joaquin Gomez is the mailroom supervisor at United Pharmaceuticals. Joaquin holds bimonthly staff meetings with his mailroom team to discuss mailroom operations and customer service issues. Joaquin makes sure his staff is prepared for any problems that arise in the mailroom and within the departments while mailroom personnel are collecting and delivering mail. Over the last two years, problems have been rare since any concerns mentioned to the staff are presented and discussed at the staff meetings. Joaquin's goal is to address the concern rather than to assign blame.

Delores Steinhoff, the copy center manager, is frustrated with the negative attitude that seems to exist within the organization about the copy center. In fact, there are constant complaints by employees about the staff's inability to meet deadlines, the poor quality of jobs, and the negative attitudes of employees. Copy center staff meetings focus on complaints about work schedules, inadequate time to meet deadlines, and unreasonable staff expectations. In an attempt to learn ways to improve copy center staff meetings, Delores has asked to sit in on Joaquin's next staff meeting. After the meeting, Delores tells Joaquin that she is impressed with the positive and productive meeting and asks for advice.

What advice can Joaquin give Delores to help her make her staff meetings more effective?

Let's Discuss

1. Describe the characteristics of an effective meeting.
2. List and describe the typical types of business meetings.
3. List the components of an effective agenda.
4. List the responsibilities of the meeting leader in conducting an effective meeting.
5. Describe the responsibilities of the administrative professional before a conference.

Critical-Thinking Activity

Carol has been in charge of the monthly staff meeting for the past six months. Although Carol has been a participant in these meetings for the last three years, her recent promotion has put her in charge. For as long as Carol can remember, the meetings have been held on the first Tuesday of the month from 10 a.m. to noon. All sales representatives assigned to Carol (about twenty) are expected to attend.

Carol believes the meetings in the past were boring, and she decides to take a new approach. She believes the meetings were too scheduled and decides to allow her staff time to chat informally before she begins the meetings. She believes the agendas were too restrictive and decides that she will allow her staff to use this meeting time to "blow off steam."

Carol believes the first meeting went well. All sales representatives were there at 10 a.m. Carol started the meeting at 10:15 a.m. after giving everyone a few minutes to chat. Several employees had questions about the health insurance policy, and Carol answered them to the best of her ability. Without the policy information in front of her, however, she found a few questions difficult to answer. Carol promised to get the answers and share them at the next meeting. Next, several individuals were interested in the new telework program that had been adopted by the organization. Although Carol had read the policy, she was not familiar with all the details. Thankfully, Alicia Greene, who was involved in the pilot program six years ago, was able to provide background information and answer specific questions about the new program. In fact, Alicia offered to prepare a presentation for next month's meeting that would explain the company's policies.

Carol thought the second meeting was productive as well. Several employees had questions about the status of recycling within the organization, and Carol was able to answer them. Staff members were also interested in the upcoming holiday party, and the details of that event were discussed as well. There were a few questions that Carol could not answer about the sexual harassment policy, but Carol suggested that the company attorney make a presentation at the next meeting.

The next few meetings were conducted in a similar open manner. Employees asked questions and Carol attempted to answer them. Unanswered questions that were asked in previous meetings were asked again, and Carol still did not have the answer. Alicia Greene continued to volunteer to make a presentation and Carol indicated that she would contact her later.

By the sixth meeting, there was an obvious change in the tone of the meeting. Most participants did not arrive until 10:20 and Carol could not get the meeting going until after 10:30. Staff members did not participate in the topic discussions, but chatted with coworkers instead. Carol listened to complaint after complaint, becoming frustrated because so little was accomplished.

What did Carol do wrong? How can Carol structure future staff meetings so that they are more productive?

Vocabulary Review

Open the *Word* file *CH15 Vocabulary* found on the Student CD. Complete the vocabulary review for Chapter 15.

English and Word Usage Drill

Complete the English and Word Usage Drill for Chapter 15 found in the *Applications Workbook*.

Workplace Applications

15-1 Prepare and Conduct a Meeting

internet

team building

(Goals 3 and 4)

1. Work with five or six classmates to complete this application. Your task is to prepare for and conduct or participate in an effective 20- to 30-minute informational meeting. The purpose of the meeting is to increase the group's knowledge about a topic that is related to the material covered in this chapter. Examples include audioconferencing, videoconferencing, online meetings, preparing an agenda, meeting types, and international meetings. Each group must select a different topic.

2. Using the Internet or other resources, conduct research on the topic of the meeting. Incorporate information from at least two articles or Websites in your meeting. (Give credit to the information sources.)

3. As a group, prepare a meeting notice, an agenda, and any written materials (handouts) that are necessary for the meeting prior to the meeting.

4. Decide which team member will lead the meeting. Conduct or participate in the meeting with your team. Submit a copy of all written materials to your instructor.

15-2 Evaluate a Meeting

(Goal 4)

1. Work with the same classmates that you worked with in Workplace Application 15-1.

2. As a team, create an appropriate evaluation form to evaluate the effectiveness of your meeting. Each team member should complete the form individually, and then the team should discuss all the forms.

3. As a team, prepare a memo to your instructor that describes the effectiveness of the meeting. Make recommendations as to changes you would make in the future to have more effective meetings. Use the *Word* file *Memo Form* found on the Student CD to prepare the memo.

team building

15-3 Attend and Evaluate a Meeting

(Goals 1, 2, and 4)

1. Attend a meeting, conference, or convention of a professional organization or group in your area.

2. Prepare a memo report to your instructor. Use the *Word* file *Memo Form* found on the Student CD to prepare the report. Address three of the following questions and add two additional questions of your own.

   - What type of meeting did you attend?

   - Was the agenda effective? Was the agenda followed?

   - Was the meeting leader effective? Why or why not?

   - Did the meeting leader effectively manage the meeting time?

   - Was the meeting room appropriate for the meeting? Why or why not?

   - Did the people attending the meeting participate effectively? Why or why not?

15-4 Create a Conference Flyer

(Goal 3)

Your supervisor, Amando Hinojosa, is in charge of his research group's annual conference next year. He has asked that you create a flyer announcing the event.

e-portfolio

1. Create a one-page flyer announcing the conference that can be distributed to prospective participants. Use the following information when preparing the flyer:

   - The event title is *Annual Research Conference*.

   - The conference will be held on the first Tuesday, Wednesday, and Thursday in April of next year.

   - The conference will be held in Dallas, Texas, at the Dallas Convention Center.

   - Several product vendors will be present on Tuesday and Wednesday.

- There will be a recognition banquet on Wednesday evening.

- A motivational keynote speaker will open the conference on Tuesday.

- The opening conference session is at 3 p.m. on Tuesday.

- Participants will be able to choose from over 30 breakout sessions.

- Several hands-on computer workshops will be available.

2. Use graphics, fonts, and other design elements to create an attractive flyer. Print the completed flyer.

Assessment of Chapter 15 Goals

Did you successfully complete the chapter goals? Evaluate yourself by filling out the form found in Chapter 15 of the *Applications Workbook*.

Travel Arrangements

Domestic Travel

The current global economy requires that business be conducted around the world, 24 hours a day, 7 days a week, 365 days a year. Although a great deal of business is now effectively and efficiently conducted through telecommunications technology as discussed in Chapter 12, many times only a face-to-face meeting will do. In these instances, whether the client or business partner is across town, across the state, across the country, or across the ocean, travel arrangements and reservations must be made.

Part of your job as an administrative professional is to make travel arrangements. To do this effectively, you must make appropriate choices with regard to travel by air, car, or rail. You must also handle reservations for hotels and restaurants and other issues related to travel. In addition, you must become familiar with the many travel services that are available. This chapter will help you understand your options and become proficient at handling travel-related tasks.

In an effort to save time, most executives prefer to travel by air. However, occasionally they must travel by car and rail. Therefore, this chapter deals mainly with air travel, with brief sections that include information about car and rail travel.

Air Travel

The flying public today is no longer made up mainly of business executives and those individuals with higher incomes. Air travel is a common mode of transportation for both business and personal travel. The business traveler, however, is a major part of the airlines' clientele, and airlines offer a variety of seating options, flight schedules, and onboard services to accommodate these customers.

FLIGHT CLASSIFICATIONS

The three classes of flight accommodations are first class, business class, and economy/coach class. Some airlines offer all three classes of flights while other airlines offer coach class only. Regional airlines, such as Southwest Airlines and American Eagle, typically offer only one class of flight.

First-class accommodations are the most expensive and luxurious of the flight classifications. First-class passengers have the most comfortable seats and receive services that are not always offered to other passengers. First-class customers have special check-in zones at the airport where they are able to board and exit the flight before other passengers. Alcoholic and non-alcoholic drinks are available immediately upon boarding the aircraft. There is no additional cost for beverages, and they are served in glass containers. Meals are not always available. However, when meals are served, cloth napkins, silverware, and china are used. Entertainment may be offered through flat-panel monitors mounted in the seatback or armrest. Headsets for listening to music may also be provided. The seats are more comfortable because they are wider and have more legroom. There are also more flight attendants per customer than in other flight classifications, which means greater attention and service for each flyer. Attendants take passengers' coats and hang them up; they also store passenger's parcels in overhead bins.

Business-class accommodations are a level of air accommodations that fall between first class and economy class. Designed specifically for passengers traveling for business purposes, this travel classification is not available on all commercial airlines or on all flights. Typically, business class is offered on long-distance flights such as those between New York and the cities on the west coast. Business-class passengers are able to board the plane before economy-class passengers and enjoy wider and more comfortable seats than those in economy class. Business services such as personal video, laptop power ports, and satellite phones may be available. Complimentary coffee, juices, and other non-alcoholic beverages are provided, and meals may be available on international flights.

Economy-class accommodations are typically the lowest-priced seats on the airplane. This accommodation classification is also called coach class or tourist class. Economy-class seats are located in the main cabin area and are typically closer together than seats found in both first class and business class. Fewer flight attendants are available to serve the needs of customers. Although complimentary soft drinks, juice, tea, and coffee may be available, other food and beverage options may be available only at a cost. In-flight entertainment may be available, but customers may be required to purchase or rent headphones or equipment.

With increased emphasis on reducing the expense of air travel, several low-fare airlines have been created that offer only economy-class accommodations. Low-fare airlines can typically fly for less because they have eliminated many of the traditional passenger services. In addition, low-fare airlines may offer limited flight schedules, fly into secondary airports, and serve fewer destinations.

TICKETING

An **e-ticket** is an electronic ticket that represents the purchase of a seat on a passenger airline, usually through a Website or by telephone. This type of ticket is quickly replacing paper tickets. Because the purchase of an e-ticket takes place online the most common method of delivering e-tickets to customers is by email or fax. E-tickets may be presented at airport ticket counters to obtain boarding passes. Also, many airports now have self-service kiosks available near ticket counters. Customers insert flight information

SECURITY MEASURES

- Watch your bags and personal belongings at all times.

- Do not accept packages from strangers.

- Report unattended bags or packages to airport security.

- Report suspicious activities and individuals to airport security.

- Be prepared to take your laptop from its case so it can be x-rayed separately.

- Check to be certain you have all your belongings before you leave the security area—wallets, keys, jewelry, cell phones, and so on.

FIGURE 16.1 Air travel requires observing several security measures.

from their e-ticket and receive a boarding pass from the machine. This option eliminates standing in lines at the airline ticket counter.

Occasionally it is necessary to change or cancel flight reservations. Travelers may be charged a penalty for changing to another flight. The policy for changes or cancellations is usually described online at the airline's Website or at the time of purchase. Some airlines will let you bank the ticket for future flights, with a small penalty charged. When a change is made because of airplane mechanical difficulty or other issues that cause the airline to change or cancel the flight, you are not charged. Since you are usually inconvenienced by such a change, the airlines attempt to make the situation as painless as possible. If the change results in your having to stay overnight, the airlines will generally pay for your hotel and give you vouchers for food.

AIRLINE SECURITY

Since the events of 9/11, America's airports have increased their levels of security. Everyone who travels by air must go through airport security checkpoints and their baggage must go through security checkpoints as well. These checkpoints were developed to help prevent passengers from bringing anything on a plane that would enable them to take it over or destroy it. A variety of security precautions are currently in place at airports across the United States. Being knowledgeable about security measures is important for business travelers. Figure 16.1 lists security measures that should be observed when a business traveler is waiting to board a flight.

The following suggestions will help the business traveler best cope with the increased security procedures at airports.

- Arrive early. Most airlines advise arriving at the airport up to two hours before your scheduled departure. If you have special needs or concerns, you may need to arrive even earlier.

- Bring proper identification. An acceptable government-issued photo identification is required. This identification may include a state-issued driver's license, state ID card, military ID card, or a passport.

- Avoid the ticket counter. A traveler can avoid the ticket counter by printing a boarding pass before arriving at the airport. Having only a carry-on bag will also allow you to bypass the ticket counter.

- Check your bags for prohibited items. A list of prohibited items is available on most airline Websites. Take the time to make sure you are following the established regulations since violating these rules is a criminal offense.

- Follow the screening guidelines. Since all passengers must be screened, it is in the traveler's best interest to help make this process go smoothly. Keep your identification and boarding pass in a convenient location. Since all metal must be identified, avoid wearing items that contain metal. Wear shoes that can be removed easily.

© Matthew Staver / Bloomberg News / Landov

Business travelers should be prepared to participate in airport security screenings.

AIRLINE CLUBS

For the frequent business traveler, membership in an airline club may be a worthwhile investment. Major airlines provide these clubs in large airports, and membership is available through the individual airlines. Membership fees vary. Some airlines offer daily passes that allow entry into any of their clubs during a 24-hour period and one-time admittance passes that allow entry into a single club. A variety of travel perks accompany an airline club, including access to the following:

- Computer equipment, fax, and copy machines
- Conference rooms and lounge space
- Reading material
- Complimentary soft drinks, juice, and coffee
- Alcoholic beverages for purchase
- Pastries and snacks
- Assistance with airline reservations
- VIP transportation to a departure terminal

PARKING SERVICES

Large airports generally provide free shuttle service from airport locations; however, you are charged for parking your car. The fee is based on the location of your car, with parking lots closer to the airport being more expensive, and the time your car is in the lot.

Because parking at an airport for an extended period can become expensive, private shuttle services in large cities occupy a profitable business niche. Shuttle buses run frequently, with generally no more than a ten-minute wait between runs.

COMPANY-OWNED AND CHARTERED PLANES

Large corporations may have their own plane or fleet of planes if the amount of travel within the company makes it advantageous to do so. Pilots employed by the organization fly the planes, which are housed adjacent to local airports.

Some small airlines specialize in privately chartered jet service. In this instance, a business would rent an entire airplane rather than seats on a commercial flight. Chartered planes are generally small, since most private chartering is for small groups of people. Sometimes called air taxis, chartered planes may be housed at locations adjacent to regular airports and use the same takeoff and landing runways as the major airlines. Food is often available on these jets for an additional cost; flight attendants are generally not available.

Ground Transportation

Once executives arrive at their destination, they may need some type of ground transportation to their hotel. That transportation may be a taxi or shuttle bus. When making arrangements, you should check taxi costs and the availability of shuttle services. Some hotels provide free shuttle services to and from the airport. Private vendors also offer shuttle services that may be less expensive than taxi services.

If executives must attend meetings at several locations during their stay, renting a car may be

Major airlines provide airline clubs in large airports that offer a variety of business amenities.

the most economical and convenient method of ground transportation. Car rental agencies are available at most airports. Cars may also be rented through airlines, travel agencies, or Websites. When renting a car, specify the make and model preferred, along with the date and time the car will be picked up and returned. Most car rental agencies have age restrictions. Check with the specific rental agency to determine the specific age requirements. For example, some may require the renter to be at least twenty-one years old; others may require the renter to be at least twenty-five years old.

Hotel Reservations

Hotel reservations can be made through travel agents or airlines at no additional cost. Hotel reservations may also be made online. Most hotels have business rooms that are equipped with computers, copiers, faxes, and so forth. However, cellular phones, PDAs, and/or laptop computers are standard equipment for many traveling executives. Meeting rooms are also available in most hotels. If you are making hotel reservations for your employer, let the hotel reservations clerk know what equipment and/or meeting rooms

are needed. If the executive is going to be arriving late, give that information to the hotel clerk. Rooms can be released at a certain hour if reservations have not been confirmed for late arrival.

Car Travel

If an executive is traveling only a few hundred miles, he or she may prefer to travel by car. Most top-level executives use company-owned or leased cars with gasoline expenses paid by the organization. Other executives are reimbursed for mileage for any business-related travel.

Your responsibilities for a trip by car may include determining the best route to follow, making hotel reservations, and identifying restaurants along the way. The American Automobile Association (AAA) provides map services along with hotel and restaurant information. However, it is necessary to be a member of AAA to get these services. As an alternative, many Internet sites are available that provide this kind of information. Some sites provide driving directions between two addresses, lists of restaurants in particular cities, temperatures, and points of interest in specific geographic locations.

© Jeff Greenberg / PhotoEdit

Hotel shuttle services are an economical alternative to taxis.

focus on Hotel Security Considerations

When staying in a hotel, it is important to pay attention to your personal security and safety. To maintain your personal safety, do not discuss your business or travel plans in public areas where they may be overheard. Additional security considerations include the following items.

- Do not allow strangers in your hotel room. If you need to meet with someone you do not know, do it in a public place such as the hotel lobby or restaurant.

- Never leave exposed or unattended valuables in your hotel room. Keep valuables (money, jewelry, airplane tickets, credit cards, or passport) with you or place them in a hotel safe deposit box or room safe.

- Familiarize yourself with escape routes in case of fire or other emergency.

- Use the door chain or bolt lock whenever you are in your room.

- Use the peephole before opening the door to visitors.

- Do not discuss your room number while standing in the lobby.

- Keep track of your room key; never leave it on restaurant or lobby tables. If you lose your key, immediately ask that your room lock be changed.

- Keep your room neat so you will notice disturbed or missing items quickly.[1]

---

[1]"Personal Security—At Home, On the Street, While Traveling," U.S. Department of State; accessed September 15, 2007; available from http://www.state.gov/m/ds/rls/rpt/19773.htm.

Rail Travel

Rail travel is not often used for business travel because it takes more time than traveling by air. However, there may be times when rail travel is necessary. Rail travel is available to some parts of the United States but often does not extend into rural areas. First-class and sleeping accommodations are available, as well as coach accommodations for more economical travel.

International Travel

Because of the increasingly global nature of business, executives often must make trips abroad. As an administrative professional, you need to be knowledgeable about the cultural differences of the countries your employer is visiting. You also must know how to make arrangements for an international trip.

Cultural Differences

A basic understanding of the culture and business customs of the people in the country where your employer is traveling will help you make appropriate travel arrangements. Additionally, such information and knowledge can be advantageous as you work in a global world and encounter people from diverse backgrounds. Information about countries can be obtained from a variety of sources, including:

- *Consulates of the country to be visited.* Consulate Websites are available. Information concerning the Counsel General of the country, basic information about the country, and how to contact the Counsel General is given on these sites.

- *Travel books.* Travel books that contain information about local customs and business practices are available in bookstores and libraries.

- *Seminars and short courses.* Local colleges and universities often provide short courses or one-day seminars on the culture of various countries and tips on conducting business in specific countries. Online courses may also be available.

- *The Internet.* A number of Websites and articles are available that discuss international cultural differences.

General guidelines for international travel are given in Figure 16.2.

Appointments

If you are involved in setting up appointments or meetings for travelers, remember to take into consideration time zone differences. **Jet lag** (a feeling of exhaustion following a flight through several time zones) is a medical condition that results in prolonged periods of fatigue. Metabolism and medication schedules are upset, as are

---

GUIDELINES FOR INTERNATIONAL TRAVEL

- Learn the appropriate greeting for the people you will be visiting.

- Learn how to say *please* and *thank you* in the language of the country.

- Do not criticize the people or customs of the country you are visiting. Show appreciation for the music, art, and culture of the country.

- Remember that generally business is conducted more formally in other countries than it is in the United States.

- Dress appropriately—generally, business suits for men and conservative dresses or suits for women. Although dress in the United States has become more casual, you cannot assume that this is true in other countries.

- Eat the food offered to you. Do not ask what you are being served. Show appreciation to the host.

- Be courteous and respectful at all times.

FIGURE 16.2 International Travel Guidelines

eating and sleeping cycles. As a result, jet lag can greatly restrict an executive's effectiveness. Give the traveler an extra day to recover from the trip before scheduling important meetings. However, if the traveler does not have the luxury of a full day to recover before appointments, certain techniques may help with jet lag. For example, when traveling west, two or three days before the flight the traveler can postpone bedtime by two or three hours. When traveling east, two or three days before the flight the traveler should retire a couple of hours earlier than normal. At the same time, the traveler can also start shifting mealtimes in the direction of those of the destination city. Although the body clock still must adapt, less jet lag occurs by using these techniques.

If possible, avoid scheduling appointments the day before the traveler leaves on a trip and the day the traveler returns from a trip. The day before a trip is usually needed for final preparations. When the traveler returns from a trip, she or he must contend with time zone changes and handle business issues that came up while she or he was away.

Business Gifts

In some countries business gifts are expected; in others business gifts are not appropriate. If a business gift is given, it should be a small item. A nice pen or memento representative of the United States could be considered. However, executives must be aware of the customs and taboos when giving gifts to avoid offending someone without knowing it. Additional details concerning gift giving are presented in Figure 16.3.

Flight Classifications

International flight classifications are the same as domestic air travel. Classes of flight are first class and economy or coach, with business class available on most international flights. Weight and size restrictions for luggage may vary

Jet lag is a medical condition that should be considered when making international appointments.

© Flying Colours Ltd / Photodisc / Getty Images

International Business Cards

Executives who frequently do business with international customers should have business cards with their information printed in English on one side of the card and the language of the country they are visiting on the other side of the card. The executives from the country visited also have cards and expect to exchange them. Different cultures have different customs associated with the exchange of business cards. For example, in Asia the exchange of cards is often quite a ceremony. Japanese executives take time to read the card and store it in a special case. The Japanese consider it rude to simply take the card and put it in a pocket.

> ## GIFT ETIQUETTE
>
> - In English-speaking countries (including Britain, Ireland, Canada, and Australia), gifts are not expected and might even be considered inappropriate. Business gifts are also rarely exchanged in Spain and France.
>
> - Gift giving is important in Hong Kong, Japan, the Philippines, Russia, and Eastern European countries.
>
> - In Filipino business culture, exchanging gifts is an essential step in solidifying business ties.
>
> - In Japan, the best time to present a gift is toward the end of your visit.
>
> - When giving gifts, be certain the gift is made in the United States. For example, do not give a gift to an individual from Japan that was made in Japan.
>
> - Appropriate gifts include pens or pen-and-pencil sets. Items from your home state and books of historical areas of your state are also appropriate.
>
> - Photo albums containing pictures of the people you met on your trip are appropriate gifts.
>
> - Flowers are not a universally acceptable gift for a host. If flowers are acceptable, the color and type of flower are important. For example, in Italy, chrysanthemums are displayed mainly at funerals. In Brazil, purple flowers signify death.

FIGURE 16.3 Observe the proper etiquette related to gifts when traveling internationally.

slightly from one airline to another. When traveling abroad, executives must arrive at the airport earlier than normal; most airlines suggest arriving two hours before the scheduled international flight. Figure 16.4 lists several international travel tips.

Passports

A **passport** is an official government document that certifies the identity and citizenship of an individual and grants the person permission to travel abroad. A passport is required in most countries outside the United States. Check with a local travel agent to determine if the country being visited requires a passport. However, even if a country does not require a passport, having one is a good idea because it shows proof of citizenship.

Passport application forms can be obtained from the Web or a passport acceptance facility, which includes federal, state, and probate courts; post offices; some public libraries; and a number of county and municipal offices located throughout the United States. When applying for your first passport, you must have two photographs of yourself, proof of U.S. citizenship, and photo identification such as a driver's license.

You can renew a passport by mail with the following stipulations:

- If the passport has not been altered or damaged
- If you received the passport within the past 15 years
- If you were over age 16 when it was issued
- If you still have the same name
- If you can legally document your name change

A passport is valid for ten years from the date of issue. As soon as the passport is received, it should be signed. Also, the information in the front pages should be completed, which includes the address of the bearer and the names to be contacted in case of an emergency. Travelers should always carry passports with them while abroad; they should never be left in hotel rooms.

Visas

A **visa** is an approval granted by a government that permits a traveler to enter and in some cases to travel within that particular country. A visa often appears as a stamped notation on a passport. Rules and restrictions for visas vary from country to country. Generally, a traveler must

---

INTERNATIONAL TRAVEL TIPS

- Register your plans with the state department so that they can assist you if there is an emergency.

- Make sure you have a signed, valid passport and a visa if required.

- Leave copies of your itinerary and passport data page with family and friends so you can be contacted if necessary.

- Check to determine if your medical insurance policy applies overseas.

- Familiarize yourself with local conditions and laws since visitors are subject to the laws of the country they are visiting.

- Take precautions to avoid being a target of crime.

Source: "Tips for Traveling Abroad," U.S. Department of State, Bureau of Consular Affairs, accessed September 14, 2007, available from http://travel. state.gov/travel/tips/tips_1232.html.

FIGURE 16.4 International Travel Tips

apply to the country being visited for a visa ahead of the travel date. Travelers may be able to find information about visas on the Website of the country for which a visa is needed. For example, the Embassy of France in the United States provides information about visas for U.S. citizens on its Website. The U.S. government provides information about obtaining a visa to travel to the United States on its Destination USA Website shown in Figure 16.5. A fee may be charged for processing visa applications.

Currency

Before leaving the United States, executives can exchange money from certain banks and currency exchange offices for the currency of the country being visited. Newspapers generally report the rate of exchange for various countries. You can also obtain rates of exchange from the Internet. If the executive prefers, he or she can exchange a small amount of money in the United States and exchange more money when arriving at the destination. Any currency left over at the end of a trip can be exchanged for U.S. currency. It is always a good idea to be aware of the exchange rates before traveling to another country and to pay attention to exchange rates once in the country. Exchange rates are not always the same; for example, the exchange rate at a bank may be more favorable than the exchange rate at an airport.

Since January 2002, the Euro has been in circulation. The **Euro** is the official currency of several countries that are members of the European Union, such as Belgium, Germany, Greece, Spain, France, Ireland, Italy, Luxembourg, the Netherlands, Austria, Portugal, Slovenia, and Finland. Other countries, such as Cyprus and Malta, may soon adopt use of the Euro. An executive traveling to any of these countries no longer needs to worry about currency exchange between the countries.

Health Precautions

Before leaving for a country abroad, the traveler should check with a physician about vaccines or necessary medications. Because the environmental factors may be different from the ones experienced in the United States, there is a possibility of developing an illness as a result of the food, water, or climate of the country. For example, a physician can prescribe medications for stomach-related illnesses or colds. Vaccinations may be required for certain countries as well.

When you are visiting a country you may wish to purchase bottled water. Tap water in another country may be safe for local residents; however, it may contain different microbes than water in the United States, which can cause digestive problems for travelers. To be safe, it is

Source: "What Is a Visa?" Destination USA, U.S. Department of State, accessed September 27, 2007, available from http://www.unitedstatesvisas.gov/whatis/index.html.

FIGURE 16.5 Destination USA Website

important to use purified water at all times, even when brushing your teeth, washing your hands, or rinsing raw foods. For the same reasons, you may want to avoid using ice that is served in drinks. Most restaurants and markets serve and sell purified water.

International Car Rental

Cars are readily available for rent at international destinations. Travel agencies can arrange for a car before the executive departs or the executive can arrange for a car after arriving in the city. In most countries, a U.S. driver's license is sufficient. Travelers may obtain an International Driver's License from AAA. Travelers should obtain appropriate insurance and become familiar with the driving regulations of the country they are visiting. Driving conditions are sometimes quite different from those in the United States. For example, in some countries you must drive on the left-hand side of the road and pass on the right-hand side. In these countries the

steering wheels are mounted on the right-hand side of the car.

International Rail Transportation

Many countries have excellent rail service (particularly in Europe). Service is frequent and inexpensive. A traveler can get from one city in Europe to another in a relatively short period of time with little inconvenience. Trains are generally clean and the accommodations are comfortable. Underground rail is also available in a number of countries in Europe.

Organizational Travel Procedures

Procedures and policies about travel arrangements vary from organization to organization. You will need to learn the specific procedures followed by your organization. Some companies use one travel agency to schedule all travel. This

To get the best exchange rate, check several sources.

agency becomes knowledgeable about the needs of the organization and is able to provide what the executives need with limited assistance. Other organizations ask that individuals make their own travel arrangements.

Regardless of how travel arrangements are made, as an administrative professional you will be involved. The first time you help plan a trip for an executive, you should talk with the person about travel preferences. Having all necessary information will help you be more effective in making appropriate travel plans. Figure 16.6 gives the important information you should know. Set up a folder to hold relevant information when the executive first tells you about an upcoming trip. You should place all notes and information relating to the trip in the folder. The folder is then available for instant referral when needed.

If an executive is traveling by air, you need to know:

- The name of the preferred airline (if the executive has a preference) as well as his or her frequent flyer program number. A **frequent flyer program** is an incentive program that provides a variety of awards after the accumulation of a certain number of points.

- Whether the flight is to be direct (if possible) or whether the executive is willing to change planes. Less expensive flights are often available if the executive is willing to change planes.

- The class of flight preferred—first class, business, or economy.

- Seating preference—aisle or window and section of plane.

- Meal preference if international flight. As you have already learned, not all airlines serve complimentary meals. Some airlines provide meals for a charge.

If you are making arrangements for more than one top-level executive to travel to the same location at the same time, company policy may dictate that the executives fly on separate airlines. With both executives on the same plane, both might be injured or killed if there were a serious accident.

Arrangements by a Travel Agency

Travel agencies can make all travel arrangements for the executive. They are especially helpful when traveling internationally. They can schedule the flight, obtain tickets, make hotel reservations, and arrange car rental. They can also deliver all necessary tickets and documentation to your organization. Part of their service includes providing an *itinerary*, a travel schedule that gives flight numbers, arrival and departure times, hotel reservations with confirmation numbers, car rental reservations, and other details.

Travel agencies receive commissions from airlines, hotels, and other service industries when they sell services. However, they may also charge the customer a minimum fee or service charge for some of the arrangements that they make.

TRAVEL INFORMATION

- Dates and times for travel

- Cities to be visited; times and locations for appointments or commitments

- Hotel preferences—price range, number of nights, size of bed (full, queen, king), smoking or nonsmoking room

- Car rental preferences—type of car, size, make, model, number of days of use, and pickup and drop-off locations

- Reimbursement—reimbursement policies of the company (per diem for meals and other travel expenses)

- Credit card number or company account number to which travel is to be billed

- Arrangements for transportation to the airport or train station

- Appointments to be made; where and when

- Materials and equipment needed—business cards, computer, cell phone

- Person in charge while the executive is away

- Correspondence and calls—how they will be handled in the executive's absence

FIGURE 16.6 Place materials related to a trip in a travel folder.

Arrangements by an Administrative Professional

As an administrative professional, you may have the responsibility of making travel arrangements for executives. Although you may telephone some airlines or hotels that you use frequently, typically the most efficient method of making reservations is to use the Web. Airlines have Websites where you can make flight reservations. Several travel Websites (that are independent from airlines) give you prices for several airlines at the same time. These sites may also provide hotel and car rental information. Hotel and car reservations can also be made online at individual hotel and car rental company Websites.

You may assist executives with travel arrangements by determining passport and visa requirements, checking on currency needs, researching health issues in the country to be visited, making hotel reservations, arranging car rental, and arranging rail transportation. In addition, you may have the following responsibilities:

- Preparing an itinerary
- Obtaining travel funds
- Preparing and organizing materials for the trip
- Checking the executive's appointments
- Determining procedures to follow in the executive's absence

PREPARE AN ITINERARY

The itinerary is a must for you and your employer. If you are working with a travel agency, the agency will prepare an itinerary that includes flight numbers, departure and arrival times, and car rental and hotel reservations. However, this itinerary will not include information about appointments and other special events. Because the executive needs to have an itinerary that includes all activities of the trip, you should prepare a complete itinerary. Copies of the itinerary should be distributed to the executive, the executive's family, and the person in charge while the executive is away. A file copy should also be retained at the office. There is no standard format for an itinerary. A sample itinerary is shown in Figure 16.7 on page 413.

OBTAIN TRAVEL FUNDS

Organizations differ in how they handle funds for trips. Airline tickets may be charged directly to the organization, or the traveler may pay for the ticket and be reimbursed by the organization. Hotel, meals, and car rental may be charged to a credit card provided by the organization. Another practice is for individuals to get a cash advance to cover expenses for a trip. To do so, the individual fills out a travel form before leaving, indicating how much money she or he will need for lodging, meals, and other expenses. The company advances the money to the employee before the person leaves on the trip. Another practice is for the executive to pay the expenses; he or she is then reimbursed by the company upon returning from the trip.

Instead of carrying large amounts of cash, an executive may carry traveler's checks. Traveler's checks may be purchased from most banks and travel agencies. Traveler's checks come with two receipts that serve as records of the checks' serial numbers. One copy of the receipt should be kept in the files at the office and the other copy should be given to the executive. Since credit cards are accepted in many locations, it may be easier for the executive to use a credit card.

PREPARE AND ORGANIZE MATERIALS

Several items may be needed for a trip. If it is an international trip, items such as passports, medications, business cards, and small gifts may be necessary. Whether the trip is domestic or international, an executive needs certain items, such as reports for meetings and presentation materials. Once the materials are prepared, the administrative assistant assembles the appropriate number of copies and gives them to the executive. The traveler needs items such as these:

- E-ticket
- Itinerary
- Calendar or appointment schedule
- Credit cards, traveler's checks, currency
- Hotel confirmation

- Special materials, reports, or presentation notes
- Reading materials
- Business cards
- Passport and visa (for international travel)
- Cell phone and PDA or smartphone, laptop computer
- Information on organizations to be visited

CHECK APPOINTMENTS

Check your employer's calendar to see if any appointments have been scheduled for the period in which the executive will be away. If so, find out whether they are to be canceled or if someone else in the company will handle them. Then, notify the people involved.

Before preparing the itinerary, write, email, or call the people your employer plans to see during the trip to confirm the appointments. Verify addresses and directions from the hotel to the location of meetings; make a note of addresses and directions on the itinerary or an appointment schedule. Some executives prefer to have their trip appointments separate from the rest of their itinerary. When this is the case, an appointment schedule is prepared. A sample appointment schedule is shown in Figure 16.8 on page 415. Although an appointment schedule can be formatted in a variety of ways, it should include the following information:

- City of the appointment
- Date and time of the appointment
- Individual or group involved in the appointment
- Telephone number
- Location (including room, building name, and street address if it is an unfamiliar location)
- Special instructions or remarks

DETERMINE PROCEDURES

Find out who will be in charge during your employer's absence. Check to see if your employer is expecting important papers that should be forwarded. Be sure you understand how to handle

ITINERARY FOR TERESA WINWRIGHT

March 1 to March 3, 20--
Grand Rapids, Michigan

MONDAY, MARCH 1	**(FORT WORTH, TEXAS, TO GRAND RAPIDS, MICHIGAN)**
9:30 a.m. CST	Leave DFW International Airport on Delta Flight 57 (e-ticket in briefcase)
2:00 p.m. EST	Arrive GRF International Airport
	Take Esteban's Transport to the Amway Grand Plaza hotel, telephone 616-555-0124 (confirmation 44038) Pickup at entrance 11-B on the lower level by baggage claim
	Hotel reservations at the Amway Grand Plaza, 187 Monroe NW, telephone 616-555-0156 (confirmation 828382)
3:30 p.m. EST	Meeting with Marcus Francisco, Room 212, Ranier Building, telephone 616-555-0129, blue folder contains papers for meeting
TUESDAY, MARCH 2	**(GRAND RAPIDS, MICHIGAN)**
10:00 a.m. EST	Meeting with Mae Wong, Conference Room A, Temple Building, telephone 616-555-0165, manila folder contains papers for meeting Lunch with Mae follows the meeting; she is making arrangements for lunch
3:00 p.m. EST	Meeting with Louis Gomez, Conference Room C, Temple Building, telephone 616-555-0166, red folder contains meeting notes
WEDNESDAY, MARCH 3	**(GRAND RAPIDS, MICHIGAN, TO FORT WORTH, TEXAS)**
9:30 a.m. EST	Meeting with Arthur Ashton, Room 220, Thurston Building, telephone 616-555-0138, yellow folder contains proposed contact language
1:30 p.m. EST	Leave GRF International Airport on Delta Flight 70 (e-ticket in briefcase)
5:00 p.m. CST	Arrive DFW International Airport

FIGURE 16.7 Itinerary

all incoming mail, both email and traditional mail. Your employer may want you to refer all mail that has a deadline to another executive within the organization. Your employer may ask that you answer the routine mail and retain other mail until he or she returns.

Duties during the Executive's Absence

Although you have worked hard and efficiently to facilitate your employer's departure, it is not appropriate to stop working when your employer is away. Your pace may be somewhat slower while your employer is out of the office, or it may accelerate. Your responsibility is to handle the work flow smoothly and efficiently during your employer's absence.

MAKE DECISIONS

You must make wise decisions within the scope of your responsibilities during your employer's absence. You should know what matters or issues to refer to someone else in the company and what matters or issues to refer directly to the executive through an email, a telephone call, or a fax. Make sure you understand your responsibilities and make appropriate decisions when necessary.

HANDLE MESSAGES, APPOINTMENTS, AND CORRESPONDENCE

Executives may email or call the office on a daily basis while they are away. If the executive prefers to call, determine the approximate time of day before he or she leaves so you can have all items that need review as well as messages ready to discuss. Always keep urgent correspondence and messages in a place where you can find them quickly.

While the executive is away, you may need to set up appointments for individuals who wish to meet with her or him after the trip. When setting up appointments, remember that your employer will have a full day of work to handle on his or her first day back. Keep the calendar appointment free on that day. Also remember that if the executive has been abroad, he or she may be experiencing some jet lag. If an appointment is absolutely necessary on the first day back, schedule it in the afternoon. Avoiding early morning appointments also will be helpful if flights are delayed.

It is important that correspondence be handled appropriately while the executive is away. If you have been given this responsibility, see that important mail is forwarded to the person in charge. You may also be responsible for handling routine mail. If so, keep a copy of the correspondence and the response for your employer to review after he or she returns. You may find it helpful to keep a listing of all items that need to

---

Professional Pointers

When preparing an itinerary, include the following information.

- **Flights.** When listing flight information, include the flight numbers and times as well as the name of the airport and the airline.

- **Hotel.** Include the name and address of the hotel, the telephone number, and confirmation number. It may also be helpful to include the type of room reserved, a list of the hotel amenities, and nearby restaurants.

- **Rental car.** If using a rental car, include the company name, telephone number, type of car, and confirmation number. Give clear instructions on where the rental office is located.

- **Transportation.** If using a transportation service include the company name, telephone number, and confirmation number.

- **Meetings or appointments.** If meetings are scheduled during the trip, include a contact name or number so the traveler can call if he or she has questions or is delayed. If the traveler is using a rental car to get to the appointment, make sure to include clear directions to the appointment.

APPOINTMENT SCHEDULE FOR TERESA WINWRIGHT

March 1 to March 3, 20--
Grand Rapids, Michigan

MONDAY, MARCH 1

3:30 p.m. EST   Meeting with Marcus Francisco, Room 212, Ranier Building, telephone 616-555-0129, blue folder contains papers for meeting

TUESDAY, MARCH 2

10:00 a.m. EST   Meeting with Mae Wong, Conference Room A, Temple Building, telephone 616-555-0165, manila folder contains papers for meeting Lunch with Mae follows the meeting; she is making arrangements for lunch

3:00 p.m. EST   Meeting with Louis Gomez, Conference Room C, Temple Building, telephone 616-555-0166, red folder contains meeting notes

WEDNESDAY, MARCH 3

9:30 a.m. EST   Meeting with Arthur Ashton, Room 220, Thurston Building, telephone 616-555-0138, yellow folder contains proposed contact language

FIGURE 16.8 Appointment Schedule

Handle messages and correspondence appropriately while the executive is away.

be discussed with your employer when he or she returns.

Post-Trip Activities

When the executive returns, you should conduct a briefing on the workplace activities during his or her absence. The executive needs the following information:

- Appointments scheduled
- Telephone calls and how they were handled
- Correspondence received
- Copies of answers to correspondence
- Email messages

Additionally, the executive needs a file of mail that does not require a response but contains information for the executive, such as informational memorandums, reports, and periodicals. Place this mail in folders by category and date.

EXPENSE REPORTS

Following a trip, many organizations require employees to prepare an expense report and turn in receipts for expenses above a certain amount. The following information is often included on an expense report.

- Employee name and department
- Date of expense
- Category of expense (meals, lodging, airfare)
- Description of the entertainment expenses (lunch with client, Tom Chung)
- Expense amount (converted to U.S. dollars if the expense is from international travel)
- Receipts if required (some organizations do not require receipts if a corporate credit card is used or if the expense is below a certain dollar amount)
- Employee signature and date
- Supervisor signature and date

The executive will usually provide you with a list of receipts from the trip, including flight, hotel, and meal receipts. Your task is to complete the expense report carefully, double-checking all individual figures and totals. Copies of the receipts are usually attached to the expense report. A sample expense report is shown in Figure 16.9.

FOLLOW-UP CORRESPONDENCE

The executive may need to write several follow-up letters after the trip. For example, she or he may want to send thank-you letters to the executives contacted on the trip. Customers or potential customers may be sent information on products or services. Contracts may be written and mailed. The executive may also need to answer correspondence that accumulated during the trip or ask you to respond to certain items.

United Pharmaceuticals
Expense Report

For the Week Ending:	1/20/20--							
Employee Name:	Melody Hoover			Destination:	Tulsa, Oklahoma			
Department:	Marketing			Purpose:	IAAP Committe Meeting			

	Monday	Tuesday	Wednesday	Thursday	Friday	Saturday	Sunday	TOTAL
Date	1/15/20--	1/16/20--	1/17/20--	1/18/20--				
Airfare								0.00
Car Rental								0.00
Local Transportation								0.00
Tolls/Parking	12.50	12.50	12.50	12.50				50.00
Miles	500	10	15	500				
Mileage Amount (.485 /mile)	242.50	4.85	7.28	242.50	0.00	0.00	0.00	497.13
Lodging	150.93	150.93	150.93	150.93				603.72
Transportation and Lodging	405.93	168.28	170.71	405.93	0.00	0.00	0.00	1,150.85
Breakfast		8.00	5.25	6.75				20.00
Lunch	10.50	15.00	12.75	15.25				53.50
Dinner	24.00		25.75					49.75
Meals	34.50	23.00	43.75	22.00	0.00	0.00	0.00	123.25
Business Meals*		105.00						105.00
Other Entertainment*								0.00
Business Entertainment	0.00	105.00	0.00	0.00	0.00	0.00	0.00	105.00
Gifts								0.00
Office Supplies			23.50					23.50
Other*								0.00
Miscellaneous	0.00	0.00	23.50	0.00	0.00	0.00	0.00	23.50
GRAND TOTAL	$440.43	$296.28	$237.96	$427.93	$0.00	$0.00	$0.00	$1,402.60

Employee Signature	*Melody Hoover*	Date:	1/23/20--
Supervisor Signature	*Teresa Winwright*	Date:	1/24/20--

Comments:
* Explanation Required   Dinner on 1/16 with Standards Review Committee members: Joan Roberts, Tom Chung, and Maria Gonzales.

FIGURE 16.9 Expense Report

Summary

To reinforce what you have learned in this chapter, study this summary.

- The current global economy requires that business be conducted around the world, necessitating travel by many business executives.

- Many executives travel by air, choosing first-class, business-class, or economy-class accommodations. Executives may also travel on company planes or chartered planes.

- Since the events of 9/11, America's airports have increased their levels of security. Being knowledgeable about security measures is important for business travelers.

- Other air travel considerations include airline clubs, parking services, ticketing, or changes or cancellations.

- Hotel and rental car reservations can be made online or through travel agents or airlines.

- Rail travel is available to some parts of the United States but often does not extend into rural areas.

- When traveling internationally, executives need to be knowledgeable about differences in the culture of the country they are visiting.

- When traveling internationally, a passport is required. Visas are also necessary in some countries.

- Travelers may need to exchange money for the currency of the country being visited either before the trip or when arriving at the destination.

- Vaccines are required prior to traveling in some countries.

- Travel policies and procedures vary from organization to organization. Travel arrangements may be made using a travel agency, or the administrative professional may make travel arrangements for executives.

- Before a trip, an administrative professional may prepare an itinerary, obtain travel funds, organize materials for the trip, and confirm or reschedule appointments for the executive.

- The administrative professional's responsibilities during the executive's absence include making decisions and handling messages, appointments, and correspondence.

- Post-trip activities may include preparing an expense report and follow-up correspondence.

What's the Problem?

Aryiana, an administrative professional for United Pharmaceuticals, works in the home office in Fort Worth, Texas. She has agreed to hold a seminar on writing effective correspondence for the administrative professionals in the Grand Rapids, Michigan, office. She has not been to the Grand Rapids facility, and she does not know any of the employees there. When making her travel arrangements, she called the Grand Rapids division and asked for directions to the office. The assistant told Aryiana that the office is only 30 minutes from the airport. Aryiana's flight is scheduled to arrive in Grand Rapids at noon. Her presentation is to begin at 2 p.m.

Aryiana's flight leaves Dallas 20 minutes late. Once she arrives in Grand Rapids, she is held on the plane for 15 minutes waiting for a gate to open. Then she must collect her luggage. When she finally gets to the taxi area, she has only 50 minutes before she is to begin her presentation. The taxi ride from the airport to the office takes 35 minutes because traffic is heavy. She rushes into the room 10 minutes before the presentation is to begin to set up her presentation slides. She begins her presentation 10 minutes late, feeling very rushed and nervous from her "ordeal."

What mistakes did Aryiana make in planning her travel arrangements?

Let's Discuss

1. List and describe the three flight classifications most commonly used for domestic travel.
2. List some security measures that passengers are requested to follow in an airport.
3. List and describe the types of resources that are available to obtain information about business customs in other countries.
4. What is the purpose of a passport? a visa?
5. What types of information should be included on an itinerary?

Critical-Thinking Activity

Two months ago Brad Venditti, a friend of yours, accepted his first full-time position as an administrative assistant for a telecommunications company. Last week Brad's employer, Elena Perez, asked him to make arrangements for her to go to Orlando. Brad received the necessary travel information from Ms. Perez and made the flight reservations. Ms. Perez requested a rental car for three days while in Florida. She indicated that she had three appointments scheduled. She gave the names and appointment times to Brad.

Brad handed Ms. Perez a handwritten list that included numbers, times, and dates of departure and return flights. Ms. Perez took one look at the list and asked about the appointment schedule; it was not on the itinerary. She asked if this was his idea of an itinerary. Brad admitted that he did not realize Ms. Perez would need anything but the flight information and that he really did not know how to prepare an itinerary.

When Ms. Perez arrived at the airport in Orlando, she called Brad and told him that the rental car agency had no record of the booking. Brad was afraid to tell Ms. Perez that he forgot to arrange for a car; he led her to believe the car rental agency made the mistake.

While Ms. Perez was away from the office, Brad thought he did not have any work to do so he spent most of his time reading a novel. Several of the employees remarked (with a smile) to Brad that they wished they had it as easy as he did.

When Ms. Perez returned from Florida, she found the mail in a stack on her desk. It had not been sorted or opened. She told Brad that he must get help in learning how to make travel arrangements. She was clear that she did not want the same problems to happen again. Brad called you asking for help.

1. How should Brad have prepared for Ms. Perez's trip?
2. What should Brad have done while Ms. Perez was away?
3. How can Brad improve the impression his employer has of him and his work?

Vocabulary Review

Open the *Word* file *CH16 Vocabulary* found on the Student CD. Complete the vocabulary review for Chapter 16.

English and Word Usage Drill

Complete the English and Word Usage Drill for Chapter 16 found in the *Applications Workbook.*

Workplace Applications

16-1 Plan Domestic Travel Arrangements

internet

e-portfolio

(Goals 1 and 3)

Your supervisor, Melody Hoover, will attend the Minnesota Business Association Convention. She has asked that you make tentative travel arrangements so that she can attend this event.

1. Open the *Word* file *CH16 Trip Plans* found in the data files. This file contains information given to you by Melody about the trip. Plan the travel arrangements as Melody requests in the memo. Note the costs for all arrangement made.

2. Create an itinerary for Melody that includes all travel arrangements you have made.

3. Write a memo to Melody Hoover providing the costs of the arrangements and any other necessary information that was not included in the itinerary. Use the *Word* file *Memo Form* found on the Student CD to prepare the memo.

16-2 Research Business Customs

internet

team building

(Goal 2)

Teresa Winwright and David Anderson are traveling to the United Pharmaceuticals location in Guangzhou, China. Your supervisor, Amando Hinojosa, asks you to conduct research to help them prepare for their trip.

1. Work with a classmate to complete this project.

2. Using the Web and/or other resources, research business customs in China including meeting behavior, business cards, professional gifts, and professional attire.

3. Prepare a summary of your findings in an unbound report. List the references you used at the end of the report on a References page.

16-3 Plan International Travel Arrangements

internet

(Goals 1 and 3)

1. Work with a classmate to complete this project.

2. Teresa Winwright and David Anderson are traveling to the United Pharmaceuticals location in Guangzhou, China. Plan all travel arrangements for their trip. Note the costs for the arrangements.

- The trip will be from April 5 through April 12.

- Make flight reservations, using the Web to get the best schedule.

- Ms. Winwright and Mr. Anderson will take a taxi from the office to the Dallas/Fort Worth airport. A representative from the China office, Cheng Xue, will meet them at the airport in Guangzhou. They will not need ground transportation while in China; the China office will provide transportation.

- Make hotel reservations for them in Guangzhou. Book two rooms with king-size beds, no smoking.

team building

3. Create an itinerary for Ms. Winwright. Include the travel arrangements you made and the appointments she has scheduled (listed below). (Use fictitious confirmation numbers for flights and the hotel.)

- April 7—meeting with Cheng Xue and Wang Chu-yu from 10 a.m. until 2 p.m., Conference Room A

- April 8—continuation of meeting with Cheng Xue and Wang Chu-yu from 11 a.m. until 3 p.m., Conference Room A

- April 9—meeting with Zhang Ping and Kwong Dong from 9 a.m. until 1 p.m., Conference Room C

- April 10—Continuation of meeting with Zhang Ping and Kwong Dong from 11 a.m. until 2 p.m., Conference Room C

4. Write a memo to Teresa Winwright providing the costs of the arrangements for her and any other necessary information that was not included in the itinerary. Use the *Word* file *Memo Form* found on the Student CD to prepare the memo.

16-4 Prepare an Expense Report

(Goal 3)

1. Melody Hoover has returned from a trip and asks you to prepare an expense report.

2. Open the *Excel* file *CH16 Expense Report* and the *Word* file *CH16 Expenses* found on the Student CD. Create the expense report using the spreadsheet file and the information provided by Melody.

Assessment of Chapter 16 Goals

Did you successfully complete the chapter goals? Evaluate yourself by filling out the form found in Chapter 16 of the *Applications Workbook*.

Career Advancement

CHAPTER 17

Job Search and Advancement

CHAPTER 18

Leadership and Management: Challenges and Characteristics

part 7

Career Profile

Office Manager

Office managers oversee the administrative support functions of organizations. Office managers work in almost all industries and for small, medium, and large companies. Office and administrative support supervisors and managers held about 1.5 million jobs in the United States in 2004.*

Office managers plan and supervise the work of office staff. This work typically includes managing schedules and records, sharing information with others by telephone and through correspondence and reports, creating presentations, conducting research, managing projects and budgets, planning meetings and travel, maintaining office equipment, and performing other tasks specific to the organization. Office managers monitor work progress to see that projects and tasks are accomplished on schedule and review completed work for quality. They may be expected to foster teamwork within their departments or work groups and help resolve interpersonal conflicts among the staff. Interviewing and evaluating prospective office employees and evaluating job performance for office employees are typically part of an office manager's duties. Office manager's may train new office employees in company policies and procedures or in duties specific to the organization.

Salaries for office managers vary by the manager's qualifications and by organization. Median annual earnings of office and administrative support supervisors and managers were $41,030 in May 2004. Office managers need strong teamwork, problem-solving, leadership, and communication skills. They must be able to organize and coordinate work efficiently, set priorities, and motivate others. Many organizations fill office manager positions by promoting administrative support workers from within their organizations. Programs in office and business administration are offered by business schools, vocational-technical institutes, and colleges. An associates degree may be required for an office manager position in a small company. In a medium or large organization, a bachelor's degree may be required. Office managers should plan to continue their education and training to stay informed about current technology and procedures.

---

*"Office and Administrative Support Worker Supervisors and Managers," *Occupational Outlook Handbook*, 2006-2007 Edition, accessed June 27, 2007, available from http://www.bls.gov/oco/ocos127.htm.

chapter 17

Job Search and Advancement

Learning Goals

1. Understand your skills, interests, and abilities as they relate to a career.

2. Determine a job search plan.

3. Identify sources of job information and research organizations of interest.

4. Prepare a resume and letter of application.

5. Demonstrate effective interview skills.

6. Develop job advancement strategies.

Understand Your Skills, Interests, and Abilities

This chapter is designed to prepare you to seek a position as an administrative professional. You can be a well-educated and skilled administrative professional and still not do well in a job search. Why? You may not have given enough time and attention to preparing yourself for the job search. You may not have determined the type of organization for which you want to work or where you want to work. You may not have given enough thought as to how you will present your skills and what you consider to be some of your strongest skills.

This chapter can be one of the most important chapters you study, one that helps you find the right position so that you may be happy and secure in your work. When you consider that you are likely to spend 40 hours per week, 5 days per week, and 50 weeks each year (allowing two weeks for vacation) on a job, you can quickly understand the importance of finding a job in which you can succeed.

As you begin to think about the job you want to hold, you must understand your interests, skills, and abilities and the type of organization for which you would like to work. You may be in the last year of your college studies, with plans to go to work as an administrative assistant in the next few months. Throughout this course, you have been developing skills and

Finding the right job, the one that matches your skills, interests, and abilities, is extremely crucial for your long-term employment success.

© Stockbyte / Getty Images

> **ESSENTIAL SKILLS AND ABILITIES FOR AN ADMINISTRATIVE ASSISTANT**
>
> - Communication
> - Human relations
> - Critical thinking
> - Decision making
> - Creative thinking
> - Teamwork
> - Technology
> - Leadership
> - Time management
> - Anger management
> - Stress management

FIGURE 17.1 Essential Skills and Abilities

abilities that will help you be an outstanding administrative professional. Now that you have almost completed this course and may be pursuing job opportunities soon, you need to give serious consideration to not only your strongest skills but also those skills that you need to develop to a greater degree before finishing this course.

Evaluate Your Skills

Figure 17.1 lists a number of skills that you will need in a job as an administrative professional. Although you have concentrated on these skills throughout this course, there are probably areas where you must continue to improve.

You will rate yourself on this list by using the Skills Rating Form in Workplace Application 17-1. Determine where you need to improve and commit to doing so during the remainder of this course. Additionally, continue to improve these skills as you assume a position as an administrative assistant. Realize that you can and must continue to grow in your administrative assistant abilities throughout your career. A prospective employer will want you to be able to answer the question *What skills do you bring to our organization?* Additionally, think about the skills and abilities that you have that do not necessarily fall under the skill category. Do you have exceptional human relations skills? Do you write well? Do you read extensively? Are you committed to continually improving the skills that you have through attending workshops?

Determine Your Interests

What interests do you have? If you have trouble identifying your interests, try asking yourself this question: *If I had the opportunity to talk about something all day long, what would it be?* In other words, what are your passions? Are you interested in the medical profession? Do you enjoy working with people who are saving lives? If so, you might want to work in a hospital, a medical doctor's office, or a pharmaceutical organization that researches new drugs.

Are you interested in the legal profession and the court systems? If so, you might want to work in an attorney's office or in the local or state judicial system. Do you speak another language proficiently? If so, you might seek a position with a multinational firm, one where you can put your language skills to use. Do you enjoy talking about religious issues? If you do, you might seek work in a church or in a church-related organization, such as a publisher of religious books. Perhaps you may be interested in an insurance company, the airline industry, or the banking industry. Are there particular businesses/industries that are flourishing now? If so, what are they? You can check the Fortune 500 companies through the Web.

Identify Your Strengths

Ask yourself this question: *What can I offer employers?* As you answer this question, think outside your technical skill sets. For example, what human relations skills do you have? Ask these questions:

- Am I self confident?
- Do I have good communication skills?
- Do I enjoy learning? Do I consistently attempt to stay current in my field?
- Am I a professional? Do I conduct myself professionally even when confronted with criticism of my work?
- Am I always open to improving my job performance?

Clarify Your Values

Values are developed early in life; they evolve from various sources, including the following:

- Parents
- Churches and religious groups

Staying current in your field is important for long-term career success.

- Societies or cultures; for example, if you were born in China you may have different values than individuals who were born in the United States

You have learned earlier in this textbook that it is important for you to clearly understand your values and how you apply them to your daily life. You have learned that you live your values every day even though you may not consciously think about what you are doing. Your values guide you through every task you undertake and through every encounter you have with other people.

As you begin a job search process, it is extremely important that you are clear about your values. If you are not clear, you may find yourself accepting a job with an organization that operates with values very different than your own. If that happens, you may often be unhappy and not understand the source of your unhappiness.

Understand Yourself

As you go about finding the right job for you, it is important that you understand who you are. An instrument used by many people for this purpose is the Myers-Briggs Type Indicator (MBTI). This personality questionnaire is based on the theories of Carl Jung, a psychiatrist. This instrument helps you understand more about your personality type, what is important to you, and how you work with others on the job. You can generally find a short version of the MBTI on the Web. If you would like to have more information about the MBTI, check your college library or book store. Several books have been written explaining the MBTI in detail.

Set Goals

Applying for a job is not easy; in fact, it is hard work. You must think through both your long-term and short-term goals. For example, your short-term goal may be to obtain a job in an organization where you can use your skills and abilities effectively. Your long-term goal might be to find an organization where you can build a successful career. If you have had very little job experience, your first job certainly may not satisfy your long-term need for building a successful career in an organization that is consistently growing and offering challenging experiences to its employees. However, very few individuals start out in an organization where they will stay for the remainder of their work life. In fact, you may want to set short-term goals of focusing on getting experiences in two or three types of organizations. Once you have broadened your work experiences, you should be ready to satisfy your long-term goal of building a successful career in a position that provides you the challenges and the monetary rewards that are important to you.

Develop a Support Team

Are there individuals in your life that you can count on to support you in stressful times? Although you have prepared yourself well for seeking a job in your professional area, you still need a support team. It is not easy to look for a job. You may find yourself being rejected for a job that you feel qualified to handle and one that you were most interested in obtaining. You need a team of good friends, a spouse, or significant other individuals in your life to support you when you are discouraged. This support team can also help you evaluate your experiences as you apply for positions. They may offer advice that will help you succeed in getting the next position that you want.

Determine Your Job Search Plan

Before you begin to look for a job, you must give careful consideration to establishing an effective search plan—one that will provide focus for you as you begin the very important task of finding a position that matches your skills and abilities. You may decide to do a **traditional job search** or a **targeted job search**. The basic differences between the two search plans are explained in the following paragraphs.

With a traditional job search, you apply for job openings that match your career goals in many organizations. You start by reviewing job openings that match your career goals from many sources. These openings may be listed in newspapers, available from employment agencies on the Web, or given to you by friends or family members who are aware of the openings. With this approach to a job search, you know that the company is hiring, and you submit your resume. You apply for a specific job—one that matches your skills and abilities. However, because the job is usually advertised in a number of venues (newspapers, employment agencies, and so forth), you may be competing with dozens of individuals. Organizations commonly receive numerous applications for one opening, particularly if the economy is in a downturn and fewer jobs are available.

A targeted job search focuses on a company rather than a position. The company may have no position currently available, but the company is one for which you would specifically like to work. For example, it may be one of the **Fortune**

500 Companies (identified by *Fortune* magazine as one of the top 500 American public corporations as measured by gross revenue), and your dream is to work for this company. You have done your research on the company, and you believe that your skills and abilities would be an asset for the company. Your task with a targeted approach is to sell yourself and your capabilities so well that the company wants to hire you.

With the targeted approach, you have the responsibility of finding companies where you want to work, regardless of whether there is an announced opening. You may find these companies through friends who work in the company and believe that it is one that is growing and replete with job opportunities for the future. Another method of finding targeted companies is through reading such publications as *Fortune* magazine, using the Web to identify the top 100 companies to work for in America, and talking with your friends or family members who work for companies that are growing and prosperous. For example, you may look for companies that are expanding their operations multinationally. You may be particularly interested in this avenue if you would like to live and work outside the United States.

You may choose to use both of these avenues as you look for a position where you can grow, learn, and feel secure in your job. Regardless of the search plan you use, there are additional considerations that are important for you to consider.

Establish Geographical Preference

Where do you want to live? If you presently live in a small town, you may decide that you want to move to a larger city that has more job opportunities available. Ask yourself these questions as you determine your geographical preferences:

- Are there numerous jobs available for administrative assistants in the area in which I live?
- If the answer is "no," where might I find jobs available in my field? Is there a metropolitan area in my home state that is home to a number of large corporations where growth opportunities for administrative assistants are available?
- Once I have established myself in my career and have developed skills that are marketable throughout the world, are there growth possibilities for me internationally?

U.S. corporations, as well as corporations with home offices in other countries, are becoming more global in their operations. General Motors, FedEx Kinko's, Marriott International, and Deloitte & Touch are examples of companies that operate globally. It is anticipated that this international job presence of corporations will continue to grow and expand. Think for a moment about the job opportunities that a worldwide corporation may provide you. For example, if you work for an international company, you may have the opportunity to work in another country. International experiences can provide tremendous growth for you in understanding our world and the people of different races and ethnicities who work in this world.

A growing number of corporations are expanding their sites to countries abroad.

Determine Search Strategies

Regardless of which search plan or strategy that you choose, there are additional avenues that you need to consider when applying for a job. Remember that an employment decision can be one of the best or worst decisions you make in your career. You need to carefully analyze your skills and abilities and be willing to take the time to determine the strategies that will work best for you and for the community in which you live. Several different strategies for obtaining information about job opportunities are presented here.

DEVELOP NETWORKS

You have already learned that you need a support team, composed of family and friends, who can help you through the sometimes stressful job search process. Additionally, you need to develop networks in the business community. **Networking** is the process of identifying and establishing a group of individuals who can assist you in the job search process or other efforts. This approach has proven to be one of the best strategies for finding a job. To begin this process, make a list of eight to ten people you know well and who have contacts in the business community.

You do not have to contact these people in person. You may find that contacting them by email is more effective. If you are contacting people that you do not know personally, you should immediately give the individual the name of the person who suggested the contact. For example, you might say, "Rebecca Edwards suggested that I contact you. I have known Rebecca for a number of years, and I called her recently concerning the names of places in our area where I might work. She suggested I contact you." Then proceed to give the person information as to your education, your work history, and the type of position you are seeking.

Once you have developed a viable network of job sources, maintain that network throughout your job search process. Use your network; you asked for their help in the job process and they willingly agreed to assist you. Keep in contact with the individuals periodically (every two or three weeks) even if it is to merely report where you are in the process. You need to keep them up to date on suggestions they have made to you and your follow-through on those suggestions. For example, if one of your network members gave you XYZ Corporation to contact and you contacted the corporation but have heard nothing from them, let your contact know. He or she may be able to offer another source or even call the contact to discuss your strengths with the individual. Remember to thank the network individuals each time you call. They are giving you their valuable time and information; the least you can do is say "thank you." When you are hired for a job, let your network know. Thank the individual that gave you the source; also report your job success to the other members of your network and thank them for their assistance throughout your search.

ENGAGE IN AN ONLINE SEARCH

Through the Web, you can research companies and organizations in which you have an interest. The Web also has a variety of other resources for job seekers, including tips for resume and cover letter preparation and interviewing. Many sites

career *tip*

Networking

As you develop your team of individuals who are willing to help you with contacts, ask these questions:

- What companies in the area are known for being a great place to work? Do you have any suggestions as to how I may obtain more information about the company?

- Do you know any companies that have openings for administrative assistants at the present time? If so, whom should I contact? May I use your name when making the contact?

- Are there other people you know that I should be contacting about job openings?

© Image Source Ltd.

Networking is one of the best strategies for finding a job.

on the Web contain job listings. These sites are sometimes called **job boards**. Job boards allow job seekers to post a resume and view job listings from many organizations. Job boards allow employers to post job openings and review resumes posted by job seekers. Many job boards are free to job seekers. Employers may be required to pay a fee to post job openings or search resumes on a job board.

USAJOBS is the official federal government job board. This Website, shown in Figure 17.2, offers listings for jobs with the federal government. Many states and some cities have Websites with information about their job listings. USAJOBS and many other job boards allow users to create **job agents**, also called job scouts. Jobs agents are programs that automatically search job listings and retrieve jobs matching criteria you set. For example, you might request jobs in a certain geographic area. The results are sent to you by email at a time period you select, such as daily or weekly.

VISIT EMPLOYMENT AGENCIES

You can search for the names of employment agencies in your area on the Web. These agencies may be state-sponsored agencies or private agencies. Typically, these agencies work with entry-level to mid-level positions. Additionally, they often have temporary assignments. These agencies charge a fee (with the exception of state agencies which do not charge). However, the fee may be paid by the company that is seeking personnel or the fee may be split between the applicant and the company. If you plan to seek assistance from an employment agency, it is a good idea to check with your trusted acquaintances to determine if the agency is a reputable one.

If you determine that you will contact an agency, be professional. Treat the person you talk with as you would a potential employer. If you decide to apply for a position with an agency, dress professionally when you go into the office.

Source: USAJOBS, U.S. Office of Personnel Management, accessed September 20, 2007, available from http://www.usajobs.gov/.

FIGURE 17.2 USAJOBS provides information about U.S. government jobs.

Even though the person you talk with at the agency will not be hiring you, this person will have contact with the company where you will have an interview. Any unprofessional behavior that you demonstrate at the agency may be reported to the prospective employer.

READ NEWSPAPERS

Although the Web has become an important information source for many people, newspapers remain an important source for employment ads. You should not ignore newspapers; scan the ads daily when you are in the search process. You need to follow every avenue that you can to find the job that fits your skills and abilities and is of interest to you. However, you do not want to spend all or most of your time in the job search on newspaper ads.

TALK WITH COLLEGE RECRUITERS

Many colleges and universities have recruiters that set up recruiting booths that students can visit. These recruiters are not hiring agents for the firm; their purpose is to look for interested

and talented individuals and then invite the individuals to the company for an interview. If you think you may be interested in the company or if you want to learn more about the company, it is a good idea to talk with the recruiters.

Research Organizations of Interest

Once you have the names of two or three firms from your networking efforts, you next step is to do some research on the companies. You may have already decided that you are going to apply to these firms, but you need to be as knowledgeable as possible in order to write a letter and develop a resume that will highlight your skills. You want to be able to intelligently discuss the company on a job interview. You also want to ask the interviewer meaningful questions concerning the company. She or he will be impressed that you took the time to learn about the company. Such an approach demonstrates your thoroughness in preparation and thought—characteristics that are needed on any job that you pursue.

Your questions will not be the same for each company where you interview. Make the questions as specific as possible; this shows the interviewer that you have done your homework. The following general questions will help you to think through various possibilities.

- Who are the company's major customers or clients?
- What are the major directions for the company for the next three years?
- Does the company plan to expand its operation by adding sites? If so, where will they be?
- Does the company plan to have international sites? If so, where?
- Do you see the company growing in the next five years? If so, what directions do you think that growth will take?
- What is the organization's service or product?
- How does the organization compare to its competitors? Is it an industry leader?
- Is the organization financially secure?
- What is the organization's stated mission?
- How long has the organization been in business?
- Does the organization have branches in more than one state within the United States?
- What are the organization's values and goals?
- Does the organization have a good reputation in the community?
- Is the organization an equal opportunity employer?

If the company is a small one, you may be able to learn about it from consulting friends, relatives, and acquaintances. Information about the organization may be available from your local chamber of commerce or your college placement office. The organization's Website and annual reports may also be good sources of information.

Review the Organization's Website

Many organizations have Websites. You may reach the Website by going to a search engine and keying the company's full name. Usually these Websites have a wealth of information about the company. Items that you may find on company Websites include the following:

- Organization's culture, mission, and values
- Employment opportunities
- Services offered
- News concerning growth plans
- Research and training
- Performance indicators
- Board of directors
- Management
- Community services
- Locations of subsidiaries
- Ownership of the company
- Affiliated entities

Obtain Annual Reports

Another good source for company information is annual reports; some companies publish their annual reports on their Websites. Tips for reading an annual report are available on the Web. Information that is usually available on an annual report includes the following:

- Letter from the chairman of the board
- Sales and marketing—covering what the company sells, how, where, and when
- Five- to ten-year summary of financial figures—allows you to determine if the company profits are growing or declining
- Management discussion and analysis—significant financial trends over a period of years
- Financial statements
- Stock price history
- List of directors and officers

Research News Stories

Investors are extremely interested in corporate America. Thus, news stories concerning good companies and bad companies appear often on television and the Web and in newspapers and magazines.

The Enron scandal of several years ago was in the news frequently, and the court cases that ensued due to the unethical and illegal practices of Enron were widely publicized. Numerous top administrators were fired and some went to prison. Conversely, positive stories often appear in newspapers, periodicals, and on the Web and TV concerning outstanding companies in corporate America.

Prepare a Resume

A **resume** is a concise statement of your background, education, skills, and work experience. Its purpose is to communicate your job skills to prospective employers. It is your personal marketing document. A well-prepared resume markets your education, skills, and experience so effectively that it sets you apart from the other candidates for the job. Both the content and the format of the resume are critical to its effectiveness. There are a number of different types of resumes. Two commonly used resumes are presented here—the chronological resume and the functional resume. Tips for determining the type of resume to prepare are given in Figure 17.3.

Chronological Resume

A **chronological resume** uses a format that gives a chronology of the applicant's work experience, starting with the most recent work experience and then listing the remainder of the experience in reverse order. Most of the resume is devoted to the section on experience or employment history, with the most recent work experience listed first. A chronological resume is appropriate if you have over five years of work experience. A disadvantage to using a chronological format is that it is easy to spot gaps between jobs. A chronological resume is shown in Figure 17.4.

Functional Resume

A **functional resume** focuses on giving the skills and qualifications of the applicant for a particular job rather than work experience. Company names and dates of employment are omitted completely or deemphasized. Position titles are deemphasized or omitted. A functional resume is appropriate for someone who is entering a new field, a person just completing his or her education and beginning to seek full-time employment, or a person who is returning to work after a period of absence. A sample functional resume for someone who is graduating from a two-year program and has little job experience is shown in Figure 17.5. Notice this resume focuses on skills rather than experience.

Electronic Resume

Some prospective employers will ask that you send an **electronic resume** (also called an e-resume). Usually an electronic resume is scanned (along with numerous other resumes) for keywords that match the keywords in the job description. Even if your resume is chosen in the initial phase, you may not be selected for an interview. The process is an intensive one of continually sorting the resumes of the most qualified individuals applying until the final number of people is selected.

TIPS FOR DETERMINING RESUME CONTENTS

- When using a functional format, highlight your skills.

- If you are a recent graduate and have held only part-time jobs, list them.

- If you have not had any paid work experience, list volunteer jobs or leadership positions you have held.

- Tailor your resume for the specific job opening, highlighting those areas of your background or work experience that fit the position you want.

- Do not use personal pronouns (I, me, you).

- Check your spelling and grammar usage carefully.

- Take advantage of professional help in writing your resume.

- Check Web sources for resume assistance.

FIGURE 17.3 Resume Tips

PATRICIA LAFAVER

1823 Corinth   plf@adm.net
Euless, TX 76039-0743   (817) 555-0125

PROFESSIONAL EXPERIENCE

September 2008 to present
Oakwood Community College
Fort Worth, Texas

Administrative assistant in the English Department
- Supervise three student assistants
- Prepare class scheduling information
- Set up files for incoming students
- Maintain filing system for the department
- Prepare and submit textbook orders for faculty
- Schedule rooms for classes
- Assist with the class schedule for each semester

September 2006 to August 2008
Brandon Bookstore
Fort Worth, Texas

Part-time cashier
Worked 20 hours per week while attending college

EDUCATION
AAS Degree, Oakwood Community College, Fort Worth, Texas

PROFESSIONAL ORGANIZATIONS
International Association of Administrative Professionals

REFERENCES
References furnished on request.

FIGURE 17.4 Chronological Resume

PATRICIA LAFAVER

1823 Corinth   plf@adm.net
Euless, TX 76039-0743   (817) 555-0125

GOAL: Administrative Assistant Position

PROFESSIONAL SKILLS
Experience in the Business Division of Oakwood Community College has allowed me to develop the following skills:

- Communication skills through working with a diverse audience of students, faculty, administrators, and community leaders
- Telephone skills through consistently communicating with faculty, administrators, and students
- Keyboarding skills through preparing syllabi, tests, and general correspondence for faculty
- Human relations skills through working with 15 faculty and approximately 50 students each semester
- Filing skills through setting up both a computer and paper filing system and maintaining the files
- Problem-solving skills through assisting students with their schedules and their degree plans
- Research skills through accessing curriculum at various community colleges
- Software application skills through using *Microsoft Office 2007* to create word processing documents, spreadsheets, databases, and electronic presentations

Experience as a part-time cashier at Brandon Bookstore while attending college helped me improve my human relations skills.

EDUCATION
AAS Degree, Oakwood Community College, Fort Worth, Texas

PROFESSIONAL ORGANIZATIONS
International Association of Administrative Professionals

REFERENCES
References furnished on request.

FIGURE 17.5 Functional Resume

Although the information you send in an electronic resume should not differ from the traditional resume, the manner in which you present the information should be different. You should not use the formats shown in Figure 17.4 and Figure 17.5 (chronological and functional resumes). Suggestions for formatting an electronic resume are as follows:

- Stick to a basic font (or fixed-width font) such as Courier; use a font size of 12 points.
- Do not use italics or underlining.
- Avoid using graphics. A resume scanner is not able to read these graphics.
- Do not use abbreviations. For example, using *AAS degree* will not be acceptable. Spell out the degree (Associate of Applied Sciences).
- Use keywords or phrases since a keyword search may be done on your resume. For example, an employer may search an employment database for an administrative assistant with experience, word processing skills, writing skills, and human relations skills.
- Do not center your name, address, email, and telephone number at the top of the page. It should be left-justified on an e-resume.
- Place keyword phrases immediately after your name and address. The most important words should be placed first, with additional keywords following in order of importance.
- Your work experience should immediately follow the keyword summary; begin with the most recent position, followed by the other positions in reverse chronological order.
- The next category on your e-resume should be education. Identify the college name, location, and year of graduation. If you are a member of any professional organization, list it.
- You may send your resume via email rather than by U.S. mail or fax. If you send it by email, paste it into the body of the message. Do not send it as an attachment unless you are asked to do so.

Figure 17.6 shows an electronic resume. Notice that it does not have bullets or italicized or underlined words. Also, notice that the heading begins at the left margin.

References

A resume reference is a person who knows your academic ability and/or work skills and habits and is willing to recommend you to employers. A reference should be able to verify part of the information you give on a resume. References are generally not listed on a resume. Instead, the phrase *References available on request* is used. Ask permission first from the person before listing him or her as a reference on a resume or job application. Three references are generally sufficient. Be prepared to give the name, job title, address, and telephone number for each reference if references are requested.

E-portfolio

An e-portfolio is designed to present your talents, experience, and accomplishments in an electronic format to a company or organization seeking employees. With an e-portfolio, you are not limited to a one- or two-page resume. The documents that you prepare for the e-portfolio provide you with additional marketing exposure. An e-portfolio can be provided on a CD or made available on the Internet. An e-portfolio should include the following:

- Technical skills
- Course work
- Professional-development workshops and seminars
- Volunteer work in the community
- Awards
- Video clips of presentations
- Your resume

A streaming audio and video clip may also be included in an e-portfolio; for example, the clip may include appropriate presentations that you have done.

Blog

A **blog** (short for Web log) is a Website that contains dated entries in reverse chronological order (most recent first) about a particular topic. A blog is often described as an online journal or diary.

PATRICIA LAFAVER

1823 Corinth
Euless, TX 76039-0743
plf@adm.net
(817) 555-0125

SUMMARY

Administrative assistant for Oakwood Community College, communication, telephone, keyboarding, human relations, filing, problem solving, research, and computer skills. Associate of Applied Sciences Degree. Proficient in Microsoft Word, Excel, PowerPoint, and Access 2007.

PROFESSIONAL EXPERIENCE

2008 to the present: Administrative assistant, Oakwood Community College, Fort Worth, Texas
Manager of three student assistants
Prepared class scheduling information
Set up files
Maintained filing system
Assisted students with questions about college programs and courses
Prepared and submitted textbook orders for faculty
Keyed syllabi
Scheduled classrooms
Assisted with class scheduling

2006-2007: Part-time cashier, Brandon Bookstore, Fort Worth, Texas

EDUCATION

Associate of Applied Sciences Degree, 2007, Oakwood Community College, Fort Worth, Texas

PROFESSIONAL ORGANIZATIONS

International Association of Administrative Professionals

REFERENCES

References furnished on request.

FIGURE 17.6 Electronic Resume

Blogs are posted by people and organizations for many different purposes. Blogs can be used to share words, text, photos, movies, and audio files to help people communicate. A blog can be used to provide prospective employers with access to information about you and your qualifications for a job. This type of blog can be an important supplement to a resume for some job seekers.

Creating a blog is not difficult; services that host a blog are available. Some of these services are free and some charge a licensing fee. Many sites have a wizard to help you with the process. Additionally, you can search for information about a company or organization through a blog. For example, a number of the Fortune 500 companies have blogs. Companies such as Cisco Systems, General Electric, Microsoft, and Texas Instruments have blogs.

Prepare a Letter of Application

Think of the letter as a sales letter—one in which your purpose is to sell your abilities. If you write a poor letter, the person receiving it is not likely to look at your resume. The basic goals of the letter are to:

- State your interest in the position.
- Provide general information about your skills (specific information appears in your resume).
- Sell your skills (let the reader know you have something to offer the organization).
- Transmit your resume and request an interview.

Figure 17.7 is a sample of the type of letter you might write. Notice that the letter has three parts: (1) stating your interest in the position, (2) providing general information concerning your skills (specific information appears in your resume), and (3) requesting an interview. If you are asked to submit a letter of application electronically, follow the same formatting guidelines you would use for an electronic resume. Keep the format simple so it can be transmitted and scanned easily.

Interview Successfully

Assume you have done well thus far in the application process. Now you have the chance to interview. A **job interview** is a meeting where a job applicant talks with an employer to determine whether the applicant is suitable for a job.

---

focus on *Preparing an Effective Blog*

Follow these suggestions to create an effective blog.

- View several blogs to note effective and ineffective layouts and features.

- Read articles online to learn more about blogs.

- Sign up with a blog hosting service to get started. Search the Internet for *blog host* to find options. Some sites offer free hosting.

- Post articles about projects you are working on—current trends in the administrative professional field, for example.

- Include summaries of professional papers that you have written; for example, significant conclusions of research that you have done.

- Include an audio presentation you have developed.

- Include a blogroll (links to your favorite blogs) of carefully screened sites.

- Maintain a professional tone in all postings.

Patricia LaFaver

1823 Corinth   plf@adm.net
Euless, TX 76039-0743   (817) 555-0125

May 15, 20--

Ms. Teresa Winwright
Vice President of Marketing
United Pharmaceuticals
1211 East Eighth Street
Fort Worth, TX 76102-5201

Dear Ms. Winwright

Your advertisement in *The Fort Worth Star Telegram* requesting an administrative assistant is most appealing to me. I am eager to talk with you about joining United Pharmaceuticals in this capacity.

My qualifications include the following:

- An associate degree in Administrative Systems from Oakwood Community College, Fort Worth, Texas
- One year of work experience in the field
- Excellent human relations and communication skills
- Knowledge of computer software, including *Microsoft Word, Excel, PowerPoint,* and *Access*

My resume, giving further details about my experiences and skills, is enclosed. May I have the opportunity to discuss my qualifications with you? I will call you next week to arrange a meeting at your convenience. I look forward to talking with you.

Sincerely

Patricia LaFaver

Patricia LaFaver

Enclosure: Resume

FIGURE 17.7 Letter of Application

Focus on your strengths when being interviewed.

Your performance during the interview process is critical. If you do not plan well and do not perform well, the job may go to someone else. You must present your strengths well in the interview in the hope that you will be offered a job that matches your skills, interests, and aspirations. Now is the time to focus on developing excellent interviewing skills. Several skills for making the interview a success are presented in the following sections.

Online Prescreening

A growing number of organizations are engaging in online prescreening of applicants. **Prescreening** involves gathering information about an applicant prior to a formal in-person interview. It allows the company to process numerous resumes quickly and efficiently. The technology used to collect screening information is called an *Applicant Tracking System* or *ATS*. The validity and reliability of prescreening is still being analyzed; however, there is some evidence that prescreening does eliminate the applicants who are unqualified. If you apply to a company that prescreens, be prepared to answer questions in the following areas:

- Salary requirements
- Present employment
- Education
- Experience in the type of job for which you are applying
- Your current employment status
- Whether or not you have ever been fired

Additionally, there may be several personality-based questions, such as:

- Are you able to work well under pressure?
- Can you multitask? (Are you able to handle several things at one time?)
- Do you finish tasks in the timeframes established?

These questions are merely a few that you may be asked. It is a good idea to have your resume with you as you answer the questions. It will help you to remember dates of employment, where employed, and similar types of information.

Remember to write a thank-you letter to the person(s) involved in the online prescreen. Just as it is important to write a thank-you letter after a face-to-face interview, it is also important to write a thank-you letter after an online interview. An example of a thank-you letter is provided later in this chapter.

Telephone Prescreening

Telephone prescreening is used by some employers to conduct an interview. If you are invited to engage in a telephone interview, here are several suggestions for handling it smoothly and effectively.

- Remember that the tone of your voice carries a lot of weight over the telephone.
- Smiling as you speak can make you sound more pleasant.
- Ask good friends, who will be honest with you, how you sound on the telephone. Do you sound cordial or aloof? Articulate or fumbling?
- Standing up while being interviewed may help. Some research indicates that you sound more self-confident and dynamic when you stand while talking over the phone.
- Be prepared for obvious questions; have your resume with you and go over the resume before the telephone call.
- Be able to respond to any items that you have on your resume. Remember that the individual calling has your resume and may be asking questions directly triggered by the resume.
- Speak so the person can hear you.
- Write a thank-you letter after the telephone interview just as you would if it were a face-to-face interview.

In-Person Interview

The in-person interview may be a second step for you after a prescreening interview. For example, you may have already been interviewed through an online prescreening process or through a telephone interview. You have done well on the previous types of interviews, and now you are ready for an in-person interview. The in-person interview can also be the first interview you have with an organization. Whatever the situation is, you need to do your homework in preparing for an in-person interview.

Review the information you found when researching the organization earlier. Do additional research if needed. The better informed you are, the better your chances of "looking great" in the interview. If the in-person is a follow up from the online or telephone screening, review what you learned from these processes. If in the past you have used social networks such as MySpace or Facebook, look back over what you have put on that site. If a stranger can find you online, so can a prospective employer. If you have put some personal information online that you feel will now embarrass you, you should take it off.

MAP THE ROUTE

Map the route that you will take to the job interview on the computer. Mapquest.com is an easy-to-use resource that can assist you in determining the best route to the job interview site. Prepare your route several days in advance of your interview; do not leave it to the last minute. Place your directions in your briefcase. Allow plenty of travel time in case the traffic is heavy at the time of your interview. It is also a good idea to drive to the location the day before and determine parking availability. You may not have parking at the building and have to park in a parking lot.

DRESS APPROPRIATELY

Dress is extremely important when interviewing. First impressions do count. Someone who is not appropriately dressed for the interview begins the session with a negative impression that is often difficult to overcome. Here are suggested guidelines for dressing for an interview.

Women should wear a two-piece business suit that is cleaned and pressed or a dress with a matching jacket. A dark blue, gray, or taupe color

Dress is extremely important when interviewing.

© Javier Pierini / Photodisc / Getty Images

For men who are interviewing, a two-piece business suit of dark blue or light to dark gray is appropriate. A black suit may be considered inappropriate due to its severity. Long-sleeved shirts should always be worn, with the color being either white or cream. A tie that complements the shirt and suit should be worn. Ties should be relatively conservative and in good condition. Dark socks that are over the calf and that will not slide down are important. A leather belt that matches the shoes should be worn. Minimum jewelry (a wedding ring or college ring) and a watch are acceptable.

ARRIVE AT THE JOB SITE

Plan to arrive several minutes before the interview time. When you arrive at the interview location, be pleasant with everyone you see—receptionists, administrative assistants, and other employees you may encounter. Keep a smile on your face, and say "thank you" often. Do not underestimate the impression you make on the receptionists and others waiting in the reception area. People in the area may be employees sent there to evaluate how job applicants react to the stress of waiting for an interview.

DEVELOP A LIST OF QUESTIONS

Before going to the interview, develop a list of questions that you might ask given the opportunity. Here are several questions that you might ask:

- What are the specific duties of the job?
- Could you tell me something about the people with whom I will be working if I am accepted for the position?
- I read on your Web page that your organization has grown over the last ten years. To what do you attribute the growth? Do you expect it to continue?
- When will you make a decision about hiring?
- What will I need to do to advance in the organization?
- Do you consider the organization to be in good financial health?

is always appropriate. A skirt is preferred over pants. The style of the suit should be conservative—not flashy. The hemline should be conservative; knee length is desirable. The color of shoes should match the clothes; a medium heel is preferable to a high heel. A closed-toe shoe is preferred over an open one. A handbag that matches the shoes is appropriate. Hose should be neutral in color and sheer. Women should wear a minimum of jewelry—nothing flashy or in poor taste. Generally, the jewelry should be gold, silver, or pearls. Small earrings are appropriate. A conservative watch is appropriate. Makeup should look subtle and natural. Nails should be clean and neatly groomed. Light polish is acceptable—pink or beige. Hair should be clean, styled appropriately for you. You should not wear hair clips or barrettes. Very light perfume is acceptable; no overpowering scent.

- What has the organization's growth been over the last five years?
- To whom would I be reporting?

DEAL WITH TOUGH QUESTIONS

When dealing with tough questions, honesty is always the best policy. However, you do not need to give all the details of each situation. Listed here are several tough questions that you might be asked. Give some thought to these and other questions that you think might come up because of your particular background or experiences. Be prepared to answer as thoughtfully and thoroughly as appropriate.

- Why did you work for this organization such a short time?
- Your salary seems extremely low in your last position. Why?
- You have moved frequently from one job to another. Why?
- Have you ever been fired?
- Did you ever have a poor relationship with your employer or employees within the organization where you worked?
- What is the biggest work-related mistake you have made?
- What would you do if your supervisor asked you to do something that is illegal?
- What would you do if your supervisor asked you to do something that conflicts with your ethics?
- If I talked with your former colleagues, what would they say about you?
- Why do you think you are qualified for the position?

Although answering such questions is not easy, here are several suggestions that may be helpful:

- Try to avoid a direct answer if the question can hurt your chance of getting the position.
- Do not say more than you need to say in answering the question. In such a situation, brevity is more important than thoroughness.
- If you have any concerns about possible skeletons in your closet, conduct a background check on yourself so that you will know what employers may discover. You do have rights in regard to background checks. Future employers must obtain prior authorization from you and give you the reason for not hiring you if it is based on negative background information.

CLOSE WITH PROFESSIONALISM

End the interview in a professional manner. Express your interest in the position, if you are interested. Ask when you may expect to hear from the company regarding the job. Thank the interviewer for his or her time.

Write a Thank-You Letter

Write a follow-up letter immediately after the interview, thanking the person for the interview. This letter also gives you the opportunity to provide the interviewer with any details that you failed to call to his or her attention. A sample thank-you letter is given in Figure 17.8.

Professional Pointers

A successful interview can lead to getting the job that's right for you. Strive to avoid these common interviewing mistakes:

- Being late
- Not making eye contact
- Criticizing past employers
- Asking questions about salary and benefits immediately
- Not answering questions concisely
- Being too self-assured (having a cocky attitude)
- Failing to demonstrate interest in the position by asking few questions
- Providing a resume with grammar and typographical errors
- Failing to bring a list of references
- Not articulating interest in the position

Patricia LaFaver

1823 Corinth   plf@adm.net
Euless, TX 76039-0743   (817) 555-0125

October 10, 20--

Mr. Alberto Rodriguez
TX Industries, Inc.
1001 East Eighth Street
Fort Worth, TX 76102-1001

Dear Mr. Rodriguez

Thank you for interviewing me this morning for the administrative assistant position in
your Human Relations Department.

I believe that my associate degree and my experience at Oakwood Community College
have prepared me well for this position. My written and oral communication skills,
along with my computer skills, are strong. Additionally, my problem-solving and people
skills will be assets to the Human Relations Department. I am pleased and excited about
the possibility of being part of your team at TX Industries, Inc.

You may reach me by calling 817-555-0125 or emailing me at plf@adm.net. I look
forward to hearing from you soon.

Sincerely

Patricia LaFaver

Patricia LaFaver

FIGURE 17.8 Thank-You Letter

Conduct an Interview Evaluation

You may do very well in an interview and still not get the job. In that case, go over the experience in your mind, playing back what happened. Jot down your thoughts about how you did. Note the questions you had trouble answering. Note any questionable reactions from the interviewer. Review your thoughts and notes with a trusted adviser. Ask her or him how you may improve. A job rejection is no reason to become depressed. Your task is to learn from each interview and maintain a positive attitude.

Evaluate a Job Offer

If you are offered a position, you need to ask yourself some questions before you decide whether to accept it. Making the right job decision is extremely important. Remember if all goes well, you will be spending a large part of your week with this company and the people in the department where you work.

As you think about the job and the work environment, ask yourself the following questions and answer them truthfully considering the interview, the people you met, and the research that you have done on the company.

- Is the work environment comfortable, challenging, and exciting?
- Will I have a chance to work with people I believe I can respect and admire?
- Will the work be interesting?
- Are the values of the organization consistent with my own?
- Are the benefits and compensation packages acceptable?
- Did the people I met seem to be pleased with their organization?
- Does there seem to be ongoing planning and goals that meet the long-term needs of the organization?

Your goal is to find the right position for you—one where you can grow and learn.

Opportunity for Advancement

Do your career goals match what the company can offer? Is there a career path that will allow you to move up in the company, assuming that you are a star performer? From your observation during the interview, your Web research, and talking with knowledgeable friends concerning the company, will you have job opportunities within the company that will allow you to grown, learn, and accept positions with a high level of responsibility and authority?

Acceptable Salary

Assume that you have answered in a positive manner the questions asked previously. Now it is time to consider your salary. Have you researched the salary ranges that are being offered in companies of like size? Do you know what is generally offered for individuals at your experience level? Do you need to accept the first offer? Are you afraid if you do not that you will lose the job offer? Most employers expect you to negotiate to some extent; however, if you really like the company, you do not want to ask for a salary that is well above the market for your experience and ability. If you have recently finished your two-year degree and have only a limited amount of actual related work experience, you cannot expect to start out at the top of the scale. Neither should you accept a salary that is too low for the position being offered. Another basic consideration concerns benefits. You need to consider carefully the benefits package. Is it in line with benefit packages being offered by other companies?

If you are offered a salary and benefits package that is below what seems to be typical in the market, you may not want to take the position. However, if the offer is attractive and meets your needs and expectations, take the offer unless you have uncovered some facts about the company that are extremely negative. If the package is not acceptable, you may make a counteroffer. However, do understand that some companies are not open to a counteroffer.

Develop Job Advancement Strategies

Your reward for completing the job search process successfully is getting the position you want. Once you have the position, maintain the same enthusiasm you had when you applied for the position. The organization selected you because you fit its needs. If you fulfill your employer's expectations and demonstrate that you are capable of accepting more responsibility, raises and promotions can be your reward. Several tips to help you succeed are presented in the next sections.

Get a Great Start

Once you have the position, maintain the same enthusiasm you had when you applied for the position. You now have the opportunity to demonstrate the skills you listed on your resume. Additionally, pay attention to what is happening in the organization and learn daily from the people with whom you work and from your experiences.

Understand the Organization's Goals

Ask about the directions of your department. If a strategic plan for the organization exists, read it. Determine how you might contribute to the strategic directions of your unit. If you have the opportunity to attend meetings of your unit or to discuss long-range and short-range goals, do so. As an administrative assistant, you may be involved in putting on paper these goals and distributing them to others within your group.

Show Initiative

Continually review the plan that you have established for yourself. Evaluate your plan every six months or so; change the plan if needed. Review your formal job description. Is there something that you need to add to your plan based on your formal job description? When you know something needs to be done, do it. Do not leave it to others to do if you are capable of the task. Welcome challenges! When you encounter a challenging opportunity, ask yourself, "What new skill do I need to develop? What do I need to learn about the job and the company? Am I constantly seeking learning opportunities? Am I helping to create goodwill in the organization?"

Listen, Observe, and Learn

Ask your boss on a regular basis for his or her feedback. Do not wait for the six-month or yearly evaluation to hear what this person might say. Ask appropriate questions when you seek feedback. A few questions that you might ask are as follows:

- What suggestions do you have for me in improving my performance?
- Are there certain skills that I should acquire?
- How can I be a better administrative assistant?

Listen to what your supervisor and co-workers tell you. Observe workplace expectations and acceptable behaviors. Ask questions when you do not understand a task you are given. Grow from feedback that is provided to you. For example, if you have performance appraisals every six months, listen carefully to any suggestions that your supervisor makes. Do not be upset by criticism. Realize that the criticism is not of you as an individual, but of skills you need to improve to perform more effectively.

Live Your Values

Throughout this course, the importance of values has been emphasized—values for the organization and values for the individual worker. After several months on the job, you need to ask yourself these questions:

- Am I living my values? If not, why not?
- Are the organization's values clear?
- Do my values mesh with those of the organization?

Do not be upset if your work performance is criticized by your employer—your task is to learn and grow.

• Is this an organization where I can continue to live my values, learn, and grow in my job?

Continue to Network

Think of your network as a living and changing one. Over time you will lose some contacts and gain others. Email or call your contacts periodically. Send thank-you notes when someone helps you. Additionally, do not think of networks as one-sided. The people within your network can help you, but you also can help them.

Handle a Job Change Appropriately

You may decide to leave a job voluntarily or you may have no choice. Whatever your reasons for leaving, you must be professional in how you handle your departure.

Layoff or Termination

With companies downsizing, layoffs are common. In such a situation, keep in mind that you did not cause the situation. Consider what you want to do next, and mobilize your resources to help you find a position that fits your needs and abilities.

Assume your job is terminated. Even though you feel rejection and insecurity, it is not a time to consider yourself a failure. It is a time to analyze why you lost your job. Listen carefully to what your employer tells you about your performance. Then determine that you will learn and grow from it. For example, if the firing is due to your lack of skills, determine what skills you need to develop as you continue to pursue your career goals.

Exit Interview

Many organizations ask employees who are leaving to complete an exit interview. An **exit interview** is a meeting that someone from the company has with an employee whose job has been terminated or who has resigned. Generally, an impartial person, perhaps a staff member in the Human Resources Department, conducts the exit interview. The purpose of an exit interview is to hear any insights the employee has that could help the company improve. Even if you are unhappy, do not make negative remarks on an exit interview. Keep in mind the old adage about not burning your bridges. You may need a reference from the organization.

Summary

To reinforce what you have learned in this chapter, study this summary.

- When preparing for a job search, think carefully about your interests, values, skill and abilities, and the type of organization for which you would like to work. Set both long-term and short-term career goals and then work toward accomplishing these goals.

- Develop a traditional or targeted job search plan.

- Develop search strategies such as developing and maintaining networks, engaging in online searches, visiting employment agencies, reading newspapers, and talking with college recruiters.

- Research companies of interest to you by viewing company Websites, reading annual reports and news stories, and talking with people about the organization.

- Prepare your resume carefully. The basic types of resumes are chronological, functional, and electronic resumes.

- A resume reference is a person who knows your academic ability and/or work skills and habits and is willing to recommend you to employers.

- An e-portfolio is designed to present your talents, experience, and accomplishments in an electronic format to a company or organization seeking employees.

- A blog can be used to provide prospective employers with access to information about you and your qualifications for a job. This type of blog can be an important supplement to a resume.

- A letter of application is generally the first contact you have with a potential employer. Its main goal is to help you get a job interview.

- A job interview is a meeting where a job applicant talks with an employer to determine whether the applicant is suitable for a job.

- Prescreening involves gathering information about an applicant prior to a formal interview and may be done online or by telephone.

- Applicants should dress appropriately for an in-person interview, develop a list of questions that can be asked, and be prepared to deal with tough questions from the interviewer.

- Applicants should write a follow-up letter thanking the interviewer and providing any details left out during the interview.

- Conduct a self-evaluation of the interview in an effort to improve performance.

- When you are offered a position, ask yourself if this is the right work environment, right company, and right job for you. Also consider the opportunity for advancement and the salary.

- Develop job advancement strategies. For example, understand the organization's goals; show initiative; and seek feedback about your performance.
- Handle a job change appropriately. If necessary, prepare yourself to deal with a layoff or job termination with grace. Be determined to find a position where you can use your skills to a greater advantage.
- Be as positive as possible during an exit interview.

What's the Problem?

Enrique has chosen to use the Web exclusively in applying for jobs. In the last three months, Enrique has applied for ten jobs online. He was invited to one interview, but he did not like the person who interviewed him. She was, in his opinion, too demanding. She repeatedly told him that his skills needed to be improved. She concentrated on telling him how little experience he had and ignored his honors from his two-year program. He was not offered the job.

In college, Enrique did very well; in fact, he was chosen as an outstanding graduate. He had a 3.5 grade point average. He enjoyed his classes and was told many times by faculty that he would do well in the business world. He is so frustrated and confused!

What suggestions do you have for Enrique as he continues his job search?

Let's Discuss

1. Make a list of your strengths as they relate to your career.
2. Make a list of your weaknesses as they relate to your career. Explain how you will try to improve your weaknesses.
3. Name four sources or ways to learn about job listings.
4. Define networking and discuss how networking can be helpful in a job search.
5. List five items of information you want to know about a company before applying for a position with the company.
6. When applying for a position, would you use a chronological or a functional resume? Explain the rationale for your answer.

Critical-Thinking Activity

Alice Chang graduated with an AAS degree two years ago. She was an A student; however, she was extremely shy. She did not take part in any extracurricular activities. After graduation, Alice decided that she would work in a variety of part-time positions before applying for a full-time job. She thought that such an approach would help her understand more about where she would like to work. For a year, she has worked in three part-time positions—one in an accounting firm, one in a legal office, and one in a college. She believes that she has learned tremendously from these jobs and is ready to pursue a position in a legal office.

Alice has applied for six jobs in the last two months; however, she has not been offered any of the jobs. When asked certain questions by the interviewers, here is how Alice responded:

- When asked about her present job, Alice said that she did not have a full-time job.
- When asked about her college experience, Alice said that she made good grades but that she held no offices. She also stated that she had not joined any clubs.
- When asked by the interviewers if she had any questions, Alice responded that she did not.
- Alice was very nervous in all interviews; however, she believes she presented herself well.
- She answered each question with the facts and was extremely polite. She thanked each interviewer and expressed her interest in the position.

Alice is discouraged. She does not know what is going wrong. She had no trouble finding part-time jobs. On each of her part-time jobs, she was asked to become a full-time employee. She refused because she thought that she had no chance to move up to positions of greater responsibility in any of the companies.

What advice would you give Alice? What is she doing wrong and how can she improve?

Vocabulary Review

Open the *Word* file *CH17 Vocabulary* on the Student CD. Complete the vocabulary review for Chapter 17.

English and Word Usage Drill

Complete the English and Word Usage Drill for Chapter 17 found in the *Applications Workbook*.

Workplace Applications

17-1 Rate Workplace Skills and Abilities

(Goal 1)

1. Open the *Word* file *CH17 Skills Form* found on the Student CD.
2. Rate yourself on the skills and abilities listed on the form. Be honest with yourself.
3. For areas where you need to improve, determine the steps you plan to take to improve. List these steps.

17-2 Plan a Job Search

(Goal 2)

1. Write an explanation of how you would conduct a job search. For example, would you search first on the Web or would you seek only jobs listed with an agency or in the newspaper? Explain why you have chosen your particular search strategy.

17-3 Research Companies

(Goal 3)

internet

1. Select three companies or organizations of interest to you. Use the Internet to do research on these companies to answer the following questions:

    • How long has the company been in business?

    • What types of products or service does the company deliver?

    • What is the possibility of growth with this company or within this industry?

2. Once you have done a comprehensive search, identify the company that you believe would be the best choice to help you achieve your career goals. Explain why you would like to work for this company.

17-4 Prepare a Resume and Letter

(Goal 4)

e-portfolio

1. Assume you are applying for a job with the company you selected in Workplace Application 17-3. Prepare a resume to use in applying to the company. Assume that there is a listing for a job for which you are qualified.

2. Prepare a letter of application to send to the company or organization with your resume.

17-5 Practice Interview Skills

(Goal 5)

team building

1. Work with two classmates on this project.

2. Each person will serve in each position—as interviewer, an observer, and as job applicant. Complete these steps to prepare for the interview:

    • Identify a job position for which you will apply when you are the applicant and share this information with your classmates.

    • Write a list of questions you will ask the applicant when you are the interviewer.

    • Write a list of items you will watch for when you are the observer.

3. Participate in two interviews (as an interviewer and as an applicant) and be an observer in one interview, each in turn. Make notes as you watch the interview when you are the observer. Be certain to point out both the strengths and the weaknesses of the applicant's performance.

17-6 Develop Job Advancement Strategies

team building

(Goal 6)

1. Work with two classmates on this project.

2. Assume you are working for the company that you identified in Activity 17-3. Develop a list of job advancement strategies that you can use on this job; be realistic in your thinking.

3. Share your strategies with your classmates. As a team, critique each person's advancement strategies and offer suggestions for improvement.

Assessment of Chapter 17 Goals

Did you successfully complete the chapter goals? Evaluate yourself by filling out the form found in Chapter 17 of the *Applications Workbook*.

chapter 18

Leadership and Management: Challenges and Characteristics

Learning Goals

1. Define *leadership* and describe leadership traits.

2. Define *management* and describe the functions of management.

3. Determine the administrative professional's job responsibilities.

4. Discuss the benefits of a healthy lifestyle, including proper diet and physical exercise.

Leadership Traits

Leadership and management are commonly used terms in and outside the workplace. People may come to respect those individuals who can help achieve the goals of the organization and who constantly demonstrate their leadership abilities through interactions with individuals within the organization. Conversely, people tend not to respect those individuals who may hold leadership positions yet never demonstrate any characteristics of a true leader. Businesses are acutely aware of the need to develop leaders, and a considerable amount of money and time is devoted to this development by organizations throughout the world. For example, development of leadership potential in the organization often occurs through the following strategies:

- Identifying potential leaders throughout the organization
- Providing on-the-job opportunities for potential leaders through mentoring, coaching, and training seminars
- Developing leaders within their current jobs or having them accept additional assignments outside their field of expertise so that they may develop skills that they do not have presently
- Providing both positive and negative feedback to the potential leaders to identify their weaknesses and turn their weaknesses into strengths

- Using a team approach, where teams of individuals are provided with growth opportunities through several weeks of intensive training
- Encouraging individuals to be leaders in their communities; for example, leaders of charities and contributors to helping schools provide enhanced opportunities for students
- Making leadership development a part of the culture of the organization

Many people belong to clubs and organizations that are headed by individuals who may or may not demonstrate leadership. These people are judged fairly quickly in their abilities to get the job done or fail in getting it done. For example, the leader who can accomplish with extraordinary skill and knowledge the goals of an organization is quickly labeled an outstanding leader by his or her constituency. Conversely, an ineffective leader may not be able to help the group coalesce around goals and thus accomplishes very little, never gaining the respect of his or her constituency and never delivering on the organizational goals.

As you grow in your knowledge and skills, you may take on several management tasks in your job. Additionally, as you develop a high level of skill and expertise, you certainly may become a leader in your administrative assistant role and garner the respect of both leadership and management within the organization. A **leader** is a person who guides or inspires others. Leaders are individuals who:

- Have great self understanding.
- Demonstrate self-management skills.
- Understand organizational culture.
- Have the ability to develop self and others within the organization.

Self Understanding

As people grow from childhood to adulthood, they have many experiences with a wide variety of individuals: parents, other relatives, friends, and acquaintances. They learn from each of these individuals, and as they grow to adulthood they develop a sense of self understanding. Without self understanding, it is impossible to lead others.

Women are assuming more positions of authority in business than ever before in the nation's history.

© Erik Snyder / Digital Vision / Getty Images

It is important that you are able to consider what you have been taught by significant others in your life. It is also important that you determine whether what you have been taught is going to guide your life in the future. Self understanding occurs when, after questioning and interpreting the knowledge that you have learned from others, you are able to:

- Interpret the statements of others.
- Test or examine the knowledge or wisdom of others.
- Learn from those who are wise.
- Clarify your own values and determine how you want to live your life.

To help you understand this concept more, take a hard look at yourself as you read the following questions.

- What do I value? What are my goals in life? What can I contribute to the work environment?
- What do I want to achieve in life?
- How will I know if I am successful? How do I evaluate success?

- What are my administrative professional strengths?
- How do I learn?
- How do I perform as a student?
- How do I believe I will perform as an administrative professional?

Self Management

Self management within an organization refers to methods, skills, and strategies by which individuals can effectively direct their own activities. In order to engage in self management, an individual must be able to answer the following questions concerning the organization and its culture.

- What are the goals of the organization?
- How may I contribute to the achievement of the goals?
- As an individual, what goals should I set for myself that support the organizational goals and also allow me to be more effective in my position?
- Do I have areas of weakness that need to be improved before I can achieve my goals? If so,

Do I understand the culture and climate of this organization?

what are these areas and how do I improve them? For example, am I as effective in my human relations skills as I should be? Do I work well with our team in the office? If my answer is "no," what do I need to do to improve the relationship with my team?

- Do I understand the culture and climate of the organization? Each organization has its own culture which is formed by the founders, its past leadership, its current leadership, its history, its size, and its climate.

Once you have answered these questions thoughtfully and thoroughly, your next step is to commit to improving yourself in the areas of weakness you have identified. Organizational growth is not limited to the organization exclusively. As you grow within an organization, you also grow in your personal abilities and in your abilities to relate to the people who are outside the workplace—your family, your friends, and others.

Organizational Culture Development

Have you ever walked into an organization for the first time and felt immediately a sense of excitement and commitment within the organization? The receptionist greeted you with warmth, enthusiasm, and caring. The personnel manager smiled and said with great enthusiasm, "Let me begin this interview by telling you about our company—our goals, our objectives, our commitment to individual growth, and our long-term plans of expansion of our organization to an international location." Your immediate response was probably a good feeling, along with the belief that maybe you had found a home—a place where you could feel part of a dynamic organization and learn and grow. You began to feel that you understood something about the culture and environment of the organization.

Organizational culture is defined as a shared group of core assumptions or beliefs learned by the people within an organization. These assumptions are determined basically by the following:

- The beliefs and values of the founders of the organization
- The learning experiences of employees
- The beliefs and values that are the result of new leaders and employees

Culture is basically the personality of the organization. It is a term that is difficult to express succinctly and efficiently, yet you know it when you observe it. The culture of the organization can be an effective or ineffective one. Just as you recognize almost immediately an effective culture, you also can recognize quickly an ineffective culture. In an ineffective culture, employees may constantly wonder if they are the next people to be laid off. There is constant confusion in the organization as to where it is headed. Trust among management and coworkers is almost nonexistent, as is trust between individual employees. **Fortress culture** is one term used for such a culture. In this culture, individuals often attempt to defend their own turf and their own job responsibilities through building a fortress strong enough to contain them until they can find another job. Usually, you can expect high turnover of personnel and frequent reorganizations within

Trust among people is almost nonexistent in an organization with a fortress culture.

such an organization. Cleary, it is not a place individuals enjoy working.

Value Recognition and Alignment

Once the organizational values and values of the people within the organization are aligned, these values are reflected in the decisions that are made in the organization. For example, the leader articulates the relationship between defined tasks and the values of the organization. As each task in the planning process is envisioned, the question asked is this: *Does the task support the stated values of the organization?* If it does not, the task does not become part of the plan. Value-driven leaders understand that success does not come from merely talking about values; these leaders understand that success comes from consistently putting values into action.

Trait Development

Effective leaders have a number of traits, including the following:

- Living by a set of values
- Developing self and others
- Serving
- Leading
- Building a shared vision
- Engendering trust
- Empowering others
- Rewarding risk taking

LIVE BY A SET OF VALUES

True leaders within an organization stand firmly on moral principles. They work within the organization to define what these principles are and to ensure that the ethical principles become a part of the daily life of the organization. When difficult decisions arise, true leaders stand on their espoused values.

If top leaders constantly espouse values, yet their daily behavior within the organization does not support these values, individuals within the organization quickly lose respect for these leaders. True leaders know that their actions must follow their words.

DEVELOP SELF

Clearly no one, no matter how intelligent and committed, can develop others without first committing to constantly developing herself or himself. If you are to be an outstanding leader, you must develop a plan for yourself that allows you to continually grow and learn. Just as a young child continues to grow and learn in an environment that is supportive and challenging, so does an effective leader continue to grow and learn. If the environment in which the leader is attempting to grow is not supportive of growth, it is time for the leader to take seriously the thought of moving to an organization that supports the growth of leaders. As a growing leader, here are several traits that you must continue to develop.

- Understand yourself—your strengths and your weaknesses.

© Image Source Ltd.

Leaders at the top of an organization must understand their values and live by them daily.

- Be a professional. Support the goals and objectives that have been mutually agreed on by the leadership of the organization.
- Be loyal to the organization. If you find you cannot be loyal to the organization due to the directions it is taking, it is time for you to move on.
- Be honest, competent, and committed.
- Understand your job and responsibilities.
- Help the people who report to you understand their jobs and responsibilities.
- Develop morale within an organization—constantly train, assist, and counsel.
- Be ever present—keep an open door, one that lets individuals know you are interested not only in the welfare of the organization but in the welfare of each person who reports to you.

SERVE

Effective leaders consider service to others as primary. In other words, effective leaders think first of how they can serve the organization, its goals, its employees, and the larger community outside the organization.

LEAD

Strong and effective leaders are not afraid to admit that a mistake has been made. For example, if a decision has been reached about an issue, strong leaders are willing to listen to people who do not agree with the decision made. In fact, strong leaders are willing to reconsider a decision if evidence is provided that the decision may be a bad one.

BUILD A SHARED VISION

Leaders of organizations must be visionary. Without a vision of what the organization should be, there may be no future for the organization. Leaders must be able to articulate the vision to those with whom they work and to get others within the organization not only to buy into the vision, but also to feel passionate about it. When individuals unite around a vision, they come together to produce a common goal. They understand and articulate their direction. They have the courage to continue to work toward their goal, no matter how difficult the process may be. For

individuals who share a vision, work becomes part of a larger purpose, affecting the climate and spirit of the organization. Risk taking and experimentation are common in such an organization.

ENGENDER TRUST

Effective leaders forge bonds of trust between themselves and the people with whom they work. In engendering this trust, leaders do what they say they will do. They consistently live the standards they set for themselves and constantly demonstrate their commitment to these standards.

- True leaders live by a stated set of values.
- They are reliable and predictable; they do what they say they will do and when they say they will do it.
- They are unshakably fair in public and in private.
- They constantly contribute to an effective organizational culture.
- They are role models of teaching and coaching.
- They do not manipulate or undermine the culture of the organization.

EMPOWER OTHERS

True leaders empower others. These leaders believe in people. They believe that people are good, honest, and well intentioned. They believe that people do the right thing when they are provided

---

Professional Pointers

Strive to develop these behaviors of effective leaders.

- **Effective leaders promote a spirit of cooperation.**
- **Effective leaders praise employees and workgroups for their contributions.**
- **Effective leaders believe the basic human needs of employees are important. (Employees must believe that an organization cares about them.)**
- **Effective leaders celebrate the success of individuals.**

the resources to accomplish a task. True leaders empower others through:

- Providing employees with access to information that will help them increase their productivity and effectiveness.
- Allowing employees a voice in decision making.
- Encouraging employees to take on greater responsibilities in their jobs.

Empowered employees feel a sense of ownership and control over their jobs. They understand they are responsible for getting their jobs done. Empowered employees usually are happier individuals; they trust the organization, feel a part of it, and enjoy the rewards the job provides.

REWARD RISK TAKING

Due to the constantly changing nature of work environments, organizations cannot take refuge in the status quo. Organizational leaders must understand that change is inevitable, and in the international economy it is important for businesses to lead in change directions rather than to follow passively. Managers, as well as employees, must be cognizant of the changes needed and have the courage to move forward with these changes.

A sign of an ineffective organizational culture is one that seeks to be free from risks. Organizations that are not willing to take risks usually do not last long. Executives who are afraid to make timely decisions can cost the organization considerable dollars. For example, if executives fail to move ahead in creative ways that not only increase the revenue of the organization but also make it an exciting and challenging place to work, both the profits earned and creativity suffer. Operating free of risk is rarely possible in the fast-based, multinational business world. What is important is a culture that stresses growth and risk taking. When people take risks they sometimes make mistakes. In a culture of innovation, some mistakes should be expected. Employees and organizations should not attempt to hide the mistakes but should attempt to grow from them. Common mistake misconceptions are shown in Figure 18.1.

Rather than adopt any of these behaviors concerning mistakes, the successful manager and the successful administrative professional realize that decisions are never free from risk. However, they do not let this fact stop them from taking risks. Neither do they defer an action that may be risky; they understand that without taking a

---

MISTAKE MISCONCEPTIONS

- If you make a mistake, you must hide it.
- Never accept that you made a mistake; put the blame on someone else.
- Do not attempt to learn from your mistakes.
- Never try a new idea or a new way of doing a task; you may be criticized if it does not work.
- Always assign blame when a mistake is made.

FIGURE 18.1 Mistake Misconceptions

© Triangle Images / Digital Vision / Getty Images

The successful manager and the successful administrative professional realize that decisions are never free from risk; they are always willing to challenge the status quo.

certain amount of risk, new ideas do not surface. They keep in mind that if they do not fail on occasion it means that they are not pushing the boundaries of innovation enough. Additionally, successful managers consistently encourage others to take risks that may help the organization to be more successful.

Similarly, the successful administrative professional is always willing to challenge the status quo and to look at new ways that work can be produced more efficiently. The individual reads consistently in the field, discovers new techniques or new equipment that can make the workplace more productive, and suggests changes that will allow the work to be produced more quickly and efficiently, thus saving the company money in the process. Leadership characteristics of risk takers are shown in Figure 18.2.

RECOGNIZE OUTSTANDING EMPLOYEES
The American culture recognizes and celebrates achievements and successes. For example, parades are held to celebrate the success of a football team that has just won a state championship game. Communities set off fireworks on July 4 to celebrate independence. Televised award ceremonies (with gift giving and congratulatory speeches) are held to honor individuals who are outstanding performers on stage and in movies. However, organizations often forget to honor individuals who contribute greatly to the success of the organization. Recognition of outstanding employees is crucial in a work environment. In addition to honoring people who have made outstanding contributions, such victory celebrations bring people together to share lessons of success, to learn from each other, and to reinforce the courage necessary to get extraordinary things done in organizations.

ESTABLISH A SPIRIT OF COMMUNITY
True leaders recognize that individuals work best when they are part of a community—a group of individuals who share common interests, beliefs, or goals. Celebrating the successes of the organization and the individuals within the organization through company-wide or department celebrations of excellence help employees to feel appreciated and part of a larger team. Additionally, individual recognition increases an employee's feeling of worth. Such celebrations also give leaders the opportunity to reinforce the shared values of the organization.

COMMIT TO CONTINUAL LEARNING
You live in a world where knowledge is increasing constantly, with change ever present. Organizations cannot take refuge in the past or conformity to the norm. These stances do not make sense if organizations are to be successful. Leadership within an organization must be willing to seek new answers to problems, try new approaches, and be flexible. Leaders must continually take risks if they are to remain a vibrant entity in the world today. Keys to successful risk taking include the following:

- Being open-minded
- Overcoming fear of mistakes
- Developing support teams
- Remaining flexible
- Going forward with confidence to achieve the essential goals of the organization

---

LEADERSHIP CHARACTERISTICS OF RISK TAKERS

Wise people who take risks engage in the following behaviors.

- Gather the appropriate information for the situation.
- Work from their strengths—not from their weaknesses.
- Prepare thoroughly for each work endeavor.
- Envision and articulate what can be gained from the project being considered.
- Are flexible.
- Recognize other individuals who take risks.
- Are open-minded.
- Have the ability to overcome fear of mistakes.

FIGURE 18.2 Leadership Characteristics of Risk Takers

ATTACK TOUGH ISSUES

Organizational life generally is not easy. The fast-paced business world offers numerous opportunities and also numerous issues. A leader realizes that it is necessary to deal with all problems, regardless of the difficulty of the problem. The work of the organization must be done. Many times there are **inhibitors** to a task—individuals who retard organizational growth or make goals and activities difficult to accomplish. Such individuals can and often do drain the organization of time and energy. They stand in the way of important goals that must be accomplished. The effective leader understands that she or he has the responsibility to remove these individuals who stand in the way of success. When leaders choose not to deal with inhibitors, the organization may fail to meet some of its major goals. Allowing incompetent individuals to stay in positions of power does not serve the leader, the organization, or, in many cases, the incompetent individual well. Although it takes courage to remove an incompetent individual, often this person realizes that he or she is not effective but does not have the courage to do something about the situation. A caring and supportive leader can help the individual address his or her incompetence and move on to another position within the organization or to another company.

CELEBRATE VICTORY

Victory celebrations within an organization are important in recognizing and rewarding those employees who consistently work hard to meet the needs of the organization and their workgroup. Why? Celebrations are significant ways to show the leader's gratitude, to foster a sense of community, and to help each person within the workgroup remember what is important to the organization. Additionally, celebrations bring people together around a common goal, producing a spirit of camaraderie and creativity within the organization.

FOLLOW AS WELL AS LEAD

Excellent leaders are also followers. They encourage new and creative methods of getting a job done. When someone comes to them with an idea that has merit, they recognize the importance of the idea and support the individual who has shared the idea. An effective leader understands clearly that all ideas do not originate with him or her. In a healthy environment, a **bilateralness** (affecting two sides equally) exists, with leaders who not only understand the importance of following, but also trust and encourage others to seek new methods of getting a job done. The excellent leader can easily take on the follower's role and bask in the accomplishments of the people with whom she or he works.

FOCUS ON CONTINUAL GROWTH

The excellent leader is continually learning and growing. This leader understands that status quo within an organization is not productive and can even lead to the demise of the company. In this information age, knowledge is constantly expanding. Continual growth requires that the leader read continually, recognize new ways of doing an old task, keep up with technological innovations that impact work, take courses if needed, and encourage people within the workgroup to engage in similar growth. Many organizations support the growth of employees through paying for relevant workshops and/or providing individuals with time off (many times with pay) to attend conferences or take college courses. Characteristics of change leaders are listed in Figure 18.3.

Definition and Functions of Management

Management is the act of directing and controlling people and resources to accomplish goals. Management may be thought of as the art of helping people be more effective than they would have been without the manager's assistance. You have already learned about the importance of leadership within an organization. Both leadership and management are crucial in an effective organization. Just as leadership cannot exist effectively without management,

FIGURE 18.3 Characteristics of Change Leaders

Continual learning is essential in our knowledge-explosion world.

© Dave & Les Jacobs / Blend Images / Jupiterimages

management cannot be effective without the support of leadership. If an organization is to be effective in reaching the goals and objectives established, both quality leadership and quality management must exist. As an administrative professional you will probably not start your career managing others. However, as you grow in your abilities and skills, you may assume a title such as *office manager*, and have several administrative professionals reporting to you.

Management includes a number of functions; eight extremely important ones are listed here.

- Creating a strategic vision
- Planning
- Organizing
- Motivating
- Delegating
- Teaching
- Recognizing and evaluating
- Discharging employees

Creating a Strategic Vision

Excellent leaders are **visionary**—able to see what is possible. They know how to set goals and motivate people to achieve these goals. When a new leader takes over a large organization, two of the first questions to be asked are: *Where is the organization going for the next five to ten years? Is there a strategic plan that focuses each unit on the objectives to be accomplished?* Without a strategic vision or plan, most organizations flounder. No one is clear on what the major tasks of the organization are and who should be accomplishing these tasks. A **strategic plan** sets the direction and goals for the organization's work, generally for the next five or fewer years. When the organization is in a constant state of change, a shorter timeframe is desirable. Additionally, numerous organizations today have sites in several different countries or have an international market for the product they produce, thus the strategic plan must be global in its perspective.

Planning

Planning is the process of thinking about the activities required to accomplish a goal—in the case of a company, the desired future of the business. Planning involves setting goals and objectives for an organization and developing plans for accomplishing these goals and objectives. The planning process of setting goals and objectives is usually done in two time frames—long-range and short-range. Many times top-level leadership (boards of directors, presidents, and vice presidents) sets the overall goals of organizations. This type of planning

The United States is part of a global society.

is referred to as strategic planning (the process of developing the organization's mission, overall goals, general strategies, and allocating resources). **Goals** generally focus on any desired changes or new directions that need to occur in the organization. Goals act as guidelines for all organization employees as to what the organization considers important work for the future. Activities established under each goal determine how the goals of the organization will be achieved. The leader of each unit of an organization is generally responsible, along with the individuals who report directly to her or him, for determining how their unit will contribute to meeting the organization's goals. Administration holds managers accountable for achieving the objectives defined. When evaluating an individual in management, one question often asked is, "Were you successful in achieving your unit's goals?" If the answer is "no" or "almost," the chief executive becomes concerned with the effectiveness of the unit and holds the manager responsible for ineffective leadership.

Organizing

Once planning occurs, the work is organized. **Organization** involves bringing together all resources—people, time, money, and projects—in the most effective way to accomplish organizational goals. Organizing around teams is common in organizations today. Few individuals within an organization can work in isolation effectively. Teams are generally more effective when the following conditions are present:

- The job to be accomplished is clear.
- People on the team work well together.
- Individuals share information.
- Teams have the authority to manage and change how work is accomplished.

Conversely, teams are not effective when these situations are present:

- The job to be accomplished is not clear.
- Resources are not available to allow the team to accomplish the task.

© Flying Colours Ltd / Digital Vision / Getty Images

focus on   *Evaluating Employees*

As a manager, you should have a carefully defined evaluation system, one that employees understand and that is adhered to by all managers. Here are several suggestions for evaluating and motivating employees.

- Maintain a job description for each job, including details of the requirements. Figure 18.4 gives a sample job description.

- Involve employees in establishing their job descriptions.

- Keep job descriptions current; ask employees to review their job descriptions at least once a year and recommend modifications if necessary.

- Establish formal evaluation procedures; involve employees in the process.

- Give a copy of the formal evaluation procedure to employees, along with the specific instrument you are using to evaluate their performance. Before the formal evaluation procedure, give employees a copy of the instrument. Ask them to do a self-evaluation and justify the ratings they give themselves.

- Evaluate performance on a daily basis. Employees should always know how they are performing. For example, if an employee prepared a report that contained grammatical errors, let the person know immediately. Do not withhold this information and then bring it up six months later during the employee's formal evaluation session.

- Allow adequate time for formal evaluation, which usually occurs every six months or every year. Set aside enough time to do it well. You may need to spend an hour or two with each employee.

- Choose an appropriate place for the evaluation. If you are using your office, ask your assistant not to interrupt you. Do not accept telephone calls, unless there is an emergency. Close the door to your office to ensure confidentiality.

- Managers are prone to micromanage.
- Employees are not empowered to do the work.
- Approval is necessary for each decision the team makes.
- Team members are not willing to take risks.

Motivating

Motivation means an inducement to act. Motivation may be **extrinsic** (coming from external factors such as salary increases or promotions) or **intrinsic** (from within the person; for example, something done because it is right and fits the person's values). The manager's job in working with a team is to know the people within the team well enough to fit each job needed to the person most likely to understand and successfully complete the task.

Delegating

Delegation is assigning tasks to others and empowering them to get the job done. One widely accepted definition of management is *getting work done through others*. Delegation requires that employees receive the proper information and training before a task is assigned. The capable manager understands the total project and delegates well. The manager takes advantage of the various strengths of the people assigned to the tasks. Additionally, the effective manager is able to identify the outcomes expected of each individual. Effective managers do not allow people to flounder in a sea of misunderstanding.

Teaching

Good managers are good teachers. These managers are well organized and good communicators.

They continually push individuals to reach new heights of competence. They do not try to solve all the problems for individuals within the organization. They attempt to build self-esteem and encourage all individuals to learn how to solve the problems that they face within the organization. They provide learning materials via the Web or in print. They hold workshops with consultants who are competent and knowledgeable of the tasks of the organization.

Evaluating and Recognizing Employees

Evaluation is important. Employees must know whether or not they are doing their jobs well. The effective manager understands the necessity of feedback and provides it continually. Feedback can be provided informally on a day-to-day basis and during formal evaluations. The Focus On feature provides more information about evaluating employees.

Leaders recognize more than the top performers in the organization; they recognize those individuals who are competently doing their jobs day after day. Making a constant effort each day to thank people (morning, noon, and at the end of the day) is part of making them feel valued. Just as the creative growth of children is promoted by parents who constantly praise, so is the growth of employees promoted by constant recognition from leaders within the organization. Figure 18.5 gives techniques that can help motivate employees.

Discharging When All Else Fails

Most managers find that it is difficult to always employ the right mix of people no matter how conscientiously they try to do so. Therefore, managers usually have the experience at least once in their work life (and probably more) of

---

JOB DESCRIPTION

Job Title: Administrative Assistant

Company: United Pharmaceuticals

Department: Human Resources

Skills

The position of administrative assistant requires these skills:

- Communication
- Time management
- Critical thinking
- Teamwork
- Computer applications (*Microsoft Office*)
- Keyboarding (accurate at 60 wpm)

Education

Associate degree or equivalent course work

Experience

Two years of workplace experience, with Human Resources Department experience preferred

Duties

- Input personnel records
- Prepare monthly personnel reports
- Compose correspondence
- Maintain a records management system
- Plan meetings
- Supervise one support staff person

FIGURE 18.4 Job Description

MOTIVATIONAL TECHNIQUES

- Set objectives.
- Give recognition.
- Develop a team.
- Delegate work.
- Pay appropriately for the job.

FIGURE 18.5 Motivational Techniques

having to discharge an employee. As you grow in your experience as an administrative professional, you may find that you occasionally have an individual who refuses or is unable to do his or her job at an acceptable level of performance.

Good managers consult with individuals who are not doing their jobs well. These managers identify the errors that are being made and offer suggestions for improvement. They also give the employee several weeks or months to improve job performance. However, if the employee fails to improve, the manager is forced to discharge the individual. Although it is never an easy task, good managers recognize that for the good of the work group and the total organization, they should not continue to employ people who are not capable of doing their jobs. When discharging an individual, follow these guidelines:

- Treat all employees fairly.
- When it becomes necessary to discharge an employee, be certain that it is for legitimate, job-related reasons.
- Keep written records of all indications of poor performance; record the date of the poor performance.
- Conduct regular, accurate, and candid performance evaluations.
- Consider the employee's feelings; if possible, discharge the person at the end of the day.
- State the reasons for discharge.
- If you anticipate problems with the employee, you may ask another manager to be in the room with you.
- Be certain that age, race, gender, and religion are not considerations when discharging an employee.
- Many states have employment at will regulations. These regulations allow you to discharge an employee for no reason. However, consult with the firm's attorney before following this path.
- Do not rehire an employee you have discharged for poor performance.

Administrative Professional Responsibilities

Throughout your educational experience, you have been obtaining knowledge and skills that will assist you in becoming a very capable administrative professional. The reliance on technology today continues to expand in offices across the world. With this expansion of technology, the role of the administrative professional has changed drastically from several years ago. There is overwhelming evidence that technology will continue to change the way people work and live.

What has the increase of technology meant for the administrative professional? One overarching answer is that due to technology, administrative professionals are assuming responsibilities that were once reserved for management. These responsibilities may include providing training and support for new administrative professionals and supervising administrative professionals. Additionally, your role in an office today will probably include many of the following job responsibilities.

- Using the Web to conduct research
- Researching, identifying, and recommending equipment needed for the office
- Providing training and support for new administrative professionals
- Researching, preparing, and presenting to administrative professionals on various topics of importance to the organization
- Supervising one or more administrative professionals
- Preparing presentation materials for your employer, including researching the subject, writing significant areas to be presented, and preparing visuals for the presentation
- Storing material on the computer and retrieving the material for dissemination to staff and clients

© Keith Brofsky / Photodisc / Getty Images

Be certain that age, race, gender, and religion are not considerations in discharging an employee.

- Organizing and maintaining paper and electronic files
- Creating spreadsheets, managing databases, and creating reports
- Arranging conference calls or Web seminars
- Working in teams with other administrative professionals
- Researching and preparing statistical reports
- Reviewing journals, such as legal or technology journals, and searching for relevant information on the Web
- Writing and posting job vacancies for administrative professionals
- Ordering supplies

This list of possible job responsibilities is not all inclusive. However, from this list you can see the magnitude and diversity of assignments that an administrative professional often handles. These job responsibilities include supervisory responsibilities—once thought to be the sole purview of management.

Live Your Values

You have already learned about the importance for leaders to understand and live their values.

Changing Responsibilities

The administrative professional's responsibilities have changed dramatically today. Continual changes that require additional management-related activities and increased technological knowledge are likely to occur in the future. These changes mean that as an administrative professional, you must:

- Continue to learn through attending appropriate seminars, becoming a member of IAAP, and constantly reading in your field and in management journals.

- Accept new responsibilities with a positive attitude.

As an administrative professional, you also must understand your values, make them known to others (particularly if you supervise employees), and constantly and consistently live your values. You gain the respect not only of your peers but also of management within the organization if you demonstrate behavior consistent with your stated values.

Plan

You have been introduced to the planning process used by managers earlier in this chapter. However, planning is not only for top-level management. If planning is to be successful, it must be understood and practiced by all individuals within an organization. Once top-level management has finished the long-range plan, it is generally distributed to all workgroups within the organization. You, as an administrative professional, may be involved in working with your supervisor and other people within your unit to help determine the long-range and short-range plans for your unit. As an administrative professional you should identify the objectives that you must accomplish in order to support the organizational plans.

DETERMINE NEEDS

An important step in planning is to determine needs for achieving goals. Assume that you presently have one assistant who reports directly to you. From your planning meetings with your employer, you know that the unit is expanding its operations in both China and India. Your employer has been clear with you that your workload will be greater. Your unit may need to employ an administrative assistant to help you with the workload.

You must think carefully through the skills that are needed. As you do so, you should consider your own skills and the set of future skills needed from you and the new employee in order to meet the needs of the organization. It is a good idea to make a list of the skills that you have

presently and the skills needed by the prospective employee. Your next step is to develop a job vacancy notice for the assistant, clearly listing the skills needed.

Where should the job vacancy notice be posted? In the newspaper? On the Web? In both places? Is this position at the level that there may be some interest from people already in your organization? If so, should you develop a job vacancy notice and advertise it first within your organization?

Will you need more space for the new assistant and the equipment? Should the office be a private one or is the space where you are located large enough for two people? If so, is it more efficient to have the assistant close to you or will efficiency increase by having the individual in a separate space?

What equipment do you need for the new assistant? Do you need a computer, a desk, a chair, and one or two filing cabinets (if you are using both electronic and paper files)?

You may want to look at equipment available on the Web to determine price ranges and equipment capacity. After you have done the Web research, you will probably want to visit two or three office equipment and furniture facilities to get a firm cost of the products and to be certain that you are recommending the right products. Through this process, you may make some discoveries that will change your mind as to the products you recommend.

PRESENT RECOMMENDATIONS

If you are satisfied that you have done your job well and pursued the appropriate avenues to get good information, present the final recommendation (job vacancy notice, space needs, and equipment details including the manufacturers and the price) to your employer. If he or she approves your recommendations, you can begin to advertise the position and to prepare purchase orders for the equipment.

Train and Supervise Assistants

Assume that the man you recommended be hired is now on the job. He has good computer and organizational skills. The individual is an independent thinker and can determine what needs to be done and do the job without you looking over his shoulder all the time. You have gone over the organization's goals and objectives with him. Additionally, you have gone over in detail your particular unit's goals and objectives and how these goals support the organization's goals. The newly hired assistant is a quick learner and has asked you for very little assistance. The work that the assistant produces is done well and quickly. You have silently congratulated yourself for accomplishing your established goals and objectives well. You are looking forward to a working unit that is productive and cohesive.

Assume that after the assistant has been on the job two months, you review the goals and objectives established by the individual. Are they being met? Are there any problems to be addressed? If the assistant is continuing to do a good job, are you offering praise? If there are areas that need to be improved, are you being honest and straightforward concerning areas of improvement?

Organize

Another skill that the administrative professional must have is organizational skill. This skill includes organization of your time, work flow, filing systems, meetings, and committees. It is not always easy to organize all the work that lands on the administrative professional's desk. For example, many organizations maintain both electronic and paper filing systems. You must make a decision as to what you will file electronically and what you will file in a paper system. Additionally, you must know the rules and use them as you file the information. Then you must be able to retrieve the information quickly upon demand by your employer.

Coordinate

The administrative assistant often has the responsibility for coordination of various activities. For example, when you have an assistant reporting to you, part of your job will be coordination of workload and schedule. What jobs will the assistant assume full-time? Are there jobs that you will need to share sometimes? For example, if you are given a rush job by your employer, you may be able to give some parts of the job to your assistant.

Maintain Physical Health and Energy

An administrative professional's job is basically a sedentary job. You will probably spend hours each day at the computer, with few breaks. Your job can also be stressful. For example, you may work in a fast-paced environment in which every job seems to be top priority. You may even find it difficult to take a break from your desk due to the press of work.

An important way to address the physical inactivity of your job is to establish an exercise program that you set as a top priority. Exercise is important not only to your physical health, but also to your mental health. Additionally, exercising provides other benefits, such as keeping your weight at a healthy level, giving you more energy and endurance, allowing you to bounce back more quickly from injury or disease, and generally helping you to maintain good health. Conversely, physical inactivity can result in increased risk for diseases such as heart disease, stroke, and osteoporosis. Physical inactivity also increases one's chances of being obese. Figure 18.6 lists a number of benefits attributable to exercise. Along with exercise, you should commit to eating a healthy diet with plenty of fruits and vegetables. Meats and other sources of fat should be kept to an appropriate level.

A number of companies throughout the United States recognize that employees need physical exercise. They know that consistent exercise has been proven to make individuals more productive on the job. These companies often provide exercise rooms that are available any time of the day. Employees may take a 30- to 60-minute break and go to the exercise room. A variety of equipment is generally provided, such as treadmills, rowing machines, exercise bikes, and barbells.

If you work for a company that does not have exercise machines, you should exercise on your own. Some studies have shown that morning is the best time to exercise. You might get up a half hour earlier each day than is your norm and jog for approximately 30 minutes. The benefits of consistent exercise far outweigh the time that it takes from your day.

In addition to exercising, it is important to eat a healthy diet that includes plenty of fruits and vegetables.

© Stockbyte / Getty Images

BENEFITS OF PHYSICAL ACTIVITY

- Reduces one's risk for heart attack, colon cancer, diabetes, stroke, and high blood pressure

- Contributes to healthy bones, muscles, and joints

- Promotes better balance that can reduce falls among older adults

- Helps to relieve the pain of arthritis

- Reduces symptoms of anxiety and depression

- Decreases the need for hospitalizations, physician visits, and medications

FIGURE 18.6 Benefits of Physical Activity

Summary

To reinforce what you have learned in this chapter, study this summary.

- Throughout the world, successful organizations spend significant dollars and organizational time in leadership development.

- A leader is a person who guides or inspires others. A leader has self understanding, demonstrates self-management skills, understands organizational culture, and has the ability to develop self and others within the organization.

- Self understanding occurs when you are able to test or examine the knowledge or wisdom of others, learn from those who are wise, clarify your own values, and determine how you want to live your life.

- Self management within an organization refers to methods, skills, and strategies by which individuals can effectively direct their own activities.

- Organizational culture is defined as a shared group of core assumptions learned by people within the organization. Understanding the organizational culture is critical for employees.

- When organizational values and the values of the people within an organization are aligned, these values are reflected in the decisions that are made.

- Effective leaders have a number of traits that help them engender trust and lead others.

- Management is the act of directing and controlling people and resources to accomplish goals. Management includes several functions such as creating a strategic vision, planning, organizing, motivating, delegating, teaching, and evaluating.

- Administrative professionals have a broad range of responsibilities, some of which were formerly considered management responsibilities.

- Successful administrative professionals understand and live by their values.

- As an administrative professional you should identify the objectives that you must accomplish in order to support the organizational plans.

- An important step in planning is to determine needs for achieving goals.

- Administrative professionals must have skills to organize their time, work flow, filing systems, meetings, and committees.

- Typically, an administrative professional position is a sedentary one. Administrative professionals should establish an exercise program that is given top priority and followed consistently.

- A number of organizations today recognize the importance of exercise for physical and mental health and provide exercise rooms and equipment for the use of employees.

What's the Problem?

As an administrative assistant, you have two employees reporting to you. Last year, you interviewed and recommended for employment Alice Kim, who you believe has excellent potential. The management of the company accepted your recommendation, and Ms. Kim has been on the job for six months. Her technical skills are excellent; however, her people skills are poor. Mr. Roberts, your supervisor, has called your attention to the fact that she does a very poor job of greeting outside visitors. In fact, he has told you that several of these visitors have remarked about her lack of helpfulness. Mr. Roberts tells you to "fix the problem" or "fire her."

What steps would you take in addressing this problem?

Let's Discuss

1. Define *leadership* and describe leadership traits.
2. Define *management* and list the functions of management.
3. List several duties of an administrative professional.
4. List guidelines to follow when discharging an employee.
5. List benefits of a healthy lifestyle, including proper diet and physical exercise.

Critical-Thinking Activity

As a new manager (of six months), you instituted a team approach to projects. You believed you were clear in your expectations about how teams should work, but nothing is going as you expected. Two team members are openly hostile, sarcastic, and abusive to each other. They use team meetings to engage in shouting matches. One of the two, Fernando, came to you to complain about the other person, Lorna. He stated that Lorna never liked him and that she uses the team meetings to criticize him. You believe him and tell him you will talk to Lorna about her behavior. However, when you talk with Lorna, she denies that she criticizes Fernando; she believes all the yelling and screaming matches are a result of his actions. You do not know how to handle the situation. You are feeling frustrated and out of control.

How can you help resolve this situation?

Vocabulary Review

Open the *Word* file *CH18 Vocabulary* on the Student CD. Complete the vocabulary review for Chapter 18.

English and Word Usage Drill

Complete the English and Word Usage Drill for Chapter 18 found in the *Applications Workbook*.

Workplace Applications

18-1 Research a Leader

(Goal 1)

1. Work with two of your classmates on this project.
2. Select one leader in the community. The leader may be in the private sector (colleges, presidents of chambers of commerce, Girl Scouts, and so forth) or the public sector (companies and corporations).

team building

3. Conduct research on the individual. For example, you might research the individual's background if it is available to you in public documents such as newspapers and the Web. If you chose to interview the president of your college or university, articles developed by the college/university or newspaper articles should be available.

4. Make an appointment to see the individual. (If the individual is not available for an interview in person, ask if she or he is available for a phone interview.) As a group, develop a list of questions. For example, you may ask the individual these types of questions:

   • How long have you been with the company or organization?

   • How long have you been in the position that you now hold?

   • What are some of the major problems you face as a leader?

   • What suggestions would you make to people who aspire to positions such as the one that you have?

   • How do you define leadership?

5. Once you have completed the interview, send the individual a thank-you letter. Write a brief summary of the interview and present your summary verbally to the class.

18-2 Research Management Functions

(Goal 2)

1. Continue to work with the group established in Application 18-1.

2. Determine the functions of management through researching the Website of two companies or organizations or by interviewing two administrators in local businesses or organizations.

3. Prepare electronic slides to summarize the main points of your findings. Present your findings verbally to the class using the slides you prepared.

18-3 Research Administrative Professional Duties

(Goal 3)

1. Work with your instructor and your classmates to select an administrative professional in your area.

2. Invite this administrative professional to discuss with the class her or his leadership responsibilities. Additionally, ask the individual to talk about her or his background, education, and experience in preparing for the responsibilities of the job.

team building

18-4 Consider Your Human Relations Skills

(Goal 3)

1. Take a moment to consider your skills in dealing with people.

   - If you have held a full-time or part-time job, were you successful in your relationships with others in the workplace?

   - If you have not had a job, do you believe you are successful in your relationships with your classmates?

2. Once you have spent time considering your human relations skills, talk with one or more of your classmates about your abilities. Ask for honest feedback from the individual(s).

3. Develop a plan to improve areas of your human relations skills that need improvement.

18-5 Develop a Diet and Exercise Plan

(Goal 4)

1. Consider your diet. Do you eat foods that will help you achieve good health? Make a list of changes you can make to your diet to promote a healthy lifestyle.

2. If you do not already have an exercise regime established, determine what type of daily exercise would be best for you. If possible, engage in this exercise routine for the next two weeks. You may want to work with a friend or classmate on this project. If you have not been exercising, having a friend to encourage you can be helpful. After the two weeks of exercise, report your progress to the class. Discuss how this exercise routine has helped you physically and mentally.

Assessment of Chapter 18 Goals

Did you successfully complete the chapter goals? Evaluate yourself by filling out the form found in Chapter 18 of the *Applications Workbook*.

This Reference Guide is a handy and easy-to-use reference to a variety of rules you will use frequently in preparing correspondence. You can use the guide to review grammar and punctuation rules. In addition, the guide includes basic formats for letters and reports. To assist you in using proper grammar and punctuation as you write and in using correct letter format, read this guide at the beginning of the course and refer to it as needed throughout the course. The parts of the Reference Guide are as follows:

Contents

Abbreviations 476

Adjectives and Adverbs 477

Bias-Free Language 477

Capitalization 478

Collective Nouns 479

Letters and Envelopes 480

Misused and Easily Confused Word and Phrases 483

Numbers 485

Parallelism 486

Plagiarism 486

Plurals and Possessives 487

Pronouns 487

Proofreaders' Marks 489

Punctuation 490

Reports 494

Spelling 501

Subject and Verb Agreement 501

Abbreviations

1. Use standard abbreviations for titles immediately before proper names.

Before the Name

Use periods in abbreviations before the name.

> Dr. Cindy Bos
>
> Mr. Michael Khirallah
>
> Rev. Thomas McIntyre

Spell out titles such as *Reverend* and *Honorable* when preceded by *the*.

> The Honorable Isabella Martinez
>
> The Reverend Elias Enderon

Abbreviate personal titles such as *Rev., Hon., Prof., Gen., Col., Capt.*, and *Lieut.* when they precede a surname and a given name. When using only the surname, spell out these titles.

> Prof. James Huddleston
>
> Professor Huddleston

After the Name

Abbreviate academic degrees with periods or eliminate the periods.

> Patricia LaFaver, Ph.D.
>
> Bryant McAnnelley, J.D.
>
> Helene Chen, MS
>
> Bryon Nichols, MD

Abbreviate civil titles in all capital letters with no periods.

> J. Hansel Zucker, CLU

2. Many companies and professional organizations use abbreviated names. Key these abbreviated names in all capital letters with no periods and no spaces between the letters.

> IBM   International Business Machines
>
> YMCA   Young Men's Christian Association

3. Abbreviate certain expressions.

> e.g.   exempli gratia (for example)
>
> etc.   et cetera (and so forth)
>
> i.e.   id est (that is)

4. Abbreviate names of countries only in tabulations or enumerations, and key these names in all capital letters. Periods may or may not be used.

> U.S.A. or USA
>
> U.S or US

Note: Spell out *United States* as a noun, and abbreviate it as an adjective.

> The people of the United States are very diverse in race and ethnicity.
>
> The median age of the U.S. population is 35.6 years.

5. Write abbreviations for government agencies in all capital letters with no periods and no spaces between the letters.

> FTC   Federal Trade Commission
>
> CIA   Central Intelligence Agency

6. Use only one period when an abbreviation containing a period falls at the end of the sentence. In sentences ending with a question mark or an exclamation mark, place the punctuation mark directly after the period.

> The play began at 8:15 p.m.
>
> Does the class start at 9:30 a.m.?

7. Avoid abbreviating the following categories of words unless these words appear in tabulations or enumerations.

- Names of territories and possessions of the United States, countries, states, and cities
- Names of months
- Days of the week
- Given names, such as *Wm.* for *William*
- Words such as *avenue, boulevard, court, street, drive, road*, and *building*
- Parts of company names (such as *Bros., Co., Corp.*) unless the words are abbreviated in the official company name

- Compass directions when they are part of an address (use *North, South, East, West*) Note: Abbreviate *NW, NE, SE,* and *SW* after a street name.

- The word *number* unless followed by a numeral

8. Use the article *a* before an abbreviation beginning with a consonant sound. Use the article *an* before an abbreviation beginning with a vowel sound.

    an IQ test

    a CPS rating

9. When an abbreviation includes an ampersand, generally, do not space before or after the ampersand.

    Texas A&M University

    P&L statement

10. Form plurals of abbreviations by adding an *s*. If it is confusing to add only an *s*, add an apostrophe *s*.

    Drs.

    A's

Adjectives and Adverbs

1. Adjectives modify nouns and pronouns.

    The *large* dog appeared hungry.

    They were *snobbish*.

    - When the word that follows a verb modifies the subject, an adjective is used.

    I feel *bad*. (not *badly*)

    - An adverb answers the question when, where, why, in what manner, or to what extent.

    The child ran *quickly*. (not *quick*)

    That tree grows *poorly* in this climate. (not *poor*)

2. Use comparative and superlative forms appropriately. Comparative forms compare two words, while superlative forms compare three words. One-syllable adjectives and adverbs add *er* and *est* to the word to form the comparative and superlative. Adjectives and adverbs with two or more syllables use *more* or *most, less* or *least*. Some two-syllable adjectives are formed either way—*friendlier* or *more friendly*.

    He is *smarter* than she is.

    She is the *most capable* person in the room.

3. Use limiting modifiers carefully. A limiting modifier is a word, phrase, or clause that limits the meaning of a preceding word or a following word. Limiting modifiers include *almost, only, merely, exactly,* and *just*. You must be careful when placing limiting modifiers. Changing the location of the modifier can change the meaning of the sentence. Notice how the placement of *only* in the following sentence changes the meaning of the sentence.

    Only he said he appreciated me.

    He *only* said he appreciated me.

    He said he *only* appreciated me.

Bias-Free Language

In the last few years, people have become more aware of the effect language can have when used to describe characteristics such as gender, race, and physical characteristics. Give careful consideration to the words you use in writing and speaking. This section offers suggestions for avoiding communication biases in three areas—gender, race, and physical characteristics.

Gender Bias

Inclusive usage in language (incorporating both sexes) is extremely important in writing. Avoid exclusive language (words that by their form or meaning discriminate on a gender basis). Examples of exclusive language include words such as *craftsman, weatherman, fireman,* and *policeman*. Other examples of exclusive language include statements such as these:

An engineer relies on his common sense.

The executive answered his phone.

Eliminate gender-bias statements when writing and speaking. For example, *weatherman* becomes *weatherperson* and *policeman* becomes *police officer*.

Do not write or say *The executive answered his phone.*

Do write or say *The executive answered the phone.*

Strategies for avoiding pronoun gender problems include the following:

- Use the plural of the noun and pronoun.
- Delete the pronoun altogether.
- Replace the masculine pronoun with an article (*the*).
- Use *he or she* (but only sparingly).

Ethnic and Racial Bias

Acceptable terms for various races and ethnicities change over time. It is the writer's and speaker's responsibility to be aware of the most acceptable terms. Presently, these terms are the most appropriate ones to use:

- *African American* (some African Americans prefer *black*)
- *Native Americans* or *American Indians*
- *Hispanic* (some individuals prefer *Latinos/ Latinas*, the masculine form ending in *o* and the feminine form ending in *a*)
- When referring to people from the eastern region of the world, *Asian* is the general term used. People of China are *Chinese*, not *Orientals*.

Biases Based on Physical Characteristics

The most recent term for individuals with disabilities is *physically challenged*. Some groups—but certainly not all—prefer to use *visually impaired* for the blind and *hearing impaired* for the deaf. Since terms do change, you should stay current with the most recent terms.

Capitalization

1. Capitalize titles of specific courses.

    He took Psychology 121 last semester.

2. Capitalize titles that precede a person's name and abbreviations after a name.

    General Schuman

    Victor Jones, Jr.

Do not capitalize titles when they follow a personal name or take the place of a personal name. Exceptions include high government titles such as *President, Attorney General, Chief Justice*, and so on when used in formal acknowledgments and lists.

    Louise Fidler, president of Dillon Industries, will speak tonight.

    The President of the United States was in Mexico in March.

3. Capitalize specific trade names of products.

    He bought a Dell computer.

4. Capitalize the first word in each line of a poem.

    Fear corrodes my dreams tonight and
        mist has greyed my hills,
    Mountains seem too tall to climb,
        December winds are chill,
    There's no comfort on the earth, I am
        a child abandoned,
    Till I feel your hand in mine
    And laugh down lonely canyons.

                                    James Kavanaugh

5. Capitalize the first word of a direct quotation.

    Kyung-soon replied, "The sky is the limit."

6. Capitalize compass directions when they refer to specific regions or when the direction is part of a specific name. Do not capitalize directions when they indicate a general location.

    We flew with Northwest Airlines.

    I grew up in the East.

    He lives on the east side of town.

7. Capitalize the first word and all words except articles, prepositions, and conjunctions in titles of books, articles, poems, and plays.

    Effective Business Communication

    The Lion King

8. Capitalize all words referring to the deity, the Bible, the books of the Bible, and other sacred books.

    the Koran

    our Lord

9. Capitalize names of organizations, political parties, religious bodies, and churches.

   Girl Scouts

   the First Presbyterian Church

10. Capitalize names of months, days of the week, holidays, holy days, and periods of history.

    Monday

    Christmas

    the Middle Ages

11. Capitalize names of divisions of a college or university.

    Business Division

    School of Medicine

12. Capitalize names of geographic sections and places: continents, countries, states, cities, rivers, mountains, lakes, and islands.

    Lake Michigan

    New York

    Africa

13. Capitalize names of specific historical events, specific laws, treaties, and departments of government.

    Vietnam War

    Department of Defense

14. Capitalize names of streets, avenues, buildings, hotels, parks, and theaters.

    The Four Seasons Hotel

    Fifth Avenue

    Theater Two

15. Capitalize only the parts of a hyphenated word that you would capitalize if the word were not hyphenated.

    mid-August

    President-elect Aguirre

16. Capitalize titles of relatives when they precede a name or when the title is used as a name. Do not capitalize family titles when they are preceded by possessive pronouns and when they describe a family relationship.

    I telephoned Uncle Ed and Aunt Mary last night.

Yesterday Mom called me about the tickets.

My cousin is in town.

17. Capitalize personifications (figures of speech in which inanimate objects or abstractions are represented with human qualities).

    In the autumn, Nature treats us to beautiful colors of gold, orange, and auburn.

18. Do not capitalize business titles when used in magazines, books, and newspapers. The internal practice of many business organizations is to capitalize the titles of company officers and managers.

    Katherine Romero, president of Computer Graphics

Collective Nouns

A collective noun is a word that is singular in form but represents a group of persons or things. For example:

    committee

    company

    department

    public

    class

    board

These rules determine the form of the verb used with a collective noun.

- When the members of a group are one unit, the verb is singular.

  The committee is unanimous in its recommendation.

- When members of the group are separate units, the verb is plural.

  The staff are not in agreement about the decision.

- If the sentence is unclear or awkward, you can address the problem by inserting the words *members of* before the collective noun and using a plural verb.

  The members of the staff are not in agreement about the decision.

Letters and Envelopes

This section provides a review of letter and punctuation styles, addressing of envelopes, and folding of letters.

Letter and Punctuation Styles

The main letter styles are block and modified block style with blocked or indented paragraphs. Figure 1 shows the block letter style with blocked paragraphs. (When using block letter style, begin each paragraph at the left margin.) Notice in the block letter style that every line begins at the left margin. Figure 2 shows modified block style with blocked paragraphs. (When using modified block style, the paragraphs may be blocked or indented.) Notice in the modified block style that the date line and the closing lines begin at the center point.

There is no punctuation after the salutation and no punctuation after the complimentary close in open punctuation. When using mixed punctuation, there is a colon after the salutation and a comma after the complimentary close. Notice the open punctuation style in Figure 1 and the mixed punctuation style in Figure 2.

Second-Page Heading

Create a header for the second page of a letter by using the Header and Footer toolbar. At the left margin of the header box, key the name of the recipient and press ENTER. Key the word *Page* and space; use the automatic numbering feature on the Header and Footer toolbar to insert the page number and press ENTER. Insert the date and press ENTER to leave a blank line between the header and the body of the letter.

Addressing of Envelopes

Your software program automatically copies the letter address from the letter on the screen to the envelope. If the return address is not pre-printed on the envelope, you must key it. You can save a return address as a default address; by following this procedure, you need to key the return address only one time.

Folding of Letters for Envelopes

Standard Size Envelopes (No. 10—4 1/8" × 9 1/2")

Fold in the manner shown below:

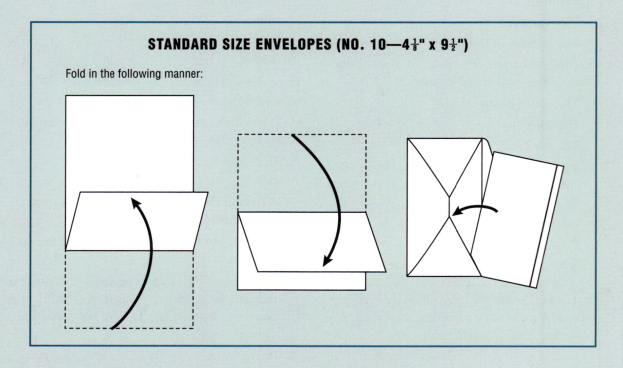

STANDARD SIZE ENVELOPES (NO. 10—4⅛" x 9½")

Fold in the following manner:

Begin at 2" or center vertically

Default 1" side margins

United
Pharmaceuticals

1211 East Eighth Street
Fort Worth, TX 76102-5201
817-555-0122

October 9, 200-

Dr. Leonard Montgomery
3418 Melrose Street
Dallas, TX 75201-9702

Dear Dr. Montgomery

Thank you for talking with me last Monday concerning our new cancer drug. At your request, I am enclosing a copy of the research studies.

You will notice that United Pharmaceuticals conducted these studies over a five-year period, using a sample group of 1,500 people. The results were excellent, and we are pleased to offer a drug that has such potential for significantly dropping the cancer mortality rate.

I will call your administrative assistant within the next few days to schedule a follow-up meeting after you have had a chance to review the studies. I look forward to discussing any questions you may have.

Sincerely

Katalina Komanie

Katalina Komanie
Sales Representative

lc

Enclosure

FIGURE 1   Block Letter Style, Open Punctuation, New Format

Begin at 2" or center vertically

Default 1" side margins

9346 Centennial Drive
Dallas, TX 76127-9312
March 3, 200-

Dr. Martin Spears
The Mathey Foundation
2895 Grapevine Road
Grapevine, TX 76051-3498

Dear Dr. Spears:

Heart disease affects the lives of many men and women in our nation. Research advances have helped thousands of individuals live longer and more fulfilling lives. Ongoing research is essential in order to reduce the number of deaths from heart disease and to give thousands of individuals a longer life.

Additional monies are necessary to fund research. A brochure detailing the various research projects you have an opportunity to support is enclosed.

Are you willing to give to this worthwhile cause? Please mail your donation today and know the satisfaction of helping others.

Sincerely,

Marcia Almonte

Marcia Almonte
Heart Charities Volunteer

Enclosure

FIGURE 2 Modified Block Letter Style, Mixed Punctuation, Traditional Format

Misused and Easily Confused Words and Phrases

1. *A* or *an* before the letter *h*

   A is used before all consonant sounds, including *h* when sounded.

   An is used before all vowel sounds, except long *u*.

   > a historic event
   >
   > an honor
   >
   > a hotel
   >
   > a useful comment

2. A while and awhile

   A while is a noun meaning a short time.

   > We plan to go home in a while.

   Awhile is an adverb meaning a short time.

   > She wrote the poem awhile ago.

3. About, at

   Use either *about* or *at*—not both.

   > He will leave about noon.
   >
   > He will leave at noon.

4. Accept, except

   To *accept* an assignment is to agree to undertake it.

   To *except* someone from an activity is to excuse that person from the activity.

5. Accessible, assessable

   If something is *accessible*, it can be reached or attained.

   An object whose value can be estimated is *assessable*.

6. Advice, advise

   Advice is a noun meaning a recommendation.

   > She did not follow my advice.

   Advise is a verb meaning to counsel.

   > The counselor will advise you.

7. All, all of

   Use *all*; *of* is redundant. If a pronoun follows *all*, reword the sentence.

   > Check all the items.
   >
   > They are all going.

8. All right, alright

   All right is the only correct usage. *Alright* is incorrect.

9. Among, between

   Use *among* when referring to three or more persons or things.

   > The inheritance was divided among the four relatives.

   Use *between* when referring to two persons or things.

   > The choice is between you and me.

10. Appraise, apprise

    Appraise means to set a value on; *apprise* means to inform.

    > He appraised the house at $300,000.
    >
    > I was apprised of the situation by Jack.

11. Bad, badly

    Bad is an adjective; *badly* is an adverb.

    > He feels bad about losing.
    >
    > The football team played badly tonight.

12. Biannual, biennial

    Biannual means occurring twice a year.

    Biennial means occurring once every two years.

13. Bimonthly, semimonthly

    Bimonthly means every two months; *semimonthly* means twice a month.

14. Can, may

    Can means to be able to; *may* means to have permission.

    > The diskette can be copied.
    >
    > You may leave when you finish your work.

15. Capital, capitol

Use *capital* unless you are referring to a building that houses a government.

> The capital of China is Columbus.
>
> We toured the United States Capitol in Washington.

16. Cite, sight, site

Cite means to quote; *sight* means vision; *site* means location.

> She cited the correct reference.
>
> That is a pleasant sight.
>
> They sighted a whale.
>
> The site for the new building will be determined soon.

17. Complement, compliment

Complement means to complete, fill, or make perfect; *compliment* means to praise.

18. Council, counsel

Council is a noun meaning a governing body.

Counsel can be a noun or a verb. As a noun, *counsel* can mean a person with whom one consults about a matter. As a verb, *counsel* means to advise.

> The council meets today.
>
> Dr. Baker's counsel helped Kim overcome her fears.
>
> Counsel was consulted on the case.
>
> He is there to counsel you.

19. Desert, dessert

Desert as a noun means a barren or arid region with low rainfall.

Desert as a verb means to abandon.

Dessert is a confection often served at the end of a meal.

> We traveled through the desert of Arizona.
>
> He deserted his family.
>
> We had ice cream for dessert.

20. Farther, further

Farther refers to distance; *further* refers to a greater degree or extent.

> The store is a mile farther down the road.
>
> We will discuss the matter further on Saturday.

21. Good, well

Good and *well* are adjectives. *Well* is used to mean in fine health; *good* is used to mean pleasant or attractive.

> I feel well.
>
> She feels good about her job.

22. Got, gotten

Got is preferred to *gotten* as the past participle of *get*. *Got* is informal when used for *must* or *ought*.

> I've got to get up at 6 a.m.
>
> Improved: I must get up at 6 a.m.

23. In, into

In means located inside an area or limits. *Into* means in the direction of the interior or toward something.

> She went into the room.
>
> She is sitting in the room.

24. Its, it's

Its is the possessive form of *it*.

It's is the contraction of *it is*.

> The family had its reunion yesterday.
>
> It's probably going to rain.

25. Percent, per cent, percentage

Percent is always written as one word; *per cent* is incorrect.

Percentage is preferred when a number is not used.

> He received 56 percent of the vote.
>
> The percentage of votes he received is not known.

26. Principal, principle

Principal as an adjective means *main*; as a noun, *principal* means the main person or a capital sum.

Principle is a noun meaning a rule, guide, or truth; *principle* never refers to a person directly.

The principal character in the play was Geoff.

The principals in the case are present.

She held steadfast to her principles.

27. Respectfully, respectively

Respectfully means in a courteous manner; *respectively* refers to being considered singly in a particular order.

She respectfully asked for her grade report.

The first, second, and third awards will go to Julio, Jody, and Chelsea, respectively.

28. Stationary, stationery

Stationary means stable or fixed; *stationery* is writing paper.

The ladder seems stationary.

Order three boxes of stationery.

29. That, which

Which and *that* are relative pronouns used to refer to places, animals, objects, ideas, and qualities. To improve clarity, many writers make this distinction: The word *which* is used to introduce nonessential information, and a comma is placed before the word. The word *that* is used to introduce a clause containing essential information, and no comma is used.

In ten minutes, Harry solved the problem that I had been working on for hours.

The presentation, which would have worked well for managers, had little appeal to the teachers.

30. Who, whom

Who is used as the subject of a verb; *whom* is used as an object of a verb or a preposition.

Ken is the one who will be at the meeting.

Lola is the person whom I will hire.

It does not matter who did what to whom.

Numbers

1. Spell out numbers one through ten; use figures for numbers above ten.

We ordered nine coats and four dresses.

The assistant keyed approximately 60 letters.

2. If a sentence contains numbers above and below ten, be consistent—either spell out all numbers or key all numbers in figures. If most of the numbers are below ten, use words. If most are above ten, use figures.

Please order 12 memo pads, 2 reams of paper, and 11 boxes of envelopes.

3. Express numbers in the millions or higher in the following manner in order to aid comprehension.

3 billion (rather than 3,000,000,000)

4. Always spell out a number that begins a sentence.

Five hundred books were in his home library.

5. If the numbers are large, rearrange the wording of the sentence so the number is not the first word of the sentence.

We had a good year in 2003.

Not: Two thousand and three was a good year.

6. Spell out indefinite numbers and amounts.

A few hundred voters came to the polls despite the inclement weather.

7. Spell out all ordinals (first, second, third, and so on) that can be expressed in words.

The store's twenty-fifth anniversary was this week.

8. Use a comma to separate adjacent numbers written in words or figures.

In 2004, 33 new products came online.

9. Write house or building numbers in figures. However, when the number one appears by itself, spell it out. Spell out numbers one through ten in street names. Write numbers above ten in figures. When using figures for the house number and the street name, use a hyphen preceded and followed by a space.

101 Building

One Main Place

21301 Fifth Avenue

122 - 33d Street

10. Spell out ages except when the age is stated exactly in years, months, and days. When presenting ages in tabular form, use figures.

    She is eighteen years old.

    He is 2 years, 10 months, and 18 days old.

Name	Age
Bauman, Dan	19
King, Jenna	21

11. Use figures to express dates written in normal month-day-year order. Do not use *th*, *nd*, or *rd* following the date.

    May 3, 2005

    Not: May 8th, 2005

12. Spell out fractions unless they are part of mixed numbers. Use a hyphen to separate the numerator and denominator of fractions written in words when the fractions stand alone or are used as compound adjectives.

    three-fourths

    one-third cup

    5¾

13. Express amounts of money in figures. Write indefinite money amounts in words.

    $1,000

    $3.27

    several hundred dollars

14. For clarity, numbers in legal documents are sometimes written in both words and figures.

    One hundred thirty-four dollars ($134)

15. Express percentages in figures; spell out the word *percent*.

    10 percent

16. To form the plural of figures, add *s*.

    The 1990s were a challenging time for Raul.

17. In times of day, use figures with a.m. and p.m.; spell out numbers with the word *o'clock*. In formal usage, spell out all times.

9 a.m.

10 p.m.

eight o'clock in the evening

Parallelism

Parts of a sentence that are parallel in meaning must be parallel in structure. Writers should balance a word with a word, a phrase with a phrase, a clause with a clause, and a sentence with a sentence. Notice the examples given below.

No   The parents tried pleading, threats, and shouting.

Yes   The parents tried pleading, threatening, and shouting.

No   In the past, orders were sent by regular mail, but now overnight delivery is used.

Yes   In the past, orders were sent by regular mail; now they are sent by overnight delivery.

Plagiarism

The dictionary definition of plagiarism is "to use and pass off as one's own (the ideas or writings of another)." The derivation of the word comes from the Latin word for kidnapper. It literally means taking someone else's work as your own—not giving credit to someone else for the person's written ideas.

Avoid plagiarism by following these steps:

- When quoting someone else's material exactly as written, use quotation marks and the appropriate documentation.

- When paraphrasing, do not use quotation marks but do document the source. Use your own words but be true to what the source says and means. Do not put your own interpretation on the paraphrase. Be certain that your paraphrasing does not distort what the originator meant.

- Do not document information that is common knowledge; i.e., information that most educated people know.

Plurals and Possessives

1. When a compound word contains a noun and is hyphenated or made up of two or more words, the principal word takes an *s* to form the plural. If there is no principal word, add an *s* to the end of the compound word.

   commanders in chief

   runners-up

2. The plural of letters is formed by adding *s* or *'s*. The apostrophe is unnecessary except where confusion might result.

   CPAs

   the do's on the list

3. Singular nouns form the possessive by adding *'s*. If a singular noun has two or more syllables and if the last syllable is not accented and is preceded by a sibilant sound (*s*, *x*, or *z*), add only the apostrophe for ease of pronunciation.

   the person's computer

   Mrs. Cross's office

   the department's rules

   Ulysses' voyage

4. Plural nouns form the possessive by adding an apostrophe if the plural ends in *s* or by adding *'s* when the plural does not end in *s*.

   ladies' wear

   the children's bicycles

5. When using a verb form ending in *ing* as a noun (gerund), a noun or pronoun before it takes the possessive form.

   Fritz's yelling was excessive.

6. To form the possessive of a compound word, add the possessive ending to the last syllable.

   Her mother-in-law's gift arrived.

   The editor-in-chief's comments were printed in the company newsletter.

7. Joint possession is indicated by adding the possessive ending to the last noun.

   We are near Jan and Keith's store.

   Drs. Edison and Sidhu's article is thought-provoking.

8. In idiomatic construction, possessive form is often used. (An idiom is defined in the dictionary as "a speech form or an expression of a given language that is peculiar to itself grammatically or cannot be understood from the individual meanings of its elements.")

   a day's work

   two weeks' vacation

9. Use the possessive form in cases where the noun modified is not expressed.

   Take it to the plumber's. (shop)

10. Write the possessive form of personal pronouns without an apostrophe.

    This book is hers.

    She will deliver yours tomorrow.

Pronouns

1. A pronoun agrees with its antecedent (the word for which the pronoun stands) in number, gender, and person.

   Carlos wants to know if *his* book is at your house.

2. A plural pronoun is used when the antecedent consists of two nouns joined by *and*.

   Diana and *Tomie* are bringing *their* stereo.

3. A singular pronoun is used when the antecedent consists of two singular nouns joined by *or* or *nor*. A plural pronoun is used when the antecedent consists of two plural nouns joined by *or* or *nor*.

   Neither *Lori* nor *Joanne* wants to do *her* part.

   Either the *men* or the *women* will do *their* share.

4. Do not confuse certain possessive pronouns with contractions that sound alike.

its (possessive)	it's (it is)
their (possessive)	they're (they are)
theirs (possessive)	there's (there is)
your (possessive)	you're (you are)
whose (possessive)	who's (who is)

As a test for the use of a possessive pronoun or a contraction, try to substitute *it is, they are, it has, there has, there is,* or *you are.* Use the corresponding possessive form if the substitution does not make sense.

Your wording is correct.

You're wording that sentence incorrectly.

Whose book is it?

Who's the owner of the laptop?

5. Use *who* and *that* when referring to persons. Use *who* when referring to an individual and *that* when referring to a group of people.

    He is the boy *who* does well in history.

    The number of people *that* will be here is more than originally thought.

6. Use *which* and *that* when referring to places, objects, and animals. Use *which* when introducing a clause containing nonessential information. Use *that* when introducing a clause containing essential information.

    The fox, *which* is very sly, caught the skunk.

    The card *that* I sent you was mailed last week.

7. A pronoun in the objective case functions as a direct object, indirect object, or the object of a preposition. Objective pronouns include *me, you, him, her, it, us, them, whom,* and *whomever.*

    The movie was an emotional experience for *her* and *me.* (The pronouns *her* and *me* are in the objective case in this sentence since they function as the object of a preposition.)

8. A linking verb connects a subject to a word that renames it. Linking verbs indicate a state of being (*am, is, are, was, were*), relate to the senses, or indicate a condition. A pronoun coming after a linking verb renames the subject, so the pronoun must be in the subjective case. Subjective pronouns include *I, you, she, he, it, we, they, who,* and *whoever.*

    It is *I* who will attend the play.

9. The pronouns *who* and *whoever* are in the subjective case and are used as the subject of a sentence or clause.

    Whoever is in charge will be required to stay late.

10. At the beginning of questions, use *who* if the question is about the subject and *whom* if the question is about the object. To help you know which is appropriate, follow these steps:

    • Delete the word *who* or *whom* from the sentence, and fill the gap in thought with *she* or *her.*

    • If *she* completes the thought, then *who* is correct.

    • If *her* completes the thought, then *whom* is correct.

    Who is going to the party?

    Give the information to *whomever* answers the telephone.

11. Reflexive pronouns reflect back to the antecedent. Reflexive pronouns include *myself, herself, himself, themselves,* and other *self* or *selves* words.

    I intend to do the painting *myself.*

Proofreaders' Marks

SYMBOL	MEANING	MARKED COPY	CORRECTED COPY
∧	Insert	two ∧people _or three_	two or three people
⎯⎯	Delete	the man ~~and~~ ~~woman~~	the man
⊏	Move to left	⊏ human relations	human relations
#	Add space	follow#these	follow these
/	Lowercase letter	in the /Fall of 2002	in the fall of 2002
⌒	Close up space	sum⌒mer	summer
⌒⌒	Transpose	when ⌒is⌒it⌒	when it is
⊐	Move to the right	⊐ skills for living	skills for living
∨	Insert apostrophe	Mac∨s book	Mac's book
∨∨	Insert quotation marks	She said, "No."	She said, "No."
⊔	Move down	falle ⎡n⎤	fallen
⊓	Move up	straigh ⎣t⎦	straight
¶	Paragraph	¶ The first and third page	The first and third page
no ¶	No new paragraph	no ¶ The first and third page	The first and third page
○ sp	Spell out	(Dr.) sp	Doctor
stet or	Let it stand; ignore correction	~~most~~ efficient worker	most efficient worker
⎯⎯	Underline	<u>Business World</u>	<u>Business World</u>
ital	Italics	<u>Newsweek</u> _ital_	_Newsweek_
⊙	Insert period	the last word⊙	the last word.

Punctuation

Punctuation is important if the reader is to interpret the writer's thoughts correctly. Correct punctuation has its base in accepted rules and principles rather than in the whims of the writer.

The Period

A period indicates a full stop and is used in the following ways:

1. At the end of a complete declarative or imperative sentence.

2. After abbreviations and after a single or double initial that represents a word.

acct.	etc.	Ph.D.
U.S.	viz.	p.m.
Dr.	i.e.	pp.

    However, abbreviations that use several initial letters do not require periods.

    FDIC (Federal Deposit Insurance Corporation)

    FEPC (Fair Employment Practices Committee)

    AAA (American Automobile Association)

    YWCA (Young Women's Christian Association)

3. Between dollars and cents. A period and cipher are not required when an amount in even dollars is expressed in figures.

    $42.65 $1.47 $25

4. To indicate a decimal.

    3.5 bushels   12.65 percent   6.25 feet

The Comma

Use a comma:

1. To separate independent clauses that are connected by coordinating conjunctions such as *and*, *but*, *or*, *for*, and *nor* unless the clauses are short and closely connected.

    We have a supply on hand, but I think we should order an additional quantity.

    She had to work late, for the auditors were examining the books.

2. To set off a subordinate clause that precedes the main clause.

    Assuming no changes are needed, I suggest that you proceed with your instructions.

3. After an introductory phrase containing a verb form. No commas are needed after introductory phrases that immediately precede the verb they modify.

    To finish his work, he remained at the office after hours.

    After planning the program, she proceeded to put it into effect.

    Six miles to the west is the downtown area.

    Between her two daughters sat the matriarch of the family.

4. To set off a nonrestrictive clause. A nonrestrictive clause adds extra or nonessential information to a sentence. In other words, the meaning of the sentence would not change if the information were deleted.

    Our group, which had never lost a debate, won the grand prize.

5. To separate from the rest of the sentence a word or a group of words that breaks the continuity of a sentence.

    The administrative professional, when his work was completed, was willing to help others.

6. To separate parenthetical expressions from the rest of the sentence.

    We have, as you know, two people who can handle the reorganization.

7. To set off names used in direct address or to set off explanatory phrases or clauses.

    I think you, Mr. Bennett, will agree with the statement.

    Ms. Linda Matsuo, our vice president, will be in your city soon.

8. To separate from the rest of the sentence expressions that, without punctuation, might be interpreted incorrectly.

    Misleading: Ever since we have filed our reports monthly.

    Better: Ever since, we have filed our reports monthly.

9. To separate words or groups of words when they are used in a series of three or more.

    Most executives agree that dependability, trustworthiness, ambition, and judgment are required of workers.

10. To set off introductory words.

    For example, the musical on Saturday was not as lyrical as the last musical I saw.

    Thus, both the man and the boy felt a degree of discrimination.

11. To separate coordinate adjectives. Coordinate adjectives are two or more adjectives that equally modify a noun.

    The large, insensitive audience laughed loudly at the mistake.

12. To set off short quotations from the rest of the sentence.

    He said, "I shall be there."

    "The committees have agreed," he said, "to work together on the project."

13. To separate the name of a city from the name of a state.

    Our southern branch is located in Atlanta, Georgia.

14. To separate abbreviations of titles from the name.

    William R. Warner, Jr.

    Ramona Sanchez, Ph.D.

15. To set off conjunctive adverbs such as *however* and *therefore*.

    I, however, do not agree with the statement.

    According to the rule, therefore, we must not penalize the student for this infraction.

16. To separate a date from a year. Within a sentence, use a comma on both sides of the year in a full date.

    The anniversary party was planned for June 18, 2005.

    He plans to attend the management seminar scheduled for April 15, 2009, at the Hill Hotel.

17. Do not use a comma in numbers in an address even when there are four or more digits.

    The house number was 3100 Edmonds Drive.

18. Do not use a comma in a date that contains the month with only a day or a year.

    The accident occurred on June 10.

    The major event for June 2003 was the ethics seminar.

The Semicolon

Use a semicolon in the following instances:

1. Between independent groups of clauses that are long or that contain parts that are separated by commas.

    He was outstanding in his knowledge of technology, including telecommunications and computers; but he was lacking in many desirable personal qualities.

2. Between independent clauses when the conjunction is omitted.

    Everyone in the group enjoyed the meal; many members of the group did not enjoy the movie.

3. To precede expressions such as *namely* or *viz.*, *for example* or *e.g.*, and *that is* or *i.e.*, when used to introduce a clause.

    We selected the machine for two reasons; namely, it is a reasonable price and it has the features we need.

    There are several reasons for changing the routine of handling mail; i.e., to reduce postage, to conserve time, and to place responsibility.

4. Before a coordinating conjunction joining independent clauses containing commas.

> When the task is difficult, the time spent is usually great; and the rewards can be equally great.

The Colon

Use a colon in the following instances:

1. After the salutation in a business letter except when open punctuation is used.

> Ladies and Gentlemen:
>
> Dear Ms. Carroll:

2. Following introductory expressions such as *the following, thus, as follows*, and other expressions that precede enumerations.

> Please send the following by parcel post: books, magazines, and newspapers.
>
> The officers elected were as follows: president, Shireen Castroneves; vice president, Malcolm Turnball; treasurer, Ronald Moline.

3. To separate hours and minutes when indicating time.

> 2:10 p.m.   4:45 p.m.   12:15 a.m.

4. To introduce a long quotation.

> This quote from Theodore Roosevelt is a favorite of mine: "It is not the critic who counts. . . ."

The Question Mark

A question mark should be used in the following instances:

1. After a direct question.

> When do you expect to arrive in Philadelphia?
>
> An exception to the foregoing rule is a sentence that is phrased in the form of a question, merely as a matter of courtesy, when it is actually a request.
>
> Will you please send us an up-to-date statement of our account.

2. After each question in a series of questions within one sentence.

> What is your opinion of the Compaq computer? the Hewlett-Packard? the Dell?

The Exclamation Point

Use an exclamation point after words or groups of words that express command, strong feeling, emotion, or an exclamation.

> Don't waste supplies!
>
> It can't be done!
>
> Stop!

The Dash

Use a dash in the following instances:

1. To indicate an omission of letters or figures.

> Dear Mr.—
>
> The dollar amounts are—

2. To indicate a definite stop or as emphasis.

> This book is not a revision of an old book— it is a totally new book.

3. To separate parenthetical expressions when unusual emphasis is desired.

> These sales arguments—and every one of them is important—should result in getting the order.

4. To separate an appositive (word or phrase that identifies the noun or pronoun that immediately precedes it) if the use of commas might cause confusion.

> Concern over terror attacks—biological warfare, attacks on cities, and attacks on government buildings and personnel—is demanding much media attention.

The Apostrophe

An apostrophe is used:

1. To indicate possession.

> The boy's coat; the ladies' dresses; the girl's book

To the possessive singular, add 's to the noun.

> man's work
>
> bird's wing
>
> hostess's plans

An exception to this rule occurs when the word following the possessive begins with an *s* sound.

> for goodness' sake
>
> for conscience' sake

To form the possessive of a plural noun ending in an *s* or *z* sound, add only the apostrophe (') to the plural noun.

> workers' rights
>
> hostesses' duties

If the plural noun does not end in *s* or *z* sounds, add 's to the plural noun.

> women's clothes
>
> alumni's donations

Proper names that end in an *s* sound form the possessive singular by adding 's.

> Josh Holtz's house
>
> Andrea Fox's automobile

Proper names ending in *s* form the possessive plural by adding the apostrophe only.

> The Walters' property faces the Balderas' swimming pool.

2. To indicate the omission of a letter or letters in a contraction.

> it's (it is), you're (you are), we'll (we will)

3. To indicate the plurals of letters, figures, words, and abbreviations.

> Don't forget to dot your i's and cross your t's.
>
> I can add easily by 2's and 4's, but I have difficulty with 6's and 8's.
>
> Direct writing is achieved in part by omitting and's and but's.
>
> Two of the speakers were Ph.D.'s.

Quotation Marks

Certain basic rules should be followed in using quotation marks. These rules are as follows:

1. When a quotation mark is used with a comma or a period, the comma or period is placed inside the quotation mark.

> She said, "I plan to complete my program in college before seeking a position."

2. When using a quotation mark with a semicolon or a colon, place the semicolon or colon outside the quotation mark.

> The treasurer said, "I plan to go by train"; others in the group stated they would go by plane.

3. When more than one paragraph of quoted material is used, quotation marks appear at the beginning of each paragraph and at the end of the last paragraph.

4. Use quotation marks in the following instances:

   - Before and after direct quotations.

     > The author states, "Too frequent use of certain words weakens the appeal."

   - To indicate a quotation within a quotation, use single quotation marks.

     > The author states, "Too frequent use of 'very' and 'most' weakens the appeal."

   - To indicate the title of a published article.

     > Have you read the article, "Anger in the Workplace"?

Omissions Marks or Ellipses

Use ellipses marks (. . .) to denote the omission of letters or words in quoted material. If the material omitted ends in a period, use four omission marks (. . . .). If the material omitted does not end in a period, use three omission marks (. . .).

> He quoted the proverb, "A soft answer turneth away wrath, but. . . ."

> She quoted Plato, "Nothing is more unworthy of a wise man . . . than to have allowed more time for trifling and useless things than they deserved."

Parentheses

Although parentheses are frequently used as a catchall in writing, they are correctly used in the following instances:

1. When amounts expressed in words are followed by figures.

   He agreed to pay twenty-five dollars ($25) as soon as possible.

2. Around words that are used as parenthetical expressions.

   Our personnel costs (including benefits) are much too high.

3. To indicate technical references.

   Sodium chloride (NaCl) is the chemical name for common table salt.

4. When enumerations are included in narrative form.

   The reasons for his resignation were three: (1) starting his own business, (2) relocating to a new area, and (3) wanting to travel.

Reports

This section provides a review of report formats for unbound and leftbound reports. Traditional formats and new formats that take advantage of the default settings of *Microsoft Office Word 2007* are shown.

Report Parts

An informal report may have only one or two parts—the body and/or an executive summary. Formal reports may contain several parts as listed below. You can eliminate certain parts, such as the executive summary, list of tables and illustrations, table of contents, and appendix, if the report is relatively short.

- Title Page
- Executive Summary
- Table of Contents
- List of Tables and Illustrations
- Body
- Documentation (endnotes/footnotes)
- Bibliography or Reference Section
- Appendix

Report Formats

Business reports are typically created in unbound or leftbound formats. A short report (fewer than five pages) is typically an unbound report. For an unbound report, side margins of 1 inch are acceptable. However, if you intend to bind the report (and most reports of more than five pages should be bound), change the left margin to at least 1.5 inches. Before making the final decision on the left margin, determine what type of binding you will use and the extra space it requires. For both unbound and leftbound reports, use a top margin of 2 inches on the Table of Contents page, the first page of the body, and the first page of other sections, such as References. Use a bottom margin of 1 inch for all pages.

Most pages of a report should be numbered. Use the header and footer options of your word processing software to insert the page numbers. The title page comes first and does not have a page number. If the report has an executive summary, it follows the title page and is numbered with a lowercase Roman numeral (ii). The table of contents comes next and has a lowercase Roman numeral (ii or iii) as a page number at the bottom of the page. The first page of the body of the report does not have a page number. The remaining pages of the body are numbered in the upper right corner. If the report has a References page, it is also numbered in the upper right corner of the page.

The following figures show formats for report pages:

Figure 3	Unbound Report, Title Page	Traditional format
Figure 4	Unbound Report, Page 1	Traditional format
Figure 5	Leftbound Report, Table of Contents	New format
Figure 6	Leftbound Report, Page 1	New format
Figure 7	Leftbound Report, Page 2	New format
Figure 8	References Page	New format

For more information about preparing reports, refer to Chapter 7, Written Communications.

VERBAL PRESENTATIONS

UNITED PHARMACEUTICALS

Maria Lopez

November 200-

FIGURE 3 Unbound Report, Title Page, Traditional Format

VERBAL PRESENTATIONS

Verbal presentations are often used in the workplace to convey information to a group of people. These presentations may be informal ones to a small group or formal ones to a large group. Individuals also may have occasion to speak at professional organization or civic group meetings.

Presenting is challenging for some people. For most people, becoming an effective presenter is a learned skill. This skill is so important to individuals and organizations that some businesses develop training to help people become effective verbal presenters. Like all skill development, one must practice presentation skills to improve them.

Plan the Presentation

Preparing a good presentation takes time and may require research or development of visual aids or handouts. The presenter may also need to learn about the audience and the setting for the presentation. Beginning preparation three weeks before the presentation is not too soon.

Determine the Purpose

The first step in planning a presentation is to define clearly the purpose of the presentation. Ask these questions to begin planning a presentation:
- Why am I giving this presentation?
- What do I want the audience to know as a result of my presentation?
- What, if anything, do I want the audience to do as a result of my presentation?

Consider the Audience

Consider the characteristics of the people who will hear the presentation. Try to determine areas of common interest to which you can relate points of information. For example, if your audience is a group of administrative professionals, you know some of their interests. You can use anecdotes or stories that have meaning for them. If you are speaking to a group of colleagues from your workplace, again you know some of their interests. You can tailor your message to meet their needs.

If you are speaking to a general audience, keep these questions in mind as you begin to plan your remarks.
- What are the ages and genders of the people who will be in the audience?
- What is education level attained by the audience members? Are they high school graduates, college graduates, or a mixture of both?
- What knowledge does the audience have about the subject of the presentation?

FIGURE 4   Unbound Report, Page 1, Traditional Format

Begin at 2"
Left margin 1.5", other margins 1"

Table of Contents

Primary Research 1
Secondary Research 1
    Clarifying Your Web Search 2
    Evaluating the Information 2
    Handling Copyrighted Information 3
Report Parts 4
    Executive Summary 4
    Title Page 4
    Table of Contents 4
    Body 5
    Documentation 5
    References or Bibliography 7
    Appendix 8
References 9

ii

FIGURE 5   Leftbound Report, Table of Contents, New Format

Begin at 2"
Left margin 1.5", other margins 1"

Preparing Reports

Most reports involve some type of research. This research may be primary research—collecting original data through surveys, observations, or experiments. The research also may be secondary research—data or material that other people have discovered and reported via the Internet, books, periodicals, and various other publications. In addition, the research may be a combination of both primary and secondary.

Primary Research

If you are conducting primary research, you must decide how you are going to gather the information. You may decide to take these steps:

- Observe situations and individuals.
- Survey or interview groups of individuals.
- Perform an experiment.

Observational research involves collecting data by observing events or actions. Survey research involves collecting data through some type of survey or interview. An interview is usually done in person; however, it may be done over the telephone. Sometimes focus groups are used. Acceptable methods of administering surveys include mailing them or giving them in person. Generally, there is a much better response rate on surveys administered in person than those done by mail.

Scientific researchers have used experimental research for years; however, business researchers are increasingly using it also (Fulton-Calkins, 2009). Such research may involve selecting two or more sample groups and exposing them to certain treatments. For example, a business may decide to test a marketing strategy before implementing a marketing campaign. Researchers select experimental groups and implement the marketing strategy. Based on the outcome of the research, the business proceeds with the marketing strategy, modifies it, or selects another one.

Secondary Research

Secondary research involves using printed information available from sources such as books, periodicals, and the Web. Doing research in libraries has these advantages:

FIGURE 6   Leftbound Report, Page 1, New Format

- Libraries carry a huge collection of materials that may offer considerable depth in the subject matter you are interested in researching.
- Libraries have materials that may not be on the Web, including historical, highly specialized, and often quite rare materials.

Clarifying Your Web Search

One of the most difficult parts of searching the Web for information is clarifying your search so you can get information you need. If you do not clarify your search sufficiently, you may find yourself looking at hundreds of articles that do not match what you need. Ask yourself these questions to assist you in clarifying your search:

- Is the Web the best place to look? If you know very little about a topic and believe you are going to need help in narrowing the field to something that fits your needs, you may decide that the library is the best place for you to do your research. There you can get the help of professionals in the field.
- What information do I want? For example, assume you are interested in finding information on ethics. Do you want a history of ethics in the United States? Do you want a history that goes back to early philosophers? Are you interested in business ethics? Are you interested in societal ethics? In other words, you need to narrow your search so you can obtain information that is helpful for the project in which you are engaged.
- When keying in your search words, enter the most descriptive word first.
- Click Help or Search Tips on the search engine to learn more about what the search engine can do.

Evaluating the Information

Evaluating the Information. Since anyone can place information on the Web, you must determine the credibility of the company or individual hosting the information and the whether the data are current. Ask yourself these questions:

- How do I know if the information is reliable? First, look for current information unless you are interested in the history of a topic. Check the dates given on the Websites.
- What organization or person is hosting the information? Is that person or company credible? If you are looking for company information, the company itself is a good resource. Check the date on the Website. Is it current? If you have information written by a particular individual, try to find out something about that individual. Is the person representing a respected organization? Has the person written in the field previously? What education does the person have? The Website may provide some helpful information about the author. If not, you can do a search of the author's name on the Web or visit the library for credentials on the individual.

FIGURE 7 Leftbound Report, Page 2, New Format

Begin at 2"

References

Patsy Fulton-Calkins and Karin Stulz, *Procedures and Theory for Administrative Professionals* (Ohio: Cengage, South-Western, 2009), 125.

Jennifer Day, "National Population Projections," U.S. Census Bureau, accessed April 15, 2009, http://www.census.gov/population/www/pop-profile/natproj.html.

Robert Levine, "You Ought to Be in Pictures," *Business 2.0*, April 2007, 90.

FIGURE 8   Leftbound Report, References Page, New Format

Spelling

1. Put *i* before *e* except after *c* or when sounded like *a* as in *neighbor* or *weigh*. Exceptions: either, neither, seize, weird, leisure, financier, conscience.

2. When a one-syllable word ends in a single consonant and when that final consonant is preceded by a single vowel, double the final consonant before a suffix that begins with a vowel or the suffix *y*.

run	running
drop	dropped
bag	baggage
skin	skinny

3. When a word of more than one syllable ends in a single consonant, when that final consonant is preceded by a single vowel, and when the word is accented on the last syllable, double the final consonant before a suffix that begins with a vowel.

begin	beginning
concur	concurrent

   When the accent does not fall on the last syllable, do not double the final consonant before a suffix that begins with a vowel.

travel	traveler
differ	differing

4. When the final consonant in a word of one or more syllables is preceded by another consonant or by two vowels, do not double the final consonant before any suffix.

look	looked
deceit	deceitful
act	acting
warm	warmly

5. Words ending in a silent *e* generally drop the *e* before a suffix that begins with a vowel.

guide	guidance
use	usable

6. Words ending in a silent *e* generally retain the *e* before a suffix that begins with a consonant unless another vowel precedes the final *e*.

hate	hateful
due	duly
excite	excitement
argue	argument

7. Words ending in *ie* drop the *e* and change the *i* to *y* before adding *ing*.

lie	lying
die	dying

8. Words ending in *ce* or *ge* generally retain the final *e* before the suffixes *able* and *ous* but drop the final *e* before the suffixes *ible* and *ing*.

manage	manageable
force	forcible

9. Words ending in *c* insert a *k* before a suffix beginning with *e*, *i*, or *y* is added.

picnic	picnicking

10. Words ending in *y* preceded by a consonant generally change the *y* to *i* before a suffix except one beginning with *i*.

modify	modifying	modifier
lonely	lonelier	

11. Words ending in *o* preceded by a vowel form the plural by adding *s*. Words ending in *o* preceded by a consonant generally form the plural by adding *es*.

folio	folios
potato	potatoes

12. Words ending in *y* preceded by a vowel form the plural by adding *s*; words ending in *y* preceded by a consonant change the *y* to *i* and add *es* to form the plural.

attorney	attorneys
lady	ladies

Subject and Verb Agreement

This section presents a review of some of the basic rules concerning subject-verb agreement.

1. When the subject consists of two singular nouns and/or pronouns connected by *or* (*either . . . or, neither . . . nor*) or *not only . . . but also*, a singular verb is required.

   Jane or *Bob has* the letter.

   Either *Ruth or Marge plans* to attend.

   Not only a *book* but also *paper is* needed.

2. When the subject consists of two plural nouns and/or pronouns connected by *or* (*either. . . or, neither . . . nor*) or *not only . . . but also*, a plural verb is required.

   Neither the *managers* nor the *administrative assistants have* access to that information.

3. When the subject is made up of both singular and plural nouns and/or pronouns connected by *or* (*either . . . or, neither . . . nor*) or *not only . . . but also*, the verb agrees with the last noun or pronoun mentioned before the verb.

   Either *Ms. Salazar* or the *assistants have* access to that information.

   Neither the *men* nor *Jo is* working.

4. Disregard intervening phrases and clauses when establishing agreement between subject and verb. *One of* is considered singular.

   One of the men *wants* to go to the convention.

5. The words *each, every, either, neither, one,* and *another* are singular. When they are used as subjects or as adjectives modifying subjects, a singular verb is required.

   Each person *is* deserving of the award.

   Neither boy *rides* the bicycle well.

6. The following pronouns are singular and require a singular verb:

   anybody everybody nobody somebody

   anyone everyone nothing something

   anything everything no one someone

   Everyone plans to attend the meeting.

   Anyone is welcome at the concert.

7. *Both, few, many, others,* and *several* are plural. When they are used as subjects or adjectives modifying subjects, a plural verb is required.

   Several members *were* appreciative of the honor.

   Both women *are* going to apply.

8. *All, none, any, some, more,* and *most* may be singular or plural depending on the noun to which they refer.

   Some of the supplies are missing.

   Some of that paper is needed.

9. *The number* has a singular meaning and requires a singular verb; *a number* has a plural meaning and requires a plural verb.

   A number of people *are* planning to attend.

   The number of requests *is* surprising.

10. Geographic locations are considered as singular and are used with a singular verb when referring to one location. When reference is made to separate islands within a geographic location, the plural form is used with a plural verb.

    The Hawaiian Islands is their vacation spot this year.

    The Caribbean Islands have distinct cultures.

A

acceptance Favorable reception; approval.

accession log Component of a numeric filing system that maintains a record of the numbers that have been assigned.

active voice When the subject of the sentence performs the action.

acute stress Occurs when an individual must respond instantaneously to a crisis situation.

agenda An outline of the procedures or the order of business to be followed during a meeting.

alternate workstation A place of work other than the employee's official duty station, such as a telecommuting center or home office.

amoral Lacking moral judgment or sensibility; neither moral nor immoral.

analog dial-up A method of connecting computer devices to a network via a modem and a public telephone network.

annotate Underline important elements or make notes on a document.

antivirus software Utility program that protects, detects, and removes viruses from a computer's memory or storage devices.

applications software Computer programs that perform a specific function or specific tasks for users.

archive records Records that have historical value to an organization and should be preserved permanently.

attitude Disposition, feelings, or moods towards things, circumstances, or people.

audioconference A type of conference in which three or more people in different locations use a voice input unit to participate in a meeting.

automatic document feeder A device that feeds a stack of original documents to be copied into the copier one by one.

B

Baby Boom Generation Individuals born between 1946 and 1964, often called *Boomers*.

balance sheet A document that shows a company's assets, liabilities, and owners' equity at a given point in time.

biases Views based on background or experiences.

bilateralness Affecting two sides equally.

blog A Website that contains dated entries in reverse chronological order about a particular topic; often described as an online journal or diary.

blue laser disk (BD) Third generation optical disk that uses blue laser technology to store and retrieve data.

Bluetooth A technology that uses short-range radio signals to connect and share data among a variety of telecommunications devices.

body language Nonverbal messages transmitted through gestures and posture using the eyes, face, hands, arms, and legs.

bond A loan that a buyer makes to a bond issuer, which may be a government or a corporation, that includes the bond issuer's promise to pay a definite sum of money at a specified time to the holder of the bond.

brainstorm A sudden clever idea; a group problem-solving technique.

broadband A form of digital data transmission that uses a wide range of frequencies to achieve added bandwidth.

budget A spending and saving plan based on expected income and expenses.

business casual dress A style of professional dress that is less formal than traditional, conservative professional dress and that varies by organization.

business-class accommodations A class of air travel accommodations between first class and economy class designed specifically for business passengers.

business continuity (BC) guide A guide or plan that provides for smooth business operations in the event of a disaster.

business ethics The study of just and unjust behavior in business.

bylaws Written policies and procedures that define how corporate board meetings are to be conducted, how officers are elected, and other procedures.

C

cable A pipeline that connects computers to a coaxial cable line to provide voice and data transmission.

call center A centralized customer contact office in an organization that handles communication through written messages, email, fax, telephone, or the company Website.

cash flow statement A document that shows a company's sources of cash received and the uses of cash for a certain time period.

change agent An individual who facilitates change and helps others accept change.

chief executive officer (CEO) A top manager of a company who reports to the board of directors and oversees company operations.

chronic stress Occurs when a distressful situation is prolonged with no rest or recuperation for the body.

chronological resume A document that focuses on a chronology of an applicant's work experience, starting with the most recent job and listing the remainder in reverse order.

coding Marking the units of the filing segment by which the record is to be stored.

Collect on Delivery (COD) A service of the U.S. Postal Service that allows the price of goods and/or postage on the item(s) ordered by the recipient to be collected by the U.S. Postal Service on delivery and given to the mailer.

committee A group established for an ongoing purpose.

community A group of individuals who share common interests, beliefs, or goals.

compressed workweek An alternative to a traditional workweek that increases the number of hours per day and decreases the number of days worked in a given time.

computer network Two or more computers and other hardware devices connected for the purpose of communication and sharing resources; examples include PANs, LANs, MANs, and WANs.

computer output microform (COM) The process of converting digital computer data to text or graphic information on microfilm without first creating printed documents.

computer virus Computer program that infects a computer and performs malicious functions.

computer vision syndrome Eye complaints related to computer work.

conciseness Expressing the necessary information in as few words as possible.

conference A meeting where discussion on certain issues or topics takes place.

confidentiality Secrecy, privacy, or discretion. The ability to receive and keep private information that is secret.

conflict A state of opposition or disagreement between persons, ideas, or interests.

continuity of operations plan (COOP) A guide or plan that provides for smooth business operations in the event of a disaster.

convention A formal annual meeting of the members of a professional group.

cookie Small text file installed on a computer when a user visits a Website that stores information about the visit.

cooperate To work or act together toward a common end or purpose.

copyright A form of protection provided by the laws of the United States to the authors of original works of authorship, such as literary, dramatic, musical, and artistic works.

corporation A type of business that is a legal entity formed by following a process of incorporation set forth by state statutes.

courteous Respectful and considerate of others.

courteousness Using good human relations skills and being considerate of others.

criticism A value judgment or statement about the worth of something.

CTDs (cumulative trauma disorders) Repetitive stress injuries that often affect muscles, tendons, and nerves.

CTS (carpal tunnel syndrome) A condition that occurs due to the compression of a large nerve in the wrist.

current ratio An indication of an organization's ability to meet its current obligations from current assets. The ratio is calculated by dividing current assets by current liabilities.

customer A person or organization that receives the services or products that are offered by an organization.

customer service The ability of an organization to consistently give customers what they want and need.

D

data conferencing Two or more people communicating and collaborating as a group in real time using computers.

decision The outcome or product of a problem or an issue that must be addressed and solved.

defined benefit plan A retirement plan for an employee that is paid for by the employer.

delegation Assigning tasks to others and empowering them to get the job done.

Delivery Confirmation A service of the U.S. Postal Service that provides the date and time a First-Class Mail, Priority Mail, or package services parcel was delivered.

dependability Trustworthiness; reliability.

digital pen An input device used to give commands or write electronically on a screen; also called a stylus or electronic pen.

digital subscriber line (DSL) Telecommunications pipeline that transmits voice and data in digital form over standard telephone lines.

direct approach A strategy wherein correspondence begins with the reason for the correspondence.

director An officer of a company who is charged with the management of its affairs and conduct. A group of directors is referred to as a board of directors.

distress Negative stress caused by factors such as sickness or a negative performance review.

dividends A share of a company's profits that are paid to stockholders.

document imaging The process of scanning paper documents and converting them to digital images.

downsizing Reducing the number of full-time employees in an organization.

downward communication Messages that flow from management to employees of an organization.

E

economy-class accommodations The least expensive class of air travel, which usually offers less comfortable accommodations and fewer amenities than other classes.

EEOC (Equal Employment Opportunity Commission) A U.S. government entity charged with ending employment discrimination.

electronic portfolio An electronic tool that allows the owner to keep a record of work or projects completed over a certain period of time; also called an *e-portfolio*.

electronic record Data stored on an electronic medium that can be readily accessed or changed.

electronic resume A resume submitted in electronic format and designed for ease of searching and scanning electronically.

empathy Showing an understanding or concern for someone's feelings or position.

empowerment Giving workers access to information they need to do a job and the authority and responsibility to do that job.

encryption Method of scrambling data or email messages, rendering them unreadable if intercepted.

ergonomics The study of the problems of people in adjusting to their environment; the science that seeks to adapt work or working conditions to fit the worker.

ethics The systematic study of moral conduct, duty, and judgment.

e-ticket An electronic ticket that represents the purchase of a seat on a passenger airline, usually through a Website or by telephone.

etiquette Code developed through customs that governs acceptable behavior.

Euro The official currency of several countries that are members of the European Union.

eustress Beneficial stress that enables individuals to strive to meet challenges.

executive summary One- or two-page summary of the document, such as a report.

exit interview A meeting that someone from the company has with an employee whose job has been terminated or who has resigned.

Express Mail The fastest delivery available from the U.S. Postal Service, offering delivery by 3 p.m. the following day to many destinations.

external customers The companies or people outside the organization who buy or use the products or services provided by the organization.

extrinsic Coming from external factors.

F

fair Being free of favoritism.

fax broadcasting Transmitting a fax to multiple locations simultaneously.

fax machine A device that electronically sends a facsimile (images and text) of an original document from one location to another via a communications network.

FDA (Food and Drug Administration) A U.S. government entity responsible for regulating food, drugs, medical products and devices, and cosmetics.

fiber optic cable Hundreds or thousands of glass threads bundled together and used to transmit data and voice.

firewall Software program that provides protection by shielding a computer or network from unauthorized access.

first-class accommodations The most expensive class of air travel, which provides the most amenities and comfortable accommodations.

First-Class Mail A mail classification from the U.S. Postal Service appropriate for sending letters, large envelopes, and packages that weight up to 13 ounces with delivery time typically being two to three days.

flash memory Nonvolatile memory where data can be electrically stored, retrieved, and erased.

flexiplace A work environment in which individuals use telecommunications technology to complete their work from places other than a traditional office.

flexiwork A work environment in which individuals use telecommunications technology to complete their work from places other than a traditional office.

flextime A variable work schedule in which all employees do not work a standard 9 a.m. to 5 p.m. day.

focus groups People brought together to talk with an interviewer about their opinions of certain products or issues.

Form W-4 Employee's Withholding Allowance Certificate; a document that shows the number of exemptions claimed for tax purposes.

fortress culture An environment in which people do not trust one another and constantly attempt to defend their positions.

Fortune 500 companies A list of the top 500 American public corporations as measured by gross revenue that is published by *Fortune* magazine.

401(k) account A tax-deferred retirement plan for employees of private companies and corporations.

403(b) account A retirement plan for employees of nonprofit organizations or educational institutions such as teachers, nurses, professors, and ministers.

frequent flyer program An incentive program that provides a variety of rewards after the accumulation of a certain number of points.

functional resume A document that focuses on giving the skills and qualifications of the applicant for a particular job rather than work experience.

G

Generation X Individuals born between 1965 and 1975.

Generation Y Individuals born between 1976 and 1981.

goals Statements of desired changes or new directions to be accomplished.

grapevine Messages that may or may not be true and that originate from an unknown source within an organization.

graphical user interface (GUI) Feature of a computer operating system that uses visual images such as icons, buttons, menus, or other graphical objects to issue commands.

graphics tablet Input device used with a digital pen to draw images and graphics on a computer.

H

hacker Individual who breaks into a computer or network to delete, steal, or alter files.

hard drive Storage device that stores computer data magnetically on permanently sealed metal disks.

heterogeneous group A group of individuals having dissimilar backgrounds and experiences.

homogeneous group A group of individuals having similar backgrounds and experiences.

honesty The trait of being genuine; not being deceptive or fraudulent.

horizontal analysis A side-by-side comparison of two or more years of financial statements showing increases and decreases in items for particular periods of time.

horizontal communication Messages that flow from coworker to coworker or from manager to manager.

hoteling Setting aside offices or cubicles for the shared use of employees who telework.

hotspot A public location that offers a Wi-Fi access point.

hypertext Text linked to other text.

I

image record A digital or photographic representation of a record on any media such as microfilm or CD.

important record A record that is necessary to the orderly continuation of a business and is replaceable only at considerable time and expense.

income statement A document that shows the company's financial results (net income or loss) over a period of time.

indexing Determining the name to be used in storing a record.

indirect approach A strategy wherein correspondence begins with an opening statement that is pleasant but neutral.

individual retirement arrangement (IRA) A personal savings plan that allows individuals to set aside money for retirement while receiving tax advantages.

inhibitor A person or thing that retards growth or stops an activity.

initiative The ability to begin and follow through on a plan or task.

inspecting Checking a record to determine whether it is ready to be filed.

instant messaging (IM) An iteration of email that flashes a message on the computer screen telling the person that he or she has a message.

internal customers Departments or employees within an organization who use the services or products provided by others within the organization.

intrinsic Coming from within.

itinerary A travel schedule that gives flight numbers, arrival and departure times, hotel reservations, car rental, and other details.

J

jet lag The feeling of exhaustion following a flight through several time zones.

job agent A program that automatically searches job listings and retrieves jobs matching criteria set by the user.

job board A Website that provides job listings and allows persons to post resumes and view job listings.

job description Document that details the duties to be performed on a job.

job interview A meeting where a job applicant talks with an employer to determine whether the applicant is suitable for a job.

job sharing An arrangement in which two or more people complete the duties of one job position.

K

key operator A person who is responsible for making simple repairs to equipment such as a copier.

L

leader A person who guides or inspires others.

Library Mail A mail classification from the U.S. Postal Service that can be used by qualifying institutions, such as schools, libraries, and museums, to mail books, sound recordings, and educational/research material.

Library of Congress U.S. national library that carries millions of books, plus other items, such as maps and manuscripts.

limited liability company (LLC) A business form that combines the tax advantages of a partnership with the limited liability of a corporation.

listen Make a conscious effort to hear and understand information.

live chat Exchanging text messages with another person in real time via methods such as computer or cell phone.

loyalty The quality of devoted attachment and affection.

M

management The act of directing and controlling people and resources to accomplish goals.

manners Standards of conduct that show us how to behave in a cultured, polite, or refined way.

Medicare A health insurance program for people age 65 or older and certain younger people such as those who have disabilities.

melting pot A term used to refer to the amalgamation of people of different ethnicities and races into one United States of America.

microform A collective term for several types of media such as roll microfilm, microfiche, and aperture cards that contain miniature images of records.

minutes A written record of a meeting.

mission statement A statement of purpose that can be used to initiate, evaluate, and refine an organization's directions.

modem Acronym that stands for modulate/demodulate; a device that converts the digital signal from a computer to an analog signal that can be transmitted along an ordinary phone line.

monotone A succession of sounds or words uttered in a single tone of voice.

moral integrity Consistent adherence to a set of ideas of right and wrong.

morality A set of ideas of right and wrong.

motivation An inducement to act.

mutual fund An investment fund that consists of stocks, bonds, and other investments focused on a strategy such as balance or growth.

N

negative stress Factors that cause emotional and mental upset.

networking Exchanging information with other people and building positive business relationships; establishing a group of individuals who can assist in the job search process or other efforts.

nonessential record A record that has no future value to an organization and may be destroyed after current use.

nonprofit corporation A corporation formed to promote a civic, charitable, or artistic purpose and whose profits benefit that purpose.

nonverbal communication Sharing information with another through the use of body language, gestures, voice quality, or proximity to another rather than by using words.

O

off-loading Contracting with individuals or companies outside the organization to complete part of the work of the organization.

online banking Handling banking transactions over the Internet.

operating system Collection of programs that manage and coordinate the computer's activities.

optical disk Lightweight plastic disk that can be used to store and retrieve data with a low-powered laser beam.

organization Bringing together resources, such as people, money, and goods, in the most effective way to accomplish goals.

organizational culture The ideas, customs, values, and skills of a particular organization.

OSHA (Occupational Safety & Health Administration) A U.S. government entity created to enforce workplace health and safety laws.

outsourcing Using an outside company or a consultant to take over the performance of a particular part of an organization's business or to complete a project.

P

P/E ratio A comparison of the profit per share earned by a company to the current price per share of the company's stock.

parallelism Use of grammatically equivalent forms.

paraphrase Restate a concept in different terms.

Parcel Post A mail classification from the U.S. Postal Service that is used for mailing packages up to 70 pounds with delivery time typically being from two to nine days.

partnership An association of two or more people as co-owners of a business.

passport An official government document certifying the identity and citizenship of an individual and granting the person permission to travel abroad.

perfectionism A propensity for setting extremely high standards and being displeased with anything else.

periodic transfer Moving materials from active files to inactive files after a stated period of time.

perpetual transfer Moving materials continuously from the active to the inactive files whenever they are no longer needed for frequent reference.

personal digital assistant (PDA) A handheld computer that allows users to manage time and information; may allow use of application programs such as word processing and access to email and Internet.

personal information management (PIM) program Computer program that allows users to manage appointments, deadlines, contacts, and tasks.

persuasive approach An indirect approach used in correspondence to convince someone to do something or to change an indifferent or negative reader's reaction.

physically challenged Having a physical handicap.

planning Thinking about the activities required to accomplish a goal.

pointing device Computer hardware that allows a user to input data through the use of an on-screen pointer such as an arrow or insertion point.

pragmatic Relating to an idea or a concept that is understood conceptually and practiced day to day.

prejudice A system of negative beliefs and feelings.

prescreening Gathering information about an applicant prior to a formal in-person interview, often done online or by telephone.

primary research Collecting original data through surveys, observations, or experiments.

Priority Mail A mail classification from the U.S. Postal Service appropriate for sending packages that weight up to 70 pounds with delivery time typically being two to three days.

procrastination Trying to avoid a task by putting it aside with the intention of doing it later.

professional image The way in which a person is perceived in the business world relating to integrity, work ethic, skills, personal appearance, and etiquette.

Protestant ethic A work ethic that began as a religious teaching in Europe in the fourteenth century and is still practiced today.

proxemics The study of personal and cultural use of space.

public relations The technique of inducing the public to have understanding for and goodwill toward a person, a firm, or an institution.

Q

quick ratio An indication of a company's ability to cover its current liabilities by its most liquid assets (without selling inventory). The quick ratio is determined by subtracting inventory from total current assets and dividing by current liabilities.

quilt A term used to describe the diversity of the United States in which people retain much of their identity and language from their cultural background.

R

racial discrimination Mistreatment or differences in treatment of people on the basis of characteristics that may be classified as racial, such as skin color or cultural heritage.

racial harassment Behavior such as offensive jokes, slurs, ridicule, insults, threats, or intimidation related to race and causing interference with work.

readability Degree of reading difficulty of a message, measured using readability indices.

record Stored information on any media created or received by an organization that is evidence of its operations or has value requiring its retention for a period of time.

records management The systematic control of records from creation to final disposition or through the record life cycle.

reduction and enlargement A copier feature that allows users to change the size of the original document.

Registered Mail A service of the U.S. Postal Service that provides security from the point of mailing to delivery and up to $25,000 insurance against loss or damage.

respect Showing regard and appreciation for someone.

response rate The number of people responding to a survey or questionnaire.

resume A document that gives a concise statement of a person's background, education, skills, and work experience.

retention period Time that records must be kept according to operational, legal, regulatory, and fiscal requirements.

role ambiguity An absence of clarity concerning work objectives and expectations.

RSIs (repetitive stress injuries) The name given to a group of conditions that are caused when over time too much stress is placed on a joint.

S

salad bowl A term used to describe the diversity of the United States in which people retain much of their identity and language from their cultural background.

satellite A device that orbits the Earth and relays signals between telecommunications stations.

scanner A device that captures an image in digital form and transfers that image to a computer.

secondary research Data or material that other people have discovered and reported via the Internet, books, periodicals, and various other publications.

self-employed A term referring to a person who works for himself/herself instead of as an employee of another person or organization, drawing income from a trade or business.

self-esteem The way a person feels about himself or herself.

self management Methods, skills, and strategies by which individuals can effectively direct their own activities.

sexual harassment Abuse or mistreatment arising from sexual conduct that is unwelcome by the recipient and that may be either physical or verbal in nature.

short message service (SMS) Text messaging; the ability to send and receive short text messages through telecommunications channels.

shredder A machine that cuts paper into strips of confetti-like material.

Silent Generation Individuals born between 1925 and 1942.

smartphone An electronic device that combines the features of a PDA and a mobile phone.

Social Security A social insurance program with its beneficiaries being retired individuals, widows and survivors, and the disabled; benefits are paid when a person retires or becomes disabled.

software piracy Illegal reproduction and distribution of software applications.

sole proprietor A single owner of unincorporated businesses.

spamming Forwarding electronic junk mail or chain letters to a mailing list.

spyware Software program that gathers personal information about the user without his or her permission; adware is spyware that randomly displays pop-up advertisements.

stakeholders People having an interest in an outcome; for example, stockholders and employees of a business who have an interest in the success of the business.

Standard Mail A mail classification from the U.S. Postal Service that offers a lower price on postage because the sender does some of the preparing and sorting.

stereotyping Holding perceptions or images of people or things that are derived from selective perception.

stock A share of ownership in a corporation.

stockholder A person who owns shares of stock in a company.

strategic plan The direction and goals for an organization's work, generally for the next five or fewer years.

stress The response of the body to a demand made upon it.

synergy The effect of two or more people or things working together to produce an effect that is greater than the sum of the individual efforts or the parts.

systems software Software programs that manage and control computer functions.

T

tablet PC Portable computer that allows input through handwriting on the screen; a tablet PC without a keyboard is called a slate.

tact Sensitivity to what is proper and appropriate in dealing with others, including the ability to speak or act without offending.

targeted job search A search that focuses on obtaining a job at a particular company.

task force A group formed to deal with a specific issue or problem.

telecenter An office space available for the use of teleworkers and located in an area that will reduce commuting time.

telecommunications The transmission of text, data, voice, video, and images from one location to another.

teleconferencing A general term applied to a variety of technology-assisted two-way (interactive) communications.

telemarketing Selling, soliciting, or promoting a product or service on the telephone.

telework Using telecommunications technology to work from somewhere other than a traditional workplace.

teleworker An individual who uses telecommunications technology to work full- or part-time at home or at some other mobile work environment.

territoriality An expression of ownership and control over a particular area or space.

time A period of duration during which something exists, happens, or acts; a limited resource.

topic sentence A sentence that contains the main idea of a paragraph.

trackball Stationary ball that can be rolled to move the cursor on the computer screen.

traditional job search A search in which you apply for job openings that match your career goals in many organizations.

Trojan horse Malicious software designed to look like something useful.

two-factor authentication System where an individual is required to provide a password and an additional item for identification purposes.

U

upward communication Messages that travel from employees to management.

useful record A record that is useful for smooth, effective operation of an organization and is inconvenient to replace.

utility program System software that performs a task related to managing a computer, its devices, or its programs.

V

values A person's deeply held beliefs.

verbal communication The process of exchanging information through the use of words.

vertical analysis A comparison used to show the relationship of each component to the total within a single financial statement.

videoconferencing A system of transmitting audio and video between individuals at two or more locations.

virtual assistant A self-employed person who uses telecommunications technology to provide administrative or technical services to clients for a fee.

visa An approval granted by a government that permits a traveler to enter and/or travel within a particular country.

visionary Able to see what is possible, having foresight.

visual aid An object or an image that a person can see to help understand a spoken or written message.

visualization The creation of a mental picture.

vital record A record that cannot be replaced and should never be destroyed.

voice over Internet protocol (VoIP) Technology that allows a user to make voice telephone calls over the Internet.

W

Wi-Fi Wireless fidelity; a medium-range radio transmission technology used in telecommunications.

WiMax A long-range wireless broadband transmission technology used in telecommunications.

work ethic Values based on the merits of hard work and diligence.

workaholic A person who is addicted to work or who has a compulsive need to work.

workplace politics Social relations involving authority or power and making decisions in the workplace.

worm Malicious, self-replicating computer program designed to cause damage to computer software or files.

NOTE to readers: Page numbers in italics indicate tables and figures.

A

Abbreviations in names, indexing, 318–319
Abilities of professionals. *See* Characteristics; Skills.
Above and Beyond 2007, 115
Acceptance, 38
Accepting responsibility. *See* Responsibility, accepting.
Accuracy, correspondence, 161
Achievement *versus* perfection, 113
Acid-test ratio, 352–353
Active listening, verbal communication, 186–187
Active voice, 158–159
Acute stress, 104–105
Administrative assistant, career profile, 3
Administrative professionals
 common teams, 37–38
 ethics (*see* Ethics, administrative professionals)
 meeting responsibilities, 382–389
Administrative professionals, responsibilities
 coordination, 469
 living your values, 467–468
 needs determination, 468
 organization, 469
 overview, 466–467
 physical health and energy, 469–470, *470*
 planning, 468
 recommendations to management, 468
 training and supervising assistants, 469
 travel arrangements (*see* Travel arrangements, by administrative professionals)
Administrative skills, in teams, 35
Advancement. *See* Job advancement.
Age differences, 6, 10–11
Agenda
 definition, 385
 example, *386*
 planning, 382
 preparing and distributing, 385
 sticking to, 390

Alcohol in the workplace, 49
Alphabetic storage, 310–311, *312*
American dining style, 94
Analog dial-up, 281
Anger
 Problem-Solving Model, 109, *109*
 purpose, 109
 relation to stress and time, 111, *112*
 resolution, 109
 stress factor, 107–108
Anger management
 audits, 111–112
 balancing work and play, 119
 diet, 117
 doing it right the first time, 113
 down time, 113
 effective communication, 116–117
 exercise, 118
 handling paper, 113
 managing large projects, 114–116
 organizational dependencies, 119
 perfection *versus* achievement, 113
 positive self-talk, 120
 relaxing, 120
 role relationships, 119
 setting priorities, 112, 114, *114*
 sleep, 118
 solving the problem, 120–121
 speed reading, 114
 talking to a friend, 120
 time management systems, 115
 to-do lists, 112
 values clarification, 112
 visualization, 118
 walking away, 120
 workstation organization, 113
Ankrum Associates, 49
Annotating mail, 264
Annual reports, job search, 432
Antivirus software, 246, *246*
Aperture cards, 336
Appearance
 body language, 83
 body piercings, 91
 first impressions, 83
 guidelines, 91, *91*
 jewelry, 91
 for a job interview, 441–442
 smile, 83
 tattoos, 91
Appearance, dress
 business attire, 89
 business casual attire, 89–90

 dressing the part, 88–89
 factors affecting, 90
 importance of, 83
 international business, 94–95
 job interviews, 441–442
 presentations, 200–201
Appendix, reports, 179
Application software, *243*, 243–244
Appointments
 effects of jet lag, 405–406
 travel arrangements, 412, 414–416, *414*
Aquinas, Thomas, 128
Archive records, 339
Arms, nonverbal communication, 191
ARPANET, 241–242
Arthur Anderson, ethics, 126
Articles in names, indexing, 320–321
ATS (Applicant Tracking System), 440
Attachments, email, 164
Attention to detail, 87
Attitude, definition, 42
Attitude clarification, 41–42
Audience considerations
 presentations, 194, 202–203
 written correspondence, 155–156
Audioconferencing, 376–377, *377*
Audits, 111–112

B

Baby Boom Generation, 6, 10–11
Back pain, 46
Balance sheets, 350–351, *351*, *355*
Balancing work and play, 119
Banking, personal, 355–356, *356*, 357
BDs (blue laser disks), 239
Bentham, Jeremy, 128
Bibliography, reports, 179
Bilateralness, 461
Billable hours agreement, 64
Blogs, job search, 436, 438
Bloopers, international correspondence, 155–156
Bluetooth, 283
Board of directors, 8–9, 375
Body language, 83, 190–192, *193*
Body piercings, 91
Body section
 presentations, 197–198
 reports, 176, 178–179

Bonds, 363–364
Books and publications
    Leadership the Challenge, 12
    Occupational Outlook Handbook, 3
    The World is Flat, 15
Boone, Garrett, 127
Bound Printed Matter, 258
Broadband, 281
Budgets, 360
Bush, George W., 129
Business attire, 89. *See also* Appearance.
Business cards
    career tips, 88
    cultural differences, 406
    international travel, 406
    for teleworkers, 75
Business casual attire, 89–90. *See also*
    Appearance.
Business-class airline travel, 400
Business dress, international, 94–95
Businesses, forms of. *See* Organizational
    structure.
Business ethics, 127. *See also* Ethics.
Business etiquette. *See* Etiquette.
Business gifts, 95, 406, *407*
Business hours, 95
Business meals, etiquette, 93–94
Business name, indexing by. *See* Indexing
    records, business names.
Business networking. *See* Networking.
Business plans, 179
Butler, David, 222
Bylaws, 374

C

Cable modem, 281
Call centers, 221–222
CAP (Certified Administrative
    Professional), 16–17
Capital, 350
Career development, 16–17
Career plans
    decision making, 23–25
    goal setting, 22–23
Career profiles
    administrative assistant, 3
    database manager, 307
    meeting planner, 372
    network administrator, 231
    office manager, 423
    service representatives, 151
Career tips
    adapting to change, 467
    business cards, 88
    certification, virtual workplace, 68
    communicating with customers, 218
    continuing education, 22
    copier key operator, 272
    effective voice messages, 288

financial goals, 359
greetings, international, 96
illegal software, 244
international business cards, 406
job search, 429
naming electronic files, 332–333
networking, 429
presentations, 202
professional organizations, virtual
    workplace, 68
speaking with credibility, 202
virtual workplace, 68
writing ethics, 173
Carpal tunnel syndrome (CTS), 45–46
Car rental, international, *409*
Car travel, domestic, 403
Cash flow statements, 352
CDs, 239
Celebrating victory, 461
Certification, 16–17, 68
Certified Administrative Professional
    (CAP), 16–17
Certified Professional Secretary (CPS),
    16–17, *17*
Chain letters, email, 165
Chairs, ergonomic, 48
Change, ethical
    evaluating effects of, 138
    factors impeding, 135–137
    practicing new behaviors, 138
    required changes, identifying, 137–
        138
    rewards for, 138
    seeking feedback, 138
    steps producing, *136*, 137–138
Change, organizational
    adapting to, 467
    crisis leadership, 14
    diversity, 5
    economic globalization, 5
    employee participation, 14
    envisioning the future, 12
    future challenges, *15*
    globalization, 5
    home offices, 6–7
    learning organizations, 11–12
    mobile offices, 6–7
    older workers, 6
    physical workplace, 6–7
    prioritization, 13
    self-employment, 7
    strategic vision, 13
    values clarification, 12
    victory celebration, 15
    virtual offices, 6–7
    workweek, 6
Change, personal
    career development, 16–17
    certification, 16–17
    continuing education, 16–17

leaving a job, 447 (*see also* Job search)
    openness to, 21
    professional organizations, 16–17
    values clarification, 15–16
Change leaders, *462*
Characteristics, of leaders. *See*
    Leadership, traits.
Characteristics, personal. *See also*
    Appearance; Skills.
    attention to detail, 87
    commitment to learning, 22
    confidentiality, 22
    courtesy, 83
    creativity, 21
    daily work, 87
    dependability, 21–22
    desk, 86–87
    honesty, 21
    initiative, 21
    integrity, 21
    motivation, 21
    openness to change, 21
    positive attitude, 84–85
    professional organization
        participation, 87–88
    punctuality, 83
    responsibility, 87
    teleworkers, 65–67
    work ethic, 85–86
    workplace, 86
Chartered planes, 402
Chronic stress, 105
Chronological resumes, 433, *434*
Citations, reports, 176, 178–179
Clarity, correspondence, 160–161
Clarity of purpose, in teams, 34
Clichés, correspondence, *162*
Clip art, presentations, 199
Closing, presentations, 198
Clothing. *See* Appearance, dress.
Coach (economy-class) airline travel, 400
COD (Collect on Delivery), 260
Coding records for storage, 314, *315*. *See
    also* Indexing.
Collaborative writing, 179–180
College recruiters, 431
Color, presentations, 199
COM (computer output to microfilm), 335
Commitment, in teams, 36
Commitment to learning. *See* Continuing
    education.
Committee meetings, 374
Common stocks, 362
Communication. *See also*
    Correspondence, written; Diversity,
    effective communication; Nonverbal
    communication; Presentations; Verbal
    communication.
        managing stress, anger, time,
            112–117, *112*

skill requirements, 18
with visitors, 39–40
Communication skills, teleworkers, 67
Community spirit, establishing, 460
Companies, forms of. *See Organizational structure.*
Company-owned planes, 402
Company Websites, job search, 432
Completeness, correspondence, 160
Compressed workweek, 6
Computer conferencing. *See Online, conferencing.*
Computer hardware
    BDs (blue laser disks), 239
    care tips, *233*
    CDs, 239
    data storage, 238–240
    digital cameras, 237
    digital pens, 235–236
    DVDs, 239
    flash memory, 239–240
    graphics tablet, 236
    handheld computers, 234–235
    hard drives, 238
    input devices, 235–237
    microcomputers, 232–233
    notebook computers, 233
    optical disks, 238–239
    PDAs (personal digital assistants), 234
    pointing devices, 235–236
    scanners, 236–237
    smartphones, 235
    speech recognition, 237, *238*
    synchronizing data, *234*
    tablet PCs, 234
    for teleworkers, 73
    touchpads, 235–236
    trackballs, 235
    types of computers, 232–235
Computer issues
    cookies, 249–250
    data protection, portable devices, 249
    firewalls, 248–249
    hackers, 247
    passwords, *248*
    privacy solutions, 250–251
    privacy threats, 249–250
    protection guidelines, 248, *250*
    security solutions, 247–249
    security threats, 246–247
    spyware, 250, *250*
    Trojan horses, 247, *248*
    two-factor authentication, 247–248
    viruses, 246, *246, 248*
    worms, 247, *248*
Computer networks
    ARPANET, 241–242
    definition, 240
    Internet, 241–242

LAN (local area network), 241
MAN (metropolitan area network), 241
PAN (personal area network), 241
WAN (wide area network), 241
WPAN (wireless personal area network), 241
WWW (World Wide Web), 242
Computer output to microfilm (COM), 335
Computer software
    antivirus, 246, *246*
    applications, *243*, 243–244
    GUIs (graphical user interfaces), 245
    illegal, 244
    OCR (optical character recognition), 236–237
    operating system, 245
    pirated, 244
    systems, 244–246
    utilities, *245*, 245–246
Computer vision syndrome, 46
Conciseness, correspondence, 161
Conferences. *See Conventions and conferences.*
Confidentiality
    definition, 22
    ethics, 144
    personal and confidential mail, 263
    in the workplace, 22
Confidential records management, 310, 339
Conflict resolution, 35–36, 189–190, *190*
Consecutive number storage, 330
Constructive criticism, ethics, 143–144
Container Store, The, 127
Continental dining style, 94
Continuing education
    career tip, 22
    commitment to learning, 68–69, 460
    coping with change, 16–17
    teleworkers, 68
Continuity of operations, telework, 60
Conventions and conferences. *See also Meetings.*
    after the event, 393
    definition, 375
    before the event, 392–393
    during the event, 393
    scope of, 391–392
Cookies, 249–250
Cooperation, 38
Coordination responsibilities, 469
Copiers
    automatic document feed, 269
    capacities and features, 268
    copy control devices, 269
    copyright, 270, *271*
    editing, 269
    ethics, 269–270

etiquette, 270–271
faxing, 269
key operator, 272
maintenance, 271–272
monitoring use of, 269
needs assessment, *268*
questions about, *268*
reduction/enlargement, 269
scanning, 269
trayless duplexing, 269
Copyright, 270, *271*
Copyrighted information, reports, 175
Corporations, structure of. *See Organizational structure.*
Correspondence. *See also specific types.*
    accuracy, 161
    clarity, 160–161
    clichés, *162*
    completeness, 160
    conciseness, 161
    courtesy, 161
    promptness, 161
    tone, positive *versus* negative, 162
    while traveling, 414, 416
    W questions, *161*
Correspondence, written. *See also Email; Letters; Mail; Memorandums; Reports.*
    audience, analyzing, 155–156
    business plans, 179
    collaboration, 179–180
    draft, final, 159
    draft, initial, 157
    editing, 157–159
    effective paragraphs, 157–158
    gathering information, 156
    general audiences, 155
    goal, determining, 154–155
    international audiences, 155–156, *157*
    organizing content, 156–157
    parallel paragraph structure, 158
    process, 159
    professional audiences, 155
    proofreading, 160, *160*
    purpose, determining, 154–155
    readability level, 159, *159*
    reader, analyzing, 155–156
    reports, 154
    sentence structure, 158
    time usage, 159
    voice, passive *versus* active, 158–159
Courtesy
    correspondence, 161
    first impressions, 83
    and manners, 92–93
Coworkers, etiquette towards, 96–97
CPS (Certified Professional Secretary), 16–17, *17*
Creative thinking, 19, *19*
Creativity, 21
Credit card numbers, email, 165

Creditworthiness, 352–353
Crisis leadership, 14
Critical, word origin, 18
Critical thinking, 18–19, *19*
Criticism, coping with, 187–188
Critiquing presentations, 203
Cross-referencing records, 314, 327, *328*, *329*
CTS (carpal tunnel syndrome), 45–46
Cultural differences. *See also* Diversity.
    business cards, 406
    business gifts, 95, 406, *407*
    business hours, 95
    correspondence audiences, 155–156, *157*
    correspondence bloopers, 155–156
    ethics, 130–131
    etiquette, 94–95
    gestures, 95
    greetings, 95–96
    holidays, 95
    international travel, 405
    meetings, 379–380
    source of information about, 405
    time, 95
Currency, international travel, 408
Current ratio, 352
Customer/client meetings, 375
Customer is always right, 213–214
Customers
    calling by name, 216
    communicating with, 218
    definition, 210
    employees as, 212
    external, 212
    future, 212
    internal, 212
Customers, bad behavior
    abusive, 220
    difficult people, 218
    inappropriate comments, 223
    racial harassment, 223
    sexual harassment, 223
    threats of bodily harm, 223
Customer service
    call centers, 221–222
    the customer is always right, 213–214
    definition, 210
    for employees, 212
    external customers, 212
    internal customers, 212
    leadership, 212
    mission statement, 211, *211*
    telemarketing, 221–222
    vision statement, 211–212
    Web-based, 222, *222*
Customer service skills
    email, 220–221
    telephone, 219–220
Customer service skills, face-to-face

admitting mistakes, 214–215
    calling customers by name, 216
    difficult people, 218
    empathy statements, 217–218
    explaining the situation, 218
    eye contact, 215
    going the extra mile, 215
    interpersonal space, 215–216
    language use, 217
    listening, 216–217, *217*
    preparing yourself, 214
    smiling, 215
    taking responsibility, 214
    visualizing success, 214

D

Database administrator, 307
Database files, 334–335
Database manager, career profile, 307
Data conferencing, 378
Data protection, portable devices, 249
Data storage, 238–240
Decision making
    career plans, 23–25
    defining the problem or purpose, 23–24
    ethics, 141
    evaluating the decision, 25
    generating alternatives, 24
    in meetings, 390
    personal skill, 19
    setting criteria, 24
    steps in, *23*, 23–25
    testing alternatives, 24–25
    travel arrangements, 414
Defined benefit plans, 360
Delegating tasks, 464
Deleting, email, 164
Delivery Confirmation, 260
Dependability, 21–22, 37
Desk, organization, 86–87
Destination USA Website, *409*
Diet, 117
Digital cameras, 237
Digital pens, 235–236
Digital portfolios, 16
Digital subscriber line (DSL), 282
Dining, 93–94
Direct approach, letters, 168, *169*
Directors, 8–9
Discharging employees, 465–466
Discipline, teleworkers, 65
Discrimination in the workplace. *See* Job discrimination.
Disposal of records, 339. *See also* Records, retention.
Disposition of electronic files, 334. *See also* Records, retention.

Distress, 104
Diversity. *See also* Cultural differences.
    age differences, 10–11
    attitude clarification, 41–42
    cultural differences, 41, *41*
    in ethical organizations, 131–134
    ethnicity, 10–11, 140–141, *141*
    generational groups, 10–11
    at Genetech, 127
    management challenges, 10–11
    melting pot analogy, 40
    negative stereotyping, 131
    at QUALCOMM, 132–134, *133*
    quilt analogy, 40
    as a resource, 40–41
    salad bowl analogy, 40
    values clarification, 41–42
    workplace changes, 5
Diversity, effective communication
    clarity, written and spoken, 44
    downward communication, 43
    ethics of, 44–45
    flexibility, 42
    formal communication, 43
    grapevine, 43
    horizontal communication, 43
    listening skills, 42
    management styles, 44
    organizational charts, 43–44
    respect, 42
    upward communication, 43
    value judgments, 42
    word interpretation, 44
Dividends, stock, 362
Documentation, reports, 176, 178–179
Document imaging, 335
Document stands, 48
Doing it right the first time, 113
Dow Jones Industrial Average, 362
Downsizing, 64
Down time, 113
Downward communication, 43
Dress. *See* Appearance, dress.
Drugs in the workplace, 49
DSL (digital subscriber line), 282
Dual-career families, stress factor, 107
Duplexing copying, 269
DVDs, 239

E

EAP (emergency action plan), 135, *135*
Economic globalization, 5, 15
Economy-class (coach) airline travel, 400
Editing
    correspondence, 157–159
    email, 164
    letters, 168

Education. *See* Continuing education.
EEOC (Equal Employment Opportunity Commission), 223
Effective listening, in teams, 35, 35–36
Electronic meetings. *See* Meetings, electronic.
Electronic portfolios, 16
Electronic records, 331–332. *See also* Records management, electronic files.
Electronic resumes, 433, 436, 437
Email. *See also* IM (instant messaging); Text messaging.
 advantages/disadvantages, 153
 all uppercase, 164
 attachments, 164
 chain letters, 165
 credit card numbers, 165
 customer service skills, 220–221
 deleting, 164
 disadvantages of, 261
 editing, 164
 effective messages, 297
 emoticons, 163
 ethics, 164–165, 297
 etiquette, 164, 297
 filing, 266–267
 formal *versus* informal, 163
 format, 165
 forwarding, 165
 graphics in, 164
 guidelines, 163–164
 junk, 165, 267
 organizing the message, 164
 personal, on office computer, 164
 proofreading, 164
 spam, 165, 267
 subject line, 163–164
 unsolicited, responding to, 164
 Windows Mail screen, 267
Emergency action plan (EAP), 135, 135
Emoticons, email, 163
Empathy statements, 217–218
Employees
 commitment to, 134
 as customers, 212
 customer service for, 212
 discharging, 465–466
 employer-sponsored retirement plans, 360–362
 empowering, 458–459
 evaluating, 465, 464
 motivating, 21, 464
 participation in change, 14
 recognizing achievements of, 460
 stock purchase plans, 360
Employer-sponsored retirement plans, 360–362
Employment agencies, 430–431
Empowering others, 458–459
Enron, ethics, 126

Envelopes
 address, example, 262
 opening, 263
 retaining, 263–264
Environmental responsibility, 130
Envisioning the future, 12
Episodic telecommuting, 59
E-portfolios, 436
Equal Employment Opportunity Commission (EEOC), 223
Ergonomics
 chairs, 48
 common injuries, 45–46
 CTS (carpal tunnel syndrome), 45–46
 definition, 45
 document stands, 48
 footrests, 48
 keyboard alternatives, 46–47
 monitor arms, 47
 mouse alternatives, 47
 preventing injuries, 46–48, 50
 problem solutions, 50, 50
 research, 48–49
 sitting position, 48–49
 task lights, 48
 work surfaces, adjustable, 47
Ethics
 Aquinas, Thomas, 128
 Arthur Anderson, 126
 Bentham, Jeremy, 128
 business, 127
 of communication, 44–45
 copiers, 269–270
 definition, 126
 email, 164–165, 297
 Enron, 126
 Kant, Immanuel, 128
 making a difference, 130
 Mills, John, 128
 Plato, 128
 Protestant ethic, 128
 reasons for, 129
 roots of, 128–129
 Socrates, 128
 stem cell research, 129
 written communication, 173
Ethics, administrative professionals
 accepting responsibility, 144
 confidentiality, 144
 constructive criticism, 143–144
 honesty, 144
 keeping the faith, 145
 loyalty, 144–145
 making decisions, 141
 negative workplace politics, 142
 supporting behavior, 141–142
Ethics, change
 evaluating effects of, 138
 factors impeding, 136–137

 practicing new behaviors, 138
 required changes, identifying, 137–138
 rewards for, 138
 seeking feedback, 138
 steps producing, 136, 137–138
Ethics, organizational
 community, commitment to, 134
 The Container Store, 127
 diversity commitment, 131–134
 employees, commitment to, 134
 environmental responsibility, 130
 ethical commitment, 131
 evaluating, 145
 Genetech, 127
 honesty, 131
 international differences, 130–131
 QUALCOMM, 132–134, 133, 134
 SC Johnson, 131
 standards, commitment to, 134
 Starbucks Coffee, 131
 Wegman's Food Markets, 127
Ethnic discrimination, 140–141, 141
E-tickets, 400
Etiquette. *See also* Telephones, etiquette.
 business dress, international, 94–95
 business gifts, 95, 406, 407
 business hours, 95
 business meals, 93–94
 business networking, 97–98
 copiers, 270–272
 courtesy, 92–93
 coworkers, 96–97
 definition, 91
 dining and restaurants, 93–94
 dining styles, 94
 email, 164, 297
 gestures, 95
 greetings, 95, 96
 holidays, 95
 IM (instant messaging), 295–297
 international differences, 94–95
 introductions, 95–96, 96
 manners, 92–93
 mobile phones, 299–300
 receiving visitors, 97, 97
 superiors, 96–97
 table manners, 93–94, 94
 telecommunications devices, 298
 time, 95
 voice messaging, 298–299
Evaluating employees, 465, 464
Evaluation form, presentations, 204
Event planning. *See* Conventions and conferences; Meetings.
Executives, meeting responsibilities, 380–383
Executive summary, reports, 175
Exemptions, income tax, 346–347
Exercise, 118

Exit interviews, 447
Expense reports, 416, *417*
Express Mail, 257
Express Mail International, 258
Extended families, stress factor, 107
External customers, 212
Extrinsic motivation, 464
Eye contact, customer service, 215
Eyes, nonverbal communication, 191

F

Face-to-face meetings, 376. *See also*
     Customer service skills, face-to-face.
Facial expressions, nonverbal
     communication, 191
Fairness, 38
Faxing, from copiers, 269
Fax machines
     definition, 273
     features and services, 273
     junk faxes, 273–274
Federal government job board, 430, *431*
Fiber optic cable, 283–284
File folders, 312–313
File guides, 312
Filenames, 332–333
File paths (electronic), 333
Filing email, 266–267. *See also* Records
     management.
Financial goals, 358–359
Financial statements, organizational
     ability to pay obligations, 352
     acid-test ratio, 352–353
     analyzing, 352–355
     balance sheets, 350–351, *351, 355*
     capital, 350
     cash flow statements, 352
     comparisons, over time, 352
     creditworthiness, 352–353
     current ratio, 352
     horizontal analysis, 352
     income statements, 352, *353*
     P/E (price/earnings) ratio, 354–355
     quick ratio, 352–353
     stockholders' equity, 350
     vertical analysis, 352
Findability, records management,
     309–310
Fired from a job, 447. *See also* Discharging
     employees.
Firewalls, 248–249
First-class airline travel, 400
First-Class Mail, 257
First Class Mail International, 258
First impressions, 83
Flash memory, 239–240
Flat rate workers, 63
Flexiplace. *See* Telework.
Flexiwork. *See* Telework.

Flextime, 6
Flight classifications, 400, 406–407
Focus on
     data protection, portable devices, 249
     effective email, 153, 220
     effective telework agreement, 71
     electronic portfolios, 16
     evaluating employees, 465
     hotel security, 404
     mail organization, 265
     messaging system safety, 296
     microforms, 335
     organizational structure, 10
     preparing an effective blog, 438
     retirement planning, 361
     understanding your organization, 10
     visual aids, 200
Folders
     electronic, 332–333, *333*
     paper, 312–313
Footnotes, reports, 178
Footrests, 48
Formal communication, 43
Formal *versus* informal email, 163
Formatting, letters, 168
Forms of organizations. *See*
     Organizational structure.
Form W-4, 346
Fortress culture, 456
Fortune 500 Companies, 428
Forwarding, email, 165
401(k) accounts, 360–361
403(b) accounts, 360–361
Frequent flyer programs, 410
Friedman, Thomas, 15
Functional resumes, 433, *435*
Furniture, for teleworkers, 75

G

General audiences, 155
Generational categories, *10*, 10–11
Generation X, 10–11
Generation Y, 10
Genetech, 127
Geographic storage system, 330
Gestures, 95
Gifts, business, 95, 406, *407*
Global Express Guaranteed, 258
Globalization, 5, 15
Goals
     career, setting, 22–23
     correspondence, determining,
          154–155
     financial, 359
     job search, 427
     personal *versus* organizational, 33
Going the extra mile, 215
Google, *196*

Governmental entities, organizational
     structure, 8
Government job board, 430, *431*
Government names, indexing
     federal, 326
     foreign, 327
     local, 325
     regional, 325
     state, 325–326
Grapevine, 43
Graphics
     in email, 164
     in reports, 176
Graphics tablets, 236
Greetings, 96, 97
Ground transportation, 402–403
Growth, focusing on, 461
GUIs (graphical user interfaces), 245

H

Hackers, 247
Hall, Edward T., 192
Handheld computers, 234–235
Handling paper, 113
Hands, nonverbal communication, 191
Hard drives, 238
Hardware, for teleworkers, 73
Headaches, 46
Health and safety. *See also* Ergonomics;
     Security.
     alcohol, 49
     back pain, 46
     computer vision syndrome, 46
     drugs, 49
     headaches, 46
     international travel, 408–409
     responsibilities, 469–470, *470*
     smoking, 49
     substance abuse, 49
     telework, safety guidelines, 73, *73*
     teleworkers, 73
     threats of bodily harm, 223
     vision problems, 46
     wrist pain, 45–46
Heterogeneous groups, 382
Holidays, 95
Home offices
     definition, 6–7
     safety guidelines, 73, *73*
     for teleworkers, 72
Homogeneous groups, 382
Honesty
     definition, 37
     ethics, 131, 144
     success quality, 21
     in teams, 37
Horizontal analysis, 352
Horizontal communication, 43
Hoteling, 59

Hotel reservations, 403
Hotel security, 404
Hotspots, 283
Hourly workers, 62–63
Humor, presentations, 196–197

I

IAAP (International Association of Administrative Assistants), 16–17
IAVOA (International Association of Virtual Office Assistants), 68
Identical names, indexing, 323
Illegal software, 244
Illustrations, lists of in reports, 176
IM (instant messaging). *See also* Email; Text messaging.
    benefits, 294–295
    definition, 294
    etiquette, 295–297
    sample screen, *294*
Image records, 331, 335–337
Images
    in email, 164
    in reports, 176
Important records, *338*
Income statements, 352, *353*
Income tax, payroll deductions
    city, 347–348
    exemptions, 346–347
    federal, *346*, 346–347
    Form W-4, 346
    local, 347–348
    Medicare, 348
    Social Security, 348, 350
    state, 347
    tax rates, 347, *347*, *348*
Independence, teleworkers, 66
Indexing records
    cross-referencing, 327, *328*, *329*
    definition, 314
    filing segments, selecting, 314
    institution names, 322
    master index, 328
    organization names, 322
Indexing records, business names
    abbreviations, 319
    articles, 320–321
    identical names, 323
    minor words, 318
    numbers, 321–322
    order of units, 317
    particles, 320–321
    possessives, 318
    prefixes, 320–321
    punctuation, 318
    single letters, 319
    symbols, 318
    titles, 320

Indexing records, government names
    federal, 326
    foreign, 327
    local, 325
    regional, 325
    state, 325–326
Indexing records, personal names
    abbreviations, 318–319
    articles, 320–321
    order of units, 317
    particles, 320–321
    possessives, 318
    prefixes, 320–321
    punctuation, 318
    single letters, 318–319
    suffixes, 319–320
    titles, 319–320
Indirect approach, letters, 168, *170*
Individual retirement arrangement (IRA), 361–362
Inhibitors, 461
Initiative, 21
Injuries in the workplace. *See* Health and safety.
Input devices, 235–237
Inspecting records for storage, 313–314
Instant messaging (IM). *See also* Email; Text messaging.
    benefits, 294–295
    definition, 294
    etiquette, 295–297
    sample screen, *294*
Institution names, indexing, 322
Integrity, 21
InteleWorks Telework Certification, 68
Internal citations, reports, 175
Internal customers, 212
International
    differences (*see* Cultural differences)
    driver's license, 409
    mail delivery, 258–259
    meetings, 379–380
    travel (*see* Travel, international)
International Association of Administrative Assistants (IAAP), 16–17
International Association of Virtual Office Assistants (IAVOA), 68
International Virtual Assistants Association (IVAA), 68
Internet, 74–75, 241–242. *See also* Web; WWW (World Wide Web).
Internet service providers (ISPs), 242
Interpersonal relationships, skill requirements, 18
Interpersonal skills, in teams, 35–36
Interpersonal space, customer service, 215–216
Interviews
    exit, 447

job application (*see* Job search, interviews)
Intrinsic motivation, 464
Introduction, presentations, 201
Introductions, etiquette, 95–97, *96*
Investing
    bonds, 363–364
    budgets, 360
    continuing education, 365
    financial goals, 358–359
    money management, 359–360
    mutual funds, 364
    needs and expenses, 358
    personal philosophy, 357–358
    portfolio evaluation, 364
    realistic choices, 359
    seeking advice, 359
Investing, for retirement
    defined benefit plans, 360
    employee stock purchase, 360
    employer-sponsored plans, 360–362
    401(k) accounts, 360–361
    403(b) accounts, 360–361
    IRA (individual retirement arrangement), 361–362
    Roth IRA, 361
    Spousal IRA, 361–362
Investing, stocks
    common, 362
    definition, 360
    dividends, 362
    Dow Jones Industrial Average, 362
    employee purchase plans, 360
    historical performance, 362
    NASDAQ, 362–363
    preferred, 362
    stock exchanges, 362–363
Investors in businesses. *See* Stockholders.
IRA (individual retirement arrangement), 361–362
ISPs (Internet service providers), 242
ITAC (The Telework Advisory Group for WorldatWork), 68
Itinerary
    definition, 410
    example, *413*
    preparing, 411–412, 414
IVAA (International Virtual Assistants Association), 68

J

Jet lag, 405–406
Jewelry, professional image, 91
Job advancement, 445–447
Job agents, 430
Job boards, 430
Job change, layoff or termination, 447. *See also* Job search.

Job discrimination
    laws prohibiting, 138–139, *139*
    racial, 140–141
    sexual harassment, 139–140, *140*, 223
    steps for handling, 141
Job insecurity, stress factor, 107
Job search
    acceptable salary, 445
    evaluating an offer, 445
    letters of application, 438, *439*
    opportunity for advancement, 445
Job search, interviews
    arriving at the site, 442
    ATS (Applicant Tracking System),
        440
    closing the interview, 443
    dressing for, 441–442
    evaluate the interview, 445
    in-person interview, 441
    mapping the route to, 441
    online prescreening, 440–441
    questions, asking and answering,
        442–443
    telephone prescreening, 441
    thank-you letter, 443, *444*
Job search, planning
    college recruiters, 431
    employment agencies, 430–431
    federal government job board, 430,
        431
    geographical preference, 428
    job agents, 430
    job boards, 430
    networking, 429
    newspapers, 431
    online search, 429–430
    search strategies, 429–431
    targeted search, 427–428
    traditional search, 427
    USAJOBS, 430, *431*
Job search, researching companies
    annual reports, 432
    company Websites, 432
    news stories, 432–433
    questions to ask, 432
Job search, resumes
    chronological, 433, *434*
    contents, *433*
    definition, 433
    electronic, 433, 436, *437*
    e-portfolio, 436
    functional, 433, *435*
    references, 436
Job search, self-assessment
    goals, 427
    interests, 425–426
    MBTI (Myers-Briggs Type Indicator),
        427
    personality assessment, 426–427
    skills, 425, *425*

strengths, 426
support team, 427
values, 426
Job sharing, 6
Junk email. *See* Spam.

K

Kant, Immanuel, 128
Keeping the faith, ethics, 145
Keyboard alternatives, 46–47
Key operator, 272

L

Labels, record storage, 313
LAN (local area network), 241
Language use
    customer service, 217
    verbal communication, 189
Layoff, 447
Leadership. *See also* Management.
    definition, 454
    leaders *versus* managers, 44
    skill requirements, 20
Leadership, traits
    ability to follow, 461
    admitting mistakes, 458
    attacking tough issues, 461
    bilateralness, 461
    building shared vision, 458
    celebrating victory, 461
    commitment to learning, 460
    dealing with inhibitors, 461
    empowering others, 458–459
    engendering trust, 458
    establishing community spirit, 460
    focus on growth, 461
    living by values, 457
    organizational culture development,
        456–457
    recognizing outstanding employees,
        460
    rewarding risk taking, 459–460
    of risk takers, *460*
    self development, 457–458
    self management, 455–456
    self understanding, 454–455
    service to others, 458
    value recognition and alignment, 457
Leadership the Challenge, 12
Leaders *versus* managers, 44
Learning, continual. *See* Continuing
    education.
Learning organizations, 11–12
Legs, nonverbal communication, 191
Letters. *See also* Correspondence.
    direct approach, 168, *169*

editing, 168
favorable information, 166
formatting, 168
indirect approach, 168, *170*
job applications, 438, *439*
negative information, 166
neutral information, 166
overview, 154
persuasive approach, 168, *171*
proofreading, 168
purpose, determining, 166, 168
types of, 166
"you" approach, 166, 168
Library Mail, 258
Life cycle, records, 308–309
Listening skills
    active listening, 186–187
    customer service, 216–217, *217*
    in diverse environments, 42
    effective listening, 35, 35–36
    role in communication, 42
    in teams, 35, 35–36
    telephone, 219–220
Lists, reports, 176
LLC (limited liability company),
    organizational structure, 8
Local area network (LAN), 241
Locating, electronic files, 332–333, *333*
Loyalty
    definition, 37
    ethics, 144–145
    in teams, 37

M

Mail. *See also* Email; USPS (United States
    Postal Service).
    envelope address, example, *262*
    in the executive's absence, 266
    incoming, 262–266
    opening, 263–264
    outgoing, 261–262
    personal and confidential items, 263
    presenting, 265–266
    reading and annotating, 264
    retaining envelopes, 263–264
    routing, 265–266
    routing slip, example, *266*
    sorting, 263
    USPS classifications, 257–258
Maintenance, electronic files, 334
MAN (metropolitan area network), 241
Management. *See also* Leadership.
    challenges, 10–11
    change leaders, *462*
    definition, 9–10, 461
    delegating tasks, 464
    discharging employees, 465–466
    effect on communication, 44

evaluating employees, 465, *464*
job description, *465*
large projects, 114–116
managers *versus* leaders, 44
motivating people, 464
organization, 463–464
planning, 462–463
skills required, 44
strategic vision, 462
supervisor's obligations in teams, 38, *38*
teaching, 464–465
Managers *versus* leaders, 44
Manners, 92–93
Master record index, 328
MBTI (Myers-Briggs Type Indicator), 427
Media Mail, 258
Medicare, 348
Meeting leader, responsibilities, 389–391
Meeting planner, career profile, 372
Meetings. *See also* Conventions and conferences.
attendees, 381–382
board of directors, 375
bylaws, 375
committee, 374
cultural differences, 379–380
customer/client, 375
date and time, confirming, 383
decision making, 390
effectiveness, 373
encouraging participation, 390
equipment, ordering, 387
evaluating the meeting, 390–391, *391*
face-to-face, 376
follow-up, 389
food and beverages, ordering, 387
heterogeneous groups, 382
homogeneous groups, 382
international, 379–380
materials, preparing, 385, 387
meeting notices, 385
meeting room, selecting and preparing, 383
minutes, recording, 387–389
necessary, 373
objectives, 381, 389–390
project team, 375
purpose, 381, 389–390
reasons for, 372
rules for managing, *374*
seating arrangement, 383–385, *384*
staff, 374
task force, 374
time and place, selecting, 382–383
time management, 390
types of, 374–376
unnecessary, 373–374
Meetings, agenda
definition, 385
example, *386*
planning, 382
preparing and distributing, 385
sticking to, 390
Meetings, electronic
audioconferencing, 376–377, *377*
data conferencing, 378
online conferencing, 378–379
pros and cons, 379
teleconferencing, 376
videoconferencing, 377–378, *379*
Meetings, roles and responsibilities
administrative professionals, 383–389
executives, 380–383
meeting leader, 389–391
participants, 391
Melting pot analogy, 40
Memorandums. *See also* Correspondence.
format, *167*
guidelines, 165–166
overview, 154
Messages, while traveling, 414, 416
Metropolitan area network (MAN), 241
Microcomputers, 232–233
Microfiche, 336
Microfilm, 336
Microforms, 335–337
Microsoft Office
Outlook, 115, *116*
Project 2007, 115
Middle digit storage system, 330
Millennials. *See* Generation Y.
Mills, John, 128
Minor words in names, indexing, 318
Minutes, recording, 387–389
Mission statement, customer service, 211, *211*
Mistakes, admitting. *See* Responsibility, accepting.
Mobile offices, 6–7, 72
Mobile phones, 285, 299–300
Modems, 281
Money
currency for international travel, 408
managing, 359–360 (*see also* Investing)
prospective salary, evaluating, 445
as stress factor, 108
Monitor arms, 47
Motivation, 21, 464
Mouse alternatives, 47
Movies, presentations, 199
Mutual funds, 364
Myers-Briggs Type Indicator (MBTI), 427

N

Naming, electronic files, 333
NASDAQ, 362–363
Necessary meetings, 373
Negative stereotyping, 131
Negative stress, 104–105
Negative workplace politics, ethics, 142
Network administrator, career profile, 231
Networking
etiquette, 97–98
job advancement, 447
job search, 429
Newspapers, job search, 431
News stories, job search, 432–433
Nonessential records, *338*
Nonjudgmental, verbal communication, 188
Nonprofit corporations, organizational structure, 8
Non-regular telecommuting, 59
Nonverbal communication
arms, 191
body language, 83, 190–192, *193*
definition, 190
eyes, 191
facial expressions, 191
hands, 191
interpreting, 193
legs, 191
posture, 191–192
proxemics, 192–193
social space, 192–193
voice quality, 192
Notebook computers, 233
Numbers in names, indexing, 321–322
Numeric records storage
advantages, 330
components, 329
consecutive number storage, 330
definition, 329
middle digit system, 330
procedures, 329–330
sequential number filing, 330
serial number filing, 330
straight number filing, 330
terminal digit system, 330
Numeric storage system, 329–330

O

Occupational Outlook Handbook, 3
Occupational Safety and Health Administration (OSHA)
EAP (emergency action plan), 135, *135*
on security programs, 49, 51
standards, 134
OCR (optical character recognition), 236–237
Office Ergonomics Training Website, 49
Office manager, 423

Office manager, career profile, 423
Office types, for teleworkers, 72
Off-loading, 64
Older workers, 6, 10–11
On-call workers, 64
Online
    banking, 355–356, *356*
    conferencing, 378–379
    job search, 429–430
    libraries, 173
    prescreening job applicants, 440–441
    USPS services, 259
Openness to change, 21
Operating system software, 245
Opportunity for advancement, 445
Optical disks, 238–239
Organization, management
    responsibilities, 463–464, 469
Organizational charts, 43–44
Organizational culture, developing, 456–457
Organizational dependencies, 119
Organizational structure. *See also*
    Workplace, organization.
    corporations, 8
    focus on, 10
    governmental entities, 8
    LLC (limited liability company), 8
    nonprofit corporations, 8
    partnerships, 7–8
    sole proprietorships, 7
Organization names, indexing, 322
Organizations, professional. *See*
    Professional organizations.
OSHA (Occupational Safety and Health
    Administration)
    EAP (emergency action plan), 135,
        135
    on security programs, 49, 51
    standards, 134
OUT folders, 316
OUT guides, 316
Outlook, 115, *116*
Outsourcing, 39

P

P/E (price/earnings) ratio, 354–355
Package Services, 258
Page numbers, reports, 176
PAN (personal area network), 241
Paper clips *versus* staples, 316
Paragraphs, effective, 157–158
Parallel paragraph structure, 158
Parcel Post, 258
Parking services, airports, 402
Particles in names, indexing, 320–321
Partnerships, organizational structure, 7–8
Passive voice, 158–159

Passports, 407
Passwords, *248*
Payroll deductions, local, 347–348
PDAs (personal digital assistants). *See also*
    PIMs (Personal Information Managers).
    description, 116
    handheld computer, 234–235
    menu options, *117*
    telecommunications, 285–286
Perfection *versus* achievement, 113
Periodic record transfer, 339
Perpetual record transfer, 339
Per project workers, 63
Personal and confidential mail, 263
Personal area network (PAN), 241
Personality assessment, 427
Personality traits of professionals. *See*
    Characteristics; Skills.
Personal name, indexing by. *See* Indexing
    records, personal names.
Persuasive approach, letters, 168, *171*
Phone service, for teleworkers, 75
Photographs, presentations, 199
Physical workplace, 6–7
Pictures
    in email, 164
    in reports, 176
Pie chart, *178*
PIMs (Personal Information Managers),
    115. *See also* PDAs (personal digital
    assistants).
Pirated software, 244
Planning
    administrative professional
        responsibilities, 468
    management responsibilities, 462–463
    skills, teleworkers, 67
Plato, 128
Pointing devices, 235–236
Politics in the workplace, ethics, 142
Portfolio evaluation, 364
Positive attitude, 84–85
Positive self-talk, 120
Possessives in names, indexing, 318
Posture, nonverbal communication, 191–192
Preferred stocks, 362
Prefixes in names, indexing, 320–321
Prescreening job applicants, 440–441
Presentations. *See also* Verbal
    communication.
    audience analysis, 194
    body, 197–198
    checking the room, 200
    clip art, 199
    closing, 198
    color, 199
    common mistakes, *201*
    connecting with the audience, 202–203

    critiquing, 203
    delivering, 201–202
    dressing the part, 200–201
    evaluation form, *204*
    humor, 196–197
    introduction, 201
    movies, 199
    nervousness, 201
    opening, 196–197
    organizing material, 195–196
    outline, *197*
    personal appearance, 200–201
    photographs, 199
    planning, 194–195
    practicing, 200–201
    purpose, determining, 194
    question-and-answer sessions, 203
    quotes, *198*
    researching, 195
    setting, 194–195
    sound clips, 199
    by teams, 203
    visual aids, 199–200
    writing, 195–198
Primary research, 172–173
Prioritizing change, 13
Priority Mail, 257–258
Priority Mail International, 258
Privacy solutions, 250–251
Privacy threats, 249–250
Problem-Solving Model, 109, *109*
Procrastination, teleworkers, 66
Professional correspondence audiences,
    155
Professional image. *See* Appearance.
Professional organizations
    IAAP (International Association of
        Administrative Assistants), 16–17
    IAVOA (International Association of
        Virtual Office Assistants), 68
    ITAC (The Telework Advisory
        Group for WorldatWork), 68
    IVAA (International Virtual
        Assistants Association), 68
    participation, 87–88
    TelCoa (The Telework Coalition), 68
    telework, 68
Professional Pointers
    anger management, 118
    behaviors of effective leaders, 458
    current technology, 237
    customer service, 213
    effective presentations, 389
    ethical behavior, 143
    handling outgoing mail, 262
    interviewing, 443
    keeping a job, 92
    preparing an itinerary, 414
    records management, 330
    stress management, 118

telecommunications etiquette, 298
time management, 118
verbal communication, 188
virtual work, 64
working with financial records, 354
working with teams, 34
written communication, 168
Project 2007, 115
Project team meetings, 375
Project teams, 34–36
Promotions. *See* Job advancement.
Promptness, correspondence, 161
Proofreading
correspondence, 160, *160*
email, 164
letters, 168
Protestant ethic, 128
Proxemics, nonverbal communication, 192–193
Public relations, in teams, 39
Public Wi-Fi access, 283
Punctuality, 83
Punctuation in names, indexing, 318

Q

QUALCOMM, 132–134, *133*, *134*
Qualities of professionals. *See*
Characteristics; Skills.
Question-and-answer sessions, presentations, 203
Quick ratio, 352–353
Quilt analogy, 40
Quotes, presentations, *198*

R

Racial discrimination, 140–141, *141*, 223
Rail travel
domestic, 405
international travel, 409–410
Readability level, 159, *159*
Reader, analyzing, 155–156
Receiving visitors, etiquette, 97, *97*
Recognizing outstanding employees, 460
Records
archive, 339
as assets, 309
categories, *338*
cross-referencing, 327, *328*, *329*
definition, 309, 336
disposal, 339
electronic, definition, 331
of historical value, 339
image, definition, 331
important, *338*
life cycle, 308–309
nonessential, *338*

periodic transfer, 339
perpetual transfer, 339
retention, 337–339
retention period, 337
transfer, 339
useful, *338*
vital, *338*
Records management
confidentiality, 310
definition, 308
effective systems, 309–310
findability, 309–310 (*see also* Indexing records)
safety, 310
security systems, 310
Records management, electronic files
aperture cards, 336
COM (computer output to microfilm), 335
creating, 332–333
database files, 335
disposition, 334
distribution, 333–334
document imaging, 335
electronic records, definition, 331
filenames, 332–333
file paths, 332
folders, 332–333, *333*
image files, managing, 335–337
image records, definition, 331
locating, 332–333, *333*
maintenance, 334
microfiche, 336
microfilm, 336
microforms, 335–337
naming, 332–333
storing, 332–333
use, 333–334
Windows Search, *334*
Records management, paper
alphabetic storage, 310–311, *312*
coding, 314, *315*
cross-referencing, 314
equipment and supplies, 311–313
file folders, 312–313
file guides, 312
geographic storage system, 330
inspection, 313–314
labels, 313
numeric storage system, 329–330
OUT folders, 316
OUT guides, 316
release marks, 313, *315*
retrieval, 316
sorting, 314, 316
staples *versus* paper clips, 316
storage cabinets, 311–312
storage procedures, 313–316
storage systems, 310, 327–331
storing, 316

subject storage system, 327–329
Recycling, 274–275
Recycling coordinator, *274*
References, for jobs, 436
Reference section, reports, 179
Registered Mail, 260
Regular telecommuting, 59
Relationships at work, stress factor, 107
Relaxing, 120
Release marks, 313, *315*
Remote work. *See* Telework.
Reports. *See also* Correspondence.
examples, *177*, *178*
pie chart, *178*
planning steps, 172
Reports, parts of
appendix, 179
bibliography, 179
body, 176, 178–179
citations, 176, 178–179
documentation, 176, 178–179
executive summary, 175
footnotes, 178
graphics, 176
internal citations, 175
lists, 176
lists of tables and illustrations, 176
page numbers, 176
reference section, 179
table of contents, 175–176
tables, 176
title page, 175
Reports, researching
copyrighted information, 175
evaluating Web information, 174–175
online libraries, 173
primary, 172–173
secondary, 173–175
Web sources, 173–175, 178–179
Researching, presentations, 195
Respect, 37, 42
Responsibility, accepting
admitting mistakes, 214–215, 458, *459*
characteristic of professionals, 87
customer service, 214
ethics, 144
Responsibility, environmental, 130
Restaurants, etiquette, 93–94
Resumes, electronic portfolios, 16
Retention, records, 337–339
Retirement. *See* Investing, for retirement;
Social Security.
Retrieving stored records, 316
Risk takers, traits of, *460*
Risk taking, rewarding, 459–460
Role ambiguity, stress factor, 106–107
Role relationships, 119
Roth IRA, 361

Routing mail, 265–266
Routing slip, example, *266*

S

Safety. *See* Health and safety.
Salad bowl analogy, 40
Salary, evaluating, 445
Satellite communication, 282
Scanners, 236–237
Scanning, from a copier, 269
SC Johnson, 131
Search engines, Windows Search, *334*
Seating arrangements, 383–385, *384*
Secondary research, 173–175
Security. *See also* Health and safety.
    airline, 401, *401*
    confidential records, 310, 339
    hotels, 404
    protective measures, 49, 51
    records management, 310
    required elements, 49, 51
    solutions, 247–249
    threats, 246–247
Security, computer
    cookies, 249–250
    data protection, portable devices, 249
    firewalls, 248–249
    hackers, 247
    passwords, *248*
    privacy solutions, 250–251
    privacy threats, 249–250
    protection guidelines, 248, *250*
    security solutions, 247–249
    security threats, 246–247
    spyware, 250, *250*
    Trojan horses, 247, *248*
    two-factor authentication, 247–248
    viruses, 246, *246*, *248*
    worms, 247, *248*
Self-confidence, teleworkers, 66
Self development, 457–458
Self-employment, workplace changes, 7
Self management, 455–456
Self-starting, teleworkers, 65–66
Self understanding, 454–455
Sentence structure, 158
Sequential number filing, 330
Serial number filing, 330
Service representatives, career profile, 151
Service to others, 458
Setting priorities, 112, 114, *114*
Sexual harassment
    description, 139–140
    EEOC guidelines, 223
    handling, *141*
    policy statement, *140*
Shared vision, building, 458
Short Message Service (SMS), 297

Shredders, 272
Silent Generation, 10–11
Single letters in names, indexing, 318–319
Single parenthood, stress factor, 107
Sitting position, 48–49
Skills. *See also* Characteristics.
    customer service (*see* Customer service skills)
    leadership (*see* Leadership, traits)
    teams (*see* Teams, skills)
Skills, personal
    communication, 18
    creative thinking, 19, *19*
    critical thinking, 18–19, *19*
    decision making, 19
    interpersonal relationships, 18
    leadership, 20
    stress management, 20–21
    teamwork, 19–20
    technology, 20
    telework, 67–69
    time management, 18
Sleep, 118
Smartphones, 116, 235
Smile, professional image, 83
Smiling, customer service, 215
Smoking, health hazards, 49
SMS (Short Message Service), 297
Social Security, 348, 350. *See also* Investing, for retirement.
Social space, 192–193
Socrates, 128
Software, for teleworkers, 73
Sole proprietorships, organizational structure, 7
Sorting mail, 263
Sorting records for storage, 314, 316. *See also* Indexing.
Sound clips, presentations, 199
Spam, 165, 267
Speaking with credibility, 202
Speech recognition, 237, *238*
Speed reading, 114
Spousal IRA, 361–362
Spyware, 250, *250*
Staff meetings, 374
Standard Mail, 258
Standards, 134. *See also* OSHA (Occupational Safety and Health Administration).
Staples *versus* paper clips, 316
Starbucks Coffee, 131
Stationary, for teleworkers, 75
Stem cell research, ethics, 129
Stock exchanges, 362–363
Stockholders, 8
Stockholders' equity, 350
Stocks. *See* Investing, stocks.
Storage cabinets, 311–312

Storing electronic files. *See* Records management, electronic files.
Storing records. *See* Records management.
Straight number filing, 330
Strategic vision, 13, 462
Stress
    acute, 104–105
    balancing, *105*
    chronic, 105
    cost of, 105–106
    definition, 104
    distress, 104
    long term, 105
    negative, 104–105
    relation to anger and time, 111, *112*
    short term, 104–105
Stress, contributing factors
    anger, 107–108
    dual-career families, 107
    extended families, 107
    job insecurity, 107
    money, 108
    relationships at work, 107
    role ambiguity, 106–107
    single parenthood, 107
    time, 108
    working conditions, 107
Stress, managing
    audits, 111–112
    balancing work and play, 119
    diet, 117
    doing it right the first time, 113
    down time, 113
    effective communication, 116–117
    exercise, 118
    handling paper, 113
    managing large projects, 114–116
    organizational dependencies, 119
    perfection *versus* achievement, 113
    positive self-talk, 120
    relaxing, 120
    role relationships, 119
    setting priorities, 112, 114, *114*
    sleep, 118
    solving the problem, 120–121
    speed reading, 114
    talking to a friend, 120
    time management systems, 115
    to-do lists, 112
    values clarification, 112
    visualization, 118
    walking away, 120
    workplace requirements, 20–21
    workstation organization, 113
Structure of organizations. *See* Organizational structure.
Subject line, email, 163–164
Subject storage system, 327–329
Substance abuse, 49

Success qualities, 21–22
Suffixes in names, indexing, 319–320
Superiors, etiquette towards, 97
Symbols in names, indexing, 318
Systems software, 244–246

T

Table manners, etiquette, 93–94, *94*
Table of contents, reports, 175–176
Tables, reports, 176
Tablet PCs, 234
Tact, 38
Targeted job search, 427–428
Task force meetings, 374
Task lights, 48
Tattoos, 91
Taxes. *See* Income tax.
Teaching, management responsibilities, 464–465
Teams
    definition, 31
    presentations, 203
    project, 34–36
    supervisor's obligations, 38, *38*
    word origin, 19
Teams, administrative professional and coworker, 37–38
    external, 37–38
    supervisor, 37
Teams, skills
    acceptance, 38
    administrative, 35
    clarity of purpose, 34
    commitment, 36
    communication with visitors, 39–40
    conflict resolution, 35–36
    cooperation, 38
    dependability, 37
    effective listening, *35*, 35–36
    fairness, 38
    honesty, 37
    interpersonal, 35–36
    loyalty, 37
    public relations, 39
    respect, 37
    tact, 38
    technology, 34–35
Teamwork
    achieving goals, 33
    skill requirements, 19–20
    understanding others, 31
    value differences, 31–32
    working together, 32–33
Technology. *See also specific technologies.*
    skill requirements, 20, 67–68
    in teams, 34–35
TelCoa (The Telework Coalition), 68
Telecenter, 59

Telecommunications, definition, 280
Telecommunications devices. *See also* Telephones.
    cell phones (*see* Mobile phones)
    mobile phones, 285
    PDAs (personal digital assistants), 285–286
    standard phones, 284
    VoIP (Voice over Internet Protocol), 286–287
Telecommunications messaging services. *See also* Email.
    IM (instant messaging), 294–297
    mobile phones, 299–300
    SMS (Short Message Service), 297
    text messaging, 297
    using safely, 296
    voice messaging, 298–299
Telecommunications pipelines
    analog dial-up, 281
    Bluetooth, 283
    broadband, 281
    cable modem, 281
    DSL (digital subscriber line), 282
    fiber optic cable, 283–284
    hotspots, 283
    modems, 281
    public Wi-Fi access, 283
    satellite, 282
    Wi-Fi (wireless fidelity), 283
    Wi-Max, 283
    wireless, 282–283
Telecommuting, 59
Teleconferencing, 376
Telemarketing, 221–222
Telephone prescreening, 441
Telephones. *See also* Telecommunications devices.
    answering calls, 287–288
    effective voice messages, 288
    placing calls, 291–292
    putting calls on hold, 289–290
    recording messages, 290
    screening calls, 288–289
    terminating calls, 290
    transferring calls, 290
Telephones, etiquette
    answering the phone, 287–288
    appropriate responses, *293*
    asking questions, 289
    being helpful, 292–293
    consider time zones, 290–291
    discretion, 292–293
    handling calls, 288–291
    identifying yourself, 287–288
    incorrect handling, example, 292
    language use, 292
    paying attention, 294
    placing calls, 291–292
    pleasant voice, 287

    putting calls on hold, 289–290
    recording messages, 290
    screening calls, 288–289
    slang expressions, *292*
    speaking distinctly, 287
    terminating calls, 290
    transferring calls, 290
    using the caller's name, 292
    your telephone personality, 292–293
Telephone skills, customer service
    abusive customers, 220
    answering professionally, 219
    listening, 219–220
Telework. *See also* Virtual assistants.
    alternate workstation, 59
    continuity of operations, 60
    definition, 58
    episodic telecommuting, 59
    in the federal government, 58–59, 60–61
    hoteling, 59
    legal mandate for, 60–61
    non-regular telecommuting, 59
    personality traits required, 65–67
    professional organizations, 68
    reasons for, 58
    regular telecommuting, 59
    skills required, 67–69
    statistics for 2007, 57–58
    suitability for, self-assessment, 64
    telecenter, 59
    telecommuting, 59
    U.S. Department of Health and Human Services, 59
    written agreements, 71
Telework, benefits to
    communities, 61, *61*
    employers, 60–61
    teleworkers, 59
Telework, challenges
    family issues, 69–70
    isolation, 69
    supervisory concerns, 70–71
    technological, 70
Telework, work environment
    business cards, 75
    computer equipment, 73
    furniture, 75
    hardware, 73
    home offices, 72
    Internet service, 74–75
    mobile offices, 72
    office types, 72
    phone service, 75
    safety guidelines, 73, *73*
    software, 73
    stationary, 75
    supplies, 74–75
    virtual offices, 72
    workspace considerations, 72–73

The Telework Advisory Group for WorldatWork (ITAC), 68
The Telework Coalition (TelCoa), 68
Teleworkers
    benefits to, 59
    commitment to learning, 68–69
    communication skills, 67
    continuing education, 68
    definition, 58
    discipline, 65
    independence, 66
    organization, 66
    personality traits required, 65–67
    planning skills, 67
    procrastination, 66
    self-confidence, 66
    self-starting, 65–66
    technology skills, 67–68
    work ethic, 67
Terminal digit storage system, 330
Termination, handling, 447. *See also* Discharging employees.
Text messaging, 297. *See also* Email; IM (instant messaging).
Thank-you letter, 443, *444*
Threats of bodily harm, 223
Ticketing, 400–401
Time
    etiquette, 95
    international differences, 95
    relation to anger and stress, 111, *112*
    as a resource, 110
    stress factor, 108
Time, managing
    audits, 111–112
    balancing work and play, 119
    diet, 117
    doing it right the first time, 113
    down time, 113
    effective communication, 116–117
    exercise, 118
    handling paper, 113
    managing large projects, 114–116
    meetings, 390
    organizational dependencies, 119
    perfection *versus* achievement, 113
    positive self-talk, 120
    relaxing, 120
    role relationships, 119
    setting priorities, 112, 114, *114*
    skill requirements, 18
    sleep, 118
    solving the problem, 120–121
    speed reading, 114
    systems for, 115
    talking to a friend, 120
    time management systems, 115
    to-do lists, 112
    values clarification, 112
    visualization, 118

    walking away, 120
    workstation organization, 113
Time, wasting
    chatter, 110
    disorganization, 110
    ineffective communication, 110
    procrastination, 111
Time zones, 290–291
Tindell, Kip, 127
Title page, reports, 175
Titles in names, indexing, 319–320
To-do lists, 112
Tone, in correspondence, 162
Touchpads, 235–236
Trackballs, 235
Traditional job search, 427
Training and supervising assistants, 469
Transferring records, 339
Travel, domestic
    car, 403
    ground transportation, 402–403
    hotel reservations, 403
    hotel security, 404
    rail, 405
Travel, domestic airlines
    business-class, 400
    chartered planes, 402
    clubs, 402
    company-owned planes, 402
    economy-class (coach), 400
    e-tickets, 400
    first-class, 400
    flight classifications, 400
    parking services, 402
    security, 401, *401*
    ticketing, 400–401
Travel, international
    airlines, 406–407
    appointments, and jet lag, 405–406
    business cards, 406
    business gifts, 406, *407*
    car rental, *409*
    cultural differences, 405
    currency, 408
    flight classifications, 406–407
    guidelines for, *405*
    health precautions, 408–409
    International Driver's License, 409
    jet lag, 405–406
    passports, 407
    rail, 409
    tips for, *408*
    visas, 407–408, *409*
Travel agencies, 410–411
Travel arrangements, by administrative professionals
    appointments, 412, 414–416, *415*
    correspondence, 414, 416
    decision making, 414
    in the executive's absence, 414–416

    expense reports, 416, *417*
    follow-up correspondence, 416
    itinerary, 411, *413*, *414*
    messages, 414, 416
    organizing materials, 412
    post-trip activities, 416
    traveler's checks, 412
    travel funds, 412
Travel arrangements, by travel agencies
    frequent flyer programs, 410
    itinerary, 410
    necessary information, *411*
Traveler's checks, 412
Trojan horses, 247, *248*
Trust, engendering, 458
Two-factor authentication, 247–248

U

United States, projected population, *213*
Unnecessary meetings, 373–374
Unsolicited email, responding to, 164
Uppercase email, 164
Upward communication, 43
U.S. Department of Health and Human Services, telework, 59
USAJOBS, 430, *431*
Useful records, *338*
USPS (United States Postal Service)
    Bound Printed Matter, 258
    COD (Collect on Delivery), 260
    Delivery Confirmation, 260
    Express Mail, 257
    Express Mail International, 258
    fastest delivery method, 257
    First-Class Mail, 257
    First Class Mail International, 258
    Global Express Guaranteed, 258
    history of, 256
    international delivery, 258–259
    Library Mail, 258
    mail classifications, 257–258
    Media Mail, 258
    online services, 259
    Package Services, 258
    Parcel Post, 258
    Priority Mail, 257–258
    Priority Mail International, 258
    Registered Mail, 260
    services, summary of, *260*
    Standard Mail, 258
Utility software, *245*, 245–246

V

Value, word origin, 31
Value judgments, effective communication, 42

Values clarification
    diversity, 41–42
    managing stress, anger, time, 112
    organizational, 12
    personal, 15–16
Verbal communication. *See also*
Presentations.
    accepting change, 188–189
    active listening, 186–187
    appropriate use of language, 189
    being nonjudgmental, 188
    coping with criticism, 187–188
    definition, 185
    factors affecting, 187
    resolving conflict, 189–190, *190*
Vertical analysis, 352
Victory celebration, 15
Videoconferencing, 377–378, *379*
Virtual Assistant Certification, 68
Virtual assistants. *See also* Telework.
    billable hours agreement, 64
    client benefits, 64
    client concerns, 64–65
    definition, 58
    description, 61–64
    downsizing, 64
    flat rate workers, 63
    hourly workers, 62–63
    off-loading, 64
    on-call workers, 64
    per project workers, 63
    suitability for, self-assessment, 64
    technical difficulties, 65
Virtual offices, 6–7, 72. *See also* Telework.
Virtual Office Temps Certification, 68
Viruses, 246, *246, 248*
Visas, 407–408, *409*

Vision problems, 46
Vision statement, customer service,
    211–212
Visual aids, presentations, 199–200
Visualization, 118
Visualizing success, customer service,
    214
Vital records, *338*
Voice, passive *versus* active, 158–159
Voice messaging, 298–299
Voice quality, nonverbal communication,
    192
VoIP (Voice over Internet Protocol),
    286–287

W

W-4 Form, 346
Walking away, 120
WAN (wide area network), 241
Web-based customer service, 222, *222*
Web conferencing. *See* Online,
    conferencing.
Web sites. *See also* Internet; WWW (World
    Wide Web).
    citing in reports, 178–179
    searching, 173–175
Wegman's Food Markets, 127
Wi-Fi (wireless fidelity), 283
Wi-Max, 283
Windows Mail screen, *267*
Windows Search, *334*
Wireless communication, 282–283
Wireless personal area network (WPAN),
    241
Workaholics, 85

Work ethic, 67, 85–86
Working conditions, stress factor, 107
Working remotely. *See* Telework.
Workplace, changes in. *See* Change,
    organizational.
Workplace, organization. *See also*
    Organizational structure.
    board of directors, 8–9
    directors, 8–9
    management, 9–11
    stockholders, 8
Workspace considerations, for
    teleworkers, 72–73
Workstation organization, 113
Work surfaces, adjustable, 47
Workweek, 6
World is Flat, The, 15
Worms, 247, *248*
WPAN (wireless personal area network),
    241
W questions, *161*
Wrist pain, 45–46
Writing, presentations, 195–198
Written communication. *See*
    Correspondence, written.
WWW (World Wide Web), 242. *See also*
    Internet; Web.

X

X Generation, 10–11

Y

"You" approach, letters, 166, 168